CENSUS OF INDIA, 1931

VOLUME VI

CALCUTTA

PARTS I & II

The publication of decennial census reports was initiated by the British Government during the middle of the nineteenth century and has been continued after independence. Questions of reliability and bias in the compilation of information as well as motivations which informed the publication of these reports have been raised and are relevant to every user of census reports. Even so, the censuses were often conducted with painstaking efforts and have preserved for us extremely wide-ranging information on the social, economic and political aspects of Indian life.

They contain information on the distribution and age structure of the population; castes and communities, patterns of occupation, patterns of land-holding and tenancy, health, migration, language, and education, etc., to name just a few aspects of the panorama of India society. For researchers interested in understanding Indian life, the reports of the decennial census complied by British officers remain, despite the problems of bias, misunderstanding or conscious distortion, an invaluable source of information.

The census reports consisted of two parts: a general social and economic profile and statistical material. The general profile contains an account of the census operations, the geographical and physical features of the area, the ethnography of caste and communities and changes in age-structure, health, education, employment, landholding pattern and tenancy, etc. The statistical part contains data on geography, rainfall, temperature, distribution of population according to different demographic criteria, caste and communities, health, education, employment and migration, and landholding and tenancy.

Census reports have, as a rule, been used by demographers, economists and economic historians, and a great deal of this use has been limited to the statistical data contained in them. Sociologists, social historians and political scientists have made very little use of these reports. These reports provide, particularly in the volumes entitled 'General Reports' which were published separately for each state as well as for India as a whole, ethnographic information on castes and tribes, describing their internal organization, social changes taking place in them, and the emerging problems of interaction among the different castes and communities. Social movements and trends towards social mobility among the castes and communities are also often discussed. Even from the viewpoint of the sociologists and social historians, therefore, the census reports are invaluable sources of information and can provide useful material on how the different sections of Indian society were responding to the processes set in motion by British rule.

The census reports are today a body of rare documents available in only a few select libraries and even these libraries do not always have all the available volumes which in an average census year extended to more than a hundred for the whole of India. This reprint of Parts I & II of Census of India 1931 for Calcutta is published in the hope that it will be welcomed by individual researchers as well as libraries.

Census of India, 1931

VOLUME VI

CALCUTTA

PARTS I & II

by

A.E. PORTER, M.A. (OXON)

Of the Indian Civil Service

Superintendent of Census Operation, Bengal

MANOHAR
2001

Rs 1250

First published 1933
Reprinted 2001

ISBN 81-7304-392-2

Published by
Ajay Kumar Jain for
Manohar Publishers & Distributors
4753/23 Ansari Road, Daryaganj
New Delhi 110 002

Printed at
Mehra Offset Press
1979, Ganj Mirkhan
Chandni Mahal, Daryaganj
New Delhi 110002

Census of India, 1931

VOLUME VI

CALCUTTA

PARTS I & II

by

A. E. PORTER, M.A., (OXON)
Of the Indian Civil Service
Superintendent of Census Operation, Bengal

CALCUTTA
CENTRAL PUBLICATION BRANCH
1933

GENERAL TABLE OF CONTENTS.

PART I.

REPORT.

PART II.

TABLES.

DETAILED TABLE OF CONTENTS OF PART I.

INTRODUCTION

The enumeration of the city of Calcutta, figures for which are included in this volume, was done under a special officer, Mr. Prafulla Chandra Sen of the Bengal Civil Service. Correspondence with the Calcutta Corporation was initiated as early as May 1930 but a more than governmental leisureliness of procedure in the municipal office made it impossible for Mr. Sen to join before the 11th August. In the meantime all that could be done was to arrange for the preparation of such maps as were available and of a list compiled from the Corporation registers showing the municipal number and situation of all premises assessed to tax. When Mr. Sen joined the date of the census was very little more than six months ahead, and it was clear that he had no grounds for expecting that his appointment would prove to be a sinecure. It soon became clear also that no better selection for the post could have been made. He threw himself into very intricate, difficult and complicated work with energy and enthusiasm. Working often in indifferent health he was entirely unsparing of himself and by tact and force of character he succeeded in getting the best possible work out of persons of every race and condition with whom the enumeration brought him into contact. It is no reflection whatever upon his ability that he failed to make headway against obstruction by one class only, viz., Marwaris and Gujarati Hindus, whose intractability has on occasion discomfited bodies more august than the census department. From the 13th of January 1931 Mr. Sen was assisted by Babu Durgapada Banarji of the Bengal Junior Civil Service whose services were so satisfactory that he was subsequently appointed a deputy superintendent of census in a post elsewhere filled by officers of the Bengal Civil Service.

The general procedure under which the census was taken is described in sufficient detail in the introduction to volume V, part i. For the census of Calcutta the same general procedure was adopted with such modifications as were rendered necessary by conditions in a great city. Municipal wards formed a convenient basis for the formation of charges. These were divided into provisional circles and the houses in each circle were numbered. So far as possible municipal premises numbers were employed and they were extended in order to show separately houses not coming under or omitted from assessment as well as the room or rooms occupied by each commensal family in a structure counting as one municipal house. After house-numbering blocks were formed and were combined into fresh circles for enumeration. During January and February a preliminary enumeration was made and on the night of the 26th February this preliminary enumeration was checked. The procedure outlined refers particularly to the municipal area. More than half the charges formed of or based on municipal wards were superintended by municipal councillors. A paid agency was employed for house-numbering but a paid enumerating agency was employed only for just over one-fifth of the 3,778 blocks of the 335 circles into which the municipal area was divided. These census divisions do not include areas for the enumeration of which special measures were taken. Within municipal limits special arrangements were made for jails, hospitals, police-stations and quarters, government and public institutions, the larger hotels and boarding houses, mills and industrial quarters and municipal institutions such as markets, etc., and the co-operation of those in charge of them was enlisted in the conduct of the enumeration. In the enumeration of the port of Calcutta several agencies co-operated. The Port Commissioners' land property was dealt with by the Estates' Superintendent and later by the Assistant Secretary of the Port Commission : the Deputy Superintendent, Port Police, Calcutta, arranged for the census of vessels lying in port and was assisted by the returns for their own vessels made by the big steamer companies of Calcutta : and both the Bengal Pilot Service and the Preventive Service of the Calcutta Customs assisted in securing the enumeration of persons on sea-going vessels. Fort William and the military areas in Hastings and Ballygunge were enumerated by the military under an officer specially deputed for that purpose. For the canals area for which the population is shown separately special arrangements were also made under officers of the Irrigation Department. In the census of railway stations, railway quarters, etc., the services of railway employees were enlisted. An acknowledgment of services rendered is owing both to those who assisted in the enumeration of special areas and also to those councillors of the Corporation and other voluntary workers who contributed to the success of the enumeration in the city. In particular acknowledgments are due to the permanent officers of the Calcutta Corporation, Messrs. J. C. Mukharji, the Chief Executive Officer, B. V. Ramiah, the Secretary, and P. L. Trivedi, the Assessor, from whom throughout the special officer has left on record that he received continuous and valuable assistance. An expression of appreciation is also due to the Calcutta Electric Supply Company, the Bengal Telephone Corporation and the Calcutta Tramways Company for the assistance which they rendered by affording publicity to the census as the date of the enumeration approached.

The compilation of the returns and preparation of the tables has been described in the introduction to volume V, part i. The final work in connection with this volume will be done by my personal assistant, Babu Bhupendra Krishna Sinha of the Bengal Civil Service, who has prepared all the tables and statements in this volume, has with his own hand drafted most of the diagrams, and has been left with the typescript of the whole volume and the duty of seeing it through the Press. An acknowledgment of service is due to the office and the staff of the Bengal Government Press in charge of census work, from whom the personal assistant received valuable assistance and co-operation.

Excluding the charges for printing this volume the cost of the census of the municipal area of Calcutta amounts in all to Rs. 51,764. This is equivalent to a cost of Rs. 446-12 per ten thousand persons or Rs. 2-9 per acre of area. The cost in 1921 was Rs. 43,002 corresponding on account of the smaller population and area then included to Rs. 491 per ten thousand inhabitants or Rs. 3-8 per acre. There has thus been a very considerable reduction in the proportionate cost at a time when conditions explained in the introduction to volume V, part i, all conspired to increase charges.

CHAPTER I

Distribution and Growth of population

1. **Introductory.**—The area covered in this part of the report includes the municipality of Calcutta with Fort William and the Maidan, the Port, the Calcutta Canal area, the two suburban municipalities, Tollygunge and South Suburban municipality in the 24-Parganas and the city of Howrah on the western side of the river Hooghly linked to Calcutta by a bridge which for many decades has been entirely inadequate to the needs of the city and is apparently still as far from replacement as ever. A map forming the frontispiece of this volume shows these areas. For the purposes of the census the Port of Calcutta has been taken to consist of (1) the waters of the river Hooghly from the Cossipore Ghat on the north to the Sandheads on the south and (2) on the left bank of the Hooghly the property of the Port Commissioners between the Cossipore Ghat on the north and the Calcutta Electric Supply Company, Metiabruz, on the south. Where comparison is made with the figures of other census counts, unless otherwise stated, the details given all refer to the areas as now constituted.

2. **Date of census and population enumerated.**—The census was taken on the evening of the 26th February 1931 and it professes to be a record of all persons actually resident in the areas concerned in the report either permanently or temporarily on the night of the 26-27th February. In certain parts of the city it proved impossible to conduct the final check of preliminary figures which generally constituted the final census. The areas concerned are given in chapter I of volume V, part i, and are here repeated in statement No. I-1. The population enumerated also includes persons who on the night of the census were within Indian territorial waters and arrived at Calcutta on some subsequent date or had left Calcutta just before the census was taken. Briefly the arrangements made ensured the inclusion in the population of the Port of all persons on the water between the Sandheads and Calcutta on the night of the census together with those further out to sea on vessels which had left a port in India before the census was there taken and did not arrive in Calcutta until after the 26th February.

STATEMENT No. I-1.

District.	Locality.	Area (sq. miles).	Population.	Date of final check.
Calcutta ..	Ward 7, 132 blocks ..	..	..	Nil.
	Ward 5, 85 blocks ..	..	..	Nil.
	Ward 29, 22 blocks ..	..	..	Nil.
	Ward 6, 32 blocks ..	1·5	49,795	Subsequently.

3. **Tables presenting the results.**—Tables corresponding to those shown in volume V, part ii, have been prepared so far as they are relevant and are shown *infra* in part ii of this volume. The narrative portion of the volume serves as an introduction to these figures and is confined as far as possible rather to indicating what they contain than to offering detailed comment on them. To most chapters there have been added subsidiary tables compiled from the tables forming part ii of the volume and from corresponding tables at previous enumerations. The figures principally discussed in this chapter are those in imperial tables I and II. Subsidiary tables printed after the chapter show—

I—the population in 1931 with percentage of variation by wards, 1872-1931 ;

II—the number of persons per acre with percentage of variation in density by wards, 1872-1931 ;

III—the average number of persons per house and houses per acre by wards, 1881-1931 ; and

IV—the extent of regular daily passenger traffic by rail between Calcutta and outlying stations, February 1931.

4. **General figures of population.**—In Calcutta with its suburbs in the 24-Parganas and Howrah the total population is 1,485,582 of which 1,196,734 is found in Calcutta including the municipal area, Fort William and the Maidan, the Port and Canals, 63,975 in the two suburban municipalities and 224,873 in the adjacent city of Howrah. It is difficult to give a confident estimate of the accuracy of the figures recorded. It is customary for a great outcry to be raised as soon as the census of Calcutta had been taken and allegations are freely made that there has been a wholesale omission of persons who should have been recorded. On the present occasion the outcry was gratifyingly less than previously and by co-operation with the newspapers to whom protests of this nature are generally sent it was possible to investigate a very large proportion of the specific allegations of omissions which were made. In the majority of cases the allegations were definitely proved to be false and particulars of the person complaining that he had been omitted were traced in the schedule. In a minority of cases it transpired that uncertainty as to the jurisdiction of a particular area or as to a premises being occupied had led to omission but, with the exception of ward 6 and ward 4, in general such omissions in each case were subsequently rectified with reference to the position on the night of the 26th February. In ward 6 and ward 4 certain areas were omitted owing to undetected defaults of the charge superintendent. Other omissions such as occurred in wards 5 and 7 where Marwaris form a considerable portion of the population were due to the intransigeance of the Marwari community and Guzrati traders who are not native to Bengal but reside here for purposes of trade and paid the city from which as immigrants they extract their material prosperity the delicate compliment of declining to be enumerated amongst its population. On the whole it is unlikely that the enumeration on the present occasion was less accurate than in 1921 and as then it is possible now also to claim that the inaccuracy does not amount to as much as 2 per mille and is probably nearer 1 per mille.

5. **Comparison with other cities.**—Calcutta contains 35 thousand more inhabitants than Bombay which is the next largest city in India. The population of the main cities of India is shown and illustrated in the accompanying diagram No. I-1. There are nearly twice as many inhabitants

DIAGRAM No. I-1.

Population in millions of the principal cities of India.

Population in millions

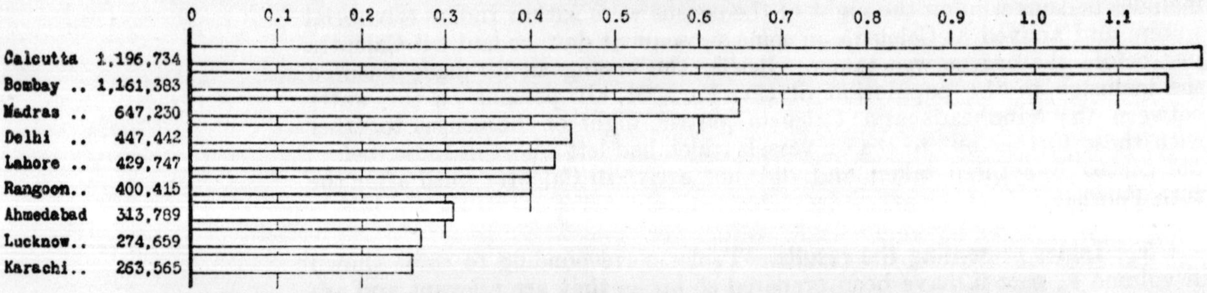

in Calcutta proper as there are in Madras and almost three times as many as there are in Rangoon. Alone of the large cities of India Bombay has recorded a decrease in population since 1921. Lahore which has expanded to more than half as large again as it was in 1921 has increased by actually a larger number during the decade than Calcutta. The same is true of Delhi and Madras which increased by 47 per cent. and 22·8 per cent. over their population of 1921. On the other hand, although the increase of 119,470 persons in the population of Calcutta during the last decade is greater than has been recorded in any of the other cities illustrated in diagram No. I-1 the percentage increase amounts to only 11·1 compared with 21·5 in Karachi, 15·9 in Rangoon, 14·5 in Ahmedabad and 14·2 in Lucknow. In comparing the size of different cities in India, however, it must be remembered that, unlike other cities with the possible exception of Bombay, Calcutta increasingly attracts a working population which daily travels in from neighbouring municipalities not included within the city itself. Figures forming subsidiary table IV give the number of season tickets current on the day on which the census was taken and show that upwards of 26 thousand persons travel daily between Calcutta and neighbouring stations. The number of these daily travellers who live within the city and travel outside it for their daily work is probably negligible, and the table suggests that in estimating the effective population of Calcutta as an industrial city, the figures should be increased by at least 2 per cent. to include suburban workers. Municipalities on the other side of the river north of Howrah, which are served by bus services, are also becoming increasingly popular as a residence for city workers. The figures given in subsidiary table IV take no account of daily passengers by these services whose numbers must be considerable.

6. **Population of wards.**—The title page to imperial table I gives full details of the present constitution of wards in Calcutta and of the changes in the municipal area which have been effected since the census of 1921. There are more than 40 thousand persons in Muchipara (80,604), Bhawanipur (79,684), Bartola (67,107), Shampukur (66,633), Garden Reach (55,872), Sukea's Street (54,101), Kalootola (48,998), Maniktala (42,399), Tollygunge (40,730) and Beniapukur (40,587). Baman Bustee with 2,679 and Park Street adjacent to it with 5,438 are the smallest wards. Figures for the individual wards of Howrah city are not given in imperial table I because no figures were forthcoming for the area of each ward, but they will be found in imperial table XVI. There are three wards in Howrah with more than 30 thousand inhabitants, viz., No. 8 (37,497), No. 6 (33,790) and No. 4 (31,882) and the ward with the smallest population is No. 2 with 6,514.

DIAGRAM No. I-2.

Changes in the density of Calcutta and Howrah, 1872-1931.

Numbers are shown by figures, rates of change by slope.

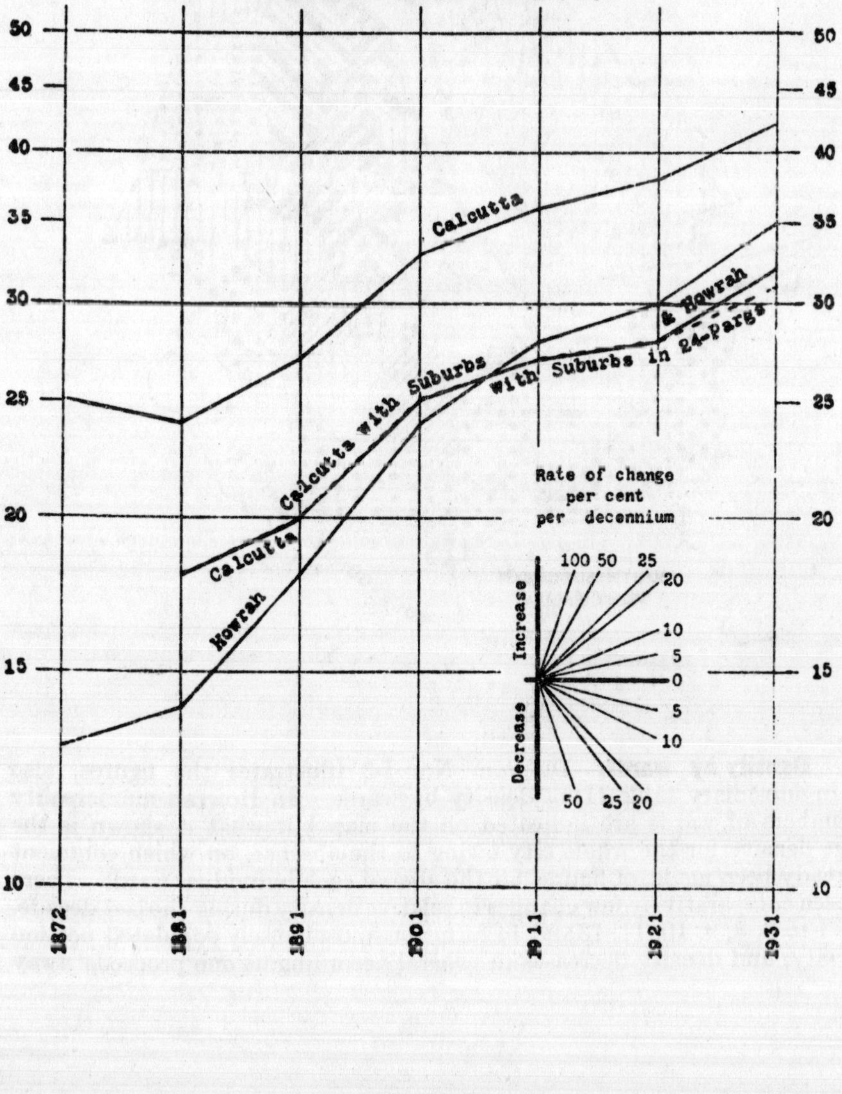

7. **Density of population with changes from 1872.**—*General.*—In the municipal area of Calcutta the average density is 58 persons to the acre. Including Fort William and the Maidan, the Port and the Canals, in which the average density is no more than 2 to 7 per acre, the density for the whole area is on the average 42 persons per acre. If the suburbs in the 24-Parganas be included, where the average density is 6 per acre, the density for greater Calcutta on the east of the river Hooghly works out at 31 per acre. In Howrah the density is 35 per acre. Changes in the density of Calcutta and Howrah are illustrated from subsidiary table II in diagram No. I-2. In Calcutta the density fell between 1872 and 1881 from 25 to 24 persons per acre, but since that date it has shown at every census an increase over that recorded in the previous census year. The rate of increase has been most rapid in Howrah where there are now 2½ times as many persons per acre as there were in 1881.

DIAGRAM No. I-3.

Density by wards of Calcutta and of the two suburban municipalities and of Howrah city.

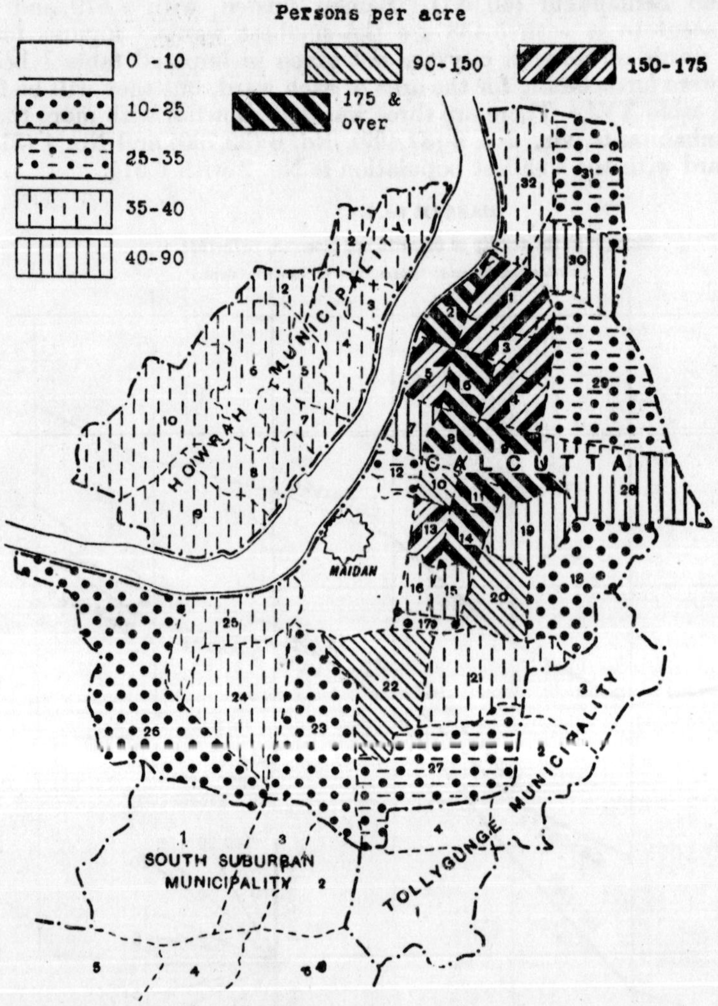

8. **Density by wards.**—Diagram No. I-3 illustrates the figures, also given in subsidiary table II, of density by wards. In Howrah municipality the numbers of wards are indicated on the map but what is shown is the average density for the whole city owing to the absence, on which comment has already been made, of figures for the area of each individual ward. There have been comparatively few changes in relative density during the last decade. Wards 1 to 6, 8, 9, 10, 11, 13 and 14 form the most densely populated portion of the city, and density decreases in general according as one proceeds away

to the outskirts of the city from these areas. There are to each acre 175 persons or over in Kumartuli, Jorasanko, Kalootola, Muchipara, Puddapukur and Taltola wards and between 150 and 175 persons in Shampukur, Bartola, Sukea's Street, Jorabagan and Fenwick Bazar. The density of population is comparatively small in the areas added to the municipal limits during the decade. Taltola (ward 14), Beniapukur (ward 20), Garden Reach (ward 26), Kalootola (ward 8), Fenwick Bazar (ward 13), Ballygunge (ward 21) are predominantly Muslim. In Kalinga (ward 15) the majority of the inhabitants are Muslims or Anglo-Indians. Park Street (ward 16), Baman Bustee (ward 17) and Ballygunge (ward 37) contain a large proportion of Europeans who are present also in large numbers in Bhawanipur (ward 22) and Alipore (ward 23). Kalootola (ward 8) contains a predominant population of Muslims and Chinese. Burrabazar (ward 7)is predominantly Marwari and there is a large proportion of Marwaris also in Jorasanko (ward 6) and in Jorabagan (ward 5), although in this last ward a majority of the population are Bengalis. Employees in Government offices are said to have a partiality for Muchipara (ward 9) and Bhawanipur (ward 22) and to avoid Jorabagan (ward 5) and Burrabazar (ward 7) as well as Kalootola (ward 8).

9. **Variations of population.**—*General.*—Variations in the population since 1872 are shown in imperial table II and illustrated for Calcutta and Howrah in diagram No. I-4. Apart from a decline of 3·1 per cent. in population between 1872 and 1881 in none of these years has there been anything but a continuous increase at each successive census from the date on which

DIAGRAM No. I-4.

Variation in the population of Calcutta and Howrah, 1872-1931.

Numbers are shown by figures, rate of change by slope.

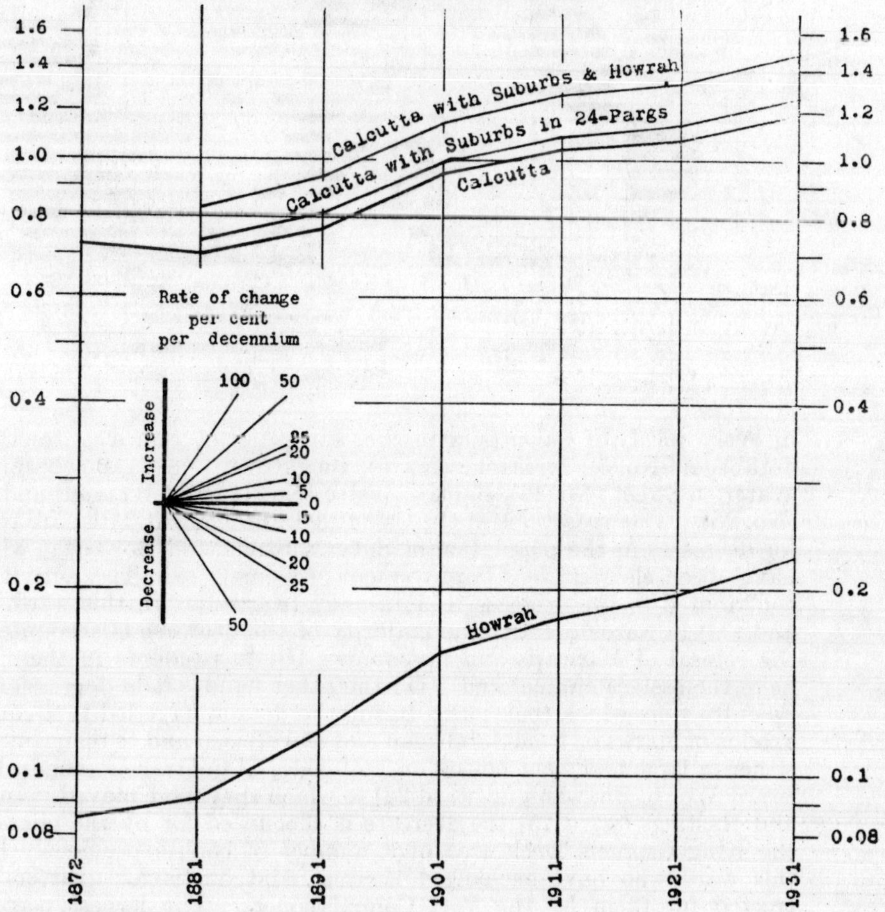

the first record was taken. Calcutta increased 11·1 per cent. during the last decade and Howrah 15·2 per cent., but the increase in the two suburban municipalities was even greater and amounted to 16·3 per cent. The increase of Calcutta with its suburbs in 24-Parganas is 11·3 per cent. The highest rate of increase occurred between 1891 and 1901 when it amounted to as much as 35·2 per cent. in Howrah and 23·6 per cent. in the municipal area of Calcutta.

10. **Variations in population by wards.**—Diagram No. I-5 illustrates similar figures for the last two decades for each ward of Calcutta and for the two suburban municipalities and Howrah city. There has been an increase

DIAGRAM No. I-5.

Variation in the population of Calcutta by wards and of the two suburban municipalities and of Howrah city, 1921-1931.

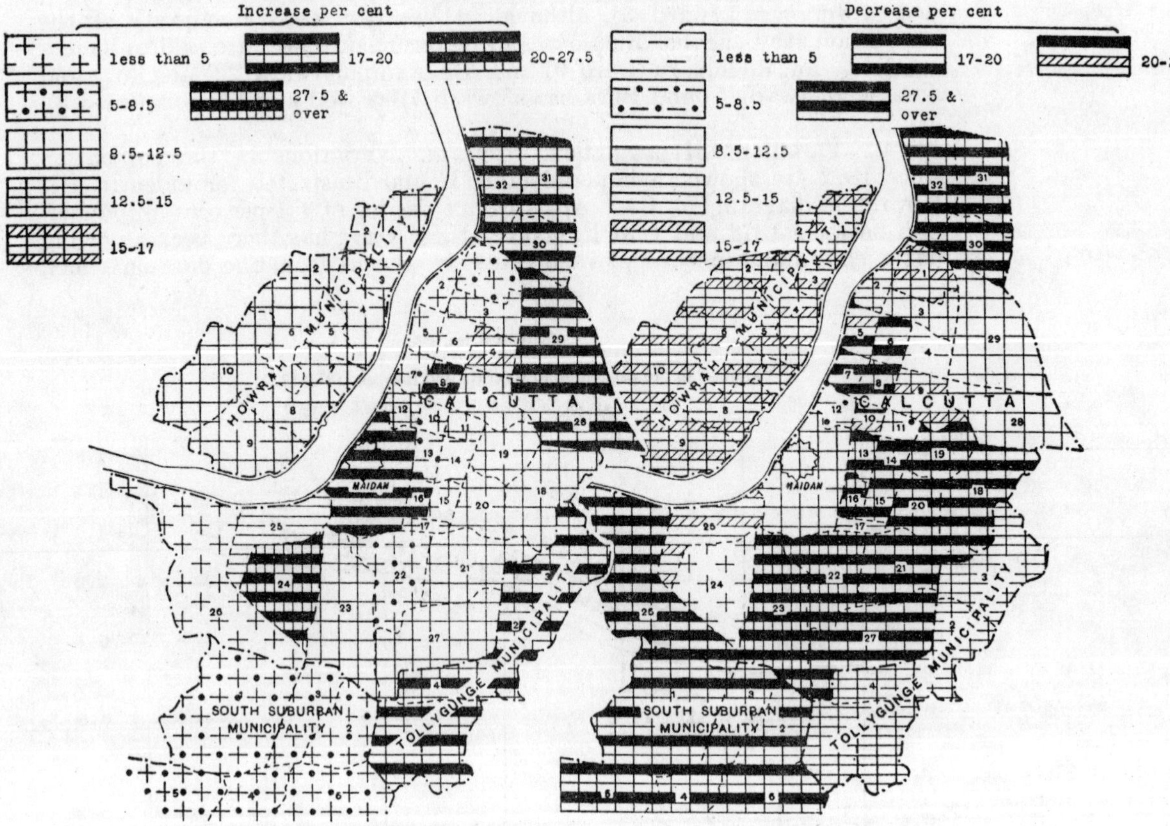

in every ward of Calcutta with the exception of Sukea's Street (No. 4), Jorabagan (No. 5), Jorasanko (No. 6), Burrabazar (No. 7), Bowbazar (No. 10), Waterloo Street (No. 12), Baman Bustee (No. 17) and Watganj and Hastings (No. 25). The operations of the Calcutta Improvement Trust are responsible for decreases in the population of Sukea's Street and Bowbazar where areas have been cleared for improvement schemes. Similar activities have contributed to the decrease in Jorasanko (ward 6). In this ward, however, and also in wards 5 and 7 the majority of the decrease is accounted for by the refusal of Marwaris and up-country Hindu residents in these wards to have themselves enumerated. On the other hand, trade depression and the Calcutta riots which took place during the decade have led to a considerable exodus of Marwaris from Jorabagan and Burrabazar and to their concentration either in large tenement houses on both sides of Central Avenue in Kalootola (ward 8) or to Bhawanipur (ward 22) to which they have moved. In Watganj and Hastings (ward 25) the decrease is accounted for by the migration into the King George's Dock area of a number of coolies previously housed in this ward who have exchanged their squalid bustis for quarters specially erected for them by the Port Commissioners. The largest percentage of increase in population has occurred in the area of the Canals and of the Port, in both of which a decrease was recorded in 1921. The increase in the Port area has already been explained. The completion and occupation of new blocks of flats in Park Street (ward 16) has led to an increase of 44 per cent. of the population there compared with a decrease in the previous decade of 28·7 per cent. The expectation in the report for 1921 that there would be a considerable increase in the population of Bhawanipur has been fulfilled by an increase of nearly 39 per cent.

11. **Houses and number of persons per house.**—There has been considerable difference in the definition of a house adopted in Calcutta at each successive census. In 1872 and 1881 the residence of a commensal family was adopted. In 1891 the definition was "each collection of houses in a single compound." In 1901 the unit was "the dwelling-place of one or more families having a separate independent entrance from the common way". In 1911 "each premises separately numbered for municipal assessment" was treated as a separate house. In 1921 a definition similar to that of 1901 was adopted. On the present occasion an attempt was made to make the maximum possible use of the municipal premises' numbers and to distinguish rooms in occupation of commensal families using the same common entrance, but separate numbers were not given to every room in clubs, hotels, boarding houses or brothels. It is, therefore, useless to endeavour to compare the figures for the number of persons in each house from year to year or to draw any deduction from them as to the relative incidence of overcrowding. Satisfactory details of the house room available per family could only be obtained in Calcutta as a result of an intensive special enquiry. As they stand the figures show a great concentration of houses in Paddapukur (ward 11), Jorasankc (ward 6), Burra Bazar (ward 7), Taltola (ward 14), Kalootola (ward 8) and Fenwick Bazar (ward 13) in all of which there are on the average at least 30 houses to the acre. As many as 8 persons per house are returned in Sukea's Street (ward 4), Jorabagan (ward 5), Muchipara (ward 9) and Bhawanipur (ward 22).

SUBSIDIARY TABLE I.—The population in 1931 with percentage of variation by wards, 1872-1931.

Wards, etc.	Population in 1931.	Percentage of variation. 1921 to 1931.	1911 to 1921.	1901 to 1911.	1891 to 1901.	1881 to 1891.	1872 to 1881.	Net variation, 1872 to 1931.
1	2	3	4	5	6	7	8	9
CALCUTTA WITH SUBURBS AND HOWRAH ..	**1,485,582**	**+11·9**	**+ 4·3**	**+11·0**	**+22·9**	**+12·5**	..	..
CALCUTTA WITH SUBURBS IN 24-PARGANAS ..	**1,260,709**	**+11·3**	**+ 3·6**	**+10·6**	**+21·1**	**+10·5**	..	..
Calcutta ..	**1,196,734**	**+11·1**	**+ 3·2**	**+ 9·9**	**+23·3**	**+10·1**	**− 3·1**	**+ 65·8**
MUNICIPAL AREA ..	**1,158,044**	**+ 9·8**	**+ 4·6**	**+ 10·7**	**+ 23·6**	**+ 11·0**	**− 5·2**	**+ 65·3**
Ward No. 1 Shampukur ..	66,633	+ 16·9	+ 7·5	+ 13·1	+ 27·1	+ 29·4	− 1·2	+ 130·6
Ward No. 2 Kumartuli ..	38,294	+ 12·7	+ 2·8	+ 9·7	+ 13·3	+ 13·6	− 24·5	+ 12·5
Ward No. 3 Bartola ..	67,107	+ 9·7	+ 12·0	+ 8·8	+ 37·8	+ 25·9	− 3·3	+ 124·3
Ward No. 4 Sukea's Street ..	54,101	− 2·3	+ 15·1	+ 14·5	+ 20·7	+ 42·7	− 2·5	+ 108·1
Ward No. 5 Jorabagan ..	39,355	− 25·1	+ 0·9	+ 6·2	+ 25·2	+ 7·9	− 7·1	+ 0·7
Ward No. 6 Jorasanko ..	46,116	− 19·5	− 3·8	+ 12·4	+ 27·2	+ 26·9	− 8·9	+ 28·0
Ward No. 30 Belgachia ..	22,252							
Ward No. 31 Satpukur ..	19,194	+ 21·6	+ 17·2	+ 18·2	+ 29·7	+ 19·5	+ 3·6	+ 170·6
Ward No. 32 Cossipore ..	27,213							
Ward No. 7 Burra Bazar ..	18,690	− 43·3	+ 8·1	− 3·4	+ 52·9	− 0·6	− 11·6	− 20·5
Ward No. 8 Kalootola ..	48,998	+ 27·2	− 32·5	− 9·6	+ 24·4	+ 7·3	− 6·9	− 3·5
Ward No. 9 Muchipara ..	80,604	+ 15·7	+ 10·0	− 1·2	+ 29·6	+ 13·5	− 0·1	+ 84·7
Ward No. 10 Bow Bazar ..	21,075	− 22·3	+ 8·4	− 7·5	+ 19·3	+ 4·8	− 8·1	− 10·5
Ward No. 11 Paddapukur ..	35,323	+ 8·2	+ 8·9	+ 6·8	+ 35·2	+ 1·2	+ 0·1	+ 72·4
Ward No. 12 Waterloo Street ..	6,711	− 5·6	+ 13·1	− 0·3	+ 6·2	+ 2·5	+ 1·4	+ 17·6
Ward No. 28 Beliaghata ..	33,235	+ 12·3	+ 25·3	+ 66·0	+ 15·0	− 41·5	− 10·9	+ 40·1
Ward No. 29 Maniktala ..	42,399							
Ward No. 13 Fenwick Bazar ..	30,975	+ 18·6	− 8·2	− 8·9	+ 10·0	+ 9·5	− 3·3	+ 15·6
Ward No. 14 Taltola ..	38,427	+ 21·4	− 1·4	− 0·4	+ 10·4	+ 12·1	− 3·9	+ 41·7
Ward No. 15 Kalinga ..	14,052	+ 19·6	+ 3·2	− 32·2	+ 26·9	+ 11·6	− 7·3	+ 10·0
Ward No. 16 Park Street ..	5,438	+ 44·0	− 28·7	− 13·4	+ 32·3	− 7·0	+ 8·8	+ 19·1
Ward No. 17 Baman Bustee ..	2,679	+ 14·9	+ 0·7	− 42·7	+ 18·6	− 24·9	− 6·7	− 59·2
Ward No. 18 Tengra ..	11,772							
Ward No. 19 Intally ..	44,224							
Ward No. 20 Beniapukur ..	40,587	+ 25·4	+ 9·2	+ 30·7	+ 17·9	+ 20·6	− 6·5	+ 137·4
Ward No. 21 Ballygunge ..	30,999							
Ward No. 27 Tollygunge ..	40,730							
Ward No. 22 Bhawanipur ..	79,684	+ 38·9	+ 5·1	+ 9·9	+ 16·6	+ 12·1	+ 2·4	+ 114·7
Ward No. 23 Alipore ..	30,020	+ 35·3	+ 12·3	+ 11·5	+ 19·7	+ 10·2	− 30·8	+ 54·6
Ward No. 24 Ekbalpore ..	32,822	+ 4·5	+ 43·7	+ 1·2	+ 40·9	− 3·3	− 12·2	+ 81·6
Ward No. 25 Watganj and Hastings ..	32,463	− 16·2	− 12·8	− 24·2	+ 17·4	+ 36·9	− 4·9	+ 15·2
Ward No. 26 Garden Reach ..	55,872	+ 22·6	+ 0·6	+ 60·6	+ 1·0	+ 124·2	+ 34·5	+ 503·5
FORT WILLIAM AND MAIDAN ..	**3,083**	**+ 11·9**	**− 37·5**	**+ 32·5**	**− 8·0**	**+ 8·4**	**+ 34·5**	**+ 24·1**
PORT ..	**33,702**	**+ 82·7**	**− 31·4**	**− 9·7**	**+ 12·0**	**− 5·7**	**+ 69·3**	**+ 102·3**
CANALS ..	**1,905**	**+ 127·0**	**− 74·3**	**− 26·6**	**+ 111·6**	**− 30·1**	**+ 70·8**	**+ 8·2**
Suburbs in 24-Parganas ..	**63,975**	**+16·3**	**+10·0**	**+27·5**	**−14·8**	**+17·4**	..	..
Tollygunge ..	24,476	+ 13·1	+ 17·4	+ 43·8	− 14·8	+ 17·4	..	..
South Suburban Municipality ..	39,499	+ 18·4	+ 5·7	+ 19·6	− 14·8	+ 17·4	..	..
HOWRAH ..	**224,873**	**+15·2**	**+9·1**	**+13·6**	**+35·2**	**+28·4**	**+8·0**	**+167·5**

SUBSIDIARY TABLE II.—The number of persons per acre with percentage of variation in density by wards, 1872 to 1931.

Wards, etc.	Density of population. 1931	1921	1911	1901	1891	1881	1872	Variation of density, increase +, decrease −. 1921-31	1911-21	1901-11	1891-1901.	1881-91	1872-81	1872-1931.
1	2	3	4	5	6	7	8	9	10	11	12	13	14	15
CALCUTTA WITH SUBURBS AND HOWRAH.	**32**	**28**	**27**	**25**	**20**	**18**	..	**+14·3**	**+3·7**	**+8·0**	**+25·0**	**+11·1**	..	..
CALCUTTA WITH SUBURBS IN 24-PARGANAS.	**31**	**28**	**27**	**25**	**20**	**18**	..	**+10·7**	**+3·7**	**+8·0**	**+25·0**	**+11·1**	..	..
Calcutta	**42**	**38**	**36**	**33**	**27**	**24**	**25**	**+10·5**	**+5·5**	**+9·1**	**+22·2**	**+ 12·5**	**− 4·0**	**+ 68·0**
MUNICIPAL AREA ..	**58**	**52**	**50**	**45**	**37**	**33**	**35**	**+ 11·5**	**+ 4·0**	**+11·1**	**+ 21·6**	**+ 12·1**	**− 5·7**	**+ 65·7**
Ward No. 1 Shampukur ..	163	139	130	115	90	70	71	+ 17·3	+ 6·9	+13·0	+ 27·8	+ 28·6	− 1·4	+ 129·6
Ward No. 2 Kumartuli ..	176	157	152	139	123	118	157	+ 12·1	+ 3·3	+ 9·4	+ 13·0	+ 4·2	− 24·8	+ 12·1
Ward No. 3 Bartola ..	167	152	136	125	90	72	74	+ 9·9	+11·8	+ 8·8	+ 38·9	+ 25·0	− 2·7	+ 125·7
Ward No. 4 Sukea's Street ..	169	173	150	131	109	76	78	− 2·3	+15·3	+14·5	+ 20·2	+ 43·4	− 2·6	+ 116·7
Ward No. 5 Jorabagan ..	162	216	214	202	161	149	161	− 25·0	+ 0·9	+ 6·0	+ 25·5	+ 8·1	− 6·8	+ 0·6
Ward No. 6 Jorasanko ..	176	219	227	202	159	125	138	− 29·6	− 3·5	+12·4	+ 27·0	+ 27·2	− 9·4	+ 27·5
Ward No. 30 Belgachia ..	40													
Ward No. 31 Satpukur ..	26	27	23	20	15	13	12	+ 22·2	+17·4	+15·0	+ 33·3	+ 15·4	+ 8·3	+ 175·0
Ward No. 32 Cossipore ..	35													
Ward No. 7 Burra Bazar ..	86	152	141	146	95	96	108	− 43·4	+ 7·8	− 3·4	+ 53·7	− 1·0	− 11·1	− 20·4
Ward No. 8 Kalootola ..	219	172	255	282	227	211	227	+ 27·3	−32·5	− 9·6	+ 24·2	+ 7·6	− 7·0	− 3·5
Ward No. 9 Muchipara ..	175	151	138	139	108	95	95	+ 15·9	+ 9·4	− 0·7	+ 28·7	+ 13·7	0	+ 84·2
Ward No. 10 Bow Bazar ..	143	184	170	184	154	147	160	− 22·3	+ 8·2	− 7·6	+ 19·5	+ 4·8	− 8·1	− 10·6
Ward No. 11 Paddapukur ..	213	197	181	169	125	124	123	+ 8·1	+ 8·8	+ 7·1	+ 35·2	+ 0·8	+ 0·8	+ 73·2
Ward No. 12 Waterloo Street ..	32	34	30	30	28	27	27	− 5·9	+13·3	0	+ 7·1	+ 3·7	0	+ 18·5
Ward No. 28 Beliaghata ..	40	31	25	15	13	22	25	+ 12·9	+24·0	+66·7	+ 15·4	− 40·9	− 12·0	+ 40·0
Ward No. 29 Maniktala ..	32													
Ward No. 13 Fenwick Bazar ..	161	136	148	163	148	135	140	+ 18·4	− 8·1	− 9·2	+ 10·1	+ 9·6	− 3·6	+ 15·0
Ward No. 14 Taltola ..	194	160	162	163	148	132	137	+ 21·2	− 1·2	− 0·6	+ 10·1	+ 12·1	− 3·6	+ 41·6
Ward No. 15 Kalinga ..	79	66	64	94	74	66	71	+ 19·7	+ 3·1	−31·9	+ 27·0	+ 12·1	− 7·0	+ 11·3
Ward No. 16 Park Street ..	36	25	35	40	30	32	30	+ 44·0	−28·6	−12·5	+ 33·3	− 6·3	+ 6·7	+ 20·0
Ward No. 17 Baman Bustee ..	21	25	24	43	36	48	51	− 16·0	+ 4·2	−44·2	+ 19·4	− 25·0	− 5·9	− 58·8
Ward No. 18 Tengra ..	12													
Ward No. 19 Intally ..	81													
Ward No. 20 Beniapukur ..	91	32	29	23	19	16	17	+ 26·0	+10·3	+26·1	+ 21·1	+ 18·7	− 5·9	+ 135·3
Ward No. 21 Ballygunge ..	37													
Ward No. 27 Tollygunge ..	29													
Ward No. 22 Bhawanipur ..	98	70	67	61	52	47	45	+ 40·0	+ 4·5	+ 9·8	+ 17·3	+ 10·6	+ 4·4	+ 11·8
Ward No. 23 Alipore ..	24	18	16	14	12	11	16	+ 33·3	+12·5	+14·3	+ 16·7	+ 9·1	− 31·2	+ 50·0
Ward No. 24 Ekbalpore ..	36	31	24	23	17	17	20	+ 5·9	+41·7	+ 4·3	+ 35·3	0	− 15·0	+ 80·0
Ward No. 25 Watganj and Hastings ..	39	46	59	52	28	39	34	− 15·2	−22·0	+13·5	+ 36·8	− 2·5	+ 14·7	+ 14·7
Ward No. 26 Garden Reach ..	15	17	21	13	13	6	4	− 11·8	−19·0	+61·5	0	+ 116·7	+ 50·0	+ 275·0
FORT WILLIAM AND MAIDAN ..	**2**	**2**	**3**	**3**	**3**	**3**	**2**	**0**	**−33·3**	**0**	**0**	**0**	**+ 50·0**	**0**
PORT ..	**5**	**3**	**4**	**4**	**4**	**4**	**2**	**+ 66·7**	**−25·0**	**0**	**0**	**0**	**+ 100·0**	**+ 150·0**
CANALS ..	**7**	**3**	**12**	**16**	**8**	**11**	**7**	**+ 133·3**	**−75·0**	**−25·0**	**+100·0**	**− 27·3**	**+ 57·1**	**0**
Suburbs in 24-Parganas	**6**	**5**	**4**	**3**	**4**	**3**	..	**+20·0**	**+25·0**	**+33·3**	**−25·0**	**+33·3**	..	..
Tollygunge	6	5	4	3	4	3	..	+ 20·0	+25·0	+33·3	− 25·0	+ 33·3	..	..
South Suburban Municipality ..	5	4	4	3	4	3	..	+ 25·0	0	[illegible]	[illegible]	[illegible]	..	..
HOWRAH ..	**35**	**30**	**28**	**24**	**18**	**14**	**13**	**+16·7**	**+7·1**	**+16·7**	**+33·3**	**+28·6**	**+7·7**	**+169·2**

SUBSIDIARY TABLE III.—The average number of persons per house and houses per acre by wards, 1881-1931.

Wards, etc.	Average number of persons per house.						Average number of houses per acre.					
	1931	1921	1911	1901	1891	1881	1931	1921	1911	1901	1891	1881
1	2	3	4	5	6	7	8	9	10	11	12	13
CALCUTTA WITH SUBURBS AND HOWRAH ..	**5**	**5**	..	..	..	..	**6**	**6**	..	..	..	..
CALCUTTA WITH SUBURBS IN 24-PARGANAS	**6**	**5**	..	..	..	..	**6**	**6**	..	..	..	..
Calcutta ..	**6**	**5**	**17**	..	..	..	**7**	**8**	**2**	..	..	..
MUNICIPAL AREA ..	**6**	**5**	**17**	..	..	..	**10**	**11**	**3**	..	..	..
Ward No. 1 Shampukur ..	7	6	18	6	9	8	24	24	7	34	11	11
Ward No. 2 Kumartuli ..	6	6	18	6	10	10	28	25	9	25	13	15
Ward No. 3 Bartola ..	6	7	19	7	8	8	28	21	7	32	11	11
Ward No. 4 Sukea's Street ..	8	6	22	6	10	8	21	30	7	44	12	11
Ward No. 5 Jorabagan ..	8	6	27	8	14	13	20	39	8	27	12	12
Ward No. 6 Jorasanko ..	4	8	21	7	13	10	33	28	11	30	14	14
Ward No. 30 Belgachia ..	6						7					
Ward No. 31 Satpukur ..	4	3	8	7	6	3	6	8	3	3	2	3
Ward No. 32 Cossipore ..	5						6					
Ward No. 7 Burra Bazar ..	3	7	24	10	10	12	30	21	6	31	12	13
Ward No. 8 Kalootola ..	5	5	34	7	17	17	45	32	8	44	16	14
Ward No. 9 Muchipara ..	8	5	19	7	11	12	23	33	7	43	10	15
Ward No. 10 Bow Bazar ..	6	5	20	9	15	15	25	37	8	25	11	12
Ward No. 11 Paddapukur ..	7	5	18	7	9	11	32	41	10	25	16	12
Ward No. 12 Waterloo Street ..	7	12	17	8	12	16	4	3	2	5	2	2
Ward No. 28 Beliaghata ..	6	4	9	5	6	..	7	8	3	3	2	..
Ward No. 29 Maniktala ..	4						9					
Ward No. 13 Fenwick Bazar ..	5	4	21	5	16	14	33	31	7	28	10	11
Ward No. 14 Taltola ..	6	4	22	6	12	13	32	37	7	31	13	11
Ward No. 15 Kalinga ..	4	3	20	5	10	12	21	19	3	17	8	6
Ward No. 16 Park Street ..	4	21	26	7	19	21	9	1	1	6	2	1
Ward No. 17 Baman Bustee ..	6	13	20	10	8	16	4	2	1	4	3	2
Ward No. 18 Tengra ..	5						2					
Ward No. 19 Intally ..	4						19					
Ward No. 20 Beniapukur ..	5	4	23	..	..	..	20	7	1	..	..	..
Ward No. 21 Ballygunge ..	6						6					
Ward No. 27 Tollygunge ..	6						5					
Ward No. 22 Bhawanipur ..	8	6	15	5	7	7	12	11	4	13	8	5
Ward No. 23 Alipore ..	7	5	26	5	6	7	4	3	1	3	2	2
Ward No. 24 Ekbalpore ..	6	4	41	4	6	..	6	9	1	6	3	..
Ward No. 25 Watganj and Hastings ..	7	4	33	..	..	..	6	11	2	..	..	..
Ward No. 26 Garden Reach ..	5	3	9	4	..	..	3	5	2	3	..	..
FORT WILLIAM AND MAIDAN ..	**5**	**27**	**7**	**7**	..	..	..	..	..	..	..	..
PORT ..	**5**	**9**	**8**	**8**	..	..	**1**	..	..	..	..	..
CANALS ..	**5**	**4**	**5**	**5**	..	..	**1**	..	..	..	..	..
Suburbs in 24-Parganas ..	**5**	**6**	..	..	..	..	**1**	**1**	..	..	..	..
Tollygunge ..	5	5	..	..	..	..	1	1	..	..	..	..
South Suburban Municipality ..	5	6	..	..	..	..	1	1	..	..	..	..
HOWRAH ..	**4**	**4**	..	..	..	..	**9**	**4**	..	..	..	..

SUBSIDIARY TABLE IV.—Extent of regular daily passenger traffic by rail between Calcutta and outlying stations (February 1931).

(Compiled from data furnished by courtesy of the railway companies.)

Stations between which tickets were issued and Railway.		Details of season tickets issued and in use on the 26th February 1931.					
		First and Second class tickets.			Intermediate and third class, vendors' and workmen's tickets.		
		From and to Calcutta.	From Calcutta.	To Calcutta.	From and to Calcutta.	From Calcutta.	To Calcutta.
1		2	3	4	5	6	7
Both Calcutta Stations and All outlying Stations.		**854**	**222½**	**631½**	**25,316**	**5,742**	**19,574**
Sealdah and all Stations.	..	**535**	**160½**	**374½**	**12,890**	**2,414½**	**10,475½**
Agarpara	E. B. ..	9	3	6	324	37	287
Akra	E. B. ..	..	..	..	99	12	87
Aranghata	E. B. ..	..	..	..	3	..	3
Badkulla	E. B. ..	..	..	..	1	..	1
Baharu	E. B. ..	..	..	..	25	1	24
Ballyganj	E. B. ..	49	12	37	974½	251½	723
Bamangachi	E. B. ..	..	..	..	154½	14	140½
Baraset	E. B. ..	3	..	3	352½	56	296½
Barrackpore	E. B. ..	62	16½	45½	457	80½	376½
Baruipur	E. B. ..	3	..	3	111	12	99
Baruipur Junction	E. B. ..	..	..	..	285	53	232
Basuldanga	E. B. ..	..	..	..	23	14	9
Belghurriah	E. B. ..	17	4	13	548½	65	483½
Birati	E. B. ..	..	..	..	94	12	82
Birnagar	E. B. ..	..	..	..	11	..	11
Bogoola	E. B. ..	..	..	..	2	..	2
Bongaon	E. B. ..	..	..	..	8	..	8
Bongaon Junction	E. B. ..	..	..	..	31	17	14
Brace Bridge	E. B. ..	1	1	..	106	70	36
Budge-Budge	E. B. ..	6	..	6	131½	34½	97
Canning	E. B. ..	2	1	1	147	2	145
Chakdaha	E. B. ..	..	..	..	3	..	3
Chakdalia	E. B. ..	..	..	..	24	5	19
Champahati	E. B. ..	1	..	1	185	31	154
Chandpara	E. B. ..	..	..	..	3	..	3
Changripota	E. B. ..	1	..	1	246	18	228
Dakshin Baraset	E. B. ..	..	..	..	37	1	36
Deula	E. B. ..	..	..	..	22	9	13
Dhakuria	E. B. ..	37	8	29	828½	224½	604
Dhamuah	E. B. ..	..	..	..	54	10	44
Dhap Dhapi	E. B. ..	..	..	..	18	2	16
Diamond Harbour	E. B. ..	..	..	..	35½	12½	23
Dogachhea	E. B. ..	..	..	..	74	2	72
Dum-Dum Cantt.	E. B. ..	94½	23	71½	673½	268	405½
Dum-Dum Junc.	E. B. ..	42	16	26	794	214½	579½
Duttapukur	E. B. ..	..	..	..	223	15	208
Fulia	E. B. ..	..	..	..	1	..	1
Garia	E. B. ..	4	1	3	217	27	190
Ghutiyari Sharif	E. B. ..	..	..	..	21	..	21
Gobardanga	E. B. ..	..	..	..	61	15	46
Gocharan	E. B. ..	..	..	..	25	..	25
Guma	E. B. ..	..	..	..	79	11	68
Habibpur	E. B. ..	..	..	..	2	..	2
Habra	E. B. ..	..	..	..	42	9	33
Halishahar	E. B. ..	..	..	..	51	5	46
Hotar	E. B. ..	..	..	..	26	15	11
Hridaipur	E. B. ..	..	..	..	119½	1	118½
Ichhapur	E. B. ..	14	7	7	248½	68½	180
Jadabpur	E. B. ..	72	36	36	649	156	493
Jaynagar-Majilpur	E. B. ..	1	..	1	80½	..	80½
Kalighat	E. B. ..	3	1	2	132½	28	104½
Kalikapur	E. B. ..	1	..	1	126	8	118
Kalyanpur	E. B. ..	..	..	..	26	7	19
Kanchrapara	E. B. ..	14	1	13	136	20	116
Kankinara	E. B. ..	13	6	7	413	54	359
Khardaha	E. B. ..	6	1	5	235½	24	211½
Krishnagar City	E. B. ..	1	..	1	20	3	17
Lakshmikantapur	E. B. ..	1	..	1	11	1	10
Madanpur	E. B. ..	..	..	..	13	..	13
Madhyamgram	E. B. ..	..	..	..	160	13	147
Magra Hat	E. B. ..	2	2	..	45	8	37
Majerhat	E. B. ..	..	..	..	33	10	23
Mallikpur	E. B. ..	..	..	..	279	30	249
Mastandapur	E. B. ..	..	..	..	9	3	6
Mathurapur Road	E. B. ..	..	..	..	23	..	23
Naihati	E. B. ..	25	9	16	481	83	398
Nangi	E. B. ..	..	..	..	36	7	29
Netra	E. B. ..	..	..	..	62	9	53
Palta	E. B. ..	1	..	1	20½	2	18½
Piali	E. B. ..	..	..	..	4	1	3
Ranaghat	E. B. ..	2	..	2	165½	27	138½
Sangrampur	E. B. ..	..	..	..	594	73	521
Santipur	E. B. ..	..	..	..	14	9	5
Santoshpur	E. B. ..	..	..	..	87	6	81
Shamnagar	E. B. ..	19	8	11	206	24	182
Shimurali	E. B. ..	..	..	..	28	5	23
Sodepur	E. B. ..	7½	2	5½	297	28	269
Sonarpur	E. B. ..	6	2	4	67	10	57
Sonarpur Junc.	E. B. ..	..	..	..	3	2	1
Surjapur	E. B. ..	..	..	..	3	1	2
Taldi	E. B. ..	..	..	..	57	..	57
Tittaghur	E. B. ..	..	..	..	157½	35	122½
Ultadanga Road	E. B. ..	15	..	15	214	32	182
Howrah and all Stations.	..	**319**	**62**	**257**	**12,426**	**3,327½**	**9,098½**
Abada	B. N. ..	..	..	..	64	2	62
Amta	H. A. ..	..	..	..	7	4	3
Andul	B. N. ..	25	4	21	746½	98	648½
Asansol	E. I. ..	..	..	..	4	4	..
Autpur	H. A. ..	..	..	..	3	3	..
Bagnan	B. N. ..	..	..	..	500	193	307
Bagnapara	E. I. ..	..	..	..	5	1	4
Bahirkhand	E. I. ..	..	..	..	16	2	14
Baidyabati	E. I. ..	9	5	4	191	24	167
Bally	E. I. ..	29	2	27	660½	52½	608
Baltikari	H. A. ..	..	..	..	32	31	1
Baluhati	H. S. ..	..	..	..	87	77	10
Bandel Junc.	E. I. ..	..	..	..	40	40	..
Bankra	H. A. ..	..	..	..	21	20	1
Bansabati	E. I. ..	3	1	2	40	6	34
Bauria Junc.	B. N. ..	..	..	..	92	44	48
Bazar Sohu	E. I. ..	..	..	..	5	..	5
Begumpur	E. I. ..	..	..	..	53	53	..
Belmuri	E. I. ..	..	..	..	15½	15½	..
Belur	E. I. ..	26	16	10	748	233	515
Bhadreswar	E. I. ..	5	4	1	91½	8½	83
Bhedia	E. I. ..	..	..	..	1	1	..
Bhogpur	B. N. ..	..	..	..	20	5	15
Bir-Shibpur	B. N. ..	..	..	..	22	..	22
Boinchee	E. I. ..	..	..	..	6	6	..
Bolpur	E. I. ..	..	..	..	7	7	..
Boragachi	H. A. ..	..	..	..	43	33	10
Burdwan Junc.	E. I. ..	..	..	..	38	13	25
Champadanga	H. A. ..	..	..	..	18	18	..
Chandanpur	E. I. ..	..	..	..	7	7	..
Chandernagore	E. I. ..	2	2	..	63	63	..
Chanditala	H. S. ..	..	..	..	13	12	1
Chengail	B. N. ..	3	..	3	55	11	44
Chinsurah	E. I. ..	2	2	..	40	40	..
Dakhinbari	H. A. ..	..	..	..	5	4	1
Dankuni	E. I. ..	6	..	6	348½	69½	279
Dearah	E. I. ..	..	..	..	4	4	..
Debipur	E. I. ..	..	..	..	5	2	3
Deulti	B. N. ..	..	..	..	262	40	222
Dumjur	H. A. ..	..	..	..	226	190	36
Echanuggurree	H. A. ..	..	..	..	4	4	..
Ekshara	H. S. ..	..	..	..	97	91	6
Fuleswar	B. N. ..	1	..	1	63½	14	49½
Galsi	E. I. ..	..	..	..	1	1	..
Garifa	E. I. ..	..	..	..	18	4	14
Guptipara	E. I. ..	..	..	..	23	4	19
Gurup	E. I. ..	..	..	..	40	4	36
Gushkara	E. I. ..	..	..	..	7	7	..
Haripal	E. I. ..	..	..	..	104	19	85
Harish-dadpur	H. A. ..	..	..	..	7	7	..
Haur	B. N. ..	..	..	..	34	8	26
Hooghly	E. I. ..	2	1	1	11	..	11
Hooghly Ghat	E. I. ..	..	..	..	18	18	..
Jagatballavpur	H. A. ..	..	..	..	7	5	2
Jalalsi	H. A. ..	..	..	..	27	18	9
Jangalpara	H. S. ..	..	..	..	26	22	4
Jangipara	H. A. ..	..	..	..	16	15	1
Jaugram	E. I. ..	..	..	..	21	6	15
Jirat	E. I. ..	1	..	1	15	1	14
Jonai	H. S. ..	..	..	..	3	..	3
Kadamtala	H. A. ..	..	..	..	40	36	4
Kaikala	E. I. ..	..	..	..	27	3	24
Kalachara	H. S. ..	..	..	..	42	30	12
Kalipur	H. S. ..	..	..	..	3	3	..
Kalna Court	E. I. ..	..	..	..	20	6	14
Kamarkunda	E. I. ..	..	..	..	86	86	..
Katwa Junc.	E. I. ..	..	..	..	2	1	1
Khamargachi	E. I. ..	..	..	..	20	1	19
Khanyan	E. I. ..	..	..	..	11	11	..
Kolaghat	B. N. ..	..	..	..	96½	24	72½
Kona	H. S. ..	..	..	..	36	31	5
Konnagar	E. I. ..	4	..	4	496½	32½	464
Kristorampur	H. S. ..	..	..	..	14	11	3
Kulgachia	B. N. ..	..	..	..	53	12	41
Lillooah	E. I. ..	9	9	..	45	45	..
Machada	B. N. ..	..	..	..	67	17	50
Magra	E. I. ..	..	..	..	132	27	105
Maju	H. A. ..	..	..	..	31	19	12
Mankardah	H. A. ..	..	..	..	245	207	38
Mankundu	E. I. ..	6	..	6	331	12	319
Memari	E. I. ..	..	..	..	48	23	25
Monirampur	E. I. ..	..	..	..	34	32	2
Mosagram	E. I. ..	..	..	..	13	5	8
Moshat	H. S. ..	..	..	..	57	53	4
Mourigram	B. N. ..	14	..	14	401½	42	359½
Munsirhat	H. A. ..	..	..	..	34	29	5
Nabadwip	E. I. ..	..	..	..	6	3	3
Nabagram	E. I. ..	..	..	..	11	..	11
Naihati Junc.	E. I. ..	..	..	..	4	4	..
Nalikul	E. I. ..	..	..	..	114	9	105
Nalpur	B. N. ..	4	..	4	45½	5	40½
Nasibpur	E. I. ..	..	..	..	31	3	28
Palla Road	E. I. ..	..	..	..	2	..	2
Panchkura	B. N. ..	..	..	..	47	5	42
Panpur	H. A. ..	..	..	..	7	6	1
Pantihal	H. A. ..	..	..	..	33	27	6
Patuli	E. I. ..	..	..	..	2	..	2
Prosadpur	H. A. ..	..	..	..	9	7	2
Pundooah	E. I. ..	..	..	..	14	14	..
Pyasara	H. A. ..	..	..	..	6	6	..
Ramrajatola	B. N. ..	27	2	25	535	59	476
Raniganj	E. I. ..	..	..	..	7	7	..
Rasulpur	E. I. ..	..	..	..	4	..	4
Rishra	E. I. ..	6	1	5	322	32	290
Sainthia	E. I. ..	..	..	..	1	1	..
Saktigarh	E. I. ..	..	..	..	1	1	..
Samudragram	E. I. ..	..	..	..	3	..	3
Sankrail	B. N. ..	..	..	..	312	31	281
Santragachi	B. N. ..	4	..	4	181½	31	150
Serampore	E. I. ..	65	5	60	1,241	86	1,155
Shalap	H. A. ..	..	..	..	126	123	3
Sheakhala	H. S. ..	..	..	..	52	39	13
Sheoraphuli Jn.	E. I. ..	3	..	3	447½	67½	380
Simlagarh	E. I. ..	..	..	..	19	4	15
Singhur	E. I. ..	1	1	..	10	10	..
Sitapurhat	H. A. ..	..	..	..	7	5	2
Somra Bazar	E. I. ..	..	..	..	2	2	..
Talandoo	E. I. ..	..	..	..	3	3	..
Talit	E. I. ..	..	..	..	21	20	1
Tarakeswar	E. I. ..	..	..	..	82	19	63
Tribeni	E. I. ..	..	..	..	2	2	..
Trishbigha	E. I. ..	..	..	..	1	1	..
Uluberia	B. N. ..	1	..	1	142½	44	98½
Uttarbantra	H. S. ..	..	..	..	2	2	..
Uttarpara	E. I. ..	61	7	54	1,036½	165½	871

Abbreviations used in column 1.—*B. N.*—Bengal Nagpur Railway: *E. B.*—Eastern Bengal Railway: *E. I.*—East Indian Railway: *H. A.*—Howrah-Amta Railway: *H. S.*—Howrah Sheakhala Railway.

CHAPTER II

Birth-place

12. **The statistics shown.**—The figures for birth-place dealt with in this chapter are contained in imperial table VI. These figures are supplemented by subsidiary tables printed at the end of this chapter and showing—

I—the numbers per 1,000 born in Bengal, in other parts of India and outside India at each census since 1901 ;

II—the numbers per 1,000 born in Bengal, in India outside Bengal and outside India by wards ; and

III—the number per 1,000 of the total population formed by immigrants born in those parts of India outside Bengal which contribute the largest numbers to the population, together with the sex ratio of such immigrants.

13. **Source of the statistics.**—The statistics were obtained from the entries made in column 13 of the general schedule. This provided for the entry of district of birth but in extracting the statistics figures were obtained only for the province or country of origin. It is, therefore, not possible on the present occasion to analyse the population of Calcutta and Howrah in order to show the contribution made by the districts of Bengal or other provinces and the treatment of the figures is therefore more summary than on previous occasions.

14. **General figures of birth-place.**—In the aggregate population of Calcutta with its suburbs in 24-Parganas and Howrah city out of a total of 1,485,582, 1,466,877 were born in India of whom 998,656 were born in Bengal. The proportionate distribution of the population is illustrated by diagram No. II-1 plotted from subsidiary table I. Somewhat surprisingly persons

DIAGRAM No. II-1.

Distribution of the total population, Calcutta with suburbs in 24-Parganas, Calcutta, Howrah and suburbs in 24-Parganas, by birth-place (born in Bengal, in India outside Bengal and outside India).

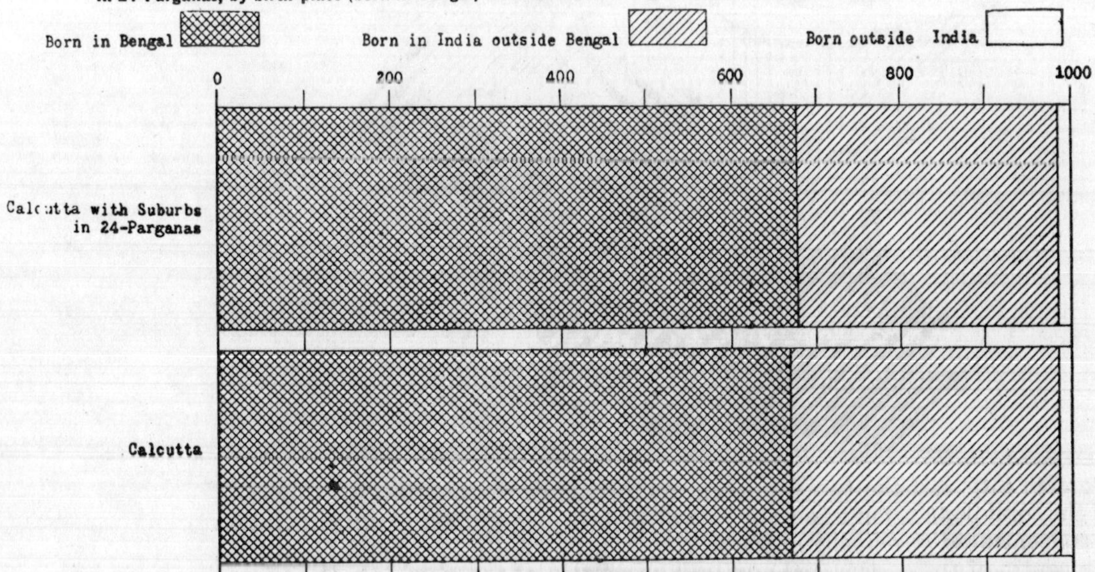

born in Bengal form a smaller proportion of the population in Howrah city than in either Calcutta proper or Calcutta with its suburbs in 24-Parganas.

In every 1,000 of the total population 644 in Howrah, 668 in Calcutta proper and 677 in Calcutta with the suburbs in 24-Parganas were born in Bengal. Those born outside India numbered in each 1,000 of the population only 7 in Howrah and 14 in Calcutta, whether the city proper be taken into consideration or also combined with it the area of its suburbs in the 24-Parganas. The immigrant population from other parts of India is in each 1,000 of the total population 349 in Howrah city, 318 in Calcutta proper and 309 in Calcutta with its suburbs. In the suburbs themselves as many as 850 in every 1,000 were born in Bengal. Calcutta with its suburbs offers greater facilities for permanent settlement than Howrah and this no doubt accounts for the larger proportion of foreign born in Howrah. In the suburbs in the 24-Parganas the higher proportion of persons born in Bengal is naturally due to the fact that in proportion to their distance from the trading centres they attract fewer immigrants who do not intend to settle down permanently and whose families consequently are more frequently born elsewhere than in Bengal.

15. **Distribution by birth-place in wards of the city.**—The proportionate distribution by birth-place shown in subsidiary table II is illustrated in the map forming diagram No. II-2. This shows in each ward of Calcutta and in

DIAGRAM No. II-2.

Number of persons per 1,000 born in Bengal to the total population, 1931.

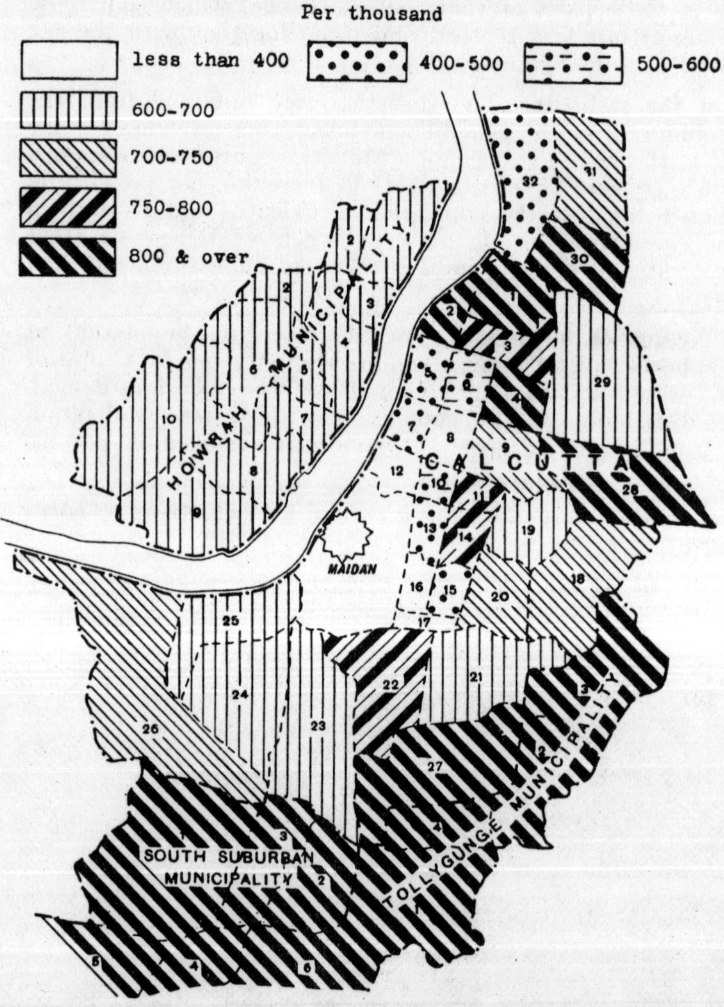

Howrah city and the two suburban municipalities the number per thousand of the total population who were born in Bengal. The foreign-born population is concentrated principally in wards 5, 6, 7, 8, 10, 12, 13, 15, 16 and 17 forming the centre of the commercial and trading portion of the city. On the fringes of the city and particularly in the suburban municipalities their proportion is relatively small but at the extreme north in the Cossipore ward they number as many as 563 in every 1,000 of the total population. Of the areas recently added to Calcutta and comprising the three old municipalities of Cossipore-Chitpore, Maniktala and Garden Reach immigrants form a comparatively small proportion of the total population in the last two in no case exceeding 33 per cent. In Kumartuli, Shampukur, Belgachia and Sukeas' Street as well as in Beliaghata and Tollygunge their proportions are even less than 20 per cent. In every 1,000 of the population Fort William and Maidan with 454, Park Street with 286 and Baman Bustee the neighbouring ward with 179 have the largest proportion of persons born outside India. Even in the suburban areas of South Calcutta the proportion of residents born outside India is comparatively small in spite of the popularity of the suburbs as a residence for Europeans.

16. **Numbers contributed by other parts of India.**—Amongst other parts of India, the province of Bihar and Orissa contributes the largest proportion of immigrants to Calcutta with suburbs in the 24-Parganas (231,151) followed by the United Provinces (104,401). As many as 10 thousand inhabitants are contributed only by two other regions in India, the Rajputana Agency (14,938) and the Punjab (12,494). In Howrah city the two principal provinces contributing immigrants are the same as in Calcutta but their order is reversed. The United Provinces contributes 38,944 and Bihar and Orissa 33,181. Madras with 2,661 and the Rajputana Agency with 1,335 follow and are the only other parts of India which contribute as many as 1,000 to the population of Howrah city. Assam, Bombay and Madras all contribute between 4,500 and 5,500 to Calcutta with its suburbs in the 24-Parganas; and to Howrah city the Punjab and the Central Provinces and Berar contribute almost 800 immigrants, a proportion similar to that of Assam and other provinces mentioned in the case of Calcutta itself. Economy prevented the extraction of details showing the principal occupation of immigrants such as were presented on the last occasion but the occupational bias of immigrants has probably changed very little. Immigrants from Orissa are still probably in the majority of cases day-labourers and domestic servants, those from Bihar day-labourers and those from the Punjab mechanics and motor-drivers. The immigrants from Rajputana are mainly traders and their employees. Madras supplies both labourers and domestic servants.

17. **Sex proportions of immigrants.**—The sex proportions amongst immigrants vary very considerably. The number of females to males is

DIAGRAM No. II-3.

Number of females per 1,000 males according to birth-place, Calcutta and Howrah.

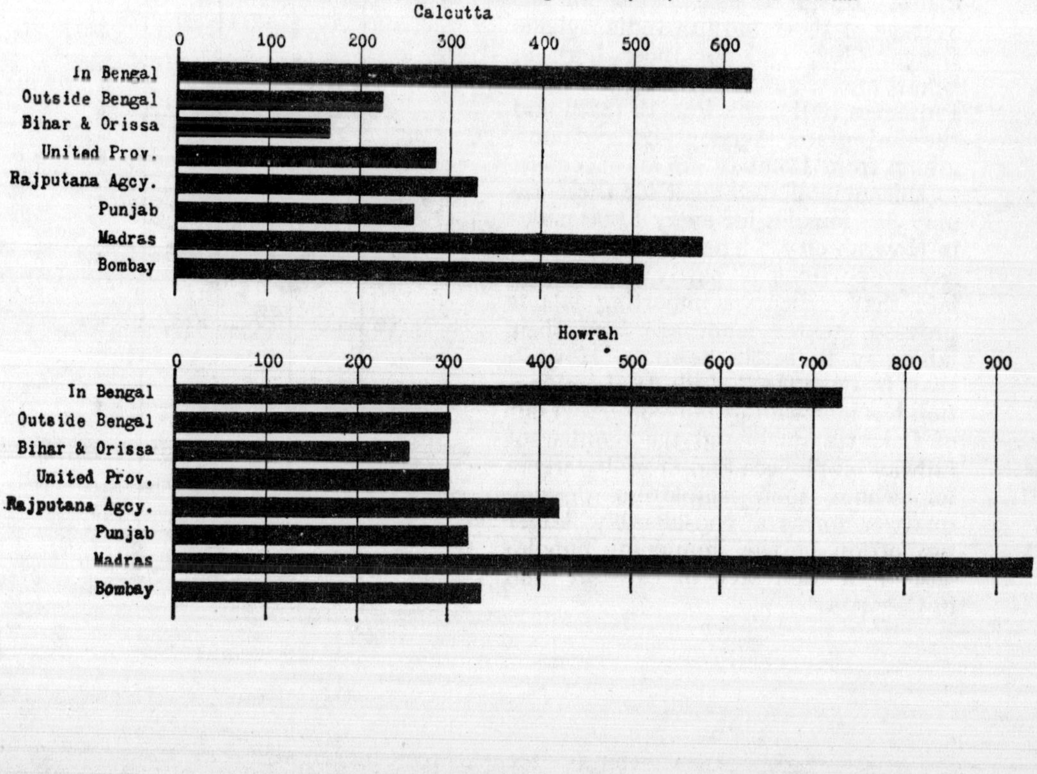

highest amongst the immigrants from the Central India Agency amongst whom females outnumber males by more than 2 to 1; and there are rather more females than males amongst the immigrants to Calcutta from the Central Provinces States. In both these instances, however, the actual numbers are relatively small. In Howrah similarly the highest proportion of females to males is found amongst those whose birth-place was not stated specifically and those from Assam States and Kashmir but the total number of immigrants concerned in these cases is only 18, 5 and 7 respectively. On the average the number of females in every 1,000 males amongst the total immigrant population is only 224 in Calcutta with its suburbs in 24-Parganas and 302 in Howrah city and in Calcutta with its suburbs there are actually more females to every 1,000 males amongst those born outside India than amongst those born in other parts of India. Diagram No. II-3 illustrates some of the figures given in columns 6 and 16 of subsidiary table III. The number of females per 1,000 males in the whole of Bengal is 924 and the rural areas is 955. In Calcutta itself amongst those born in Bengal there are 630 females in every 1,000 males but this figure is approached amongst those provinces which supply any considerable number of males only in the case of Madras and Bombay. From Madras there are 579 female immigrants for every 1,000 males and from Bombay there are 512. The immigrant from Orissa in general leaves his women-folk behind and this contributes to the very small proportion of females to males, viz., 168 to every 1,000 amongst the immigrants to Calcutta from Bihar and Orissa. A rather larger proportion of females comes with the male immigrants from the Punjab (260), the United Provinces (284) and the Rajputana Agency (331). In Howrah the proportion of females to males in the total population is 488 per 1,000. Those born in Bengal show proportions (731 per 1,000 considerably in excess of those in similar conditions in Calcutta and in general for each of the areas illustrated in diagram No. IV-3 the proportion of females to males is higher. It is most markedly higher in the case of immigrants from Madras amongst whom there are 940 females in every 1,000 males. But it is also higher for the average of those born in India outside Bengal (302) and for those born in Bihar and Orissa (257), the United Provinces (301), the Punjab (322) and the Rajputana Agency (422). Immigrants from Bombay are an exception to this general statement for there are only 337 females for every 1,000 males in Howrah city. The difference in the sex proportions is partly due to the fact that industries importing labour provide greater facilities for their labourers to settle down in Howrah than in Calcutta. Industrial production has increasingly moved further out of Calcutta itself and the number of railway employees and of mill workers for whom their employers provide quarters forms a considerably larger proportion of the immigrant population from each area in Howrah than in Calcutta.

DIAGRAM No. II-4.

Proportion of total population in Calcutta and Howrah who were born outside Bengal, in other parts of India and outside India, 1901-1931.

NOTE.—The scale shows units for those born outside India and hundreds for others.

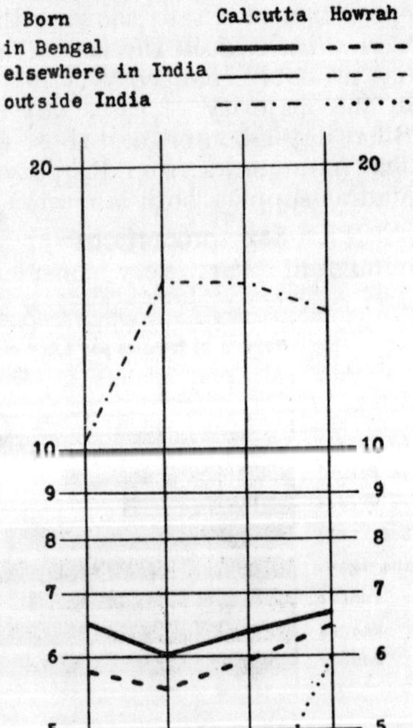

18. **Variations in proportions of immigrants from census to census.**—Diagram No. IV-4 illustrates the figures given in subsidiary table No. I for the proportion of immigrants at successive census years. The diagram illustrates the proportion of persons born in Bengal, in other parts of India and outside India both in Calcutta and Howrah at each census since and including 1901. Between 1901 and 1911 the number of immigrants increased in both cities at the expense of those born in Bengal with the exception of persons in Howrah born outside India. Since then the proportion of native born inhabitants has consistently increased in both cities and there has been a corresponding decline in the numbers born outside Bengal whether in or outside India with the exception of persons born outside India and enumerated in Howrah city. Between 1911 and 1931 their numbers increased from 3 first to 4 and then to 7 per 1,000. Some part of the decrease in the numbers returned as immigrants is due to permanent settlement by previous immigrants from other places in India and a comparison of subsidiary table I with imperial table XV illustrates this. In Calcutta there are over 150 thousand persons returned as having been born in Bengal more than those who speak Bengali as their mother tongue. In Howrah also more than 23,600 persons less speak Bengali as their mother tongue than the number returned as having been born in Bengal. The actual numbers of immigrants indeed have not declined during the last decade. There are now actually more than 66 thousand immigrants from other parts of India in Calcutta in excess of the number returned in 1921. In Howrah city on the other hand, there has been a decrease of less than 500 and here there was also a decrease in the decade 1911-1921. In this decade there was also a decrease in Calcutta but the figures of 1931 are almost 37 thousand in excess of those in 1911. Immigrants from outside India have in each case continuously increased their numbers since 1901. They numbered then something over 10 thousand in Calcutta and 682 in Howrah and their numbers are now almost 17 thousand in Calcutta and approaching 1,500 in Howrah. There are more immigrants from Europe in Calcutta than there were in 1921 but less in Howrah. In Calcutta immigrants from France are now fewer than they were in 1921 but those from Germany, Holland and Italy have increased and there has also been an increase in the number of persons born in Great Britain and Ireland. There has been a similar increase in immigrants from other Asiatic countries than India in Calcutta and there has also been an increase in immigrants from those countries in Howrah principally contributed by persons born in Nepal. Immigrants from Nepal have also almost doubled in numbers in Calcutta with suburbs.

SUBSIDIARY TABLE I.—Number and ratio (per 1,000 of the total population) of persons born in Bengal, in other parts of India and outside India, 1901 to 1931.

Area.	1901		1911		1921		1931	
	Number.	Per 1,000.	Number.	Per 1,000.	Number.	Per 1,000.	Number.	Per 1,000.
1	2	3	4	5	6	7	8	9
BORN IN BENGAL.								
CALCUTTA WITH SUBURBS IN 24-PARGANAS AND HOWRAH ..	**709,837**	**641**	**730,054**	**597**	**847,257**	**638**	**998,656**	**672**
CALCUTTA WITH SUBURBS IN 24-PARGANAS ..	**619,280**	**652**	**630,810**	**605**	**731,832**	**646**	**853,792**	**677**
Calcutta ..	548,685	648	539,374	602	579,564	639	799,408	668
Howrah ..	90,557	575	99,244	554	115,425	591	144,864	644
Suburbs in 24-Parganas ..	70,595	696	91,436	621	152,268	679	54,384	850
BORN IN OTHER PARTS OF INDIA.								
CALCUTTA WITH SUBURBS IN 24-PARGANAS AND HOWRAH ..	**385,875**	**349**	**478,192**	**391**	**464,756**	**350**	**468,221**	**315**
CALCUTTA WITH SUBURBS IN 24-PARGANAS ..	**319,520**	**337**	**399,017**	**382**	**385,733**	**341**	**389,657**	**309**
Calcutta ..	289,043	340	343,689	384	314,480	346	380,428	318
Howrah ..	66,355	421	79,175	442	79,023	405	78,564	349
Suburbs in 24-Parganas ..	30,477	301	55,328	376	71,253	318	9,229	144
BORN OUTSIDE INDIA.								
CALCUTTA WITH SUBURBS IN 24-PARGANAS AND HOWRAH ..	**11,026**	**10**	**14,067**	**12**	**15,534**	**12**	**18,705**	**13**
CALCUTTA WITH SUBURBS IN 24-PARGANAS ..	**10,344**	**11**	**13,480**	**13**	**14,681**	**13**	**17,260**	**14**
Calcutta ..	10,068	12	13,004	15	13,807	15	16,898	14
Howrah ..	682	4	587	3	853	4	1,445	7
Suburbs in 24-Parganas ..	276	3	476	3	874	4	362	6

SUBSIDIARY TABLE II.—Number and ratio (per thousand of the total population) of persons born in Bengal, in other parts of India and outside India, by wards, 1931.

Area.	Total population.	Born in Bengal.		Born outside Bengal.					
				All places.		In India.		Outside India.	
		No.	Per 1,000.	No.	Per 1,000.	No.	Per 1,000.	No.	Per 1,000.
1	2	3	4	5	6	7	8	9	10
CALCUTTA WITH SUBURBS AND HOWRAH ..	**1,485,582**	**998,656**	**672**	**486,926**	**328**	**468,221**	**315**	**18,705**	**13**
CALCUTTA WITH SUBURBS IN 24-PARGANAS ..	**1,260,709**	**853,792**	**677**	**406,917**	**323**	**389,657**	**309**	**17,260**	**14**
Calcutta ..	***1,196,734**	***799,408**	**668**	***397,326**	**332**	***380,428**	**318**	***16,898**	**14**
MUNICIPAL AREA ..	**1,155,133**	**786,373**	**682**	**368,760**	**318**	**356,416**	**307**	**12,344**	**11**
District No. I—									
Ward No. 1 Shampukur ..	66,632	56,571	849	10,061	151	9,980	150	81	1
Ward No. 2 Kumartuli ..	38,291	31,481	822	6,810	178	6,779	177	31	1
Ward No. 3 Bartola ..	67,100	52,801	787	14,299	213	14,157	211	142	2
Ward No. 4 Sukea's Street ..	54,096	44,070	815	10,026	185	9,991	184	35	1
Ward No. 5 Jorabagan ..	39,351	19,069	484	20,282	516	20,244	515	38	1
Ward No. 6 Jorasanko ..	46,097	24,589	533	21,508	467	21,490	467	18	..
Ward No. 30 Belgachia ..	22,237	18,534	833	3,703	167	3,621	163	82	4
Ward No. 31 Satpukur ..	19,163	14,006	731	5,157	269	4,861	253	296	16
Ward No. 32 Cossipore ..	27,201	11,899	437	15,302	563	15,224	560	78	3
District No. II—									
Ward No. 7 Burra Bazar ..	18,684	7,679	411	11,005	589	10,698	572	307	17
Ward No. 8 Kalootola ..	48,459	13,660	282	34,799	718	33,235	686	1,564	32
Ward No. 9 Muchipara ..	80,563	59,698	740	20,865	260	20,590	257	275	3
Ward No. 10 Bow Bazar ..	20,499	11,533	563	8,966	437	8,297	404	669	33
Ward No. 11 Puddapukur ..	35,283	27,004	765	8,279	235	8,094	230	185	5
Ward No. 12 Waterloo Street ..	6,338	1,751	276	4,587	724	4,175	659	412	65
Ward No. 28 Beliaghata ..	33,232	27,048	816	6,184	184	6,150	183	34	1
Ward No. 29 Maniktala ..	42,397	28,732	678	13,665	322	13,664	322	1	..
District No. III—									
Ward No. 13 Fenwick Bazar ..	30,810	15,114	491	15,696	509	14,750	479	946	30
Ward No. 14 Taltola ..	38,248	28,798	753	9,450	247	9,152	240	298	7
Ward No. 15 Kalinga ..	14,014	6,746	483	7,268	517	6,657	472	611	45
Ward No. 16 Park Street ..	5,408	1,506	279	3,902	721	2,351	435	1,551	286
Ward No. 17 Baman Bustee ..	2,643	981	371	1,662	629	1,188	450	474	179
Ward No. 18 Tengra .	11,715	8,370	715	3,345	285	3,300	281	45	4
Ward No. 19 Intally ..	44,150	30,688	695	13,462	305	13,259	300	203	5
Ward No. 20 Beniapukur ..	40,575	29,242	720	11,333	280	11,059	272	274	8
Ward No. 21 Ballygunge ..	30,900	19,960	646	10,940	354	9,983	323	957	31
District No. IV—									
Ward No. 27 Tollygunge ..	40,709	32,941	810	7,768	190	7,356	180	412	10
Ward No. 22 Bhawanipur ..	79,615	59,979	753	19,636	247	18,849	237	787	10
Ward No. 23 Alipore ..	29,880	19,855	665	10,025	335	9,328	312	697	23
Ward No. 24 Ekbalpore ..	32,781	20,298	619	12,483	381	12,166	371	317	10
Ward No. 25 Watganj & Hastings ..	32,345	20,371	631	11,874	369	11,518	358	356	11
Ward No. 26 Garden Reach ..	55,817	41,399	742	14,418	258	14,250	255	168	3
FORT WILLIAM AND MAIDAN ..	**3,064**	**463**	**151**	**2,601**	**849**	**1,209**	**395**	**1,392**	**454**
PORT ..	**33,185**	**9,869**	**297**	**23,316**	**703**	**21,953**	**662**	**1,363**	**41**
CANALS ..	**1,905**	**1,407**	**739**	**498**	**261**	**498**	**261**	..	..
Suburbs in 24-Parganas ..	**63,975**	**54,384**	**850**	**9,591**	**150**	**9,229**	**144**	**362**	**6**
HOWRAH ..	**224,873**	**144,864**	**644**	**80,009**	**356**	**78,564**	**349**	**1,445**	**7**

*The figures against each detailed area under Calcutta exclude the figures for Buddhists and Tribals. Details of locality of birth for these are given below:—

Total population	..	3,447
Born in Bengal	..	1,296
Born in India	..	352
Born outside India	..	1,799

SUBSIDIARY TABLE III.—Number and ratio (per 1,000 of the total population) of persons born outside Bengal with the number of females per 1,000 males in the immigrant population from each area.

Area of birth.	Enumerated in: Calcutta—Population = 1,196,734.					Calcutta with Suburbs in 24-Parganas—Population = 1,260,709.					Howrah City—Population = 224,873.				
	Both sexes.	Males.	Females.	Per 1,000 of total population.	Females per 1,000 of males.	Both sexes.	Males.	Females.	Per 1,000 of total population.	Females per 1,000 of males.	Both sexes.	Males.	Females.	Per 1,000 of total population.	Females per 1,000 of males.
1	2	3	4	5	6	7	8	9	10	11	12	13	14	15	16
Outside Bengal ..	**397,326**	**324,528**	**72,798**	332	224	**406,917**	**332,500**	**74,417**	323	224	**80,009**	**61,445**	**18,564**	356	302
Other parts of India ..	**380,428**	**312,140**	**68,288**	318	219	**389,657**	**319,880**	**69,777**	309	218	**78,564**	**60,323**	**18,241**	349	302
Outside India ..	**16,898**	**12,388**	**4,510**	14	364	**17,260**	**12,620**	**4,640**	14	368	**1,445**	**1,122**	**323**	7	288
Ajmer-Merwara **Province** ..	197	115	82	..	713	197	115	82	..	713	11	7	4	..	571
Andamans & Nicobars **Province** ..	3	3	..	..	..	3	3	..	..	..	..	..	..	..	..
Assam **Province** ..	4,616	3,918	698	4	178	4,629	3,928	701	4	178	97	70	27	..	386
Beluchistan (Districts and Administered Territory) **Province** ..	..	..	..	..	..	..	..	..	..	..	2	2	..	..	..
Bihar and Orissa **Province** ..	223,698	191,531	32,167	187	168	231,151	197,955	33,196	183	168	33,181	26,393	6,788	148	257
Bombay **Province** ..	4,467	2,955	1,512	4	512	4,505	2,981	1,524	4	511	226	169	57	1	337
Burma **Province** ..	1,461	1,125	336	1	299	1,476	1,128	348	1	309	47	27	20	..	741
Central Provinces & Berar ..	3,000	2,187	813	3	372	3,148	2,277	871	3	382	794	459	335	4	730
Coorg **Province** ..	2	2	..	..	..	2	2	..	..	..	..	..	..	..	..
Delhi **Province** ..	1,558	1,307	251	1	192	1,558	1,307	251	1	192	53	33	20	..	606
Madras **Province** ..	5,287	3,348	1,939	4	579	5,300	3,350	1,950	4	582	2,661	1,372	1,289	12	940
N. W. F. P. (Districts and Administered Territory) **Province** ..	611	439	172	1	392	618	446	172	..	386	26	19	7	..	368
Punjab **Province** ..	12,445	9,879	2,566	10	260	12,494	9,912	2,582	10	260	797	603	194	4	322
U. P. of Agra & Oudh ..	103,032	80,215	22,817	86	284	104,401	81,259	23,142	83	285	38,944	29,945	8,999	173	301
Assam **States** ..	203	170	33	..	194	203	170	33	..	194	5	2	3	..	1,500
Beluchistan **States** ..	79	72	7	..	97	79	72	7	..	97	..	..	..	..	..
Baroda **States** ..	233	171	62	..	363	233	171	62	..	363	..	..	..	..	..
Bihar and Orissa **States** ..	1,053	917	136	1	148	1,120	966	154	1	159	181	135	46	1	341
Bombay **States** ..	88	81	7	..	86	88	81	7	..	86	..	..	..	..	..
Central India Agency ..	186	60	126	..	2,100	186	60	126	..	2,100	5	4	1	..	250
Central Provinces States ..	26	12	14	..	1,167	26	12	14	..	1,167	..	..	..	..	..
Gwalior State ..	908	718	190	1	265	908	718	190	1	265	145	114	31	1	272
Hyderabad State ..	380	283	97	..	343	380	283	97	..	343	22	15	7	..	467
Kashmir State ..	93	69	24	..	348	93	69	24	..	348	7	3	4	..	1,333
Madras States (including Cochin and Travancore) ..	48	30	18	..	600	48	30	18	..	600	..	..	..	..	..
Cochin State ..	23	14	9	..	643	23	14	9	..	643	..	..	..	..	..
Travancore State ..	8	8	..	..	..	8	8	..	..	..	..	..	..	..	..
Mysore State ..	171	108	63	..	583	171	108	63	..	583	..	..	..	..	..
Punjab States Agency ..	258	194	64	..	330	258	194	64	..	330	..	..	..	..	..
Rajputana Agency ..	14,881	11,180	3,701	12	331	14,938	11,232	3,706	12	330	1,335	939	396	6	422
Sikkim State ..	313	171	142	..	830	313	171	142	..	830	6	5	1	..	200
United Provinces States ..	246	136	110	..	809	246	136	110	..	809	..	..	..	..	..
India unspecified ..	24	21	3	..	143	24	21	3	..	143	18	6	12	..	2,000
French and Portuguese settlement ..	861	723	138	1	191	861	723	138	1	191	1	1	..	..	..

CHAPTER III

Age, sex and marital condition

19. **Introductory.**—The statistics to which this chapter is an introduction are contained in the imperial tables showing details of sex, age and marital condition by religions (No. VII) and by selected castes (No. VIII). Subsidiary tables printed after this chapter show the following :—

I—the number of females per thousand males, by wards, 1911, 1921 and 1931 ;

II—the distribution by age-groups of 1,000 persons of each sex, 1911, 1921 and 1931 ;

III—the number of females per 1,000 males of the same age, with the number of females per 1,000 females, all ages, expressed as a percentage of the number of males of the same age per 1,000 males, all ages, 1911, 1921 and 1931 ;

IV—the numbers of children and aged persons per 100 of the population with number of married females aged 15-40 per 100 females of all ages and number of children under 10 years old per 100 married females aged 15-40 ;

V—estimates of the population of Calcutta on the 1st January of each year, 1921 to 1930 ;

VI—the number of births reported in Calcutta with birth rate (per 1,000) and ratio of female births and birth rate to male births and birth rate annually, 1921 to 1930 ;

VII—the number of deaths reported in Calcutta with death rate (per 1,000) and ratio of female deaths and death rate to male deaths and death rate annually, 1921 to 1930 ;

VIII—the number of deaths annually reported in Calcutta by sexes at age-groups, 1921 to 1930 ;

IX—the number of deaths reported in Calcutta with death rate (per 1,000) from selected causes and with percentages on deaths from all causes annually, 1921 to 1930 ; and

X—the numbers in each marital condition (per 1,000) of the same sex and age-group by religions, 1911, 1921 and 1931.

Part I—Sex

20. **General sex distribution.**—In Calcutta with suburbs in the 24-Parganas out of a total population of 1,260,709 persons 851,931 are males and 408,778 are females. In Calcutta proper the figures are respectively for both sexes 1,196,734, for males 814,948 and for females 381,786. In Howrah city out of a total population of 224,873, males number 145,120 and females 79,753. These figures give a proportion of females for every thousand males amounting to 480 for Calcutta with suburbs in 24-Parganas, 469 in Calcutta proper and 550 in Howrah city. The variations in the sex proportions at every census year from 1911 are shown in subsidiary table I. In Calcutta there are hardly more than half as many females to a given number of males as in the whole of Bengal and considerably less than that proportion compared with the rural part of Bengal. Full details of the proportion of females per 1,000 males in various areas including Calcutta at every census since 1872 will be found shown and illustrated in diagram No. II-5 of volume V, part I. Since the year 1881 the proportion of females to males in the whole of Bengal has shown a continuous and steady decline. It amounted to 994 in 1881, 973 in 1891, 960 in 1901, 945 in 1911, 932 in 1921 and 924 in 1931. In Calcutta the figures were 500 in 1881, 526 in 1891, 495 in 1911, 488 in 1921 and have now further declined to the figure already given. The ratios here given for years before 1911 refer to Calcutta as constituted at previous census enumerations, whereas those given in subsidiary table I refer to the area

now forming Calcutta, and this accounts for the difference in the figures from those given for 1911 and 1921 in diagram No. II-5 to which reference has already been made. The marked disparity in the proportion of females to

DIAGRAM No. III-1.

Number of females per thousand males, 1931.

Per thousand

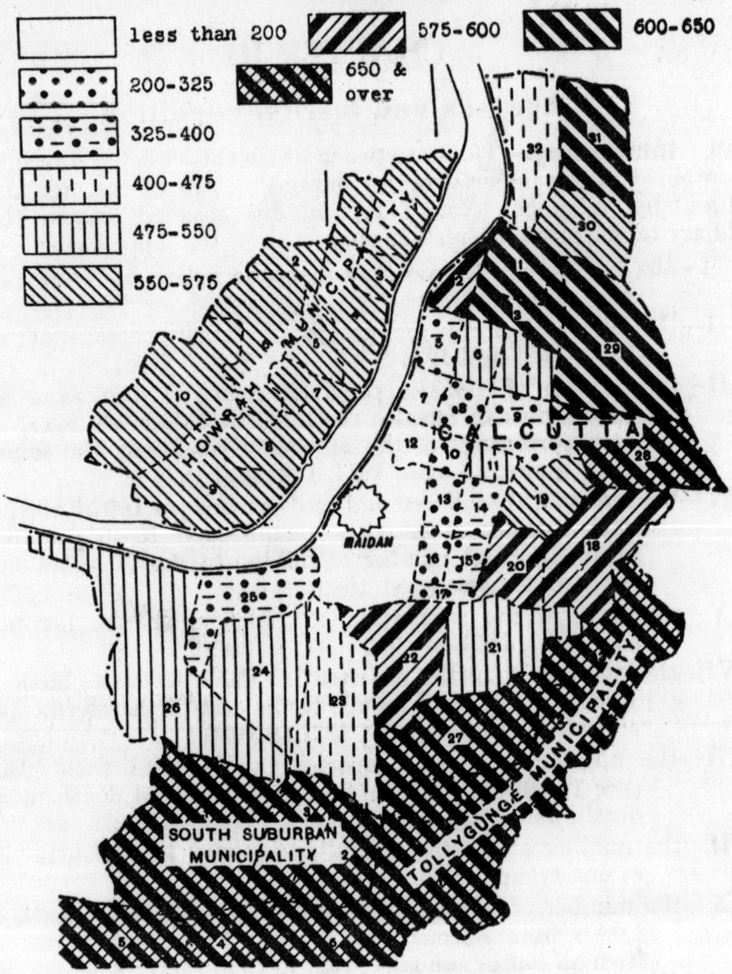

males is a feature of all town populations in Bengal. The numbers of females per thousand males are 787 in non-industrial towns and 526 in industrial towns. The proportions to some extent indicate the degree to which the population living in towns is resident there not permanently but merely for the purpose of earning its living. The worker in Calcutta and other industrial towns does not find conditions convenient for bringing his family to live with him.

21. **Sex ratios by wards.**—The sex ratios shown in subsidiary table I are illustrated for the wards of Calcutta in diagram No. III-1. The municipalities on the southern confines of the city and Beliaghata forming a part of the old municipality of Maniktala added to the city during the decade have the largest percentage of females to males, but it is no higher in each thousand than 781 in the south suburban municipality and is as low as 654 in Tollygunge. Roughly speaking the proportion of females decreases as one proceeds inward from the perimeter of the city and is also less in those wards largely or principally inhabited by others than Bengalis. Thus the highest proportion of females to males is found in the old Cossipore-Chitpur Municipality in what is now Satpukur ward which is principally inhabited by Bengalis.. Here the proportion is 609 per thousand males and there are between 600 and 650 in every thousand males also in Shampukur, Bartola,

and Maniktala and between 575 and 600 in Kumartuli, Tengra, Beniapukur and Bhawanipur. Ballygunge with exactly one female to every two males has an unexpectedly low proportion in the belt in which the proportions are otherwise relatively high. There is less than one female to every five males in Burra Bazar and Waterloo Street as well as in Fort William, the Port and the Canals. The indication for Howrah Municipality given on the diagram is the average for the whole city and must not be interpreted as referring to each individual ward.

Part II—Age

22. **Method of constructing age-groups and effect on comparison with figures of previous year.**—Full details have been given in volume V of the method for obtaining the quinquennial groups shown in imperial table VII and only a summary is necessary of what is there given in full. Reason was found to believe that the figures of 1921 actually represented ages to the nearest and not as they purported to be at the last birthday. It was determined to take advantage of this peculiarity of the actual returns and the enumerators were directed to record age at nearest birthday. A further peculiarity of the census figures in 1921 was that there was a very marked preference for certain digits in returning ages. The Actuary to the Government of India estimated that by obtaining ages to the nearest birthday and grouping them in alternate ternary and septenary groups (4-6, 7-13, 14-16, 17-23, etc.) the groups obtained would each include a larger percentage than can be obtained on any other grouping of the persons whose actual age fell within the group but who were induced by preference for particular digits to mis-state their ages. The returns obtained to the nearest birthday were consequently sorted into the alternate ternary and septenary groups proposed and the results shown in the table have been obtained by combining together to form quinary groups one half of two adjacent groups so formed. The method assumes that in any particular sorter's group there are as many persons actually aged less than as over the central point and this is clearly not an absolutely accurate assumption, but the error introduced by it is negligible compared with the increased accuracy in the total figures obtained by correcting them for the tendency to return ages at nearest birthday and for such minor mis-statements of age as were deduced from the returns of the previous years. In comparing the figures given on the present occasion with those of previous years it is consequently necessary to bear in mind that the actual composition of corresponding groups in 1921 and 1911 actually includes persons who on the average are at least six months younger than on the present occasion. In other words each quinary group on the present occasion contains a number of persons who in 1921 and previous years would have been shown in the next higher group because they gave their age as the year forming the lower limit of the group but were actually less than that age.

23. **General age distribution.**—The proportionate distribution of the population at ages by sexes in successive census years is shown in subsidiary table II and illustrated for each sex for Calcutta with suburbs in the 24-Parganas in diagram No. III-2. The diagram brings out clearly the features which were to be expected from the considerations adduced in the previous paragraph. There is in both sexes a considerable decrease in the proportions aged 60 and over and a considerable increase in the proportions aged less than 5. The other most notable characteristic of the age distribution which is brought out clearly in the diagram is the enormous preponderance in the proportions of females at the early ages as well as in the higher age-groups. In an equal number of each sex there are 127 females aged 0-5 for every 67 males, 110 aged 5-10 for every 67 males, 104 aged 10-15 for every 73 males, 22 aged 55-60 for every 17 males and 41 aged 60 and over for every 26 males. At every age below 40 the proportions of the total population are higher amongst females than amongst males. But between the ages of 15 and 55 which contains almost exactly 75 per cent. of the male population the numbers of females form less than 60 per cent. of the total females. The discrepancy is perhaps most marked in the age-groups 25-30 and 30-35 in which in equal numbers of both sexes there are almost half as many more men as women.

24. **Discrepancies in proportions at age-groups in each sex.**—In diagram No. III-3 the discrepancies in the proportions at age-groups are illustrated both for the total population and for the three most numerous religions, Hindu, Muslim and Christian, in the same area as is illustrated in diagram No. III-2. The curves for Muslims and Hindus show comparatively little variation and as Hindus constitute the largest proportion of the population their curve naturally follows very closely that for all religions. There is a very marked preponderance in the proportion of females amongst Muslims up to the age-group 15-20 and at every age-group after 20-25 the deficiency in their proportion is much more marked. The distribution of Christians varies considerably from that of the other two religions. There are very wide discrepancies in the proportions and they are most defective amongst females at the age-group 45-50, some 15 years after the corresponding stage is reached on the curve for the other religions. Diagram No. III-3 illustrates statcment No. III-1.

DIAGRAM No. III-2.

Distribution by age-groups of 100 of each sex, Calcutta with suburbs in 24-Parganas, 1921 and 1931.

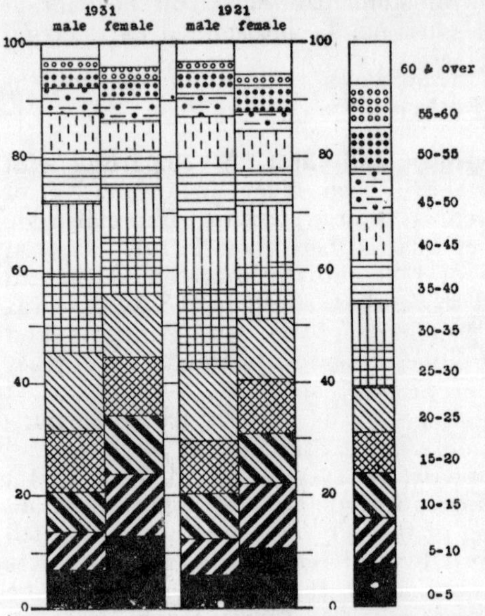

DIAGRAM No. III-3.

Number of females by age-groups per 1,000 females all ages, as a percentage of males at the same age per 1,000 males, all ages, by religions, Calcutta with suburbs in 24-Parganas, 1931.

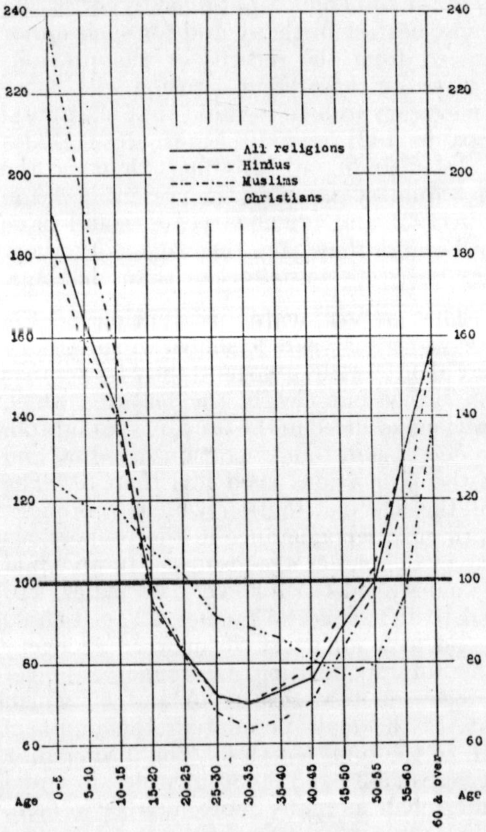

STATEMENT No. III-1.

Number of females at age groups per 1,000 females all ages, as a percentage of the number of males at the same age groups per 1,000 males all ages by main religions, Calcutta with suburbs in 24-Parganas, 1931.

Age-group.	All religions.	Hindus.	Muslims.	Christians.
0—5 ..	**189**	182	237	116
5—10 ..	**164**	158	187	119
10—15 ..	**142**	140	156	118
15—20 ..	**95**	94	100	108
20—25 ..	**82**	82	82	102
25—30 ..	**72**	72	68	91
30—35 ..	**70**	70	64	89
35—40 ..	**73**	74	66	86
40—45 ..	**76**	79	70	81
45—50 ..	**89**	93	83	77
50—55 ..	**100**	103	97	80
55—60 ..	**129**	128	124	96
60 and over	**158**	158	154	137

25. **Age distribution by sexes, 1921 and 1931.**—The accompanying statement No. III-2 shows by sexes the numbers of and over the age given in every thousand of the same sex in Calcutta and its suburbs in the 24-Parganas in 1921 and 1931. These figures are illustrated in diagram No. III-4. The diagram brings out very clearly the decrease in the numbers of or over any particular age which has resulted from a more accurate distribution of the age-returns. At the age 10-15 amongst males the discrepancy

is comparatively small but it increases particularly between the ages of 20-30 and again between the ages of 35-55. The result is the same

STATEMENT No. III-2.

Numbers in each 1,000 of the same sex of and over the age shown, Calcutta with suburbs in 24-Parganas, 1921 and 1931.

Aged and over.		Calcutta with suburbs in 24-Parganas. 1921. Male.	1921. Female.	1931. Male.	1931. Female.
3	..	1,000	1,000	1,000	1,000
5	..	943	894	933	873
10	..	878	779	866	763
15	..	798	689	793	659
20	..	705	596	684	555
25	..	574	488	546	442
30	..	440	387	405	341
35	..	311	287	280	254
40	..	222	224	191	189
45	..	135	155	120	135
50	..	92	121	75	95
55	..	51	75	43	63
60	..	36	57	26	41

DIAGRAM No. III-4.

Distribution of 100 of each sex of and over the age shown in Calcutta with suburbs in 24-Parganas, 1921 and 1931.

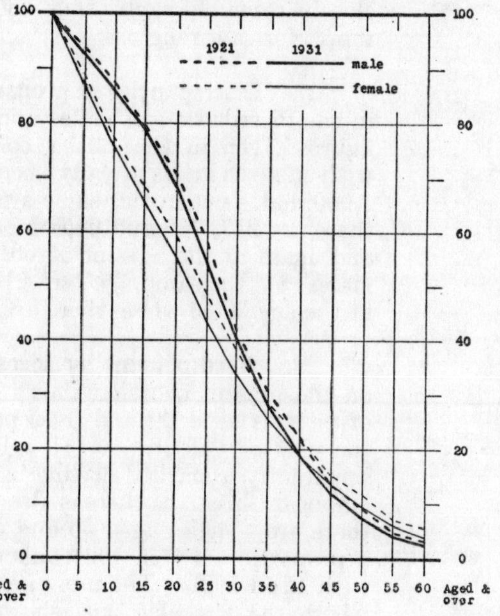

in each sex. There are approximately an equal number of the population above and below the age of about 26 or 27 amongst males and 22 or 23 amongst females and in both sexes the age at and above which there are one-quarter of the total population falls in the age-group 35-40. Approximately 50 per cent. of the male population is between the ages of about 17 and 37 and amongst females some 50 per cent. are aged 10 to 35 or 36 years old.

26. **Age distribution by religions.**—Statement No. III-3 and diagram No. III-5 illustrating it show a similar distribution of the three principal religions. In the diagram the curve for Hindu females follows so closely

DIAGRAM No. III-5.

Numbers in 100 of each sex of and over the age shown by principal religions, Calcutta with suburbs in 24-Parganas, 1931.

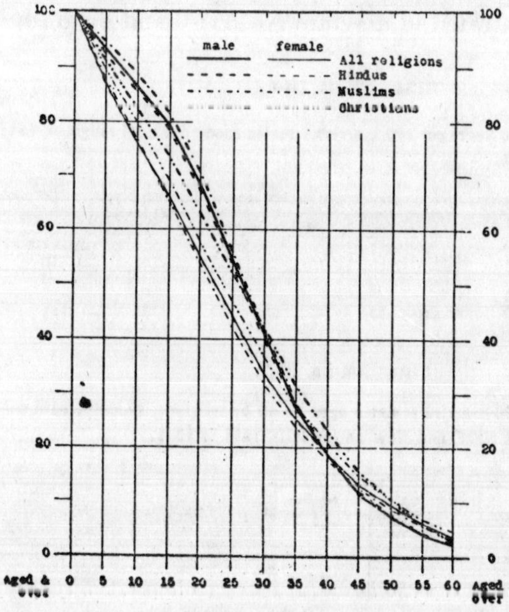

STATEMENT No. III-3.

Numbers in each 1,000 of each sex who are of and over the age shown in each principal religion, Calcutta with suburbs in 24-Parganas, 1931.

Aged and over.		Hindu. Male.	Hindu. Female.	Muslim. Male.	Muslim. Female.	Christian. Male.	Christian. Female.
0	..	1,000	1,000	1,000	1,000	1,000	1,000
5	..	928	869	949	879	912	898
10	..	859	760	888	765	828	798
15	..	780	658	817	654	737	691
20	..	678	557	706	543	634	580
25	..	542	446	560	423	525	469
30	..	402	345	412	323	416	370
35	..	277	257	293	240	316	281
40	..	188	191	201	179	235	211
45	..	118	136	130	129	160	150
50	..	75	96	84	91	103	106
55	..	43	63	43	61	59	71
60	..	26	41	26	40	35	48

that for females of all religions as to be practically indistinguishable from it. Christians show in both sexes the most regular progression and amongst males up to the age of about 27 they have a smaller percentage above any age chosen than is found in any other religion. Beyond this age, however, until the age of about 50 they have a larger proportion of and over any age taken. Christian females, on the other hand, at all ages have a higher proportion aged and over the age taken than in any other religion. The main differences occur about the ages 5-30 and particularly at the ages 10-15 and 15-20, but beyond the age of 30 the Hindu and Muslim proportions closely resemble each other and in the diagram are indistinguishable from those for all religions.

27. **Discrepancies in proportions at ages in each sex.**—The discrepancies in the distribution of males and females at age-groups is also seen from the figures given in the earlier columns of subsidiary table III. In Calcutta with suburbs it has already been said that there are only 480 females to every 1,000 males but in this same area at the ages 0-5, 5-10 and 10-15 respectively there are 917, 786 and 685 females for every 1,000 males of the same age, and again at the ages of 55-60 and 60 and over the proportions per 1,000 males of the same age are 611 and 765. The discrepancy is most marked at the age 30-35 where there are less than one-third as many females as males.

28. **Aged persons by sexes.**—The correction of the age-groups effected on the present occasion shows itself also in the reduction of the proportion of persons aged 60 and over per hundred of the same sex aged 15-40. In the city of Calcutta, in all religions except Christians, there is since 1921 apparently a marked decline in the percentage amongst both sexes and even amongst Christians there is also a decline amongst the males. On the average there are 4 males aged 60 and over for every 100 aged 15-40 compared with a proportion of 6 in 1921. Amongst the females the average is 9 compared with 12 in 1921. The most notable decrease occurs amongst Muslim females where the figure is now shown to be 8 compared with 13 in the previous year. The preponderance of persons of middle age amongst males and their deficiency amongst females compared with the figures for all Bengal is similarly brought out by these proportions. On the average in all religions in each sex there are 8 persons aged 60 and over for every hundred aged 15-40, but in Calcutta this average is increased in the case of females and halved in the case of males. The proportions for males are exactly the same (4 per 100) amongst both Hindus and Muslims but the figure for Muslim females (8) is lower than that for Hindu females (9).

29. **Young children per 100 married females aged 15-40.**—Subsidiary table IV also gives figures for the number of children of both sexes aged under 10 per 100 married females aged 15-40. For each successive census year these figures are illustrated in diagram No. III-6 and diagram No. III-7

DIAGRAM No. III-6.

Number of children aged under 10 years per 100 married females aged 15-40, all religions, 1911 to 1931.

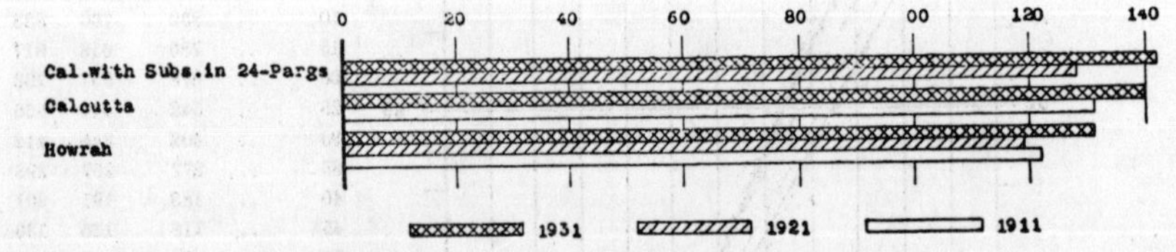

DIAGRAM No. III-7.

Number of children under 10 years per 100 married females aged 15-40 by religions, Calcutta with suburbs in 24-Parganas (on right) and Howrah (on left), 1911 to 1931.

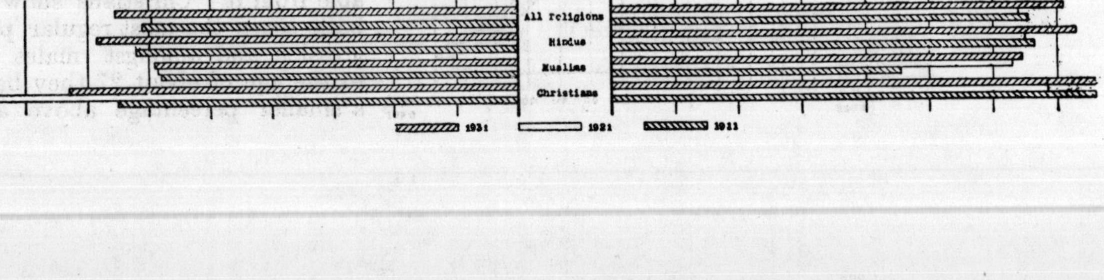

illustrates the figures for Howrah and for Calcutta with its suburbs in the 24-Parganas for each of the three principal religions. In general the proportion of children is highest amongst Christians followed by Hindus and of the three religions chosen the proportion is lowest amongst Muslims. On the whole, however, the proportion of children is very considerably less than in the whole of Bengal. Thus for every 100 married females aged 15-40 in Calcutta with suburbs there are only 142 children compared with 170 in the whole of Bengal. The figures for Hindus are 146 compared with 163 and those for Muslims are 129 compared with 174 in all Bengal where their proportion is higher than the average for all religions and considerably higher than for Hindus.

DIAGRAM No. III-8.

Number of reported female births per 1,000 male births annually in Calcutta, 1921 to 1930.

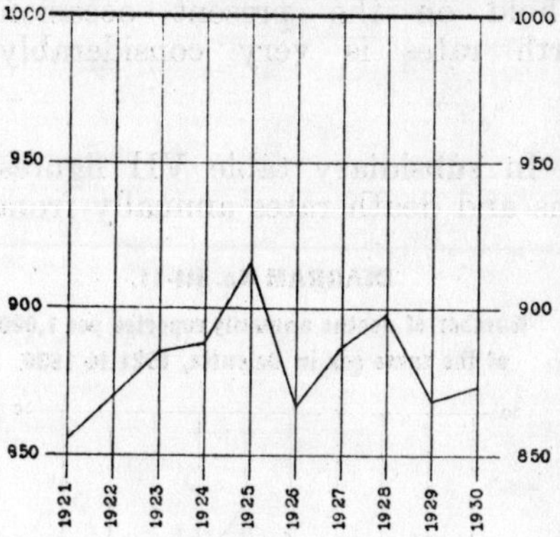

30. **Annual reported births.**—Figures of the annual reported births by sexes with averages for the whole decade are shown for Calcutta in subsidiary table VI which also gives figures of the birth-rate. Diagram No. III-8 illustrates from column 10 of this table the variations from year to year in the number of females born per thousand males. During the decade the reported average is 881. The average figure is very low and is less than the lowest figure recorded in Bengal in any division during the 30 years from 1901 to 1930. The lowest figure was 884 for 1,000 males in the Chittagong Division in 1927. The highest figure recorded in Calcutta in 1925 is 916 only.

31. **Annual birth rates.**—The birth rates shown in subsidiary table VI have been calculated on two methods. The first is that previously adopted under which the ratios are calculated upon the population at the last preceding census, but as this introduces an increasing exaggeration in the ratios towards the end of a decade in which a population is increasing they have also been calculated and are shown in columns 6 and 7 upon the estimated population on 1st January of each year, computed on the assumption that the population changed at a regular annual rate. In the same way the ratios given in columns 8 and 9 for the number of births reported per 1,000 married females aged 15-40 are calculated on the estimated number of married females of this age on 1st January of each year, also assuming that their numbers between each census changed at a similar uniform rate. The figures by sexes given in columns 6 and 7 which are illustrated in diagram No. III-9 are of very little interest because of the entirely abnormal distribution of the population by sexes in Calcutta. It is of more interest to compare those in columns 8 and 9 with the corresponding figures for all Bengal shown in statement No. IV-12 in chapter IV of volume V, part i. The annual average in Calcutta was 39·1 male births and 34·4 female births for every 100 married females aged between 15-40. The average for Bengal is in each case more than twice as high and amounts for males to 84·9 and for females to 78·5. The discrepancy is interesting particularly as the curves for the actual ratios in Calcutta are all generally of the same form as those for all Bengal at least up to about the year 1928. Up to this period in both areas peaks in the birth rate were shown in 1923 and 1925 and a marked depression in 1927, but beyond this period

DIAGRAM No. III-9.

Number of annual reported births per 1,000 of the same sex, Calcutta, 1921 to 1930.

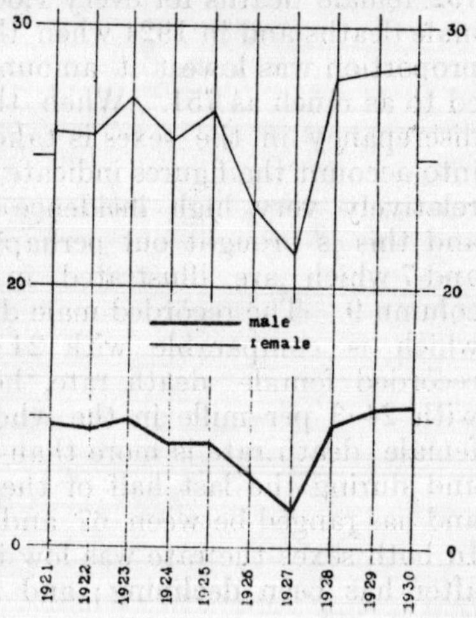

the rate in both sexes has increased in Calcutta whereas for the whole of Bengal after a spurt in 1928 there has been again a falling off. The fact that Calcutta is a permanent residence for comparatively few of its inhabitants probably helps to account for a very much smaller birth rate calculated on the total number of married females aged 15-40, since a certain proportion of the children born to them will be born in their mother's native village. The actual number of births recorded, however, in Bengal as a whole is very far short of the numbers actually born and there does not appear to be any satisfactory way of estimating exactly the extent to which the lower birth rate in Calcutta is due to an even greater inaccuracy in the recorded births. The tendency in cities appears to be for the birth rate to be lower than in other areas and it appears to be established that mere density of population in itself in general has an effect in reducing the birth rate. In 1921 it was reported that during the previous decade births had been rather more accurately reported in Calcutta than in other parts of Bengal and if the same conditions hold on the present occasion the discrepancy between the actual birth rates is very considerably increased.

32. **Annual deaths and death rates.**—In subsidiary table VII figures are given for the number of reported deaths and death rates annually from

DIAGRAM No. III-10.

Number of female deaths per 1,000 male deaths annually reported in Calcutta, 1921 to 1930.

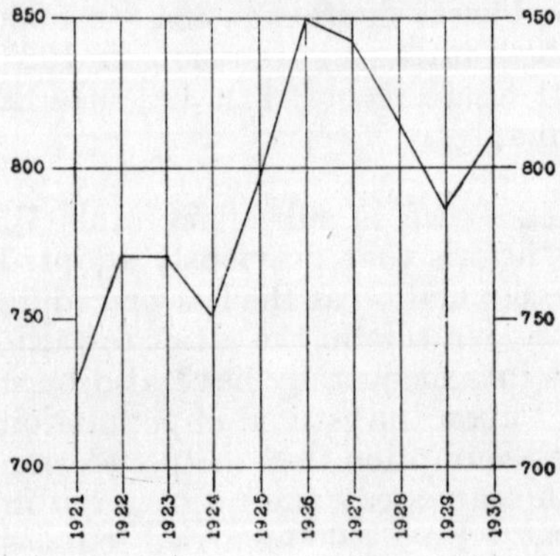

DIAGRAM No. III-11.

Number of deaths annually reported per 1,000 of the same sex in Calcutta, 1921 to 1930.

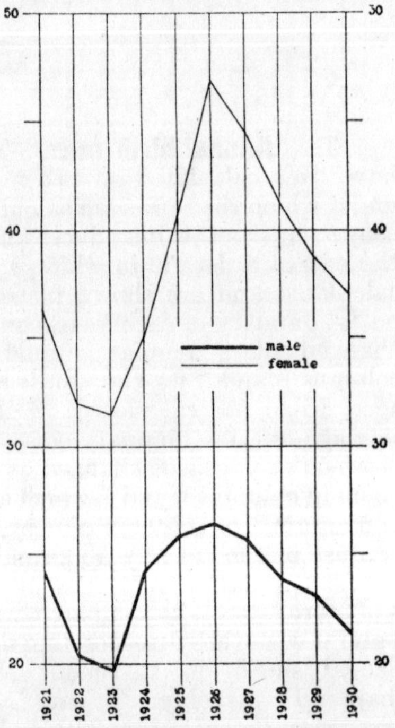

1921 to 1930. The figures for the sex ratios in the death rate given in column 8 of this table are illustrated in diagram No. III-10. The average during the decade is 792 female deaths for every 1,000 male deaths and in 1924 when the proportion was lowest it amounted to as much as 751. When the discrepancy in the sexes is taken into account the figures indicate a relatively very high incidence of mortality amongst females in Calcutta and this is brought out perhaps more strikingly in the figures in columns 6 and 7 which are illustrated in diagram No. III-11 and by the figures in column 9. The recorded male death rate on the average was 23·5 per mille which is comparable with 24·9 per mille, the rate for all Bengal. The recorded female death rate, however, on the average was 38·6 compared with 24·3 per mille in the whole of Bengal. On an average the recorded female death rate is more than 64 per cent. higher than the male death rate and during the last half of the decade the discrepancy has been increased and has ranged between 67 and 77 per cent. higher than amongst males. In both sexes the rate was low in 1922 and 1923 but rose in 1926 and thereafter has been declining; and this tendency offers an interesting contrast with that for all Bengal where the highest rate was recorded in 1921 and with slight setbacks amongst males in 1924 and amongst females in 1923 and in 1927 and 1928 has steadily decreased in every year since then. Assuming that the relative accuracy with which deaths are reported is the same in each sex, one explanation of the heavier incidence of mortality amongst females in Calcutta may be sought in the fact that the male population is to such a large extent composed of men in the prime of life who in most cases survive until they leave the city and return to their homes whereas a very much larger proportion of the female population may be taken to be permanent residents, who are not attracted to the city by the opportunities of earning a living and the need to support a family left behind in their native villages.

33. **Annual deaths at age-groups in each sex.**—In subsidiary table VIII figures are given of the number of deaths recorded annually in each sex by age-groups from 1921 to 1930, but no attempt has been made to work out age-specific death rates owing to the extreme uncertainty of the age constitution of the population at each intercensal year. On the average the largest number of deaths is recorded in both sexes in the age-group 0-5 in which in each case well over one-quarter of the total deaths occurring took place. One seventh of the deaths are recorded for males in each of the age-groups 20-30, 30-40 and 60 and over. Amongst females more than one-sixth of the deaths occur at the ages of 60 and over and more than one-eighth at the ages 20-30.

34. **Deaths from selected causes.**—Subsidiary table IX shows figures by sexes for deaths and death rates from various causes. On the average nearly 6 thousand males and over 4 thousand females annually die from respiratory diseases which account for one-third of the deaths in each sex and carry off in each thousand of the same sex annually almost 8 males and more than 11 females. Fevers are recorded as the cause of death annually of nearly 2,500 males and over 2,000 females; they carry off annually more than 3 per mille males and 5½ per mille females and account in all for 14 per cent. of the total deaths of females and 13 per cent. of the total deaths of males. Dysentery and diarrhœa amongst the seven causes shown in the table are the next most fertile sources of mortality: they carry off annually over 2 males and 4 females in every 1,000 of the same sex and contribute nearly 10 per cent. of the male deaths and more than 11 per cent. of the female deaths. The figures offer an interesting comparison with those given in subsidiary tables XI and XII of chapter IV in volume V, part i. The deaths from respiratory diseases in Calcutta account proportionately for almost thirteen times the proportion of deaths due to these causes in all Bengal; but the porportion of deaths from fevers which is higher than from any other cause in the whole of Bengal is only one-fifth or one-sixth as large in Calcutta.

Part III—Marital Condition

35. **Effect on figures of marital condition of the method of composing age-groups.**—In chapter VI of volume V, part i, there is a discussion at some length of the effect upon the figures for marital condition by ages of the method of constructing the quinary groups in which they are presented. Put in its briefest form the expected effect would be a tendency at the lower ages to exaggerate the numbers married and widowed and to minimise the numbers unmarried and at the higher ages to exaggerate the numbers married and minimise the numbers widowed. The exaggerations in each case may generally be taken to be due to the inclusion in a lower age-group of persons who ought properly to be included in the higher group. But the proposition is stated in very general terms and for some of the rather complicated factors which may be taken to have operated the reader must refer in detail to the chapter in volume V already quoted. For comparison

with a similar statement in volume V, part i, the original sorters' groups have been reconstructed for each marital condition by sex and are shown in the accompanying statement No. III-4.

STATEMENT No. III-4.

Numbers unmarried, married and widowed in each sex by age-groups to nearest birthday, 1931.

Age-groups.	All marital conditions.			Unmarried.			Married.			Widowed.		
	Both sexes.	Males.	Females.	Both sexes.	Males.	Females.	Both sexes.	Males.	Females.	Both sexes.	Males.	Females.
1	2	3	4	5	6	7	8	9	10	11	12	13
ALL RELIGIONS.												
All ages ..	**1,196,734**	**814,948**	**381,786**	**409,491**	**283,099**	**126,392**	**695,871**	**509,722**	**186,149**	**91,372**	**22,127**	**69,245**
0—3 ..	**71,589**	**37,281**	**34,308**	**70,747**	36,821	33,926	**818**	453	365	**25**	7	18
4—6 ..	**59,676**	**31,434**	**28,242**	**57,840**	30,576	27,264	**1,689**	840	849	**147**	18	129
7—13 ..	**131,100**	**75,562**	**55,538**	**115,490**	68,308	47,182	**15,311**	7,176	8,135	**299**	78	221
14—16 ..	**65,502**	**41,532**	**23,970**	**38,912**	31,356	7,556	**26,037**	10,074	15,963	**553**	102	451
17—23 ..	**190,958**	**135,428**	**55,530**	**74,638**	69,688	4,950	**112,077**	64,884	47,193	**4,243**	856	3,387
24—26 ..	**122,574**	**91,568**	**31,006**	**23,634**	22,010	1,624	**93,919**	68,342	25,577	**5,021**	1,216	3,805
27—33 ..	**189,216**	**142,794**	**46,422**	**16,054**	14,272	1,782	**161,755**	125,580	36,175	**11,407**	2,942	8,465
34—36 ..	**84,004**	**64,048**	**19,956**	**3,670**	3,160	510	**72,843**	58,882	13,961	**7,491**	2,006	5,485
37—43 ..	**111,566**	**82,112**	**29,454**	**4,118**	3,484	634	**93,447**	75,272	18,175	**14,001**	3,356	10,645
44—46 ..	**44,010**	**32,122**	**11,888**	**1,214**	980	234	**35,189**	29,204	5,985	**7,607**	1,938	5,669
47—53 ..	**58,230**	**40,032**	**18,198**	**1,476**	1,132	344	**42,933**	35,630	7,303	**13,821**	3,270	10,551
54 and over	**68,309**	**41,035**	**27,274**	**1,698**	1,312	386	**39,853**	33,385	6,468	**26,757**	6,338	20,419
HINDU.												
All ages ..	**822,293**	**547,846**	**274,447**	**287,294**	**198,309**	**88,985**	**463,488**	**333,835**	**129,653**	**71,511**	**15,702**	**55,809**
0—3 ..	**53,039**	**27,375**	**25,664**	**52,457**	27,069	25,388	**566**	302	264	**17**	4	13
4—6 ..	**43,158**	**22,674**	**20,484**	**42,057**	22,158	19,899	**1,023**	504	519	**78**	12	66
7—13 ..	**90,986**	**51,548**	**39,438**	**80,377**	46,708	33,669	**10,391**	4,788	5,603	**218**	52	166
14—16 ..	**43,950**	**27,416**	**16,534**	**25,681**	20,946	4,735	**17,853**	6,416	11,437	**416**	54	362
17—23 ..	**129,340**	**90,356**	**38,984**	**51,523**	49,100	2,423	**74,451**	40,682	33,769	**3,366**	574	2,792
24—26 ..	**82,064**	**60,024**	**22,040**	**16,635**	15,714	921	**61,269**	43,518	17,751	**4,160**	792	3,368
27—33 ..	**130,382**	**96,698**	**33,684**	**10,755**	9,816	939	**110,087**	84,820	25,267	**9,540**	2,062	7,478
34—36 ..	**56,398**	**41,986**	**14,412**	**2,371**	2,056	315	**48,009**	38,556	9,453	**6,018**	1,374	4,644
37—43 ..	**76,704**	**55,184**	**21,520**	**2,865**	2,536	329	**62,535**	50,168	12,367	**11,304**	2,480	8,824
44—46 ..	**29,402**	**20,732**	**8,670**	**697**	590	107	**22,911**	18,764	4,147	**5,794**	1,378	4,416
47—53 ..	**39,714**	**26,522**	**13,192**	**873**	718	155	**28,215**	23,432	4,783	**10,626**	2,372	8,254
54 and over	**47,156**	**27,331**	**19,825**	**1,003**	898	105	**26,178**	21,885	4,293	**19,974**	4,548	15,426
MUSLIM.												
All ages ..	**311,155**	**229,311**	**81,844**	**91,287**	**66,352**	**24,935**	**203,359**	**157,550**	**45,809**	**16,509**	**5,409**	**11,100**
0—3 ..	**14,399**	**7,674**	**6,725**	**14,233**	7,571	6,662	**161**	101	60	**5**	2	3
4—6 ..	**13,137**	**6,978**	**6,159**	**12,540**	6,714	5,826	**534**	258	276	**63**	6	57
7—13 ..	**32,641**	**20,116**	**12,525**	**28,088**	17,958	10,130	**4,482**	2,140	2,342	**71**	18	53
14—16 ..	**17,285**	**11,714**	**5,571**	**9,728**	8,350	1,378	**7,434**	3,314	4,120	**123**	50	73
17—23 ..	**52,031**	**39,354**	**12,677**	**17,320**	16,732	588	**33,908**	22,356	11,552	**803**	266	537
24—26 ..	**35,165**	**28,188**	**6,977**	**4,846**	4,746	100	**29,554**	23,040	6,514	**765**	402	363
27—33 ..	**50,007**	**40,432**	**9,575**	**2,914**	2,782	132	**45,522**	36,866	8,656	**1,571**	784	787
34—36 ..	**23,663**	**19,500**	**4,163**	**546**	528	18	**21,858**	18,428	3,430	**1,259**	544	715
37—43 ..	**28,839**	**23,062**	**5,777**	**536**	484	52	**26,074**	21,856	4,218	**2,229**	722	1,507
44—46 ..	**12,041**	**9,660**	**2,381**	**170**	162	8	**10,346**	9,048	1,298	**1,525**	450	1,075
47—53 ..	**15,017**	**11,244**	**3,773**	**190**	166	24	**12,142**	10,340	1,802	**2,685**	738	1,947
54 and over	**16,930**	**11,389**	**5,541**	**176**	159	17	**11,344**	9,803	1,541	**5,410**	1,427	3,983

36. **Marital condition by sex.**—Figures for the proportionate distribution by marital condition in each sex for the principal religions in Calcutta

STATEMENT No. III-5.

Distribution by marital condition of 1,000 of each sex in the principal religions, Calcutta and Howrah, 1921 and 1931.

Religion.	Calcutta. 1931 Unmarried.		Married.		Widowed.		Calcutta. 1921. Unmarried.		Married.		Widowed.	
	Male.	Female.	Male.	Female.	Male.	Female.	Male.	Female.	Male.	Female.	Male.	Female.
1	2	3	4	5	6	7	8	9	10	11	12	13
All religions ..	**347**	**331**	**626**	**488**	**27**	**181**	**369**	**302**	**596**	**475**	**35**	**223**
Hindu ..	362	324	609	473	29	203	374	284	589	467	37	249
Muslim ..	289	305	687	559	24	136	327	298	643	533	30	169
Christian ..	536	506	439	398	25	96	559	507	412	379	29	114

Religion.	Howrah. 1931. Unmarried.		Married.		Widowed.		Howrah. 1921. Unmarried.		Married.		Widowed.	
	Male.	Female.	Male.	Female.	Male.	Female.	Male.	Female.	Male.	Female.	Male.	Female.
1	14	15	16	17	18	19	20	21	22	23	24	25
All religions ..	**341**	**321**	**630**	**513**	**29**	**166**	**364**	**266**	**594**	**516**	**42**	**218**
Hindu ..	350	331	621	487	29	182	374	255	581	499	42	246
Muslim ..	300	280	609	610	31	110	323	295	635	582	42	123
Christian ..	517	434	457	464	26	102	560	427	414	460	26	113

and Howrah are shown for 1921 and 1931 in the accompanying statement No. III-5 and are illustrated in diagram No. III-12. In both

Calcutta and Howrah there has been an increase in the proportion married amongst males and there has been a similar increase in Calcutta amongst females also. In both Calcutta and Howrah there has been a marked decrease in the proportion widowed in both sexes in all religions and there

DIAGRAM No. III-12.

Proportionate distribution by marital condition of each sex in the main religions, Calcutta and Howrah, 1921 (lower column) and 1931 (upper column).

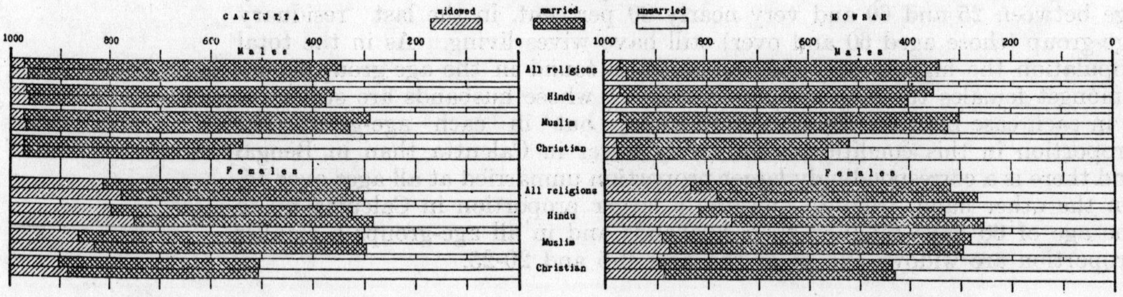

has been also a decrease in the proportion of males unmarried but an increase in the proportion of females unmarried compared with 1921. The general tendencies compared with 1921 are the same in all religions with the sole exception that there has been a decrease in the proportion of Muslim spinsters in Howrah and of Christian spinsters in Calcutta compared with the proportion of 1921. In both cities amongst the religions shown the highest married ratio is displayed in both sexes by the Muslims and the lowest by the Christians. Amongst Christian males, both in Calcutta and in Howrah, the proportions widowed are practically the same as in 1921, but in both cities in each sex of all the other religions shown there is a distinct decrease in the proportions widowed which points to a definite increase in the extent to which marriage is being postponed amongst women or widow remarriage is being practised, and the decrease is most notable in the case of females amongst whom in general there has actually been an increase in the proportions unmarried, so that the increased proportion of those whose husbands are still alive must in general be ascribed to this cause.

37. **Marital condition ratios at age-groups by sexes.**—The proportionate distribution of the population at age-groups by marital conditions is

STATEMENT No. III-6.

Distribution by marital condition of 1,000 of the same age-group in each sex, Calcutta, 1931.

	Unmarried.		Married.		Widowed.	
Ages.	Male.	Female.	Male.	Female.	Male.	Female.
0—5 ..	983	982	17	16	..	2
5—10 ..	924	889	75	107	1	4
10—15 ..	850	688	148	303	2	9
15—20 ..	571	157	424	795	5	48
20—25 ..	404	76	587	841	9	83
25—30 ..	155	44	827	798	18	158
30—35 ..	84	35	892	755	24	210
35—40 ..	45	23	918	650	37	327
40—45 ..	39	21	915	584	46	395
45—50 ..	29	19	899	442	72	539
50—55 ..	28	18	883	384	89	598
55—60 ..	22	13	847	282	131	705
60 and over	40	14	778	194	182	792

shown in subsidiary table X. For Calcutta a somewhat more detailed distribution is shown in the accompanying statement No. III-6 illustrated by diagram No. III-13.

DIAGRAM No. III-13.

Distribution by marital condition of 100 of the same sex and age-group in the population of Calcutta, 1931.

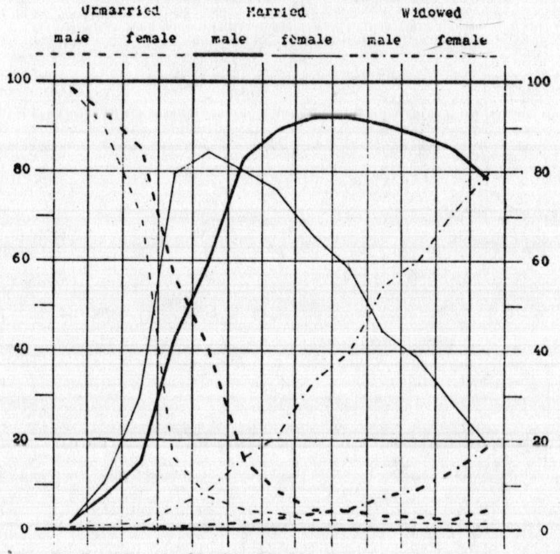

More than half the males in Calcutta remain unmarried up to the age of 20, but whereas as many as 69 per cent. are unmarried amongst females in the age-group 10-15, by the next age-group, or at an average age something over 17½, fewer than 16 per cent. remain unmarried and of the remaining 84 per cent. nearly 5 have already married and lost their husbands. The age distribution of males by marital condition is remarkably consonant with that for the whole province and practically displays no relevant difference with the exception of a rather larger proportion unmarried at the later ages. Over 80 per cent. of the male population are married at any age between 25 and 60 and very nearly 80 per cent. in the last residuary age-group (those aged 60 and over) still have wives living. As in the total population the highest proportion married is found in the age-group 35-40. Amongst females the largest number married whose husbands are still alive is in each case between the ages of 15 to 30, but in each age-group the proportion in this condition is distinctly lower in Calcutta than in Bengal and there is a correspondingly larger proportion unmarried at all ages over 15. On the other hand, from 35 onwards a larger proportion in Calcutta up to the age of 60 have retained their husbands and in all age-groups a smaller proportion are widows except at the ages 0-5 and 20-25.

SUBSIDIARY TABLE I.—Number of females per 1,000 males, by wards, 1911, 1921 and 1931.

Wards, etc.	Number of females per 1,000 males.		
	1931.	1921.	1911.
1	2	3	4
CALCUTTA WITH SUBURBS AND HOWRAH ..	**490**	**500**	**512**
CALCUTTA WITH SUBURBS IN 24-PARGANAS ..	**480**	**496**	**504**
Calcutta ..	**469**	**488**	**495**
MUNICIPAL AREA ..	**487**	**502**	**519**
Ward No. 1 Shampukur ..	642	640	635
Ward No. 2 Kumartuli ..	598	604	565
Ward No. 3 Bartola ..	634	631	666
Ward No. 4 Sukea's Street ..	536	559	623
Ward No. 5 Jorabagan ..	390	462	441
Ward No. 6 Jorasanko ..	545	590	579
Ward No. 30 Belgachia ..	564		
Ward No. 31 Satpukur ..	609	556	565
Ward No. 32 Cossipore ..	418		
Ward No. 7 Burra Bazar ..	111	201	207
Ward No. 8 Kalootola ..	239	304	358
Ward No. 9 Muchipara ..	393	427	478
Ward No. 10 Bow Bazar ..	315	337	343
Ward No. 11 Paddapukur ..	523	544	571
Ward No. 12 Waterloo Street ..	145	103	111
Ward No. 28 Beliaghata ..	701	643	694
Ward No. 29 Maniktala ..	638		
Ward No. 13 Fenwick Bazar ..	206	228	248
Ward No. 14 Taltola ..	389	419	472
Ward No. 15 Kalinga ..	397	414	412
Ward No. 16 Park Street ..	320	348	182
Ward No. 17 Baman Bustee ..	303	272	234
Ward No. 18 Tengra ..	582		
Ward No. 19 Intally ..	572	567	608
Ward No. 20 Beniapukur ..	583		
Ward No. 21 Ballygunge ..	500	643	683
Ward No. 27 Tollygunge ..	669		
Ward No. 22 Bhawanipur ..	576	600	653
Ward No. 23 Alipore ..	406	412	428
Ward No. 24 Ekbalpore ..	515	476	679
Ward No. 25 Watganj and Hastings ..	359	417	391
Ward No. 26 Garden Reach ..	546	551	637
FORT WILLIAM AND MAIDAN ..	**159**	**92**	**125**
PORT ..	**59**	**1**	**4**
CANALS ..	**4**	**1**	..
Suburbs in 24-Parganas ..	**730**	**697**	**731**
Tollygunge ..	654	624	624
South Suburban Municipality ..	781	747	747
HOWRAH ..	**550**	**520**	**562**

SUBSIDIARY TABLE II.—Distribution by age-groups

Age-group.	Numbers at age-groups shown per 1,000 persons of the same									
	Calcutta with suburbs in 24-Parganas.				Calcutta.					
	1931.		1921.		1931.		*1921.		1911.	
	Males.	Females.	Males.	Females.	Males.	Females.	Males.	Females.	Males.	Females.
1	2	3	4	5	6	7	8	9	10	11
										ALL
0—5	67	127	57	106	65	127	57	105	56	106
5—10	67	110	65	115	66	110	65	115	61	111
10—15	73	104	80	90	72	104	80	90	73	83
15—20	109	104	93	93	108	104	92	93	91	91
20—25	138	113	131	108	139	113	131	109	139	109
25—30	141	101	134	101	144	101	134	100	145	100
30—35	125	87	129	100	127	87	130	102	133	98
35—40	89	65	89	63	90	65	89	63	85	59
40—45	71	54	87	69	70	54	88	69	85	74
45—50	45	40	43	34	44	40	43	34	38	35
50—55	32	32	41	46	32	32	41	46	41	50
55—60	17	22	15	18	17	22	15	18	15	19
60 and over	26	41	36	57	26	41	35	56	38	65
										HIN
0—5	72	131	57	105	71	131	..	..	56	104
5—10	69	109	64	113	68	109	..	..	60	108
10—15	73	102	78	87	72	102	..	..	71	79
15—20	108	101	93	93	107	101	..	..	92	91
20—25	136	111	135	108	137	111	..	..	141	107
25—30	140	101	135	101	143	101	..	..	146	99
30—35	125	88	131	99	126	88	..	..	134	97
35—40	89	66	88	63	89	66	..	..	85	61
40—45	70	55	87	70	69	55	..	..	86	76
45—50	43	40	42	36	43	40	..	..	38	38
50—55	32	33	41	48	32	33	..	..	40	52
55—60	17	22	16	20	17	22	..	..	15	21
60 and over	26	41	33	57	26	41	..	..	36	65
										MUS
0—5	51	121	52	107	49	120	..	..	53	112
5—10	61	114	65	121	59	114	..	..	61	122
10—15	71	111	82	91	69	111	..	..	75	89
15—20	111	111	91	88	111	111	..	..	90	89
20—25	146	120	123	107	147	120	..	..	131	113
25—30	148	100	133	100	150	101	..	..	145	100
30—35	129	83	127	105	131	83	..	..	134	100
35—40	92	61	91	59	93	61	..	..	84	51
40—45	71	50	91	70	71	50	..	..	87	71
45—50	46	38	44	30	46	38	..	..	38	28
50—55	31	30	44	49	31	30	..	..	44	47
55—60	17	21	14	13	17	21	..	..	13	13
60 and over	26	40	43	60	26	40	..	..	45	65
										CHRIS
0—5	88	102	75	91	87	102	..	..	84	101
5—10	84	100	76	105	83	100	..	..	75	102
10—15	91	107	95	120	91	107	..	..	77	107
15—20	103	111	90	104	104	111	..	..	81	101
20—25	109	111	120	105	109	111	..	..	137	114
25—30	109	99	112	106	109	99	..	..	140	106
30—35	100	89	103	96	101	89	..	..	107	87
35—40	81	70	90	71	82	70	..	..	89	69
40—45	75	61	83	57	75	61	..	..	63	62
45—50	57	44	86	40	57	44	..	..	51	40
50—55	44	35	40	36	44	35	..	..	38	37
55—60	24	23	22	20	24	23	..	..	21	21
60 and over	35	48	38	49	34	48	..	..	37	53

*The figures in columns 8 and 9 for Calcutta

of 1,000 persons of each sex, 1911, 1921 and 1931.

sex all ages.

Howrah.						Variation : Increase+, Decrease−.					
						Calcutta with suburbs in 24-Parganas.		Howrah.			
1931.		1921.		1911.		1921-1931.		1921-1931.		1911-1921.	
Males.	Females.	Males.	Females.	Males.	Females.	Males.	Females.	Males.	Females.	Males.	Females.
12	13	14	15	16	17	18	19	20	21	22	23
RELIGIONS.											
77	126	59	101	67	109	+ 14,026	+ 12,464	+ 3,608	+ 3,305	− 147	− 252
74	104	69	115	68	106	+ 8,302	+ 1,631	+ 1,863	+ 599	+ 1,012	+ 859
76	108	83	89	80	80	+ 1,796	+ 8,727	+ 438	+ 2,676	+ 1,467	+ 756
101	112	91	95	90	92	+ 22,548	+ 7,609	+ 2,994	+ 2,619	+ 1,439	+ 393
128	117	126	115			+ 18,281	+ 5,654	+ 2,305	+ 1,612		
137	102	132	97	481	375	+ 19,259	+ 3,400	+ 2,854	+ 1,666	+ 6,869	+ 1,553
124	83	133	111			+ 9,057	− 2,334	+ 921	− 835		
91	64	90	62			+ 8,786	+ 2,888	+ 1,693	+ 1,024		
72	54	90	71			− 6,108	− 3,726	− 1,059	− 494		
45	38	40	33	179	180	+ 5,354	+ 3,251	+ 1,432	+ 764	+ 2,920	− 556
33	32	40	44			− 4,132	− 4,168	− 471	− 345		
25	22	13	17			+ 2,942	+ 2,170	+ 809	+ 641		
17	38	34	50	35	58	− 4,837	− 4,377	− 739	− 308	+ 346	− 364
DU.											
67	127	58	98	64	104	+ 11,504	+ 10,426	+ 2,871	+ 2,842	+ 242	+ 150
73	102	66	114	64	103	+ 6,186	+ 1,757	+ 1,588	+ 484	+ 1,120	+ 948
75	110	82	90	78	79	+ 1,180	+ 6,725	+ 374	+ 2,221	+ 1,465	+ 844
104	114	95	99	93	94	+ 13,296	+ 4,793	+ 2.192	+ 2,011	+ 1,393	+ 611
130	116	132	113			+ 7,796	+ 3,722	+ 1,528	+ 1,384		
139	101	135	92	491	367	+ 10,225	+ 2,871	+ 2,244	+ 1,485	+ 6,193	+ 2,112
126	81	132	112			+ 3,355	− 884	+ 1,060	− 738		
91	64	89	61			+ 4,985	+ 2,382	+ 1,449	+ 823		
72	53	88	72			− 5,202	− 2,481	− 605	− 404		
53	37	39	34	177	192	+ 2,837	+ 2,251	+ 1,005	+ 550	+ 2,463	− 411
31	33	40	45			− 3,076	− 3,048	− 374	− 264		
16	23	13	18			+ 1,447	+ 1,283	+ 512	+ 489		
23	39	31	52	33	61	− 2,429	− 3,032	− 472	− 284	+ 298	− 231
LIM.											
76	121	60	110	75	123	+ 1,595	+ 1,540	+ 684	+ 422	− 372	− 385
76	112	75	123	82	114	+ 1,513	− 339	+ 263	+ 101	− 144	− 77
77	102	84	88	87	85	+ 306	+ 1,836	+ 61	+ 441	− 57	− 102
94	105	78	80	79	86	+ 8,160	+ 2,279	+ 748	+ 580	+ 39	− 230
121	119	107	123			+ 10,363	+ 1,430	+ 765	+ 209		
132	107	125	111	452	398	+ 8,807	+ 363	+ 605	+ 166	+ 708	− 566
120	90	138	110			+ 5,419	− 1,540	− 161	− 98		
93	66	95	61			+ 3,706	+ 321	+ 225	+ 214		
75	54	99	69			− 1,095	− 1,510	− 467	− 99		
50	37	41	28	183	146	+ 2,132	+ 803	+ 436	+ 213	+ 462	− 174
36	30	43	41			− 1,328	− 1,183	− 103	− 90		
20	20	12	13			+ 1,275	+ 743	+ 288	+ 148		
30	37	43	44	42	48	− 2,485	− 1,531	− 287	− 18	+ 68	− 137
TIAN.											
116	129	91	109	110	129	+ 616	+ 530	+ 39	+ 35	− 12	− 17
96	90	99	80	76	95	+ 525	+ 230	+ 2	+ 21	+ 40	− 13
90	81	99	76	62	58	+ 283	+ 113	− 8	+ 15	+ 58	+ 19
96	104	86	100	76	85	+ 723	+ 495	+ 19	+ 16	+ 23	+ 17
97	123	107	117			+ 162	+ 479	− 9	+ 21		
97	111	110	107	445	435	+ 344	+ 193	− 13	+ 17	0	− 11
98	86	104	103			+ 344	+ 146	− 4	− 5		
84	63	82	90			+ 115	+ 204	+ 6	− 19		
77	60	73	60			+ 119	+ 263	+ 9	+ 7		
54	51	65	53	196	152	+ 236	+ 205	− 12	+ 5	+ 26	+ 17
42	40	41	33			+ 276	+ 111	+ 3	+ 11		
18	21	18	20			+ 137	+ 120	+ 1	+ 3		
35	41	25	52	35	46	+ 50	+ 122	+ 15	− 6	− 9	+ 6

refer to the area as constituted in 1921.

SUBSIDIARY TABLE III.—Number of females per 1,000 males of the same age, with the number of females per 1,000 females of all ages, expressed as a percentage of the number of males of the the same age per 1,000 males of all ages, 1911, 1921 and 1931.

Age-group.	Number of females per 1,000 males at the same age.								Number of females at ages per 1,000 females all ages as a percentage of number of males same age per 1,000 all ages.						
	Calcutta with suburbs.		Calcutta.			Howrah.			Calcutta with suburbs.		Calcutta.		Howrah.		
	1931.	1921.	1931.	1921.	1911.	1931.	1921.	1911.	1931.	1921.	1931.	1911.	1931.	1921.	1911.
1	2	3	4	5	6	7	8	9	10	11	12	13	14	15	16
ALL RELIGIONS.															
0—5 ..	917	927	914	917	941	905	898	914	189·4	185·9	195·4	189·3	163·6	171·2	162·7
5—10 ..	786	885	783	876	904	778	875	878	164·2	176·9	166·7	182·0	140·5	172·7	155·9
10—15 ..	685	560	679	546	569	781	561	568	142·5	112·5	144·4	113·7	142·1	107·2	100·0
15—20 ..	459	498	471	462	495	609	541	579	95·4	100·0	96·3	100·0	110·9	104·4	122·2
20—25 ..	392	407	381	372	390	503	475		81·9	83·4	81·3	78·4	91·4	91·3	
25—30 ..	343	374	330	350	340	408	379	438	71·6	75·4	70·1	69·0	74·5	73·5	78·0
30—35 ..	332	387	321	352	363	365	402		69·6	77·5	68·5	73·7	66·9	83·5	
35—40 ..	347	349	338		343	387			73·1	70·8	72·2	69·4	70·3	68·9	
40—45 ..	369	391	362	375	428	406	420		76·1	79·3	77·1	87·1	75·0	78·9	
45—50 ..	427	397	417		458	459			88·9	79·1	90·9	92·1	84·4	82·5	
50—55 ..	485	554	471	537	597	547	588	562	100·0	112·2	100·0	121·9	97·0	110·0	100·6
55—60 ..	611	580	598		647	704			129·4	120·0	129·4	126·7	88·0	131·2	
60 and over ..	765	790	749	770	836	847	774	932	157·7	158·3	157·7	171·0	223·5	147·0	165·7
HINDU.															
0—5 ..	932	942	928	939	948	927	895	907	181·9	184·2	184·5	185·7	189·5	169·0	162·5
5—10 ..	809	906	807	902	905	784	900	911	158·0	176·6	160·3	180·0	139·7	172·7	160·9
10—15 ..	712	569	709	562	563	812	574	573	139·7	111·6	141·7	111·3	146·7	109·8	101·3
15—20 ..	478	511	471	487	504	617	546	565	93·5	100·0	94·4	98·9	109·6	104·2	101·1
20—25 ..	416	409	406	385	384	495	450		81·6	80·0	81·0	75·9	89·2	85·6	
25—30 ..	370	383	356	367	345	402	358	416	72·1	74·8	70·6	67·8	72·7	68·1	74·7
30—35 ..	360	391	347	369	369	357	411		70·4	75·6	69·8	72·4	64·3	84·8	
35—40 ..	378	367	370		364	391			74·2	71·6	74·2	71·8	70·3	68·5	
40—45 ..	403	412	398	407	448	414	442		78·6	80·5	79·7	88·4	73·6	81·8	
45—50 ..	472	430	463		509	577		602	93·0	85·7	93·0	100·0	69·8	87·2	108·5
50—55 ..	533	600	519	591	653	582	619		103·1	117·1	103·1	130·0	106·4	112·5	
55—60 ..	677	641	663		725	766			127·7	125·0	127·7	140·0	143·8	138·5	
60 and over ..	826	886	807	879	928	926	875	1,052	157·7	172·7	157·7	180·6	169·6	167·7	184·8
MUSLIM.															
0—5 ..	880	867	879	818	929	827	909	932	237·3	205·8	144·9	211·3	159·2	183·3	164·0
5—10 ..	695	804	690	753	885	766	813	795	186·9	186·2	193·2	200·0	147·4	164·0	139·0
10—15 ..	580	478	568	419	524	683	517	547	156·3	111·0	160·9	118·7	132·5	104·8	97·7
15—20 ..	371	413	358	322	435	573	505	618	100·0	96·7	100·0	98·9	111·7	102·6	108·9
20—25 ..	303	373	291	293	381	506	563		82·2	87·0	81·6	86·3	98·3	115·0	
25—30 ..	250	320	241	261	305	418	442	498	67·6	75·2	67·3	69·0	81·1	88·8	88·1
30—35 ..	237	349	229	265	330	384	362		64·3	82·7	63·4	74·6	75·0	79·7	
35—40 ..	243	275	234		268	365			66·3	64·8	65·6	60·7	71·0	64·2	
40—45 ..	260	328	249	266	363	370	343		70·4	76·9	70·4	81·6	72·0	69·7	
45—50 ..	305	288	294		326	381		451	82·6	68·2	82·6	73·7	74·0	68·3	79·8
50—55 ..	353	435	339	364	475	434	483		96·8	111·4	96·8	106·8	83·3	95·3	
55—60 ..	446	384	433		444	523			123·5	92·9	123·5	100·0	100·0	183·3	
60 and over ..	570	583	558	517	651	636	503	649	153·9	139·5	153·9	144·5	123·3	102·3	114·3
CHRISTIAN.															
0—5 ..	955	986	954	977	917	677	871	919	115·9	121·3	117·2	120·2	111·2	119·8	126·4
5—10 ..	965	1,125	974	1,129	1,034	926	590	979	119·0	138·2	120·5	136·0	93·8	80·8	125·0
10—15 ..	945	1,016	954	1,032	1,060	709	570	727	118·3	126·3	117·6	139·0	90·0	76·8	93·6
15—20 ..	867	932	865	944	949	846	846	872	107·8	115·6	106·7	124·7	108·3	116·3	111·8
20—25 ..	829	704	827	689	636	993	788		101·8	87·5	101·8	83·2	126·8	109·3	
25—30 ..	732	755	731	751	574	898	707	767	90·9	94·6	82·6	75·7	114·4	97·3	97·8
30—35 ..	713	755	712	699	616	696	748		89·0	93·2	88·1	81·3	87·8	99·0	
35—40 ..	697	637	553		592	593			86·4	78·9	85·4	77·5	75·0	109·8	
40—45 ..	657	559	653	571	753	604	594		81·3	68·7	81·3	98·4	77·9	82·2	
45—50 ..	622	576	619		603	750		605	77·2	46·5	77·2	78·4	94·4	81·5	77·6
50—55 ..	646	731	642	736	729	746	663		79·5	90·0	79·5	97·4	95·2	80·5	
55—60 ..	763	732	766		752	920			95·8	90·9	95·8	100·0	116·7	111·1	
60 and over ..	1,110	1,034	1,119	1,027	1,103	918	1,500	1,047	137·1	128·9	141·2	143·2	117·1	208·0	131·4

SUBSIDIARY TABLE IV.—Numbers of children and aged persons per 100 of the population with number of married females aged 15---40 per 100 females of all ages and number of children under 10 years old per 100 married females aged 15—40.

Religion.	Number of children both sexes aged under 10 per 100.						Persons aged 60 and over per 100 same sex, aged 15—40.						Married females aged 15—40 per 100 females of all ages.		
	Persons aged 15—40.			Married females aged 15—40.			1931.		1921.		1911.				
	1931.	1921.	1911.	1931.	1921.	1911.	Males.	Females.	Males.	Females.	Males.	Females.	1931.	1921.	1911.
1	2	3	4	5	6	7	8	9	10	11	12	13	14	15	16
CALCUTTA WITH SUBURBS.															
All religions ..	**30**	**29**	..	**142**	**128**	..	**4**	**9**	**6**	**12**	..	..	**36**	**31**	..
Hindus ..	32	29	..	146	130	..	4	9	6	8	..	..	35	35	..
Muslims ..	25	28	..	129	126	..	4	8	8	13	..	..	42	40	..
Christians ..	38	34	..	152	137	..	7	10	7	10	..	..	27	28	..
CALCUTTA.															
All religions ..	**29**	**27**	**27**	**140**	**130**	**131**	**4**	**9**	**6**	**12**	**6**	**14**	**37**	**36**	**35**
Hindus ..	31	28	27	144	131	133	4	9	5	12	6	14	36	35	33
Muslims ..	24	24	20	128	126	91	4	8	7	13	8	14	42	40	39
Christians ..	37	33	34	151	134	152	7	10	8	10	7	11	27	28	27
HOWRAH.															
All religions ..	**32**	**29**	**31**	**131**	**119**	**122**	**4**	**8**	**6**	**11**	**6**	**12**	**38**	**39**	**37**
Hindus ..	31	28	29	137	120	124	4	8	5	11	6	13	36	38	35
Muslims ..	34	32	36	118	117	116	5	8	8	9	8	9	45	43	27
Christians ..	45	46	39	146	172	130	7	8	5	10	7	9	34	32	36

SUBSIDIARY TABLE V.—Estimates of the population in thousands on the 1st January of each year 1921 to 1930.

Year.		Calcutta with suburbs in 24-Parganas.		Calcutta.		Howrah.	
		Males.	Females.	Males.	Females	Males.	Females.
1		2	3	4	5	6	7
Population recorded at the census of—							
1921	..	**756·7**	**375·6**	**724·2**	**353·0**	**128·5**	**66·8**
1931	..	**851·9**	**408·8**	**814·9**	**381·8**	**145·1**	**79·3**
Estimated population on 1st January of each year at a uniform annual rate of change.							
Average 1921-30	..	**797·5**	**390·0**	**763·1**	**365·4**	**135·5**	**72·4**
1921	..	756·0	375·4	723·7	352·8	128·2	66·8
1922	..	765·0	378·6	732·2	355·6	129·7	68·0
1923	..	774·0	381·7	740·8	358·4	131·3	69·2
1924	..	783·1	385·0	749·0	361·1	133·0	70·4
1925	..	792·4	388·2	758·3	363·9	134·6	71·6
1926	..	801·8	391·5	767·2	366·8	136·2	72·9
1927	..	811·2	394·8	776·2	369·6	137·8	74·2
1928	..	820·8	398·1	785·3	372·5	139·5	75·5
1929	..	830·5	401·5	794·5	375·4	141·2	76·8
1930	..	840·3	404·9	804·0	378·0	143·0	78·1
Estimated population on 1st January of each year calculated from the returns of vital statistics.							
1921	..	*	*	723·7	352·8	*	*
1922	..	*	*	716·0	348·2	*	*
1923	..	*	*	710·3	344·8	*	*
1924	..	*	*	705·4	342·1	*	*
1925	..	*	*	697·6	337·7	*	*
1926	..	*	*	688·6	331·9	*	*
1927	..	*	*	678·1	323·2	*	*
1928	..	*	*	667·0	314·2	*	*
1929	..	*	*	659·8	309·3	*	*
1930	..	*	*	653·5	305·4	*	*
1931	..	*	*	648·7	302·2	*	*

* Not available.

SUBSIDIARY TABLE VI.—Number of births reported with birth rate (per 1,000) and ratio of female birth and births rate to male births and birth rate annually, 1921 to 1930.

Year.		Actual number of births reported.		Number of births reported per 1,000. Of each sex, census figures, 1921.		Of each sex estimated population on 1st January each year.		Married females aged 15—40 on the 1st January.		Number of female births per 1,000 male births.	Female birth rate (column 7) as a percentage of male birth rate (column 6).
		Males.	Females.	Males.	Females.	Males.	Females.	Males.	Females.		
1		2	3	4	5	6	7	8	9	10	11
CALCUTTA.											
Average 1921-30		**10,812**	**9,516**	**14·8**	**26·9**	**14·1**	**26·0**	**39·1**	**34·4**	**881**	**184·0**
1921	..	10,673	9,128	14·7	25·9	14·7	25·9	41·5	35·5	855	176·2
1922	..	10,631	9,205	14·7	26·1	14·5	25·8	40·7	35·2	870	178·0
1923	..	11,011	9,740	15·2	27·6	14·9	27·2	41·5	36·8	885	182·6
1924	..	10,421	9,245	14·4	26·2	13·9	25·6	38·6	34·2	888	184·2
1925	..	10,631	9,715	14·7	27·5	14·0	26·7	38·8	35·4	916	190·7
1926	..	9,747	8,452	13·5	23·9	12·7	23·0	34·9	30·3	867	181·1
1927	..	8,869	7,871	12·3	22·3	11·4	21·3	31·3	27·8	887	186·8
1928	..	11,580	10,421	14·6	29·5	14·7	28·0	40·2	36·2	898	190·5
1929	..	12,187	10,602	16·8	30·0	15·3	28·3	41·6	36·2	869	185·0
1930	..	12,372	10,779	17·1	30·5	15·4	28·5	41·5	36·2	874	185·0

SUBSIDIARY TABLE VII.—Number of deaths reported with death rate (per 1,000) and ratio of female deaths and death rate to male deaths and death rate annually, 1921 to 1930.

Year.	Actual number of deaths reported.		Number of deaths reported per 1,000 of each sex calculated on the population. Recorded at the census of 1921.		Estimated on the 1st January each year at a uniform annual rate of change.		Number of female deaths per 1,000 male deaths.	Female death rate (column 7) as a percentage of male death rate (column 6).
	Males.	Females.	Males.	Females.	Males.	Females.		
1	2	3	4	5	6	7	8	9
CALCUTTA.								
Average 1921-30 ..	**17,955**	**14,250**	**25·9**	**42·5**	**23·5**	**38·6**	**792**	**164·1**
1921* ..	17,588	12,807	28·4	44·1	24·3	36·3	727	149·4
1922* ..	14,901	11,408	24·1	39·6	20·4	32·0	771	157·0
1923* ..	14,584	11,250	23·6	38·7	19·7	31·4	771	159·4
1924 ..	18,219	13,662	25·1	38·7	24·3	35·1	751	144·4
1925 ..	19,641	15,554	27·1	44·0	25·9	42·7	796	164·9
1926 ..	20,212	17,164	27·9	48·6	26·4	46·8	850	177·3
1927 ..	19,976	16,844	27·6	47·7	25·7	44·5	843	177·0
1928 ..	18,781	15,338	25·9	43·4	23·9	41·2	816	172·4
1929 ..	18,462	14,519	25·5	41·1	23·2	38·7	787	166·8
1930 ..	17,183	13,952	23·7	39·5	21·4	36·9	811	172·4

*Death figures for Cossipore-Chitpore, Maniktola and Garden Reach are not on record for 1921, 1922 and 1923.

SUBSIDIARY TABLE VIII.—Number of deaths annually reported by sexes at age-groups, 1921 to 1930.

Age-group.	Average 1921-30.		Actual number of deaths reported. *1921.		*1922.		*1923.		1924.	
	Males.	Females.	Males.	Females.	Males.	Females.	Males.	Females.	Males.	Females.
1	2	3	4	5	6	7	8	9	10	11
CALCUTTA.										
All ages ..	**17,955**	**14,257**	***17,588**	***12,807**	***14,901**	***11,480**	***14,584**	***11,250**	**18,219**	**13,662**
0—5 ..	**4,890**	**4,364**	4,581	3,995	3,876	3,450	4,076	3,715	5,146	4,501
5—10 ..	**733**	**686**	623	550	576	504	517	470	709	649
10—15 ..	**659**	**511**	566	382	555	432	517	378	621	455
15—20 ..	**800**	**775**	661	645	626	588	648	650	736	760
20—30 ..	**2,581**	**1,863**	2,365	1,557	2,027	1,494	1,992	1,352	2,516	1,717
30—40 ..	**2,340**	**1,434**	2,505	1,195	2,086	1,133	1,912	1,060	2,374	1,326
40—50 ..	**1,949**	**1,060**	2,141	866	1,721	823	1,619	752	2,013	881
50—60 ..	**1,426**	**869**	1,496	708	1,211	638	1,145	611	1,399	724
60 and over ..	**2,577**	**2,684**	2,650	2,909	2,223	2,418	2,158	2,262	2,705	2,649

Age-group.	Actual number of deaths reported. 1925.		1926.		1927.		1928.		1929.		1930.	
	Males.	Females.	Males.	Females.	Males.	Females.	Males.	Females.	Males.	Females.	Males.	Females
	12	13	14	15	16	17	18	19	20	21	22	23
CALCUTTA.												
All ages ..	**19,641**	**15,554**	**20,212**	**17,164**	**19,976**	**16,844**	**18,781**	**15,338**	**18,462**	**14,519**	**17,183**	**13,952**
0—5 ..	5,433	5,221	5,556	5,227	4,847	4,734	4,936	4,446	5,124	4,194	5,322	4,158
5—10 ..	850	852	800	836	974	1,011	784	726	707	647	788	714
10—15 ..	650	551	617	575	868	718	750	539	652	469	791	615
15—20 ..	781	867	846	925	1,057	903	841	780	772	768	1,031	867
20—30 ..	2,836	1,926	2,764	2,156	2,948	2,048	2,610	1,905	2,704	1,987	3,047	2,483
30—40 ..	2,593	1,451	2,603	1,659	2,528	1,766	2,402	1,529	2,531	1,660	1,870	1,563
40—50 ..	2,200	1,042	2,261	1,205	2,254	1,551	1,938	1,460	2,028	916	1,318	1,106
50—60 ..	1,500	770	1,664	1,031	1,496	1,167	1,579	1,242	1,419	808	1,348	994
60 and over ..	2,798	2,874	3,101	3,550	3,004	2,946	2,941	2,711	2,525	3,070	1,668	1,452

*Death figures for Cossipore-Chitpore, Maniktola and Garden Reach are not on record for 1921, 1922 and 1923.

SUBSIDIARY TABLE IX.—Number of deaths reported with death rate (per 1,000) from selected causes with percentages on deaths from all causes annually, 1921 to 1930.

Cause of death.	Year.	Actual number reported.		Number of deaths per 1,000 total population.				Number of deaths per 1,000 deaths from all causes.	
				Recorded at the census of 1921.		Calculated at a uniform rate of change.			
		Males.	Females.	Males.	Females.	Males.	Females.	Males.	Females.
1	2	3	4	5	6	7	8	9	10
Cholera.	**Average 1921-30** ..	**1,166**	**556**	**1·7**	**1·6**	**1·5**	**1·5**	**64**	**40**
	1921 ..	1,392	605	2·3	2·1	2·3	2·1	79	47
	1922 ..	885	384	1·4	1·3	1·3	1·2	59	34
	1923 ..	602	312	1·0	1·1	0·9	1·0	41	38
	1924 ..	848	402	1·2	1·1	1·1	1·1	47	29
	1925 ..	670	326	0·9	0·9	0·9	0·9	34	21
	1926 ..	1,114	597	1·5	1·7	1·4	1·6	55	35
	1927 ..	1,488	683	2·0	1·9	1·9	1·9	74	41
	1928 ..	1,708	876	2·4	2·5	2·2	2·4	91	57
	1929 ..	1,744	827	2·4	2·3	2·2	2·2	95	57
	1930 ..	1,211	544	1·7	1·5	1·5	1·4	70	39
Small-pox.	**Average 1921-30** ..	**630**	**520**	**0·9**	**1·5**	**0·8**	**1·4**	**33**	**34**
	1921 ..	59	30	0·1	0·1	0·1	0·1	2	2
	1922 ..	247	203	0·4	0·7	0·4	0·7	17	18
	1923 ..	97	60	0·1	0·2	0·1	0·2	7	5
	1924 ..	185	131	0·2	0·4	0·2	0·4	10	10
	1925 ..	2,185	1,738	3·0	4·9	2·9	4·8	111	111
	1926 ..	536	398	0·7	1·1	0·7	1·1	27	23
	1927 ..	1,514	1,346	2·1	3·8	2·0	3·7	76	80
	1928 ..	295	263	0·4	0·7	0·4	0·7	16	17
	1929 ..	208	185	0·3	0·5	0·3	0·5	11	13
	1930 ..	972	846	1·3	2·4	1·2	2·3	57	60
Fever.	**Average 1921-30** ..	**2,422**	**2,027**	**3·5**	**6·0**	**3·2**	**5·5**	**130**	**141**
	1921 ..	2,312	1,596	3·7	5·5	3·7	5·5	90	124
	1922 ..	1,882	1,478	3·0	5·1	2·9	5·0	126	129
	1923 ..	2,159	1,577	3·5	5·4	3·4	5·4	148	139
	1924 ..	3,093	2,283	4·3	6·5	4·2	6·4	170	166
	1925 ..	2,922	2,531	4·0	7·2	3·9	6·95	149	162
	1926 ..	2,915	2,588	4·0	7·3	3·8	7·1	144	150
	1927 ..	2,577	2,306	3·5	6·5	3·3	6·2	129	137
	1928 ..	2,502	2,296	3·4	6·5	3·2	6·2	133	150
	1929 ..	2,051	1,946	2·8	5·5	2·6	5·2	111	134
	1930 ..	1,807	1,674	2·5	4·7	2·3	4·4	105	119
Dysentery and Diarrhoea.	**Average 1921-30** ..	**1,710**	**1,586**	**2·5**	**4·7**	**2·2**	**4·3**	**95**	**111**
	1921 ..	1,778	1,373	2·9	4·7	2·9	4·7	101	107
	1922 ..	1,370	1,303	2·2	4·5	2·2	4·5	92	114
	1923 ..	1,478	1,256	2·4	4·3	2·3	4·3	101	111
	1924 ..	1,816	1,542	2·5	4·4	2·4	4·3	100	112
	1925 ..	1,639	1,493	2·3	4·2	2·2	4·1	83	96
	1926 ..	1,979	2,023	2·7	5·7	2·6	5·5	98	117
	1927 ..	1,925	1,920	2·7	5·4	2·5	5·2	92	114
	1928 ..	1,852	1,775	2·6	5·0	2·4	4·8	98	116
	1929 ..	1,700	1,548	2·3	4·4	2·1	4·1	92	106
	1930 ..	1,561	1,627	2·2	4·6	1·9	4·3	91	116
Respiratory diseases.	**Average 1921-30** ..	**5,765**	**4,152**	**8·3**	**12·4**	**7·5**	**11·3**	**315**	**303**
	1921 ..	6,086	4,147	9·9	14·3	9·9	14·3	345	323
	1922 ..	5,072	3,596	8·2	12·4	8·2	12·4	340	315
	1923 ..	4,916	3,546	7·9	12·2	7·8	12·1	338	315
	1924 ..	5,864	4,153	8·1	11·8	8·0	11·6	322	303
	1925 ..	5,822	4,050	8·0	11·5	7·8	11·2	297	260
	1926 ..	6,261	4,816	8·6	13·6	8·2	13·1	238	280
	1927 ..	5,961	4,504	8·2	12·8	7·7	12·2	298	268
	1928 ..	6,147	4,486	8·5	12·7	7·8	12·0	327	293
	1929 ..	6,141	4,250	8·5	12·0	7·7	11·3	333	293
	1930 ..	5,383	3,972	7·4	11·2	6·7	10·5	313	284
Suicide.	**Average 1921-30** ..	**34**	**23**	**0·04**	**0·07**	**0·04**	**0·07**	**1·7**	**1·7**
	1921 ..	22	23	0·03	0·07	0·03	0·07	1·3	1·7
	1922 ..	22	23	0·03	0·07	0·03	0·07	1·5	2·0
	1923 ..	29	27	0·04	0·08	0·04	0·08	3·0	2·4
	1924 ..	46	34	0·06	0·10	0·05	0·09	2·5	2·5
	1925 ..	44	42	0·06	0·12	0·06	0·12	2·2	2·7
	1926 ..	32	28	0·04	0·08	0·04	0·08	1·6	1·6
	1927 ..	36	15	0·05	0·04	0·05	0·04	1·8	0·9
	1928 ..	15	10	0·02	0·03	0·02	0·03	0·8	0·7
	1929 ..	15	7	0·02	0·02	0·02	0·02	0·8	0·5
	1930 ..	34	23	0·05	0·07	0·04	0·06	2·0	1·6
Plague.	**Average 1921-30** ..	**23**	**7**	**0·04**	**0·02**	**0·03**	**0·02**	**1·5**	**0·6**
	1921 ..	30	7	0·01	0·02	0·04	0·02	1·7	0·5
	1922 ..	103	41	0·2	0·1	0·18	0·1	6·9	3·6
	1923 ..	59	18	0·1	0·1	0·08	0·05	4·1	1·6
	1924 ..	29	4	0·04	0·01	0·04	0·01	1·6	0·3
	1925 ..	8	1	0·01	0·003	0·01	0·003	0·4	0·1
	1926 ..	..	..	..	..	..	..	..	..
	1927 ..	1	..	0·001	..	0·001	..	0·05	..
	1928 ..	4	..	0·005	..	0·005	..	0·2	..
	1929 ..	..	..	..	..	..	..	..	..
	1930 ..	..	..	..	..	..	..	..	..

NOTE.—Death figures for Cossipore-Chitpore, Maniktola and Garden Reach are not on record for 1921, 1922 and 1923.

SUBSIDIARY TABLE X.—Numbers in each marital condition (per 1,000) of the same sex and age-group by religions, 1911, 1921 and 1931.

Religion.	Age period.	Number per 1,000 of the same sex.																	
		Unmarried.						Married.						Widowed.					
		1931.		1921.		1911.		1931.		1921.		1911.		1931.		1921.		1911.	
		Males.	Females.	Males.	Females.	Males.	Females.	Males.	Females.	Males.	Females.	Males.	Females.	Males.	Females.	Males.	Females.	Males.	Females.
	1	2	3	4	5	6	7	8	9	10	11	12	13	14	15	16	17	18	19
	***CALCUTTA WITH SUBURBS IN 24-PARGANAS.**																		
All religions.	0—5 ..	985	983	989	991	..	..	15	15	11	8	..	..	..	2	..	1	..	..
	5—10 ..	928	886	976	957	..	..	71	110	23	41	..	..	1	4	1	2	..	..
	10—15 ..	856	683	897	577	..	..	143	308	101	405	..	..	1	9	2	18	..	..
	15—20 ..	571	152	732	829	..	..	424	797	261	109	..	..	5	51	7	62	..	..
	20—40 ..	187	48	217	40	..	..	793	768	755	758	..	..	20	184	28	202	..	..
	40—60 ..	32	18	36	19	..	..	895	448	885	416	..	..	73	534	79	565	..	..
	60 and over ..	40	15	30	47	..	..	778	193	774	147	..	..	182	792	196	806	..	..
Hindu.	0—5 ..	987	985	989	992	..	..	13	14	11	7	..	..	..	1	..	1	..	..
	5—10 ..	932	890	978	958	..	..	67	106	21	40	..	..	1	4	1	2	..	..
	10—15 ..	862	679	903	515	..	..	137	310	94	462	..	..	1	11	3	23	..	..
	15—20 ..	593	124	746	50	..	..	402	816	247	876	..	..	5	60	7	74	..	..
	20—40 ..	196	36	220	31	..	..	783	743	751	725	..	..	21	221	29	244	..	..
	40—60 ..	31	11	36	16	..	..	891	415	877	375	..	..	78	574	87	609	..	..
	60 and over ..	43	5	30	9	..	..	762	171	755	130	..	..	195	824	215	861	..	..
Muslim.	0—5 ..	980	978	988	990	..	..	19	19	12	9	..	..	1	3	..	1	..	..
	5—10 ..	914	855	969	949	..	..	85	139	30	48	..	..	1	6	1	3	..	..
	10—15 ..	830	635	865	627	..	..	168	358	133	363	..	..	2	7	2	10	..	..
	15—20 ..	495	104	677	107	..	..	499	862	317	854	..	..	6	34	6	39	..	..
	20—40 ..	140	20	178	18	..	..	841	879	795	875	..	..	19	101	27	107	..	..
	40—60 ..	16	5	23	7	..	..	926	515	916	518	..	..	58	480	61	475	..	..
	60 and over ..	16	4	21	4	..	..	829	237	827	205	..	..	155	759	152	791	..	..
Christian.	0—5 ..	970	973	1,000	1,000	..	..	30	25	..	..	..	..	..	2	..	..	..	..
	5—10 ..	960	963	992	987	..	..	39	36	8	12	..	..	1	1	..	1	..	..
	10—15 ..	947	918	986	980	..	..	52	78	13	18	..	..	1	4	1	2	..	..
	15—20 ..	829	641	935	775	..	..	170	345	65	213	..	..	1	14	..	12	..	..
	20—40 ..	422	298	476	238	..	..	562	633	507	682	..	..	16	69	17	80	..	..
	40—60 ..	132	143	124	131	..	..	802	602	811	548	..	..	66	255	65	321	..	..
	60 and over ..	124	149	109	85	..	..	697	268	656	247	..	..	179	583	235	668	..	..
	CALCUTTA.																		
All religions.	0—5 ..	983	982	988	990	995	995	17	16	12	9	5	4	..	2	..	1	0·1	1
	5—10 ..	924	889	974	962	978	949	75	107	25	36	22	48	1	4	1	2	0·3	3
	10—15 ..	850	688	891	615	889	483	148	303	107	368	109	498	2	9	2	17	2	19
	15—20 ..	571	157	735	131	686	101	424	795	259	809	308	824	5	48	6	60	6	75
	20—40 ..	187	48	224	46	186	51	793	775	750	752	787	727	20	177	26	202	27	222
	40—60 ..	32	19	37	23	37	27	898	457	887	423	886	376	70	524	76	554	77	597
	60 and over ..	40	14	33	13	32	18	778	194	777	163	773	133	182	792	190	824	195	849
Hindu.	0—5 ..	986	984	987	990	995	995	14	15	13	9	5	5	..	1	..	1	0·1	0·2
	5—10 ..	928	894	977	963	980	948	71	102	22	35	20	50	1	4	1	2	0·3	2
	10—15 ..	857	687	900	550	887	381	142	304	98	429	111	595	1	9	2	21	2	24
	15—20 ..	595	129	747	57	679	41	400	814	246	872	314	871	5	57	7	71	7	88
	20—40 ..	197	36	225	35	173	40	784	752	748	725	798	690	21	212	27	240	29	270
	40—60 ..	32	11	36	18	37	25	890	425	880	387	876	332	78	564	84	595	87	643
	60 and over ..	44	5	33	10	33	16	764	172	761	142	752	110	192	823	206	848	215	874
Muslim.	0—5 ..	979	977	987	985	995	993	20	20	13	14	5	5	1	3	..	1	..	2
	5—10 ..	910	854	962	949	969	944	89	140	38	47	31	53	1	6	..	4	0·4	3
	10—15 ..	827	636	849	681	880	584	171	357	149	308	118	403	2	7	2	11	2	13
	15—20 ..	492	108	679	139	669	78	503	858	315	822	326	870	5	34	6	39	5	52
	20—40 ..	140	19	188	21	166	20	841	885	787	870	810	855	19	96	25	109	24	125
	40—60 ..	17	6	23	7	23	8	928	526	919	523	923	490	55	468	58	470	54	502
	60 and over ..	17	4	22	4	15	8	829	244	829	215	833	181	154	752	149	781	152	811
Christian.	0—5 ..	972	972	1,000	1,000	999	998	28	26	..	..	1	2	..	2	..	..	..	..
	5—10 ..	959	963	994	988	995	995	40	36	6	12	5	3	1	1	..	..	..	2
	10—15 ..	946	918	985	981	983	970	53	78	14	17	16	28	1	4	1	2	1	2
	15—20 ..	828	640	936	784	960	723	171	346	64	206	39	261	1	14	..	10	1	16
	20—40 ..	423	298	482	243	552	269	562	634	503	678	428	645	15	68	15	79	20	86
	40—60 ..	134	143	127	133	155	132	805	604	809	548	752	496	61	253	64	319	93	372
	60 and over ..	127	151	112	86	131	108	694	267	652	251	605	195	179	582	236	663	264	697
	HOWRAH.																		
All religions.	0—5 ..	969	981	995	993	998	995	30	18	5	7	2	·5	1	1	..	..	..	1
	5—10 ..	926	846	958	941	980	912	73	150	41	56	19	81	1	4	1	3	1	..
	10—15 ..	856	635	899	473	857	377	142	356	98	501	139	600	2	9	3	26	4	4
	15—20 ..	540	176	720	76	645	51	453	779	273	868	344	881	7	45	7	56	11	13
	20—40 ..	155	48	194	16	173	16	822	803	771	789	787	778	23	149	35	195	40	33
	40—60 ..	21	24	34	9	38	8	907	455	870	431	863	365	72	521	96	560	99	91
	60 and over ..	16	8	25	5	26	5	803	229	785	158	743	110	181	763	190	837	231	222
Hindu.	0—5 ..	970	982	996	993	997	997	30	16	4	7	3	3	..	2	..	..	..	..
	5—10 ..	931	848	951	941	981	923	68	147	49	55	18	70	1	5	..	4	1	7
	10—15 ..	868	646	910	450	871	330	130	344	86	520	125	644	2	10	4	30	4	26
	15—20 ..	565	202	746	33	668	50	428	747	248	905	322	870	7	51	6	62	10	80
	20—40 ..	165	55	205	12	181	14	813	771	761	754	780	733	22	174	34	234	39	253
	40—60 ..	22	29	37	8	44	7	903	413	864	384	848	324	75	558	99	608	108	669
	60 and over ..	17	8	31	4	34	4	787	207	755	124	709	93	196	785	214	872	257	903
Muslim.	0—5 ..	966	967	989	994	999	989	33	32	10	5	1	11	1	1	1	1	..	..
	5—10 ..	905	826	979	938	977	878	94	72	19	62	23	116	1	2	2	..	..	6
	10—15 ..	811	572	857	524	816	481	186	421	140	462	181	504	3	7	3	14	3	15
	15—20 ..	424	48	601	214	551	20	563	931	390	753	434	947	13	21	9	33	15	33
	20—40 ..	115	13	145	14	138	9	857	918	815	913	817	903	28	69	40	73	45	88
	40—60 ..	13	5	22	8	18	5	922	605	893	602	909	522	65	390	85	390	73	473
	60 and over ..	4	2	10	10	9	3	853	309	860	292	819	164	143	689	130	698	172	833
Christian.	0—5 ..	982	1,000	1,000	991	1,000	1,000	12	..	..	9	..	..	6	..	..	..	..	..
	5—10 ..	978	980	985	987	1,000	1,000	22	20	15	13	..	..	..	..	..	..	..	..
	10—15 ..	945	956	978	933	961	1,000	47	44	22	67	39	..	8	..	..	..	..	..
	15—20 ..	816	521	974	677	936	561	177	470	26	293	64	427	7	9	..	30	..	12
	20—40 ..	315	193	431	214	405	185	672	746	542	701	573	735	13	61	27	85	22	80
	40—60 ..	108	47	79	61	115	95	817	642	865	689	811	442	75	311	56	250	74	468
	60 and over ..	184	67	88	20	23	89	673	333	765	333	814	232	143	600	147	647	163	689

*Figures for Tollygunge and South Suburbs are not on record for 1911.

CHAPTER IV

Infirmities

38. **The statistics shown.**—The statistics to which this chapter is an introduction are contained in imperial table IX. They are supplemented by subsidiary tables printed at the end of this chapter and showing—

I—the number in each 100,000 of the same sex who are insane, deaf-mute, blind and leper ;

II—the distribution by age-groups of 10,000 of each sex returned as insane, deaf-mute, blind or leper at each census from 1891 to 1931 ; and

III—the number in each 100,000 of the same sex and age who are insane, deaf-mute, blind and leper with the number of females afflicted per 1,000 males by age-groups.

39. **Source and accuracy of the figures.**—The infirmities recorded at the present census are the same as on previous occasions, namely, insanity, deaf-mutism, blindness and leprosy. The statistics presented were compiled from the entry made in column 18 of the census schedule. Details are given in part I of imperial table IX by age and in part II by wards both in Calcutta and in Howrah. For full details of the compilation of these figures and general comments upon the accuracy to be expected, attention is directed to chapter VII of volume V, part I. It is expedient, however, to repeat the warning there given that the figures claim no absolute accuracy and are principally of importance for purposes of comparison between one locality and another at the same time or in different years.

40. **Census infirmities from year to year.**—Figures for the incidence of each infirmity at different census years from 1891 are illustrated in diagram

DIAGRAM No. IV-1.

Numbers insane, deaf-mute, blind and leper in each 100,000 of the same sex 1891 to 1931 for Calcutta and 1921 to 1931 for Howrah

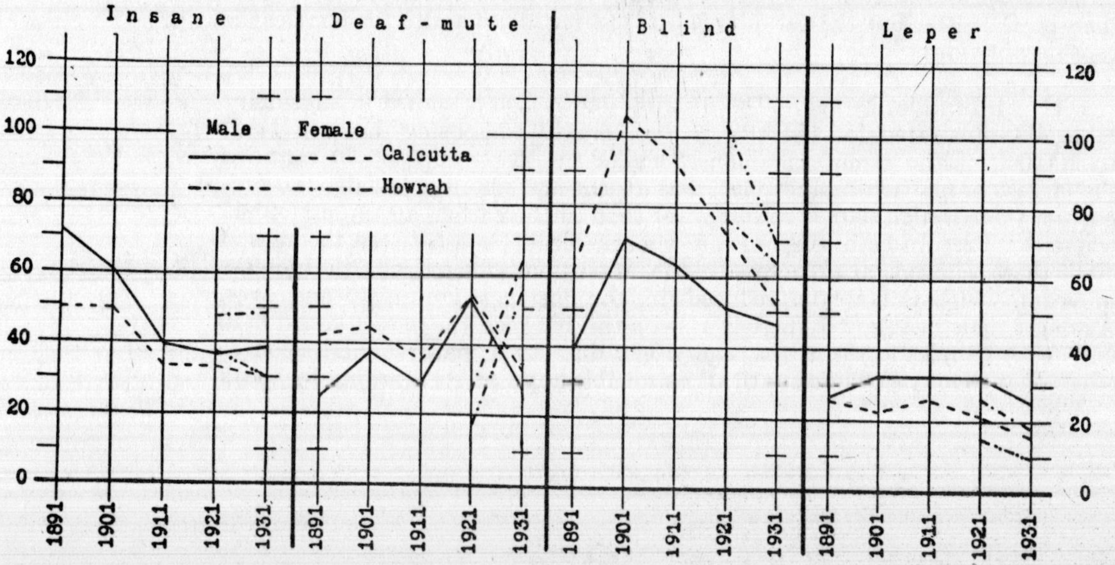

No. IV-1 plotted from the figures given in the accompanying statement No. IV-1. In Calcutta, with the exception of insanity amongst males, there has been a decrease during the last decade in the proportionate incidence reported in each of the four census infirmities. In Howrah there has been a slight increase in the incidence of insanity amongst males and a marked increase in both sexes in the reported incidence of deaf-mutism. It is unsafe, however, to draw any deduction from these tendencies since it is apprehended that the figures for all infirmities are considerably less accurate for Calcutta and Howrah than for rural parts of the province. Scientific intensive study by trained medical workers dealing with leprosy reveals over limited areas throughout the province an incidence of leprosy amounting in some cases to five or even more times that of the census return. The figures in rural areas, however, are likely to be, if anything, rather more accurate than those in Calcutta, since the enumerator is there often personally acquainted with the majority, if not all, of the persons he enumerates and moreover has very much more leisure and can afford very much more patience than the enumerator in the city. Taking the figures as they stand, however, the returns for insanity show in Calcutta amongst males a decline from 71 per 100,000 in 1891 to 38 on the present occasion, and amongst females a decline from 49 in 1891 and 1901 to 30 on the present occasion. Amongst deaf-mutes the tendency has not been so markedly in the direction of a decrease but has shown considerable variations amongst males. The figure for males was 24 in 1891 ; it rose to 37 in 1901, declined to 28 in 1911, rose again to 52 in 1921 and now stands at 27—practically the same as in 1911. The female ratio for deaf-mutes has shown similar though rather less pronounced variations and is now 32 compared with 42 in 1891. Amongst the blind in Calcutta the proportion rose considerably both amongst males (from 38 to 70) and amongst females (from 60 to 105) between 1891 and 1901, but has subsequently at each successive census shown a decline and now stands for males at 49 and for females at 53. The leprosy ratio has shown the least variation. Amongst males it was 26 in 1911, rose and stood steady at 32 in 1901, 1911 and 1921 and has now declined to 25. The female ratio which was 25 in 1891 has steadily declined with the exception of an increase between 1901 and 1911 and now stands at 15. Insanity and leprosy are not admitted in Calcutta to be so prevalent amongst females as males, but the proportions of females deaf-mute and blind are in each case higher than those for males. Comparative figures for Howrah are available only for 1921 and 1931. A slight increase in insanity has already been commented upon amongst males and there is an increase in the proportion of deaf-mutes per 100,000 from 26 to 63 amongst males and from 16 to 54 amongst females. In each sex the proportions returned in Howrah as insane, deaf-mute and blind are higher than in Calcutta, but the ratio for lepers (18 for males and 9 for females) is considerably lower.

STATEMENT No. IV-1.

Numbers per 100,000 insane, deaf-mute, blind and lepers in each sex from census to census.

Year.	Insane.		Deaf-mute.		Blind.		Leper.	
	Males.	Females.	Males.	Females.	Males.	Females.	Males.	Females.
CALCUTTA.								
1891 ..	71	49	24	42	38	60	26	25
1901 ..	60	49	37	44	70	105	32	22
1911 ..	39	33	28	35	63	92	32	26
1921 ..	36	33	52	35	51	72	32	21
1931 ..	38	30	27	32	47	53	25	15
HOWRAH.								
1921 ..	47	37	26	16	76	103	26	15
1931 ..	48	30	63	54	64	70	18	9

41. **Infirmities by age.**—The distribution by age is shown in subsidiary table III illustrated for Calcutta in four curves composing diagram IV-2. In 100,000 of the same sex amongst males the age-groups 65-70 contains the largest proportion insane (119), but at this age amongst females the proportion though high (90) is rather lower than in the earlier age-groups 40-45 where it is 92. In both sexes with a remarkable decline between the ages of 40-65 there is in general an increase in the proportions afflicted with the increase in years, which is however reduced in the last age-groups 70 and over. Amongst male deaf-mutes there is a steep rise between the ages 0-5 and 5-10 and with females again in the age 10-15 due to a natural hesitation to admit that a child is afflicted until all reasonable hope of its learning to speak

late in life has been lost. In both sexes there is then a fairly sharp decline which is in accordance with expectation owing to the fact that deaf-mutes generally are short-lived, but there are marked irregularities in the curve after

DIAGRAM No. IV-2.

Numbers insane, deaf-mute, blind and leper per 100,000 of the same sex and age-group in Calcutta.

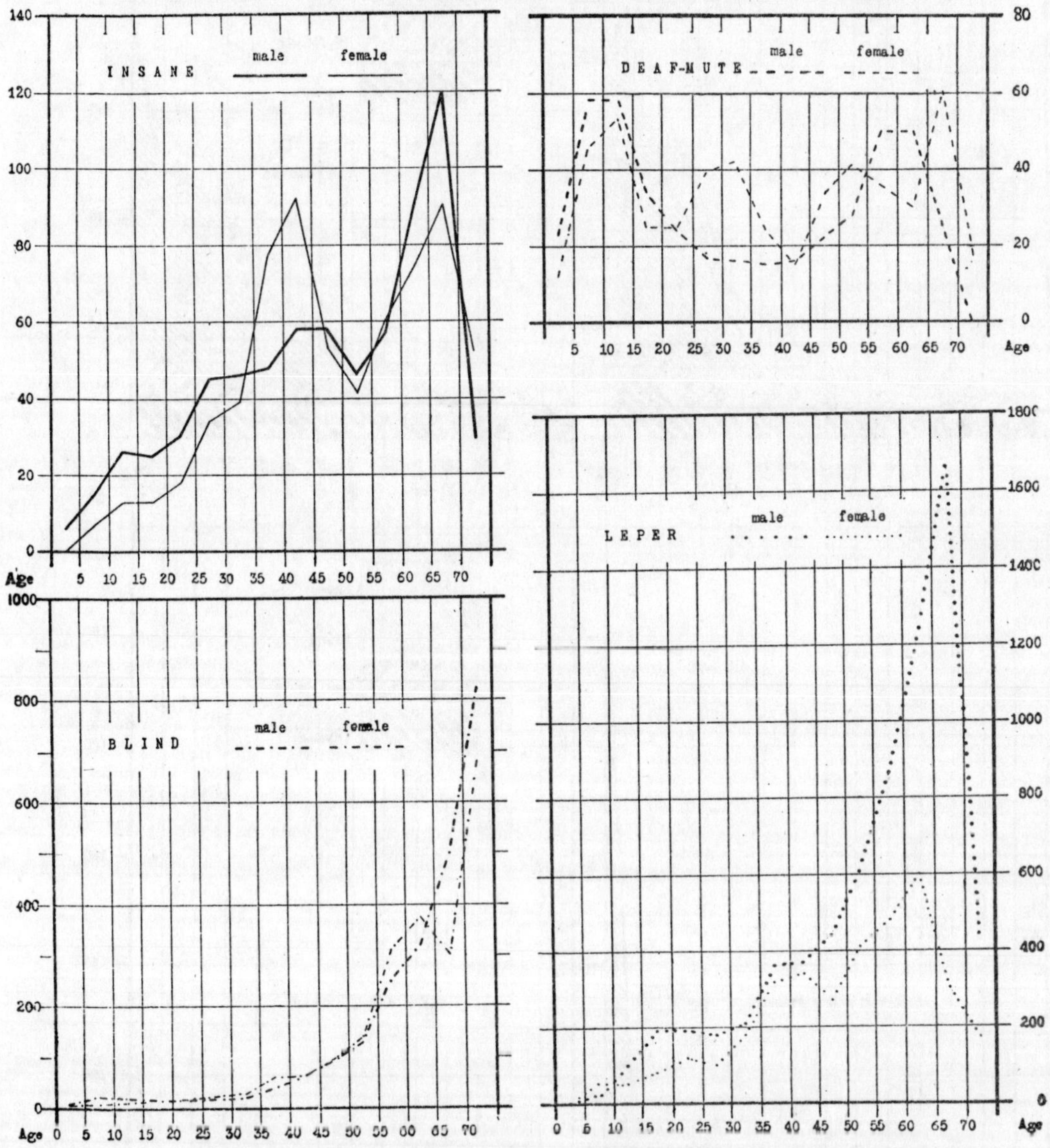

the age of 20 to 25 in the case of females and in both sexes the very considerable increase with the increase in years points to the incorrect inclusion of persons who have lost their hearing late in life. The census returns are not restricted specifically to persons deaf and dumb from birth but deaf-mutism is nevertheless a congenital disease and those suffering from it in a large majority of cases succumb to the stress of puberty. As is to be expected the figures for the blind are comparatively low at each age-groups up to 45. The proportions then show a marked increase which is accentuated after the average age of 52½. Amongst females blindness returned at each age-group is comparatively less prevalent than amongst males except between the ages of 25 to 30 and 35 to 40 and again between the ages of 50 to 55 and 60 to 65. The curve for leprosy shows an enormous increase after the age of 45 in both sexes, but particularly amongst males, and this is probably a genuine feature of the incidence of the disease since it may lie dormant until the prime of

DIAGRAM No. IV-3.

Distribution by infirmities of the total number afflicted per 100,000 of the same sex and age in Calcutta and Howrah.

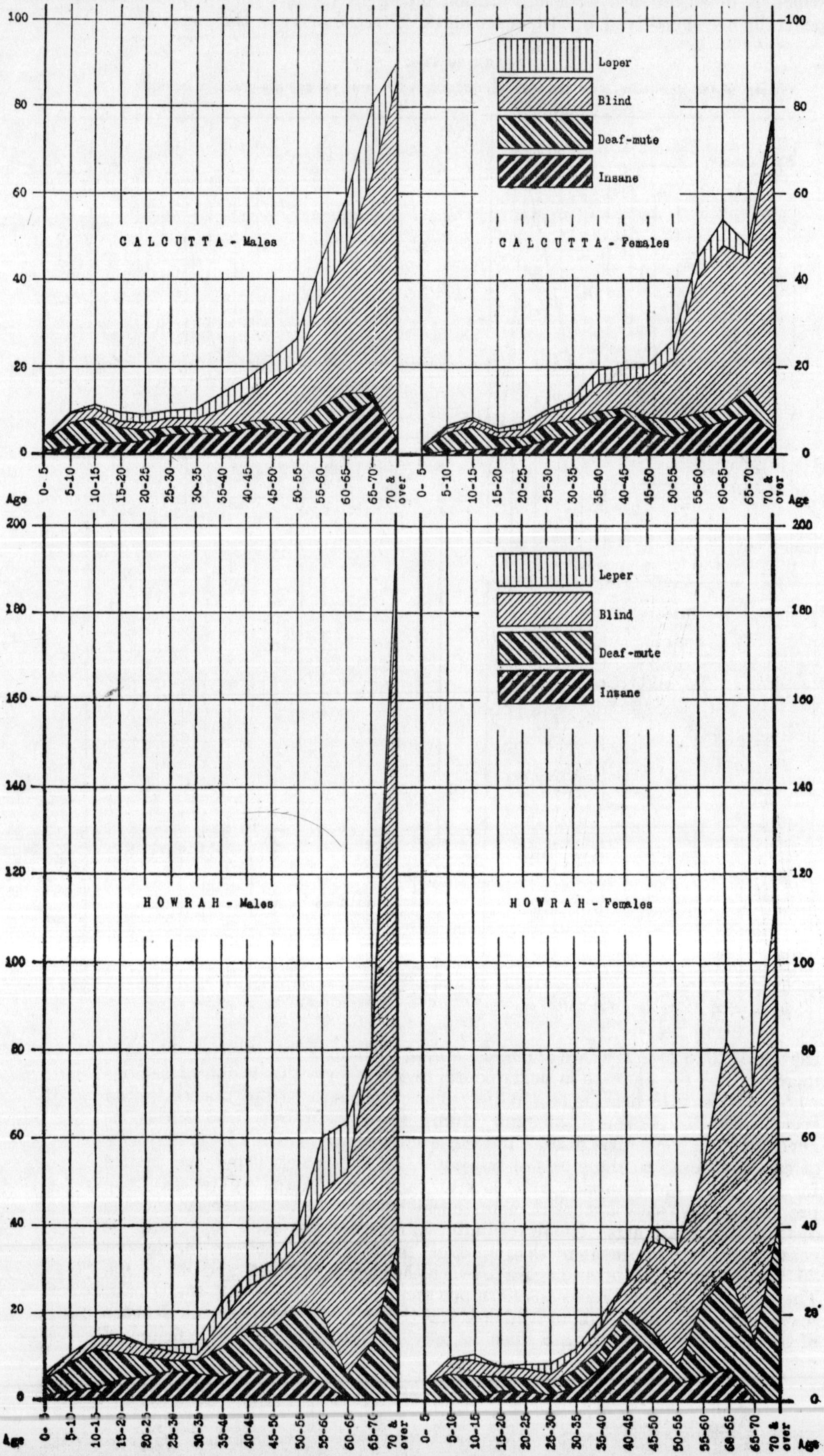

life is passed and failing powers make it impossible to offer as vigorous a resistance to it as in earlier years. Except in the two earliest age-groups the figures for leprosy for females are less in every period than those for males. This characteristic is displayed in general in the figures for all Bengal but it is doubtful if it is a reflection of the actual conditions since females are liable to the influence of predisposing causes from which males are free, and which would be expected to give the disease a greater opportunity to develop.

42. **Numbers afflicted aggregate at age-groups.**—The figures discussed in the previous paragraph are further illustrated in diagram No. IV-3 in which the figures for Howrah are also shown. In these diagrams the totals afflicted in each age-groups are shown with the numbers suffering from each specific affliction. The cumulative figures are shown in statement No. IV-2 annexed. These figures are not strictly accurate for Calcutta owing to the

STATEMENT No. IV-2.

Numbers in each sex by age-groups suffering from all four census infirmities in Calcutta and Howrah.

Age group.	Calcutta.								Howrah.							
	Insane.		Insane and deaf-mute.		Insane, deaf-mute and blind.		Insane, deaf-mute, blind and leper.		Insane.		Insane and deaf-mute.		Insane, deaf-mute and blind.		Insane, deaf-mute, blind and leper.	
	Males.	Females.	Males.	Females.	Males.	Females.	Males.	Females.	Males.	Females.	Males.	Females.	Males.	Females.	Males.	Females.
1	2	3	4	5	6	7	8	9	10	11	12	13	14	15	16	17
0—5 ..	6	..	29	12	35	14	35	14	9	..	45	40	63	40	63	40
5—10 ..	15	7	73	52	94	59	96	64	19	..	85	60	104	96	104	96
10—15 ..	26	13	84	66	104	79	114	84	27	..	118	58	145	93	145	105
15—20 ..	25	13	59	38	76	53	95	61	48	22	109	55	143	77	150	77
20—25 ..	30	18	54	43	72	61	91	73	54	21	97	53	124	74	124	85
25—30 ..	45	34	62	73	82	96	100	106	65	12	90	37	110	62	125	87
30—35 ..	46	39	62	81	82	111	103	129	61	30	89	75	106	105	128	120
35—40 ..	48	77	63	101	103	162	139	194	53	78	121	117	181	175	219	194
40—45 ..	58	92	74	107	137	170	174	204	67	164	162	211	257	281	286	281
45—50 ..	58	53	80	86	174	179	218	206	61	100	168	167	290	367	321	400
50—55 ..	46	41	73	82	203	221	264	262	64	39	212	78	360	349	402	349
55—60 ..	57	60	107	96	357	407	443	455	40	57	201	228	482	514	603	514
60—65 ..	90	75	140	105	459	479	579	539	..	74	58	297	520	817	635	817
65—70 ..	119	90	143	150	642	449	808	479	..	..	132	141	791	705	791	705
70 and over ..	29	52	29	69	853	750	897	767	..	..	361	403	1,805	1,108	1,895	1,108

inclusion within figures for each infirmity of persons suffering from more than one but their numbers are so small as to have no effect on the proportions indicated on the diagram, and there are none in Howrah returned as suffering from more than one infirmity. The diagram brings out clearly the distribution of the total afflicted in each age-group. In Howrah no increase of leprosy in either sex was returned at the later ages as in Calcutta. On the other hand, the almost certainly unreal increase of deaf-mutes in Howrah at the later ages has no parallel in the figures for Calcutta. The marked increase of blindness associated with the increase in age is a feature of both curves. In Howrah there has clearly been considerable inaccuracy in the return of leprosy particularly amongst females.

43. **Age distribution of the afflicted by sexes.**—The accompanying statement No. IV-3 illustrates the numbers in each sex suffering from each

STATEMENT No. IV-3.

Numbers under the age shown suffering from each census infirmity in Calcutta and Howrah.

Aged under.	Calcutta.								Howrah.							
	Insane.		Deaf-mute.		Blind.		Leper.		Insane.		Deaf-mute.		Blind.		Leper.	
	Males.	Females.	Males.	Females.	Males.	Females.	Males.	Females.	Males.	Females.	Males.	Females.	Males.	Females.	Males.	Females.
1	2	3	4	5	6	7	8	9	10	11	12	13	14	15	16	17
All ages	**10,000**	**10,000**	**10,000**	**10,000**	**10,000**	**10,000**	**10,000**	**10,000**	**10,000**	**10,000**	**10,000**	**10,000**	**10,000**	**10,000**	**10,000**	**10,000**
5	97	..	548	488	79	50	..	..	145	..	440	930	215	..	..	..
10	357	263	1,964	2,033	367	199	50	358	435	..	1,209	2,093	430	536	..	..
15	844	702	3,516	3,740	681	448	349	716	870	..	2,308	3,256	753	1,072	..	1,429
20	1,558	1,141	4,886	4,553	1,074	747	1,195	1,252	1,884	833	3,297	3,954	1,291	1,429	385	1,429
25	2,662	1,843	6,119	5,447	1,598	1,145	2,240	2,145	3,333	1,666	4,176	4,652	1,829	1,786	385	2,858
30	4,384	2,983	7,032	6,667	2,200	1,503	3,285	2,850	5,218	2,083	4,725	5,117	2,259	2,143	1,539	5,713
35	5,942	4,123	7,808	7,805	2,750	2,090	4,380	3,929	6,812	2,916	5,274	5,815	2,582	2,500	3,077	7,142
40	7,078	5,789	8,310	8,293	3,509	2,836	5,674	5,357	7,826	4,583	6,263	6,280	3,442	3,036	5,000	8,571
45	8,149	7,455	8,721	8,437	4,451	3,483	6,719	6,607	8,840	7,499	7,362	6,745	4,516	3,572	6,154	8,571
50	8,831	8,157	9,086	8,943	5,341	4,180	7,515	7,321	9,420	8,749	8,131	7,210	5,376	4,643	6,923	10,000
55	9,221	8,596	9,406	9,449	6,231	5,026	8,311	8,214	9,855	9,166	8,900	7,442	6,129	5,893	7,692	10,000
60	9,481	9,035	9,726	9,593	7,147	6,320	8,907	8,928	10,000	9,583	9,340	8,140	6,882	6,786	8,846	10,000
65	9,773	9,474	9,954	9,756	7,985	7,564	9,503	9,642	10,000	10,000	9,450	8,838	7,742	8,036	9,615	10,000
70	9,935	9,737	10,000	9,919	8,535	8,061	9,851	9,821	10,000	10,000	9,560	9,070	8,280	8,750	9,615	10,000

affliction who are under the age shown and for both Calcutta and Howrah these figures are illustrated in diagram No. IV-4. Except in the case of deaf-mutes and lepers in Howrah, the return in general suggests either a greater

DIAGRAM No. IV-4.

Numbers under the age shown amongst 100 of the insane, deaf-mute, blind, lepers in each sex in Calcutta and Howrah.

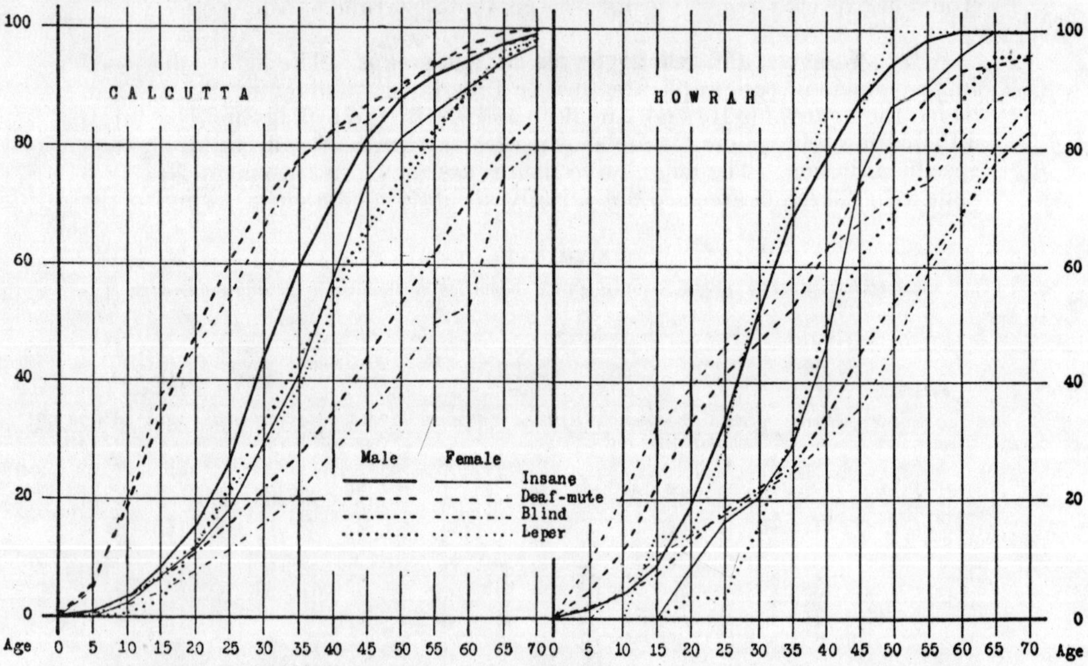

longevity amongst females afflicted than males, or a greater reluctance to reveal the existence of infirmities at earlier ages. Thus at any age chosen there is in general below that age a smaller percentage of females afflicted than of males. For instance, there are 40 per cent. female insane below the age of about 35 but this percentage has already been reached by the time the male insane reach the age of 30. In Calcutta again only 40 per cent. of the blind are under about 42½ years of age, but it is not until nearly 50 that 40 per cent. of the female blind are reached. The curve shown for deaf-mutes in Howrah brings out clearly the inaccuracies in the return to which reference has already been made. Curves for the four infirmities for Calcutta show a fairly close analogy with those for the whole of the province which will be found illustrated in chapter VII of Volume V. Deviations from the general order in which the curves of each infirmity for each sex occur in Howrah as compared with Calcutta suggest the direction in which inaccuracies have entered into the figures of Howrah.

44. **Distribution of infirmities by wards.**—Tengra, South Suburban Municipality, Ekbalpur and Bhawanipur contribute the largest number of persons afflicted with all infirmities amongst the localities shown in imperial table IX, part II. The highest proportionate incidence of insanity per 100,000 is found amongst males in Tengra (255) and the two suburban municipalities, Tollygunj (115) and South Suburban Municipality (113). Amongst females Tengra and Puddapukur with an incidence of 208 and 107 per 100,000 respectively show the highest insanity ratio. Deaf-mutism is most prevalent in Ekbalpur amongst males (88 per 100,000) but the incidence in this ward is little more than one-fourth of that amongst females in Tengra (323 per 100,000) and is considerably less than the incidence amongst females in Puddapukur (107). Tengra has the highest incidence of blindness amongst males (322 per 100,000) and with the exception of Fort William and the Maidan the highest incidence amongst females also (208 per 100,000). The actual figure in Fort William however amounts to no more than one person and the high proportion is due to the very small population of this area.

Blindness is prevalent in the South Suburban Municipality where amongst 100,000 of the same sex 284 females and 156 males are afflicted and in Ekbalpur where the figures respectively are 161 and 115. Tengra contributes more than one-half of the total lepers of Calcutta proper and the incidence is as high as almost 1·6 per cent. amongst males and 0·6 per cent. amongst females. No figures proportionate to these are to be found in any other ward and in Ekbalpur where the proportion is next highest the total numbers afflicted are only one-third of those in Tengra and the proportion in each 100,000 of the same sex is 143 for males and 152 for females. The high proportion of lepers in Tengra is of course due to the existence in that ward of the Albert Victor Gobra Leper Asylum. In Howrah blindness and deaf-mutism are the infirmities most prevalent. The highest return of insanity is made in ward No. 6 which also contributes the next highest number of deaf-mutes after ward No. 8, and the next highest number of blind after ward No. 5. Ward No. 4 in Howrah contributed the largest number of lepers.

SUBSIDIARY TABLE I.—Number insane, deaf-mute, blind and leper per 100,000 of the same sex by locality.

Name of Ward, etc.	Insane.		Deaf-mute.		Blind.		Leper.	
	Males.	Females.	Males.	Females.	Males.	Females.	Males.	Females.
1	2	3	4	5	6	7	8	9
CALCUTTA WITH SUBURBS AND HOWRAH	**42**	**31**	**33**	**38**	**54**	**58**	**23**	**13**
CALCUTTA WITH SUBURBS IN 24-PARGANAS	**41**	**31**	**28**	**34**	**53**	**56**	**24**	**14**
Calcutta	**38**	**30**	**27**	**32**	**47**	**53**	**25**	**15**
MUNICIPAL AREA ..	**40**	**30**	**28**	**32**	**49**	**52**	**26**	**15**
Ward No. 1 Shampukur ..	25	19	12	19	37	54	10	4
Ward No. 2 Kumartuli ..	50	28	46	28	50	56	..	..
Ward No. 3 Bartola ..	39	12	34	35	49	42	2	4
Ward No. 4 Sukea's Street ..	..	..	3	11	3	11	..	11
Ward No. 5 Jorabagan ..	14	18	14	18	39	9	21	..
Ward No. 6 Jorasanko ..	74	31	17	25	37	31	7	..
Ward No. 30 Belgachia ..	35	37	28	37	56	62	21	..
Ward No. 31 Satpukur ..	59	41	25	..	75	165	..	..
Ward No. 32 Cossipore ..	36	25	26	25	42	87	21	12
Ward No. 7 Burra Bazar ..	12	..	..	..	30	..	..	..
Ward No. 8 Kalootola ..	13	..	13	42	30	21	23	..
Ward No. 9 Muchipara ..	38	22	29	26	38	62	7	..
Ward No. 10 Bow Bazar ..	6	59	31	20	37	20	..	..
Ward No. 11 Paddapukur ..	60	107	52	107	47	..	..	..
Ward No. 12 Waterloo Street ..	..	..	..	..	17	..	..	..
Ward No. 28 Beliaghata ..	36	44	61	51	56	80	10	7
Ward No. 29 Maniktala ..	35	18	12	30	50	79	..	6
Ward No. 13 Fenwick Bazar ..	19	..	16	38	27	38	..	..
Ward No. 14 Taltola ..	18	..	7	..	87	..	..	..
Ward No. 15 Kalinga ..	..	25	10	50	40	25	..	..
Ward No. 16 Park Street ..	..	..	..	..	24	..	..	..
Ward No. 17 Baman Bustee ..	..	..	..	..	49	..	..	..
Ward No. 18 Tengra ..	255	208	54	323	322	208	1,585	578
Ward No. 19 Entally ..	78	37	46	62	50	50	18	19
Ward No. 20 Beniapukur ..	47	27	58	27	94	60	16	7
Ward No. 21 Ballygunge ..	29	48	29	10	53	39	5	..
Ward No. 27 Tollygunge ..	49	18	33	18	33	55	..	..
Ward No. 22 Bhawanipur ..	51	27	38	34	47	38	4	..
Ward No. 23 Alipore ..	37	23	23	12	9	35	5	..
Ward No. 24 Ekbalpore ..	88	72	88	9	115	161	143	152
Ward No. 25 Watganj and Hastings ..	46	35	29	35	33	23	8	12
Ward No. 26 Garden Reach ..	55	41	22	25	77	86	3	10
FORT WILLIAM AND MAIDAN						**237**		
PORT ..	..	..	**6**	..	**3**	**53**	**3**	..
Suburbs in 24-Parganas	**114**	**44**	**51**	**67**	**178**	**104**	**3**	**4**
Tollygunge ..	115	52	27	52	20	10	..	..
South Suburban Municipality ..	113	40	68	75	284	156	5	6
HOWRAH ..	**48**	**30**	**63**	**54**	**64**	**70**	**18**	**9**

SUBSIDIARY TABLE II.—Distribution by age-groups of 10,000 of each sex

Age.	Insane. Males. 1931	1921	1911	1901	1891	Insane. Females. 1931	1921	1911	1901	1891
1	2	3	4	5	6	7	8	9	10	11
CAL										
All ages	**10,000**	**10,000**	**10,000**	**10,000**	**10,000**	**10,000**	**10,000**	**10,000**	**10,000**	**10,000**
0—5	97	45	43	30	126	..	105	..	144	261
5—10	260	315	171	60	126	263	211	..	216	174
10—15	487	270	214	239	126	439	..	426	432	435
15—20	714	586	726	269	377	439	316	319	791	522
20—25	1,104	1,036	940	1,493	1,038	702	1,158	1,064	1,223	348
25—30	1,722	1,577	1,496	1,791	1,509	1,140	1,368	1,277	935	783
30—35	1,558	1,532	1,624	1,642	1,447	1,140	1,684	957	1,367	522
35—40	1,136	1,171	983	1,731	1,635	1,666	1,158	1,170	1,079	2,522
40—45	1,071	1,441	1,239	895	1,164	1,666	947	1,915	1,367	1,217
45—50	632	405	855	478	1,006	702	1,263	957	1,007	1,217
50—55	390	631	769	537	503	439	421	851	504	956
55—60	260	270	427	328	566	439	316	319	288	608
60—65	292					439				
65—70	162	721	513	507	377	263	1,053	745	647	435
70 & over	65					263				
SUBURBS IN										
All ages	**10,000**	**10,000**	**10,000**	**10,000**	*	**10,000**	**10,000**	**10,000**	**10,000**	*
0—5	..	225	..	..		..	213	714	..	
5—10	476	..	..	..		..	..	..	..	
10—15	476	449	526	..		833	426	..	1,000	
15—20	952	674	351	1,177		..	851	714	..	
20—25	1,430	1,011	1,930	2,353		..	638	357	1,000	
25—30	1,905	1,236	2,456	2,941		1,667	851	1,429	2,000	
30—35	1,667	1,798	1,754	1,176		2,500	1,064	2,143	2,000	
35—40	952	1,011	526	1,177		2,500	638	714	1,000	
40—45	952	787	702	..		1,667	1,489	1,429	1,000	
45—50	476	787	1,404	588		833	638	357	..	
50—55	476	1,011	176	..		..	426	357	2,000	
55—60	..	449	..	588		..	213	..	..	
60—65	..					..				
65—70	..	562	175	..		..	2,553	1,786	..	
70 & over	238					..				

Age.	Blind. Males. 1931	1921	1911	1901	1891	Blind. Females. 1931	1921	1911	1901	1891
1	22	23	24	25	26	27	28	29	30	31
CAL										
All ages	**10,000**	**10,000**	**10,000**	**10,000**	**10,000**	**10,000**	**10,000**	**10,000**	**10,000**	**10,000**
0—5	79	32	208	202	351	50	144	..	167	213
5—10	288	319	494	177	234	149	239	151	67	213
10—15	314	733	520	328	585	249	335	340	166	355
15—20	393	637	364	556	585	299	96	38	367	71
20—25	524	478	545	404	468	398	335	377	333	284
25—30	602	446	701	758	351	448	335	604	333	142
30—35	550	732	701	1,439	468	497	526	491	467	567
35—40	759	541	571	328	585	746	383	302	400	142
40—45	942	764	1,013	1,111	818	647	574	792	833	993
45—50	890	955	571	631	702	697	526	566	433	851
50—55	890	733	1,039	783	1,286	846	1,005	1,207	967	1,489
55—60	916	382	338	379	2,748	1,294	574	453	667	2,269
60—65	838					1,244				
65—70	550	3,248	2,935	2,904	819	497	4,928	4,679	4,800	2,411
70 & over	1,465					1,939				
SUBURBS IN										
All ages	**10,000**	**10,000**	**10,000**	**10,000**	*	**10,000**	**10,000**	**10,000**	**10,000**	*
0—5	..	430	714	232		..	128	667	500	
5—10	1,061	107	714	465		1,071	..	334	..	
10—15	1,818	322	714	465		1,786	128	167	..	
15—20	2,423	323	1,072	930		2,144	385	167	..	
20—25	1,818	753	357	233		1,429	128	333	250	
25—30	303	860	357	232		357	256	333	250	
30—35	..	538	357	698		714	641	833	750	
35—40	152	215	536	698		..	128	333	1,000	
40—45	303	968	357	930		..	1,026	500	500	
45—50	..	430	536	465		357	385	500	500	
50—55	152	968	179	233		357	897	1,000	1,750	
55—60	303	1,183	357	..		357	898	333	750	
60—65	303					357				
65—70	303	2,903	3,750	4,419		714	5,000	4,500	3,750	
70 & over	1,061					357				

*Not

returned as insane, deaf-mute, blind or leper at each census from 1891 to 1931.

Deaf-mute.									
Males.					Females.				
1931	1921	1911	1901	1891	1931	1921	1911	1901	1891
12	13	14	15	16	17	18	19	20	21
CUTTA.									
10,000	10,000	10,000	10,000	10,000	10,000	10,000	10,000	10,000	10,000
548	279	636	333	561	488	581	392	80	505
1,416	774	1,098	905	841	1,545	710	1,765	1,040	707
1,552	1,177	1,445	1,048	561	1,707	903	784	1,040	909
1,370	1,268	1,272	952	935	813	645	1,177	1,280	202
1,233	960	983	1,143	935	894	710	1,177	800	404
913	867	809	905	841	1,220	839	882	640	404
776	681	1,041	762	1,215	1,138	968	1,079	400	1,010
502	619	462	619	934	488	516	882	480	505
411	867	694	857	654	144	710	686	720	1,111
365	526	462	571	654	506	322	98	320	606
320	464	578	667	654	506	645	294	720	808
320	434	173	286	467	144	451	..	320	1,414
228					163				
46	1,084	347	952	748	163	2,000	784	2,160	1,415
..					81				
24-PARGANAS.									
10,000	10,000	10,000	10,000		10,000	10,000	10,000	10,000	
526	1,064	833	833		2,222	..	..	1,177	
2,105	1,277	2,778	..		1,667	1,818	4,286	1,176	
2,632	1,277	1,667	2,500		2,222	909	1,429	1,177	
1,053	851	833	..		1,111	1,818	1,428	..	
526	1,277	278	833		1,111	..	..	588	
1,053	638	555	417		1,111	1,364	..	1,765	
1,053	851	1,389	833		..	455	2,143	588	
526	1,277	556	834		..	909	..	..	
..	425	..	833		556	455	714	588	
..	425	..	417		..	454	..	..	
..	213	1,111	1,250		..	..	..	1,177	
526	..	..	417		..	..	..	588	
..					..				
..	425	..	833		..	1,818	..	1,176	
..					..				

Leper.									
Males.					Females.				
1931	1921	1911	1901	1891	1931	1921	1911	1901	1891
32	33	34	35	36	37	38	39	40	41
CUTTA.									
10,000	10,000	10,000	10,000	10,000	10,000	10,000	10,000	10,000	10,000
..	152	51	..	174	..	..	..	..	345
50	101	51	56	174	358	323	..	161	345
299	..	300	111	348	358	323	..	161	862
846	305	306	667	435	536	645	400	323	517
1,045	355	306	1,000	783	893	645	400	968	862
1,045	1,624	1,735	1,333	869	714	1,613	1,333	645	..
1,095	1,574	1,531	1,222	1,130	1,070	806	934	1,290	862
1,294	1,777	765	1,111	1,826	1,428	806	1,733	1,613	517
1,045	1,218	1,735	1,333	1,478	1,250	806	1,333	1,129	862
796	863	663	667	522	714	968	400	823	1,035
796	812	1,225	1,167	696	893	968	1,200	968	690
596	305	357	333	435	714	..	267	1,935	1,724
596					714				
348	914	969	1,000	1,130	179	2,097	2,000	484	1,379
149					179				
24-PARGANAS.									
10,000	10,000	10,000	10,000		10,000	10,000	10,000	10,000	
..	..	..	..		..	..	..	..	
..	..	..	..		..	..	..	..	
..	370	588	714		..	..	..	..	
..	1,111	..	..		..	..	..	..	
..	1,111	..	714		..	..	..	..	
..	741	588	715		..	6,667	..	..	
..	741	1,765	714		..	..	..	..	
10,000	..	1,765	714		..	..	2,000	2,500	
..	2,963	1,765	1,429		..	..	..	2,500	
..	370	588	..		..	..	..	..	
..	741	588	1,429		..	..	4,000	2,500	
..	..	588	..		10,000	..	..	2,500	
..					..				
..	1,852	1,765	3,571		..	3,333	4,000	..	
..					..				

available.

SUBSIDIARY TABLE II.—Distribution by age-groups of 10,000 of each sex returned as insane, deaf-mute, blind or leper at each census from 1891 to 1931.

Age.	Insane.				Deaf-mute.				Blind.				Leper.			
	Males.		Females.		Males.		Females.		Males.		Females.		Males.		Females.	
	1931	1921	1931	1921	1931	1921	1931	1921	1931	1921	1931	1921	1931	1921	1931	1921
1	2	3	4	5	6	7	8	9	10	11	12	13	14	15	16	17
HOWRAH.																
All ages	**10,000**	**10,000**	**10,000**	**10,000**	**10,000**	**10,000**	**10,000**	**10,000**	**10,000**	**10,000**	**10,000**	**10,000**	**10,000**	**10,000**	**10,000**	**10,000**
0—5	145	..	..	..	440	294	930	2,728	215	412	..	..	..	..	..	..
5—10	290	492	..	..	769	2,059	1,163	909	215	516	536	580	..	..	..	..
10—15	435	164	..	400	1,099	1,765	1,163	1,818	323	1,031	536	290	..	..	1,429	..
15—20	1,014	656	833	1,200	989	882	698	909	538	309	357	290	385	294	..	2,000
20—25	1,449	1,639	333	800	879	..	698	..	538	103	357	725	..	1,471	1,429	..
25—30	1,885	1,147	417	1,600	549	1,177	465	909	430	206	357	145	1,154	1,765	2,855	4,000
30—35	1,594	2,951	833	1,200	549	1,471	698	..	323	1,237	357	435	1,538	882	1,429	..
35—40	1,014	820	1,667	800	989	294	465	909	860	206	536	869	1,923	1,471	1,429	1,000
40—45	1,014	1,311	2,916	1,600	1,099	..	465	909	1,074	928	536	1,159	1,154	588	..	..
45—50	580	164	1,250	..	769	588	465	..	860	619	1,071	580	769	882	1,429	1,000
50—55	435	656	417	800	769	588	232	909	753	1,134	1,250	869	769	1,471	..	2,000
55—60	145	..	417	..	440	294	698	..	753	309	893	580	1,154	294	..	..
60—65	..		417		110		698		860		1,250		769		..	
65—70	..	..	..	1,600	110	588	232	..	538	2,990	714	3,478	..	882	..	..
70 & over	..		..		440		930		1,720		1,250		385		..	

SUBSIDIARY TABLE III.—Number insane, deaf-mute, blind and leper in each 100,000 of the same sex and age with number of females afflicted per 1,000 males of the same age.

	Age.	Number afflicted per 100,000.								Number of females afflicted per 1,000 males.			
		Insane.		Deaf-mute.		Blind.		Leper.					
		Males.	Females.	Males.	Females.	Males.	Females.	Males.	Females.	Insane.	Deaf-mute.	Blind.	Leper.
	1	2	3	4	5	6	7	8	9	10	11	12	13
CALCUTTA.	**All ages**	**38**	**30**	**27**	**32**	**47**	**53**	**25**	**15**	**370**	**562**	**526**	**279**
	0—5	6	..	23	12	6	2	..	..	..	500	333	..
	5—10	15	7	58	45	21	7	2	5	375	613	273	2,000
	10—15	26	13	58	53	20	13	10	5	333	618	417	333
	15—20	25	13	34	25	17	15	19	8	227	333	400	176
	20—25	30	18	24	25	18	18	19	12	235	407	400	238
	25—30	45	34	17	39	20	23	18	10	245	750	391	190
	30—35	46	39	16	42	20	30	21	18	271	824	476	273
	35—40	48	77	15	24	40	61	36	32	543	545	517	308
	40—45	58	92	16	15	63	63	37	34	576	333	361	333
	45—50	58	53	22	33	94	93	44	27	381	625	412	250
	50—55	46	41	27	41	130	139	61	41	417	714	500	312
	55—60	57	60	50	36	250	311	86	48	625	429	743	333
	60—65	90	75	50	30	319	374	120	60	555	400	781	333
	65—70	119	90	24	60	499	299	166	30	600	2,000	476	143
	70 & over	29	52	..	17	824	681	44	17	1,500	..	696	333
SUBURBS.	**All ages**	**114**	**44**	**51**	**67**	**178**	**104**	[illegible]	[illegible]	[illegible]	[illegible]	[illegible]	[illegible]
	0—5	..	..	26	108	..	..	..	..	..	4,000	..	..
	5—10	55	..	110	100	192	100	..	..	..	750	429	..
	10—15	56	36	140	145	335	181	..	..	500	800	417	..
	15—20	97	..	48	74	387	221	..	..	..	1,000	375	..
	20—25	137	..	23	69	274	138	..	..	..	2,000	333	..
	25—30	239	77	60	77	60	39	..	..	250	1,000	500	..
	30—35	217	133	62	..	..	89	..	..	429	..	..	..
	35—40	129	175	32	..	32	..	32	..	750	..	..	..
	40—45	136	133	..	67	68	..	..	..	500	..	..	..
	45—50	110	88	..	..	..	88	..	..	500	..	..	..
	50—55	174	..	..	..	87	107	..	..	..	..	1,000	..
	55—60	..	..	134	..	269	157	..	157	..	..	500	..
	60—65	..	..	..	..	381	187	..	..	..	..	500	..
	65—70	..	..	..	..	893	763	..	..	..	..	1,000	..
	70 & over	280	..	..	..	1,961	264	..	..	..	..	143	..
HOWRAH.	**All ages**	**48**	**30**	**63**	**54**	**64**	**70**	**18**	**9**	**348**	**473**	**602**	**269**
	0—5	9	..	36	40	18	..	..	..	..	1,000	..	..
	5—10	19	..	66	60	19	36	..	..	..	714	1,500	..
	10—15	27	..	91	58	27	35	..	12	..	500	1,000	..
	15—20	48	22	61	33	34	22	7	..	286	333	400	..
	20—25	54	21	43	32	27	21	..	11	200	375	400	..
	25—30	65	12	25	25	20	25	15	25	77	400	500	667
	30—35	61	30	28	45	17	30	22	15	182	600	667	250
	35—40	53	78	68	39	60	58	38	19	571	222	375	200
	40—45	67	164	95	47	95	70	29	..	1,000	200	300	..
	45—50	61	100	107	67	122	200	31	33	750	286	750	500
	50—55	64	39	148	39	148	271	42	..	333	143	1,000	..
	55—60	40	57	161	171	281	286	121	..	1,000	750	714	..
	60—65	..	74	58	223	462	520	115	..	..	3,000	875	..
	65—70	..	..	132	141	659	564	..	..	..	1,000	800	..
	70 & over	..	..	361	403	1,444	705	90	..	..	1,000	438	..

CHAPTER V

Occupation

45. **The statistics shown.**—The statistics to which this chapter is an introduction are contained in imperial tables X showing occupation or means of livelihood and XI showing occupations of selected castes or similar groups. The contents of the tables together with a comparison between the details presented in 1921 and on the present occasion are sufficiently described in the title page to each table and are not here repeated. Subsidiary tables printed at the end of this chapter show—

I—the numbers of workers by sex and occupation in 1911, 1921 and 1931; and

II—the numbers of workers engaged in each occupation per 10,000 of the total population of the same sex, 1911, 1921 and 1931.

46. **Source of the statistics and particularity of the returns.**—General comment on the method in which the statistics were obtained is given in detail in chapter VIII of volume V, part i, to which the reader is referred. A detailed comment on the scheme of classification adopted is also given there. In Calcutta the largest proportion and in Howrah the second largest proportion is contributed to the returns by persons whose means of livelihood was not described with sufficient precision to permit its being included in one of the specific occupational categories, and all comment on the occupational distribution is made with the reservation that the figures in some groups, presumably falling mainly under Industry or Trade, should be higher than they actually are.

47. **Dependence.**—In Calcutta 586,367 males and 46,972 females are workers and the corresponding numbers in Howrah are 72,208 males and 8,742 females. In every 10,000 males consequently 6,883 are workers in Calcutta and 4,976 in Howrah and in a corresponding number of females there are 1,149 workers in Calcutta with suburbs in 24-Parganas and 1,097 in Howrah. In each sex and in both cities there has been a considerable decline in the proportion but not in the actual number returned as workers. In 1921, amongst 10,000 males there were 7,686 workers in Calcutta with suburbs in 24-Parganas and 7,595 in Howrah and the corresponding figures amongst females were 1,810 and 1,827. The figures are given in the accompanying statement No. V-1 and illustrated in diagram No. V-1. The proportion of

STATEMENT No. V-1.

Numbers per 10,000 of each sex who are workers (distinguished in 1931 as "earners" and "working dependents") and non-working dependents, in Calcutta with suburbs in 24-Parganas and in Howrah, 1921 and 1931.

	Calcutta with suburbs in 24-Parganas.				Howrah.			
	1921		1931		1921		1931	
	Males.	Females.	Males.	Females.	Males.	Females.	Males.	Females.
Workers	7,686	1,810	6,883	1,149	7,595	1,827	4,976	1,097
Earners	..	..	6,841	1,146	..	..	4,957	1,092
Working dependents	..	..	42	3	..	..	19	5
Non-working dependents	2,314	8,190	3,117	8,851	2,405	8,173	5,024	8,903

DIAGRAM No. V-1.

Proportionate distribution of workers and non-working dependents in Calcutta with suburbs in 24-Parganas and in Howrah, 1921 and 1931.

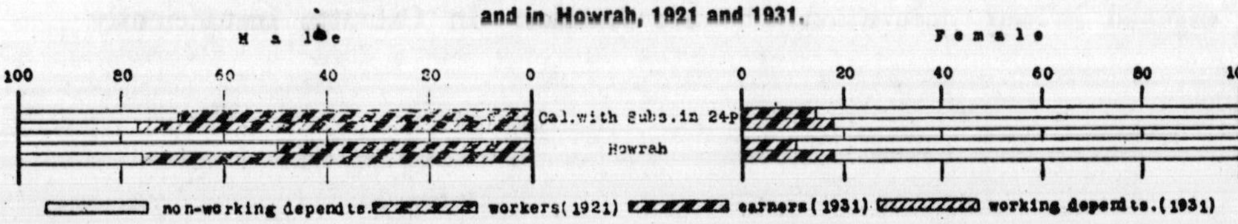

workers who contribute their labour for the assistance of other members of their family without obtaining any direct return in cash or kind for it, is very low and can be indicated on the scale shown on the diagram only in one instance. In every 10,000 of the same sex working dependents amount amongst males to 42 in Calcutta with suburbs in 24-Parganas and to 19 in Howrah, and amongst females to 3 in Calcutta with suburbs in 24-Parganas and to 5 in Howrah. In chapter VIII of volume V, part i, the opinion is expressed that the decline in the proportion of workers is most probably due principally to the innovation under which separate statistics have been obtained for working dependents, and that the figures shown on the present occasion for earners may probably be taken in general as reasonably accurate. As has been suggested for Bengal as a whole this explanation receives here also support from the figures for some of the occupational sub-classes in which it is unlikely that dependents should render any assistance. The proportion of the population occupied in the category of public force is almost exactly the same in 1931 as in 1921 and there is a considerable increase in the proportions of those employed, amongst males, as public servants or in domestic service and of those living on their income. An increase is also shown amongst females living on their income, but at the same time there has been a noticeable increase in the number whose means of livelihood was not sufficiently described.

48. **Occupational distribution by sub-classes and sex.**—Diagram No. V-2 illustrates statement No. V-2 and shows, for Calcutta with suburbs in 24-Parganas and for Howrah, the numbers and percentages of the total

DIAGRAM No. V-2.

Distribution of workers by occupational sub-classes, in Calcutta with suburbs in 24-Parganas and Howrah, 1921 and 1931.

NOTE.—For explanation see text.

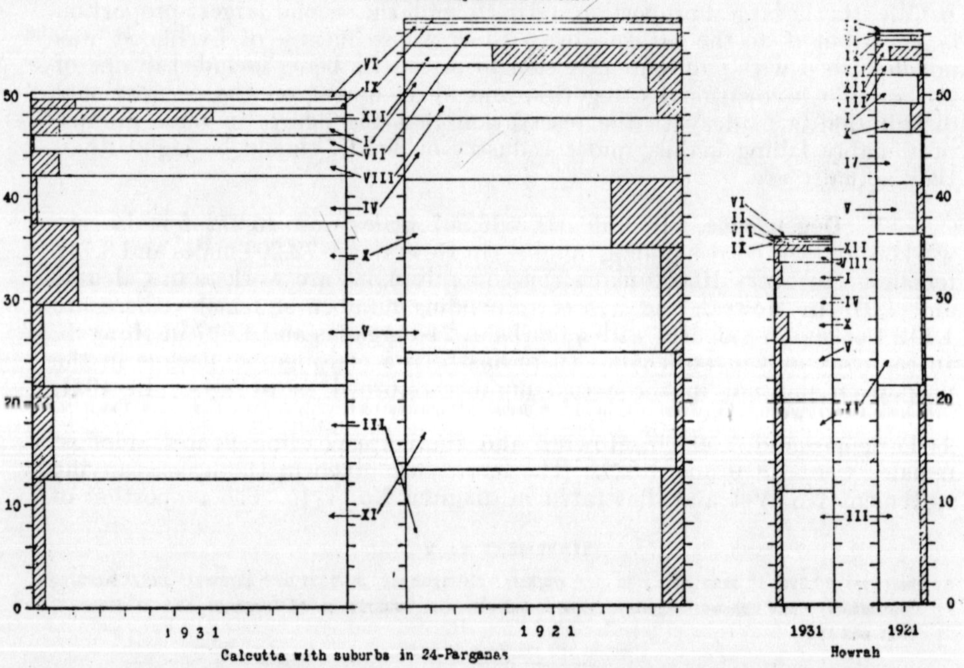

population employed in each of the main sub-classes in the occupational scheme. In the diagram each interval marked on the base represents a total population of 100,000 and each interval marked vertically represents 2 per cent. of the total population. The total area covered by each rectangle, therefore, is proportionate to the total number of workers and its height represents the proportion of workers to the total population. The diagram also indicates in the shaded portions the relative numbers of those engaged in any occupation who are females. In Calcutta insufficiently described occupations are the means of livelihood of the largest proportion of the working population and industry of the next largest group. In Howrah the very large number of persons employed in industry reverses the order of

STATEMENT No. V-2.

Numbers of workers in each occupational sub-class with percentage on total population and percentage of workers who are females in Calcutta with suburbs in 24-Parganas and Howrah, 1921 and 1931.

Occupational sub-class.	Calcutta with suburbs in 24-Parganas.						Howrah.					
	1931—Population 1,260,709			1921—Population 1,132,246			1931—Population 224,873			1921—Population 195,301		
	No. of workers.	Per cent. of total population.	Per cent. of workers who are females.	No. of workers.	Per cent. of total population.	Per cent. of workers who are females.	No. of workers.	Per cent. of total population.	Per cent. of workers who are females.	No. of workers.	Per cent. of total population.	Per cent. of workers who are females.
I—Exploitation of animals and vegetation	17,017	1·34	9·43	27,389	2·42	11·95	4,752	2·11	11·61	5,436	2·78	9·32
II—Exploitation of minerals ..	93	0·01	6·45	78	0·01	2·56	285	0·13	3·15	46	0·02	21·73
III—Industry	113,786	9·03	6·38	150,899	13·33	7·60	25,228	11·22	9·43	42,100	21·56	11·72
IV—Transport	57,629	4·57	1·58	68,583	6·06	1·59	6,253	2·78	1·99	9,754	4·99	1·70
V—Trade	100,609	7·98	3·67	115,962	10·24	7·55	12,652	5·63	8·29	9,860	5·05	13·45
VI—Public force	7,545	0·60	..	6,727	0·59	..	190	0·08	..	647	0·33	..
VII—Public administration ..	21,058	1·67	0·59	16,873	1·49	1·35	434	0·19	11·75	1,207	0·62	0·41
VIII—Professions and liberal arts ..	30,353	2·41	9·03	29,734	2·63	8·51	2,588	1·15	5·40	2,775	1·42	4·68
IX—Persons living on their income	11,877	0·94	14·02	5,084	0·45	33·73	576	0·26	22·22	1,037	0·53	26·71
X—Domestic service	100,304	7·96	14·63	75,576	6·67	25·74	6,720	2·99	22·45	5,644	2·89	26·87
XI—Insufficiently described occupations	157,923	12·53	3·54	129,264	11·42	2·71	20,099	8·94	10·63	28,745	14·72	5·60
XII—Unproductive	15,145	1·20	57·34	23,397	2·07	68·19	1,173	0·52	56·35	2,536	1·30	68·05

these two categories. Domestic service and transport in both cities follow in descending order. In Howrah as many as 2·1 per cent. of the population have an agricultural occupation compared with 1·34 per cent. in Calcutta. Professions and the liberal arts offer employment to 1·15 per cent. of the population of Howrah and 2·4 per cent. of the population of Calcutta and other occupations provide for a comparatively small proportion only. In Howrah the relative proportions engaged in each occupational sub-class appear in practically the same order both in 1921 and 1931 with the exception that persons living on their income now form a larger portion of the population than public servants, and those engaged in transport a smaller proportion than those employed as domestic servants. In Calcutta there are somewhat greater deviations. Industry, specifically and sufficiently described, now accounts for a smaller proportion of the population than insufficiently described occupations and the proportion employed in public service is now greater either than those employed in pasture and agriculture or those following unproductive occupations. Amongst persons following unproductive occupations in both cities in both years there is an actual preponderance of females owing to the fact that prostitutes contribute a very considerable proportion of the occupations grouped in this category. In both cities in each year those employed in domestic service or living on their income as well as those occupied in sub-class XII already mentioned include a proportion of females which is considerably higher than in other categories. A comparatively large proportion of workers are women also amongst those whose occupation is agriculture, public service, insufficiently described occupations, industry and trade in Howrah. In Calcutta the proportion of women workers to the total is less than in Howrah in every instance except the negligible numbers employed in mining, those engaged in professions and liberal arts and those following unproductive occupations.

49. **Proportionate distribution of occupations by sexes.**—Diagram No. V-3 illustrating statement No. V-3 shows the total proportions in each sex engaged in each sub-class in Calcutta with suburbs in 24-Parganas and in Howrah. Comment on this diagram has largely been offered in advance in dealing with diagram No. V-2, but additional information is conveyed as to the relative popularity in each sex of the different occupational categories. It is, for instance, interesting that in Calcutta with suburbs in 24-Parganas more than half as many females again are living on unproductive occupations as on insufficiently described occupations and 2½ times as many as on domestic

service and that industry supports, apart from those returned under undefined designations, almost exactly half as many females as live on

DIAGRAM No. V-3.

Number of workers by sexes in each occupational sub-class per 100 of the same sex in Calcutta with suburbs in 24-Parganas and in Howrah, 1921 and 1931.

NOTE.—The figures in 1931 for sub-class XII (males) for Calcutta with suburbs in 24-Parganas are incorrectly represented and should be 76 and 42 instead of 118 and 42.

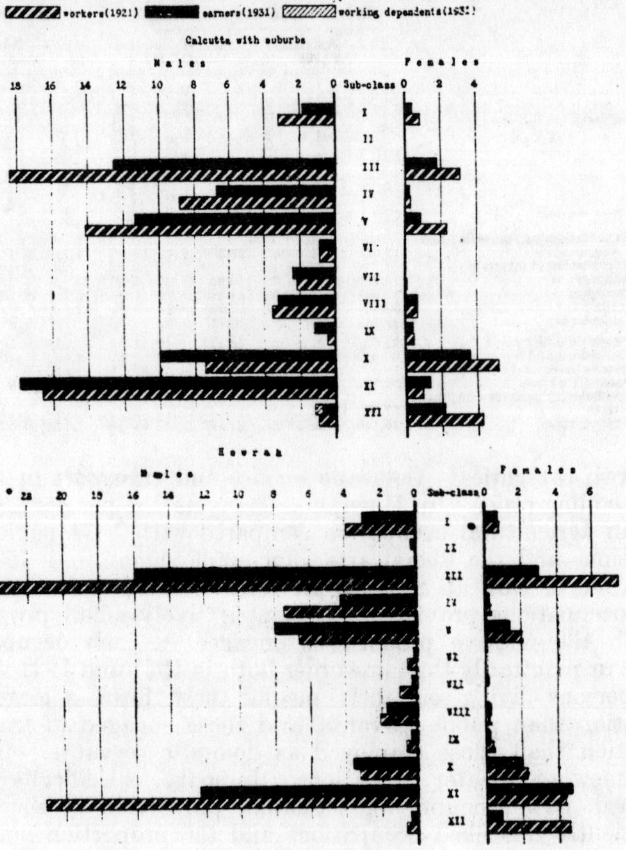

domestic service. The figures for Howrah are different. More than half as many females again are supported by industry properly returned as are living

STATEMENT No. V-3.

Numbers of workers by occupational sub-classes per 10,000 of each sex in Calcutta with suburbs in 24-Parganas and in Howrah, 1921 and 1931.

NOTE.—The figures in brackets are of working dependents included with earners in those which they follow.

Occupational sub-class.	Calcutta with suburbs in 24-Parganas. 1931 Males.	1931 Females.	1921 Males.	1921 Females.	Howrah. 1931 Males.	1931 Females.	1921 Males.	1921 Females.
All sub-classes	**6,883 (42)**	**1,149 (3)**	**7,686**	**1,810**	**4,976 (19)**	**1,097 (5)**	**7,595**	**1,827**
I—Exploitation of animals and vegetation	181	39	319	87	290 (4)	69	384	76
II—Exploitation of minerals ..	1	..	1	..	19	1	3	1
III—Industry	1,250	178	1,842	305	1,574 (6)	298	2,893	739
IV—Transport	666	22	892	29	423 (4)	16	746	25
V—Trade	1,138	90	1,417	233	799 (1)	132 (2)	664	198
VI—Public force	88	..	89	..	13	..	50	..
VII—Public administration ..	246	3	220	6	26	6	94	1
VIII—Professions and liberal arts ..	324	67	360	67	169	18	206	19
IX—Persons living on their income	120	41	45	46	31	16	59	41
X—Domestic service ..	1,005	359 (1)	742	518	359	190 (3)	321	227
XI—Insufficiently described occupations	1,788	137	1,662	93	1,238	268	2,112	241
XII—Unproductive	76 (42)	212 (2)	98	425	36 (4)	83	63	258

on domestic service and nearly an equal excess was returned compared with insufficiently described occupations most of which probably would fall under some industrial group or trade.

50. **Distribution by broad occupational categories.**—Perhaps a more convenient way of considering the occupational distribution is that shown for Calcutta in diagram No. V-4 illustrating statement No. V-4. In this statement

DIAGRAM No. V-4.

Distribution of workers showing also the subsidiary occupations of earners in Calcutta with suburbs in 24-Parganas, 1931.

NOTE.—For explanation of occupational categories see statement No. V-4.

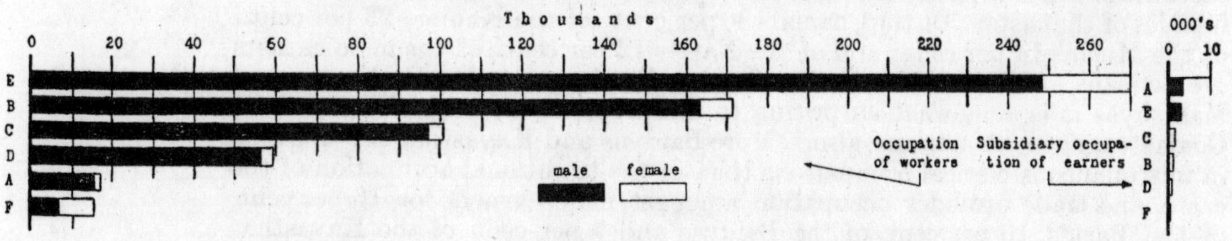

occupations are grouped in six broad categories which are described in the heading of the statement and the figures are separately given for those who follow occupations in each category as a subsidiary occupation. The numbers of these are small and on the scale of the diagram in some cases can scarcely

STATEMENT No. V-4.

Distribution of earners and working dependents and of earners, subsidiary occupation, in Calcutta with suburbs in 24-Parganas, 1931.

NOTE.—The occupational categories shown in the statement are as follows :—

(A) Pasture and agriculture (sub-class I),
(B) Industries including Mines and Transport (sub-classes II to IV),
(C) Trade and Commerce (sub-class V),
(D) Public Administration and Professions (sub-classes VI to VIII),
(E) Miscellaneous (sub-classes IX to XI),
(F) Unproductive (sub-class XII).

Categories.	Earners and working dependents.			Earners, subsidiary occupation.		
	Both sexes.	Males.	Females.	Both sexes.	Males.	Females.
A	**17,017**	15,411	1,606	**2,964**	2,931	33
B	**171,508**	163,328	8,180	**821**	791	30
C	**100,609**	96,916	3,693	**1,129**	1,107	22
D	**58,956**	56,089	2,867	**320**	310	10
E	**270,104**	248,163	21,941	**2,795**	2,616	179
F	**15,145**	6,460	8,685	**82**	2	80

be perceived. Sub-class XII, Unproductive occupations, employs the fewest number of workers and agriculture the next fewest although agriculture is the most numerous subsidiary occupation. Of the total workers $42\frac{1}{2}$ per cent. are employed under the category shown as "miscellaneous" which include persons living on their income, domestic service and insufficiently described occupations most of which, however, would probably properly be ascribed to one of the groups included under the category industry or trade. Over 27 per cent. are employed in occupations specifically returned as industries, mines and transport and nearly 16 per cent. in trade and commerce. The remaining category, public administration and the professions, accounts for rather more than 9 per cent. of the workers. Apart from agriculture the only subsidiary occupations followed by as many as 4 per mille of the total number of workers fall into the miscellaneous group mainly consisting of occupations insufficiently described.

51. **Caste and occupation.**—Some indication of the extent to which castes confine themselves to their traditional occupation is given in the figures shown as imperial table XI. Many of the groups there shown have comparatively few earners. Amongst those with the most considerable numbers it is only natural that the castes of a strongly marked occupational character should show the largest numbers following the traditional occupation. Taking only males the caste occupation provides a means of livelihood for 74 per cent. of Dhobis, 59 per cent. of Muchis, 44 per cent. of Napits and 20 per cent. of Chamars. As a contrast to these figures the traditional occupation supplies a means of livelihood only to 7 per cent. of the Brahman earners and 8 per cent. of the Mahishyas and these two classes

consequently show a most notable versatility in the other occupations which they adopt. Occupation is found amongst Brahman earners for 24 per cent. in clerical and other miscellaneous occupations, 18 per cent. in domestic service and even for 12 per cent. in trade and 6 per cent. as artisans. Amongst Mahishya male earners a means of livelihood is provided for 23 per cent. as artisans, 15 per cent. in trade, 13 per cent. as labourers, nearly 13 per cent. in miscellaneous undefined clerical occupations and 12 per cent. as domestic servants in which capacity there are employed also a considerable number of the females of the caste. Of the Chamars 30 per cent., of the Kamars 23 per cent., of the Muchis 14 per cent., and of the Napits 12 per cent., of the male earners are artisans and in addition to the figures already given for Brahmans and Mahishyas it is somewhat surprising to find as many as 15 per cent. of the Goalas engaged as artisans also. More Baidyas and Kayasthas are engaged in miscellaneous clerical occupations than in the traditional occupation of the caste, and trade provides occupation amongst male earners for 16 per cent. of the Baruis, 10 per cent. of the Baidyas and 7 per cent. of the Kayasthas in addition to the proportion already mentioned for Brahmans and Mahishyas. Domestic service provides an occupation for 22 per cent. of the Goala earners, 11 per cent. of the Napit earners and 10 per cent. of the Kayastha earners. The conditions of town life no doubt account for the fact that agriculture, in general the most popular occupation after the caste occupation in the whole of Bengal, for the groups chosen provides a means of livelihood to so small a number of the earners of each caste who are found in Calcutta.

SUBSIDIARY TABLES

SUBSIDIARY TABLE I.—Numbers of workers by

NOTE.—On account of reconstitution and re-arrangement of groups, orders, etc., of 1921 and 1911, the total of groups does not

Group No.	Occupation (**CLASS, sub-class, ORDER** and group).	Calcutta with suburbs in 24-Parganas. 1931 Earners, principal occupation and working dependents. Males.	Females.	Earners subsidiary occupation. Males.	Females.	1921 Workers. Males.	Females.	1911* Workers. Males.	Females.
1	2	3	4	5	6	7	8	9	10
	ALL OCCUPATIONS ..	**586,367**	**46,972**	**7,757**	**354**	**581,566**	**68,000**	**551,125**	**72,914**
	A.—PRODUCTION OF RAW MATERIALS ..	**15,498**	**1,612**	**2,931**	**33**	**24,192**	**3,275**	**17,855**	**2,029**
	I.—Exploitation of animals and vegetation ..	**15,411**	**1,606**	**2,931**	**33**	**24,116**	**3,273**	**17,624**	**2,028**
	1.—PASTURE AND AGRICULTURE ..	**15,036**	**1,559**	**2,893**	**33**	**23,371**	**3,223**	**16,667**	**1,741**
	(a) Ordinary cultivation ..	**12,867**	**1,526**	**2,862**	**33**	**19,911**	**2,799**	**10,813**	**1,604**
1	Non-cultivating proprietors taking rent in money or kind	6,905	1,161	1,428	22	9,606	2,360	5,973	1,315
2	Estate agents and managers of private owners ..	23	..	..	..				
3	Estate agents and managers of Government ..	4	..	..	..	2,090	..	1,270	..
4	Rent collectors, clerks, etc. ..	1,870	..	8	..				
5	Cultivating owners ..	2,182	168	979	..	5,509	292	2,705	145
6	Tenant cultivators ..	111	71	64	7				
7	Agricultural labourers ..	1,772	126	383	4	2,706	147	865	144
	(b) Cultivation of special crops, fruit, etc. (Planters, managers, clerks and labourers) ..	**1,459**	**9**	**20**	..	**2,821**	**385**	**3,329**	**47**
9, 10, 11, 12	Cinchona, Cocoanut, Coffee, Ganja ..	..	..	..	..	72	2	103	29
13†	*Pan*-vine ..	113	7	2	..	2,749	383	3,226	18
15‡	Tea ..	12	1	..	..	‡	‡	‡	‡
16	Market gardeners, flower and fruit growers ..	1,334	1	18	..	†	†	†	†
	(c) Forestry ..	**376**	..	..	..	**329**	**20**	**1,713**	**52**
17	Forest officers, rangers, guards, etc. ..	100	..	..	..	6	..	1	..
18	Wood cutters and charcoal burners ..	203	..	..	..	323	20	1,712	52
19	Collectors of forest produce ..	73	..	..	..				
	(d) Stock raising ..	**333**	**24**	**11**	..	**310**	**19**	**812**	**38**
21	Cattle and buffalo breeders and keepers ..	189	24	9	..	3	..	561	32
22	Breeders of transport animals ..	13	..	..	..	307	19	251	6
23	Herdsmen, shepherds and breeders of other animals ..	131	..	2	..				
	(e) Raising of small animals and insects ..	**1**	..	..	..	..	..	..	..
26	Lac cultivation ..	1	..	..	..	..	..	..	..
	2.—FISHING AND HUNTING ..	**375**	**47**	**38**	..	**745**	**50**	**957**	**287**
27	Fishing and pearling ..	366	47	38	..	716	50	944	286
28	Hunting ..	9	..	..	..	29	..	13	1
	II.—Exploitation of minerals ..	**87**	**6**	..	..	**76**	**2**	**231**	**1**
	3.—METALLIC MINERALS ..	..	..	..	..	..	..	**1**	..
29, 30, 31, 32, 33, 34	Gold, Iron, Lead, silver and zinc, Manganese, Tin and wolfram, Other metallic minerals ..	..	..	..	..	..	..	1	..
	4.—NON-METALLIC MINERALS ..	**87**	**6**	..	..	**76**	**2**	**230**	..
35	Coal ..	84	2	..	..	67	2	39	..
38	Mica ..	2	4	..	..	9	..	1	..
40	Salt, saltpetre and other saline substances ..	1	..	..	..	..	..	190	..
	B.—PREPARATION AND SUPPLY OF MATERIAL SUBSTANCES ..	**260,157**	**11,867**	**1,898**	**52**	**314,116**	**21,328**	**319,691**	**20,945**
	III.—Industry ..	**100,526**	**7,260**	**705**	**29**	**139,428**	**11,471**	**134,865**	**11,929**
	5.—TEXTILES ..	**14,306**	**1,647**	**88**	**2**	**26,130**	**3,067**	**23,796**	**4,055**
42	Cotton ginning, cleaning and pressing ..	218	7	2	..	166	3	28	..
43	Cotton spinning, sizing and weaving ..	502	42	5	..	2,275	560	2,422	588
44	Jute pressing, spinning and weaving ..	13,272	1,577	81	2	22,372	2,374	19,955	3,360
44A	*Jute pressing* ..	*3,194*	*201*	..	..	*15,076*	*1,335*	..	..
45	Rope, twine, string and other fibres ..	49	11	..	..	959	89	861	76
46	Wool carding, spinning and weaving ..	5	..	..	..	18	2	29	2
47	Silk spinning and weaving ..	26	..	..	..	106	3	181	6
48	Hair (horse-hair), etc. ..	..	..	..	..	..	..	31	3
49	Dyeing, bleaching, printing, preparation and sponging of textiles ..	137	..	..	..	184	6	185	6
50	Lace, crepe, embroideries, fringes, etc., and insufficiently described textile industries ..	97	10	..	..	50	30	104	14
	6.—HIDES, SKINS AND HARD MATERIALS FROM THE ANIMAL KINGDOM ..	**210**	..	..	..	**988**	**61**	**588**	**28**
51	Workers in leather ..	210	..	..	..	777	22	471	2
52	Furriers and persons occupied with feathers and bristles, brush makers ..	..	..	..	..	51	..	..	..
53	Workers (except button makers) in bone, ivory, horn shell, etc. ..	..	..	..	..	160	39	117	26
	7.—WOOD ..	**12,292**	**171**	**78**	..	**15,009**	**422**	**10,046**	**483**
54	Sawyers ..	302	..	..	..	294	1	9,232	17
55	Carpenters, turners and joiners, etc. ..	9,728	43	59	..	13,498	106		
56	Basket-makers and other workers in woody materials (including leaves) and thatchers and builders working with bamboo, reeds or similar materials ..	2,262	128	19	..	1,217	315	814	466
	8.—METALS ..	**3,915**	**15**	**58**	..	**7,779**	**79**	**7,297**	**139**
57	Smelting, forging and rolling of iron and other metals ..	140	..	..	..	1,118	7	202	14
58	Makers of arms, guns, etc. ..	76	..	..	..	365	..	59	..
59	Blacksmiths, other workers in iron and makers of implements ..	2,950	3	..	..	3,447	24	3,391	21
60	Workers in brass, copper and bell metal ..	247	5	..	..	1,122	37	1,639	69
61	Workers in other metals (except precious metals) ..	426	7	10	..	1,633	11	1,817	26
62	Workers in mints, die-sinkers, etc. ..	76	..	..	..	94	..	189	..

* The figures refer to the
† Included in group 13.
‡ Groups 14 and 15 are

sex and occupation in 1911, 1921 and 1931.

add up to the figures against the order or sub-order (in same cases) for these years. Similarly for figures against sub-classes.

Calcutta.								Howrah.						
1931				1921*		1911*		1931				1921		
Earners, principal occupation and working dependents.		Earners subsidiary occupation.		Workers.		Workers.		Earners, principal occupation and working dependents.		Earners subsidiary occupation.		Workers.		Gouup No.
Males.	Females.	Males.	Females.	Males.	Females.	Males.	Females.	Males.	Females.	Males.	Females.	Males.	Females.	
11	12	13	14	15	16	17	18	19	20	21	22	23	24	25
565,875	**43,916**	**6,210**	**334**	**476,034**	**52,660**	**482,277**	**61,177**	**72,208**	**8,742**	**2,670**	**124**	**97,576**	**12,211**	
12,151	**1,266**	**1,861**	**22**	**17,432**	**2,430**	**14,774**	**1,579**	**4,476**	**561**	**561**	**24**	**4,965**	**517**	
12,065	**1,264**	**1,861**	**22**	**17,356**	**2,428**	**14,543**	**1,578**	**4,200**	**552**	**540**	**24**	**4,929**	**507**	
11,714	**1,235**	**1,828**	**22**	**16,977**	**2,401**	**13,965**	**1,438**	**3,042**	**381**	**538**	**24**	**4,756**	**446**	
9,897	**1,202**	**1,823**	**22**	**14,556**	**2,170**	**9,245**	**1,316**	**2,835**	**330**	**535**	**24**	**4,450**	**427**	
6,538	1,084	1,098	18	8,698	1,988	5,636	1,171	891	239	191	20	873	242	1
19	..	..	..					18	..	..	..			2
4	..	..	..	1,817	..	1,169	..	..	..	..	..	207	..	3
1,327	..	7	..					283	3	..	..			4
1,350	59	525	..	3,490	134	2,192	111	646	33	330	4	2,095	128	5
1	..	..	..					436	17	10	..			6
658	59	193	4	551	48	248	34	561	38	4	..	1,275	57	7
1,298	**9**	**2**	..	**1,947**	**214**	**2,526**	**38**	**151**	**3**	**1**	..	**149**	**1**	
..	..	..	..	67	2	103	29	..	..	..	..	..	..	9, 10, 11, 12
113	7	2	..	1,880	212	2,423	9	..	..	..	..	149	1	13
10	1	..	..	‡	‡	‡	‡	21	..	..	..	‡	‡	15
1,175	1	..	..	†	†	†	†	130	3	1	..	†	†	16
319	..	..	..	**254**	**15**	**1,509**	**48**	**6**	..	..	..	**37**	..	
100	..	..	..	4	..	1	..	..	..	..	..	..	..	17
146	..	..	..	250	15	1,508	48	6	..	..	..	37	..	18
73	..	..	..					..	..	..	..			19
199	**24**	**3**	..	**220**	**2**	**685**	**36**	**50**	**48**	**2**	..	**120**	**18**	
87	24	3	..	3	..	556	32	28	30	..	..	30	..	21
13	..	..	..	217	2	129	4	..	..	..	..	90	18	22
99	..	..	..					22	18	2	..			23
1	..	..	..	..	..	..	..	..	..	..	..	..	..	
1	..	..	..	..	..	..	..	..	..	..	..	..	..	26
351	**29**	**33**	..	**379**	**27**	**578**	**140**	**1,158**	**171**	**2**	..	**173**	**61**	
342	29	33	..	354	27	567	139	1,158	171	2	..	173	61	27
9	..	..	..	25	..	11	1	..	..	..	..	..	..	28
86	**2**	..	..	**76**	**2**	**231**	**1**	**276**	**9**	**21**	..	**36**	**10**	
..	..	..	..	..	..	**1**	..	..	..	..	..	..	..	
..	..	..	..	..	..	1	..	..	..	..	..	..	..	29, 30, 31, 32, 33, 34
86	**2**	..	..	**76**	**2**	**230**	**1**	**276**	**9**	**21**	..	**36**	**10**	
83	2	..	..	67	2	39	1	276	9	21	..	36	10	35
2	..	..	..	9	..	1	..	..	..	..	..	..	..	38
1	..	..	..	..	..	190	..	..	..	..	..	..	..	40
251,637	**10,246**	**1,565**	**43**	**243,728**	**13,512**	**271,491**	**14,883**	**40,578**	**3,555**	**1,225**	**25**	**55,285**	**6,429**	
102,093	**6,133**	**508**	**21**	**92,722**	**6,190**	**104,808**	**7,814**	**22,848**	**2,380**	**511**	**10**	**37,164**	**4,936**	
13,906	**1,441**	**87**	**2**	**7,890**	**719**	**10,104**	**1,744**	**16,330**	**1,090**	**239**	**2**	**20,542**	**3,566**	
210	7	2	..	158	3	18	..	50	..	..	..	3	105	42
454	37	4	..	484	32	450	88	1,263	3	6	..	442	42	43
12,965	1,376	81	2	6,880	635	9,138	1,612	14,902	1,686	232	2	19,962	3,295	44
3,012	..	..	..	*3,603*	*183*	..	..	*5,881*	*482*	*67*	*1*	*912*	*172*	*44A*
49	11	..	..	160	9	147	23	60	1	1	..	132	124	45
5	..	..	..	..	2	28	..	9	..	..	..	..	..	46
14	..	..	..	30	2	11	..	..	..	..	..	3	..	47
..	..	..	..	..	..	31	3	5	..	..	..	..	..	48
137	..	..	..	128	6	184	6	2	..	..	..	..	..	49
72	10	..	..	50	30	97	12	48	..	..	..	..	..	50
69	..	..	..	**235**	**2**	**467**	**2**	**1**	..	..	..	..	..	
69	..	..	..	156	2	460	2	1	..	..	..	..	..	51
..	..	..	..	51	..	..	..	..	..	..	..	..	..	52
..	..	..	..	28	..	7	..	..	..	..	..	..	..	53
11,606	**161**	**21**	..	**12,787**	**337**	**8,864**	**444**	**261**	**51**	**7**	**3**	**1,546**	**80**	
302	..	..	..	214	..	8,102	11	..	..	..	..	24	..	54
9,354	43	21	..	11,503	90			228	21	7	3	1,264	11	55
1,950	118	..	..	1,070	247	762	433	33	30	..	..	258	69	56
3,592	**11**	**20**	..	**5,001**	**62**	**5,897**	**101**	**90**	**26**	..	..	**3,828**	**37**	
127	..	..	..	522	2	117	..	47	2	..	..	2,854	..	57
76	..	..	..	82	..	57	..	..	..	..	..	..	..	58
2,666	2	9	..	2,231	16	2,580	7	99	22	..	..	810	33	59
241	2	1	..	944	33	1,356	68	1	..	..	..	162	4	60
406	7	10	..	1,154	11	1,610	26	3	1	..	..	2	..	61
76	..	..	..	68	..	177	..	..	..	..	..	..	..	62

area as then constituted.

included within groups 9, 10, 11 and 12.

SUBSIDIARY TABLE I.—Numbers of workers by

Group No.	Occupation (**CLASS, sub-class, ORDER** and group).	Calcutta with suburbs in 24-Parganas. 1931 Earners, principal occupation and working dependents. Males.	1931 Earners, principal occupation and working dependents. Females.	1931 Earners subsidiary occupation. Males.	1931 Earners subsidiary occupation. Females.	1921 Workers. Males.	1921 Workers. Females.	1911* Workers. Males.	1911* Workers. Females.
1	2	3	4	5	6	7	8	9	10
	III.—Industry—*concld.*								
	9.—CERAMICS ..	**1,245**	**192**	**32**	..	**3,513**	**558**	**1,636**	**245**
63	Potters and makers of earthenware ..	399	37	17	..	1,101	264	612	105
64	Brick and tile makers ..	539	152	15	..	2,346	292	927	129
65	Other workers in ceramics ..	307	3	..	..	66	2	97	11
	10.—CHEMICAL PRODUCTS PROPERLY SO-CALLED AND ANALOGOUS ..	**1,340**	**81**	..	**4**	**2,620**	**122**	**3,766**	**189**
66	Manufacture of matches, fireworks and other explosives	542	39	..	4	65	..	307	..
67	Manufacture of aerated and mineral waters and ice ..	92	1	..	..	87	..	43	..
68	Manufacture and refining of vegetable oils ..	353	24	..	..	1,519	64 }	2,566	77
69	Manufacture and refining of mineral oils ..	..	..	..	..	..	.. }		
70	Other chemical manufactures ..	353	17	..	..	949	58	850	112
	11.—FOOD INDUSTRIES ..	**7,695**	**1,210**	**75**	**5**	**7,266**	**1,622**	**5,917**	**1,147**
71	Rice pounders and huskers and flour grinders ..	1,721	1,040	25	2	1,067	1,119	680	730
72	Grain parchers, etc. ..	20	1	..	..	67	142	225	117
73	Butchers ..	1,179	18	..	..	2,384	180	1,760	147
74	Makers of sugar, molasses and *gurh* ..	205	..	..	..	396	3	568	8
75	Sweetmeat and condiment makers ..	652	16	..	..	787	43	625	9
76	Toddy drawers ..	3	2	..	..	83	..	64	..
77	Brewers and distillers ..	..	..	..	..	30	..	3	..
78	Manufacturers of tobacco ..	3,377	129	50	3 }				
79	Manufacturers of opium ..	..	..	..	.. }	1,140	114	606	119
80	Manufacturers of *ganja* ..	..	..	..	.. }				
81	Other food industries ..	538	4	..	..	1,312	21	1,386	17
	12.—INDUSTRIES OF DRESS AND THE TOILET ..	**26,817**	**1,783**	**229**	**1**	**29,188**	**1,887**	**32,336**	**1,595**
82	Boot, shoe, sandal and clog makers ..	7,626	987	20	1	9,868	259	11,958	78
83	Tailors, milliners, dressmakers and darners ..	8,659	276	139	.. }	10,513	526	11,301	324
84	Embroiderers and makers of hats and other articles of wear ..	630	5	..	.. }				
85	Washermen and cleaners ..	6,208	409	39	..	5,392	934	4,860	880
86	Barbers, hair dressers and wig-makers ..	3,694	106	31	..	3,415	168	4,192	312
87	Other industires connected with the toilet ..	..	..	..	..	..	..	25	1
	13.—FURNITURE INDUSTRIES ..	**1,404**	**19**	..	..	**1,225**	**18**	**720**	**12**
88	Cabinet-makers, carriage-painters, etc. ..	1,379	19	..	..	1,220	18	711	11
89	Upholsterers, tent-makers, etc. ..	25	..	..	..	5	..	9	1
	14.—BUILDING INDUSTRIES ..	**11,762**	**990**	**75**	**2**	**15,483**	**1,375**	**19,244**	**1,623**
90	Lime burners, cement workers, excavators and well sinkers, stone-cutters and dressers, brick-layers and masons, builders (other than of buildings made of bamboo or similar materials), painters, house-decorators, tilers, plumbers, etc. ..	11,762	990	75	2	15,483	1,375	19,244	1,623
	15.—CONSTRUCTION OF MEANS OF TRANSPORT ..	**1,921**	**1**	..	..	**4,531**	**85**	**759**	..
91	Manufacture assembly or repair of motor vehicles or cycles ..	1,085	1	..	..	1,003	2	..	..
92	Makers of carriages, carts, *palkis*, etc., and wheel-wrights	128	..	..	..	220	..	491	..
93	Ship, boat and aeroplane builders ..	708	..	..	..	3,308	83	268	..
	16.—PRODUCTION AND TRANSMISSION OF PHYSICAL FORCE ..	**2,300**	**1**	..	..	**2,295**	**44**	**2,621**	**15**
94	Heat, light, electricity, motive power, etc. (gas works and electric light and power) ..	2,300	1	..	..	2,295	44	2,621	15
	17.—MISCELLANEOUS AND UNDEFINED INDUSTRIES ..	**21,319**	**1,150**	**70**	**15**	**23,401**	**2,131**	**26,139**	**2,407**
95	Printers, engravers, book-binders, etc. ..	10,709	9	30	..	9,640	228	10,059	64
96	Makers of musical instruments ..	588	..	..	..	203	66	320	..
97	Makers of clocks and surgical or scientific instruments, etc. ..	327	..	1	..	590	7	663	3
98	Makers of jewellery and ornaments ..	3,382	30	21	..	6,369	81	6,877	73
99	Other miscellaneous and undefined industries (toy-making, taxidermy, etc.) ..	22	19	..	..	67	13	131	20
100	Scavenging ..	6,291	1,092	18	15	6,414	1,731	7,645	2,073
	IV.—Transport ..	**56,715**	**914**	**86**	**1**	**67,488**	**1,095**	**87,406**	**567**
	19.—TRANSPORT BY WATER ..	**22,112**	**38**	**30**	..	**27,250**	**40**	**41,859**	**173**
102	Ship-owners, boat-owners and their employees, officers, mariners, etc., ships' brokers, boatmen and towmen ..	19,083	5	27	..	25,423	3	34,877	..
102A	*Ship-owners, boat-owners and their employees, officers, mariners, etc., ships' brokers, boatmen and towmen of inland water transport* ..	*12,080*	*5*	*27*	..	*15,042*	*3*	..	..
103	Persons (other than labourers) employed in harbours, docks, rivers and canals, including pilots ..	1,700	33	3	..	390	31 }	6,982	173
104	Labourers employed on harbours, docks, rivers and canals ..	1,329	..	..	..	1,437	6 }		
	20.—TRANSPORT BY ROAD ..	**24,844**	**731**	**53**	**1**	**27,678**	**498**	**33,244**	**266**
105	Persons (other than labourers) employed on the construction and maintenance of roads and bridges ..	..	..	..	..	10	.. }	666	44
106	Labourers employed on the construction of roads and bridges ..	2,082	705	..	..	243	.. }		
107	Owners, managers and employees (excluding personal servants) connected with mechanically driven vehicles (including trams) ..	7,774	4	14	1	5,727	20 }	27,979	217
108	Owners, managers and employees (excluding personal servants) connected with other vehicles ..	8,725	1	32	..	15,740	72 }		
109	Owners and bearers of *palkis*, etc. ..	1,258	16	..	..	560	..	847	..
110	Owners and drivers of pack elephants, camels, mules, asses and bullocks ..	5	..	..	..	42	..	..	..
111	Porters and messengers ..	5,000	5	7	..	5,356	406	3,752	5
	21.—TRANSPORT BY RAIL ..	**6,571**	**121**	..	..	**9,162**	**447**	**9,831**	**50**
112	Railway employees of all kinds other than coolies ..	5,005	119	..	..	6,831	145	9,831	50
113	Labourers employed on railway construction and maintenance and coolies and porters employed on railway premises ..	1,566	2	..	..	2,331	302	..	..
	22.—POST OFFICE, TELEGRAPH AND TELEPHONE SERVICES ..	**3,188**	**24**	**3**	..	**3,398**	**110**	**2,472**	**78**
114	Post office, telegraph and telephone services ..	3,188	24	3	..	3,398	110	2,472	78

* The figures refer to the

sex and occupation in 1911, 1921 and 1931.

Calcutta.								Howrah.						Group No.
1931				1921*		1911*		1931				1921		
Earners, principal occupation and working dependents.		Earners subsidiary occupation.		Workers.		Workers.		Earners, principal occupation and working dependents.		Earners subsidiary occupation.		Workers.		
Males.	Females.	Males.	Females.	Males.	Females.	Males.	Females.	Males.	Females.	Males.	Females.	Males.	Females.	
11	12	13	14	15	16	17	18	19	20	21	22	23	24	25
987	14	1	..	985	111	685	77	192	21	10	..	978	15	
296	8	..	..	530	75	419	49	139	4	10	..	258	11	63
384	3	1	..	392	34	183	18	51	16	..	..	720	4	64
307	3	..	..	63	2	83	10	2	1	..	..	..	..	65
1,299	74	..	4	2,006	60	2,597	46	110	..	..	..	216	46	
542	39	..	4	25	..	11	..	3	..	..	..	..	..	66
90	1	..	..	64	..	11	..	3	..	..	..	..	..	67
348	23	..	..	1,289	30	2,071	32	104	..	..	..	216	46	68
..	..	..	..					..	..	..	..			69
319	11	..	..	628	30	504	14	..	..	..	..	..	..	70
6,853	564	50	5	4,331	889	4,729	704	397	45	66	2	2,093	139	
1,003	412	..	2	438	583	669	474	22	15	10	2	1,349	119	71
19	..	..	..	27	99	117	73	11	..	..	..	23	5	72
1,153	17	..	..	1,373	119	1,401	83	89	1	..	..	11	..	73
205	..	..	..	203	..	131	..	..	..	..	..	..	..	74
652	16	..	..	277	35	623	9	..	..	..	..	291	3	75
2	2	..	..	12	..	61	..	7	..	..	..	..	..	76
..	..	..	..	2	..	3	..	..	..	..	..	..	..	77
3,284	113	50	3					229	29	54	..			78
..	..	..	..	900	39	470	49	..	..	..	..	269	11	79
..	..	..	..					..	..	..	..			80
535	4	..	..	1,099	14	1,254	16	39	..	2	..	150	1	81
25,605	1,753	200	..	22,626	1,300	27,596	1,304	2,816	193	110	2	3,212	371	
7,543	984	19	..	9,138	249	11,427	71	441	19	12	..	483	26	82
7,910	271	131	..	6,283	197	8,251	289	728	11	22	..	1,031	91	83
626	5	..	..					102	3	4	..			84
5,958	387	30	..	4,351	723	4,080	696	1,008	130	68	..	1,052	209	85
3,568	106	20	..	2,854	131	3,813	247	537	30	4	2	646	45	86
..	..	..	..	..	..	25	1	..	..	..	..	..	..	87
1,404	19	..	..	1,135	13	706	11	..	..	..	..	..	..	
1,379	19	..	..	1,130	13	699	10	..	..	..	..	..	..	88
25	..	..	..	5	..	7	1	..	..	..	..	..	..	89
11,389	978	59	2	10,718	870	15,786	1,184	1,128	44	23	..	2,906	155	
11,389	978	59	2	10,718	870	15,786	1,184	1,128	44	23	..	2,906	155	90
1,885	..	..	..	2,219	6	714	..	48	..	17	..	22	..	
1,060	..	..	..	876	1	..	..	45	..	15	..	..	..	91
117	..	..	..	192	..	457	..	..	..	2	..	..	..	92
708	..	..	..	1,151	5	257	..	3	..	..	..	22	..	93
2,277	1	..	..	1,858	36	2,435	14	364	..	3	..	25	..	
2,277	1	..	..	1,858	36	2,435	14	364	..	3	..	25	..	94
21,221	1,117	70	8	20,931	1,785	24,228	2,183	1,102	310	36	1	1,796	527	
10,676	9	30	..	9,101	132	9,532	53	92	..	2	..	12	..	95
588	..	..	..	130	28	276	..	2	..	..	..	..	..	96
320	..	1	..	532	7	625	3	143	..	3	..	4	..	97
3,382	30	21	..	5,180	75	6,048	52	281	..	3	..	431	4	98
22	16	..	..	52	4	97	12	..	5	..	..	..	..	99
6,233	1,062	18	8	5,879	1,534	7,210	1,889	584	305	28	1	1,349	523	100
55,955	748	84	1	59,013	987	78,581	539	6,128	125	131	..	9,588	166	
22,054	37	29	..	26,554	37	40,084	173	382	1	16	..	1,303	1	
19,025	4	26	..	24,773	..	34,219	..	356	1	16	..	422	1	102
12,022	*4*	*26*	..	*14,711*	..	..	..	*494*	*1*	*16*	..	*407*	*1*	*102A*
1.700	33	3	..	353	31	5,865	173	22	..	..	..	678	..	103
1.329	..	..	..	1,428	6			4	..	..	..	203	..	104
24,236	569	52	1	22,377	412	28,316	239	1,605	42	48	..	1,140	10	
..	..	..	..	3	..	382	28	1	..	..	..	..	..	105
1,948	544	..	..	91	..			425	42	..	..	3	..	106
7,707	4	14	1	4,971	20	23,585	206	125	..	..	..	7	..	107
8,338	..	31	..	11,718	36			898	..	27	..	936	8	108
1,244	16	..	..	410	..	809	..	29	..	..	..	194	2	109
5	..	..	..	29	..	..	..	..	..	..	..	..	..	110
4,994	5	7	..	5,155	356	3,540	5	127	..	19	..	..	..	111
6,498	118	..	..	7,103	423	7,802	49	3,861	81	67	..	6,771	155	
4,974	116	..	..	4,983	138	7,802	49	2,848	54	67	..	5,163	19	112
1,524	2	..	..	2,120	290	..	..	1,010	27	..	..	1,608	136	113
3,167	24	3	..	2,979	110	2,379	78	280	1	2	..	374	..	
3,167	24	3	..	2,979	110	2,379	78	280	1	2	..	374	..	114

area as then constituted.

SUBSIDIARY TABLE I.—Numbers of workers by

Group No.	Occupation (CLASS, sub-class, ORDER and group).	Calcutta with suburbs in 24-Parganas.							
		1931				1921		1911*	
		Earners, principal occupation and working dependents.		Earners subsidiary occupation.		Workers.		Workers.	
		Males.	Females.	Males.	Females.	Males.	Females.	Males.	Females.
1	2	3	4	5	6	7	8	9	10
	V.—Trade ..	**96,916**	**3,693**	**1,107**	**22**	**107,200**	**8,762**	**97,420**	**8,449**
	23.—BANKS, ESTABLISHMENTS OF CREDIT, EXCHANGE AND INSURANCE ..	**2,875**	**31**	**131**	**2**	**3,190**	**296**	**3,919**	**315**
115	Bank-managers, money-lenders, exchange and insurance agents, money changers and brokers and their employees ..	2,875	31	131	2	3,190	296	3,919	315
	24.—BROKERAGE, COMMISSION AND EXPORT ..	**5,154**	**40**	**32**	**2**	**9,620**	**90**	**6,435**	**42**
116	Brokers, commission agents, commercial travellers, warehouse owners and employees ..	5,154	40	32	2	9,620	90	6,435	42
	25.—TRADE IN TEXTILES ..	**4,509**	**51**	**70**	**3**	**6,452**	**212**	**12,605**	**243**
117	Trade in piece goods, jute, wool, cotton, silk, hair and other textiles ..	4,509	51	70	3	6,452	212 }	12,605	243
117A	*Trade in jute* ..	*131*	..	*34*	..	*692*	*2* }		
	26.—TRADE IN SKINS, LEATHER AND FURS ..	**1,304**	**10**	**15**	..	**2,318**	**61**	**3,483**	**46**
118	Trade in skins, leather, furs, feathers, horn, etc. and articles made therefrom ..	1,304	10	15	..	2,318	61	3,483	46
	27.—TRADE IN WOOD ..	**914**	**26**	**3**	..	**1,521**	**31**	**1,648**	**147**
119	Trade in wood (not firewood) ..	848	9	3	.. }	1,521	31	1,648	147
120	Trade in barks ..	29	..	..	.. }				
121	Trade in bamboos and canes ..	24	17	..	.. }				
122	Trade in thatches and other forest produce ..	13	..	..	.. }				
	28.—TRADE IN METALS ..	**501**	**8**	**2**	..	**959**	**35**	**1,827**	**20**
123	Trade in metals, machinery, knives, tools, etc. ..	501	8	2	..	959	35	1,827	20
	29.—TRADE IN POTTERY, BRICKS AND TILES ..	**106**	**1**	..	..	**72**	**1**	**175**	**34**
124	Trade in pottery, bricks and tiles ..	106	1	..	..	72	1	175	34
	30.—TRADE IN CHEMICAL PRODUCTS ..	**423**	**6**	**13**	..	**884**	**42**	**1,632**	**22**
125	Drugs, dyes, paints, petroleum, explosives, etc. ..	423	6	13	..	884	42	1,632	22
	31.—HOTELS, CAFES, RESTAURANT, ETC. ..	**4,167**	**103**	**8**	..	**4,794**	**623**	**3,594**	**149**
126	Vendors of wine, liquors, ærated waters and ice ..	465	7	..	..	1,125	59	2,334	30
127	Owners and managers of hotels, cook shops, *sarais*, etc. (and employees) ..	3,649	96	8	.. }	3,669	564	1,260	119
128	Hawkers of drink and foodstuffs ..	53	..	..	.. }				
	32.—OTHER TRADE IN FOOD STUFFS ..	**30,917**	**2,113**	**511**	**10**	**29,686**	**4,301**	**36,423**	**5,737**
129	Grain and pulse dealers ..	2,842	177	21	..	3,049	497	6,428	800
130	Dealers in sweetmeats, sugar and spices ..	2,368	79	47	..	16,094	1,873	20,587	2,930
131	Dealers in dairy products, eggs and poultry ..	4,229	497	48	2	4,052	792	4,307	844
132	Dealers in animals for food ..	149	3	..	..	2,353	938	1,329	826
133	Dealers in fodder for animals ..	328	7	..	..	872	13	1,353	110
134	Dealers in other food stuffs ..	19,364	1,343	395	8	..	..	..	..
135	Dealers in tobacco ..	931	7	..	.. }	3,266	188	2,419	227
136	Dealers in opium ..	106	..	..	.. }				
137	Dealers in *ganja* ..	600	..	..	.. }				
	33.—TRADE IN CLOTHING AND TOILET ARTICLES	**1,988**	**23**	**6**	..	**3,113**	**50**	**5,331**	**67**
138	Trade in ready-made clothing and other articles of dress and the toilet (hats, umbrellas, socks, ready-made shoes, perfumes, etc.) ..	1,988	23	6	..	3,113	50	5,331	67
	34.—TRADE IN FURNITURE ..	**816**	**4**	**5**	..	**1,481**	**39**	**2,071**	**80**
139	Trade in furniture, carpets, curtains and bedding ..	230	3	..	..	499	9	386	8
140	Hardware, cooking utensils, porcelain, crokery, glassware, bottles, articles for gardening, etc. ..	586	1	5	..	982	30	1,685	72
	35.—TRADE IN BUILDING MATERIALS ..	**171**	**7**	**3**	..	**240**	**5**	**351**	**11**
141	Trade in building materials (other than bricks, tiles and woody materials) ..	171	7	3	..	240	5	351	11
	36.—TRADE IN MEANS OF TRANSPORT ..	**274**	**3**	**2**	..	**492**	..	**729**	**14**
142	Dealers in and hirers of mechanical transport motors, cycles, etc. ..	152	..	2	..	65	.. }	729	14
143	Dealers in and hirers of other carriages, carts, boats, etc. ..	4	..	..	..	85	.. }		
144	Dealers in and hirers of elephants, camels, horses, cattle, asses, mules, etc. ..	118	3	..	..	342	.. }		
	37.—TRADE IN FUEL ..	**1,491**	**104**	**1**	**3**	**2,476**	**1,037**	**2,235**	**895**
145	Dealers in firewood, charcoal, coal, cowdung, etc. ..	1,491	104	1	3	2,476	1,037	2,235	895
	38.—TRADE IN ARTICLES OF LUXURY AND THOSE PERTAINING TO LETTERS AND THE ARTS AND SCIENCES	**4,859**	**68**	**59**	..	**5,401**	**278**	**5,563**	**230**
146	Dealers in precious stones, jewellery (real and imitation), clocks, optical instruments, etc. ..	1,451	16	33	..	2,007	40	1,500	14
147	Dealers in common bangles, bead necklaces, fans, small articles, toys, hunting and fishing tackle, flowers, etc.	188	14	..	..	514	103	1,490	144
148	Publishers, book-sellers, stationers, dealers in music, pictures, musical instruments and curiosities ..	3,220	38	26	..	2,880	135	2,573	72
	39.—TRADE OF OTHER SORTS ..	**36,447**	**1,095**	**246**	**2**	**34,501**	**1,661**	**9,399**	**397**
149	Dealers in rags, stable refuse, etc. ..					1	2	83	..
150	General store-keepers and shop-keepers otherwise unspecified ..	31,393	919	206	2	31,184	1,519	6,814	267
151	Itinerant traders, pedlars and hawkers (of other than food, etc.) ..	5,046	176	40	..	3,231	140	2,188	120
152	Other traders (including farmers of pounds, tolls and markets) ..	8	..	..	..	85	..	115	7
	C.—PUBLIC ADMINISTRATION AND LIBERAL ARTS ..	**56,089**	**2,867**	**310**	**10**	**50,575**	**2,759**	**47,512**	**6,017**
	VI.—Public Force ..	**7,545**	..	**4**	..	**6,727**	..	**8,856**	..
	40.—ARMY ..	**1,753**	..	..	..	**2,123**	..	**4,263**	..
153	Imperial Army ..	1,753	..	..	..	2,123	..	4,252	..
154	Indian States Armies ..	..	..	..	..	..	..	11	..
	41.—NAVY ..	**9**	..	..	..	**14**	..	..	..
155	Navy ..	9	..	..	..	14	..	..	..

* The figures refer to the

sex and occupation in 1911, 1921 and 1931.

Calcutta.								Howrah.						
1931				1921*		1911*		1931				1921		
Earners, principal occupation and working dependents.		Earners subsidiary occupation.		Workers.		Workers.		Earners, principal occupation and working dependents.		Earners subsidiary occupation.		Workers.		Gouup No.
Males.	Females.	Males.	Females.	Males.	Females.	Males.	Females.	Males.	Females.	Males.	Females.	Males.	Females.	
11	12	13	14	15	16	17	18	19	20	21	22	23	24	25
93,589	**3,365**	**976**	**21**	**91,993**	**6,335**	**88,102**	**6,530**	**11,602**	**1,050**	**583**	**15**	**8,533**	**1,327**	
2,791	**27**	**124**	**2**	**2,507**	**265**	**3,616**	**268**	**105**	**11**	**1**	**1**	**386**	**47**	
2,791	27	124	2	2,507	265	3,616	268	105	11	1	1	386	47	115
5,125	**40**	**30**	**2**	**9,245**	**70**	**6,208**	**41**	**330**	**6**	**2**	..	**175**	..	
5.125	40	30	2	9,245	70	6,208	41	330	6	2	..	175	..	116
4,486	**51**	**70**	**3**	**5,685**	**173**	**11,957**	**225**	**489**	**15**	**34**	..	**985**	**9**	
4,486	51	70	3	5,685	173	11,957	225	489	15	34	..	985	9	117
131	..	*34*	..	*446*	..			*4*	..	..	..	*574*	..	*117A*
1,106	**7**	**15**	..	**1,658**	**45**	**3,324**	**46**	**5**	**1**	..	..	..	..	
1,106	7	15.	..	1,658	45	3,324	46	5	1	..	..	..	..	118
759	**25**	**3**	..	**1,069**	**25**	**1,489**	**146**	**86**	**2**	**29**	..	**16**	**3**	
693	8	3	..	1,069	25	1,489	146	67	2	29	..	16	3	119
29	..	..	..					8	..	..	..			120
24	17	..	..					3	..	..	..			121
13	..	..	..					8	..	..	..			122
501	**8**	**2**	..	**844**	**25**	**1,619**	**14**	**81**	..	**3**	..	**48**	..	
501	8	2	..	844	25	1,619	14	81	..	3	..	48	..	123
106	**1**	..	..	**56**	**1**	**162**	**28**	**23**	..	**1**	..	..	..	
106	1	..	..	56	1	162	28	23	..	1	..	..	..	124
423	**6**	**13**	..	**773**	**32**	**1,522**	**18**	**53**	..	**3**	..	**251**	..	
423	6	13	..	773	32	1,522	18	53	..	3	..	251	..	125
3,928	**97**	**8**	..	**3,726**	**456**	**3,159**	**139**	**460**	**7**	**6**	..	**519**	**10**	
276	1	..	..	756	22	1,941	23	111	1	2	..	205	6	126
3,649	96	8	..	2,970	434	1,218	116	349	6	4	..	314	4	127
3	..	..	..					..	..	..	..			128
29,596	**1,850**	**402**	**10**	**23,435**	**2,658**	**31,401**	**4,221**	**3,323**	**612**	**145**	**11**	**4,676**	**1,146**	
2,767	142	20	..	2,265	182	5,371	480	197	126	2	3	634	95	129
2,294	72	47	..	13,395	1,346	18,081	2,360	588	61	9	3	2,849	547	130
3,938	397	32	2	2,892	485	3,735	677	400	128	31	1	520	184	131
149	3	..	..	1,543	514	1,056	590	1	..	..	..	277	265	132
327	7	..	..	545	13	1,188	15	16	1	..	..	190	45	133
18,517	1,222	303	8	..	..	..	..	2,090	293	99	4	..	..	134
898	7	..	..	2,795	118	2,060	99	20	3	1	..	206	10	135
106	..	..	..					4	..	..	..			136
600	..	..	..					7	..	..	..			137
1,983	**23**	**6**	..	**2,673**	**41**	**5,201**	**40**	**131**	..	**1**	..	**218**	**3**	
1,983	23	6	..	2,673	41	5,201	40	131	..	1	..	218	3	138
797	**4**	**2**	..	**1,127**	**16**	**1,887**	**49**	**26**	**2**	..	..	**90**	..	
230	3	..	..	375	..	366	5	4	1	..	..	10	..	139
567	1	2	..	752	16	1,521	44	22	..	..	..	80	..	140
140	**7**	..	..	**145**	**4**	**295**	**11**	**14**	..	..	..	**9**	..	
148	7	..	..	145	4	295	11	14	..	..	..	9	..	141
244	**2**	**2**	..	**143**	..	**276**	**2**	**33**	..	..	..	..	..	
149	..	2	..	56	..	276	2	14	..	..	..	..	..	142
4	..	..	..	28	..			8	..	..	..			143
91	2	..	..	59	..			11	..	..	..			144
1,433	**88**	**1**	**3**	**1,898**	**860**	**1,963**	**763**	**413**	**45**	**63**	..	**317**	**55**	
1,433	88	1	3	1,898	860	1,963	763	413	45	63	..	317	55	145
4,527	**64**	**52**	..	**4,678**	**152**	**5,167**	**161**	**444**	**87**	**80**	..	**273**	**38**	
1,209	14	26	..	1,884	8	1,466	13	134	4	1	..	..	..	146
183	12	..	..	324	47	1,311	82	10	32	..	..	23	12	147
3,135	38	26	..	2,470	97	2,390	66	300	51	79	..	250	26	148
35,636	**1,065**	**246**	**1**	**32,278**	**1,512**	**8,766**	**358**	**5,586**	**262**	**215**	**3**	**570**	**16**	
				1	..	75	..					..	..	149
30,586	889	206	1	29,250	1,395	6,418	237	5,083	241	215	3	206	..	150
5,044	176	40	..	2,951	117	1,990	112	495	19	..	..	364	16	151
6	..	..	..	76	..	103	6	8	2	..	..	..	..	152
54,298	**2,755**	**221**	**10**	**46,648**	**2,546**	**44,159**	**5,140**	**3,021**	**191**	**206**	**3**	**4,494**	**135**	
7,140	..	**4**	..	**6,234**	..	**8,568**	..	**190**	..	**3**	..	**647**	..	
1,753	..	..	..	**2,115**	..	**4,225**	..	**1**	..	..	..	**5**	..	
1,753	..	..	..	2,115	..	4,225	..	1	..	..	..	5	..	153
..	..	..	..	..	..	..	..	..	..	..	..	..	..	154
9	..	..	..	**14**	..	..	..	..	..	..	..	..	..	
9	..	..	..	14	..	..	..	..	..	..	..	..	..	155

area as then constituted.

SUBSIDIARY TABLE I.—Numbers of workers by

Group No.	Occupation (CLASS, sub-class, ORDER and group).	Calcutta with suburbs in 24-Parganas. 1931 Earners, principal occupation and working dependents. Males.	1931 Earners, principal occupation and working dependents. Females.	1931 Earners subsidiary occupation. Males.	1931 Earners subsidiary occupation. Females.	1921 Workers. Males.	1921 Workers. Females.	1911* Workers. Males.	1911* Workers. Females.
1	2	3	4	5	6	7	8	9	10
	VI.—Public Force—*concld.*								
	42.—AIR FORCE ..	**3**	..	..	..	..	..	..	..
156	Air Force ..	3	..	..	..	..	..	..	..
	43.—POLICE ..	**5,780**	..	**4**	..	**4,590**	..	**4,593**	..
157	Police ..	5,759	..	4	..	4,574	..	4,593	..
158	Village watchmen ..	21	..	..	..	16	..	..	..
	VII.—Public Administration ..	**20,933**	**125**	**89**	..	**16,645**	**228**	**14,183**	**219**
	44.—PUBLIC ADMINISTRATION ..	**20,933**	**125**	**89**	..	**16,645**	**228**	**14,183**	**219**
159	Service of the State ..	14,395	77	83	..	8,741	92	9,334	18
160	Service of Indian and foreign states ..	..	..	..	..	9	..	23	..
161	Municipal and other local (not village) service ..	6,538	48	6	..	7,895	136	4,826	201
162	Village officials and servants other than watchmen ..	..	..	..	..	..	..	..	..
	VIII.—Professions and Liberal Arts ..	**27,611**	**2,742**	**217**	**10**	**27,203**	**2,531**	**20,263**	**2,990**
	45.—RELIGION ..	**5,392**	**210**	**60**	**1**	**5,477**	**209**	**6,999**	**1,195**
163	Priests, ministers, etc. ..	4,841	188	60	1	4,623	141	4,956	212
164	Monks, nuns, religious mendicants ..	321	9	..	..	522	27	1,587	868
165	Other religious workers ..	4	..	..	..	59	38	148	98
166	Servants in religious edifices, burial and burning grounds, pilgrim conductors, circumcisers, etc. ..	226	13	..	..	273	3	308	17
	46.—LAW ..	**9,096**	..	**30**	..	**6,590**	..	**3,016**	..
167	Lawyers of all kinds, including *kazis*, law agents, and *mukhtears* ..	5,173	..	16	..	3,221	..	1,947	..
168	Lawyers' clerks, petition-writers, etc. ..	3,923	..	14	..	3,369	..	1,069	..
	47.—MEDICINE ..	**6,004**	**1,248**	**36**	**7**	**4,503**	**1,251**	**3,397**	**836**
169	Registered medical practitioners including oculists ..	2,593	159	7	1 }				
170	Other persons practising the healing arts without being registered ..	1,277	38	12	.. }	3,176	79	2,658	83
171	Dentists ..	612	1	..	.. }				
172	Midwives, vaccinators, compounders, nurses, masseurs, etc. ..	1,491	1,050	17	6	1,327	1,172	739	753
173†	Veterinary surgeons ..	31	..	..	..	†	†	†	†
	48.—INSTRUCTION ..	**4,621**	**893**	**63**	**1**	**3,745**	**616**	**2,814**	**502**
174	Professors and teachers of all kinds ..	4,498	866	57	1	3,661	612 }	2,814	502
175	Clerks and servants connected with education ..	123	27	6	..	84	4 }		
	49.—LETTERS, ARTS AND SCIENCES (OTHER THAN 44) ..	**2,498**	**391**	**28**	**1**	**6,888**	**455**	**4,037**	**457**
176	Public scribes, stenographers, etc. ..	294	182	..	..	747	126	269	239
177	Architects, surveyors, engineers and their employees (not being state servants) ..	124	..	..	..	1,735	23	1,697	16
178	Authors, editors, journalists and photographers ..	276	6	12	.. }				
179	Artists, sculptors and image-makers ..	923	9	6	.. }				
180	Scientists (astronomers, botanists, etc.) ..	2	..	..	.. }	6,597	6,290	908	47
181	Horoscope casters, astrologers, fortune-tellers, wizards, witches and mediums ..	75	1	..	.. }				
182	Musicians (composers and performers other than military), actors, dancers, etc. ..	738	191	4	1	1,223	265	1,315	161
183	Managers and employees of places of public entertainments, race courses, societies, clubs, etc. ..	61	..	..	..	118	5	292	168
184	Conjurors, acrobats, recitors, exhibitors of curiosities and wild animals, etc. ..	5	2	6	..	108	15	199	3
	D.—MISCELLANEOUS ..	**254,623**	**30,626**	**2,618**	**259**	**192,683**	**40,638**	**166,067**	**43,923**
	IX.—Persons living on their income ..	**10,211**	**1,666**	**772**	**35**	**3,369**	**1,715**	**4,210**	**2,808**
	50.—PERSONS LIVING PRINCIPALLY ON THEIR INCOME ..	**10,211**	**1,666**	**772**	**35**	**3,369**	**1,715**	**4,210**	**2,808**
185	Proprietors (other than of agricultural land) fund and scholarship holders and pensioners ..	10,211	1,666	772	35	3,369	1,715	4,210	2,808
	X.—Domestic Service ..	**85,629**	**14,675**	**597**	**125**	**56,116**	**19,460**	**62,490**	**22,409**
	51.—DOMESTIC SERVICE ..	**85,629**	**14,675**	**597**	**125**	**56,116**	**19,460**	**62,490**	**22,409**
186	Private motor drivers and cleaners ..	2,147	3	4	..	514	..	..	..
187	Other domestic servants ..	83,482	14,672	593	125	55,602	19,460	62,490	22,409
	XI.—Insufficiently described occupations ..	**152,323**	**5,600**	**1,247**	**19**	**125,756**	**3,508**	**96,352**	**4,051**
	52.—GENERAL TERMS WHICH DO NOT INDICATE A DEFINITE OCCUPATION ..	**152,323**	**5,600**	**1,247**	**19**	**125,756**	**3,508**	**96,352**	**4,051**
188	Manufacturers, businessmen and contractors otherwise unspecified ..	3,407	14	30	..	2,929	137	1,494	9
189	Cashiers, accountants, book-keepers, clerks and other employees in unspecified offices, warehouses and shops	87,990	1,522	885	12	75,798	522	35,879	290
190	Mechanics otherwise unspecified ..	4,769	1	12	..	3,458	7	3,527	37
191	Labourers and workmen otherwise unspecified ..	56,157	4,063	320	7	43,571	2,842	55,452	3,715
	XII.—Unproductive ..	**6,460**	**8,685**	**2**	**80**	**7,442**	**15,955**	**7,225**	**17,463**
	53.—INMATES OF JAILS, ASYLUMS AND ALMS-HOUSES ..	**4,290**	**84**	..	..	**3,892**	**173**	**4,089**	**488**
192	Inmates of jails, asylums and alms-houses ..	4,290	84	..	..	3,892	173	4,089	488
	54.—BEGGARS, VAGRANTS AND PROSTITUTES ..	**2,169**	**8,601**	**2**	**80**	**3,522**	**15,782**	**3,136**	**16,975**
193	Beggars and vagrants ..	2,169	1,094	2	1	3,522	6,264 }	3,136	16,975
194	Procurers and prostitutes ..	..	7,507	..	79	..	9,518 }		
	55.—OTHER UNCLASSIFIED NON-PRODUCTIVE INDUSTRIES ..	**1**	..	..	..	**28**	..	..	..
195	Other unclassified non-productive industries ..	1	..	..	..	28	..	..	..

*The figures refer to the
†Included in groups 169,

sex and occupation in 1911, 1921 and 1931.

Calcutta. 1931. Earners, principal occupation and working dependents. Males.	Calcutta. 1931. Earners, principal occupation and working dependents. Females.	Calcutta. 1931. Earners subsidiary occupation. Males.	Calcutta. 1931. Earners subsidiary occupation. Females.	Calcutta. 1921*. Workers. Males.	Calcutta. 1921*. Workers. Females.	Calcutta. 1911*. Workers. Males.	Calcutta. 1911*. Workers. Females.	Howrah. 1931. Earners, principal occupation and working dependents. Males.	Howrah. 1931. Earners, principal occupation and working dependents. Females.	Howrah. 1931. Earners subsidiary occupation. Males.	Howrah. 1931. Earners subsidiary occupation. Females.	Howrah. 1921. Workers. Males.	Howrah. 1921. Workers. Females.	Gouup No.
11	12	13	14	15	16	17	18	19	20	21	22	23	24	25
3	..	..	..	..	..	..	..	..	..	..	..	..	..	
3	..	..	..	..	..	..	..	..	..	..	..	..	..	156
5,375	..	**4**	..	**4,105**	..	**4,343**	..	**189**	..	**3**	..	**642**	..	
5,372	..	4	..	4,105	..	4,343	..	148	..	..	..	565	..	157
3	..	..	..	..	..	..	..	41	..	3	..	77	..	158
20,261	**116**	**44**	..	**15,351**	**178**	**12,926**	**176**	**383**	**51**	**64**	..	**1,202**	**5**	
20,261	**116**	**44**	..	**15,351**	**178**	**12,926**	**176**	**383**	**51**	**64**	..	**1,202**	**5**	
13,753	77	40	..	8,067	92	8,564	18	305	..	20	..	904	5	159
..	..	..	..	9	..	23	..	..	..	..	..	..	..	160
6,508	39	4	..	7,275	86	4,339	158	74	51	44	..	298	..	161
..	..	..	..	..	..	..	..	4	..	..	..	..	..	162
26,897	**2,639**	**173**	**10**	**25,063**	**2,368**	**18,800**	**2,735**	**2,448**	**140**	**139**	**3**	**2,645**	**130**	
5,253	**203**	**41**	**1**	**4,926**	**190**	**6,321**	**983**	**806**	**16**	**18**	..	**1,075**	..	
4,704	181	41	1	4,158	131	4,624	205	755	15	18	..	1,071	..	163
320	9	..	..	494	23	1,261	681	1	..	..	..	..	..	164
4	..	..	..	33	36	140	80	..	..	..	..	..	..	165
225	13	..	..	241	..	296	17	50	1	..	..	4	..	166
8,969	..	**29**	..	**6,301**	..	**2,865**	..	**287**	..	**2**	..	**463**	..	
5,093	..	16	..	3,078	..	1,862	..	181	..	..	..	369	..	167
3.876	..	13	..	3,223	..	1,003	..	106	..	2	..	94	..	168
5,793	**1,202**	**26**	**7**	**4,001**	**1,171**	**3,103**	**803**	**485**	**66**	**21**	**3**	**528**	**79**	
2,516	137	7	1					283	5	9	..			169
1,256	38	6	..	2,862	70	2,433	80	145	4	10	3	271	8	170
612	1	..	..					3	..	..	..			171
1,389	1,026	13	6	1,139	1,101	670	723	52	57	2	..	257	71	172
20	..	..	..	†	†	†	†	2	..	..	..	†	†	173
4,449	**868**	**55**	**1**	**3,350**	**562**	**2,603**	**497**	**727**	**51**	**57**	..	**243**	**42**	
4,334	841	49	1	3,270	558	2,603	497	726	51	57	..	243	42	174
115	27	6	..	80	4			1	..	..	..			175
2,433	**366**	**22**	**1**	**6,485**	**445**	**3,908**	**452**	**143**	**7**	**41**	..	**336**	**9**	
294	182	..	..	727	125	269	239	2	..	..	..	..	..	176
120	..	..	..	1,613	23	1,642	16	31	..	..	..	145	..	177
274	6	12	..					27	..	..	..			178
895	9	6	..	5,465	4,170	892	46	25	5	39	..	917	427	179
2	..	..	..					..	..	..	..			180
65	1	..	..					15	1	..	..			181
726	166	4	1	1,134	264	1,256	157	24	1	2	..	43	8	182
52	..	..	..	57	5	289	168	..	..	..	..	..	..	183
5	2	..	..	85	15	180	3	19	..	..	..	..	1	184
247,789	**29,649**	**2,560**	**259**	**168,226**	**34,172**	**151,853**	**39,575**	**24,133**	**4,435**	**678**	**72**	**32,832**	**5,130**	
10,112	**1,622**	**769**	**35**	**3,115**	**1,405**	**3,865**	**2,229**	**448**	**128**	**42**	**14**	**760**	**277**	
10,112	**1,622**	**769**	**35**	**3,115**	**1,405**	**3,865**	**2,229**	**448**	**128**	**42**	**14**	**760**	**277**	
10,112	1,622	769	35	3,115	1,405	3,865	2,229	448	128	42	14	760	277	185
83,851	**14,270**	**587**	**125**	**51,819**	**17,205**	**58,553**	**21,011**	**5,211**	**1,509**	**95**	**33**	**4,127**	**1,517**	
83,851	**14,270**	**587**	**125**	**51,819**	**17,205**	**58,553**	**21,011**	**5,211**	**1,509**	**95**	**33**	**4,127**	**1,517**	
1,975	1	4	..	363	..	..	..	552	2	10	..	139	..	186
81,876	14,269	583	125	51,456	17,205	58,553	21,011	4,659	1,507	85	33	3,988	1,517	187
147,468	**5,239**	**1,202**	**19**	**106,836**	**2,360**	**86,626**	**3,208**	**17,962**	**2,137**	**528**	**16**	**27,135**	**1,610**	
147,468	**5,239**	**1,202**	**19**	**106,836**	**2,360**	**86,626**	**3,208**	**17,962**	**2,137**	**528**	**16**	**27,135**	**1,610**	
3,380	14	30	..	2,278	136	1,419	9	182	1	7	..	438	47	188
86,769	1,448	885	12	69,720	511	33,724	290	3,641	790	228	2	12,973	812	189
4,347	..	..	..	1,902	6	2,556	36	2,950	3	25	..	3,927	..	190
52,972	3,777	287	7	32,936	1,707	48,927	2,873	11,189	1,343	268	14	9,797	751	191
6,358	**8,518**	**2**	**80**	**6,456**	**13,202**	**6,674**	**15,356**	**512**	**661**	**13**	**9**	**810**	**1,726**	
4,290	**84**	..	..	**3,892**	**173**	**4,089**	**487**	**132**	..	..	..	**41**	**3**	
4,290	84	..	..	3,892	173	4,089	487	132	..	..	..	41	3	192
2,067	**8,434**	**2**	**80**	**2,539**	**13,029**	**2,585**	**14,869**	**365**	**661**	**13**	**9**	**769**	**1,723**	
2,067	994	2	1	2,539	4,152	2,585	14,869	365	198	13	1	769	427	193
..	7,440	..	79	..	8,877				463	..	8	..	1,296	194
1	..	..	..	**25**	..	..	..	**15**	..	..	..	..	..	
1	..	..	..	25	..	..	..	15	..	..	..	..	..	195

area as then constituted.
170 and 171.

SUBSIDIARY TABLE II.—Numbers of workers engaged in each occupation

NOTE.—On account of reconstitution and rearrangement of groups, order, etc., of 1921 and 1911 the total of groups does not

Group No.	Occupation (**CLASS, sub-class, ORDER** and group).	Calcutta with suburbs in 24-Parganas.									
		1931.						1921.		1911.	
		Earners principal occupation.		Working dependents.		Earners subsidiary occupation.		Workers.		Workers.	
		Male.	Female.	Male.	Female.	Male.	Female.	Male.	Female.	Male.	Female.
1	2	3	4	5	6	7	8	9	10	11	12
	ALL OCCUPATIONS ..	**6,841**	**1,146**	**42**	**3**	**91**	**9**	**7,686**	**1,810**	**7,897**	**2,111**
	A.—PRODUCTION OF RAW MATERIALS ..	**182**	**39**	..	..	**34**	**1**	**320**	**87**	**256**	**59**
	I.—Exploitation of animals and vegetation ..	**181**	**39**	..	..	**34**	**1**	**319**	**87**	**253**	**59**
	1.—PASTURE AND AGRICULTURE ..	**176**	**38**	..	..	**34**	**1**	**309**	**86**	**239**	**50**
	(a) Ordinary Cultivation ..	**151**	**37**	..	..	**34**	**1**	**263**	**75**	**155**	**46**
1	Non-cultivating proprietors taking rent in money or kind ..	81	28	..	..	17	1	127	63	86	38
2	Estate agents and managers of private owners ..	..	..	..	..	..	..				
3	Estate agents and managers of government ..	..	..	..	..	..	..	28	..	18	..
4	Rent collectors, clerks, etc. ..	22	..	..	..	..	..				
5	Cultivating owners ..	26	4	..	..	11	..	73	8	39	4
6 & 8	Tenant cultivators and cultivators of *jhum*, *taungya* and other shifting areas ..	1	2	..	..	1	..				
7	Agricultural labourers ..	21	3	..	..	4	..	36	4	12	4
	(b) Cultivation of special crops, fruit, etc. (Planters, managers, clerks and labourers) ..	**17**	..	..	..	..	..	**37**	**10**	**48**	**1**
9	Cinchona ..										
10	Cocoanut ..										
11	Coffee ..	..	..	..	..	..	..	1	..	1	1
12	Ganja ..										
13	*Pan*-vine ..	1	..	..	..	..	..	..	..	..	..
14	Rubber ..	..	..	..	..	..	..	36	10	46	1
15	Tea ..	..	..	..	..	..	..				
16	Market gardeners, flower and fruit growers ..	16	..	..	..	..	..	..	..	..	..
	(c) Forestry ..	**4**	..	..	..	..	..	**4**	**1**	**25**	**2**
17	Forest officers, rangers, guards, etc. ..	1	..	..	..	..	..	..	..	..	..
18	Wood cutters and charcoal burners ..	2	..	..	..	..	..	4	1		
19	Collectors of forest produce ..	1	..	..	..	..	..			25	2
20	Collectors of lac ..	..	..	..	..	..	..	..	..		
	(d) Stock raising ..	**4**	**1**	..	..	..	..	**4**	..	**12**	**1**
21	Cattle and buffalo breeders and keepers ..	2	1	..	..	..	..	..	..	8	1
22	Breeders of transport animals ..	..	..	..	..	..	..	..	..	4	..
23	Herdsmen, shepherds and breeders of other animals ..	2	..	..	..	..	..				
	2.—FISHING AND HUNTING ..	**4**	**1**	..	..	..	..	**10**	**1**	**14**	
27	Fishing and pearling ..	4	1	..	..	..	..	10	1	14	
	II.—Exploitation of minerals ..	**1**	..	..	..	..	..	**1**	..	**3**	..
	4.—NON-METALLIC MINERALS ..	**1**	..	..	..	..	..	**1**	..	**3**	..
35	Coal ..	1	..	..	..	..	..	1	..	1	..
36	Petroleum ..	..	..	..	..	..	..	..	..	..	..
37	Building materials (including stone, materials for cement manufacture and clays).										
38	Mica										
39	Precious and semi-precious stones ..	..	..	..	..	..	..	..	..	3	..
40	Salt, saltpetre and other saline substances ..										
41	Other non-metallic minerals ..										
	B.—PREPARATION AND SUPPLY OF MATERIAL SUBSTANCES ..	**3,054**	**290**	..	..	**22**	**1**	**4,151**	**568**	**4,581**	**606**
	III.—Industry ..	**1,250**	**178**	..	..	**8**	**1**	**1,842**	**305**	**1,933**	**345**
	5.—TEXTILES ..	**168**	**40**	..	..	**1**	..	**345**	**82**	**341**	**117**
42	Cotton ginning, cleaning and pressing ..	3	..	..	..	..	..	2	..	..	..
43	Cotton spinning, sizing and weaving ..	6	1	..	..	..	..	30	15	35	17
44	Jute pressing, spinning and weaving ..	156	39	..	..	1	..	296	63	286	97
44A	*Jute pressing* ..	*37*	*5*	..	..	..	..	*199*	*36*	..	..
45	Rope, twine, string and other fibres ..	1	..	..	..	..	..	13	2	12	2
46	Wool carding, spinning and weaving ..	..	..	..	..	..	..	..	..	..	..
47	Silk spinning and weaving ..	..	..	..	..	..	..	1	..	3	..
48	Hair (horse-hair), etc. ..	..	..	..	..	..	..	..	..	..	..
49	Dyeing, bleaching, printing, preparation and sponging of textiles ..	2	..	..	..	..	..	2	..	3	..
50	Lace, crepe, embroideries, fringes, etc., and insufficiently described textile industries ..	1	..	..	..	..	..	1	1	1	..
	6.—HIDES, SKINS AND HARD MATERIALS FROM THE ANIMAL KINGDOM ..	**2**	..	..	..	..	..	**13**	**2**	**8**	**1**
51	Workers in leather ..	2	..	..	..	..	..	10	1	7	..
52	Furriers and persons occupied with feathers and bristles, brush makers ..	..	..	..	..	..	..	1	..	..	..
53	Workers (except button makers) in bone, ivory, horn shell, etc. ..	..	..	..	..	..	..	2	1	2	1
	7.—WOOD ..	**144**	**4**	..	..	**1**	..	**198**	**11**	**144**	**14**
54	Sawyers ..	4	..	..	..	..	..	4	..	132	1
55	Carpenters, turners and joiners, etc. ..	114	1	..	..	1	..	178	3		
56	Basket-makers and other workers in woody materials (including leaves) and thatchers and builders working with bamboo, reeds or similar materials ..	27	3	..	..	..	..	16	8	12	13
	8.—METALS ..	**46**	..	..	..	**1**	..	**103**	**2**	**105**	**4**
57	Smelting, forging and rolling of iron and other metals ..	2	..	..	..	..	..	15	..	3	..
58	Makers of arms, guns, etc. ..	1	..	..	..	..	..	5	..	1	..
59	Blacksmiths, other workers in iron and makers of implements ..	35	..	..	..	1	..	46	1	49	1
60	Workers in brass, copper and bell metal ..	3	..	..	..	..	..	15	1	23	2
61	Workers in other metals (except precious metals) ..	5	..	..	..	..	..	22	..	26	1
62	Workers in mints, die-sinkers, etc. ..	1	..	..	..	..	..	1	..	3	..
	9.—CERAMICS ..	**15**	**5**	..	..	..	..	**46**	**15**	**23**	**7**
63	Potters and makers of earthenware ..	5	1	..	..	..	..	15	7	9	3
64	Brick and tile makers ..	6	4	..	..	..	..	31	8	13	4
65	Other workers in ceramics ..	4	..	..	..	..	..	1	..	1	..

per 10,000 of the total population of the same sex, 1911, 1921 and 1931.

add up to the figures against the order or sub-order (in some cases) for these years. Similarly for figures against sub-classes.

Calcutta.										Howrah.								
1931.						1921.		1911.		1931.						1921.		Group No.
Earners principal occupation.		Working dependents.		Earners subsidiary occupation.		Workers.		Workers.		Earners principal occupation.		Working dependents.		Earners subsidiary occupation.		Workers.		
Male.	Female.	Male.	Female.	Male.	Female.	Male.	Female.	Male.	Female.	Male.	Female.	Male.	Female.	Male.	Female.	Male.	Female.	
13	14	15	16	17	18	19	20	21	22	23	24	25	26	27	28	29	30	
6,900	**1,147**	**44**	**3**	**76**	**9**	**7,708**	**1,814**	**7,936**	**2,121**	**4,957**	**1,092**	**19**	**5**	**184**	**16**	**7,595**	**1,827**	
149	**33**	..	..	**23**	**1**	**282**	**84**	**243**	**55**	**305**	**70**	**4**	..	**39**	**3**	**386**	**77**	
148	**33**	..	..	**23**	**1**	**281**	**84**	**239**	**55**	**286**	**69**	**4**	..	**37**	**3**	**384**	**76**	
144	**32**	..	..	**22**	**1**	**275**	**83**	**230**	**50**	**206**	**48**	**3**	..	**37**	**3**	**370**	**67**	
121	**31**	..	..	**22**	**1**	**236**	**75**	**152**	**46**	**192**	**41**	**3**	..	**37**	**3**	**346**	**64**	
80	28	..	..	13	..	141	69	93	41	61	30	..	..	13	3	68	36	1
..	..	..	..	..	..					1	..	..	..	..	..			2
..	..	..	..	..	..	29	..	19	..	..	..	..	..	..	..	16	..	3
16	..	..	..	..	..					19	..	..	..	..	..			4
17	2	..	..	6	..					45	4	..	..	23	1	163	19	5
..	..	..	..	..	..	56	5	36	4	30	2	..	..	1	..			6 & 8
8	1	..	..	2	..	9	2	4	1	36	5	3	..	..	..	99	9	7
16	..	..	..	..	..	**32**	**7**	**42**	**1**	**10**	..	..	..	..	..	**12**	..	
..	..	..	..	..	..	1	..	2	1	..	..	..	..	..	..	..	..	9, 10, 11, 12
1	..	..	..	..	..	..	..	..	..	..	..	..	..	..	..	..	..	13
..	..	..	..	..	..	30	7	40	..	..	..	..	..	..	..	12	..	14
..	..	..	..	..	..					1	..	..	..	..	..			15
14	..	..	..	..	..	..	..	..	..	9	..	..	..	..	..	..	..	16
4	..	..	..	..	..	**4**	**1**	**25**	**2**	..	..	..	..	..	..	**3**	..	
1	..	..	..	..	..	..	..	..	..	..	..	..	..	..	..	..	..	17
2	..	..	..	..	..	4	1			..	..	..	..	..	..			18
1	..	..	..	..	..			25	2	..	..	..	..	..	..	3	..	19
..	..	..	..	..	..	..	..			..	..	..	..	..	..			20
2	**1**	..	..	..	..	**4**	..	**11**	**1**	**3**	**6**	..	..	..	..	**9**	**3**	
1	1	..	..	..	..		..	9	1	2	4	..	..	..	..	2	..	21
..	..	..	..	..	..	4	..	2	..	..	..	..	..	..	..	7	3	22
1	..	..	..	..	..		..	..		2	2	..	..	..	..			23
4	**1**	..	..	..	..	**6**	**1**	**9**	**5**	**79**	**21**	..	..	..	..	**14**	**9**	
4	1	..	..	..	..	6	1	9	5	79	21	..	..	..	..	14	9	27
1	..	..	..	..	..	**1**	..	**4**	..	**19**	**1**	..	..	**1**	..	**3**	**1**	
1	..	..	..	..	..	**1**	..	**4**	..	**19**	**1**	..	..	**1**	..	**3**	**1**	
1	..	..	..	..	..	1	..	1	..	19	1	..	..	1	..	3	1	35
..	..	..	..	..	..	..	..	..	..	..	..	..	..	..	..	..	..	36
..	..	..	..	..	..	..	..	3	..	..	..	..	..	..	..	..	..	37, 38, 39, 40, 4
3,088	**268**	..	..	**19**	**1**	**3,946**	**466**	**4,468**	**516**	**2,785**	**444**	**11**	**2**	**84**	**3**	**4,303**	**962**	
1,253	**160**	..	..	**6**	**1**	**1,501**	**213**	**1,725**	**271**	**1,568**	**298**	**6**	..	**35**	**1**	**2,893**	**739**	
171	**38**	..	..	**1**	..	**128**	**25**	**166**	**60**	**1,126**	**212**	..	..	**16**	..	**1,599**	**534**	
3	..	..	..	..	..	3	..	..	..	3	..	..	..	..	..	..	16	42
6	1	..	..	..	..	8	1	7	3	87	..	..	..	..	..	34	6	43
159	36	..	..	1	..	111	22	150	56	1,027	211	..	..	16	..	1,554	493	44
37	..	..	..	..	..	*58*	*6*	..	..	*405*	*60*	..	..	*5*	..	*71*	*26*	44A
1	..	..	..	..	..	3	..	2	1	4	..	..	..	..	..	10	19	45
..	..	..	..	..	..	..	..	1	..	1	..	..	..	..	..	..	..	46
..	..	..	..	..	..	..	..	..	..	..	..	..	..	..	..	..	..	47
..	..	..	..	..	..	..	..	1	..	..	..	..	..	..	..	..	..	48
2	..	..	..	..	..	2	..	0	..	..	..	..	..	..	..	..	..	49
1	..	..	..	..	..	1	1	2	..	3	..	..	..	..	..	..	..	50
1	..	..	..	..	..	**4**	..	**8**	..	..	..	..	..	..	..	..	..	
1	..	..	..	..	..	3	..	8	..	..	..	..	..	..	..	..	..	51
..	..	..	..	..	..	1	..	..	..	..	..	..	..	..	..	..	..	52
..	..	..	..	..	..	..	..	..	..	..	..	..	..	..	..	..	..	58
142	**4**	..	..	..	..	**207**	**12**	**146**	**15**	**18**	**6**	..	..	..	..	**120**	**12**	
4	..	..	..	..	..	3	..	133	..	..	..	..	..	..	..	2	..	54
115	1	..	..	..	..	186	3	..	..	16	3	..	..	..	..	98	2	55
24	3	..	..	..	..	17	9	13	15	2	4	..	..	..	..	20	10	56
44	..	..	..	..	..	**81**	**2**	**97**	**4**	**6**	**3**	..	..	..	..	**298**	**6**	
2	..	..	..	..	..	8	..	2	..	3	..	..	..	..	..	222	..	57
1	..	..	..	..	..	1	..	1	..	..	..	..	..	..	..	..	..	58
33	..	..	..	..	..	36	1	42	..	3	3	..	..	..	..	63	5	59
3	..	..	..	..	..	15	1	22	2	..	..	..	..	..	..	13	1	60
5	..	..	..	..	..	19	..	26	1	..	..	..	..	..	..	..	..	61
1	..	..	..	..	..	1	..	3	..	..	..	..	..	..	..	..	..	62
12	..	..	..	..	..	**16**	**4**	**11**	**3**	**13**	**3**	..	..	**1**	..	**76**	**2**	
4	..	..	..	..	..	9	3	7	2	10	1	..	..	1	..	20	2	63
5	..	..	..	..	..	6	1	3	1	3	2	..	..	..	..	56	1	64
4	..	..	..	..	..	1	..	..	..	..	..	..	..	..	..	..	..	65

SUBSIDIARY TABLE II.—Numbers of workers engaged in each occupation

Group No.	Occupation (CLASS, sub-class, ORDER and group).	Calcutta with suburbs in 24-Parganas.									
		1931.						1921.		1911.	
		Earners principal occupation.		Working dependents.		Earners subsidiary occupation.		Workers.		Workers.	
		Male.	Female.	Male.	Female.	Male.	Female.	Male.	Female.	Male.	Female.
1	2	3	4	5	6	7	8	9	10	11	12
	III.—Industry—*concld.*										
	10.—CHEMICAL PRODUCTS PROPERLY SO CALLED AND ANALOGOUS ..	**16**	**2**	..	..	..	..	**35**	**3**	**54**	**5**
66	Manufacture of matches, fireworks and other explosives ..	6	1	..	..	..	..	1	..	4	..
67	Manufacture of aerated and mineral waters and ice ..	1	..	..	..	..	..	1	..	1	..
68	Manufacture and refining of vegetable oils ..	4	1	..	..	..	..	20	2	37	2
69	Manufacture and refining of mineral oils ..	..	..	..	..	..	..	..	..	..	..
70	Other chemical manufactures ..	4	..	..	..	..	..	13	2	12	3
	11.—FOOD INDUSTRIES ..	**90**	**30**	..	..	**1**	..	**96**	**43**	**85**	**33**
71	Rice pounders and huskers and flour grinders ..	20	25	..	..	..	..	14	30	10	21
72	Grain parchers, etc. ..	..	..	..	..	..	..	1	4	3	3
73	Butchers ..	14	..	..	..	..	..	32	5	25	4
74	Makers of sugar, molasses and *gurh* ..	2	..	..	..	..	..	5	..	8	..
75	Sweetmeat and condiment makers ..	8	..	..	..	..	..	10	1	9	..
76	Toddy drawers ..	..	..	..	..	..	..	1	..	1	..
78	Manufacturers of tobacco ..	40	3	..	..	1	.. }				
79	Manufacturers of opium ..	..	..	..	..	..	.. }	15	3	9	3
80	Manufacturers of *ganja* ..	..	..	..	..	..	.. }				
81	Other food industries ..	6	..	..	..	..	..	17	1	20	1
	12.—INDUSTRIES OF DRESS AND THE TOILET ..	**315**	**44**	..	..	**3**	..	**386**	**50**	**463**	**46**
82	Boot, shoe, sandal and clog makers ..	90	24	..	..	..	..	130	7	171	8
83	Tailors, milliners, dressmakers and darners ..	102	7	..	..	2	.. }	139	14	162	4
84	Embroiderers and makers of hats and other articles of wear ..	7	..	..	..	..	.. }				
85	Washermen and cleaners ..	73	10	..	..	..	..	71	25	70	25
86	Barbers, hair-dressers and wig-makers ..	43	3	..	..	..	..	45	4	60	9
	13.—FURNITURE INDUSTRIES ..	**16**	..	..	..	..	..	**16**	..	**10**	..
88	Cabinet-makers, carriage-painters, etc. ..	16	..	..	..	..	..	16	..	10	..
	14.—BUILDING INDUSTRIES ..	**138**	**24**	..	..	**1**	..	**205**	**37**	**276**	**47**
90	Lime-burners, cement-workers, excavators and well-sinkers, stone-cutters and dressers, brick-layers and masons, builders (other than of buildings made of bamboo or similar materials), painters, house-decorators, tilers, plumbers, etc. ..	138	24	..	..	1	..	205	37	276	47
	15.—CONSTRUCTION OF MEANS OF TRANSPORT	**23**	..	..	..	..	..	**60**	**2**	**11**	..
91	Manufacture assembly or repair of motor vehicles or cycles ..	13	..	..	..	..	..	13	..	..	..
92	Makers of carriages, carts, *palkis*, etc. and wheel-wrights ..	2	..	..	..	..	..	3	..	7	..
93	Ship, boat and aeroplane builders ..	8	..	..	..	..	..	44	2	4	..
	16.—PRODUCTION AND TRANSMISSION OF PHYSICAL FORCE ..	**27**	..	..	..	..	..	**30**	**1**	**38**	..
94	Heat, light, electricity, motive power, etc. (gas works and electric light and power) ..	27	..	..	..	..	..	30	1	38	..
	17.—MISCELLANEOUS AND UNDEFINED INDUSTRIES ..	**250**	**28**	..	..	**1**	..	**309**	**57**	**375**	**70**
95	Printers, engravers, book-binders, etc. ..	126	..	..	..	..	..	127	6	144	2
96	Makers of musical instruments ..	7	..	..	..	..	..	3	2	5	..
97	Makers of clocks and surgical or scientific instruments, etc. ..	4	..	..	..	..	..	8	..	9	..
98	Makers of jewellery and ornaments ..	40	1	..	..	..	..	84	2	99	2
99	Other miscellaneous and undefined industries (toy-making, taxidermy, etc.) ..	..	..	..	..	..	..	1	..	2	1
100	Scavenging ..	74	27	..	..	..	..	85	46	110	60
	IV.—Transport ..	**666**	**22**	..	..	**1**	..	**892**	**29**	**1,252**	**16**
	19.—TRANSPORT BY WATER ..	**260**	**1**	..	..	..	..	**360**	**1**	**600**	**5**
102	Ship-owners, boat-owners and their employees, officers, mariners, etc., ships' brokers, boatmen and towmen ..	224	..	..	..	..	..	336	..	500	..
102A	*Ship-owners, boat-owners and their employees, officers, mariners, etc., ships' brokers, boatmen and towmen of inland water transport* ..	*142*	..	..	..	..	..	*199*	..	..	..
103	Persons (other than labourers) employed in harbours, docks, rivers and canals, including pilots ..	90	1	..	..	..	..	5	1 }	100	5
104	Labourers employed on harbours, docks, rivers and canals ..	16	..	..	..	..	..	19	.. }		
	20.—TRANSPORT BY ROAD ..	**292**	**18**	..	..	**1**	..	**356**	**13**	**476**	**8**
105	Persons (other than labourers) employed on the construction and maintenance of roads and bridges ..	..	..	..	..	..	..	..	.. }	10	1
106	Labourers employed on the construction of roads and bridges ..	24	17	..	..	..	..	3	.. }		
107	Owners, managers and employees (excluding personal servants) connected with mechanically driven vehicles (including trams) ..	91	..	..	..	..	..	76	1 }	401	6
108	Owners, managers and employees (excluding personal servants) connected with other vehicles ..	102	..	..	..	..	..	208	2 }		
109	Owners and bearers of *palkis*, etc. ..	15	..	..	..	..	..	7	..	12	..
110	Owners and drivers of pack elephants, camels, mules, asses and bullocks ..	..	..	..	..	..	..	1	..	..	..
111	Porters and messengers ..	59	..	..	..	..	..	71	11	54	..
	21.—TRANSPORT BY RAIL ..	**77**	**3**	..	..	..	..	**121**	**12**	**141**	**1**
112	Railway employees of all kinds other than coolies ..	59	3	..	..	..	..	90	4	141	1
113	Labourers employed on railway construction and maintenance and coolies and porters employed on railway premises ..	18	..	..	..	..	..	31	8	..	..
	22.—POST-OFFICE, TELEGRAPH AND TELEPHONE SERVICES ..	**37**	**1**	..	..	..	..	**45**	**3**	**35**	**2**
114	Post-office, telegraph and telephone services ..	37	1	..	..	..	..	45	3	35	2
	V.—Trade ..	**1,138**	**90**	..	..	**13**	**1**	**1,417**	**233**	**1,396**	**245**
	23.—BANKS, ESTABLISHMENTS OF CREDIT, EXCHANGE AND INSURANCE ..	**34**	**1**	..	..	**2**	..	**42**	**8**	**56**	**9**
115	Bank-managers, money-lenders, exchange and insurance agents, money changers and brokers and their employees ..	34	1	..	..	2	..	42	8	56	9
	24.—BROKERAGE COMMISSION AND EXPORT ..	**61**	**1**	..	..	..	..	**127**	**2**	**92**	**1**
116	Brokers, commission agents, commercial travellers, warehouse owners and employees ..	61	1	..	..	..	..	127	2	92	1

per 10,000 of the total population of the same sex, 1911, 1921 and 1931.

Calcutta.										Howrah.								Group No.
1931.						1921.		1911.		1931.						1921.		
Earners principal occupation.		Working dependents.		Earners subsidiary occupation.		Workers.		Workers.		Earners principal occupation.		Working dependents.		Earners subsidiary occupation.		Workers.		
Male.	Female.	Male.	Female.	Male.	Female.	Male.	Female.	Male.	Female.	Male.	Female.	Male.	Female.	Male.	Female.	Male.	Female.	
13	14	15	16	17	18	19	20	21	22	23	24	25	26	27	28	29	30	
16	**2**	..	..	..	..	**32**	**2**	**43**	**2**	**8**	..	..	..	..	..	**17**	**7**	
7	1	..	..	..	..	..	..	..	..	..	..	..	..	..	..	..	..	66
1	..	..	..	..	..	1	..	..	..	..	..	..	..	..	..	..	..	67
4	1	..	..	..	..	21	1	34	1	7	..	..	..	..	..	17	7	68
..	..	..	..	..	..	..	..	..	..	..	..	..	..	..	..	..	..	69
4	..	..	..	..	..	10	1	8	1	..	..	..	..	..	..	..	..	70
84	**15**	..	..	**1**	..	**70**	**31**	**78**	**24**	**27**	**6**	..	..	**5**	..	**163**	**21**	
12	11	..	..	..	..	7	20	11	16	2	2	..	..	1	..	105	18	71
..	..	..	..	..	..	..	3	2	2	1	..	..	..	..	..	2	1	72
14	..	..	..	..	..	22	4	23	3	6	..	..	..	..	..	1	..	73
3	..	..	..	..	..	3	..	2	..	..	..	..	..	..	..	..	..	74
8	..	..	..	..	..	4	1	10	..	..	..	..	..	..	..	23	..	75
..	..	..	..	..	..	..	..	1	..	..	..	..	..	..	..	..	..	76
{ 40	3	..	..	1	.. }				2{	16	4	..	..	4	.. }		{	78
..	..	..	..	..	..	15	1	8		..	..	..	..	..	..	21	2{	79
..	..	..	..	..	..					..	..	..	..	..	..			80
7	..	..	..	..	..	18	..	21	1	3	..	..	..	..	..	12	..	81
314	**46**	..	..	**2**	..	**366**	**45**	**454**	**45**	**188**	**24**	**6**	..	**8**	..	**250**	**56**	
93	26	..	..	..	..	148	9	188	2	30	2	..	..	1	..	38	4	82
{ 97	7	..	..	2	.. }	102	7	136	10	45	1	5	..	2	.. }	80	14	{83
8	..	..	..	..	..					7	16	..	..	..	..			84
73	10	..	..	..	..	70	25	67	24	69	4	..	..	5	..	82	31	85
44	3	..	..	..	..	46	5	63	9	37	..	..	..	..	..	50	7	86
17	..	..	..	..	..	**18**	..	**12**	..	..	..	..	..	..	..	..	..	
17	..	..	..	..	..	18	..	12	..	..	..	..	..	..	..	..	..	88
140	**26**	..	..	**1**	..	**173**	**30**	**260**	**41**	**78**	**6**	..	..	**2**	..	**226**	**23**	
140	26	..	..	1	..	173	30	260	41	78	6	..	..	2	..	226	23	90
23	..	..	..	..	..	**36**	..	**12**	..	**3**	..	..	..	**1**	..	**2**	..	
13	..	..	..	..	..	14	..	..	..	3	..	..	..	1	..	..	..	91
1	..	..	..	..	..	3	..	8	..	..	..	..	..	..	..	..	..	92
9	..	..	..	..	..	19	..	4	..	..	..	..	..	..	..	2	..	93
28	..	..	..	..	..	**30**	**1**	**40**	..	**25**	..	..	..	..	..	**2**	..	
28	..	..	..	..	..	30	1	40	..	25	..	..	..	..	..	2	..	94
260	**29**	..	..	**1**	..	**339**	**61**	**399**	**76**	**76**	**39**	..	..	**2**	..	**140**	**79**	
131	..	..	..	..	..	147	5	157	2	6	..	..	..	..	..	1	..	95
7	..	..	..	..	..	2	1	5	..	..	..	..	..	..	..	..	..	96
4	..	..	..	..	..	9	..	10	..	10	..	..	..	..	..	..	..	97
42	1	..	..	..	..	84	3	100	2	19	..	..	..	..	..	34	1	98
..	..	..	..	..	..	1	..	2	..	..	1	..	..	..	..	..	..	99
76	28	..	..	..	..	95	53	119	65	40	38	..	..	2	..	105	78	100
687	**20**	..	..	**1**	..	**955**	**34**	**1,293**	**19**	**419**	**16**	**4**	..	**9**	..	**746**	**25**	
271	**1**	..	..	..	..	**430**	**1**	**660**	**6**	**24**	..	**2**	..	**1**	..	**102**	..	
233	..	..	..	..	..	401	..	568	..	22	..	2	..	1	..	33	..	102
148	..	..	..	..	..	*235*	..	..	..	*32*	..	*8*	..	*1*	..	*32*	..	*102A*
{ 21	1	..	..	..	..	6	1 }	96	6{	2	..	..	..	..	..	53	..	103
16	..	..	..	..	..	23	..			..	..	..	..	..	..	16	..	104
297	**15**	..	..	**1**	..	**362**	**14**	**466**	**8**	**111**	**5**	..	..	**3**	..	**89**	**1**	
{ ..	..	..	..	..	..	..	.. }	6	1{	..	..	..	..	..	..	..	..	105
24	14	..	..	..	..	1	..			29	5	..	..	..	..	..	..	106
{ 95	..	..	..	..	..	80	1 }	388	7{	9	..	..	..	..	..	1	..	107
102	..	..	..	..	..	190	1			62	..	..	..	2	..	73	1	108
15	..	..	..	..	..	7	..	13	..	2	..	..	..	..	..	15	..	109
..	..	..	..	..	..	..	..	..	..	..	..	..	..	..	..	..	..	110
61	..	..	..	..	..	83	12	58	..	9	..	..	..	1	..	..	..	111
80	**3**	..	..	..	..	**115**	**15**	**128**	**2**	**265**	**10**	**1**	..	**5**	..	**528**	**23**	
61	3	..	..	..	..	81	5	128	2	196	7	..	..	5	..	402	3	112
19	..	..	..	..	..	34	10	..	..	69	3	1	..	..	..	126	21	113
39	**1**	..	..	..	..	**48**	**4**	**39**	**3**	**19**	..	..	..	..	..	**29**	..	
39	1	..	..	..	..	48	4	39	3	19	..	..	..	..	..	29	..	114
1,148	**88**	..	..	**12**	**1**	**1,489**	**218**	**1,451**	**226**	**798**	**130**	**1**	**2**	**40**	**2**	**664**	**198**	
34	**1**	..	..	**2**	..	**41**	**9**	**59**	**9**	**7**	**1**	..	..	..	..	**30**	**7**	
34	1	..	..	2	..	41	9	59	9	7	1	..	..	..	..	30	7	115
63	**1**	..	..	..	..	**150**	**2**	**102**	**1**	**23**	**1**	..	..	..	..	**14**	..	
63	1	..	..	..	..	150	2	102	1	23	1	..	..	..	..	14	..	116

SUBSIDIARY TABLE II.—Numbers of workers engaged in each occupation

Group No.	Occupation (CLASS, sub-class, ORDER and group).	Calcutta with suburbs in 24-Parganas. 1931. Earners principal occupation. Male.	Female.	Working dependents. Male.	Female.	Earners subsidiary occupation. Male.	Female.	1921. Workers. Male.	Female.	1911. Workers. Male.	Female.
1	2	3	4	5	6	7	8	9	10	11	12
	V.—Trade—*concld.*										
	25.—TRADE IN TEXTILES ..	**53**	**1**	..	..	**1**	..	**85**	**6**	**181**	**7**
117	Trade in piece goods, jute, wool, cotton, silk, hair and other textiles	53	1	..	..	1	..	85	6	181	7
117A	*Trade in jute* ..	*2*	..	..	..	..	..	*9*	..	..	..
	26.—TRADE IN SKINS, LEATHER AND FURS ..	**15**	..	..	..	..	..	**31**	**2**	**50**	**1**
118	Trade in skins, leather, furs, feathers, horn, etc., and articles made therefrom ..	15	..	..	..	..	..	31	2	50	1
	27.—TRADE IN WOOD ..	**11**	**1**	..	..	..	..	**20**	**1**	**24**	**4**
119	Trade in wood (not firewood) ..	10	..	..	..	..	..	}			
120	Trade in barks ..	..	..	..	..	..	..	20	1	24	4
121	Trade in bamboos and canes ..	..	..	..	..	..	..				
122	Trade in thatches and other forest produce ..	..	..	..	..	..	..				
	28.—TRADE IN METALS ..	**6**	..	..	..	..	..	**13**	**1**	**26**	**1**
123	Trade in metals, machinery, knives, tools, etc. ..	6	..	..	..	..	..	13	1	26	1
	29.—TRADE IN POTTERY, BRICKS AND TILES ..	**1**	..	..	..	..	..	**1**	..	**3**	**1**
124	Trade in pottery, bricks and tiles ..	1	..	..	..	..	..	1	..	3	1
	30.—TRADE IN CHEMICAL PRODUCTS ..	**5**	..	..	..	..	..	**12**	**1**	**23**	**1**
125	Drugs, dyes, paints, petroleum, explosives, etc. ..	5	..	..	..	..	..	12	1	23	1
	31.—HOTELS, CAFES, RESTAURANT, ETC. ..	**49**	**3**	..	..	..	..	**63**	**17**	**51**	**4**
126	Vendors of wine, liquors, aerated waters and ice ..	5	..	..	..	..	..	15	2	33	1
127	Owners and managers of hotels, cook shops, *serais*, etc. (and employees)	43	2	..	..	..	..	} 48	15	18	3
128	Hawkers of drink and food stuffs ..	1	..	..	..	..	..				
	32.—OTHER TRADE IN FOOD STUFFS ..	**363**	**52**	..	..	**6**	..	**392**	**115**	**522**	**166**
129	Grain and pulse dealers ..	33	4	..	..	..	..	40	13	92	23
130	Dealers in sweetmeats, sugar and spices ..	28	2	..	..	1	..	213	50	295	85
131	Dealers in dairy products, eggs and poultry ..	50	12	..	..	1	..	54	21	62	24
132	Dealers in animals for food ..	2	..	..	..	..	..	31	25	19	24
133	Dealers in fodder for animals ..	4	..	..	..	..	..	11	..	19	3
134	Dealers in other food stuffs ..	227	33	..	..	5	..	..	..	..	..
135	Dealers in tobacco ..	11	..	..	..	..	..	}			
136	Dealers in opium ..	1	..	..	..	..	..	43	5	35	7
137	Dealers in *ganja* ..	7	..	..	..	..	..				
	33.—TRADE IN CLOTHING AND TOILET ARTICLES ..	**23**	**1**	..	..	..	..	**41**	**1**	**76**	**2**
138	Trade in ready-made clothing and other articles of dress and the toilet (hats, umbrellas, socks, ready-made shoes, perfumes, etc.) ..	23	1	..	..	..	..	41	1	76	2
	34.—TRADE IN FURNITURE ..	**10**	..	..	..	..	..	**20**	**1**	**30**	**2**
139	Trade in furniture, carpets, curtains and bedding ..	3	..	..	..	..	..	7	..	6	..
140	Hardware, cooking utensils, porcelain, crokery, glass-ware, bottles, articles for gardening, etc. ..	7	..	..	..	..	..	13	1	24	2
	35.—TRADE IN BUILDING MATERIALS ..	**2**	..	..	..	..	..	**3**	..	**5**	..
141	Trade in building materials (other than bricks, tiles and woody materials) ..	2	..	..	..	..	..	3	..	5	..
	36.—TRADE IN MEANS OF TRANSPORT ..	**3**	..	..	..	..	..	**7**	..	**10**	..
142	Dealers in and hirers of mechanical transport-motors, cycles, etc. ..	2	..	..	..	..	..	1	.. }		
143	Dealers in and hirers of other carriages, carts, boats, etc. ..	..	..	..	..	..	..	1	..	10	..
144	Dealers in and hirers of elephants, camels, horses, cattle, asses, mules, etc. ..	1	..	..	..	..	..	5	..		
	37.—TRADE IN FUEL ..	**18**	**3**	..	..	..	..	**33**	**28**	**32**	**26**
145	Dealers in firewood, charcoal, coal, cowdung, etc. ..	18	3	..	..	..	..	33	28	32	26
	38.—TRADE IN ARTICLES OF LUXURY AND THOSE PERTAINING TO LETTERS AND THE ARTS AND SCIENCES ..	**57**	**2**	..	..	**1**	..	**71**	**7**	**80**	**7**
146	Dealers in precious stones, jewellery (real and imitation), clocks, optical instruments, etc. ..	17	..	..	..	..	..	27	1	22	..
147	Dealers in common bangles, bead necklaces, fans, small articles, toys, hunting and fishing tackle, flowers, etc. ..	2	..	..	..	..	..	7	3	21	4
148	Publishers, book-sellers, stationers, dealers in music, pictures, musical instruments and curiosities ..	38	1	..	..	..	..	38	4	37	2
	39.—TRADE OF OTHER SORTS ..	**428**	**27**	..	..	**3**	..	**456**	**44**	**135**	**11**
149	Dealers in rags, stable refuse, etc. ..	..	..	..	..	..	..	..	..	1	..
150	General store-keepers and shop-keepers otherwise unspecified ..	368	22	..	..	2	..	412	40	98	8
151	Itinerant traders, padlars and hawkers (of other than food, etc.) ..	59	4	..	..	1	..	43	4	31	3
152	Other traders (including farmers of pounds, tolls and markets) ..	..	..	..	..	..	..	1	..	2	..
	C.—PUBLIC ADMINISTRATION AND LIBERAL ARTS	**658**	**70**	..	..	**4**	..	**668**	**73**	**681**	**174**
	VI.—Public Force ..	**88**	..	..	..	..	..	**89**	..	**127**	..
	40.—ARMY ..	**21**	..	..	..	..	..	**28**	..	**61**	..
153	Imperial Army ..	21	..	..	..	..	..	28	..	61	..
	43.—POLICE ..	**68**	..	..	..	..	..	**61**	..	**66**	..
157	Police ..	68	..	..	..	..	..	60	..	66	..
158	Village watchmen ..	..	..	..	..	..	..	1	..	..	..
	VII.—Public Administration ..	**246**	**3**	..	..	**1**	..	**220**	**6**	**203**	**6**
	44.—PUBLIC ADMINISTRATION ..	**246**	**3**	..	..	**1**	..	**220**	**6**	**203**	**6**
159	Service of the State ..	169	2	..	..	1	..	116	2	134	1
160	Service of Indian and foreign states ..	..	..	..	..	..	..	..	..	..	..
161	Municipal and other local (not village) service ..	77	1	..	..	..	..	104	4	69	6

per 10,000 of the total population of the same sex, 1911, 1921 and 1931.

Calcutta.										Howrah.								Group No.
1931.						1921.		1911.		1931.						1921.		
Earners principal occupation.		Working dependents.		Earners subsidiary occupation.		Workers.		Workers.		Earners principal occupation.		Working dependents.		Earners subsidiary occupation.		Workers.		
Male.	Female.	Male.	Female.	Male.	Female.	Male.	Female.	Male.	Female.	Male.	Female.	Male.	Female.	Male.	Female.	Male.	Female.	
13	14	15	16	17	18	19	20	21	22	23	24	25	26	27	28	29	30	
55	1	..	..	1	..	92	6	197	8	34	2	..	..	2	..	77	1	
55	1	..	..	1	..	92	6	197	8	34	2	..	..	2	..	77	1	117
2	..	..	..	..	..	7	..	..	..	..	..	..	..	..	..	45	..	117A
14	..	..	..	..	..	27	2	55	2	..	..	..	..	..	..	..	..	
14	..	..	..	..	..	27	2	55	2	..	..	..	..	..	..	..	..	118
9	1	..	..	..	..	17	1	25	5	6	..	..	..	2	..	1	..	
9	..	..	..	..	..	17	1	25	5	5	..	..	..	2	..	1	..	119
..	..	..	..	..	..					1	..	..	..	..	..			120
..	..	..	..	..	..					..	..	..	..	..	..			121
..	..	..	..	..	..					1	..	..	..	..	..			122
6	..	..	..	..	..	14	1	27	..	6	..	..	..	..	..	4	..	
6	..	..	..	..	..	14	1	27	..	6	..	..	..	..	..	4	..	123
1	..	..	..	..	..	1	..	3	1	2	..	..	..	..	..	..	..	
1	..	..	..	..	..	1	..	3	1	2	..	..	..	..	..	..	..	124
5	..	..	..	..	..	13	1	25	1	4	..	..	..	..	..	20	..	
5	..	..	..	..	..	13	1	25	1	4	..	..	..	..	..	20	..	125
48	3	..	..	..	..	60	16	52	5	31	1	..	..	..	..	40	1	
3	..	..	..	..	..	12	1	32	1	7	..	..	..	..	..	16	1	126
45	3	..	..	..	..	48	15	20	4	24	1	..	..	..	..	24	1	127, 128
363	48	..	..	5	..	379	92	518	146	229	75	..	2	10	1	364	171	
34	4	..	..	..	..	37	6	88	17	14	16	..	..	..	..	49	14	129
28	2	..	..	1	..	217	46	297	82	40	7	..	..	1	..	222	82	130
48	10	..	..	..	..	47	17	61	23	28	16	..	..	2	..	40	28	131
2	..	..	..	..	..	25	18	17	20	..	..	..	..	..	..	22	40	132
4	..	..	..	..	..	9	..	20	1	1	..	..	..	..	..	15	7	133
227	32	..	..	4	..	..	..	..	..	144	36	..	1	7	1	..	..	134
11	..	..	..	..	..	45	4	34	3	1	..	..	..	..	..	16	1	135
1	..	..	..	..	..					..	..	..	..	..	..			136
7	..	..	..	..	..					..	..	..	..	..	..			137
24	1	..	..	..	..	43	1	86	1	9	..	..	..	..	..	17	..	
24	1	..	..	..	..	43	1	86	1	9	..	..	..	..	..	17	..	138
10	..	..	..	..	..	18	1	31	2	2	..	..	..	..	..	7	..	
3	..	..	..	..	..	6	..	6	..	..	..	..	..	..	..	1	..	139
7	..	..	..	..	..	12	1	25	2	2	..	..	..	..	..	6	..	140
2	..	..	..	..	..	2	..	5	..	1	..	..	..	..	..	1	..	
2	..	..	..	..	..	2	..	5	..	1	..	..	..	..	..	1	..	141
3	..	..	..	..	..	2	..	5	..	2	..	..	..	..	..	..	..	
2	..	..	..	..	..	1	..	5	..	1	..	..	..	..	..	..	..	142
..	..	..	..	..	..	..	..		..	1	..	..	..	..	..	..	..	143
1	..	..	..	..	..	1	..		..	1	..	..	..	..	..	..	..	144
18	2	..	..	..	..	31	30	32	26	28	6	..	..	4	..	25	8	
18	2	..	..	..	..	31	30	32	26	28	6	..	..	4	..	25	8	145
56	2	..	..	1	..	76	5	85	6	31	11	..	..	6	..	21	6	
15	..	..	..	..	..	31	..	24	..	9	1	..	..	..	..	..	..	146
2	..	..	..	..	..	5	2	22	3	1	4	..	..	..	..	2	2	147
38	1	..	..	..	..	40	3	30	2	21	6	..	..	6	..	19	4	148
437	28	..	..	3	..	523	52	144	12	384	33	1	..	15	..	44	2	
..	..	..	..	..	..	..	..	1	..	..	..	..	..	..	..	..	..	149
375	23	..	..	3	..	474	48	106	8	350	30	1	..	15	..	16	..	150
62	5	..	..	..	..	48	4	33	4	34	2	..	..	..	..	28	2	151
..	..	..	..	..	..	1	..	2	..	1	..	..	..	..	..	..	..	152
666	72	..	..	3	..	755	88	727	178	208	24	..	..	14	..	350	20	
88	..	..	..	..	..	101	..	141	..	13	..	..	..	..	..	50	..	
22	..	..	..	..	..	34	..	70	..	..	..	..	..	..	..	..	..	
22	..	..	..	..	..	34	..	70	..	..	..	..	..	..	..	..	..	153
66	..	..	..	..	..	66	..	71	..	13	..	..	..	..	..	50	..	
66	..	..	..	..	..	66	..	71	..	10	..	..	..	..	..	44	..	157
..	..	..	..	..	..	..	..	..	..	3	..	..	..	..	..	6	..	158
249	3	..	..	1	..	248	6	213	6	26	6	..	..	4	..	94	1	
249	3	..	..	1	..	248	6	213	6	26	6	..	..	4	..	94	1	
169	2	..	..	..	..	131	3	141	1	21	..	..	..	1	..	70	1	159
..	..	..	..	..	..	..	..	..	..	..	..	..	..	..	..	..	..	160
80	1	..	..	..	..	118	3	71	5	5	6	..	..	3	..	23	..	161

SUBSIDIARY TABLE II.—Numbers of workers engaged in each occupation

Group No.	Occupation (CLASS, sub-class, ORDER and group).	Calcutta with suburbs in 24-Parganas. 1931. Earners principal occupation. Male.	1931. Earners principal occupation. Female.	1931. Working dependents. Male.	1931. Working dependents. Female.	1931. Earners subsidiary occupation. Male.	1931. Earners subsidiary occupation. Female.	1921. Workers. Male.	1921. Workers. Female.	1911. Workers. Male.	1911. Workers. Female.
1	2	3	4	5	6	7	8	9	10	11	12
	VIII.—Professions and Liberal Arts ..	**324**	**67**	..	..	**3**	..	**360**	**67**	**290**	**87**
	45.—RELIGION ..	**63**	**5**	..	..	**1**	..	**72**	**6**	**100**	**35**
163	Priests, ministers, etc. ..	57	5	..	..	1	..	61	4	71	6
164	Monks, nuns, religious mendicants ..	4	..	..	..	..	..	7	1	23	25
165	Other religious workers ..	..	..	..	..	..	..	1	1	2	3
166	Servants in religious edifices, burial and burning grounds, pilgrim conductors, circumcisers, etc. ..	3	..	..	..	..	..	4	..	4	..
	46.—LAW ..	**107**	..	..	..	..	..	**87**	..	**43**	..
167	Lawyers of all kinds, including *kazis*, law agents, and *mukhtears* ..	61	..	..	..	..	..	43	..	28	..
168	Lawyers' clerks, petition-writers, etc. ..	46	..	..	..	..	..	44	..	15	..
	47.—MEDICINE ..	**70**	**31**	..	..	..	..	**60**	**33**	**49**	**24**
169	Registered medical practitioners including oculists ..	30	4	..	..	..	..				
170	Other persons practising the healing arts without being registered ..	15	1	..	..	..	..	42	2	38	2
171	Dentists ..	7	..	..	..	..	..				
172	Midwives, vaccinators, compounders, nurses, masseurs, etc. ..	18	26	..	..	..	..				
173	Veterinary surgeons ..	..	..	..	..	..	..	18	31	11	22
	48.—INSTRUCTION ..	**54**	**22**	..	..	**1**	..	**49**	**16**	**40**	**15**
174	Professors and teachers of all kinds ..	53	21	..	..	1	..	48	16	40	15
175	Clerks and servants connected with education ..	1	1	..	..	..	..	1	..		
	49.—LETTERS, ARTS AND SCIENCES (OTHER THAN 44) ..	**29**	**10**	..	..	..	..	**91**	**12**	**58**	**13**
176	Public scribes, stenographers, etc. ..	3	4	..	..	..	..	10	3	4	7
177	Architects, surveyors, engineers and their employees (not being state servants) ..	1	..	..	..	..	..	23	1	24	1
178	Authors, editors, journalists and photographers ..	3	..	..	..	..	..				
179	Artists, sculptors and image-makers ..	11	..	..	..	..	..				
180	Scientists (astronomers, botanists, etc.) ..	..	..	..	..	..	..	87	167	13	1
181	Horoscope casters, astrologers, fortune-tellers, wizards, witches and mediums ..	1	..	..	..	..	..				
182	Musicians (composers and performers other than military) actors, dancers, etc. ..	9	5	..	..	..	..	16	7	19	5
183	Managers and employees of places of public entertainments, race courses, societies, clubs, etc. ..	1	..	..	..	..	..	2	..	4	5
184	Conjurors, acrobats, recitors, exhibitors of curiosities and wild animals, etc. ..	..	..	..	..	..	..	1	..	3	..
	D.—MISCELLANEOUS ..	**2,947**	**747**	**42**	**3**	**31**	**6**	**2,546**	**1,082**	**2,380**	**1,272**
	IX.—Persons living on their income ..	**120**	**41**	..	..	**9**	**1**	**45**	**46**	**60**	**81**
	50.—PERSONS LIVING PRINCIPALLY ON THEIR INCOME ..	**120**	**41**	..	..	**9**	**1**	**45**	**46**	**60**	**81**
185	Proprietors (other than of agricultural land), fund and scholarship holders and pensioners ..	120	41	..	..	9	1	45	46	60	81
	X.—Domestic service ..	**1,005**	**358**	..	**1**	**7**	**3**	**742**	**518**	**895**	**649**
	51.—DOMESTIC SERVICE ..	**1,005**	**358**	..	**1**	**7**	**3**	**742**	**518**	**895**	**649**
186	Private motor drivers and cleaners ..	25	..	..	..	..	..	7	..	..	..
187	Other domestic servants ..	980	358	..	1	7	3	735	518	895	649
	XI.—Insufficiently described occupations ..	**1,788**	**137**	..	..	**15**	..	**1,662**	**93**	**1,381**	**117**
	52.—GENERAL TERMS WHICH DO NOT INDICATE A DEFINITE OCCUPATION ..	**1,788**	**137**	..	..	**15**	..	**1,662**	**93**	**1,381**	**117**
188	Manufacturers, business men and contractors otherwise unspecified	40	..	..	..	..	..	39	4	21	..
189	Cashiers, accountants, book-keepers, clerks, and other employees in unspecified offices, warehouses and shops ..	1,033	37	..	..	10	..	1,002	14	514	8
190	Mechanics otherwise unspecified ..	56	..	..	..	..	..	46	..	51	1
191	Labourers and workmen otherwise unspecified ..	659	99	..	..	4	..	576	76	794	108
	XII.—Unproductive ..	**34**	**210**	**42**	**2**	..	**2**	**98**	**425**	**104**	**506**
	53.—INMATES OF JAILS, ASYLUMS AND ALMS HOUSES ..	**8**	..	**42**	**2**	..	..	**51**	**5**	**59**	**14**
192	Inmates of jails, asylums and alms houses ..	8	..	42	2	..	..	51	5	59	14
	54.—BEGGARS, VAGRANTS AND PROSTITUTES ..	**26**	**210**	..	..	..	**2**	**47**	**420**	**45**	**491**
193	Beggars and vagrants ..	26	27	..	..	..	..	47	167	45	491
194	Procurers and prostitutes ..	..	184	..	..	..	2	..	253		

per 10,000 of the total population of the same sex, 1911, 1921 and 1931.

Calcutta.										Howrah.								
1931.						1921.		1911.		1931.						1921.		Group No.
Earners principal occupation.		Working dependents.		Earners subsidiary occupation.		Workers.		Workers.		Earners principal occupation.		Working dependents.		Earners subsidiary occupation.		Workers.		
Male.	Female.	Male.	Female.	Male.	Female.	Male.	Female.	Male.	Female.	Male.	Female.	Male.	Female.	Male.	Female.	Male.	Female.	
13	14	15	16	17	18	19	20	21	22	23	24	25	26	27	28	29	30	
330	**69**	..	..	**2**	..	**406**	**82**	**309**	**95**	**169**	**18**	..	..	**10**	..	**206**	**19**	
64	**5**	..	..	**1**	..	**80**	**7**	**104**	**34**	**55**	**2**	..	..	**1**	..	**84**	..	
58	5	..	..	1	..	67	5	76	7	52	2	..	..	1	..	84	..	163
4	..	..	..	..	..	8	1	21	24	..	..	..	..	..	..	..	..	164
..	..	..	..	..	..	1	1	2	3	..	..	..	..	..	..	..	..	165
3	..	..	..	..	..	4	..	5	1	3	..	..	..	..	..	..	..	166
110	..	..	..	..	..	**102**	..	**47**	..	**20**	..	..	..	..	..	**36**	..	
62	..	..	..	..	..	50	..	31	..	12	..	..	..	..	..	29	..	167
47	..	..	..	..	..	52	..	16	..	7	..	..	..	..	..	7	..	168
71	**31**	..	..	..	..	**65**	**40**	**51**	**28**	**33**	**8**	..	..	**1**	..	**41**	**12**	
31	4	..	..	..	..					20	1	..	..	1	..			169
15	1	..	..	..	..	45	2	40	3	10	1	..	..	1	..	21	1	170
8	..	..	..	..	..					..	..	..	..	..	..			171
17	27	..	..	..	..					4	7	..	..	..	..			172
..	..	..	..	..	..	18	38	11	25	..	..	..	..	..	..	20	11	173
55	**23**	..	..	**1**	..	**54**	**19**	**43**	**17**	**50**	**6**	..	..	**4**	..	**19**	**6**	
53	22	..	..	1	..	53	19	43	17	50	6	..	..	4	..	19	6	174
1	1	..	..	..	..	1	..			..	..	..	..	..	..	..	..	175
30	**10**	..	..	..	..	**105**	**15**	**64**	**16**	**10**	**1**	..	..	**3**	..	**26**	**1**	
4	5	..	..	..	..	12	4	4	8	..	..	..	..	..	..	..	..	176
1	..	..	..	..	..	26	1	27	1	2	..	..	..	..	..	11	..	177
3	..	..	..	..	..					2	..	..	..	..	..			178
11	..	..	..	..	..					2	1	..	..	3	..			179
..	..	..	..	..	..	88	144	15	2	..	..	..	..	..	..	71	64	180
1	..	..	..	..	..					1	..	..	..	..	..			181
9	4	..	..	..	..	18	9	21	5	2	..	..	..	..	..	3	1	182
1	..	..	..	..	..	1	..	5	6	..	..	..	..	..	..	..	..	183
..	..	..	..	..	..	1	1	3	..	1	..	..	..	..	..	..	..	184
2,997	**774**	**44**	**3**	**31**	**7**	**2,724**	**1,177**	**2,499**	**1,372**	**1,659**	**553**	**4**	**3**	**47**	**9**	**2,556**	**768**	
124	**42**	..	..	**9**	**1**	**50**	**48**	**64**	**77**	**31**	**16**	..	..	**3**	**2**	**59**	**41**	
124	**42**	..	..	**9**	**1**	**50**	**48**	**64**	**77**	**31**	**16**	..	..	**3**	**2**	**59**	**41**	
124	42	..	..	9	1	50	48	64	77	31	16	..	..	3	2	59	41	185
1,029	**373**	..	**1**	**7**	**3**	**839**	**593**	**963**	**729**	**359**	**187**	..	**3**	**7**	**4**	**321**	**227**	
1,029	**373**	..	**1**	**7**	**3**	**839**	**593**	**963**	**729**	**359**	**187**	..	**3**	**7**	**4**	**321**	**227**	
24	..	..	..	..	..	6	..	..	..	38	..	..	..	1	..	11	..	186
1,004	373	..	1	7	3	833	593	963	729	321	187	..	3	6	4	310	227	187
1,810	**137**	..	..	**15**	..	**1,730**	**81**	**1,426**	**111**	**1,238**	**268**	..	..	**36**	**2**	**2,112**	**241**	
1,810	**137**	..	..	**15**	..	**1,730**	**81**	**1,426**	**111**	**1,238**	**268**	..	..	**36**	**2**	**2,112**	**241**	
41	..	..	..	..	..	37	5	23	..	13	..	..	..	..	..	34	7	188
1,064	38	..	..	11	..	1,129	18	555	10	251	99	..	..	16	..	1,010	122	189
53	..	..	..	..	..	31	..	42	1	203	..	..	..	2	..	306	..	190
650	99	..	..	4	..	533	59	805	100	771	168	..	..	18	2	762	112	191
34	**221**	**44**	**2**	..	**2**	**105**	**455**	**110**	**532**	**32**	**83**	**4**	..	**1**	**1**	**63**	**258**	
9	..	**44**	**2**	..	..	**63**	**6**	**67**	**17**	**5**	..	**4**	..	..	..	**3**	..	
9	..	44	2	..	..	63	6	67	17	5	..	4	..	..	..	3	..	192
25	**221**	..	..	..	**2**	**41**	**449**	**43**	**515**	**25**	**83**	..	..	**1**	**1**	**60**	**258**	
25	26	..	..	..	..	41	143	43	515	25	25	..	..	1	..	60	64	193
..	195	..	..	..	2	..	306			..	58	..	..	..	1	..	194	194

per 10,000 of the total population of the same sex, 1911, 1921 and 1931

CHAPTER VI

Literacy

52. **The statistics discussed.**—This chapter serves as an introduction to the figures for literacy given by religions in imperial table XIII and by selected castes and other groups in imperial table XIV. Subsidiary tables printed at the end of this chapter show—

I—the number literate (by age-groups), illiterate and literate in English per 1,000 of the same sex in each religion;

II—literacy ratios in successive census years;

III—the numbers literate per 1,000 and literate in English per 10,000 of the same sex in selected castes or other groups, 1911, 1921 and 1931; and

IV—the number of institutions and pupils according to the returns of the Education Department in Calcutta and Howrah, 1901, 1911, 1921 and 1931.

53. **Source of the statistics.**—The reader is referred to chapter IX of volume V, part i, for a full description of the method in which the information here discussed was obtained and tabulated. It is there explained that the omission from the statistics of one-half the total number of the returns of those literate and aged 4-6 at the nearest birthday on the assumption that they were less than 5 years old has probably resulted in the omission from the tables of a certain number of persons who should have been included in the group of literates aged 5-10 years. In statement No. VI-1 details are given for the principal religions in Calcutta of the numbers thus excluded from the total of literates, who might perhaps more properly be included on the assumption that they are over 5 years of age.

STATEMENT No. VI—1.

Numbers of each sex in each principal religions aged 4-6 and returned as literates but treated as illiterates for the purpose of table XIII.

Religion.	Males.	Females.
All religions ..	**2,115**	**1,610**
Hindus ..	1,605	1,175
Muslims ..	231	144
Christians ..	226	248
Buddhists ..	4	7
Tribals ..	1	..

54. **General literacy.**—In the population of Calcutta proper 473,589 persons (male—362,558, female—111,031) are literate. The corresponding numbers in the suburbs in the 24-Parganas are 14,062 (male—11,294, female—2,768), and in Howrah city 72,569 (male—55,013, female—17,556). The total number therefore in Calcutta with its suburbs in 24-Parganas and Howrah is 560,220 (male—428,865, female—131,355). The proportions literate of both sexes per 1,000 aged 5 and over are 432 in Calcutta, 356 in Howrah and 423 in Calcutta with its suburbs in the 24-Parganas. The male literacy ratio on similar figures calculated on the total number of males only aged 5 and over is 476 in Calcutta, 411 in Howrah and 470 in Calcutta with its suburbs in 24-Parganas. More than one in every three females is literate in Calcutta and more than one in every four in Howrah and the ratio per 1,000 in Calcutta with its suburbs in the 24-Parganas is 319. The figures for English literacy give totals for Calcutta of 227,858 (male—190,620, female—37,238), for the suburbs in the 24-Parganas 5,562 (male—4,943, female—619) and for Howrah 25,718 (male—22,898, female—2,820) giving a total for Calcutta with its suburbs in the 24-Parganas and Howrah of 259,137 (male—218,460, female—40,677). On the total population of the same sex aged 5 and over these figures work out to a proportion per 1,000 in both sexes of 208 in Calcutta, 203 in Calcutta with suburbs in the 24-Parganas and 126 in Howrah. The male ratios are considerably higher and are 250 in Calcutta, 246 in Calcutta with its suburbs in the 24-Parganas and 171 in Howrah. The female figures are considerably smaller particularly in Howrah and amount to 112 in Calcutta,

106 in Calcutta with suburbs in the 24-Parganas and 40 in Howrah. The average level of literacy is considerably higher in Calcutta than in the whole of Bengal. In an equal number of the same sex nearly ten times as many females and three times as many males are literate in Calcutta with suburbs in the 24-Parganas as in Bengal as a whole and in both sexes together the proportions are very nearly four to one. The discrepancy is even more pronounced in literacy in English. Taking equal numbers again there are literate in Calcutta with suburbs in 24-Parganas eight times as many of both sexes, nearly six times as many males and twenty-one times as many females as in the whole of Bengal.

55. **Literacy by religions.**—Taking both sexes together by religions the order of literacy in Calcutta with suburbs in the 24-Parganas is as follows: Christians with 77·7 per cent. literate come first followed by Zoroastrians (Parsis) with 71·3, Jews with 69·3, Jains with 58·2, Buddhists with 57·4, Sikhs with 48·4, Hindus with 44·5, Confucians with 36·8, Muslims with 31·0 and those professing tribal religions with 8·5 per cent. Amongst males the proportions literate are in the same order with the exception that the Muslim literacy ratio is higher than the Confucian. Amongst Christians there is almost an equal proportion of literates in both sexes but in every other religion there is some considerable discrepancy and the order of literacy amongst females differs in some respects from that for the total population. The literacy ratio for Confucian females (561 per 1,000) is actually higher than that for males (328 per 1,000), and Muslim females with only about 2 literates to every five males in an equal number of each sex have a literacy ratio higher only than those professing tribal religions. The literacy ratio amongst Hindu females on the other hand is higher than that amongst Jains though the male literacy amongst Jains is considerably higher than amongst Hindus. Jews who come third in male literacy stand second with a proportion of 670 per mille of female literacy and Parsis come below them with 650 though their male literacy ratio is 758 per mille compared with 716 amongst Jews. The comparatively large proportion of Europeans and Anglo-Indians in the population of the city and its suburbs results in Christians showing very much the highest literacy ratio in English. In every 1,000 of the same sex there are 694 males, 704 females and 698 of both sexes literate in English amongst Christians. Parsis and Jews follow at some distance. The ratios are amongst Parsis 645 for males, 555 for females and 607 for both sexes combined and amongst the Jews 547 for males, 485 for females and 517 for both sexes taken together. Hindus and Buddhists who follow have ratios scarcely one-half that of the Jews and amongst Muslims with ratios of 127 amongst males, 20 amongst females and an average if both sexes of 100 per 1,000 there are considerably less than half the proportion literate than amongst Hindus.

56. **Changes of literacy ratios and growth of numbers attending schools.**—Subsidiary table IV illustrates the growth both in Calcutta and Howrah of educational institutions and the numbers of scholars during the last three decades. The total undergoing education of any kind in Calcutta is nearly three times as many now as it was in 1901 and in Howrah almost five times as many are now undergoing educational courses of some kind as in that year. Only in the figures of collegiate education in Calcutta has there at any time been a decrease in any census year compared with the previous census year. In 1921 there were 14,260 students undergoing collegiate education but in 1931, though there are 23 colleges for 18 in that year, the number of students is no more than 13,979. In Calcutta the figures of literacy for both sexes increased at each census compared with the last between 1901 and 1921 when they reached the proportion of 450 in every 1,000, but they have now decreased to 432 in every 1,000, a result particularly attributable to the fact that in 1921 all persons returned as literate were assumed to be aged 5 and over whereas on the present occasion a number of persons returned as literate and probably aged 5 and over have been excluded from the group of literates on the assumption that they were less

than five years old. In Howrah there has not been any such decline in the proportions which have continuously increased from 164 in 1901 to 261 in 1911, 259 in 1921 and now to 356 per 1,000 in 1931. The decrease in Calcutta is entirely amongst males. The female literacy ratio has increased from 271 in 1921 to 333 on the present occasion whereas the male literacy ratio which was 530 per 1,000 in 1921 is now only 476. In Howrah, on the other hand, the increase shown by both sexes is reflected in the figures for each individual sex and there are now 411 males in every 1,000 literate for 325 in 1921 and 252 females for 127 in 1921. The figures for English literacy show the same variations between Calcutta and Howrah although in Calcutta the increase in female literacy in English from 80 per 1,000 to 112 has so far counterbalanced the decrease in male literacy from 262 to 250 per 1,000 as to result in an actual increase in the literacy proportions in both sexes together from 206 in 1921 to 208 on the present occasion. In Howrah the figures are very much smaller but show a continuous increase after the decrease recorded between 1901 and 1911. The figures in 1921 were 106 for both sexes, 146 for males and 24 for females; and by the present census these had risen to 126 for both sexes, 171 for males and 40 for females.

57. **Literacy by age—general.**—The statement No. VI-2 below illustrated for Calcutta and suburbs in the 24-Parganas by diagram No. VI-1 overleaf shows the distribution of the total population aged and over 5, 10, 15 and 20

STATEMENT No. VI—2.

Distribution by age and literacy of 10,000 of the population of each sex.

Age.	Calcutta with suburbs in 24-Parganas and Howrah City.						Calcutta with suburbs in 24-Parganas.					
	Males.			Females.			Males.			Females.		
	Total.	Literate.	Literate in English.	Total.	Literate.	Literate in English.	Total.	Literate.	Literate in English.	Total.	Literate.	Literate in English.
1	2	3	4	5	6	7	8	9	10	11	12	13
ALL AGES ..	**10,000**	**4,302**	**2,191**	**10,000**	**1,213**	**832**	**10,000**	**4,388**	**2,295**	**10,000**	**2,786**	**925**
5 and over ..	**9,318**	4,302	2,191	**8,727**	1,213	832	**9,333**	4,388	2,295	**8,725**	2,786	925
10 and over ..	**8,638**	4,071	2,082	**7,639**	924	748	**8,662**	4,161	2,184	**7,627**	2,487	833
15 and over ..	**7,904**	3,743	1,905	**6,592**	540	623	**7,933**	3,832	2,004	**6,587**	2,095	696
20 and over ..	**6,827**	3,204	1,606	**5,539**	163	493	**6,846**	3,275	1,688	**5,548**	1,698	554

years according to literacy by sex. The figures illustrate but not so markedly a feature to which attention has been directed in volume V, part i, viz., the fact that literacy continues to be acquired at comparatively late ages. Literates form an increasing proportion of the male population up to the age of 15 and over and literacy in English is acquired in a number of cases even at a later date, since the proportion of the population returned as literate in English is at each successive quinquennial period greater amongst those of or over the age chosen right up to the age of 20 and over. Amongst females literacy, if not acquired before the age of 10, is comparatively rarely acquired later, since at 15 and over and 20 and over the numbers literate in any language or English form a smaller proportion of the total population at the same age than they do at 10 and over.

58. **Literacy by age—by localities.**—The numbers literate at each age-group per 1,000 of the same sex and age are shown by locality in subsidiary table II. Literacy is highest amongst the age-groups chosen in both sexes at the age of 15-20 principally because in both sexes at that age the majority of those who will be literate at all have already acquired literacy whilst a group comprising all persons aged 20 and over includes in the later ages an increasingly larger proportion of persons who had no opportunity to acquire literacy in youth and have not acquired it since. In the

figures for Calcutta the decrease in the proportions literate at all ages is shown to be distributed between each of the four age-groups taken, and is most pronounced in the age-group 10-15, a result to which some contribution has most probably been made by the fact that amongst the very large number who achieve literacy between the ages of 10 and 15 a proportion has been omitted from this group and placed in the lower group 5-10 which in turn has lost a number aged 5 and over who have been omitted on the assumption that their real age is probably less than 5. This deduction is borne out by the figures for female literacy which were 396 per 1,000 aged 10-15 in 1921 and are now only 393 although there has been more than a 20 per cent. increase in the proportions of literacy at all ages and there is an increase recorded in every other age-group. The figures for literacy in English similarly bear out this conclusion. Whereas amongst males there has been a decrease in the proportions literate at every other age-group, there is a considerable increase in the numbers at the age of 5-10. By the majority of persons literacy in English is acquired probably at a rather later date than vernacular literacy so that there will be fewer returned as literate in English and aged 4-6 at their nearest birthday; the age-group 5-10 is therefore not likely to have suffered any corresponding decrease to set off the increase derived by the inclusion of a number of literates really falling properly within the next higher group. Amongst females the increase in English literacy has been sufficient to result in an increased proportion at every age-group. The figures here discussed are illustrated in diagram No. VI-2.

DIAGRAM No. VI—1.

Numbers amongst each 100 in each sex of and over the age shown (males on left, females on right) who are illiterate, literate and literate in English (Calcutta with Suburbs in 24-Parganas), 1931.

NOTE.—The hatchings show from bottom to top those literate in English, those literate in other languages than English and those illiterate.

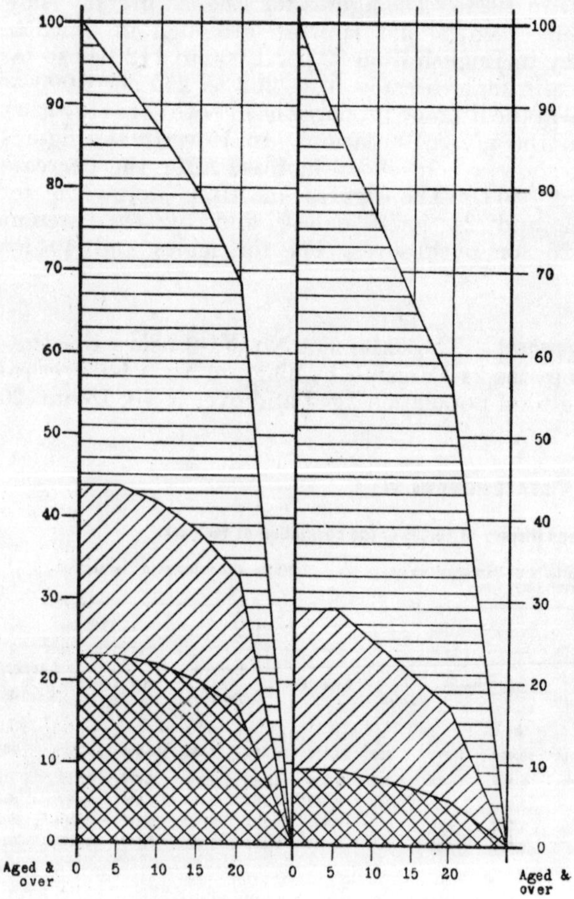

DIAGRAM No. VI—2.

Numbers literate per 100 of the same sex and age-group (males on left, females on right), Calcutta with Suburbs in 24-Parganas, 1921 (hatched) and 1931 (plain).

NOTE.—The deeply shaded portion represents literacy in English.

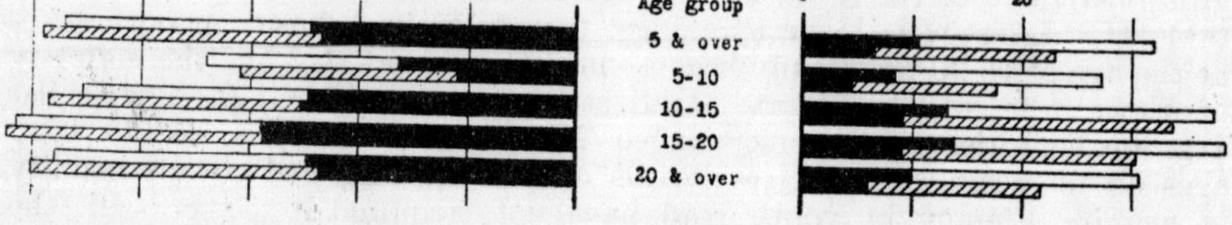

59. **Literacy by age—by religion.**—The figures for literacy at age-groups by religions are given in subsidiary table I and are illustrated in diagram No. VI-3 for the principal religions in Calcutta with suburbs in the 24-Parganas. The proportion of literacy at every age-group is highest amongst the Christians in both males and females alike and lowest, amongst the five individual religions shown, in the Muslims. Only amongst Christians and Sikhs is the proportion literate at ages 20 and over higher than at other age-groups, a circumstance which may indicate one of two things, either that literacy is acquired progressively beyond the age of 20 with greater frequency amongst these two religions or more probably that these two religious communities have for a very much longer time in the past achieved a high standard of literacy at an early age, so that amongst those aged 20 and over the proportions who acquired literacy before that age form a larger proportion of the population. Amongst females a similar condition is shown only by the Jains and in every other case including the Christians the proportion literate aged 20 and over is less than that at the ages 15 to 20. The general order of literacy by age-groups is in each sex the same at each age-group throughout all the age-groups taken except that Sikh males whose literacy ratio at 5-10 years is lower than the average surpass the average at ages 10-15 and again at 20 and over, whilst the increase in the

DIAGRAM No. VI—3.

Numbers literate per thousand of the same sex and age-group (males on left, females on right), by religions, Calcutta with Suburbs in 24-Parganas, 1931.

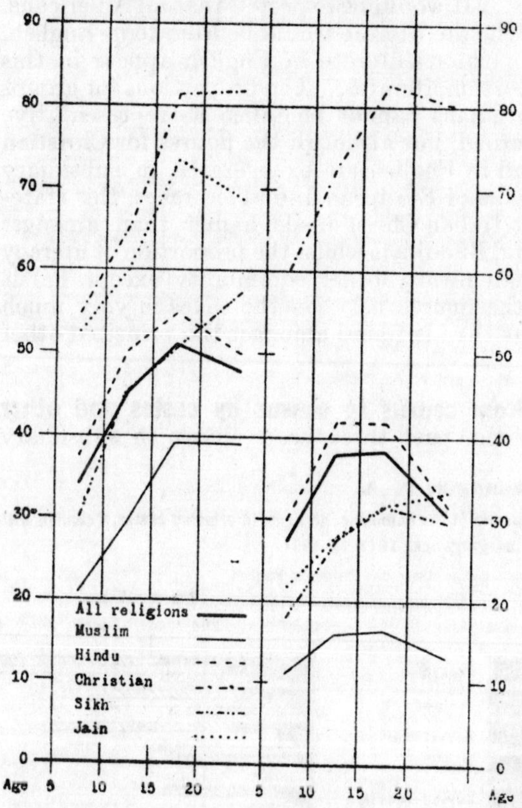

STATEMENT No. VI—3.

Literacy of Christians by race, Calcutta with Suburbs in 24-Parganas and Howrah.

Race.	Number literate per 1,000 of the same sex all ages.			Number literate in English per 10,000 of the same sex all ages.		
	Both sexes.	Males.	Females.	Both sexes.	Males.	Females.
1	2	3	4	5	6	7
Asiatic Christians—						
Chinese ..	707	671	740	6,395	5,714	7,013
Indian ..	543	545	539	3,756	4,795	3,702
Japanese ..	608	651	548	5,811	6,047	5,484
Malayan ..	474	750	273	2,632	5,000	909
Persian ..	800	842	769	7,556	8,421	6,923
Siamese ..	833	..	833	6,667	..	6,667
Anglo-Indian Christians ..	745	738	751	7,240	7,110	7,366
European Christians*—						
American ..	801	790	823	7,068	6,667	7,903
Armenian ..	564	447	713	5,054	4,043	6,341
Australian ..	719	529	933	7,188	5,294	9,333
Belgian ..	625	600	1,000	6,250	6,000	10,000
Dutch ..	765	821	550	7,449	8,077	5,000
English ..	868	895	828	8,631	8,898	8,218
French ..	797	797	798	6,892	6,271	7,596
German ..	912	921	892	8,761	8,816	8,649
Greek ..	472	828	233	4,722	8,275	2,326
Irish ..	771	785	750	7,293	7,212	7,409
Italian ..	591	561	659	5,699	5,427	7,241
Norwegian ..	56	56	..	555	555	..
Portuguese ..	689	655	746	6,648	6,195	7,460
Russian ..	708	545	846	7,083	5,454	8,461
Scotch ..	847	847	847	8,165	8,060	8,404
South African ..	563	556	572	5,000	4,444	5,720
Spanish ..	196	54	778	1,957	540	7,778
Swiss ..	909	875	1,000	9,048	8,125	10,000
Welsh ..	788	771	1,000	7,990	7,742	10,000

*And Allied races.

literacy of Jain females at and over the age of 20 brings them above the average and also above the proportion for Hindus which at every other age-group is higher than amongst this community.

60. **Christian literacy by race.**—The literacy proportions amongst Christians distinguished by races is shown in statement No. VI-3 overleaf although some of the figures there given for European Christians and Christians of allied races appear to be surprising. It would be expected that all Americans, Englishmen, Irishmen and Scots who are literate would be literate in English, but in all of these cases the proportions literate in English appear in this statement less than the total proportion literates. The proportions for groups such as Persian and Chinese Christians cannot be taken as representative owing to the small numbers concerned, but although the figures for Christian literacy both in the vernacular and in English are exaggerated in subsidiary table I by the inclusion of Christians of European and allied races, this statement shows that literacy amongst Indian Christians is higher than amongst others except Parsis, Jews, Jains and Buddhists whilst the proportion of literacy in English is similarly higher than in any other community except Parsis and Jews. The discrepancy in the figures between the sexes is very much less amongst the Indian Christians than is found amongst the principal other communities.

61. **Variations of literacy from census to census by castes and other groups.**—Figures of literacy for the past three years shown in subsidiary

DIAGRAM No. VI—4.

Numbers literate and literate in English per thousand of the same sex, all ages, in selected castes, Calcutta with Suburbs in 24-Parganas, 1911 to 1931.

NOTE.—The heavily shaded portion shows literacy in English.

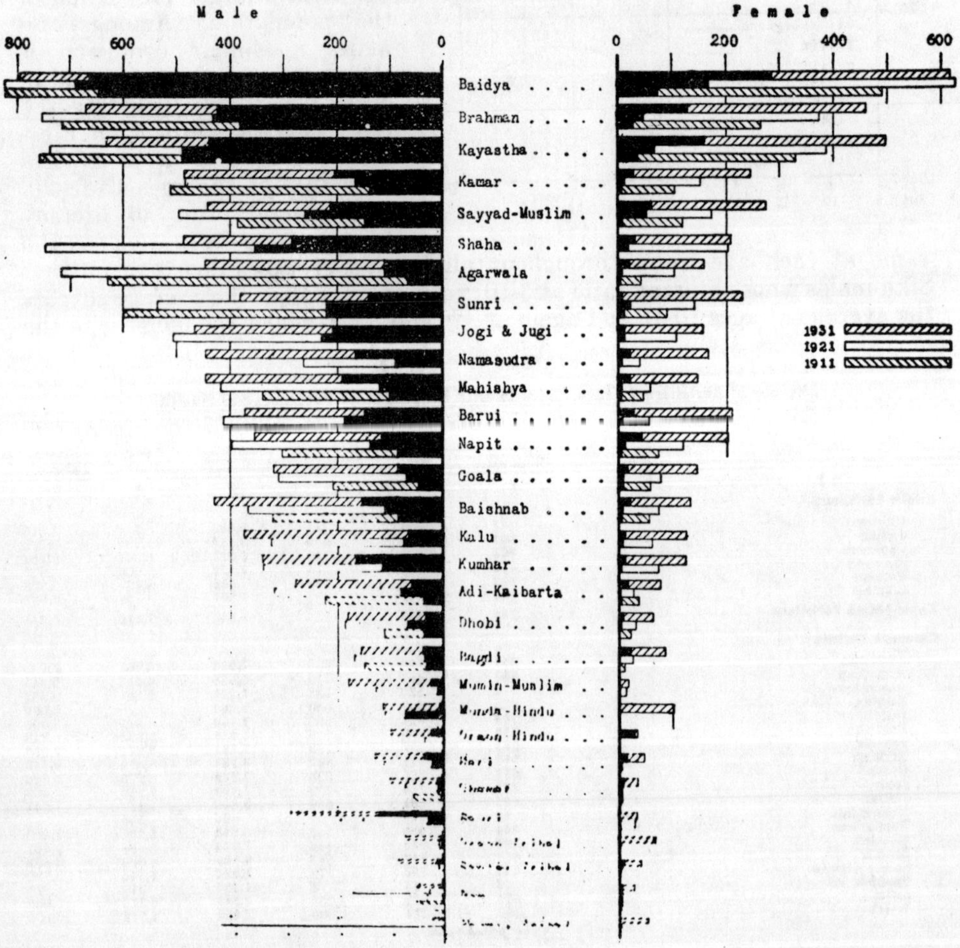

table III are illustrated for selected castes and other groups in diagram No. VI-4. Baidyas, Brahmans and Kayasthas are the three upper castes of Hindu society in Bengal and head the list both for males and females. Amongst males in all three castes and amongst Baidya females the proportions literate in 1931 show a decrease on those recorded in 1921. There is similarly a decrease in the English literacy ratio for males compared with 1921, but amongst the females of each caste there has been a marked increase in the English literacy ratio and there has also been a distinct increase in the proportions literate in any language among Brahman and Kayastha females. The lowest literacy ratios are shown amongst aboriginals and members of the lower classes of Hindus. The Kamars with a literacy ratio of 485 per thousand amongst males appear to be somewhat surprisingly high in the list. They are above Sayyads whose male literacy ratio stands now at 440 compared with 494 per thousand in 1921 and even above the trading classes like the Shahas, Agarwalas and Sunris whose male literacy ratios are respectively 484, 446 and 379 per thousand. Speaking generally, the literacy ratio amongst males has increased only amongst the classes whose literacy ratio is comparatively low, although groups like the Kumhars and Mahishyas, as well as the Namasudras, all of which have literacy ratios between 34 and 45 per cent., have also acquired a considerable increase of literacy during the past decade. Baidyas, Brahmans and Kayasthas lead in English literacy followed by Shahas, Sayyads, Jogis and Kamars. The highest proportion of English literacy amongst females is in the Baidya, Kayastha and Brahman castes and in the Mundas and Oraons—the figures for whom, however, can hardly be taken as typical owing to the small numbers of these castes actually found in Calcutta.

SUBSIDIARY TABLE I.—Number literate (by age-groups), illiterate and literate in English per 1,000 of the same sex in each religion.

Religion.	Number per 1,000 of the same sex and age who are—								
	Literate.								
	Aged 5 and over.			5—10		10—15		15—20	
	Both sexes.	Male.	Female.	Male.	Female.	Male.	Female.	Male.	Female.
1	2	3	4	5	6	7	8	9	10
CALCUTTA WITH SUBURBS IN 24-PARGANAS.									
All religions ..	**423**	**470**	**319**	**339**	**272**	**451**	**377**	**513**	**382**
Hindu ..	**445**	497	338	373	298	502	419	549	417
Muslim ..	**310**	369	135	208	111	290	157	390	164
Christian ..	**777**	778	776	547	606	653	734	815	827
Sikh ..	**484**	540	283	298	181	453	276	507	315
Jain ..	**582**	668	304	516	218	586	279	717	316
Buddhist ..	**574**	617	393	314	291	581	391	645	526
Jew ..	**693**	716	670	591	714	698	774	706	771
Zoroastrian ..	**713**	758	650	394	623	427	679	636	563
Confucian ..	**368**	328	561	767	500	746	640	457	645
Tribal ..	**85**	93	56	57	105	125	91	130	107
CALCUTTA.									
All religions ..	**432**	**476**	**333**	**348**	**283**	**462**	**393**	**520**	**398**
Hindu ..	**456**	503	354	383	312	514	439	560	435
Muslim ..	**316**	373	140	215	115	297	164	392	170
Christian ..	**779**	780	779	555	607	661	733	814	827
Sikh ..	**483**	539	283	298	189	455	276	507	315
Jain ..	**582**	668	304	516	218	586	279	717	316
Buddhist ..	**585**	622	422	329	296	588	409	648	545
Jew ..	**693**	715	670	591	714	698	774	706	771
Zoroastrian ..	**713**	758	650	394	623	427	679	636	563
Confucian ..	**368**	328	561	767	500	746	640	457	645
Tribal ..	**117**	148	..	..	..	71	..	114	..
HOWRAH.									
All religions ..	**356**	**411**	**252**	**340**	**239**	**426**	**285**	**426**	**280**
Hindu ..	**387**	444	278	386	275	478	316	457	305
Muslim ..	**222**	274	115	163	91	223	125	284	131
Christian ..	**846**	845	848	743	670	866	900	875	904
Sikh ..	**449**	492	240	167	667	200	333	500	333
Jain ..	**519**	659	77	..	...	250	..	500	..
Buddhist ..	**851**	975	143	..	..	..	..	1,000	..
Zoroastrian ..	**890**	1,000	500	1,000	1,000	1,000	..	1,000	750
Tribal ..	**141**	193	70	..	..	..	1,000	167	100

Religion.	Number per 1,000 of the same sex and age who are—							
	Literate.		Illiterate.			Literate in English.		
	20 and over.		Aged 5 and over.			Aged 5 and over.		
	Male.	Female.	Both sexes.	Male.	Female.	Both sexes.	Male.	Female.
1	11	12	13	14	15	16	17	18
CALCUTTA WITH SUBURBS IN 24-PARGANAS.								
All religions ..	**478**	**306**	**577**	**530**	**681**	**203**	**246**	**100**
Hindu ..	500	316	**555**	503	662	**214**	276	85
Muslim ..	388	130	**690**	631	865	**100**	127	20
Christian ..	820	804	**223**	222	224	**698**	694	704
Sikh ..	575	295	**516**	460	717	**101**	115	50
Jain ..	678	334	**418**	332	696	**191**	234	52
Buddhist ..	629	389	**426**	383	607	**213**	247	95
Jew ..	752	623	**307**	284	330	**517**	547	485
Zoroastrian ..	886	663	**287**	242	350	**607**	645	555
Confucian ..	260	496	**632**	672	439	**209**	242	44
Tribal ..	89	37	**915**	907	944	**7**	9	..
CALCUTTA.								
All religions ..	**482**	**319**	**568**	**524**	**667**	**208**	**250**	**112**
Hindu ..	505	332	**544**	497	646	**220**	281	90
Muslim ..	391	135	**684**	627	860	**102**	129	21
Christian ..	821	808	**221**	220	221	**703**	699	708
Sikh ..	575	295	**517**	461	717	**101**	115	50
Jain ..	678	333	**418**	332	696	**192**	234	53
Buddhist ..	634	424	**415**	378	578	**222**	250	101
Jew ..	751	623	**307**	285	330	**516**	546	485
Zoroastrian ..	886	663	**287**	242	350	**607**	645	555
Confucian ..	260	496	**632**	672	439	**209**	242	44
Tribal ..	166	..	**883**	852	1,000	**19**	23	..
HOWRAH.								
All religions ..	**414**	**242**	**644**	**589**	**748**	**126**	**171**	**40**
Hindu ..	441	265	**613**	556	722	**143**	200	37
Muslim ..	291	115	**778**	726	885	**31**	44	3
Christian ..	854	858	**154**	155	152	**805**	798	814
Sikh ..	567	125	**551**	508	760	**109**	131	..
Jain ..	759	100	**481**	341	923	**185**	244	..
Buddhist ..	1,000	143	**149**	125	857	**128**	150	..
Zoroastrian ..	1,000	400	**110**	..	500	**617**	702	**313**
Tribal ..	225	33	**858**	807		**20**	18	**28**

SUBSIDIARY TABLE II.—Progress of Education—Literacy ratios in successive census years.

Year.	Number per 1,000 of the same age and sex who are— Literate and aged. 5 and over†.			5—10‡		10—15		15—20		20 and over	
	Both sexes.	Male.	Female.	Male.	Female.	Male.	Female.	Male.	Female.	Male.	Female.
1	2	3	4	5	6	7	8	9	10	11	12
CALCUTTA WITH SUBURBS IN 24-PARGANAS.											
1931 ..	**423**	470	319	339	272	451	377	513	382	478	**306**
1921 ..	**406**	489	230	309	176	484	337	522	304	501	**213**
CALCUTTA*.											
1931 ..	**432**	476	333	348	283	462	393	520	398	482	**319**
1921 ..	**450**	530	271	359	214	534	396	559	355	540	**251**
1911 ..	**321**	396	164	153	78	444	273	470	260	419	**166**
1901 ..	**248**	316	115	129	62	390	189	425	204	323	**108**
HOWRAH.											
1931 ..	**356**	411	252	340	239	426	285	426	280	414	**242**
1921 ..	**259**	325	127	244	103	369	175	377	188	320	**115**
1911 ..	**261**	354	96	182	59	386	222	406	200	376	**77**
1901 ..	**164**	234	43	82	18	258	64	292	78	252	**42**

Year.	Number per 1,000 of the same age and sex who are— Literate in English and aged. 5 and over†.			5—10‡		10—15		15—20		20 and over.	
	Both sexes.	Male.	Female.	Male.	Female.	Male.	Female.	Male.	Female.	Male.	Female.
1	13	14	15	16	17	18	19	20	21	22	23
CALCUTTA WITH SUBURBS IN 24-PARGANAS.											
1931 ..	**203**	246	106	165	84	247	132	291	137	247	100
1921 ..	**180**	234	64	111	44	254	93	289	90	235	60
CALCUTTA*.											
1931 ..	**208**	250	112	173	89	257	139	298	144	249	**105**
1921 ..	**206**	262	80	138	56	291	114	319	112	262	**74**
1911 ..	**142**	183	56	48	19	219	74	232	67	175	**52**
1901 ..	**103**	132	46	50	26	191	70	100	66	130	**44**
HOWRAH.											
1931 ..	**126**	171	40	137	39	203	54	197	53	167	**36**
1921 ..	**106**	146	24	76	14	194	21	198	28	141	**25**
1911 ..	**59**	85	12	20	6	117	9	136	19	87	**14**
1901 ..	**120**	170	31	80	27	197	80	213	59	181	**23**

* Figures are for Calcutta as it existed at each census year shown.
† All ages for 1911 and earlier years.
‡ 0—10 for 1911 and 1901.

SUBSIDIARY TABLE III.—Literacy of selected caste or other groups—Numbers literate per 1,000 and literate in English per 10,000 of the same sex, 1911, 1921 and 1931.

Caste or other group and religion.		Numbers literate per 1,000 of the same sex all ages. Calcutta with Suburbs in 24-Parganas and Howrah. 1931			1921			1911*		
		Both sexes.	Male	Female.	Both sexes.	Male.	Female.	Both sexes.	Male.	Female.
1		2	3	4	5	6	7	8	9	10
Adi Kaibarta—Hindu	..	**185**	277	75	**191**	318	26	**137**	223	36
Agarwala—Hindu	..	**342**	446	157	**494**	716	103	**415**	627	39
Bagdi—Hindu	..	**121**	156	85	**97**	168	23	**75**	148	8
Baidya—Hindu	..	**719**	793	614	**745**	823	626	**690**	821	487
Baishnav—Hindu	..	**276**	431	131	**209**	367	73	**169**	322	55
Barui—Hindu	..	**310**	372	207	**313**	412	55	..	..	..
Bauri—Hindu	..	**82**	293	30	**115**	155	27	..	..	..
Bhumij—Tribal	..	**28**	19	53	**379**	429	..	..	..	..
Brahman—Hindu	..	**596**	669	457	**625**	749	372	**572**	713	266
Chamar—Hindu	..	**85**	102	132	**53**	75	3	**44**	57	3
Dhobi—Hindu	..	**139**	179	62	**131**	186	31	**79**	110	21
Dom—Hindu	..	**41**	51	25	**93**	175	2	**32**	54	2
Goala—Hindu	..	**278**	319	143	**253**	309	74	**172**	208	58
Hari—Hindu	..	**91**	130	44	**58**	112	1	..	..	..
Jogi or Jugi—Hindu	..	**327**	465	156	**323**	506	106	..	..	..
Kalu—Hindu	..	**268**	376	123	**225**	324	60	..	..	..
Kamar—Hindu	..	**394**	485	244	**365**	483	152	**312**	456	103
Kayastha—Hindu	..	**582**	631	495	**612**	736	386	**596**	755	328
Kumhar—Hindu	..	**259**	341	122	**236**	339	72	..	..	..
Mahishya—Hindu	..	**322**	446	143	**262**	417	57	**226**	341	45
Munda—All religions	..	**238**	241	230	..	..	..	..	..	..
—Hindu	..	**112**	114	101	**71**	109	..	..	..	..
Mumin (Jolaha)—Muslim	..	**120**	180	15	**93**	128	11	..	..	..
Namasudra—Hindu	..	**326**	444	165	**177**	262	41	..	..	..
Napit—Hindu	..	**305**	355	200	**304**	398	117	**224**	303	72
Oraon—All religions	..	**179**	172	198	..	..	..	..	..	..
—Hindu	..	**95**	101	32	**27**	34	..	..	..	..
—Tribal	..	**73**	76	65	**8**	10	..	..	..	..
Santal—All religions	..	**217**	169	283	..	..	..	..	..	..
—Hindu	..	..	..	..	**30**	52	6	..	..	..
—Tribal	..	**72**	87	38	**5**	11	..	..	..	..
Sayyad—Muslim	..	**389**	440	273	**395**	494	169	**310**	384	117
Shaha—Hindu	..	**387**	484	208	**593**	745	202	..	..	..
Sunri—Hindu	..	**328**	379	229	**405**	536	140	**431**	598	90

Caste or other group and religion.		Numbers literate in English per 10,000 all ages of the same sex. Calcutta with Suburbs in 24-Parganas and Howrah. 1931			1921			1911*		
		Both sexes.	Male.	Female.	Both sexes.	Male.	Female.	Both sexes.	Male.	Female.
1		11	12	13	14	15	16	17	18	19
Adi Kaibarta—Hindu	..	**410**	610	169	**459**	797	16	**216**	369	34
Agarwala—Hindu	..	**785**	1,110	206	**789**	1,119	67	**439**	672	25
Bagdi—Hindu	..	**295**	374	215	**185**	353	7	**148**	302	..
Baidya—Hindu	..	**5,065**	6,633	2,857	**4,819**	6,897	1,653	**4,224**	6,476	739
Baishnav—Hindu	..	**841**	1,520	210	**539**	1,111	45	**389**	863	35
Barui—Hindu	..	**1,027**	1,474	289	**1,353**	1,853	49	..	..	..
Bauri—Hindu	..	**242**	220	..	**206**	298	..	..	..	..
Bhumij—Tribal	..	..	..	..	..	..	..	..	..	..
Brahman—Hindu	..	**3,239**	4,266	1,286	**3,053**	4,320	471	**2,706**	3,831	271
Chamar—Hindu	..	**85**	111	31	**69**	98	2	**21**	28	..
Dhobi—Hindu	..	**235**	324	65	**449**	679	27	**230**	347	8
Dom—Hindu	..	**30**	33	27	**149**	281	..	**12**	21	..
Goala—Hindu	..	**691**	851	162	**548**	701	62	**349**	441	60
Hari—Hindu	..	**244**	348	121	**99**	198	..	..	..	..
Jogi or Jugi—Hindu	..	**1,191**	2,084	94	**1,296**	2,315	84	..	..	..
Kalu—Hindu	..	**411**	644	100	**492**	749	65	..	..	..
Kamar—Hindu	..	**1,375**	2,040	279	**1,109**	1,657	118	**845**	1,386	56
Kayastha—Hindu	..	[illegible]	[illegible]	[illegible]	[illegible]	[illegible]	[illegible]	[illegible]	[illegible]	[illegible]
Kumhar—Hindu	..	**1,078**	1,656	112	**726**	1,168	25	..	..	..
Mahishya—Hindu	..	**1,210**	1,903	212	**702**	1,192	50	**632**	1,011	35
Munda—All religions	..	**1,071**	1,010	1,250	..	..	..	..	..	..
—Hindu	..	**53**	65	..	**476**	727	..	..	..	..
Mumin (Jolaha)—Muslim	..	**143**	226	..	**79**	113	..	..	..	..
Namasudra—Hindu	..	**1,031**	1,640	194	**569**	892	45	..	..	..
Napit—Hindu	..	**917**	1,149	421	**954**	1,388	102	**578**	863	28
Oraon—All religions	..	**1,136**	1,034	1,450	..	..	..	..	..	..
—Hindu	..	**217**	208	323	..	..	..	..	..	..
—Tribal	..	**52**	69	..	**40**	50	..	..	..	..
Santal—All religions	..	**969**	1,089	806	..	..	..	..	..	..
—Hindu	..	..	..	..	**27**	52	..	..	..	..
—Tribal	..	**110**	133	54	..	..	..	..	..	..
Sayyad—Muslim	..	**1,674**	2,126	631	**1,968**	2,592	537	**1,086**	1,475	65
Shaha—Hindu	..	**1,955**	2,861	292	**2,598**	3,537	173	..	..	..
Sunri—Hindu	..	**951**	1,412	62	**1,548**	2,202	224	**1,523**	2,228	94

*Figures for 1911 are for Calcutta with the Municipalities of Cossipore-Chitpore, Maniktala and Garden Reach.

SUBSIDIARY TABLE IV.—Number of Institutions and pupils according to the Returns of the Education Department.

—	Calcutta.							
	1931		1921		1911		1901	
	Institutions.	Scholars.	Institutions.	Scholars.	Institutions.	Scholars.	Institutions.	Scholars.
1	2	3	4	5	6	7	8	9
GRAND TOTAL ..	**950**	**124,875**	**635**	**73,771**	**554**	**54,334**	**398**	**42,200**
Collegiate Education ..	**23**	**13,979**	**18**	**14,260**	**22**	**7,193**	**25**	**6,237**
Colleges ..	23	13,979	18	14,260	22	7,193	25	6,237
School Education, General ..	**773**	**102,043**	**529**	**56,626**	**368**	**40,462**	**342**	**33,989**
High English Schools ..	110	43,904	69	28,269	56	19,767	47	15,650
Middle English Schools ..	28	4,312	27	4,111	23	3,670	16	2,165
Middle Vernacular Schools ..	3	492	9	1,191	8	1,260	16	1,816
Primary Schools ..	632	53,335	424	23,055	281	15,765	263	14,358
School Education*—Other ..	**154**	**8,853**	**88**	**2,885**	**164**	**6,679**	**31**	**1,974**
Training Schools ..	9	301	10	128	6	150	5	351
Other Schools ..	145	8,552	78	2,757	158	6,529	26	1,623

—	Howrah.							
	1931		1921		1911		1901	
	Institutions.	Scholars.	Institutions.	Scholars.	Institutions.	Scholars.	Institutions.	Scholars.
1	10	11	12	13	14	15	16	17
GRAND TOTAL ..	**222**	**17,264**	**156**	**9,957**	**99**	**6,296**	**55**	**3,650**
Collegiate Education ..	**1**	**145**	..	..	..	..	..	..
Colleges ..	1	145	..	..	..	..	..	..
School Education, General ..	**195**	**16,528**	**141**	**9,786**	**91**	**6,220**	**48**	**3,596**
High English Schools ..	14	5,444	9	3,024	7	2,357	5	1,535
Middle English Schools ..	3	686	3	603	3	618	3	575
Middle Vernacular Schools ..	..	..	1	132	..	..	..	..
Primary Schools ..	178	10,398	128	6,027	81	3,245	40	1,486
School Education*—Other ..	**26**	**591**	**15**	**171**	**8**	**76**	**7**	**54**
Training Schools ..	1	39	..	..	..	..	..	..
Other Schools ..	25	552	15	171	8	76	7	54

*Including special and training schools.

CHAPTER VII

Language

62. **The statistics shown.**—The statistics to which this chapter forms an introduction are shown in imperial table X in part ii of this volume. Figures for mother tongue only are there printed and for subsidiary languages in detail reference must be made to volume V, part ii. The figures for subsidiary languages, however, have been summarised in some of the subsidiary tables printed after this chapter. These show:

I—the numerical distribution of the population by wards speaking Bengali, Hindustani and English in 1931 with proportions, 1931 and 1921;

II—the numerical distribution of languages on a philological classification at successive census years with proportions in 1931;

III—the prevalence of subsidiary languages, 1931, and

IV—Bi-lingualism by mother tongue, 1931.

63. **General distribution of mother tongues.**—Bengali is the mother tongue of 648,451 persons or 54·3 per cent. in Calcutta and of 121,240 persons or 53·9 per cent. in Howrah. In Calcutta, Hindustani is spoken as mother tongue by 436,123 persons forming 36·6 per cent. of the population and in Howrah by 90,877 persons forming a considerably larger proportion of this population, viz., 40·4 per cent. Oriya is spoken by 38,135 persons in Calcutta and 5,513 persons in Howrah and any language other than a language of India is the mother tongue of no more than 39,422 persons in Calcutta and 2,221 persons in Howrah. English is spoken as mother tongue by 32,393 persons in Calcutta and 2,012 persons in Howrah and those speaking English form respectively 2·7 and rather less than 1 per cent. of the total population. In diagram No. VII-1 these figures also shown in statement No. VII-1 are graphically represented. The total area bounded by each circumference is proportionate to the

DIAGRAM No. VII-1.

Distribution of the population by language in Calcutta and Howrah, 1931.

NOTE.—For explanation see text.

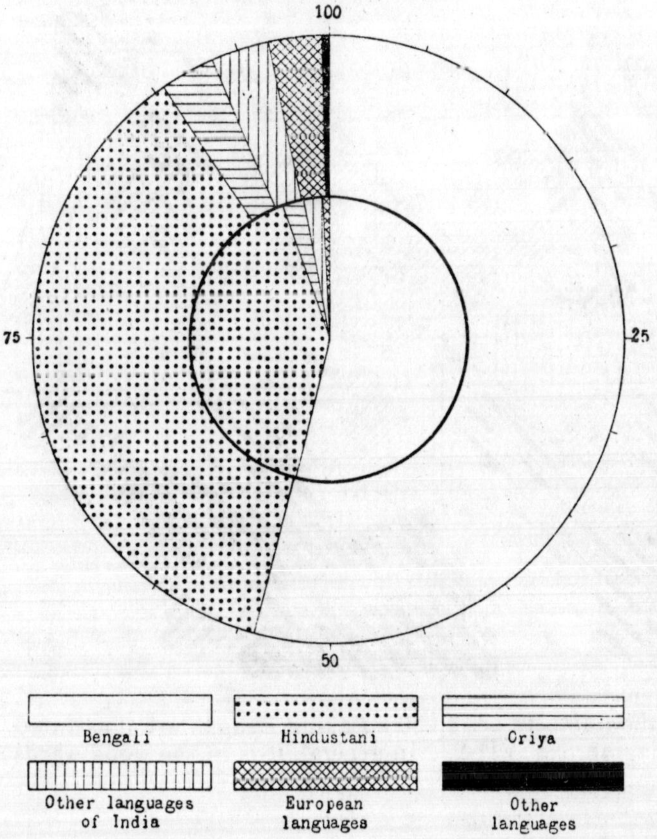

total population of Calcutta and Howrah respectively and a segment based upon each division marked on the circumference of the outer circle would represent 5 per cent. of the total population. As an estimate of the actual numbers speaking each language shown it would be necessary in the case of Calcutta to imagine each radius of the segment produced to the centre, but for comparison of proportions the points at which the radii of the segment for Howrah cut the outer circumference may be compared with the corresponding radii for Calcutta city. In Calcutta Bengali is the mother tongue of a rather larger proportion of the population than in Howrah and Hindustani somewhat surprisingly of nearly 4 per cent. less. In Howrah the percentage of persons speaking English is considerably less than in Calcutta and the number speaking any language except the five principally illustrated in the diagram is negligible. Both in Calcutta and in Howrah, Bengali is now the mother tongue of a larger percentage of the population than in 1921 and in both cities the percentage speaking Hindustani as mother tongue has declined. Those speaking English have remained constant in proportion in Calcutta and have declined by 1 per mille in Howrah.

STATEMENT No. VII-1.

Numbers (in thousands) and proportions speaking selected languages as mother tongue—Calcutta and Howrah, 1931.

	Calcutta.		Howrah.	
	Number.	Percentage.	Number.	Percentage.
All languages ..	**1,197**	**100·0**	**225**	**100·0**
Bengali ..	649	54·3	121	53·9
Hindustani ..	436	36·6	91	40·4
Oriya ..	38	3·1	6	2·6
Other languages of India ..	35	2·8	5	2·2
European languages ..	33	2·7	2	0·9
Other languages ..	6	0·5	..	..

64. **Distribution of Bengali by wards.**—Subsidiary table I illustrates the numbers and proportions speaking Bengali, Hindustani and English in each

DIAGRAM No. VII-2.

Numbers speaking Bengali as mother tongue in 1921 (left) and 1931 (right) per 1,000 of the total population by wards.

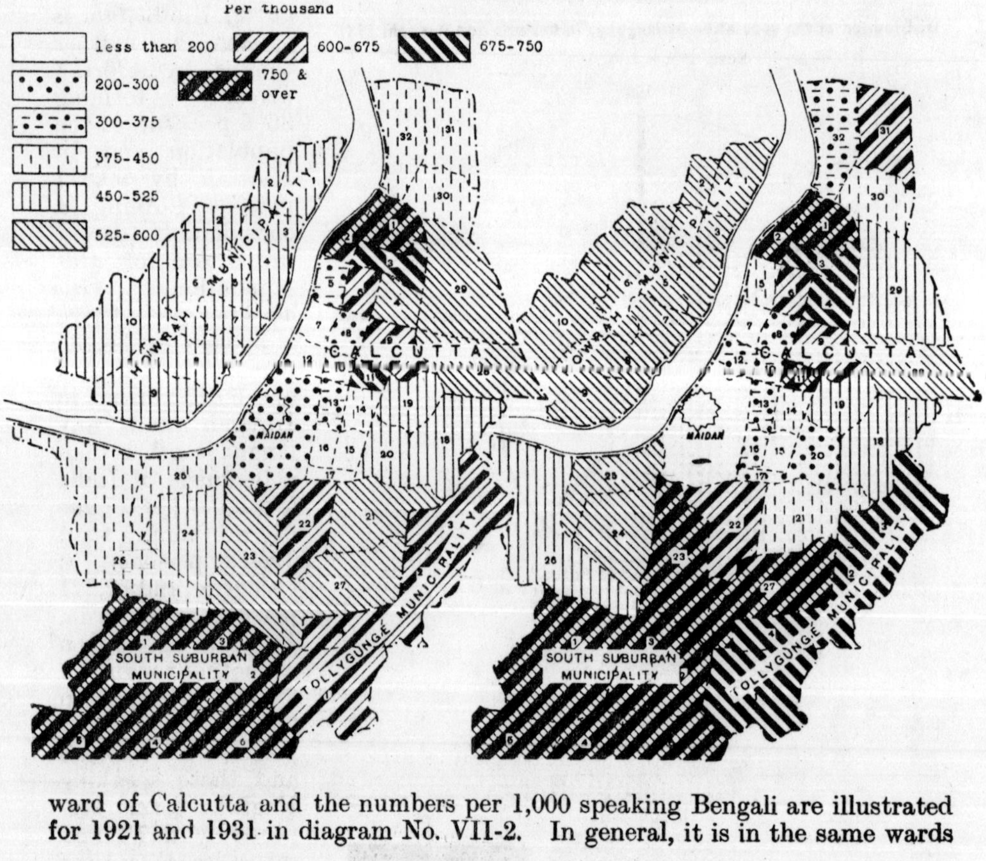

ward of Calcutta and the numbers per 1,000 speaking Bengali are illustrated for 1921 and 1931 in diagram No. VII-2. In general, it is in the same wards that Bengali is most prevalent now as in 1921. In the suburban municipalities it is spoken by almost three-quarters of the total population and in adjacent wards such as Alipore and Tollygunge it is the mother tongue actually of more than three-quarters of the population, although in 1921 no more than 60 per cent. of the population in these two wards spoke Bengali. In the Garden Reach ward, similarly, the proportion has risen from 44 to 47½ per cent. and also in Ekbalpore and in Watganj and Hastings between 52½ and 53 per cent. of the inhabitants now speak Bengali where less than half spoke it in 1921. In the north of Calcutta there has been a considerable increase in the proportion in Sukeas' Street (ward 4) where almost three-quarters of the population now use Bengali as their mother tongue and also in Paddapukur where the proportion was nearly 70 in 1921 but is now more than 76 per cent. The division into three municipal wards of the old Cossipore-Chitpore municipality shows the highest concentration of persons speaking Bengali in the part which now forms Satpukur (ward No. 31), and in what was the municipality of Maniktala the division into Beliaghata and Maniktala wards shows that there is a higher concentration of Bengali speakers in Beliaghata. Decreases in the proportion are returned in Burra Bazar, Kalootola, Muchipara and Bow Bazar, as well as in Fenwick Bazar, and the decrease in Kalootola is to be compared with a considerable increase in the proportion speaking Hindi as mother tongue no doubt due to the migration into this ward of numbers of upcountry Hindus and Marwaris to which a reference has been made in chapter I.

65. **Distribution of Hindustani by wards.**—The distribution by wards of the proportion speaking Hindustani is illustrated from subsidiary table I in diagram No. VII-3, but the series of hatchings used differs from those

DIAGRAM No. VII-3.

Numbers speaking Hindustani as mother tongue in 1921 (left) and 1931 (right) per 1,000 of the total population by wards.

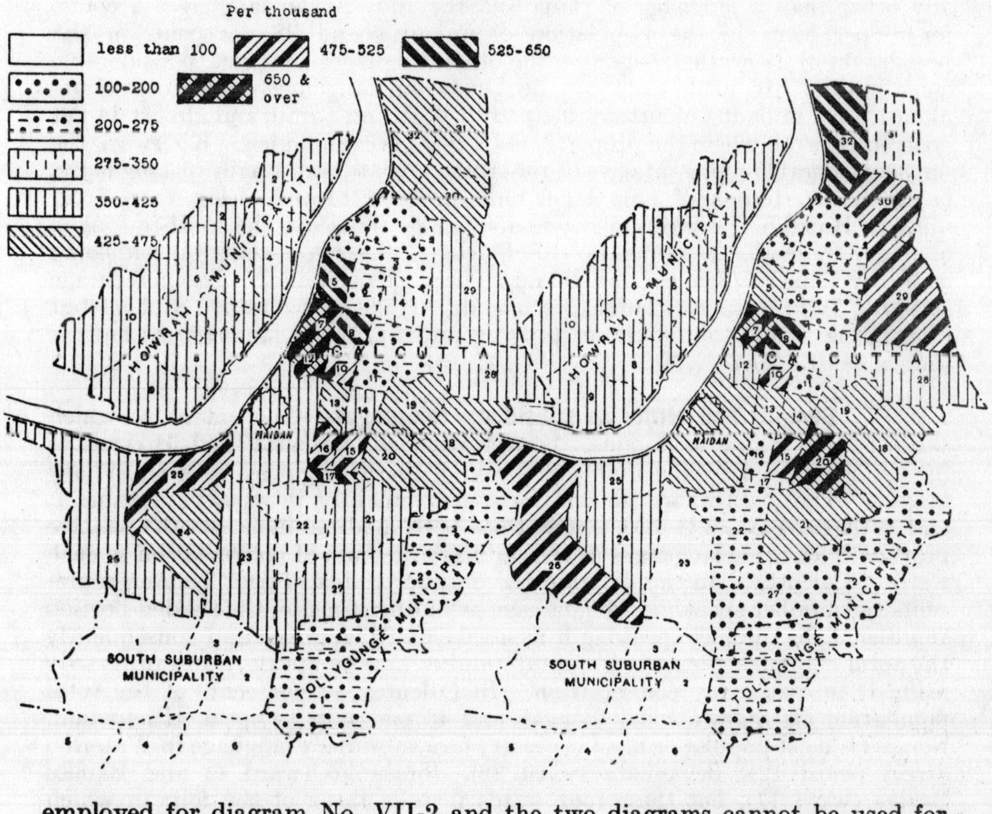

employed for diagram No. VII-2 and the two diagrams cannot be used for comparison at a glance. Burra Bazar (ward 7) and Beniapukur (ward 20) contain a population in which 65 per cent. or over speak Hindustani. A similar percentage also spoke it in Waterloo Street (ward 12) in 1921, but the proportion there has now fallen to 41 per cent. Migration of Marwaris and upcountry men as well as their non-co-operation in Jorabagan (ward 5) is sufficient to explain the decrease from 56 to 43 per cent. in the proportion speaking Hindi as mother tongue. The division of the old municipalities of Cossipore-Chitpore and Maniktala shows a high concentration of persons speaking Hindustani in the complementary wards to those in which the proportion speaking Bengali is high. Thus in Cossipore ward more than 63 per cent. of the population speak Hindi as mother tongue and in Belgachia and Maniktala (wards 30 and 29) the proportion is between 47½ and 52½. There has been an increase in Kalootola (ward 8) from 55 to 64 per cent. which is concealed by the fact that the same hatching covers both and is to be ascribed, as has already been indicated in the last paragraph, to the influx of Marwaris and upcountry men into tenement houses along Central Avenue. There has been a decrease in the proportion speaking Hindustani in Watganj and Hastings and an increase in Garden Reach attributable to the migration to which reference has been made in chapter I of upcountry coolies employed under the Port Commissioners. Decreases in Park Street and Baman Bustee correspond to considerable increases in the proportion speaking Bengali as mother tongue in these wards and suggest that the Hindustani speaking population has shifted eastward into Beniapukur where a considerable increase has been commented upon as well as to Ballygunge (ward 21), where there has been an apparent increase possibly due, however, to the redistribution of the old combined ward Ballygunge and Tollygunge.

66. **A philological distribution.**—In imperial table X languages are arranged in an order explained in the title page in that table. But in subsidiary tables II and III a scientific classification upon a philological scheme has been attempted. Full details of the scheme are to be found in chapter X of volume V, part i, and are not here repeated. Only 33 per cent. of the inhabitants of Calcutta and 9 per cent. of the inhabitants of Howrah speak any other than a language of India and the Indo-Aryan languages account for 96 per cent. in the population of Calcutta and 98 per cent. in the population of Howrah. Amongst the other languages of India considerable contributions are made only by the Dravidian languages which contribute almost 6 per mille in Calcutta, principally Telegu and Tamil, and almost 14 per cent. in Howrah where the proportion of Telegu is even higher. Kherwari, the only considerable representative of the Austro-Asiatic sub-family of languages, is the mother tongue of only 1 per mille in Calcutta and of less than 7 per mille in Howrah. Asiatic languages foreign to India are the mother tongue of 5 per mille in the population of Calcutta, the main contribution being made by Chinese (2·5 per mille) and Hebrew (1 per mille). The percentage speaking Indo-European languages has already been mentioned and all but a negligible proportion of those speaking any European language as mother tongue use English.

67. **Bengali and Hindi as subsidiary languages.**—The extent to which Bengali and Hindi monopolise conversation in Calcutta and Howrah is further illustrated by the numbers speaking these languages as a subsidiary tongue. The figures are shown most conveniently in subsidiary table I, and in diagram No. VII-4 an attempt has been made to illustrate the relative prevalence of these languages as the ordinary medium of conversation in each ward of Calcutta. In the diagram the unshaded area of each column represents the number speaking the language as mother tongue, the shaded portion represents the number speaking it as a subsidiary language and consequently the total column represents the total number able to speak it and ordinarily using it in every day conversation. In Calcutta 56 per cent. of the total population are able to speak Bengali and 40 per cent. to speak Hindustani. Bengali is most popular or most necessary as a subsidiary language in Waterloo Street (ward 12), Beliaghata (ward 28), Jorasanko (ward 6) and Baman Bustee (ward 17), but these four wards include three of the four in which Hindustani also is most frequently used as a medium of conversation

subsidiary to the mother tongue, viz., Park Street (ward 16), Waterloo Street (ward 12), Jorasanko (ward 6) and Baman Bustee (ward 17). As a subsidiary language more than half as many persons again use Hindustani

DIAGRAM No. VII-4.

Numbers per 1,000 speaking Bengali (on left) and Hindustani (on right) by wards, 1931.

NOTE.—For explanation see text.

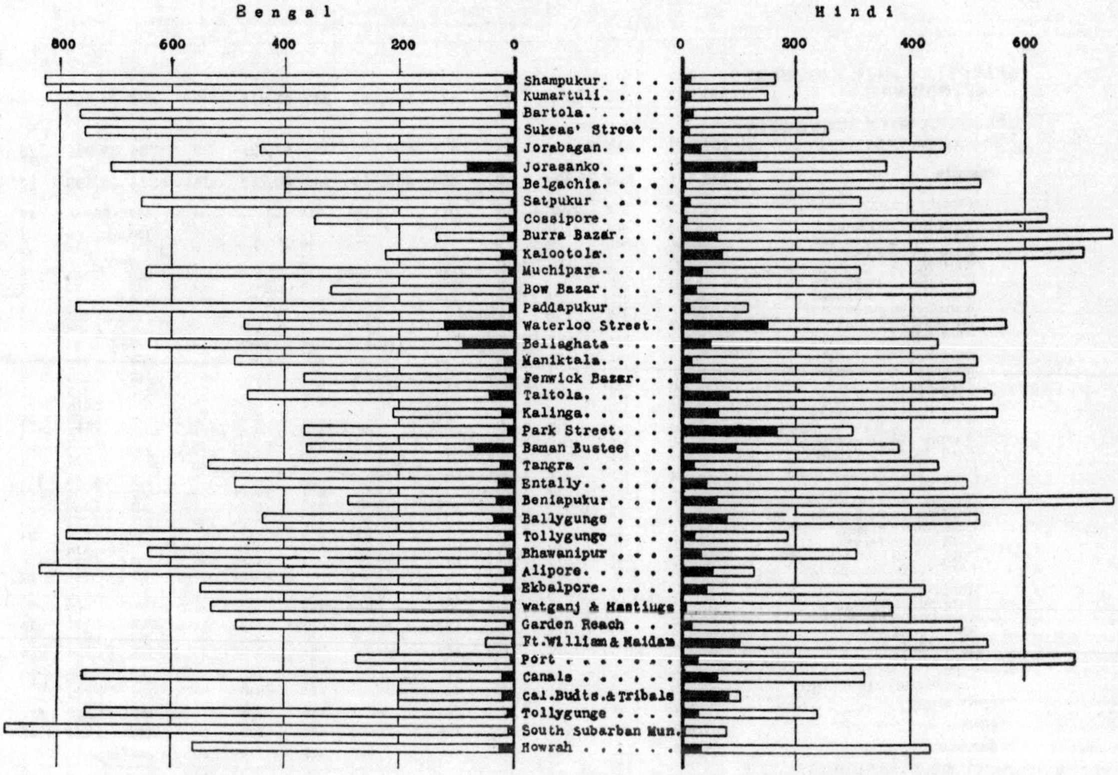

as Bengali. The extent to which English is shown as a subsidiary language is hardly an indication of its prevalence as a medium of intercourse; and there have probably been omissions particularly as the main object of the enquiry into subsidiary languages was to elicit details primarily of the interaction of languages of Asia.

SUBSIDIARY TABLE I.—Numerical distribution of the population by wards speaking Bengali, Hindustani and English, 1931, with proportions, 1931 and 1921.

Locality.	Bengali.					Hindustani.					English.				
	1931.				1921.	1931.				1921.	1931.				1921.
	As mother tongue.		As subsidiary language.		As mother tongue.	As mother tongue.		As subsidiary language.		As mother tongue.	As mother tongue.		As subsidiary language.		As mother tongue.
	No.	Per 1,000.	No.	Per 1,000.	Per 1,000.	No.	Per 1,000.	No.	Per 1,000.	Per 1,000.	No.	Per 1,000.	No.	Per 1,000.	Per 1,000.
1	2	3	4	5	6	7	8	9	10	11	12	13	14	15	16
CALCUTTA WITH SUBURBS AND HOWRAH ..	**822,861**	**555**	**29,541**	**20**	**533**	**535,023**	**361**	**48,415**	**33**	**372**	**34,953**	**24**	**9,825**	**7**	**23**
CALCUTTA WITH SUBURBS IN 24-PARGANAS ..	**701,621**	**558**	**24,112**	**19**	**538**	**444,146**	**353**	**41,425**	**33**	**363**	**32,941**	**26**	**9,408**	**7**	**25**
Calcutta ..	**648,451**	**543**	**23,675**	**20**	**490**	**436,123**	**366**	**40,712**	**34**	**374**	**32,393**	**27**	**8,979**	**8**	**27**
MUNICIPAL AREA ..	**637,335**	**552**	**23,421**	**20**	**523**	**412,190**	**357**	**39,221**	**34**	**368**	**29,548**	**26**	**8,701**	**8**	**26**
Ward No. 1 Shampukur ..	53,797	807	1,150	17	765	10,224	153	603	9	153	5	..	428	6	1
Ward No. 2 Kumartuli ..	31,320	818	138	4	775	5,318	139	350	9	155	10	..	263	7	1
Ward No. 3 Bartola ..	49,705	741	1,487	22	735	14,880	222	784	12	218	7	..	307	5	1
Ward No. 4 Sukea's Street ..	40,344	746	302	6	589	13,293	246	387	7	303	105	2	8	..	1
Ward No. 5 Jorabagan ..	17,191	437	339	9	349	16,889	429	1,117	28	560	59	1	..	..	1
Ward No. 6 Jorasanko ..	28,907	627	3,739	81	617	10,408	226	5,891	128	257	11	..	7	..	1
Ward No. 30 Belgachia ..	8,848	398	24	1		11,538	519	50	2		627	28	..	..	
Ward No. 31 Satpukur ..	12,388	647	98	5	403	5,787	302	164	9	451	100	5	..	..	7
Ward No. 32 Cossipore ..	9,271	341	179	7		17,245	634	101	4		86	3	49	2	
Ward No. 7 Burra Bazar ..	2,340	125	161	9	189	12,982	695	1,065	57	700	452	24	9	..	5
Ward No. 8 Kalootola ..	9,781	202	1,063	22	225	30,853	637	3,181	66	545	326	7	585	12	25
Ward No. 9 Muchipara ..	51,080	634	887	11	657	22,747	282	2,346	29	222	846	11	991	12	13
Ward No. 10 Bow Bazar ..	6,507	317	42	2	352	10,096	492	399	19	485	2,678	131	96	5	142
Ward No. 11 Paddapukur ..	26,845	761	239	7	697	3,567	101	383	11	154	1,575	45	264	7	51
Ward No. 12 Waterloo Street ..	2,234	353	753	119	62	2,623	414	958	151	668	1,157	183	1	..	192
Ward No. 28 Beliaghata ..	18,372	553	2,909	88	547	13,306	400	1,594	48	403	9	..	1,784	54	5
Ward No. 29 Maniktala ..	19,999	472	775	18		21,274	502	506	12		27	1	188	4	
Ward No. 13 Fenwick Bazar ..	10,934	355	295	10	365	13,989	464	897	29	465	3,466	113	468	15	108
Ward No. 14 Taltola ..	16,185	423	1,604	42	379	17,765	464	2,942	77	407	2,892	76	961	25	81
Ward No. 15 Kalinga ..	2,630	188	289	21	177	6,853	489	855	61	482	2,759	197	213	15	202
Ward No. 16 Park Street ..	1,920	355	59	11	58	715	132	895	165	522	2,323	430	49	9	370
Ward No. 17 Baman Bustee ..	775	293	176	67	75	756	286	241	91	530	856	324	238	90	377
Ward No. 18 Tengra ..	5,999	512	269	23		5,039	430	198	17		119	10	5	..	
Ward No. 19 Intally ..	20,341	461	1,130	26	516	20,280	459	1,724	39	437	2,315	52	335	8	26
Ward No. 20 Beniapukur ..	10,423	257	1,275	31		28,282	697	2,319	57		906	22	141	3	
Ward No. 21 Ballygunge ..	12,486	404	1,028	33	567	13,777	446	2,280	74	398	1,119	36	231	7	18
Ward No. 27 Tollygunge ..	31,285	770	526	13		6,859	169	705	17		205	5	157	4	
Ward No. 22 Bhawanipur ..	50,042	628	891	11	608	21,721	273	2,471	31	326	1,134	14	605	8	18
Ward No. 23 Alipore ..	24,450	818	430	14	563	2,249	75	1,523	51	383	1,082	36	191	6	31
Ward No. 24 Ekbalpore ..	17,422	531	563	17	499	12,600	384	1,320	40	426	1,258	38	67	2	23
Ward No. 25 Watganj and Hastings ..	16,972	526	50	2	427	11,711	363	126	4	489	825	26	19	1	22
Ward No. 26 Garden Reach ..	26,542	475	551	10	445	26,564	476	846	15	359	209	4	41	1	3
FORT WILLIAM AND MAIDAN	**142**	**46**	**2**	**1**	**268**	**1,337**	**436**	**310**	**100**	**360**	**1,263**	**412**	..	..	**329**
PORT ..	**8,937**	**269**	**158**	**5**	**364**	**22,030**	**664**	**788**	**24**	**580**	**1,575**	**47**	**18**	**1**	**44**
CANALS ..	**1,405**	**737**	**33**	**17**	**665**	**496**	**260**	**114**	**60**	**326**	..	..	**58**	**30**	..
Calcutta Buddhists and Tribal	632	183	61	18	..	70	20	279	81	..	7	2	202	59	..
Suburbs in 24-Parganas ..	**53,170**	**831**	**437**	**7**	**795**	**8,023**	**125**	**713**	**11**	**155**	**548**	**9**	**429**	**7**	**1**
Tollygunge ..	18,144	741	247	10	668	5,212	213	604	25	246	174	7	405	17	2
South Suburban Municipality ..	35,026	886	190	5	878	2,811	71	109	3	95	374	9	24	1	..
HOWRAH ..	**121,240**	**539**	**5,429**	**24**	**509**	**90,877**	**704**	**6,990**	**31**	**414**	**2,012**	**9**	**417**	**2**	**10**

SUBSIDIARY TABLE II

SUBSIDIARY TABLE II.—Numerical distribution of languages on a

NOTE.—Figures for Calcutta in 1931 and 1911 are for the city as now constituted and in 1921 are for the city as then

Language.	Persons speaking the language — Calcutta with Suburbs in 24-Parganas. 1931. Actual numbers. Both sexes.	Males.	Females.	1931. Percentage. Both sexes.	1921. Both sexes.
1	2	3	4	5	6
ALL LANGUAGES ..	**1,260,709**	**851,931**	**408,778**	*1,000*	**1,132,246**
Languages of India ..	**1,220,905**	**828,794**	**392,111**	*968*	**1,097,782**
AUSTRIC FAMILY ..	**1,617**	**974**	**643**	*1·3*	**1,157**
Austro-Asiatic Sub-family ..	**1,617**	**974**	**643**	*1·3*	**1,157**
(1) Mon-khmer Branch ..	**124**	**120**	**4**	*0·1*	**4**
(a) Palaung-Wa Group ..	..	..	..	..	**1**
Palaung ..	..	..	..	..	**1**
(b) Khasi Group ..	**124**	**120**	**4**	*0·1*	**3**
Khasi ..	**124**	120	4	*0·1*	**3**
(2) Munda Branch ..	**1,493**	**854**	**639**	*1·2*	**1,153**
Kherwari ..	**1,493**	854	639	*1·2*	**1,153**
TIBETO-CHINESE FAMILY ..	**227**	**179**	**48**	*0·18*	**150**
Tibeto-Burman Sub-family ..	**227**	**179**	**48**	*0·18*	**150**
(1) Tibeto-Himalayan Branch ..	**83**	**61**	**22**	*0·07*	**38**
(a) Tibetan Group ..	**55**	**37**	**18**	*0·04*	**35**
Bhotia of Tibet or Tibetan ..	**39**	26	13	*0·03* }	**35**
Bhotia (others) ..	**16**	11	5	*0·01* }	
(b) Pronominalised Himalayan Group ..	**2**	**2**	..	*0·00*	..
Khambu ..	**2**	2	..	*0·00*	..
(c) Non-pronominalised Himalayan Group ..	**26**	**22**	**4**	*0·02*	**3**
Gurung ..	**2**	2	..	*0·002*	..
Murmi ..	**7**	5	2	*0·006*	..
Magari ..	..	..	..	..	..
Newari ..	**8**	8	..	*0·006*	..
Rong or Lepcha ..	**9**	7	2	*0·007*	**3**
(2) Assam-Burmese Branch ..	**143**	**117**	**26**	*0·11*	**112**
(a) Baro Bodo Group ..	..	..	..		**9**
Garo ..	..	..	..	..	**9**
Rabha ..	..	..	..	..	..
Baro Bodo ..	...	..	..	..	..
(b) Kuki Chin Group ..	**24**	**24**	..	*0·02*	**3**
(i) Meithei Sub-group ..	**24**	**24**	..	*0·02*	**3**
Meithei ..	**24**	24	..	*0·02*	**3**
(c) Central Chin Group ..	..	..	..	..	**2**
Lushei ..	..	..	..	..	**2**
(d) Kachin Group ..	..	..	..	..	**2**
Kachin ..	..	..	..	..	**2**
(e) Burma Group ..	**119**	**93**	**26**	*0·09*	**96**
Burmese ..	**107**	81	26	*0·08*	**84**
Arakanese ..	**12**	12	..	*0·01*	**12**
(3) Unclassed ..	**1**	**1**	..	*0·00*	..
Mro (Mru) ..	**1**	1	..	*0·00*	..
Tai Chinese Sub-family ..	..	..	..	..	..
Tai Branch (Tai Group) ..	..	..	..	..	..
Siamese ..	..	..	..	..	..
DRAVIDIAN FAMILY ..	**6,945**	**4,386**	**2,559**	*5·5*	**4,950**
(a) Dravida Group ..	**2,829**	**1,618**	**1,211**	*2·2*	**1,949**
Tamil ..	**2,554**	1,401	1,153	*2·0*	**1,906**
Malayalam ..	**236**	192	44	*0·2*	**16**
Kanarese ..	**39**	25	14	*0·03*	**27**
(b) Intermediate Group ..	**723**	**542**	**181**	*0·6*	**915**
Kurukh (Oraon) ..	**723**	542	181	*0·6*	**915**
(c) Andhra langauge ..	**3,393**	**2,226**	**1,167**	*2·7*	**2,086**
Telegu ..	**3,393**	2,226	1,167	*2·7*	**2,086**
INDO-EUROPEAN FAMILY ..	**1,212,116**	**823,255**	**388,861**	*961*	**1,091,525**
Aryan Sub-family ..	**1,212,116**	**823,255**	**388,861**	*961*	**1,091,525**
(1) Ernian Branch ..	**1,074**	**902**	**172**	*0·85*	**1,133**
(a) Eastern Group ..	**1,074**	**902**	**172**	*0·85*	**1,133**
Pashto ..	**741**	693	48	*0·59*	**622**
Persian ..	**333**	209	124	*0·26*	**511**
(2) Dardic Branch ..	**39**	**37**	**2**	*0·03*	**54**
Dard Group ..	**39**	**37**	**2**	*0·03*	**54**
Kashmiri ..	**39**	37	2	*0·03*	**54**
(3) Indo-Aryan Branch ..	**1,211,003**	**822,316**	**388,687**	*960*	**1,090,338**
(i) Outer Sub-branch ..	**1,009,109**	**670,291**	**338,818**	*800*	**908,184**
(a) North-Western Group ..	**359**	**286**	**73**	*0·3*	**179**
Sindhi ..	**359**	286	73	*0·3*	**179**
(b) Southern Group ..	**1,072**	**869**	**203**	*0·85*	**556**
Marathi ..	**1,072**	869	203	*0·86*	**556**
Konkani ..	*35*	*14*	*21*	*0·03*	..

philological classification at successive census years with proportions in 1931.

constituted before the addition of the municipalities of Cossipore-Chitpore, Maniktala and Garden Reach.

shown in column 1 as mother tongue.

Calcutta.						Howrah.				
1931.				1921.	1911.	1931.				1921.
Actual numbers.			Percentage.			Actual numbers.			Percentage.	
Both sexes.	Males.	Females.	Both sexes.	Both sexes.	Both sexes.	Both sexes.	Males.	Females.	Both sexes.	Both sexes.
7	8	9	10	11	12	13	14	15	16	17
1,196,734	**814,948**	**381,786**	*1,000*	**907,851**	**1,043,307**	**224,873**	**145,120**	**79,753**	*1,000*	**195,301**
1,157,645	**792,214**	**365,431**	*967*	**874,444**	**1,009,656**	**222,734**	**143,980**	**78,754**	*991*	**193,280**
1,272	727	545	1·1	822	124	145	86	59	6·5	113
1,272	727	545	1·1	822	124	145	86	59	6·5	..
124	120	4	0·1	4	21	..	..	..	..	..
..	..	..	..	1	..	..	..	..	..	..
..	..	..	..	1	..	..	..	..	..	..
124	120	4	0·1	3	21	..	..	..	..	..
124	120	4	0·1	3	21	..	..	..	..	..
1,148	607	541	1·0	818	103	145	86	59	6·5	113
1,148	607	541	1·0	818	103	145	86	59	6·5	113
227	179	48	0·2	144	260	1	..	1	0·00	205
227	179	48	0·2	144	254	1	..	1	0·00	205
83	61	22	0·07	37	75	1	..	1	0·00	96
55	37	18	0·04	34	72	..	..	..	..	93
39	26	13	0·03 }	34	72	..	..	..	.. }	93
16	11	5	0·01 }		..	..	..	..	.. }	
2	2	..	0·00	..	..	..	..	..	..	..
2	2	..	0·00	..	..	..	..	..	..	..
26	22	4	0·02	3	3	1	..	1	0·00	3
2	2	..	0·002	..	..	..	..	..	..	..
7	5	2	0·006	..	..	..	..	..	..	..
..	..	..	..	..	..	..	..	..	..	3
8	8	..	0·006	..	..	..	..	..	..	..
9	7	2	0·007	3	3	1	..	1	0·00	..
143	117	26	0·12	107	179	..	..	..	..	109
..	..	..	..	6	..	..	..	..	..	108
..	..	..	..	6	..	..	..	..	..	2
..	..	..	..	..	..	..	..	..	..	9
..	..	..	..	..	..	..	..	..	..	97
24	24	..	0·02	..	..	..	..	..	..	..
24	24	..	0·02	3	..	..	..	..	..	..
24	24	..	0·02	3	..	..	..	..	..	..
..	..	..	..	..	..	..	..	..	..	..
..	..	..	..	..	..	..	..	..	..	..
..	..	..	..	..	..	..	..	..	..	..
..	..	..	..	..	..	..	..	..	..	..
119	93	26	0·1	96	179	..	..	..	..	1
107	81	26	0·09	84	179	..	..	..	..	1
12	12	..	0·01	12	..	..	..	..	..	..
1	1	..	0·00	..	..	..	..	..	..	..
1	1	..	0·00	..	..	..	..	..	..	..
..	..	..	..	..	6	..	..	..	..	..
..	..	..	..	..	6	..	..	..	..	..
..	..	..	..	..	6	..	..	..	..	..
6,623	4,121	2,502	5·5	3,492	3,383	3,038	1,644	1,394	13·5	2,855
2,829	1,618	1,211	2·4	1,895	1,852	199	95	104	0·9	105
2,554	1,401	1,153	2·1	1,855	1,701	190	92	98	0·86	105
236	192	44	0·2	13	150	7	3	4	0·03	..
39	15	14	0·03	27	1	2	..	2	0·01	..
405	279	126	0·3	7	62	217	181	36	1·0	101
405	279	126	0·3	7	62	217	181	36	1·0	101
3,389	2,224	1,165	2·8	1,590	1,469	2,622	1,368	1,254	11·7	2,649
3,389	2,224	1,165	2·8	1,590	1,469	2,622	1,368	1,254	11·7	2,649
1,149,523	787,187	362,336	960	869,986	1,005,882	219,550	142,250	77,300	977	190,107
1,149,523	787,187	362,336	960	869,986	1,005,882	219,550	142,250	77,300	977	190,107
1,043	871	172	0·87	897	1,415	97	91	6	0·43	62
1,043	871	172	0·87	897	1,415	97	91	6	0·43	62
710	662	48	0·59	398	624	15	15	..	0·07	40
333	209	124	0·28	499	791	82	76	6	0·36	22
39	37	2	0·03	54	25	..	..	..	..	..
39	37	2	0·03	54	25	..	..	..	..	..
39	37	2	0·03	54	25	..	..	..	..	..
1,148,441	786,279	362,162	959	869,035	1,004,442	219,453	142,159	77,294	976	190,045
949,816	636,785	313,025	793	718,753	816,028	181,330	113,989	67,341	806·5	156,928
359	286	73	0·3	179	179	22	16	6	0·1	..
359	286	73	0·3	179	179	22	16	6	0·1	..
1,031	835	196	0·86	547	523	29	20	9	0·13	38
1,031	835	196	0·86	547	523	29	20	9	0·13	38
35	*14*	*21*	*0·03*	..	*298*	..	..	..	..	..

SUBSIDIARY TABLE II.—Numerical distribution of languages on a

NOTE.—Figures for Calcutta in 1931 and 1911 are for the city as now constituted and in 1921 are for the city as then

Language.		Persons speaking the language				
		Calcutta with Suburbs in 24-Parganas.				
		1931.				1921.
		Actual numbers.			Percentage.	
		Both sexes.	Males.	Females.	Both sexes.	Both sexes.
1		2	3	4	5	6
(c) Eastern Group	..	**1,007,678**	**669,136**	**338,542**	*799*	**907,449**
Oriya	..	**39,409**	36,612	2,797	*31·3*	**51,659**
Bengali	..	**701,621**	430,580	271,041	*556·5*	**608,797**
Assamese	..	**160**	132	28	*0·1*	**232**
Bihari (60 per cent. of Hindustani)	..	**266,488**	201,812	64,676	*211·3*	**246,761**
(ii) Mediate Sub-branch	..	**155,451**	**117,724**	**37,727**	*123*	**143,944**
Mediate Group	..	**155,451**	**117,724**	**37,727**	*123*	**143,944**
Eastern Hindi (35 per cent. of Hindustani)	..	**155,451**	117,724	37,727	*123*	**143,944**
(iii) Inner Sub-branch	..	**46,443**	**34,301**	**12,142**	*36·8*	**38,210**
(a) Central Group	..	**42,711**	**31,571**	**11,140**	*33·9*	**36,939**
Western Hindi (5 per cent. of Hindustani)	..	**22,207**	16,818	5,389	*17·6*	**20,563**
Rajasthani	..	**7,399**	4,956	2,443	*5·9*	**7,359**
Gujarati	..	**3,884**	2,535	1,349	*3·1*	**6,033**
Panjabi	..	**9,221**	7,262	1,959	*7·3*	**2,984**
(b) Pahari Group	..	**3,732**	**2,730**	**1,002**	*3·0*	**1,271**
Eastern Paharia, Khaskura or Naipali	..	**3,732**	2,730	1,002	*3·0*	**1,271**
(4) Unclassed Languages	..	..	..	..	..	..
Andamanese	..	..	..	..	..	..
Language foreign to India	..	**39,804**	**23,137**	**16,667**	*32*	**34,464**
Vernaculars of other Asiatic countries and Africa	..	**6,211**	**4,410**	**1,801**	*4·9*	**5,176**
INDO-EUROPEAN FAMILY	..	**532**	**223**	**309**	*0·42*	**196**
Aryan Sub-family	..	**532**	**223**	**309**	*0·42*	**196**
Indo-Aryan Branch	..	**15**	**15**	..	*0·01*	**38**
Outer Sub-branch	..	**15**	**15**	..	*0·01*	**38**
Southern Group	..	**15**	**15**	..	*0·01*	**38**
Singhalese	..	**15**	15	..	*0·01*	**38**
Eranian Branch	..	**517**	**208**	**309**	*0·41*	**158**
Armenian Group	..	**517**	**208**	**309**	*0·41*	**158**
Armenian	..	**517**	208	309	*0·41*	**158**
TIBETO-CHINESE FAMILY	..	**3,184**	**2,558**	**626**	*2·53*	**3,574**
Tai Chinese Sub-family	..	**3,184**	**2,558**	**626**	*2·53*	**3,574**
Chinese Branch	..	**3,184**	**2,558**	**626**	*2·53*	**3,574**
Chinese Group	..	**3,184**	**2,558**	**626**	*2·53*	**3,574**
Chinese	..	**3,184**	2,558	626	*2·53*	**3,574**
SEMITIC FAMILY	..	**1,959**	**1,222**	**737**	*1·55*	**1,043**
Arabic	..	**764**	629	135	*0·60*	**424**
Hebrew	..	**1,195**	593	602	*0·95*	**619**
HEMITIC FAMILY	..	..	..	..	..	..
Somali	..	..	..	..	..	..
MONGOLIAN FAMILY	..	**536**	**407**	**129**	*0·43*	**361**
Ural-Altaic Group	..	**3**	..	**3**	..	**1**
Turkish	..	**3**	..	3	..	**1**
Japanese Group	..	**533**	**407**	**126**	*0·43*	**360**
Japanese	..	**533**	407	126	*0·43*	**360**
EUROPEAN LANGUAGES	..	**33,593**	**18,727**	**14,866**	*26·7*	**29,290**
INDO-EUROPEAN FAMILY	..	**33,593**	**18,727**	**14,866**	*26·7*	**29,290**
Greek Group	..	**59**	**17**	**42**	*0·05*	**59**
Greek	..	**59**	17	42	*0·05*	**59**
Romance Group	..	**440**	**270**	**170**	*0·35*	**387**
Italian	..	**157**	142	15	*0·12*	**18**
French	..	**161**	66	95	*0·13*	**128**
Spanish	..	**38**	35	3	*0·03*	**11**
Portuguese	..	**84**	27	57	*0·07*	**230**
Celtic Group	..	**8**	**8**	..	*0·01*	..
Gaelic	..	**8**	8	..	*0·01*	..
Balto-Slavonic Group	..	**33**	**16**	**17**	*0·03*	**4**
Russian	..	**33**	16	17	*0·03*	**4**
Polish	..	..	..	..	..	..
Roumanian	..	..	..	..	..	..
Teutonic Group	..	**33,052**	**18,415**	**14,637**	*26·2*	**28,840**
English	..	**32,941**	18,342	14,599	*26·1*	**28,807**
Dutch	..	**64**	56	8	*0·05*	**16**
Flemish	..	**2**	2	..	*0·00*	..
Norwegian	..	..	..	..	..	**3**
Swedish	..	**1**	..	1	*0·00*	**8**
Danish	..	**2**	2	..	*0·00*	**3**
German	..	**42**	13	29	*0·03*	**2**
MONGOLIAN FAMILY	..	**1**	**1**	..	*0·00*	..
Ural-Altaic Group	..	**1**	**1**	..	*0·00*	..
Hungarian	..	**1**	1	..	*0·00*	..

philological classification at successive census years with proportions in 1931.

constituted before the addition of the municipalities of Cossipore-Chitpore, Maniktala and Garden Reach.

shown in column 1 as mother tongue.

Calcutta.						Howrah.				
1931.				1921.	1911.	1931.				1921.
Actual numbers.			Percentage.			Actual numbers.			Percentage.	
Both sexes.	Males.	Females.	Both sexes.	Both sexes.	Both sexes.	Both sexes.	Males.	Females.	Both sexes.	Both sexes.
7	8	9	10	11	12	13	14	15	16	17
948,420	**635,664**	**312,756**	*792*	**718,027**	**815,326**	**181,279**	**113,953**	**67,326**	*806·3*	**156,890**
38,135	35,400	2,735	*31·8*	**39,556**	**41,153**	**5,513**	4,755	758	*24·5*	**9,911**
648,451	402,043	246,408	*541·6*	**477,957**	**512,579**	**121,240**	68,990	52,250	*539·3*	**98,407**
160	132	28	*0·1*	**216**	**56**	..	..	..	..	**8**
261,674	198,089	63,585	*218·5*	**200,298**	**261,538**	**54,526**	40,208	14,318	*242·5*	**48,564**
152,643	**115,552**	**37,091**	*127·5*	**116,841**	**152,564**	**31,807**	**23,454**	**8,353**	*141·5*	**28,329**
152,643	**115,552**	**37,091**	*127·5*	**116,841**	**152,564**	**31,807**	**23,454**	**8,353**	*141·5*	**28,329**
152,643	115,552	37,091	*127·5*	**116,841**	**152,564**	**31,807**	23,454	8,353	*141·4*	**28,329**
45,988	**33,942**	**12,046**	*38·4*	**33,441**	**35,850**	**6,316**	**4,716**	**1,600**	*28·1*	**4,788**
42,295	**31,248**	**11,047**	*35·3*	**32,393**	**35,338**	**5,296**	**3,933**	**1,363**	*23·6*	**4,602**
21,806	16,508	5,298	*18·2*	**16,691**	**21,795**	**4,544**	3,351	1,193	*20·2*	**4,047**
7,397	4,956	2,441	*6·2*	**7,249**	**8,998**	**82**	71	11	*0·4*	**296**
3,883	2,534	1,349	*3·2*	**5,817**	**2,802**	**237**	182	55	*1·1*	**152**
9,209	7,250	1,959	*7·7*	**2,636**	**1,743**	**433**	329	104	*1·9*	**107**
3,693	**2,694**	**999**	*3·1*	**1,048**	**512**	**1,020**	**783**	**237**	*4·5*	**186**
3,693	2,694	999	*3·1*	**1,048**	**512**	**1,020**	783	237	*4·5*	**186**
..	..	..	..	..	**7**	..	..	..	..	..
..	..	..	..	..	**7**	..	..	..	..	..
39,089	**22,734**	**16,355**	*33*	**33,407**	**33,651**	**2,139**	**1,140**	**999**	*9·5*	**2,021**
6,055	**4,312**	**1,743**	*5·1*	**5,095**	**4,285**	**100**	**36**	**64**	*0·4*	**49**
532	**223**	**309**	*0·44*	**188**	**313**	**3**	..	**3**	*0·01*	..
532	**223**	**309**	*0·44*	**188**	**313**	**3**	..	**3**	*0·01*	..
15	**15**	..	*0·01*	**38**	**6**	..	..	..	..	..
15	**15**	..	*0·01*	**38**	**6**	..	..	..	..	..
15	**15**	..	*0·01*	**38**	**6**	..	..	..	..	..
15	15	..	*0·01*	**38**	**6**	..	..	..	..	..
517	**208**	**309**	*0·43*	**150**	**307**	**3**	..	**3**	*0·01*	**1**
517	**208**	**309**	*0·43*	**150**	**307**	**3**	..	**3**	*0·01*	**1**
517	208	309	*0·43*	**150**	**307**	**3**	..	3	*0·01*	**1**
3,028	**2,460**	**568**	*2·53*	**3,510**	**2,611**	**42**	**35**	**7**	*0·19*	**45**
3,028	**2,460**	**568**	*2·53*	**3,510**	**2,611**	**42**	**35**	**7**	*0·19*	**45**
3,028	**2,460**	**568**	*2·53*	**3,510**	**2,611**	**42**	**35**	**7**	*0·19*	**45**
3,028	**2,460**	**568**	*2·53*	**3,510**	**2,611**	**42**	**35**	**7**	*0·19*	**45**
3,028	2,460	568	*2·53*	**3,510**	**2,611**	**42**	35	7	*0·19*	**45**
1,959	**1,222**	**737**	*1·64*	**1,037**	**1,258**	**53**	..	**53**	*0·24*	..
764	629	135	*0·64*	**418**	**656**	**53**	..	53	*0·24*	..
1,195	593	602	*1·00*	**619**	**602**	..	..	..	..	..
..	..	..	..	..	**5**	..	..	..	..	..
..	..	..	..	..	**5**	..	..	..	..	..
536	**407**	**129**	*0·45*	**360**	**98**	**2**	**1**	**1**	*0·01*	**3**
3	..	**3**	*0·00*	**1**	**5**	..	..	..	..	..
3	..	3	*0·00*	**1**	**5**	..	..	..	..	..
533	**407**	**126**	*0·45*	**359**	**93**	**2**	**1**	**1**	*0·01*	**3**
533	407	126	*0·45*	**359**	**93**	**2**	1	1	*0·01*	**3**
33,034	**18,422**	**14,612**	*27·6*	**28,312**	**29,366**	**2,039**	**1,104**	**935**	*9·07*	**1,972**
33,034	**18,422**	**14,612**	*27·6*	**28,312**	**29,366**	**2,039**	**1,104**	**935**	*9·07*	**1,972**
59	**17**	**42**	*0·05*	**39**	**80**	..	..	..	..	..
59	17	42	*0·05*	**39**	**80**	..	..	..	..	..
433	**266**	**167**	*0·36*	**379**	**450**	**11**	**8**	**3**	*0·05*	**5**
157	142	15	*0·13*	**18**	**82**	**2**	2	..	*0·01*	**5**
154	62	92	*0·13*	**121**	**110**	**9**	6	3	*0·04*	..
38	35	3	*0·03*	**11**	**4**	..	..	..	..	..
84	27	57	*0·07*	**229**	**254**	..	..	..	..	..
8	**8**	..	*0·01*	..	..	..	..	..	..	..
8	8	..	*0·01*	..	..	..	..	..	..	..
33	**16**	**17**	*0·03*	**4**	**54**	**4**	**3**	**1**	*0·02*	**2**
33	16	17	*0·03*	**4**	**46**	**4**	3	1	*0·02*	..
..	..	..	..	..	**1**	..	..	..	..	**2**
..	..	..	..	..	**7**	..	..	..	..	..
32,500	**18,114**	**14,386**	*27·14*	**27,890**	**28,782**	**2,024**	**1,093**	**931**	*9·00*	**1,965**
32,393	18,043	14,350	*27·05*	**27,857**	**28,430**	**2,012**	1,086	926	*8·95*	**1,965**
60	54	6	*0·05*	**16**	**25**	**1**	1	..	*0·00*	..
2	2	..	*0·00*	..	..	..	..	..	..	..
..	..	..	..	**3**	**5**	**1**	1	..	*0·00*	..
1	..	1	*0·00*	**9**	**9**	..	..	..	..	..
2	2	..	*0·00*	**3**	**1**	..	..	..	..	..
42	13	29	*0·04*	**2**	**312**	**10**	5	5	*0·04*	..
1	**1**	..	*0·00*	..	..	..	..	..	..	..
1	**1**	..	*0·00*	..	..	..	..	..	..	..
1	1	..	*0·00*	..	..	..	..	..	..	..

SUBSIDIARY TABLE III.—Prevalence of subsidiary languages, 1931.

Language.	Number speaking the languages shown in column 1 as subsidiary language.											
	Calcutta with suburbs in 24-Parganas.				Calcutta.				Howrah.			
	Actual numbers.			Per 1,000.	Actual numbers.			Per 1,000.	Actual numbers.			Per 1,000.
	Both sexes.	Males.	Fe-males	Both sexes.	Both sexes.	Males.	Fe-males.	Both sexes.	Both sexes.	Males.	Fe-males.	Both sexes.
1	2	3	4	5	6	7	8	9	10	11	12	13
ALL LANGUAGES	**76,621**	**59,119**	**17,502**	**60·8**	**75,026**	**57,817**	**17,209**	**62·7**	**12,933**	**9,182**	**3,751**	**57·5**
Langauge of India	**66,786**	**50,388**	**16,398**	**53·0**	**65,626**	**49,498**	**16,128**	**54·8**	**12,461**	**8,779**	**3,682**	**55·4**
TIBETO-CHINESE FAMILY	..	..	..	..	..	..	..	..	**1**	**1**	..	**0·00**
TIBETO-BURMAN SUB-FAMILY	..	..	..	..	..	..	..	..	**1**	**1**	..	**0·00**
Assam-Burmese Branch	..	..	..	..	..	..	..	..	**1**	**1**	..	**0·00**
Burma Group	..	..	..	..	..	..	..	..	**1**	**1**	..	**0·00**
Burmese	..	..	..	..	..	..	..	..	1	1	..	0·00
DRAVIDIAN FAMILY	**76**	**34**	**42**	**0·06**	**76**	**34**	**42**	**0·06**	**17**	**11**	**6**	**0·08**
(a) Dravid Group	**24**	**18**	**6**	**0·02**	**24**	**18**	**6**	**0·02**	**3**	**3**	..	**0·01**
Tamil	24	18	6	0·02	24	18	6	0·02	2	2	..	0·01
Malayalam	..	..	..	..	..	..	..	..	1	1	..	0·00
(b) Intermediate Group	..	..	..	..	..	..	..	..	**4**	**4**	..	**0·02**
Kurukh (Oraon)	..	..	..	..	..	..	..	..	4	4	..	0·02
(c) Andhra Language	**52**	**16**	**36**	**0·04**	**52**	**16**	**36**	**0·04**	**10**	**4**	**6**	**0·04**
Telegu	52	16	36	0·04	52	16	36	0·04	10	4	6	0·04
INDO-EUROPEAN FAMILY	**66,710**	**50,354**	**16,356**	**52·9**	**65,550**	**49,464**	**16,086**	**54·7**	**12,443**	**8,767**	**3,676**	**55·3**
ARYAN SUB-FAMILY	**66,710**	**50,354**	**16,356**	**52·9**	**65,550**	**49,464**	**16,086**	**54·7**	**12,443**	**8,767**	**3,676**	**55·3**
(1) Eranian Branch	**510**	**510**	..	**0·4**	**510**	**510**	..	**0·4**	**1**	**1**	..	**0·0**
(a) Eastern Group	**510**	**510**	..	**0·4**	**510**	**510**	..	**0·4**	**1**	**1**	..	**0·0**
Pashto	10	10	..	0·01	10	10	..	0·01	..	..	..	..
Persian	500	500	..	0·39	500	500	..	0·41	1	1	..	0·00
(2) Indo-Aryan Branch	**66,200**	**49,844**	**16,356**	**52·5**	**65,040**	**48,954**	**16,086**	**54·3**	**12,442**	**8,766**	**3,676**	**55·3**
(i) Outer Sub-branch	**49,357**	**37,445**	**11,912**	**39·1**	**48,482**	**36,781**	**11,701**	**40·5**	**9,638**	**6,814**	**2,824**	**42·9**
(a) Southern Group	**3**	**2**	**1**	**0·00**	**3**	**2**	**1**	**0·00**	..	..	..	..
Marathi	3	2	1	0·00	3	2	1	0·00	..	..	..	..
(b) Eastern Group	**49,354**	**37,443**	**11,911**	**39·1**	**48,479**	**36,779**	**11,700**	**40·5**	**9,638**	**6,814**	**2,824**	**42·9**
Oriya	386	244	142	0·31	376	236	140	0·31	15	13	2	0·07
Bengali	24,112	18,845	5,267	19·13	23,675	18,528	5,147	19·77	5,429	3,874	1,555	24·15
Bihari (60 per cent. of Hindustani)	24,856	18,354	6,502	19·71	24,428	18,015	6,413	20·41	4,194	2,927	1,267	18·65
(ii) Mediate Sub-branch	**14,499**	**10,706**	**3,793**	**11·5**	**14,249**	**10,508**	**3,741**	**11·9**	**2,446**	**1,707**	**739**	**10·9**
Mediate Group	**14,499**	**10,706**	**3,793**	**11·5**	**14,249**	**10,508**	**3,741**	**11·9**	**2,446**	**1,707**	**739**	**10·9**
Eastern Hindi (35 per cent. of Hindustani)	14,499	10,706	3,793	11·5	14,249	10,508	3,741	11·9	2,446	1,707	739	10·9
(iii) Inner Sub-branch	**2,344**	**1,693**	**651**	**1·86**	**2,309**	**1,665**	**644**	**1·93**	**358**	**245**	**113**	**1·59**
(a) Central Group	**2,341**	**1,690**	**651**	**1·86**	**2,306**	**1,662**	**644**	**1·93**	**352**	**245**	**107**	**1·56**
Western Hindi (5 per cent. of Hindustani)	2,070	1,529	541	1·64	2,035	1,501	534	1·70	350	244	106	1·55
Rajasthani	98	5	93	0·08	98	5	93	0·08	..	..	..	..
Gujarati	98	88	10	0·08	98	88	10	0·08	..	..	..	..
Panjabi	75	68	7	0·06	75	68	7	0·06	2	1	1	0·01
(b) Pahari Group	**3**	**3**	..	**0·00**	**3**	**3**	..	**0·00**	**6**	..	**6**	**0·03**
Eastern Paharia (Kashkura or Naipali)	3	3	..	0·00	3	3	..	0·00	6	..	6	0·03
Language Foreign to India	**9,835**	**8,731**	**1,104**	**7·8**	**9,400**	**8,319**	**1,081**	**7·9**	**472**	**403**	**69**	**2·1**
Vernaculars of other Asiatic countries	**427**	**399**	**28**	**0·34**	**421**	**399**	**22**	**0·35**	**48**	**32**	**16**	**0·21**
SEMITIC FAMILY	**427**	**399**	**28**	**0·34**	**421**	**399**	**22**	**0·35**	**48**	**32**	**16**	**0·21**
Arabic	427	399	28	0·34	421	399	22	0·35	48	32	16	0·21
European Languages	**9,408**	**8,332**	**1,076**	**7·46**	**8,979**	**7,920**	**1,059**	**7·50**	**424**	**371**	**53**	**1·89**
INDO-EUROPEAN FAMILY	**9,408**	**8,332**	**1,076**	**7·46**	**8,979**	**7,920**	**1,059**	**7·50**	**424**	**371**	**53**	**1·89**
Romance Group	..	..	..	..	..	..	..	..	**6**	**4**	**2**	**0·03**
French	..	..	..	..	..	..	..	..	6	4	2	0·03
Teutonic Group	**9,408**	**8,332**	**1,076**	**7·46**	**8,979**	**7,920**	**1,059**	**7·50**	**418**	**367**	**51**	**1·86**
English	9,408	8,332	1,076	7·46	8,979	7,920	1,059	7·50	417	367	50	1·86
German	..	..	..	..	..	..	..	..	1	..	1	0·00

SUBSIDIARY TABLE IV.—Bi-lingualism by mother tongue, 1931.

MOTHER TONGUE with subsidiary language.	Numbers per 1,000 speaking the mother tongue shown in column 1 who are bi-lingual in the language also shown in column 1.					
	Calcutta with suburbs in 24-Parganas.		Calcutta.		Howrah.	
	Males.	Females.	Males.	Females.	Males.	Females.
1	2	3	4	5	6	7
BENGALI						
Any language	51	26	52	28	58	27
Hindustani	42	24	44	26	56	27
English	12	2	12	2	4	0·4
HINDUSTANI						
Any language	45	46	45	46	51	59
Bengali	37	44	37	44	50	58
English	7	2	7	2	0·8	0·5
ORIYA						
Any language	151	138	154	137	149	387
Bengali	124	82	126	79	100	194
Hindustani	64	59	66	60	52	191
PANJABI						
Any language	258	98	259	98	258	144
Bengali	20	5	20	5	..	..
Hindustani	255	91	255	91	225	144
RAJASTHANI						
Any language	372	191	372	191	..	..
Bengali	192	..	192	..	..	..
Hindustani	371	191	371	191	..	..
GUJARATI						
Any language	282	168	283	168	319	327
Bengali	4	1	4	1	11	18
Hindustani	241	140	242	140	214	145
English	43	28	43	28	[illegible]	104
NAIPALI						
Any language	306	159	301	159	264	4
Bengali	48	10	49	10	5	..
Hindustani	289	150	284	150	258	[illegible]

CHAPTER VIII

Religion

68. **The statistics shown.**—This chapter discusses the figures for religion presented in imperial table XVI. Subsidiary tables printed at the end of the chapter show :—

I—the general distribution of population by religion with percentage of variation, 1901-1931 ;

II—the number of Hindus per 10,000 of the total population, 1901-1931, with percentage of variation ;

III—the number of Muslims per 10,000 of the total population, 1901-1931, with percentage of variation ; and

IV—the number of Christians per 10,000 of the total population, 1901-1931, with percentage of variation.

69. **General strength of religions.**—Calcutta with suburbs and Howrah contains 1,045,599 Hindus, 371,919 Muslims, 50,990 Christians and less than 5,000 adherents of any other religion. In Calcutta with its suburbs in the 24-Parganas the numbers are 871,986 Hindus, 323,633 Muslims and 48,473 Christians. An innovation of the present census was an attempt to obtain sects of Hindus. No returns of sect however were made by all but a nearly negligible proportion of the population. Out of the total number of 1,045,599 Hindus in Calcutta with its suburbs no fewer than 1,022,226 made no return of their caste and although figures are given in the title page to imperial table XVI for those who returned their sect the very small proportion of Hindus who did so makes it unprofitable to offer any comment upon them. The variations in the figures returned for Calcutta with suburbs in 24-Parganas at every census since 1901 shown in subsidiary table I are illustrated in diagram No. VIII-1.

DIAGRAM No. VIII-1.

Numbers of Hindus, Muslims, Christians and those of other religions in Calcutta and its suburbs in the 24-Parganas in 1901, 1911, 1921 and 1931.

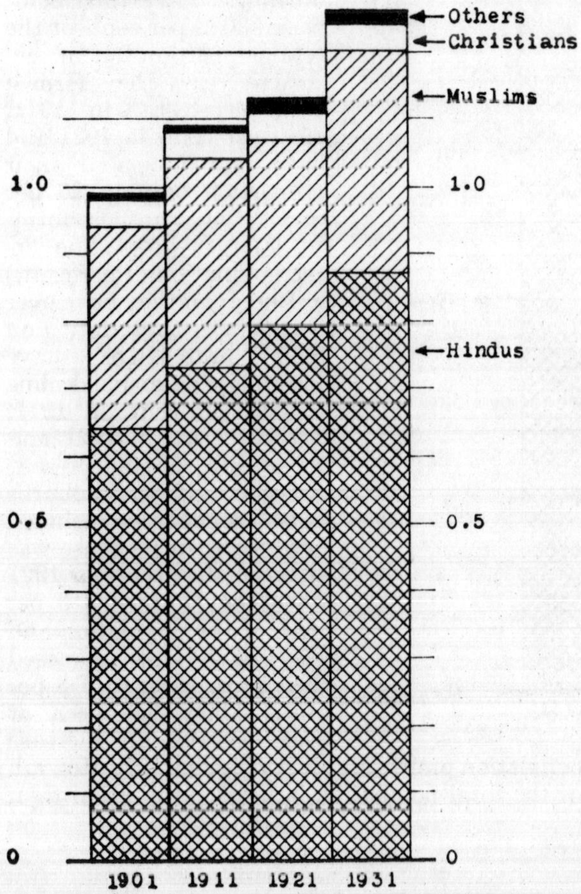

Hindus numbered 643,176 in 1901 and have steadily increased at every successive census. Muslims numbered 297,643 in 1901, 311,730 in 1911 and

282,053 in 1921. Their numbers on the present occasion show an increase of 14·7 per cent. over the figure of 1921 which showed a decrease of nearly 30 thousand over the figure in the previous census year, 1911. The number of Christians has steadily increased from 38,910 in 1901 to the present figure already noted and the rate of increase during the last decade (17·6 per cent.) is the highest recorded since 1901. There was a considerable increase in the numbers of persons professing other religions than these three between the years 1901 when they numbered 8,610 and 1921 when they numbered 17,743 but their numbers on the present occasion have declined and they amounted in all only to 16,617.

70. **General distribution of religions in Howrah.**—In Howrah 173,613 of the total population are Hindus, 48,286 are Muslims and 2,517 are Christians including 1 person of indefinite belief. There are 164 Sikhs but less than a hundred persons of any other religion except those following tribal beliefs who however have declined from 194 in 1921 to 103 in 1931. The numbers of all three principal religions in Howrah city have increased since 1921. In that year there were 149,606 Hindus, 43,040 Muslims and 2,348 Christians.

71. **Proportionate distribution by religions.**—The proportionate distribution of the three principal religions in Calcutta is illustrated from subsidiary tables II to IV in diagram No. VIII-2. The proportion of Hindus in the population steadily increased from 1901 when it was 64·9 per cent. to 1921 when it had reached 69·6 per cent. But in 1931 Hindus form a rather smaller proportion than in 1921 amounting to 68·7 per cent. in the total population. In 1901 Muslims formed a larger proportion of the population than they do now. They then comprised 30·2 per cent. of the total population but in successive years they formed 28·7 per cent. in 1911, 25·0 per cent. in 1921 and have now increased their proportion only to 26 per cent. Christians also formed a larger proportion on the population (4 per cent.) in 1901 than they have ever done since that date and their proportions have shown a progressive decline to 3·9 per cent. in 1911, 3·7 per cent. in 1921 and 4 per cent. on the present occasion. If the suburbs in 24-Parganas be included however their decrease was arrested after the year 1921 when they formed 3·6 per cent. of the population and they have now increased their proportion to 3·8 per cent. There has been at every census an increase in the proportion in the total population professing other religions. In Howrah Hindus form 77·2 per cent. of the total population, a larger proportion than

DIAGRAM No. VIII-2.

Religious distribution of 100 of the population of Calcutta and suburbs in 24-Parganas at each census, 1901 to 1931.

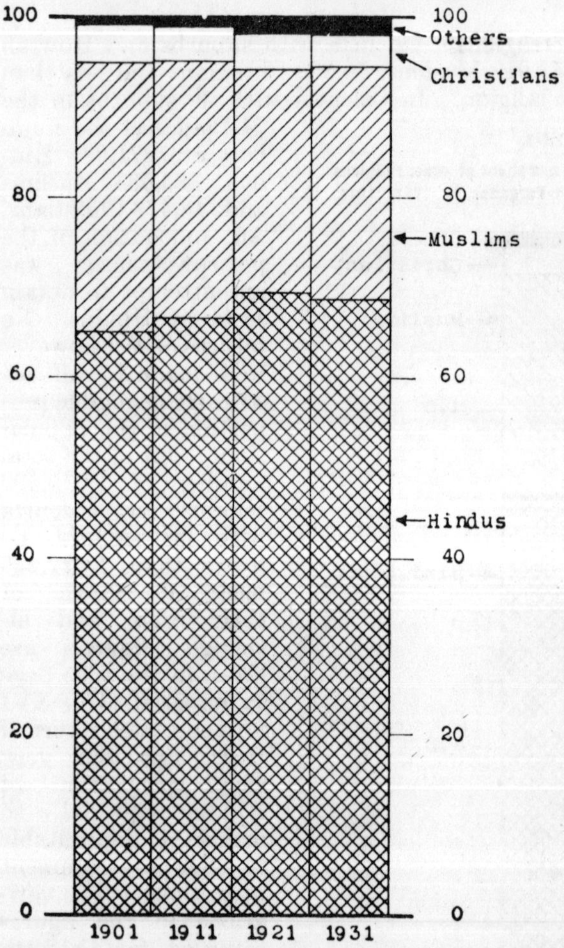

in any previous year since 1901 and the proportionate increase in their numbers was 14·1 per cent. between 1901 and 1911, 13 per cent. between 1911 and 1921 and 16 per cent. between 1921 and 1931. As in Calcutta so also in Howrah the proportion of Muslims has declined since 1901 when they formed 24·9 per cent. of the population and after forming 24·6 per cent. in 1911 and 22·0 per cent. in 1921 they now form 21·5 per cent. only. Their actual numbers showed a decrease between 1911 and 1921 amounting to 2·2 per cent. but although they have now increased by 12·2 per cent. their increase has not been sufficient to constitute them a larger proportion of the total population than in 1921. As with Muslims with Christians also there has been a continuous decrease in the proportions recorded at each census since 1901. In that year they formed 1·5 per cent. of the total population which had fallen to 1·2 in 1911 and 1921 and is now 1·1 in spite of increases in actual numbers between 1911 and 1921 of 6·4 per cent. and between 1921 and 1931 of 7·2 per cent.

72. **Distribution of Hindus by locality.**—Diagram No. VIII-3 illustrates from subsidiary table II the numbers of Hindus per 1,000 in each ward of

DIAGRAM No. VIII-3.

Numbers of Hindus per thousand of the total population in each ward of Calcutta and Howrah and in the two suburban municipalities, 1931.

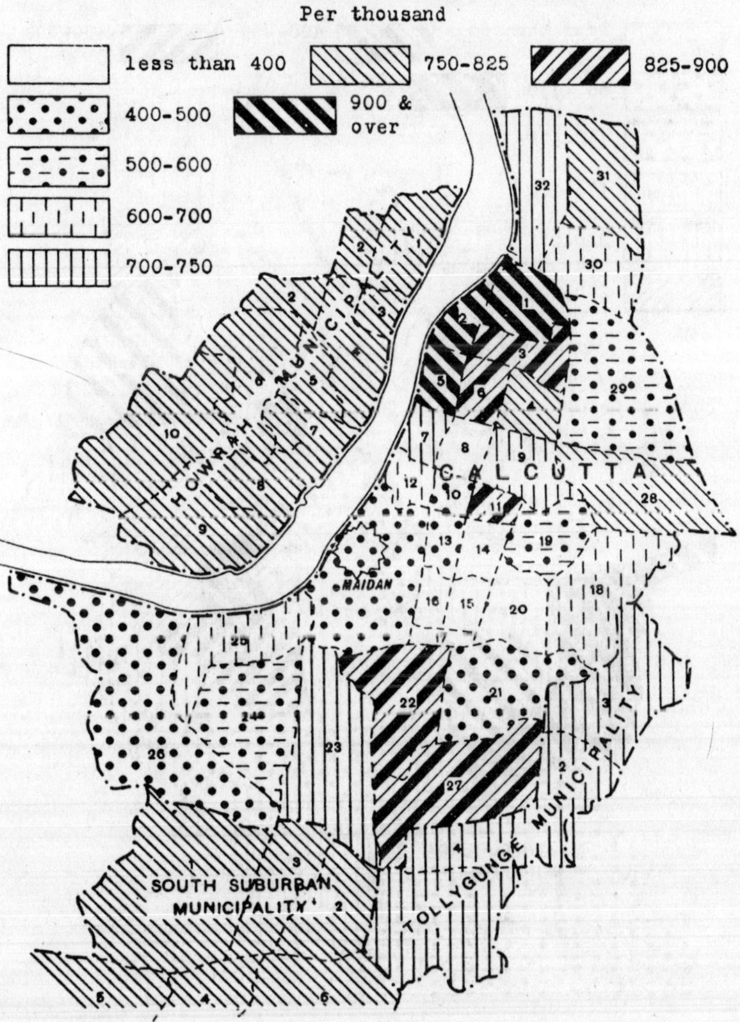

Calcutta but although figures are separately shown in imperial table XVI for their numbers in each ward of Howrah the same proportions have not

been indicated in the map. They form the largest proportion of the population in Jorabagan and Kumartuli (97 ·5 per cent.) and in Shampukur (94 per cent). They are also very numerous in Jorasanko (89 per cent.) and Bartola (88 ·5 per cent.) and in the wards of Tollygunge (89 ·3 per cent.) and Bhawanipur (88 ·7 per cent.). Their numbers are between 75 and 82 ·5 per cent. in Satpukur, Sukeas' Street, Beliaghata and the South Suburban Municipality and they form 77 ·2 per cent. of the total population of Howrah Municipality. They are less than 40 per cent. of the population in the area about Park Street, viz., Baman Bustee, Park Street, Kalinga, Beniapukur and Taltola and also in Kalootola ward. A comparison with their distribution in 1921 shows that they are relatively strong generally in the same areas as before but their proportions have decreased in Maniktala and the redistribution of wards shows their main concentration to be in the Tollygunge portion of what used to be the Tollygunge-Ballygunge ward.

73. **Local distribution of Muslims.**—Diagram No. VIII-4 illustrated from subsidiary table III a similar local distribution of Muslims. They are

DIAGRAM No. VIII-4.

Numbers of Muslims per thousand of the total population in each ward of Calcutta and in Howrah and in the two suburban municipalities, 1931.

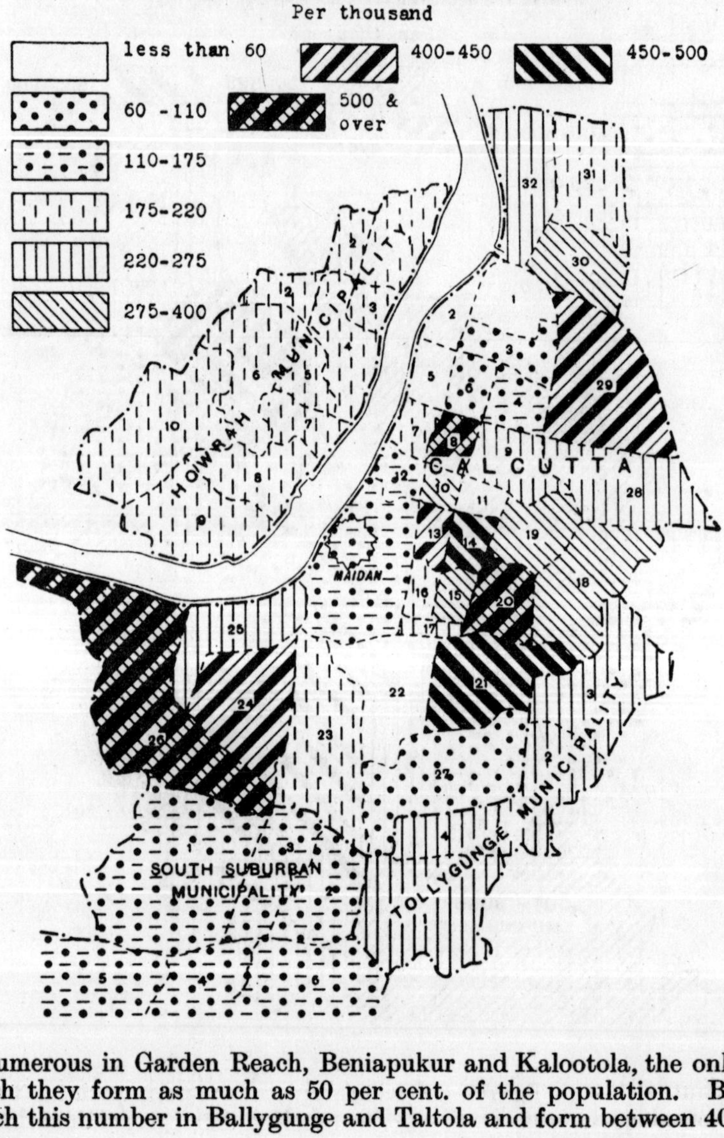

most numerous in Garden Reach, Beniapukur and Kalootola, the only areas in which they form as much as 50 per cent. of the population. But they approach this number in Ballygunge and Taltola and form between 40 and 45 per cent. of the population also in Ekbalpur, Fenwick Bazar and Maniktala. They are naturally least numerous in Shampukur, Kumartuli and Bartola where the Hindus predominate and also in Puddapukur and Bhawanipur. In all these five wards they form less than 6 per cent. of the total population. Their distribution corresponds in general with that of 1921 but they form a smaller proportion of the population in the predominantly Hindu areas though they have increased their proportions in other wards except Shampukur, Kumartuli, Bartola, Sukeas' Street, Jorabagan, Bow Bazar, Bhawanipur and Watganj and Hastings as well as in Fort William and the Maidan. They formed 22 per cent. of the population of Howrah in 1921 but only 21·5 per cent. on the present occasion.

74. **Local distribution of Christians.**—Diagram No. VIII-5 plotted from subsidiary table IV shows for Christians figures similar to those discussed above for Muslims and Hindus. They form a larger proportion of the population in the Fort and Maidan and the wards immediately adjoining it than in any

DIAGRAM No. VIII-5.

Numbers of Christians per thousand of the total population in each ward of Calcutta and in Howrah and in the two suburban municipalities, 1931.

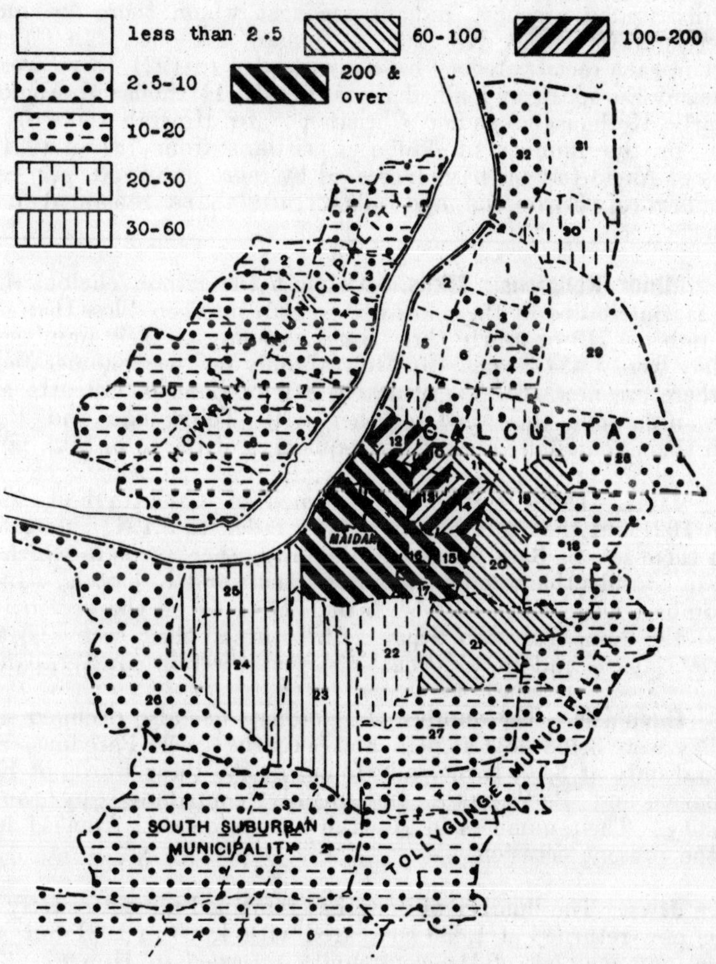

other part and in Park Street and Fort William and the Maidan they make up between 45 and 50 per cent. of the total population. They are more than 20 per cent. of the population also in Baman Bustee and Kalinga adjoining Park Street ward and between 10 and 20 per cent. in the neighbouring wards of Taltola, Fenwick Bazar, Bow Bazar and Waterloo Street. In the two suburban municipalities and also in Tollygunge ward their proportions are between one and two per cent. but they are more numerous in Ballygunge, Beniapukur, Entally and Puddapukur on the fringe of the area where they are mostly concentrated and in these wards their proportions are between 6 and 10 per cent. of the total population. They form a smaller percentage of the population than they did in 1921 in Jorasanko, Kalootola, Bow Bazar, Waterloo Street and Fenwick Bazar as well as in Park Street, Baman Bustee, Bhawanipur and Garden Reach.

75. **Christians by sect and race.**—Figures of Christians by the principal sects and races are shown in the supplement No. II to imperial table XVI. The restricted sort has confined the display of sects to four groups: Roman Catholic, Romo Syrian, Other Syrian and Others. In 1921 three racial classes only were shown but on the present occasion the racial distinctions adopted are (*a*) European and allied races; (*b*) Anglo-Indians; (*c*) Indians; and (*d*) Others. Anglo-Indians form the largest number of Christians and are nearly 17 thousand strong in Calcutta itself. European and allied races number nearly 16 thousand and Indians more than 14 thousand. In Howrah the proportions are somewhat similar and there are 1,218 Anglo-Indians, 822 Europeans and 476 Indians. Nearly two-thirds of the Anglo-Indian Christians are Roman Catholics and rather more than the same proportion of European and allied races are Protestant. The proportions are more evenly distributed amongst Indians amongst whom there are more than 9 Protestants for rather less than 6 Roman Catholics. In Calcutta the numbers in each racial category have increased. In 1921 there were nearly 13 thousand European and allied races, nearly 14 thousand Anglo-Indians and nearly 13 thousand Indian Christians. In Howrah there has been a decrease in the number of Indian Christians from 781 in 1921 but the numbers of Anglo-Indians have increased by more than 50 per cent. and the numbers of Europeans and allied races have remained practically the same.

76. **Minor Religions: Sikhs.**—Amongst the minor religions the largest number is contributed by the Sikhs who in 1921 numbered less than the Jains. They number 4,713 or nearly three times as many as their numbers in 1921 when they were 1,484 strong. In Howrah only one was enumerated in 1921 where there are now 164. Very nearly half of them in Calcutta are found in Bhawanipur and this ward together with Tollygunge and Ballygunge between them contribute almost three-quarters of the total Sikh population.

77. **Jains.**—There were 5,670 returned in Calcutta and suburbs as Jains in 1921 but their numbers have now fallen to 3,194. More than one-third of them live in Bara Bazar and the only other wards in which they are present in considerable numbers are Bow Bazar and Kalootola. In Howrah their numbers have increased from 8 in 1921 to 57 on the present occasion. Amongst the Jains less than 9 per cent. returned their sect. Of these 139 were Swetambaris and an additional 135 were Swetambari Terapanthis.

78. **Buddhists.**—The number of Buddhists has also declined since 1921 when they were 3,468 in Calcutta and suburbs in 24-Parganas and they now stand only at 3,178 principally found in the three wards of Kalootola, Bow Bazar and Puddapukur and mainly contributed by the Chinese community. Their numbers in Howrah have increased from 47 in 1921 to 49 on the present occasion.

79. **Jews.**—The number of Jews has remained almost exactly constant and it is now returned at 1,830 compared with 1,820 in 1921 but in neither year was any member of the community returned in Howrah. They are principally found in Bow Bazar and Kalootola which between them contribute more than half of the total community and more than one hundred of the community are found also only in Fenwick Bazar, Kalinga and Park Street.

80. **Confucians.**—Confucians as in 1921 are most numerous in Kalootola which contains all but a very small proportion of the total number recorded on the present occasion and is the residence of many Chinese. Their number is 1,363 which is almost identical with their number in 1921 which was 1,361.

81. **Zoroastrians.**—Zoroastrians shown as Parsis in 1921 are returned in almost double the numbers then recorded and they are now exactly four times as many in Howrah city as they were then. In Calcutta they are principally found in Kalootola, Fenwick Bazar, Bow Bazar and Taltola wards.

82. **Tribal Religions.**—The numbers returning tribal beliefs have declined from 1,271 in 1921 to 1,140 and there has been a similar decline in Howrah from 194 to 103. They are principally found in the two suburban municipalities which contain two-thirds of their numbers.

SUBSIDIARY TABLE I.—General distribution of the population by religion, with percentage of variation, 1901-1931.

A : General distribution.

Religion.	Calcutta with suburbs in 24-Parganas.					Calcutta.					Municipal area.				
	Actual population of 1931.	Number per 10,000 of the total population.				Actual population of 1931.	Number per 10,000 of the total population.				Actual population of 1931.	Number per 10,000 of the total population.			
		1931.	1921.	1911.	1901.		1931.	1921.	1911.	1901.		1931.	1921.	1911.	1901.
1	2	3	4	5	6	7	8	9	10	11	12	13	14	15	16
Hindu ..	871,986	6,917	6,988	6,672	6,508	822,293	6,871	6,961	6,647	6,485	806,169	6,961	7,061	6,772	6,617
Muslim ..	323,633	2,567	2,491	2,851	3,012	311,155	2,600	2,505	2,866	3,019	292,601	2,527	2,416	2,756	2,906
Christian ..	48,473	384	364	376	394	47,558	397	375	388	406	44,307	383	366	371	374
Sikh ..	4,713	37	13	9	2	4,705	39	14	9	2	4,542	39	11	10	1
Jain ..	3,194	25	50	17	13	3,185	27	53	17	13	3,149	27	54	18	14
Buddhist ..	3,178	25	31	23	30	3,021	25	32	24	31	2,562	22	31	22	29
Jew ..	1,830	15	16	18	19	1,829	15	17	18	20	1,803	16	17	19	21
Confucian ..	1,363	11	12	10	11	1,363	12	13	10	2	1,363	12	13	10	2
Zoroastrian ..	1,199	10	5	4	3	1,199	10	6	5	3	1,199	10	6	5	3
Tribal ..	1,140	9	11	7	*	426	4	7	1	*	349	3	7	1	*

*Not available.

B : Percentage variation in actual number, 1901-31.

(Increase +, Decrease –.)

Religion.	Calcutta with suburbs in 24-Parganas.				Calcutta.				Municipal area.			
	1921-31.	1911-21.	1901-11.	1901-31.	1921-31.	1911-21.	1901-11.	1901-31.	1921-31.	1911-21.	1901-11.	1901-31.
1	2	3	4	5	6	7	8	9	10	11	12	13
Hindu ..	+ 10·2	+ 8·5	+ 13·4	+ 35·6	+ 9·7	+ 8·1	+ 12·7	+ 33·6	+ 8·2	+ 9·1	+ 13·3	+ 33·7
Muslim ..	+ 14·7	– 9·5	+ 4·7	+ 8·7	+ 15·3	– 9·7	+ 4·3	+ 8·6	+ 14·8	– 8·3	+ 4·9	+ 10·5
Christian ..	+ 17·6	+ 0·4	+ 5·5	+ 24·6	+ 17·8	– 0·3	+ 5·2	+ 23·5	+ 14·7	+ 3·1	+ 9·8	+ 29·8
Sikh ..	+217·6	+ 51·4	+504·9	+ 2,809·2	+217·0	+ 51·4	+504·9	+ 2,804·3	+283·6	+ 21·7	+969·2	+ 4,891·2
Jain ..	– 43·7	+212·7	+ 46·1	+ 157·4	– 43·8	+ 212·7	+ 46·1	+ 156·6	– 44·3	+ 212·0	+ 46·1	+ 153·7
Buddhist ..	– 8·4	+ 40·0	– 16·5	+ 7·1	– 12·9	+ 40·9	– 17·1	+ 1·8	– 21·6	+ 44·0	– 15·3	– 4·4
Jew ..	+ 0·5	– 5·4	+ 1·8	– 3·1	+ 0·5	– 5·2	+ 1·6	– 3·2	– 0·9	– 5·2	+ 2·4	– 3·8
Confucian ..	– 3·4	+ 34·8	..	+ 30·2	– 1·4	+ 32·1	+488·2	+ 665·7	+ 4·0	+ 25·1	+488·2	+ 665·7
Zoroastrian ..	+ 93·4	+ 31·9	+ 59·3	+ 306·4	+ 93·4	+ 31·9	+ 59·3	+ 306·4	+ 94·0	+ 31·5	+ 59·3	+ 306·4
Tribal ..	– 10·3	+ 75·3	*	*	– 44·5	+1,343·3	*	*	– 54·4	+ 1,060·6	*	*

*Not available.

SUBSIDIARY TABLE II.—Numbers of Hindus per 10,000 of the total population, 1901-1931, with percentage variation.

NOTE.—Figures for 1901-1921 exclude Aryas and Brahmos.

Ward, etc.	Numbers per 10,000 of the total population in—				Percentage variation in actual strength, increase +, decrease −.			
	1931.	1921.	1911.	1901.	1921-31.	1911-21.	1901-11.	1901-31.
1	2	3	4	5	6	7	8	9
CALCUTTA	**6,871**	**6,961**	**6,647**	**6,485**	**+ 9·7**	**+ 8·1**	**+12·7**	**+33·6**
Ward No. 1 Shampukur	9,412	9,205	8,817	8,481	+ 19·5	+ 12·2	+ 17·6	+ 82·9
Ward No. 2 Kumartuli	9,747	9,710	9,627	9,592	+ 13·0	+ 3·6	+ 10·1	+ 29·0
Ward No. 3 Bartola	8,853	8,602	8,324	7,894	+ 12·7	+ 15·8	+ 14·7	+ 80·2
Ward No. 4 Sukea's Street	8,149	7,876	7,672	7,611	+ 1·1	+ 18·2	+ 15·4	+ 71·9
Ward No. 5 Jorabagan	9,750	9,529	9,489	9,347	− 23·4	+ 1·1	+ 7·8	− 16·3
Ward No. 6 Jorasanko	8,895	8,849	8,359	8,221	− 19·6	+ 1·8	+ 14·2	− 5·8
Ward No. 30 Belgachia	6,649							
Ward No. 31 Satpukur	7,967	7,143	7,147	7,130	+ 32·7	+ 17·2	+ 18·5	+ 73·4
Ward No. 32 Cossipore	7,461							
Ward No. 7 Burra Bazar	7,304	7,343	7,577	7,216	− 43·5	+ 4·8	+ 1·4	− 40·1
Ward No. 8 Kalootola	3,488	4,611	4,380	4,199	− 3·8	− 28·8	− 5·7	− 35·6
Ward No. 9 Muchipara	7,047	7,127	6,745	6,212	+ 13·6	+ 62·2	+ 7·3	+ 63·3
Ward No. 10 Bow Bazar	4,856	4,383	4,239	3,883	− 14·0	+ 12·0	+ 0·9	− 2·6
Ward No. 11 Paddapukur	8,871	8,961	8,643	8,432	+ 7·1	+ 12·5	+ 9·5	+ 32·4
Ward No. 12 Waterloo Street	6,128	6,457	5,600	5,395	− 10·4	+ 30·4	+ 2·0	+ 19·2
Ward No. 28 Beliaghata	7,734	6,265	6,123	7,037	+ 20·5	+ 28·2	+ 44·4	+ 9·8
Ward No. 29 Maniktala	5,932							
Ward No. 13 Fenwick Bazar	4,054	4,755	4,920	5,139	+ 1·1	− 11·2	− 12·8	− 21·7
Ward No. 14 Taltola	3,731	4,149	3,892	3,713	+ 11·6	+ 2·6	+ 4·4	+ 19·7
Ward No. 15 Kalinga	3,272	3,741	3,736	4,093	+ 4·3	+ 3·3	− 38·1	− 33·1
Ward No. 16 Park Street	2,770	2,879	5,013	4,116	+ 36·5	− 5·9	+ 5·2	− 40·3
Ward No. 17 Baman Bustee	3,189	3,896	4,246	5,771	− 31·1	− 7·6	− 58·1	− 73·1
Ward No. 18 Tengra	6,806							
Ward No. 19 Intally	5,968	5,243	5,229	5,337	+ 2·5	− 0·9	+ 21·7	+ 33·8
Ward No. 20 Beniapukur	3,130							
Ward No. 21 Ballygunge	4,441							
		6,079	5,442	5,443	+ 61·8	+ 37·7	+ 46·8	+238·6
Ward No. 27 Tollygunge	8,931							
Ward No. 22 Bhawanipur	8,873	8,828	8,577	8,217	+ 39·1	+ 8·2	+ 14·8	+ 73·3
Ward No. 23 Alipore	7,452	7,605	7,579	7,643	+ 32·6	+ 7·6	+ 10·6	+ 65·2
Ward No. 24 Ekbalpore	5,053	5,836	3,933	4,448	− 9·6	+113·0	− 10·5	+ 72·5
Ward No. 25 Watganj and Hastings	6,864	6,835	6,849	6,632	− 15·9	− 21·6	+ 20·3	− 20·7
Ward No. 26 Garden Reach	4,594	5,326	4,699	4,318	+ 5·7	+ 14·0	+ 74·6	+110·7
FORT WILLIAN AND MAIDAN	**4,154**	**3,784**	**3,906**	**3,972**	**+ 23·0**	**− 39·5**	**− 6·0**	**− 30·0**
PORT	**4,128**	**1,707**	**2,569**	**2,787**	**+ 29·9**	**+ 54·5**	**− 16·7**	**+ 67·2**
CANALS	**5,082**	**6,400**	**5,360**	**4,893**	**+ 78·0**	**− 69·9**	**− 19·6**	**− 55·5**
Suburbs in 24-Parganas	**7,767**	**7,530**	**7,200**	**7,063**	**+20·0**	**+15·1**	**+30·0**	**+ 79·5**
Tollygunge	7,038	6,805	6,427	5,865	+ 17·0	+ 24·3	+ 57·5	+129·1
South Suburban Municipality	8,217	8,001	7,652	7,646	+ 21·7	+ 10·6	+ 19·7	+ 61·0
HOWRAH	**7,720**	**7,660**	**7,397**	**7,361**	**+16·0**	**+13·0**	**+14·1**	**+50·0**

SUBSIDIARY TABLE III.—Numbers of Muslims per 10,000 of the total population, 1901-1931, with percentage variation.

Ward, etc.	Numbers per 10,000 of the total population in—				Percentage variation in actual strength, increase +, decrease −.			
	1931.	1921.	1911.	1901.	1921-31.	1911-21.	1901-11.	1901-31.
1	2	3	4	5	6	7	8	9
CALCUTTA	**2,600**	**2,505**	**2,866**	**3,019**	**+15·3**	**− 9·7**	**+ 4·3**	**+ 8·6**
Ward No. 1 Shampukur	554	769	1,157	1,505	− 15·9	− 28·5	− 13·1	− 8·7
Ward No. 2 Kumartuli	236	277	363	402	− 4·0	− 21·4	− 1·0	− 25·3
Ward No. 3 Bartola	1,092	1,322	1,622	2,069	− 9·4	− 8·7	− 14·8	+101·6
Ward No. 4 Sukea's Street	1,741	1,934	2,130	2,221	− 12·1	+ 4·6	+ 9·8	+132·8
Ward No. 5 Jorabagan	108	286	372	448	− 48·4	− 22·6	− 11·8	− 64·6
Ward No. 6 Jorasanko	1,054	922	1,533	1,668	− 7·9	− 42·1	+ 3·3	− 45·0
Ward No. 30 Belgachia	3,019							
Ward No. 31 Satpukur	1,941	2,713	2,706	2,784	+ 10·6	+ 17·6	+ 15·0	+ 49·3
Ward No. 32 Cossipore	2,389							
Ward No. 7 Burra Bazar	1,765	1,346	1,793	2,082	− 25·6	− 18·8	− 16·9	− 49·8
Ward No. 8 Kalootola	5,761	4,277	4,792	5,022	+ 71·3	− 39·8	− 13·8	− 11·0
Ward No. 9 Muchipara	2,706	2,569	2,920	3,484	+ 21·8	− 3·3	− 17·2	+ 35·7
Ward No. 10 Bow Bazar	2,994	3,334	3,522	3,735	− 30·1	+ 2·6	− 12·8	− 37·5
Ward No. 11 Paddapukur	429	403	430	718	+ 14·9	+ 2·2	06·1	25·0
Ward No. 12 Waterloo Street	1,216	1,160	1,536	2,170	− 1·0	− 14·6	− 30·5	− 41·2
Ward No. 28 Beliaghata	2,202	3,640	3,842	2,937	0·2	+ 18·7	−117·1	− 20·7
Ward No. 29 Maniktala	4,046							
Ward No. 13 Fenwick Bazar	4,399	3,650	3,674	3,678	+ 43·1	− 8·8	− 9·1	+ 18·6
Ward No. 14 Taltola	4,718	4,451	4,820	5,161	+ 28·6	− 8·9	− 7·0	+ 9·0
Ward No. 15 Kalinga	3,900	3,776	3,992	4,719	+ 23·6	− 2·4	− 42·6	− 30·8
Ward No. 16 Park Street	2,050	1,385	2,050	3,589	+113·0	− 52·1	− 50·4	− 49·3
Ward No. 17 Baman Bustee	2,284	1,862	2,013	2,669	+ 4·4	− 6·8	− 57·2	− 58·3
Ward No. 18 Tengra	2,970							
Ward No. 19 Intally	3,094	4,101	4,164	4,109	+ 16·8	− 2·4	+ 25·8	+ 49·7
Ward No. 20 Beniapukur	6,115							
Ward No. 21 Ballygunge	4,651							
		3,483	4,210	4,171	− 0·1	+ 5·3	+ 48·5	+ 55·9
Ward No. 27 Tollygunge	802							
Ward No. 22 Bhawanipur	557	689	1,056	1,524	+ 1·3	− 31·4	− 23·8	− 41·2
Ward No. 23 Alipore	2,017	1,983	2,080	2,143	+ 37·6	− 0·8	+ 16·8	+ 59·4
Ward No. 24 Ekbalpore	4,443	3,884	5,646	5,231	+ 19·6	− 1·2	+ 9·3	+ 29·0
Ward No. 25 Watganj and Hastings	2,727	2,840	2,876	3,140	− 19·4	− 22·4	+ 6·7	− 33·3
Ward No. 26 Garden Reach	5,307	4,595	5,234	5,593	+ 41·6	− 11·7	+ 50·2	+ 87·8
FORT WILLIAM AND MAIDAN	**1,106**	**1,880**	**2,344**	**2,602**	**− 34·2**	**− 50·1**	**− 13·9**	**− 71·6**
PORT	**5,128**	**7,651**	**6,839**	**6,123**	**+ 22·5**	**− 23·3**	**+ 0·9**	**− 5·2**
CANALS	**4,918**	**3,528**	**4,640**	**5,073**	**+217·0**	**− 80·2**	**− 32·8**	**− 58·5**
Suburbs in 24-Parganas	**1,950**	**2,220**	**2,551**	**2,824**	**+ 2·2**	**− 4·2**	**+15·2**	**+12·7**
Tollygunge	2,578	2,992	3,289	4,070	− 0·2	+ 6·8	+ 16·2	+ 23·7
South Suburban Municipality	1,524	1,719	2,119	2,218	+ 5·1	− 14·2	+ 14·2	+ 2·9
HOWRAH	**2,147**	**2,204**	**2,458**	**2,490**	**+12·2**	**− 2·2**	**+12·2**	**+23·1**

SUBSIDIARY TABLE IV.—Numbers of Christians per 10,000 of the total population, 1901-1931, with percentage variation.

Ward, etc.	Numbers per 10,000 of the total population in—				Percentage variation in actual strength, increase +, decrease −.			
	1931.	1921.	1911.	1901.	1921-31.	1911-21.	1901-11.	1901-31.
1	2	3	4	5	6	7	8	9
CALCUTTA ..	**397**	**375**	**388**	**406**	**+17·8**	**− 0·3**	**+ 5·2**	**+23·5**
Ward No. 1 Shampukur	8	8	5	7	+ 19·2	+ 61·5	− 25·7	+ 92·3
Ward No. 2 Kumartuli	3	2	5	2	+ 71·4	− 58·8	+240·0	+140·0
Ward No. 3 Bartola	33	30	39	30	+ 13·9	− 8·0	+ 41·3	+124·2
Ward No. 4 Sukea's Street	100	94	119	135	+ 4·3	− 10·1	+ 1·2	+ 2·1
Ward No. 5 Jorabagan	19	10	12	12	+ 40·9	− 14·3	+ 6·8	+ 28·8
Ward No. 6 Jorasanko	24	34	32	39	− 43·1	+ 2·1	− 9·6	− 47·4
Ward No. 30 Belgachia	299							
Ward No. 31 Satpukur	7	143	126	83	+ 54·3	+ 6·2	+ 80·2	+195·3
Ward No. 32 Cossipore	70							
Ward No. 7 Burra Bazar	264	64	157	193	+132·2	− 56·0	− 21·2	− 19·2
Ward No. 8 Kalootola	83	303	352	450	− 65·6	− 42·1	− 29·3	− 85·8
Ward No. 9 Muchipara	227	227	267	249	+ 15·0	− 6·3	+ 6·0	+ 51·0
Ward No. 10 Bow Bazar	1,303	1,514	1,295	1,915	− 34·7	− 3·3	− 18·2	− 47·0
Ward No. 11 Paddapukur	661	610	875	833	+ 20·7	− 24·2	+ 12·2	+ 0·04
Ward No. 12 Waterloo Street	1,837	1,910	2,191	1,963	− 92·0	− 1·4	+ 9·6	− 1·8
Ward No. 28 Beliaghata	47	70	31	21	− 55·5	+187·8	+152·3	− 62·2
Ward No. 29 Maniktala	12							
Ward No, 13 Fenwick Bazar	1,328	1,379	1,226	1,121	+ 14·3	+ 3·2	− 0·5	+ 17·4
Ward No. 14 Taltola	1,408	1,406	1,242	1,096	+ 21·4	+ 11·7	+ 12·8	+ 53·1
Ward No. 15 Kalinga	2,638	2,359	2,221	1,158	+ 33·8	+ 9·6	+ 30·0	+ 90·7
Ward No. 16 Park Street	4,702	5,453	2,860	2,195	+ 25·2	+ 36·0	+ 12·6	+ 91·6
Ward No. 17 Baman Bustee	3,960	3,994	3,651	1,434	− 15·6	+ 10·2	+ 44·6	+ 34·5
Ward No. 18 Tengra	166							
Ward No. 19 Intally	879	629	590	532	+ 26·3	+ 6·6	+ 37·9	+108·2
Ward No. 20 Beniapukur	728							
Ward No. 21 Ballygunge	674	338	299	380	+ 46·1	+ 44·2	+ 15·5	+143·1
Ward No. 27 Tollygunge	110							
Ward No. 22 Bhawanipur	294	368	338	243	+ 10·9	+ 14·5	+ 52·7	+ 93·7
Ward No. 23 Alipore	457	324	217	566	+ 75·7	+ 82·5	+ 35·0	+332·8
Ward No. 24 Ekbalpore	486	274	420	312	+ 85·3	− 6·2	+ 36·0	+136·3
Ward No. 25 Watganj and Hastings	340	280	254	226	− 2·8	− 13·6	+ 31·0	+ 10·1
Ward No. 26 Garden Reach	48	49	41	65	+ 23·7	+ 17·6	0·0	+ 45·5
FORT WILLIAM AND MAIDAN	**4,485**	**3,233**	**3,729**	**3,501**	**+ 55·2**	**− 45·8**	**+ 4·2**	**− 12·4**
PORT	**554**	**472**	**519**	**938**	**+115·5**	**− 37·9**	**− 50·0**	**− 33·1**
CANALS	..	..	..	**34**	..	..	**−100·0**	**−100·0**
Suburbs in 24-Parganas ..	**143**	**153**	**111**	**101**	**+ 9·1**	**+50·9**	**+40·7**	**+131·6**
Tollygunge	109	104	68	35	+ 19·2	+ 79·2	+177·8	+493·3
South Suburban Municipality	164	185	137	133	+ 5·4	+ 42·7	+ 23·1	+ 85·1
HOWRAH ..	**113**	**120**	**120**	**153**	**+ 7·2**	**+ 6·4**	**− 3·3**	**+10·3**

CHAPTER IX

Caste, Tribe, Race or Nationality

83. **The statistics shown.**—This chapter discusses the figures shown in imperial tables XVII and XIX. Two subsidiary tables printed at the end of the chapter show :—

I—the variations of selected castes and tribes from 1901 to 1931 ; and

II—the variations in the numbers of Europeans and Anglo-Indians in different parts of the city from 1911 to 1931.

84. **Source of the figures.**—The method in which the caste returns were elicited has been described in volume V, part I, chapter XII. The same instructions were issued for the census of Calcutta, but in sorting statistics were extracted in rather greater detail than for Bengal as a whole. The title page to imperial table XVII explains the difficulties of bringing the returns received under any single consistent classification and what is actually shown in the tables is a differentiation by more than one criterion.

85. **Castes of Hindus.**—The Hindu castes which number as many as 10,000 in Calcutta city itself are shown in order in statement No. IX-1. In the city itself Kayasthas, Brahmans and Mahishyas contribute a larger

STATEMENT No. IX-1.

Hindu castes with more than 10,000 in Calcutta city, 1931.

Name of Caste.	Numbers in Calcutta city.			Numbers in Howrah city.		
	Both sexes.	Males.	Females.	Both sexes.	Males.	Females.
1	2	3	4	5	6	7
Kayastha ..	160,630	103,354	57,276	17,473	10,445	7,028
Brahman ..	159,104	105,886	53,218	29,652	18,524	11,128
Mahishya ..	46,215	28,128	18,087	19,984	11,772	8,212
Subarnabanik ..	33,745	19,668	14,077	2,494	1,167	1,327
Goala ..	30,770	24,051	6,719	6,709	4,970	1,739
Rajput ..	30,673	25,734	4,939	5,129	4,335	794
Chamar ..	24,867	18,920	5,947	6,896	5,364	1,532
Tanti and Tatwa ..	20,170	11,161	9,009	3,400	2,260	1,140
Baidya ..	17,498	10,167	7,331	1,055	680	375
Kahar and Rawani Kahar ..	17,296	13,888	3,408	3,653	2,801	852
Kalu and Teli ..	15,864	10.750	5,114	4,264	2,519	1,745
Baishnab ..	13,895	6,760	7,135	2,962	1,346	1,616
Sadgop ..	13,851	7,496	6,355	2,872	1,618	1,254
Muchi ..	12,943	10,422	2,521	1,540	1,064	476
Napit ..	12,208	8,534	3,674	2,969	1,945	1,024
Shaha ..	11,673	7,495	4,178	665	494	171
Dhobi ..	11,252	7,463	3,789	2,301	1,369	932
Gandhabanik ..	10,239	6,630	3,609	1,855	1,319	536

share than any other caste in the total population. There are larger numbers of Brahmans living in the suburbs in 24-Parganas than Kayasthas with the result that although Brahmans head the list for Calcutta with suburbs and 24-Parganas their place is taken in Calcutta proper by the Kayasthas. In Howrah also the three most numerous Hindu castes are Brahmans, Mahishyas and Kayasthas. After Mahishyas the Subarnabaniks now command the largest number in the Calcutta city and also in the city with suburbs in 24-Parganas : they now outnumber the Goalas and Chamars who surpassed them in number in 1921. The Chamars have also fallen below the Rajputs, who now come after the Goalas both in the town proper and also in the town suburbs, but are not a very definite group and undoubtedly include a number who are Kshattriyas only on their own claim. The figures for Kalus and Telis exclude those for Tili included in 1921 but are shown together with them in subsidiary table I for comparison, with the result that the oil-pressing castes figure lower in statement No. IX-1 than in the corresponding statement of 1921 in which the figures were for Calcutta with suburbs in 24-Parganas. The small caste of Baidyas numbers in Calcutta itself 17,498 and in Calcutta with suburbs 17,957 so that more than 16 per cent. of the total numbers in the province have gravitated to the city and its neighbourhood. Kayasthas and Baidyas between them contribute about 176 thousand to the population of Calcutta itself or rather more than one-fifth the total number of Hindus. These two castes are exclusively Bengali and must contribute a very considerable proportion of the Bengali Hindu inhabitants of the city. There are a number of Brahmans of other provinces included within the total and if Brahmans are added to Kayasthas and Baidyas the aggregate amounts to 350 thousand and forms 40 per cent. of the total number of Hindus in the city proper. Subarnabaniks, Shahas and Gandhabaniks representing indigenous Bengali trading classes, contribute more than 10,000 each to the population of Calcutta proper. Of these three groups the first two have increased both in Calcutta proper and in greater Calcutta, but the increase of Shahas is no doubt partly the result of a decrease in the number of Sunris and the number of Gandhabaniks has declined since 1921. As in 1921 the functional classes Goalas, Chamars, Doms, Kalus, Muchis, Napits and Dhobas, all contribute as many as 10,000 to the total population in the city proper. Apart from the Mahishyas there are comparatively few representatives of the great cultivating classes of Bengal, although there has been a considerable increase in the number of Namasudras particularly in the suburbs in 24-Parganas. The Pods, on the other hand, have somewhat surprisingly increased in numbers within the city but have decreased in the city taken together with its suburbs partly possibly on account of the ambition of this caste to get itself returned under some Kshattriya synonym. The primitive peoples from Bihar and Orissa are very few in numbers. Thus there are less than 4 thousand contributed in the aggregate by Agarias, Bahelias, Bhuiyas, Bhumij, Ghatwals, Kewats, Kharias, Mundas, Oraons and Santals. On the other hand Kahars, another Bihar caste, are present in considerable strength, though their numbers have declined since 1921 both in Calcutta with or without its suburbs and also in Howrah partly no doubt on account of the return of some Kshattriya synonym by the members of this caste. Karans and Khandaits contribute over 7 thousand to Calcutta itself of whom more than six times as many Khandaits and more than 30 times as many Karans are males as females. It is almost impossible to estimate the extent of the migration to Calcutta of groups originating in Nepal. Only one solitary male returned his caste as Khas and the remainder have no doubt either enlisted themselves in the ranks of the Khattris, Khettris or Chetries (whose numbers however have decreased by nearly 8,500 in Calcutta with its suburbs) or more likely have contributed to the very considerable increase of Rajputs whose numbers have in Calcutta proper increased by more than 2½ times and probably include most of those persons who returned themselves as Kshattriyas and whose actual caste it was not possible to ascertain. In Calcutta itself there is an unexpectedly small proportion of Hindus who did not return their castes or returned them under an inadequate term, but the numbers are more than 10 thousand in Howrah where no return of caste was elicited from almost 6 per cent. of Hindus.

86. **Muslim groups.**—Figures are given in table XVII for Saiyad, Shekh, Mogal, Pathan and "Mumin" (Jolahas) amongst the Muslims. The greatest number were returned as Shekh, but a considerable number (14,683) were also returned as Pathans and more than 6 thousand as Saiyad. In both cases the numbers are smaller than in 1921. The use of a more dignified title for the Jolahas has not led to any increase in the numbers and they are now returned as less than one-fourth of what they were in 1921. A not inconsiderable number of Muslims were returned also as Mogals (3,135 in Calcutta).

87. **Variations in selected groups.**—For some of the caste referred to in preceding paragraphs as also for Jalia Kaibarttas, Jains and Indian Christians the numbers at successive census enumerations since 1901 are illustrated from subsidiary table No. I in diagram No. IX-1. The diagram shows the figures for Calcutta with suburbs and 24-Parganas. Brahmans, Baidyas and Kayasthas have during the whole three decades shown a fairly similar rate of increase. Mahishyas also have consistently increased. On the other hand Jalia Kaibarttas have been reduced to less than half their numbers in 1921 and the figures for "Mumin" (Jolahas) continue and accentuate the rate of decrease recorded between 1911 and 1921. The decline in the number of Agarwalas commented upon in 1921 has been continued but at a somewhat retarded rate. Jains after an increase between 1901 and 1911 and also between 1911 and 1921 when their numbers increased to more than 3 times what they were in 1911 are now scarcely more than one-half and very considerably less than two-thirds of what they were in 1921. Indian Christians who contribute over 14 thousand to Calcutta alone have shown a continuous increase most marked during 1911 to 1921, but amounting, during the last decade, in Calcutta to 7·9 per cent. and in Calcutta with suburbs in the 24-Parganas to 15·2 per cent.

DIAGRAM No. IX-1.

Changes in the numbers of selected castes and other groups in Calcutta with suburbs in 24-Parganas, 1901-31.

The scale shows hundreds for Mumin and Jalia Kaibarttas, thousands for Agarwalas, Baidyas and Jains and ten thousands for other groups.

NOTE.—In the diagram, *read* Mumin for Murmi.

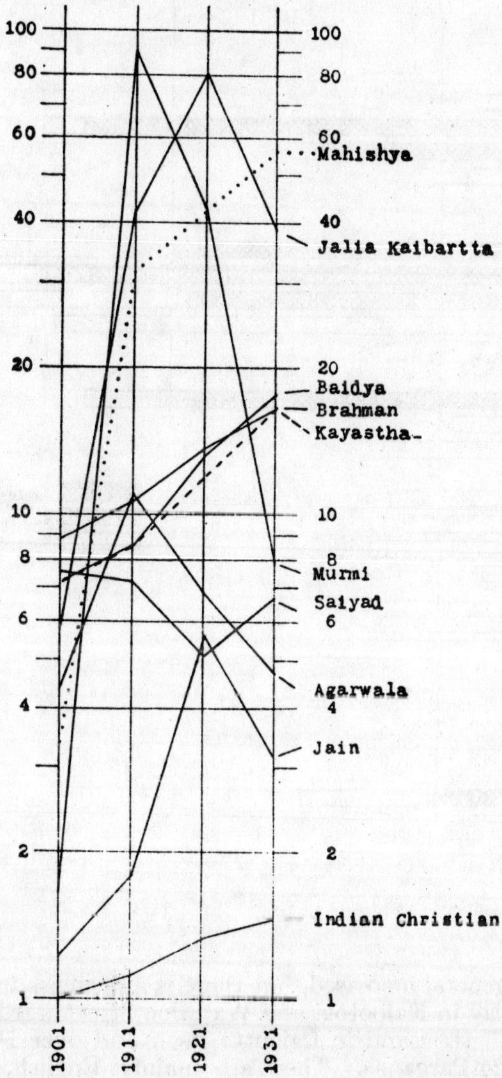

88. **Europeans and Anglo-Indians.**—Over 16 thousand Europeans and allied races including Armenians (who however are shown amongst the Asiatic races in table XVII), were returned in Calcutta with suburbs in 24-Parganas and of these all but about 170 were returned in Calcutta itself. Diagram IX-2 overleaf prepared from imperial table XIX shows their distribution in the wards of Calcutta and Howrah and distinguishes European British subjects from other Europeans. Anglo-Indians number nearly 17 thousand in Calcutta proper and rather more than 17 thousand in Calcutta with its suburbs and their numbers have increased by over 2½ thousand since 1921. They are most numerous in Taltola, Bow Bazar, Intally, Fenwick Bazar and Kalinga. In Howrah they reside principally in ward No. 4. Decreases in their number have been recorded since 1921 in Kalootola and Bow Bazar and also in Park Street and Bamanbustee where the total numbers were not considerable. Europeans are most numerous in Park Street, Fenwick Bazar, Ballygunge, Fort William and Maidan and the Port area, in each of which localities they number more than 1,000.

DIAGRAM No. IX-2.

Number of sAnglo-Indians and of Europeans (distinguished as British subjects and others) by wards of Calcutta and Howrah, 1921.

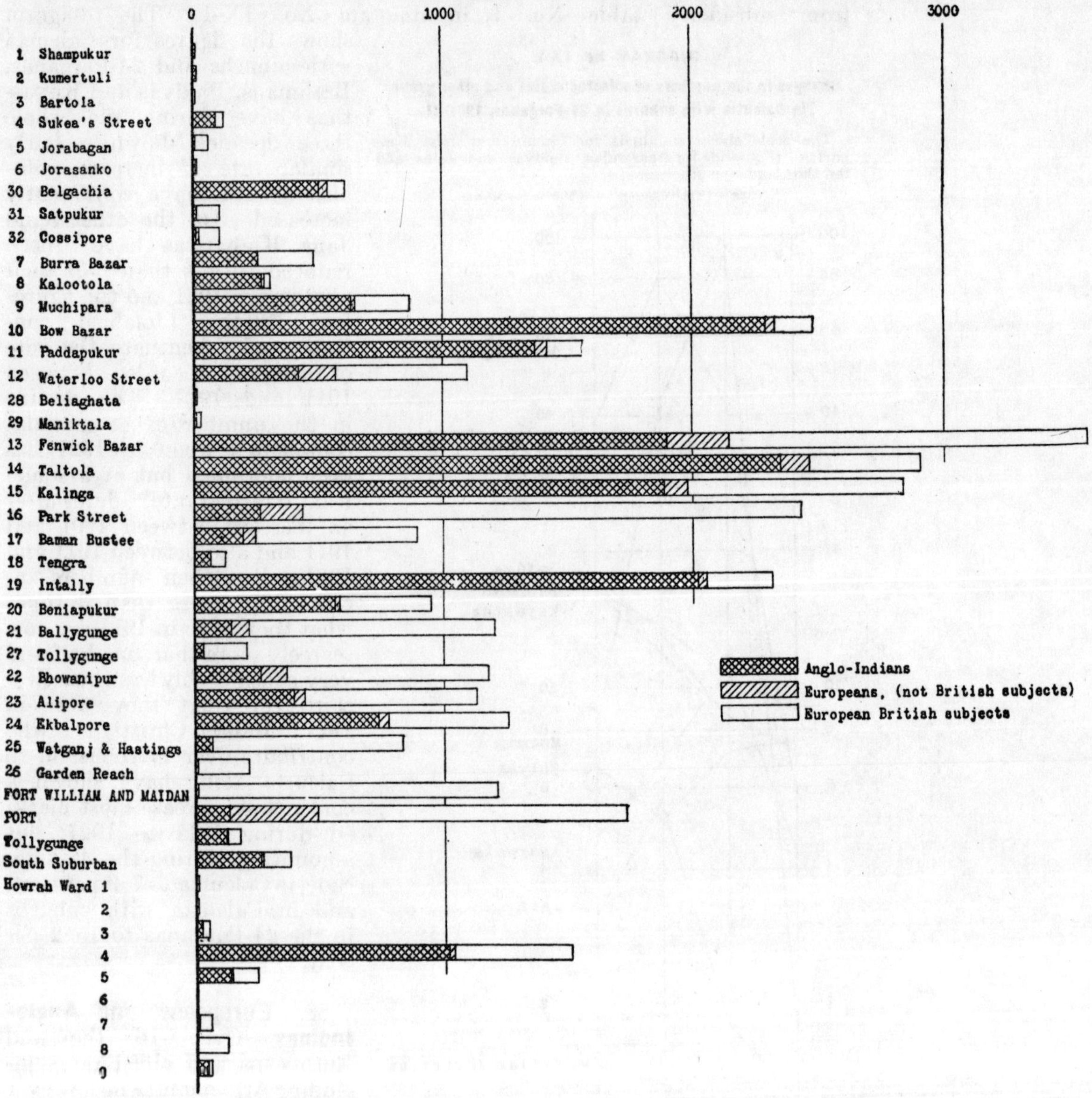

Their numbers have in general increased, but there is a decrease in municipal district No. II particularly in Kalootola and Waterloo Street wards. British subjects number over 13 thousand in Calcutta itself and over 14 thousand in Calcutta with the 24-Parganas. They are mainly English, but small numbers in each case (considerably less than in 1921) were returned as Scotch, Irish and Welsh, and it is possible that amongst the 846 persons who returned themselves as Europeans without specifying nationality some proportion are also British subjects born in Great Britian and Ireland. Over 2 thousand inhabitants of Calcutta are Europeans other than British subjects or belong to cognate races such as Americans, the French, Italian, Portuguese, Armenian and German nations; each contribute more than 100 to the population of Calcutta. Germans and Italians number more now than in 1921 and the Americans exactly the same as then, but there has been a decrease in the numbers of the other nationalities. Armenians, who numbered 987 in Calcutta with its suburbs in 1921, now number 738 and are less numerous than they have been at any time since 1901.

SUBSIDIARY TABLE I

SUBSIDIARY TABLE I.—Variations in

	Caste, tribe, race, etc.	Calcutta with suburbs in 24-Parganas. Actual numbers recorded at the census.				Variation per cent., Increase +, Decrease −.			
		1931.	1921.	1911.	1901.	1921-31.	1911-21.	1901-11.	1901-31.
	1	2	3	4	5	6	7	8	9
	A—ASIATIC RACES.								
1	Agarwala ..	4,698	6,948	10,916	4,383	− 32·4	− 36·4	+ 149·1	+ 7·2
2	Aguri ..	701	244	1,744	2,093	+ 187·3	− 86·0	− 16·7	− 66·5
3	Armenian ..	738	987	832	792	− 25·2	+ 18·6	+ 5·1	− 6·8
4	Bagdi ..	6,814	9,086	9,086	11,076	− 25·0	..	− 18·0	− 38·5
5	Baidya ..	17,957	13,417	8,693	7,290	+ 33·8	+ 54·3	+ 19·2	+ 146·3
6	Baishnab ..	15,328	17,016	16,997	17,942	− 9·9	+ 0·1	− 5·3	− 14·6
7	Barui ..	1,859	1,935	2,043	1,906	− 3·9	− 5·3	+ 7·2	− 2·5
8	Bhuiya ..	1,526	2,641	2,820	1,022	− 42·2	− 6·3	+ 175·9	+ 49·3
9	Brahman ..	167,631	136,930	107,141	88,610	+ 22·4	+ 27·8	+ 20·9	+ 89·2
10	Brahmo ..	1,554	1,785	1,560	1,812	− 12·9	+ 14·4	− 13·9	− 14·2
11	Chamar ..	25,549	29,657	33,808	29,610	− 13·9	− 12·3	+ 14·2	− 13·7
12	Chasadhoba ..	146	140	1,746	683	+ 4·3	− 92·0	+ 155·6	− 78·6
13	Chinese ..	3,005	3,542	2,560	1,640	− 15·2	+ 38·4	+ 56·1	+ 83·2
14	Dhobi ..	11,886	11,221	10,981	11,190	+ 5·9	+ 2·2	− 1·9	+ 6·2
15	Dom ..	3,837	4,444	6,024	10,546	− 13·7	− 26·3	− 42·9	− 63·6
16	Dosadh ..	6,562	7,324	10,716	8,740	− 10·4	− 31·7	+ 22·6	− 24·9
17	Gandhabanik ..	10,441	19,767	7,636	10,070	− 47·2	+ 158·9	− 24·2	+ 3·7
18	Goala ..	33,702	31,437	31,480	26,284	+ 7·2	− 0·1	+ 19·8	+ 28·2
19	Halwai ..	1,035	1,482	1,824	1,753	− 30·2	− 18·8	+ 4·1	− 41·0
20	Hari ..	1,099	1,152	3,352	1,668	− 4·6	− 65·6	+ 101·0	− 34·1
21	Indian Christian ..	14,637	13,570	11,226	10,047	+ 7·9	+ 20·9	+ 11·7	+ 45·7
22	Jain (caste unspecified) ..	3,194	5,670	1,813	1,241	− 43·7	+ 212·8	+ 46·1	+ 157·4
23	Jalia Kaibartta (Adi Kaibartta) ..	3,933	8,069	4,218	584	− 51·3	+ 91·3	+ 622·3	+ 573·5
24	Japanese ..	577	385	92	66	+ 49·9	+ 318·5	+ 39·4	+ 774·2
25	Jew ..	1,830	1,820	1,920	1,889	+ 0·5	− 5·2	+ 1·6	− 3·1
26	Jogi or Jugi ..	4,232	4,340	2,895	3,581	− 2·5	+ 49·9	− 19·2	+ 18·2
27	Kahar and Rawani Kahar ..	17,498	20,738	24,006	20,281	− 15·6	− 13·6	+ 18·4	− 13·7
28	Koiri ..	3,048	3,918	5,222	4,387	− 22·2	− 25·0	+ 19·0	− 30·5
29	Kalu ..	2,146	4,120	4,178	4,721	− 47·9	− 1·4	− 11·5	− 54·5
30	Kamar ..	8,921	8,964	8,140	7,587	− 0·5	+ 10·1	+ 7·3	+ 17·6
31	Kandu ..	987	1,546	2,455	2,167	− 36·2	− 37·0	+ 13·3	− 54·5
32	Kansari ..	4,693	4,205	4,533	3,939	+ 11·6	− 7·2	+ 15·1	+ 19·1
33	Kaora ..	4,833	5,512	4,531	3,705	− 12·3	+ 21·7	+ 22·3	+ 30·4
34	Kayastha ..	165,101	120,722	86,644	71,757	+ 36·8	+ 39·3	+ 20·7	+ 130·1
35	Khandait ..	7,942	13,208	11,409	6,306	− 39·9	+ 15·8	+ 80·9	+ 25·9
36	Khetri ..	1,025	8,646	3,914	5,563	− 88·1	+ 120·9	− 29·6	− 81·6
37	Kumhar ..	4,456	4,624	3,430	2,439	− 3·6	+ 34·8	+ 40·6	+ 82·7
38	Kurmi ..	9,999	8,479	9,429	7,143	+ 17·9	− 10·1	+ 32·0	+ 40·0
39	Lalbegi ..	2,459	1,615	1,804	3,125	+ 52·3	− 10·5	− 42·3	− 21·3
40	Lohar ..	567	1,143	1,429	674	− 50·4	− 20·0	+ 112·0	− 15·9
41	Mahasri ..	130	1,827	2,637	1,004	− 92·9	− 30·7	+ 162·6	− 87·0
42	Mahishya ..	56,454	43,145	31,961	3,359	+ 30·8	+ 35·0	+ 851·4	+ 1,580·7
43	Mali ..	1,510	1,893	1,719	1,758	− 20·2	+ 10·1	− 2·2	− 14·1
44	Mallah ..	2,325	2,094	2,927	3,883	+ 11·0	− 28·5	− 24·6	− 40·1
45	Moyra ..	8,744	7,422	6,644	7,331	+ 17·8	+ 11·7	− 9·4	+ 19·3
46	Muchi ..	13,512	15,003	12,703	9,425	− 9·9	+ 18·1	+ 34·8	+ 43·4
47	Mumin (Jolaha)—Muslim ..	791	4,255	8,864	166	− 81·4	− 52·0	+ 5,239·8	+ 376·5
48	Namasudra ..	4,103	2,965	2,084	1,782	+ 38·4	+ 42·3	+ 16·9	+ 130·2
49	Napit ..	13,068	12,678	12,630	13,465	+ 3·1	+ 0·4	− 6·2	− 2·9
50	Nuniya ..	2,526	2,060	1,969	1,370	+ 22·6	+ 4·6	+ 43·7	+ 84·4
51	Pasi ..	3,041	2,842	2,705	2,134	+ 7·0	+ 5·1	+ 26·8	+ 42·5
52	Pathan—Muslim ..	14,683	14,469	21,025	14,531	+ 1·5	− 31·2	+ 44·7	+ 1·0
53	Pod ..	5,630	5,704	2,379	2,490	− 1·3	+ 139·7	− 4·5	+ 126·1
54	Rajput ..	31,455	13,052	14,731	9,414	+ 141·0	− 11·4	+ 56·5	+ 234·1
55	Rajwar ..	905	1,236	1,083	529	− 26·8	+ 14·1	+ 104·7	+ 71·1
56	Sadgop ..	14,523	14,163	13,924	13,649	+ 2·5	+ 1·7	+ 2·0	+ 6·4
57	Sayyad—Muslim ..	6,798	5,100	7,254	7,586	+ 33·3	− 29·7	− 4·4	− 10·4
58	Shaha ..	11,748	8,054	2,399 }	7,610 {	+ 45·9	+ 235·7 }	− 4·8	+ 85·3
	Sunri ..	2,351.	2,710	4,848 }		− 13·2	− 44·1 }		
59	Shekh—Muslim ..	285,948	247,018	257,170	262,087	+ 15·8	− 3·9	− 1·9	+ 9·1
60	Sikh (caste unspecified) ..	4,713	1,484	980	162	+ 217·6	+ 51·4	+ 504·9	+ 2,809·3
61	Sonar ..	2,492	4,236	4,865	4,691	− 41·2	− 12·9	+ 3·7	− 46·9
62	Subarnabanik ..	34,022	29,444	28,780	26,526	+ 15·5	+ 2·3	+ 8·5	+ 28·3
63	Sutradhar ..	5,522	6,105	6,461	6,191	− 9·5	− 5·5	+ 4·4	− 10·8
64	Tambuli ..	3,299	2,882	3,136	5,265	+ 14·5	− 8·1	− 40·4	− 37·3
65	Tanti and Tatwa ..	20,422	23,314	21,751	22,482	− 12·4	+ 7·2	− 3·3	− 9·2
66	Teli and Tili ..	[illegible]	[illegible]	[illegible]	16,378	[illegible]	[illegible] 3·9	+ 26·1	+ 41·7
67	Tiyar ..	801	1,220	1,757	1,406	− 34·3	− 30·6	+ 25·0	− 43·0
	B—NON-ASIATIC RACES.								
	(i) British subjects.								
68	Anglo-Indian ..	17,251	14,136	14,469	14,663	+ 22·0	− 2·3	− 1·3	+ 17·7
69	Australian ..	31	134	109	4	− 76·9	+ 22·9	+ 2,625·0	+ 675·0
70	Canadian ..	7	101	21	11	− 93·1	+ 381·0	+ 90·9	− 36·4
71	English ..	11,909	9,364	9,423	8,490	+ 27·2	− 0·6	+ 11·0	+ 40·3
72	Irish ..	488	614	996	1,648	− 20·5	− 38·4	− 39·6	− 70·4
73	Maltese ..	1	1	2	2	..	− 50·0	..	− 50·0
74	New Zealander ..	1	20	2	3	− 95·0	+ 900·0	− 33·3	− 66·7
75	Scotch ..	894	1,091	1,668	1,179	− 18·1	− 34·6	+ 41·5	− 24·2
76	South African ..	16	12	8	..	+ 33·3	+ 50·0	..	..
77	Welsh ..	66	139	83	76	− 52·5	+ 67·5	+ 9·2	− 13·2
	(ii) Other than British subjects.								
78	American ..	173	177	111	205	− 2·3	+ 59·5	− 45·9	− 15·6
79	Austrian ..	7	7	69	145	..	− 89·9	− 52·4	− 95·2
80	Belgian ..	32	12	39	103	+ 166·7	− 69·2	− 62·1	− 68·9
81	Dane ..	5	2	19	20	+ 150·0	− 89·5	− 5·0	− 75·0
82	Dutch ..	96	43	62	37	+ 123·3	− 30·6	+ 67·6	+ 159·5
83	French ..	212	214	215	198	− 0·9	− 0·5	+ 8·6	+ 7·1
84	German ..	103	16	282	222	+ 543·7	− 94·3	+ 27·0	− 53·6
85	Greek ..	72	114	131	122	− 36·8	− 13·0	+ 7·4	− 41·0
86	Italian ..	190	78	106	61	+ 143·5	− 26·4	+ 73·8	+ 211·5
87	Norwegian ..	17	10	9	49	+ 70·0	+ 11·1	− 81·6	− 65·3
88	Portuguese ..	175	278	254	178	− 37·0	+ 9·4	+ 42·7	− 1·7
89	Russian ..	20	33	36	67	− 39·4	− 8·3	− 46·3	− 70·1
90	Spaniard ..	46	28	23	35	+ 64·3	+ 21·7	− 34·3	+ 31·4
91	Swede ..	36	23	22	71	+ 56·5	+ 4·5	− 69·0	− 49·3
92	Swiss ..	22	12	39	9	+ 83·3	− 69·2	+ 333·3	+ 144·4

selected castes, tribes, etc., 1901-31.

Calcutta.								Howrah.		
Actual numbers recorded at the census.				Variation per cent., Increase+, Decrease−.				Actual numbers recorded at the census.		Variation per cent., Increase +, Decrease −.
1931.	1921.	1911.	1901.	1921-31.	1911-21.	1901-11.	1901-31.	1931.	1921.	1921-31.
10	11	12	13	14	15	16	17	18	19	20
4,694	6,826	10,729	4,303	− 31·2	− 36·4	+ 149·3	+ 9·1	551	490	+ 12·4
699	235	1,671	2,012	+ 197·4	− 85·9	− 16·9	− 65·3	88	129	− 31·8
738	966	815	777	− 23·6	+ 18·5	+ 4·9	− 5·0	8	19	− 57·9
5,365	3,628	4,866	7,182	+ 47·9	− 25·4	− 32·2	− 25·3	2,112	2,735	− 22·8
17,498	12,633	8,418	6,909	+ 38·5	+ 50·1	+ 21·8	+ 153·3	1,055	684	+ 54·2
13,895	10,429	12,793	14,079	+ 33·2	− 18·5	− 9·1	− 1·3	2,962	3,171	− 6·6
1,817	1,555	1,877	1,774	+ 16·8	− 17·2	+ 5·8	+ 2·4	1,081	1,000	+ 8·1
1,439	1,976	2,126	1,022	− 27·2	− 7·1	+ 108·0	+ 40·8	991	317	+ 212·6
159,104	120,270	99,301	82,539	+ 32·3	+ 21·1	+ 20·3	+ 92·8	29,652	22,295	+ 33·0
1,554	1,759	1,529	1,799	− 11·7	+ 15·0	− 15·0	− 13·6	..	36	..
24,867	20,259	27,073	24,586	+ 22·7	− 25·2	+ 10·1	+ 1·1	6,896	5,168	+ 33·4
142	65	1,634	563	+ 118·5	− 96·0	+ 190·2	− 74·8	206	340	− 39·4
2,849	3,479	2,437	1,577	− 18·1	+ 42·8	+ 54·5	+ 80·7	41	3	+ 1,266·7
11,252	8,594	9,217	9,826	+ 30·9	− 6·8	− 6·2	+ 14·5	2,301	2,382	− 3·4
3,757	3,928	5,490	9,625	− 4·4	− 28·5	− 43·0	− 61·0	755	745	+ 1·3
6,324	5,894	8,803	7,787	+ 7·3	− 33·0	+ 13·0	− 18·8	1,919	1,733	+ 10·7
10,239	18,493	7,184	9,468	− 44·6	+ 157·4	− 24·1	+ 8·1	1,855	3,366	− 44·9
30,770	24,121	26,556	22,945	+ 27·6	− 9·2	+ 15·7	+ 34·1	6,709	5,579	+ 20·3
1,010	1,269	1,651	1,582	− 20·4	− 23·1	+ 4·4	− 36·2	141	132	+ 6·8
1,073	992	2,999	1,581	+ 8·2	− 66·9	+ 89·7	− 32·1	337	1,695	− 80·1
14,280	12,394	10,901	9,908	+ 15·2	+ 13·7	+ 10·0	+ 44·1	476	781	− 39·1
3,185	5,524	1,797	1,241	− 42·3	+ 207·4	+ 44·8	+ 156·6	57	8	+ 612·5
3,756	6,423	3,476	476	− 41·5	+ 84·8	+ 630·3	+ 689·1	4,052	8,112	− 50·0
577	384	92	66	+ 50·3	+ 317·4	+ 39·4	+ 774·2	2	2	..
1,829	1,820	1,919	1,889	+ 0·5	− 5·2	+ 1·6	− 3·2	..	..	..
3,297	2,802	2,430	2,923	+ 17·7	+ 15·3	− 16·9	− 12·8	736	636	+ 15·7
17,296	18,906	22,085	19,253	− 8·5	− 14·4	+ 14·7	− 10·2	3,653	3,670	− 0·5
2,861	2,517	3,905	3,552	+ 13·7	− 35·5	+ 9·9	− 19·5	985	1,083	− 9·1
1,758	2,871	3,764	4,314	− 38·8	− 23·7	− 12·7	− 59·2	894	802	+ 11·5
8,468	7,603	7,283	7,103	+ 11·4	+ 4·4	+ 2·5	+ 19·2	1,506	1,494	+ 0·8
960	1,149	1,898	1,870	− 16·4	− 39·5	+ 1·5	− 48·7	567	801	− 29·2
4,692	4,087	4,449	3,909	+ 14·8	− 8·1	+ 13·8	+ 20·0	131	187	− 29·9
2,907	3,449	4,177	3,302	− 15·7	− 17·4	+ 26·5	− 12·0	908	814	+ 11·5
160,630	106,088	79,244	67,140	+ 51·4	+ 33·9	+ 18·0	+ 139·2	17,473	14,686	+ 19·0
7,081	9,940	9,785	5,834	− 28·8	+ 1·6	+ 67·7	+ 21·4	1,781	2,177	− 18·2
1,025	7,710	3,818	5,259	− 86·7	+ 101·9	− 27·4	− 81·5	23	842	− 97·3
3,177	1,992	2,403	2,127	+ 59·5	− 17·1	+ 13·0	+ 49·4	554	612	− 9·5
9,628	7,288	8,395	6,320	+ 32·1	− 13·2	+ 32·8	+ 52·4	2,967	2,315	+ 28·2
2,433	1,596	1,757	3,048	+ 52·4	− 9·2	− 42·4	− 20·2	112	8	+ 1,300·0
559	898	1,192	625	− 37·8	− 24·7	+ 90·7	− 10·6	229	357	− 35·9
130	1,749	2,605	1,004	− 92·6	− 32·9	+ 159·5	− 87·0	8	5	+ 60·0
46,215	24,472	23,921	2,123	+ 88·8	+ 2·3	+ 1,026·8	+ 2,076·9	19,984	13,882	+ 44·0
1,437	1,554	1,581	1,574	− 7·5	− 1·7	+ 0·4	− 8·7	752	371	+ 102·7
2,322	1,928	2,766	3,802	+ 20·4	− 30·3	− 27·2	− 38·9	614	825	− 25·6
8,484	6,230	5,948	6,758	+ 36·2	+ 4·7	− 12·0	+ 25·5	1,244	1,193	+ 4·3
12,943	12,271	10,516	8,477	+ 5·5	+ 16·7	+ 24·1	+ 52·7	1,540	2,049	− 24·8
788	3,302	7,145	166	− 76·1	− 53·8	+ 4,204·2	+ 374·7	3,115	1,251	+ 149·0
3,808	1,804	1,141	1,313	+ 111·1	+ 58·1	− 13·1	+ 190·0	176	181	− 2·8
12,208	9,932	11,120	12,162	+ 22·9	− 10·7	− 8·6	+ 0·4	2,969	2,558	+ 16·1
2,208	1,150	1,607	1,180	+ 92·0	− 28·4	+ 36·2	+ 87·1	470	342	+ 37·4
2,451	1,311	1,743	1,542	+ 87·0	− 24·8	+ 13·0	+ 58·9	1,060	1,100	+ 14·2
14,683	10,857	17,160	12,555	+ 35·2	− 36·7	+ 36·7	+ 16·9	..	3,482	..
2,015	1,415	1,455	2,187	+ 42·4	− 2·7	− 33·5	− 7·9	759	602	+ 26·1
30,673	11,145	12,905	8,408	+ 175·2	− 13·6	+ 53·5	+ 264·8	5,129	3,157	+ 62·5
868	1,145	980	517	− 24·2	+ 16·8	+ 89·6	+ 67·9	81	43	+ 88·4
13,851	10,761	10,835	11,757	+ 28·7	− 0·7	− 7·8	+ 17·8	2,872	2,658	+ 8·1
6,600	3,981	6,175	6,798	+ 65·8	− 35·5	− 9·2	− 2·9	495	583	− 15·1
{ 11,673	7,432	2,169 }	7,024 {	+ 57·1	+ 242·6 }	− 10·2	+ 98·0	{ 665	124	+ 436·3
2,236	2,120	4,140		+ 5·5	− 48·8			494	567	− 12·9
285,948	180,632	207,275	228,741	+ 58·3	− 12·9	− 9·4	+ 25·0	..	37,360	..
4,705	1,372	932	153	+ 242·9	+ 47·2	+ 509·2	+ 2,975·2	164	1	+ 16,300·0
2,349	3,604	4,385	4,194	− 34·8	− 17·8	+ 4·6	− 44·0	625	804	− 22·3
33,745	28,593	28,205	25,190	+ 18·0	+ 1·4	+ 12·0	+ 34·0	2,494	2,059	+ 21·1
5,477	5,048	5,516	5,656	+ 8·5	− 8·5	− 2·5	− 3·2	889	837	+ 6·2
8,264	2,603	2,904	4,932	+ 25·4	− 10·4	− 41·1	− 33·8	306	378	− 19·0
20,170	19,285	19,424	20,692	+ 4·0	− 0·7	− 6·1	− 2·5	3,400	4,108	− 17·2
22,413	17,865	18,466	14,825	+ 25·5	− 3·3	+ 24·6	+ 51·2	8,432	6,651	+ 26·8
275	272	798	954	+ 1·1	− 65·9	− 16·4	− 71·2	243	457	− 46·8
16,863	13,621	14,177	14,482	+ 23·8	− 3·9	− 2·1	+ 16·4	1,218	750	+ 62·4
31	130	107	..	− 76·2	+ 21·5	..	..	1	8	− 87·5
7	86	21	11	− 91·9	+ 309·5	+ 90·9	− 36·4	1	..	..
11,750	9,086	9,215	8,330	+ 29·3	− 1·4	+ 10·6	+ 41·1	605	447	+ 35·3
488	598	990	1,629	− 18·4	− 39·6	− 39·2	− 70·0	44	42	+ 4·8
1	1	2	2	..	50·0	..	− 50·0	..	..	..
1	20	1	3	− 95·0	+ 1,900·0	− 66·7	− 66·7	..	..	..
894	997	1,584	1,127	− 10·3	− 37·1	+ 40·6	− 20·7	114	189	− 39·7
16	12	8	..	+ 33·3	+ 50·0	..	..	..	..	..
66	138	82	73	− 52·2	+ 68·3	+ 12·3	− 9·6	..	7	..
173	173	111	205	..	+ 55·9	− 45·9	− 15·6	18	15	+ 20·0
7	1	69	144	+ 600·0	− 98·5	− 52·1	− 95·1	..	..	..
32	12	39	103	+ 166·7	− 69·2	− 62·1	− 68·9	..	4	..
5	2	19	20	+ 150·0	− 89·5	− 5·0	− 75·0	..	..	..
92	39	62	37	+ 135·9	− 37·1	+ 67·6	+ 148·6	2	7	− 71·4
205	207	212	198	− 1·0	− 2·4	+ 7·1	+ 3·5	10	19	− 47·1
103	16	280	220	+ 543·7	− 94·3	+ 27·3	− 53·2	10	1	+ 900·0
72	91	115	108	− 20·9	− 20·9	+ 6·5	− 33·3	..	1	..
190	78	106	61	+ 143·5	− 26·4	+ 73·8	+ 211·5	3	6	− 50·0
17	10	9	49	+ 70·0	+ 11·1	− 81·6	− 65·3	1	1	..
175	276	254	178	− 36·6	+ 8·7	+ 42·7	− 1·7	1	..	..
20	29	36	67	− 31·0	− 19·4	− 46·3	− 70·1	4	..	..
46	28	23	35	+ 64·3	+ 21·7	− 34·3	+ 31·4	..	..	..
36	16	22	71	+ 125·0	− 27·3	− 69·0	− 49·3	..	..	..
22	12	39	9	+ 83·3	− 69·2	+ 333·3	+ 144·4	..	..	..

SUBSIDIARY TABLE II.—Variation in the numbers of Europeans and Anglo-Indians, 1911-31.

Ward, etc.	A.—Europeans and allied races (including Armenians). Actual number recorded at the census of			Variation, per cent., increase +, decrease −.			B.—Anglo-Indians. Actual number recorded at the census of			Variation, per cent., increase +, decrease −.		
	1931.	1921.	1911.	1921-31.	1911-21.	1911-31.	1931.	1921.	1911.	1921-31.	1911-21.	1911-31.
1	2	3	4	5	6	7	8	9	10	11	12	13
CALCUTTA WITH SUBURBS AND HOWRAH ..	**16,980**	**14,198**	*	+ **20**	*	*	**18,469**	**14,886**	*	+ **24**	*	*
CALCUTTA WITH SUBURBS IN 24-PARGANAS ..	**16,157**	**13,381**	*	+ **21**	*	*	**17,251**	**14,136**	*	+ **22**	*	*
Calcutta ..	**15,987**	**13,328**	**14,640**	+ **20**	− **9**	+ **9**	**16,863**	**14,128**	**14,469**	+ **19**	− **2**	+ **17**
MUNICIPAL AREA ..	**13,170**	**11,758**	**12,130**	+ **12**	− **3**	+ **9**	**16,728**	**14,106**	**14,342**	+ **19**	− **2**	+ **17**
District No. I ..	**393**	**373**	**308**	+ **5**	+ **21**	+ **28**	**611**	**270**	**402**	+ **126**	− **33**	+ **52**
Ward No. 1 Shampukur ..	1	10	..	− 90	..	..	4	3	2	+ 33	+ 50	+ 100
Ward No. 2 Kumartuli ..	2	6	8	− 67	− 25	− 75	8	1	8	+ 700	− 87	..
Ward No. 3 Bartola ..	6	16	7	− 62	+ 129	− 14	1	8	11	− 87	− 27	− 91
Ward No. 4 Sukea's Street ..	30	32	62	− 6	− 48	− 52	76	19	125	+ 300	− 85	− 39
Ward No. 5 Jorabagan ..	56	37	32	+ 51	+ 16	+ 75	3	11	16	− 73	− 31	− 81
Ward No. 6 Jorasanko ..	5	53	3	− 91	+ 1,667	+ 67	6	..	..	..	..	..
Ward No. 30 Belgachia ..	103						500					
Ward No. 31 Satpukur ..	92	219	196	+ 34	+ 12	+ 49	8	228	240	+ 125	− 5	+ 114
Ward No. 32 Cossipore ..	98						5					
District No. II ..	**1,589**	**2,277**	**3,062**	− **30**	− **26**	− **48**	**5,246**	**5,864**	**6,920**	− **11**	− **15**	− **24**
Ward No. 7 Burra Bazar ..	223	150	181	+ 49	− 17	+ 23	254	51	248	+ 398	− 79	+ 2
Ward No. 8 Kalootola ..	35	304	230	− 88	+ 32	− 85	269	555	1,530	− 52	− 64	− 82
Ward No. 9 Muchipara ..	240	360	266	− 33	+ 35	− 10	629	535	734	+ 18	− 27	− 14
Ward No. 10 Bow Bazar ..	185	253	765	− 27	− 67	− 76	2,296	3,412	2,987	− 33	+ 14	− 23
Ward No. 11 Paddapukur ..	196	211	452	− 7	− 53	− 57	1,370	704	1,190	+ 95	− 41	+ 15
Ward No. 12 Waterloo Street ..	686	924	1,131	− 26	− 18	− 39	415	346	201	+ 20	+ 72	+ 106
Ward No. 28 Beliaghata ..	5	75	37	− 68	+ 103	− 35	5	261	30	− 95	+ 770	− 57
Ward No. 29 Maniktala ..	19						8					
District No. III ..	**7,862**	**6,865**	**6,669**	+ **14**	+ **3**	+ **18**	**9,370**	**6,852**	**6,006**	+ **37**	+ **14**	+ **56**
Ward No. 13 Fenwick Bazar ..	1,670	1,498	1,364	+ 11	+ 10	+ 22	1,901	1,207	1,271	+ 57	− 5	+ 50
Ward No. 14 Taltola ..	557	544	734	+ 2	− 26	− 24	2,349	1,902	1,760	+ 23	+ 8	+ 33
Ward No. 15 Kalinga ..	947	1,249	1,336	− 24	− 7	− 29	1,883	880	904	+ 114	− 3	+ 108
Ward No. 16 Park Street ..	2,167	1,682	1,305	+ 29	+ 29	+ 66	259	272	100	− 5	+ 172	+ 159
Ward No. 17 Baman Bustee ..	712	704	869	+ 1	− 19	− 18	192	313	174	− 39	+ 80	+ 10
Ward No. 18 Tengra ..	61						61					
Ward No. 19 Intally ..	291	174	329	+ 67	− 47	− 12	2,020	1,692	1,333	+ 19	+ 27	+ 52
Ward No. 20 Beniapukur ..	394	244	203	+ 61	+ 20	+ 94	561	472	380	+ 19	+ 24	+ 48
Ward No. 21 Ballygunge ..	1,063	770	529	+ 38	+ 46	+ 101	144	114	84	+ 26	+ 36	+ 71
District No. IV ..	**3,326**	**2,243**	**2,091**	+ **48**	+ **7**	+ **59**	**1,501**	**1,120**	**1,014**	+ **34**	+ **10**	+ **48**
Ward No. 27 Tollygunge ..	170	810	738	+ 13	+ 10	+ 24	35	210	243	+ 24	− 14	+ 7
Ward No. 22 Bhawanipur ..	916						261					
Ward No. 23 Alipore ..	740	465	291	+ 59	+ 60	+ 154	391	210	37	+ 86	+ 468	+ 957
Ward No. 24 Ekbalpore ..	526	370	326	+ 42	+ 13	+ 61	740	279	366	+ 165	− 24	+ 102
Ward No. 25 Watganj & Hastings ..	773	471	626	+ 64	− 25	+ 23	66	403	346	− 84	+ 16	− 81
Ward No. 26 Garden Reach ..	201	127	110	+ 58	+ 15	+ 83	8	18	22	− 56	− 18	− 64
FORT WILLIAM AND MAIDAN ..	**1,217**	**877**	**1,457**	+ **39**	− **40**	− **16**	**1**	**7**	**49**	− **86**	− **86**	− **98**
PORT ..	**1,600**	**693**	**1,053**	+ **131**	− **34**	+ **52**	**134**	**15**	**78**	+ **793**	− **81**	+ **72**
Suburbs in 24-Parganas ..	**170**	**53**	*	+ **221**	*	*	**388**	**8**	*	+ **4,750**	*	*
Tollygunge ..	53	49	*	+ 8	*	*	123	6	*	+ 1,950	*	*
South Suburban Municipality ..	117	4	*	+ 2,825	*	*	265	2	*	+ 13,150	*	*
HOWRAH ..	**823**	**817**	*	+ **1**	*	*	**1,218**	**750**	*	+ **62**	*	*

*Not available.

N.B.—In 1921 and 1911 Hastings was a separate ward, but during this census Hastings has been amalgamated with Watganj forming a single ward Hastings-Watganj.

The figures for Hastings have been shown against Hastings-Watganj.

In previous census years Ballygunge-Tollygunge was a combined ward, but in the present census they have been separated: previous figures for Ballygunge-Tollygunge have been shown against Ballygunge.

PART II

TABLES

DETAILED TABLE OF CONTENTS.

PART II.

TABLES.

IMPERIAL TABLE I.—Area, occupied houses, population and persons per acre.

This table corresponding to imperial table I of 1921 shows for Calcutta by municipal districts and wards, Fort William and the Maidan, Calcutta Port and Canals, suburbs of Calcutta in 24-Parganas district and Howrah City the area in acres with the number of occupied houses, population and number of persons per acre. The addition of figures for municipal districts in Calcutta City, with a consequent irregularity in the presentation of wards in the order of their serial numbers, is an innovation intended to make the tables of more use in the actual administration of the city.

2. For the area of localities in this table no more recent or more reliable figures are known than those which have previously appeared in the census reports and which, for the wards of Calcutta Municipality, are those ascertained at a plane-table survey conducted in connection with the census of 1901. The figures given in 1921 have consequently been taken as the basis on which those now shown are calculated. By the Calcutta Municipal Act (Bengal Act III of 1923) the municipalities of Cossipore-Chitpore (2,093 acres), Maniktala (2,182 acres) and Garden Reach (2,752 acres) were added to the municipal limits and in 1924 the Ballygunge Pumping Station and High Level Outfall Sewer (about 160 acres) and some 960 acres of South Suburban Municipality fell under the Calcutta Corporation. The total area thus added to the Calcutta Municipality is 8,147 acres and by this amount all figures in which the Calcutta Municipality is included exceed the figures given for the same areas in 1921. Wards 1—17 and 22—25 remain as in 1921 though ward 17 is known now as Baman Bustee instead of Victoria Terrace, but wards 18—21 have suffered changes of boundary and the areas newly absorbed in and after 1923 have been differently distributed. Cossipore-Chitpore Municipality now forms wards 30, 31 and 32 : wards 28 and 29 cover what was the municipality of Maniktala : wards 19 (Entally) and 20 (Beniapukur) of 1921 are now wards 18, 19 and 20 : and the double ward Ballygunge-Tollygunge (No. 21 of 1921) with the addition of the pumping station is now divided into wards 21 and 27. Finally Garden Reach ward (No. 26) comprises not only the old Garden Reach Municipality but also the area of 960 acres taken from the South Suburban Municipality. Ward 26, therefore, is shown to be of the same area as its two component parts together, but in the other cases no accurate figures exist. Those firnished by the municipal authorities did not agree with the totals adopted for the reason already stated and were based on nothing more reliable than planimetre calculations from a small scale map : and in reaching the figures of area given in this table for wards 18—21 and 27—32 the figures adopted from the report of 1921 have been divided in the same proportion as the figures of area for the same wards calculated by the corporation. The statement below shows how this distribution has been effected : areas are shown in acres :—

No. and name of ward.	Area in 1921.	Area as given by the Calcutta Corporation.	Area adopted in Imperial table I.
1	2	3	4
18	1,111	919	953
19		526	546
20		429	444
21	2,067	810	838
27		1,344	1,389
28	2,182	836	839
29		1,335	1,343
30	2,093	548	559
31		734	750
32		765	784

3. No figures have been forthcoming for the area of individual wards in Howrah. The population of each ward by sexes is shown in columns 2—4 of imperial table XVI, *infra*.

IMPERIAL TABLE I.—Area, occupied houses, population and persons per acre.

Name of ward, etc.	Area in acres.	Number of occupied houses.	Population.			Number of persons per acre.
			Both sexes.	Males.	Females.	
1	2	3	4	5	6	7
CALCUTTA WITH SUBURBS AND HOWRAH	**46,655**	**281,130**	**1,485,582**	**997,051**	**488,531**	**32**
CALCUTTA WITH SUBURBS IN 24-PARGANAS	**40,191**	**223,162**	**1,260,709**	**851,931**	**408,778**	**31**
Calcutta ..	**28,694**	**210,686**	**1,196,734**	**814,948**	**381,786**	**42**
MUNICIPAL AREA ..	**20,101**	**203,231**	**1,158,044**	**778,559**	**379,485**	**58**
District No. I ..	**3,947**	**60,940**	**380,265**	**244,356**	**135,909**	**96**
Ward No. 1 Shampukur ..	409	9,619	**66,633**	40,571	26,062	163
Ward No. 2 Kumartuli ..	217	6,105	**38,294**	23,968	14,326	176
Ward No. 3 Bartola ..	403	11,305	**67,107**	41,066	26,041	167
Ward No. 4 Sukea's Street ..	320	6,758	**54,101**	35,227	18,874	169
Ward No. 5 Jorabagan ..	243	4,931	**39,355**	28,320	11,035	162
Ward No. 6 Jorasanko ..	262	8,568	**46,116**	29,847	16,269	176
Ward No. 30 Belgachia ..	559	3,958	**22,252**	14,228	8,024	40
Ward No. 31 Satpukur ..	750	4,648	**19,194**	11,934	7,260	26
Ward No. 32 Cossipore ..	784	5,048	**27,213**	19,195	8,018	35
District No. II ..	**3,607**	**54,658**	**287,035**	**204,746**	**82,289**	**80**
Ward No. 7 Burra Bazar ..	217	6,464	**18,690**	16,815	1,875	86
Ward No. 8 Kalootola ..	224	10,154	**48,998**	39,545	9,453	219
Ward No. 9 Muchipara ..	460	10,599	**80,604**	57,880	22,724	175
Ward No. 10 Bow Bazar ..	147	3,723	**21,075**	16,029	5,046	143
Ward No. 11 Paddapukur ..	166	5,243	**35,323**	23,191	12,132	213
Ward No. 12 Waterloo Street ..	211	938	**6,711**	5,860	851	32
Ward No. 28 Beliaghata ..	839	5,927	**33,235**	19,541	13,694	40
Ward No. 29 Maniktala ..	1,343	11,610	**42,399**	25,885	16,514	32
District No. III ..	**3,631**	**44,485**	**219,153**	**151,464**	**67,689**	**60**
Ward No. 13 Fenwick Bazar ..	192	6,419	**30,975**	25,686	5,289	161
Ward No. 14 Taltola ..	198	6,292	**38,427**	27,660	10,767	194
Ward No. 15 Kalinga ..	179	3,763	**14,052**	10,063	3,989	79
Ward No. 16 Park Street ..	153	1,281	**5,438**	4,121	1,317	36
Ward No. 17 Baman Bustee ..	128	464	**2,679**	2,056	623	21
Ward No. 18 Tengra ..	953	2,321	**11,772**	7,444	4,328	12
Ward No. 19 Intally ..	546	10,255	**44,224**	28,125	16,099	81
Ward No. 20 Beniapukur ..	444	8,821	**40,587**	25,648	14,939	91
Ward No. 21 Ballygunge ..	838	4,869	**30,999**	20,661	10,338	37
District No. IV ..	**8,916**	**43,148**	**271,591**	**177,993**	**93,598**	**30**
Ward No. 27 Tollygunge ..	1,389	6,370	**40,730**	24,400	16,330	29
Ward No. 22 Bhawanipur ..	816	10,120	**79,684**	50,564	29,120	98
Ward No. 23 Alipore ..	1,241	4,614	**30,020**	21,350	8,670	24
Ward No. 24 Ekbalpore ..	921	5,762	**32,822**	21,664	11,158	36
Ward No. 25 Watganj and Hastings ..	837	4,624	**32,463**	23,884	8,579	39
Ward No. 26 Garden Reach ..	3,712	11,658	**55,872**	36,131	19,741	15
FORT WILLIAM AND MAIDAN ..	**1,283**	**610**	**3,083**	**2,661**	**422**	**2**
PORT ..	**7,040**	**6,485**	**33,702**	**31,831**	**1,871**	**5**
CANALS ..	**270**	**360**	**1,905**	**1,897**	**8**	**7**
Suburbs in 24-Parganas ..	**11,497**	**12,476**	**63,975**	**36,983**	**26,992**	**6**
Tollygunge ..	3,977	4,864	**24,476**	14,800	9,676	6
South Suburban Municipality ..	7,520	7,612	**39,499**	22,183	17,316	5
HOWRAH ..	**6,464**	**57,968**	**224,873**	**145,120**	**79,753**	**35**

IMPERIAL TABLE II.—Variation in population since 1872.

This table corresponds to imperial table II of 1921 and shows the population at each census since 1872. Figures are given for the same areas as are shown in table I with the following exceptions :—

(*a*) What are now wards 30, 31 and 32 were previously the municipality of Cossipore-Chitpore.

(*b*) What are now wards 28 and 29 were previously the municipality of Maniktala.

(*c*) What are now wards 18, 19 and 20 were previously two wards only, Intally and Beniapukur.

(*d*) What are now wards 21 and 27 were previously the single ward Ballygunge-Tollygunge.

No satisfactory estimate can be framed of the previous population in areas into which these original units have been partitioned. In each of these cases the total population against the area concerned has been shown for years up to and including 1921. The fact that the present wards formed out of the old Ballygunge-Tollygunge ward fall into two districts makes it also impossible to give district totals for districts III and IV.

2. There was an intermediate enumeration of Calcutta in 1876 and figures are given below :—

Name of ward, etc.	Persons recorded in 1876.			Variation (increase +, decrease −).	
	Both sexes.	Males.	Females.	1876 to 1881.	1872 to 1876.
1	2	3	4	5	6
Calcutta	**684,710**	**432,472**	**252,238**	+ **14,472**	− **36,918**
MUNICIPAL AREA	**662,018**	**410,217**	**251,801**	+ **2,818**	− **38,706**
District No. I	**205,302**	**123,726**	**81,576**	..	..
Ward No. 1 Shampukur	27,620	15,200	12,420	+ 891	− 1,228
Ward No. 2 Kumartuli	32,482	20,608	11,874	− 6,800	− 1,542
Ward No. 3 Bartola	28,652	16,194	12,458	+ 283	− 1,271
Ward No. 4 Sukea's Street	24,014	13,918	10,096	+ 391	− 1,022
Ward No. 5 Jorabagan	37,305	24,955	12,350	− 987	− 1,771
Ward No. 6 Jorasanko	34,395	20,301	14,094	− 1,571	− 1,634
Ward No. 30 Belgachia Ward No. 31 Satpukur Ward No. 32 Cossipore	20,834	12,550	8,284	+ 5,460	− 4535
District No. II	**201,468**	**130,880**	**70,588**	..	..
Ward No. 7 Burra Bazar	22,438	17,464	4,974	− 1,669	− 1,065
Ward No. 8 Kalootola	48,502	31,444	17,058	− 1,179	− 2,303
Ward No. 9 Muchipara	41,815	25,445	16,370	+ 1,766	− 1,824
Ward No. 10 Bow Bazar	22,476	15,030	7,446	− 849	− 1,067
Ward No. 11 Paddapukur	19,557	11,448	8,109	+ 959	− 929
Ward No. 12 Waterloo Street	5,445	4,901	544	+ 340	− 259
Ward No. 28 Beliaghata Ward No. 29 Maniktala	41,235	25,148	16,087	+ 6,890	− 12,757
District No. III					
Ward No. 13 Fenwick Bazar	25,573	19,360	6,213	+ 325	− 1,214
Ward No. 14 Taltola	25,883	15,683	10,200	+ 180	− 1,229
Ward No. 15 Kalinga	12,194	7,910	4,284	− 354	− 579
Ward No. 16 Park Street	4,358	3,498	860	+ 610	− 208
Ward No. 17 Baman Bustee	6,269	4,766	1,503	− 144	− 299
Ward No. 18 Tengra Ward No. 19 Intally Ward No. 20 Beniapukur	46,692	27,167	19,525	− 868	− 868
Ward No. 21 Ballygunge **District No. IV** Ward No. 27 Tollygunge	21,876	12,401	9,475	− 1,453	− 1,453
Ward No. 22 Bhowanipur	37,560	21,053	16,507	+ 442	+ 442
Ward No. 23 Alipore	16,429	10,632	5,797	− 2,991	− 2,990
Ward No. 24 Ekbalpore	16,972	9,380	7,592	− 1,103	− 1,102
Ward No. 25 Watganj and Hastings	30,585	17,753	12,832	+ 2,450	+ 2,402
Ward No. 26 Garden Reach	10,857	6,008	4,849	+ 1,599	+ 1,599
FORT WILLIAM AND MAIDAN	**2,612**	**2,292**	**320**	+ **727**	+ **129**
PORT	**17,696**	**17,643**	**53**	+ **10,504**	+ **1,036**
CANALS	**2,384**	**2,320**	**64**	+ **623**	+ **623**

The figures here shown separately for Cossipore-Chitpore and Maniktala (i.e., for wards 30, 31 and 32 and 28 and 29) are estimated from the recorded totals for the 2 wards together. They have been framed on the assumption that (*a*) the ratio borne by females in Cossipore-Chitpore to those in Maniktala which is the same in 1872 and 1881 remained the same in 1876 and (*b*) the corresponding ratios for males changed at a uniform rate between 1872 and 1881. These assumptions yield figures which make the ratio of males to females in each area approximate closely to what it would on the assumption that this ratio also had changed in each area at a uniform rate between 1872 and 1881.

IMPERIAL TABLE II.—Variation in population since 1872.

Name of ward, etc.	Persons. 1931.	1921.	1911.	1901.	1891.	1881.	1872.	Variation (increase +, decrease −). 1921-1931.	1911-1921.	1901-1911.	1891-1901.	1881-1891.	1872-1881.
1	2	3	4	5	6	7	8	9	10	11	12	13	14
CALCUTTA WITH SUBURBS AND HOWRAH ..	**1,485,582**	**1,327,547**	**1,272,279**	**1,145,933**	**932,440**	**829,197**	..	**+ 158,035**	**+ 55,268**	**+ 126,346**	**+ 213,493**	**+ 103,243**	..
CALCUTTA WITH SUBURBS IN 24-PARGANAS	**1,260,709**	**1,132,246**	**1,093,273**	**988,339**	**815,834**	**738,384**	..	**+ 128,463**	**+ 38,973**	**+ 104,934**	**+ 172,505**	**+ 77,450**	..
Calcutta ..	**1,196,734**	**1,077,264**	**1,043,307**	**949,144**	**769,813**	**699,182**	**721,628**	**+ 119,470**	**+ 33,957**	**+ 94,163**	**+ 179,331**	**+ 70,631**	**− 22,446**
MUNICIPAL AREA ..	**1,15[illegible],044**	**1,055,228**	**1,008,741**	**9[illegible]1,599**	**737,503**	**664,636**	**700,724**	**+ 102,816**	**+ 46,487**	**+ 97,142**	**+ 174,096**	**+ 72,867**	**− 36,088**
District No. I—Total ..	**380,265**	**373,868**	**348,664**	**312,099**	**247,018**	**202,969**	**218,305**	**+ 6,397**	**+ 25,204**	**+ 36,565**	**+ 65,081**	**+ 44,049**	**− 15,336**
Ward No. 1 Shampukur ..	6[illegible],633	57,006	53,036	46,887	36,885	28,511	28,848	+ 9,627	+ 3,970	+ 6,149	+ 10,002	+ 8,374	− 337
Ward No. 2 Kumartuli ..	38,294	33,984	33,073	30,155	26,614	25,682	34,024	+ 4,310	+ 911	+ 2,918	+ 3,541	+ 932	− 8,342
Ward No. 3 Bartola ..	67,107	61,183	54,610	50,216	36,431	28,935	29,923	+ 5,924	+ 6,573	+ 4,394	+ 13,785	+ 7,496	− 988
Ward No. 4 Sukea's Street ..	5[illegible],101	55,372	48 112	42,034	34,828	24,405	25,036	− 1,271	+ 7,260	+ 6,078	+ 7,206	+ 10,423	− 631
Ward No. 5 Jorabagan ..	3[illegible],355	52,573	52,114	49,069	39,180	36,318	39,076	− 13,218	+ 459	+ 3,045	+ 9,889	+ 2,862	− 2,758
Ward No. 6 Jorasanko ..	43,116	57,276	59,541	52,988	41,657	32,824	36,029	− 11,160	− 2,265	+ 6,553	+ 11,331	+ 8,833	− 3,205
Ward No. 30 Belgachia ..	22,252												
Ward No. 31 Satpukur ..	1[illegible],194	56,474	48,178	40,750	31,423	26,294	25,369	+ 12,185	+ 8,296	+ 7,428	+ 9,327	+ 5,129	+ 925
Ward No. 32 Cossipore ..	2[illegible],218												
District No. II—Total ..	**28[illegible],035**	**275,365**	**265,982**	**252,661**	**198,421**	**207,726**	**221,672**	**+ 11,670**	**+ 9,383**	**+ 13,321**	**+ 54,240**	**− 9,305**	**− 13,946**
Ward No. 7 Burra Bazar ..	1[illegible],690	32,959	30,495	31,574	20,646	20,769	23,503	− 14,269	+ 2,464	− 1,079	+ 10,928	− 123	− 2,734
Ward No. 8 Kalootola ..	4[illegible],998	38,510	57,094	63,170	50,781	47,323	50,805	+ 10,488	− 18,584	− 6,076	+ 12,389	+ 3,458	− 3,482
Ward No. 9 Muchipara ..	8[illegible],604	69,670	63,362	64,116	49,472	43,581	43,639	+ 10,934	+ 6,308	− 754	+ 14,644	+ 5,891	− 58
Ward No. 10 Bow Bazar ..	2[illegible],075	27,110	25,014	27,052	22,668	21,627	23,543	− 6,035	+ 2,096	− 2,038	+ 4,384	+ 1,041	− 1,916
Ward No. 11 Paddapukur ..	3[illegible],323	32,638	29,966	28,060	20,761	20,516	20,486	+ 2,685	+ 2,672	+ 1,906	+ 7,299	+ 245	− 30
Ward No. 12 Waterloo Street ..	[illegible],711	7,106	6,284	6,302	5,932	5,785	5,704	− 395	+ 822	− 18	+ 370	+ 147	+ 81
Ward No. 28 Beliaghata ..	3[illegible],235	67,372	53,767	32,387	28,161	48,125	53,992	+ 8,262	+ 13,605	+ 21,380	+ 4,226	− 19,964	− 5,867
Ward No. 29 Maniktala ..	4[illegible],399												
District No. III—Total ..	**21[illegible],153**												
Ward No. 13 Fenwick Bazar ..	3[illegible],975	26,111	28,436	31,208	28,366	25,898	26,787	+ 4,864	− 2,325	− 2,772	+ 2,842	+ 2,468	− 889
Ward No. 14 Taltola ..	38,427	31,664	32,112	32,237	29,207	26,063	27,112	+ 6,763	− 448	− 125	+ 3,030	+ 3,144	− 1,049
Ward No. 15 Kalinga ..	14,052	11,747	11,385	16,780	13,218	11,840	12,773	+ 2,305	+ 362	− 5,395	+ 3,562	+ 1,378	− 933
Ward No. 16 Park Street ..	5,438	3,776	5,294	6,110	4,620	4,968	4,566	+ 1,662	− 1,518	− 816	+ 1,490	− 348	+ 402
Ward No. 17 Baman Bustee ..	2,679	3,147	3,125	5,454	4,598	6,125	6,568	− 468	+ 22	− 2,329	+ 856	− 1,527	− 443
Ward No. 18 Tengra ..	11,772												
Ward No. 19 Intaly ..	44,224	83,385	82,953	66,828	56,912	45,824	47,560	+ 13,198	+ 432	+ 16,125	+ 9,916	+ 11,088	− 1,736
Ward No. 20 Beniapukur ..	40,587												
Ward No. 21 Ballygunge ..	30,999												
District No. IV—Total ..	**271,591**	50,854	39,952	27,207	22,331	20,423	23,329	+ 20,875	+ 10,902	+ 12,745	+ 4,376	+ 2,408	− 2,906
Ward No. 27 Tollygunge ..	40,730												
Ward No. 22 Bhowanipur ..	79,684	57,378	54,569	49,641	42,591	38,002	37,118	+ 22,306	+ 2,809	+ 4,928	+ 7,050	+ 4,589	+ 884
Ward No. 23 Alipore ..	30,020	22,184	19,749	17,718	14,804	13,438	19,419	+ 7,836	+ 2,435	+ 2,031	+ 2,914	+ 1,366	− 5,981
Ward No. 24 Ekbalpore ..	32,322	31,420	21,869	21,608	15,340	15,869	18,074	+ 1,402	+ 9,551	+ 261	+ 6,268	− 529	− 2,205
Ward No. 25 Watganj and Hastings ..	32,463	38,762	49,356	43,837	31,653	33,035	28,183	− 6,299	− 10,594	+ 5,519	+ 12,184	− 1,382	+ 4,852
Ward No. 26 Garden Reach ..	55,372	45,567	45,295	28,211	27,924	12,456	9,258	+ 10,305	+ 272	+ 17,084	+ 287	+ 15,468	+ 3,198
FORT WILLIAM AND MAIDAN ..	**3,[illegible]83**	**2,756**	**4,411**	**3,330**	**3,619**	**3,339**	**2,483**	**+ 327**	**− 1,655**	**+ 1,081**	**− 289**	**+ 280**	**+ 856**
PORT ..	**33,[illegible]02**	**18,441**	**26,890**	**29,768**	**26,589**	**28,200**	**16,660**	**+ 15,261**	**− 8,449**	**− 2,878**	**+ 3,179**	**− 1,611**	**+ 11,540**
CANALS ..	**1,[illegible]05**	**839**	**3,265**	**4,447**	**2,102**	**3,007**	**1,761**	**+ 1,066**	**− 2,426**	**− 1,182**	**+ 2,345**	**− 905**	**+ 1,246**
Suburbs in 24-Parganas ..	**63,975**	**54,982**	**49,966**	**39,195**	**46,021**	**39,202**	..	**+ 8,993**	**+ 5,016**	**+ 10,771**	**− 6,826**	**+ 6,819**	..
Tollygunge ..	24,476	21,637	18,433	12,821	15,054	12,824	..	+ 2,839	+ 3,204	+ 5,612	− 2,233	+ 2,930	..
South Suburban Municipality ..	39,499	33,345	31,533	26,374	30,967	26,378	..	+ 6,154	+ 1,812	+ 5,159	− 4,593	+ 4,589	..
HOWRAH ..	**224,873**	**195,301**	**179,006**	**157,594**	**116,606**	**90,813**	**84,069**	**+ 29,572**	**+ 16,295**	**+ 21,412**	**+ 40,988**	**+ 25,793**	**+ 6,744**

IMPERIAL TABLE II.—Variation in population since 1872.

Name of ward, etc.	Net variation in period 1872 to 1931 Increase(+) Decrease(−)	Males. 1931.	Males. 1921.	Males. 1911.	Males. 1901.	Males. 1891.	Males. 1881.	Males. 1872.	Females. 1931.	Females. 1921.	Females. 1911.	Females. 1901.	Females. 1891.	Females. 1881.	Females. 1872.
1	15	16	17	18	19	20	21	22	23	24	25	26	27	28	29
CALCUTTA WITH SUBURBS AND HOWRAH ..	..	**997,051**	**885,129**	**841,299**	**746,152**	**595,194**	..	..	**488,531**	**442,418**	**430,980**	**399,781**	**337,246**	..	..
CALCUTTA WITH SUBURBS IN 24-PARGANAS	..	**851,931**	**756,657**	**726,733**	**646,248**	**524,717**	..	..	**408,778**	**375,589**	**366,540**	**342,091**	**291,117**	..	..
Calcutta ..	+ 475,106	**814,948**	**724,248**	**697,867**	**624,855**	**499,599**	**444,525**	**461,505**	**381,786**	**353,016**	**345,440**	**324,289**	**270,214**	**254,657**	**260,123**
MUNICIPAL AREA ..	+ 457,320	**778,559**	**702,462**	**663,897**	**587,709**	**467,746**	**410,496**	**441,006**	**379,485**	**352,766**	**344,844**	**323,890**	**269,757**	**254,140**	**259,718**
District No. I—Total ..	+ 161,960	**244,356**	**237,264**	**220,659**	**193,245**	**150,527**	**122,221**	**133,646**	**135,909**	**136,604**	**128,005**	**118,854**	**96,491**	**80,748**	**84,659**
Ward No. 1 Shampukur ..	+ 37,785	40,571	34,766	32,438	28,004	21,491	16,042	16,191	26,062	22,240	20,598	18,883	15,394	12,469	12,657
Ward No. 2 Kumartuli ..	+ 4,270	23,968	21,191	21,134	19,029	16,178	15,680	22,070	14,326	12,793	11,939	11,126	10,436	10,002	11,954
Ward No. 3 Bartala ..	+ 37,184	41,066	37,521	32,787	29,324	21,020	16,248	17,246	26,041	23,662	21,823	20,892	15,411	12,687	12,677
Ward No. 4 Sukea's Street ..	+ 29,065	35,227	35,514	29,645	25,291	20,633	14,198	14,786	18,874	19,858	18,467	16,743	14,195	10,207	10,250
Ward No. 5 Jorabagan ..	+ 279	28,320	35,951	36,155	33,005	26,411	24,324	26,726	11,035	16,622	15,959	16,064	12,769	11,994	12,350
Ward No. 6 Jorasanko ..	+ 10,087	29,847	36,032	37,707	32,403	25,370	19,649	21,741	16,269	21,244	21,834	20,585	16,287	13,175	14,288
Ward No. 30 Belgachia ..		14,228							8,024						
Ward No. 31 Satpukur ..	+ 43,290	11,934	36,289	30,793	26,189	19,424	16,080	14,886	7,260	20,185	17,385	14,561	11,999	10,214	10,483
Ward No. 32 Cossipore ..		19,195							8,018						
District No. II—Total ..	+ 65,363	**204,736**	**194,636**	**185,245**	**172,998**	**133,967**	**134,257**	**146,626**	**82,289**	**80,729**	**80,737**	**79,663**	**64,454**	**73,469**	**75,046**
Ward No. 7 Burra Bazar ..	− 4,813	16,845	27,436	25,259	24,985	16,226	16,122	18,703	1,875	5,523	5,236	6,589	4,420	4,647	4,800
Ward No. 8 Kalootola ..	− 1,807	39,545	29,538	42,036	44,770	35,315	31,606	33,675	9,453	8,972	15,058	18,400	15,466	15,717	17,130
Ward No. 9 Muchipara ..	+ 36,965	57,880	48,818	42,859	41,933	31,976	26,488	27,087	22,724	20,852	20,503	22,183	17,496	17,093	16,552
Ward No. 10 Bow Bazar ..	− 2,468	16,029	20,275	18,625	19,075	15,880	14,398	16,096	5,046	6,835	6,389	7,977	6,788	7,229	7,447
Ward No. 11 Paddapukur ..	+ 14,837	23,191	21,133	19,073	17,347	12,715	12,126	12,260	12,132	11,505	10,893	10,713	8,046	8,390	8,226
Ward No. 12 Waterloo Street ..	+ 1,007	5,860	6,440	5,658	5,746	5,437	5,220	5,249	851	666	626	556	495	565	455
Ward No. 28 Beliaghata ..	+ 21,642	19,541	40,996	31,735	19,142	16,418	28,297	33,556	13,694	26,376	22,032	13,245	11,743	19,828	20,436
Ward No. 29 Maniktala ..		25,885							16,514						
District No. III—Total ..		**151,464**							**67,689**						
Ward No. 13 Fenwick Bazar ..	+ 4,188	25,686	21,258	22,777	23,833	21,829	19,494	20,734	5,289	4,853	5,659	7,375	6,537	6,404	6,053
Ward No. 14 Taltola ..	+ 11,315	27,660	22,314	21,820	20,706	18,579	15,452	16,796	10,767	9,350	10,292	11,531	10,628	10,611	10,316
Ward No. 15 Kalinga ..	+ 1,279	10,063	8,305	8,064	11,084	8,897	7,594	8,471	3,989	3,442	3,321	5,696	4,321	4,246	4,302
Ward No. 16 Park Street ..	+ 872	4,121	2,801	4,479	4,775	3,725	3,933	3,746	1,317	975	815	1,335	895	1,035	820
Ward No. 17 Baman Bustee ..	− 3,889	2,056	2,474	2,533	4,504	3,552	4,596	5,104	623	673	592	950	1,046	1,529	1,464
Ward No. 18 Tengra ..		7,444							4,328						
Ward No. 19 Intally ..	+ 49,023	28,125	53,225	51,585	40,703	34,080	26,857	27,477	16,099	30,160	31,368	26,125	22,832	18,967	20,083
Ward No. 20 Beniapukur ..		25,648							14,939						
Ward No. 21 Ballygunge ..		20,661							10,338						
District No. IV—Total ..	+ 48,400	**177,993**	30,951	23,740	15,606	13,018	11,744	13,058	**93,598**	19,903	16,212	11,601	9,813	8,679	10,271
Ward No. 27 Tollygunge ..		24,400							16,330						
Ward No. 22 Bhowanipur ..	+ 12,566	50,564	35,868	33,006	28,747	24,232	21,035	21,072	29,120	21,510	21,563	20,894	18,359	16,967	16,046
Ward No. 23 Alipore ..	+ 10,601	21,350	15,708	13,827	12,052	9,854	9,012	12,252	8,670	6,476	5,922	5,666	4,950	4,426	7,167
Ward No. 24 Ekbalpore ..	+ 14,748	21,664	21,287	13,031	12,832	8,297	8,117	10,643	11,158	10,133	8,838	8,776	7,043	7,752	7,431
Ward No. 25 Watganj and Hastings ..	+ 4,280	23,884	26,998	35,466	29,696	20,594	19,489	16,060	8,579	11,764	13,890	14,141	11,059	13,546	12,128
Ward No. 26 Garden Reach ..	+ 46,614	36,131	29,373	27,665	16,928	16,595	6,695	5,321	19,741	16,194	17,630	11,283	11,329	5,761	3,937
FORT WILLIAM AND MAIDAN ..	+ 600	**2,681**	**2,524**	**3,921**	**3,111**	**3,265**	**3,070**	**2,182**	**422**	**232**	**490**	**219**	**354**	**269**	**301**
PORT ..	+ 17,042	**31,831**	**18,424**	**26,784**	**29,598**	**26,516**	**28,037**	**16,599**	**1,871**	**17**	**106**	**170**	**73**	**163**	**61**
CANALS ..	+ 144	**1,897**	**838**	**3,265**	**4,437**	**2,072**	**2,922**	**1,718**	**8**	**1**	..	**10**	**30**	**85**	**43**
Suburbs in 24-Parganas ..	..	**36,983**	**32,409**	**28,866**	**21,393**	**25,118**	..	..	**26,992**	**22,573**	**21,100**	**17,802**	**20,903**	..	..
Tollygunge ..	..	14,800	13,326	11,183	7,222	8,479	..	..	9,676	8,311	7,250	5,599	6,575	..	..
South Suburban Municipality ..	..	22,183	19,083	17,683	14,171	16,639	..	..	17,316	14,262	13,850	12,203	14,328	..	..
HOWRAH ..	+ 140,804	**145,120**	**128,472**	**114,566**	**99,904**	**70,477**	**52,337**	**46,514**	**79,753**	**66,829**	**64,440**	**57,690**	**46,129**	**38,476**	**37,555**

IMPERIAL TABLES III, IV AND V.

The Statistics for these tables are contained in Imperial Tables I and II and are not repeated.

IMPERIAL TABLE VI.—Birthplace.

This table shows the birthplace of persons enumerated in Calcutta, its suburbs in 24-Parganas and Howrah City. It corresponds to imperial table XI of 1921, but public economy has dictated a restriction of the particulars shown by the exclusion of districts of birth.

2. In the interests of space and for oonvenience of reference entries for any birthplace totalling less than 100 have been combined in the table in the next larger area within which they fall. Details of the entries thus combined are given in the supplement to the table printed below :

SUPPLEMENT TO IMPERIAL TABLE VI.—Details of entries not shown separately in the table.

REFERENCE TO TABLE VI with details of Birthplace and locality of enumeration.	Both sexes.	Males.	Females.
1	2	3	4
28.—OTHER BRITISH TERRITORY not adjacent to Bengal	7	7	..
1. Andaman and Nicobar Islands			
Calcutta ..	3	3	..
2. Beluchistan (Districts and Administered Territories)			
Howrah City ..	2	2	..
3. Coorg			
Calcutta ..	2	2	..
39.—OTHER STATES not adjacent to Bengal.	241	195	46
4. Beluchistan States			
Calcutta ..	79	72	7
5. Bombay States			
Calcutta ..	88	81	7
6. Central Provinces States			
Calcutta ..	26	12	14
7. Madras States (including Cochin and Travancore)			
Calcutta ..	48	30	18
8. *Cochin State*			
Calcutta ..	*23*	*14*	*9*
9. *Travancore State*			
Calcutta ..	*8*	*8*	..
42.—FRENCH SETTLEMENTS.	22	6	16
10. Chandernagore			
Howrah ..	1	1	..
11. Elsewhere unspecified			
Calcutta ..	21	5	16
45.—BRITISH DOMINIONS IN OTHER ASIATIC COUNTRIES.	142	102	40
12. Ceylon.			
All Cities ..	67	45	22
Calcutta ..	65	45	20
Suburbs in 24-Parganas.	1	..	1
Howrah ..	1	..	1
13. Hongkong			
Calcutta ..	32	22	10
14. Straits Settlements and Malaya			
Calcutta ..	43	35	8
53.—ELSEWHERE IN ASIATIC COUNTRIES OUTSIDE BRITISH DOMINIONS.	207	143	64
15. Armenia			
Calcutta ..	53	31	22
16. Bhutan			
Calcutta ..	9	6	3
53.—ELSEWHERE IN ASIATIC COUNTRIES OUTSIDE BRITISH DOMINIONS (continued)			
17. Iraq			
Calcutta ..	7	..	7
18. Java			
Calcutta ..	42	41	1
19. Philippine Islands			
Calcutta ..	8	7	1
20. Siam			
Calcutta ..	4	4	..
21. Tibet			
Calcutta ..	35	26	9
22. Turkey in Asia			
Calcutta ..	49	28	21
60.—BRITISH POSSESSIONS IN EUROPE.	17	10	7
23. Gibraltar			
Calcutta ..	1	1	..
24. Malta			
Calcutta	16	9	7
66.—ELSEWHERE IN CONTINENTAL EUROPE.	406	286	120
25. Austria			
Calcutta ..	23	16	7
26. Belgium			
All Cities ..	67	41	26
Calcutta	62	37	25
Suburbs in 24-Parganas.	2	2	..
Howrah ..	3	2	1
27. Bulgaria			
Calcutta ..	4	..	4
28. Czechoslovakia			
All Cities ..	4	2	2
Calcutta ..	2	2	..
Howrah ..	2	..	2
29. Denmark			
Calcutta ..	24	23	1
30. Greece			
Calcutta ..	32	29	3
31. Norway			
All Cities ..	66	65	1
Calcutta ..	64	63	1
Howrah ..	2	2	..
32. Portugal			
Calcutta ..	16	16	..
33. Rumania			
Calcutta ..	1	..	1
66.—ELSEWHERE IN CONTINENTAL EUROPE (continued)			
34. Soviet Russia			
All Cities ..	61	20	41
Calcutta ..	60	19	41
Howrah ..	1	1	..
35. Spain			
Calcutta ..	30	19	11
36. Sweden			
Calcutta ..	41	37	4
37. Switzerland			
Calcutta ..	35	17	18
38. Turkey in Europe			
Calcutta ..	2	1	1
69.—BRITISH DOMINIONS IN AFRICA.	9	6	3
39. Cape Colony			
Calcutta ..	1	1	..
40. Kenya (British East Africa)			
Suburbs in 24-Parganas.	1	..	1
41. Mauritius			
Calcutta ..	3	3	..
42. Natal			
Calcutta ..	4	2	2
73.—BRITISH DOMINIONS IN AMERICA.	25	15	10
43. Canada			
Calcutta	22	13	9
44. British West Indies			
Calcutta ..	3	2	1
77.—BRITISH DOMINIONS IN AUSTRALASIA.	94	47	47
45. Australia			
All Cities ..	73	32	41
Calcutta ..	68	28	40
Suburbs in 24-Parganas.	1	1	..
Howrah ..	4	3	1
46. Fiji			
Calcutta ..	1	..	1
47. New Zealand			
Calcutta ..	20	15	5

IMPERIAL TABLE VI.—Birthplace.

	Province, State or Country of Birth.	Calcutta with Suburbs in 24-Parganas and Howrah City.			Calcutta.			Suburbs in 24-Parganas.			Howrah City.		
		Both sexes.	Males.	Females.	Both sexes.	Males.	Females.	Both sexes.	Males.	Fe-males.	Both sexes.	Males.	Fe-males.
	1	2	3	4	5	6	7	8	9	10	11	12	13
1	**TOTAL POPULATION** ..	**1,485,582**	**997,051**	**488,531**	**1,196,734**	**814,948**	**381,786**	**63,975**	**36,983**	**26,992**	**224,873**	**145,120**	**79,753**
2	**A. Born in India** ..	**1,466,877**	**983,309**	**483,568**	**1,179,836**	**802,560**	**377,276**	**63,613**	**36,751**	**26,862**	**223,428**	**143,998**	**79,430**
3	**I. Born in Bengal** ..	**998,656**	**603,106**	**395,550**	**799,408**	**490,420**	**308,988**	**54,384**	**29,011**	**25,373**	**144,864**	**83,675**	**61,189**
4	(1) British Districts ..	**995,083**	600,563	394,520	**795,903**	487,933	307,970	**54,352**	28,982	25,370	**144,828**	83,648	61,180
5	(2) States ..	**3,573**	2,543	1,030	**3,505**	2,487	1,018	**32**	29	3	**36**	27	9
6	Cooch Behar ..	**1,063**	377	686	**1,052**	371	681	..	..	..	**11**	6	5
7	Tripura ..	**2,510**	2,166	344	**2,453**	2,116	337	**32**	29	3	**25**	21	4
8	**II. Born in other parts of India** ..	**468,221**	**380,203**	**88,018**	**380,428**	**312,140**	**68,288**	**9,229**	**7,740**	**1,489**	**78,564**	**60,323**	**18,241**
9	(*a*) Provinces and States adjacent to Bengal.	**272,409**	230,950	41,459	**231,344**	197,832	33,512	**7,548**	6,486	1,062	**33,517**	26,632	6,885
10	(1) British Territory ..	**270,581**	229,501	41,080	**229,775**	196,574	33,201	**7,481**	6,437	1,044	**33,325**	26,490	6,835
11	Assam ..	**4,726**	3,998	728	**4,616**	3,918	698	**13**	10	3	**97**	70	27
12	Bihar and Orissa ..	**264,332**	224,348	39,984	**223,698**	191,531	32,167	**7,453**	6,424	1,029	**33,181**	26,393	6,788
13	Burma ..	**1,523**	1,155	368	**1,461**	1,125	336	**15**	3	12	**47**	27	20
14	(2) States ..	**1,828**	1,449	379	**1,569**	1,258	311	**67**	49	18	**192**	142	50
15	Assam States ..	**208**	172	36	**203**	170	33	..	..	..	**5**	2	3
16	Bihar and Orissa States ..	**1,301**	1,101	200	**1,053**	917	136	**67**	49	18	**181**	135	46
17	Sikkim State ..	**319**	176	143	**313**	171	142	..	..	..	**6**	5	1
18	(*b*) Other Provinces and States in India	**194,908**	148,502	46,406	**148,199**	113,564	34,635	**1,681**	1,254	427	**45,028**	33,684	11,344
19	(1) British Territory ..	**175,740**	134,261	41,479	**130,602**	100,450	30,152	**1,624**	1,202	422	**43,514**	32,609	10,905
20	Ajmere-Merwara ..	**208**	122	86	**197**	115	82	..	..	..	**11**	7	4
21	Bombay ..	**4,731**	3,150	1,581	**4,467**	2,955	1,512	**38**	26	12	**226**	169	57
22	Central Provinces and Berar	**3,942**	2,736	1,206	**3,000**	2,187	813	**148**	90	58	**794**	459	335
23	Delhi ..	**1,611**	1,340	271	**1,558**	1,307	251	..	..	..	**53**	33	20
24	Madras ..	**7,961**	4,722	3,239	**5,287**	3,348	1,939	**13**	2	11	**2,661**	1,372	1,289
25	North West Frontier Province (Districts and Administered Territory).	**644**	465	179	**611**	439	172	**7**	7	..	**26**	19	7
26	Punjab ..	**13,291**	10,515	2,776	**12,445**	9,879	2,566	**49**	33	16	**797**	603	194
27	United Provinces of Agra and Oudh.	**143,345**	111,204	32,141	**103,032**	80,215	22,817	**1,369**	1,044	325	**38,944**	29,945	8,999
28	Elsewhere ..	**7**	7	..	**5**	5	..	..	..	..	**2**	2	..
29	(2) States and Agencies ..	**19,168**	14,241	4,927	**17,597**	13,114	4,483	**57**	52	5	**1,514**	1,075	439
30	Baroda State ..	**233**	171	62	**233**	171	62	..	..	..	..	..	..
31	Central India Agency ..	**191**	64	127	**186**	60	126	..	..	..	**5**	4	1
32	Gwalior State ..	**1,053**	832	221	**908**	718	190	..	..	..	**145**	114	31
33	Hyderabad State ..	**402**	298	104	**380**	283	97	..	..	..	**22**	15	7
34	Kashmir State ..	**100**	72	28	**93**	69	24	..	..	..	**7**	3	4
35	Mysore State ..	**171**	108	63	**171**	108	63	..	..	..	..	..	..
36	Punjab States Agency ..	**258**	194	64	**258**	194	64	..	..	..	..	..	..
37	Rajputana Agency ..	**16,273**	12,171	4,102	**14,881**	11,180	3,701	**57**	52	5	**1,335**	939	396
38	United Provinces States ..	**246**	136	110	**246**	136	110	..	..	..	..	..	..
39	Other States ..	**241**	195	46	**241**	195	46	..	..	..	..	..	..
40	(*c*) India, unspecified ..	**42**	27	15	**24**	21	3	..	..	..	**18**	6	12
41	(*d*) French and Portuguese Settlements.	**862**	724	138	**861**	723	138	..	..	..	**1**	1	..
42	(1) French Settlements ..	**22**	6	16	**21**	5	16	..	..	..	**1**	1	..
43	(2) Portuguese Settlements (unspecified).	**840**	718	122	**840**	718	122	..	..	..	..	..	..
44	**B. Born in other Asiatic Countries.**	**8,822**	**7,085**	**1,737**	**7,548**	**6,068**	**1,480**	**194**	**141**	**53**	**1,080**	**876**	**204**
45	(1) Within British Dominions ..	**142**	102	40	**140**	102	38	**1**	..	1	**1**	..	1
46	(2) Outside British Dominions ..	**8,680**	6,983	1,697	**7,408**	5,966	1,442	**193**	141	52	**1,079**	876	203
47	Afganistan ..	**529**	519	10	**446**	437	9	**15**	15	..	**68**	67	1
48	Arabia ..	**110**	83	27	**108**	81	27	..	..	..	**2**	2	..
49	China ..	**2,801**	2,359	442	**2,627**	2,240	387	**133**	85	48	**41**	34	7
50	Japan ..	**527**	411	116	**525**	410	115	..	..	..	**2**	1	1
51	Nepal ..	**3,715**	2,985	730	**2,715**	2,176	539	**45**	41	4	**955**	768	187
52	Persia ..	**791**	483	308	**780**	479	301	..	..	..	**11**	4	7
53	Elsewhere ..	**207**	143	64	**207**	143	64	..	..	..	..	..	..
54	**C. Born in Europe** ..	**9,479**	**6,429**	**3,050**	**8,971**	**6,108**	**2,863**	**165**	**89**	**76**	**343**	**232**	**111**
55	(1) Great Britain and Ireland ..	**8,434**	5,659	2,775	**7,960**	5,359	2,601	**154**	83	71	**320**	217	103
56	England and Wales ..	**6,839**	4,553	2,286	**6,588**	4,406	2,182	**87**	44	43	**164**	103	61
57	Scotland ..	**1,071**	786	285	**898**	662	236	**27**	15	12	**146**	109	37
58	Northern Ireland ..	**519**	316	203	**469**	287	182	**40**	24	16	**10**	5	5
59	United Kingdom (unspecified)	**5**	4	1	**5**	4	1	..	..	..	..	..	..
60	(2) British possessions in Europe	**17**	10	7	**17**	10	7	..	..	..	..	..	..
61	(3) Continental Europe ..	**1,026**	760	266	**992**	739	253	**11**	6	5	**23**	15	8
62	France ..	**138**	58	80	**125**	53	72	**8**	4	4	**5**	1	4
63	Germany ..	**140**	104	36	**135**	100	35	..	..	..	**5**	4	1
64	Holland ..	**128**	121	7	**123**	117	6	**1**	..	1	**4**	4	..
65	Italy ..	**214**	191	23	**213**	190	23	..	..	..	**1**	1	..
66	Elsewhere ..	**406**	286	120	**396**	279	117	**2**	2	..	**8**	5	3
67	(4) Europe (unspecified) ..	**2**	..	2	**2**	..	2	..	..	..	..	..	..
68	**D. Born in Africa** ..	**72**	**48**	**24**	**64**	**43**	**21**	**1**	..	**1**	**7**	**5**	**2**
69	(1) Within British Dominions ..	**9**	6	3	**8**	6	2	**1**	..	1	..	..	..
70	(2) *Outside British Dominions ..	**7**	4	3	**7**	4	3	..	..	..	..	..	..
71	(3) Africa (unspecified) ..	**56**	38	18	**49**	33	16	..	..	..	**7**	5	2
72	**E. Born in America** ..	**238**	**133**	**105**	**226**	**126**	**100**	**1**	**1**	..	**11**	**6**	**5**
73	(1) Within British Dominions ..	**25**	15	10	**25**	15	10	..	..	..	..	..	..
74	(2) Outside British Dominions (United States).	**9**	9	..	**9**	9	..	..	..	..	..	..	..
75	(3) America (unspecified) ..	**204**	109	95	**192**	102	90	**1**	1	..	**11**	6	5
76	**F. Born in Australasia** ..	**94**	**47**	**47**	**89**	**43**	**46**	**1**	**1**	..	**4**	**3**	**1**
77	(1) Within British Dominions ..	**94**	47	47	**89**	43	46	**1**	1	..	**4**	**3**	1

***Persons were recorded who were born in Egypt only amongst the countries in Africa outside British Dominions.**

IMPERIAL TABLE VII.—Age, sex and marital condition by religion.

This table corresponds to imperial table VII of 1921. It is divided into three parts. Part A gives figures for Calcutta, part B for Suburbs in 24-Parganas and part C for Howrah City. In all three parts figures are given for the religions by quinquennial age-groups up to 70 with additional figures for the groups 0—1, 1—2, 2—3, 3—4 and 4—5. Figures for sects of Hindus are an innovation of the present census.

2. In addition to the sects shown for Hindus in Calcutta one Saiva was returned, male, widowed and aged 60—65. Hindus for whom no returns under a separate sect are given did not return any sect.

3. The majority of Muslims in Calcutta are Sunnis. The only other sect for which details are given is that of the Shias. Figures for Shias in Howrah are shown below : none were returned as widowed :—

SHIAS IN HOWRAH CITY.

Age.	Unmarried.			Married.		
	Both sexes.	Males.	Females.	Both sexes.	Males.	Females.
1	2	3	4	5	6	7
All ages ..	**19**	**16**	**3**	**21**	**14**	**7**
0—5 ..	**3**	3	..	..	..	..
1—2 ..	*1*	*1*	..	..	..	..
2—3 ..	*2*	*2*	..	..	..	..
5—10 ..	**5**	3	2	**1**	1	..
10—15 ..	**4**	3	1	**1**	..	1
15—20 ..	**1**	1	..	**4**	3	1
20—25 ..	**1**	1	..	**4**	2	2
25—30 ..	**1**	1	..	**3**	2	1
30—35 ..	**2**	2	..	**3**	2	1
35—40 ..	**1**	1	..	**1**	1	..
40—45 ..	**1**	1	..	**3**	2	1
55—60 ..	..	..	..	**1**	1	..

4. The figures for Christians include persons of indefinite belief as under :—

	Both sexes.	Males.	Females.
Calcutta ..	**74**	64	10
Howrah City ..	**1**	1	..

5. No sect was returned by Jains for whom figures under separate sects are not shown.

6. One Jew, male, married, of age 45—50, was returned in Suburbs in 24-Parganas.

IMPERIAL TABLE VII.—Age, sex and marital condition by religion.

Part A.—Calcutta.

Age-group.	All marital conditions.			Unmarried.			Married.			Widowed.		
	Both sexes.	Males.	Females.	Both sexes.	Males.	Females.	Both sexes.	Males.	Females.	Both sexes.	Males.	Females.
1	2	3	4	5	6	7	8	9	10	11	12	13
ALL RELIGIONS.												
All ages	**1,196,734**	**814,948**	**381,786**	**409,491**	**283,099**	**126,392**	**695,871**	**509,722**	**186,149**	**91,372**	**22,127**	**69,245**
0—5	101,427	52,998	48,429	99,667	52,109	47,558	1,662	873	789	98	16	82
0—1	*22,186*	*11,956*	*10,230*	*22,001*	*11,850*	*10,151*	*180*	*104*	*76*	*5*	*2*	*3*
1—2	*17,500*	*9,070*	*8,430*	*17,300*	*8,958*	*8,342*	*195*	*110*	*85*	*5*	*2*	*3*
2—3	*21,077*	*10,770*	*10,307*	*20,786*	*10,617*	*10,169*	*282*	*152*	*130*	*9*	*1*	*8*
3—4	*20,772*	*10,724*	*10,048*	*20,300*	*10,492*	*9,808*	*442*	*227*	*215*	*30*	*5*	*25*
4—5	*19,892*	*10,478*	*9,414*	*19,280*	*10,192*	*9,088*	*563*	*280*	*283*	*49*	*6*	*43*
5—10	95,388	53,498	41,890	86,665	49,442	37,223	8,500	4,008	4,492	223	48	175
10—15	98,301	58,547	39,754	77,201	49,832	27,369	20,674	8,625	12,049	426	90	336
15—20	128,230	88,480	39,750	56,775	50,522	6,253	69,057	37,479	31,578	2,398	479	1,919
20—25	156,766	113,498	43,268	49,136	45,849	3,287	102,998	66,613	36,385	4,632	1,036	3,596
25—30	155,895	117,181	38,714	19,844	18,141	1,703	127,837	96,961	30,876	8,214	2,079	6,135
30—35	136,610	103,421	33,189	9,862	8,716	1,146	117,299	92,231	25,068	9,449	2,474	6,975
35—40	97,785	73,080	24,705	3,894	3,322	572	83,145	67,077	16,068	10,746	2,681	8,065
40—45	77,788	57,117	20,671	2,666	2,232	434	64,318	52,238	12,080	10,804	2,647	8,157
45—50	51,120	36,077	15,043	1,345	1,056	289	39,061	32,417	6,644	10,714	2,604	8,110
50—55	38,319	26,053	12,266	953	729	224	27,721	23,012	4,709	9,645	2,312	7,333
55—60	22,339	13,976	8,363	422	312	110	14,193	11,833	2,360	7,724	1,831	5,893
60—65	16,701	10,023	6,678	316	229	87	9,843	8,263	1,580	6,542	1,531	5,011
65—70	7,549	4,206	3,343	170	123	47	3,837	3,248	589	3,542	835	2,707
70 & over	12,516	6,793	5,723	575	485	90	5,726	4,844	882	6,215	1,464	4,751
MUSLIM.												
All ages	**311,155**	**229,311**	**81,844**	**91,287**	**66,352**	**24,935**	**203,359**	**157,550**	**45,809**	**16,509**	**5,409**	**11,100**
0—5	20,967	11,163	9,804	20,503	10,928	9,575	428	230	198	36	5	31
0—1	*4,187*	*2,342*	*1,845*	*4,151*	*2,315*	*1,836*	*35*	*27*	*8*	*1*	..	*1*
1—2	*3,469*	*1,825*	*1,644*	*3,442*	*1,810*	*1,632*	*27*	*15*	*12*	..	..	..
2—3	*4,442*	*2,318*	*2,124*	*4,379*	*2,281*	*2,098*	*61*	*36*	*25*	*2*	*1*	*1*
3—4	*4,490*	*2,352*	*2,138*	*4,351*	*2,284*	*2,067*	*127*	*66*	*61*	*12*	*2*	*10*
4—5	*4,379*	*2,326*	*2,053*	*4,180*	*2,238*	*1,942*	*178*	*86*	*92*	*21*	*2*	*19*
5—10	22,889	13,547	9,342	20,314	12,336	7,978	2,508	1,199	1,309	67	12	55
10—15	24,963	15,915	9,048	18,908	13,154	5,754	5,958	2,727	3,231	97	34	63
15—20	34,658	25,534	9,124	13,524	12,541	983	20,671	12,835	7,836	463	158	305
20—25	43,598	33,771	9,827	11,083	10,739	344	31,731	22,698	9,033	784	334	450
25—30	42,586	34,310	8,276	3,880	3,764	116	37,538	29,953	7,585	1,168	593	575
30—35	36,835	29,966	6,869	1,730	1,655	75	33,690	27,647	6,043	1,415	664	751
35—40	26,251	21,281	4,970	541	506	35	23,966	20,142	3,824	1,744	633	1,111
40—45	20,440	16,361	4,079	353	323	30	18,210	15,452	2,758	1,877	586	1,291
45—50	13,529	10,452	3,077	180	164	16	11,244	9,694	1,550	2,105	594	1,511
50—55	9,602	7,172	2,430	110	99	11	7,685	6,577	1,108	1,807	496	1,311
55—60	5,675	3,959	1,716	49	45	4	4,053	3,520	533	1,573	394	1,179
60—65	4,343	2,920	1,423	38	33	5	2,935	2,546	389	1,370	341	1,029
65—70	1,735	1,124	611	20	16	4	1,078	938	140	637	170	467
70 & over	3,084	1,836	1,248	54	49	5	1,664	1,392	272	1,366	395	971
SHIA.												
All ages	*274*	*247*	*27*	*91*	*86*	*5*	*176*	*155*	*21*	*7*	*6*	*1*
0—5	*7*	*1*	*6*	*4*	*1*	*3*	*3*	..	*3*	..	..	..
0—1	*2*	*1*	*1*	*2*	*1*	*1*	..	..	..	..	..	..
1—2	*1*	..	*1*	*1*	..	*1*	..	..	..	..	..	..
2—3	*1*	..	*1*	*1*	..	*1*	..	..	..	..	..	..
3—4	*1*	..	*1*	..	..	..	*1*	..	*1*	..	..	..
4—5	*2*	..	*2*	..	..	..	*2*	..	*2*	..	..	..
5—10	*6*	*3*	*3*		*3*	*1*	*2*	..	*2*	..	..	..
10—15	*8*	*7*	*1*	*6*	*6*	..	*2*	*1*	*1*	..	..	..
15—20	*29*	*25*	*4*	*18*	*17*	*1*	*11*	*8*	*3*	..	..	..
20—25	*59*	*56*	*3*	*32*	*32*	..	*26*	*23*	*3*	*1*	*1*	..
25—30	*55*	*54*	*1*	*20*	*20*	..	*34*	*33*	*1*	*1*	*1*	..
30—35	*31*	*30*	*1*	*3*	*3*	..	*26*	*25*	*1*	*2*	*2*	..
35—40	*28*	*26*	*2*	*2*	*2*	..	*25*	*23*	*2*	*1*	*1*	..
40—45	*23*	*20*	*3*	..	..	..	*23*	*20*	*3*	..	..	..
45—50	*12*	*12*	..	*1*	*1*	..	*10*	*10*	..	*1*	*1*	..
50—55	*10*	*9*	*1*	*1*	*1*	..	*8*	*8*	..	*1*	..	*1*
55—60	*3*	*3*	..	..	..	..	*3*	*3*	..	..	..	..
60—65	*1*	*1*	..	..	..	..	*1*	*1*	..	..	..	..
65—70	..	..	..	..	..	..	..	..	..	..	..	..
70 & over	*2*	..	*2*	..	..	..	*2*	..	*2*	..	..	..
HINDU.												
All ages	**822,293**	**547,846**	**274,447**	**287,294**	**198,309**	**88,985**	**463,488**	**333,835**	**129,653**	**71,511**	**15,702**	**55,809**
0—5	74,618	38,712	35,906	73,485	38,148	35,337	1,077	554	523	56	10	46
0—1	*16,600*	*8,860*	*7,740*	*16,476*	*8,792*	*7,684*	*121*	*66*	*55*	*3*	*2*	*1*
1—2	*13,033*	*6,704*	*6,329*	*12,881*	*6,618*	*6,263*	*147*	*84*	*63*	*5*	*2*	*3*
2—3	*15,479*	*7,832*	*7,647*	*15,281*	*7,733*	*7,548*	*192*	*99*	*93*	*6*	..	*6*
3—4	*15,120*	*7,758*	*7,362*	*14,828*	*7,619*	*7,209*	*276*	*137*	*139*	*16*	*2*	*14*
4—5	*14,386*	*7,558*	*6,828*	*14,019*	*7,386*	*6,633*	*341*	*168*	*173*	*26*	*4*	*22*
5—10	67,072	37,111	29,961	61,217	34,433	26,784	5,707	2,646	3,061	148	32	116
10—15	67,468	39,482	27,986	53,029	33,827	19,202	14,122	5,602	8,520	317	53	264
15—20	86,645	58,886	27,759	38,602	35,023	3,579	46,152	23,549	22,603	1,891	314	1,577
20—25	105,702	75,190	30,512	34,079	32,407	1,672	67,860	42,100	25,760	3,763	683	3,080
25—30	106,223	78,361	27,862	13,695	12,765	930	85,678	64,169	21,509	6,850	1,427	5,423
30—35	93,390	69,342	24,048	6,563	5,936	627	79,048	61,688	17,360	7,779	1,718	6,061
35—40	66,551	48,585	17,966	2,618	2,296	322	55,272	44,362	10,910	8,661	1,927	6,734
40—45	53,053	37,958	15,095	1,781	1,563	218	42,723	34,466	8,257	8,549	1,929	6,620
45—50	34,558	23,627	10,931	785	654	131	25,563	21,098	4,465	8,210	1,875	6,335
50—55	26,366	17,361	9,005	551	454	97	18,350	15,214	3,136	7,465	1,693	5,772
55—60	15,309	9,205	6,104	217	187	30	9,279	7,679	1,600	5,813	1,339	4,474
60—65	11,347	6,541	4,806	158	136	22	6,335	5,298	1,037	4,854	1,107	3,747
65—70	5,309	2,841	2,468	87	76	11	2,542	2,155	387	2,680	610	2,070
70 & over	8,682	4,644	4,038	427	404	23	3,780	3,255	525	4,475	985	3,490

IMPERIAL TABLE VII.—Age, sex and marital condition by religion.

Part A.—Calcutta.

Age-group.	All marital conditions.			Unmarried.			Married.			Widowed.		
	Both sexes.	Males.	Females.	Both sexes.	Males.	Females.	Both sexes.	Males.	Females.	Both sexes.	Males.	Females.
1	2	3	4	5	6	7	8	9	10	11	12	13
						SAKTA.						
All ages	6,196	3,479	2,717	2,604	1,579	1,025	2,871	1,693	1,178	721	207	514
0—5	687	306	381	671	296	375	13	10	3	3	..	3
0—1	158	74	84	158	74	84	..	..	..	..	..	..
1—2	118	47	71	117	46	71	1	1	..	..	..	..
2—3	137	55	82	137	55	82	..	..	..	..	..	..
3—4	133	60	73	128	57	71	4	3	1	1	..	1
4—5	141	70	71	131	64	67	8	6	2	2	..	2
5—10	651	297	354	586	269	317	61	28	33	4	..	4
10—15	624	278	346	505	251	254	113	27	86	6	..	6
15—20	669	389	280	347	304	43	299	81	218	23	4	19
20—25	758	468	290	311	296	15	415	166	249	32	6	26
25—30	653	409	244	113	102	11	491	298	193	49	9	40
30—35	593	401	192	40	38	2	449	305	144	104	58	46
35—40	462	318	144	11	10	1	341	245	96	110	63	47
40—45	340	217	123	9	7	2	269	196	73	62	14	48
45—50	226	129	97	4	2	2	152	113	39	70	14	56
50—55	193	103	90	4	2	2	118	90	28	71	11	60
55—60	113	58	55	1	1	..	58	51	7	54	6	48
60—65	89	45	44	2	1	1	41	39	2	46	5	41
65—70	58	27	31	..	..	..	24	21	3	34	6	28
70 & over	80	34	46	..	..	..	27	23	4	53	11	42
						VAISHNAVA.						
All ages	3,948	1,856	2,092	1,450	862	588	1,778	926	852	720	68	652
0—5	432	192	240	427	191	236	5	1	4	..	..	..
0—1	102	41	61	102	41	61	..	..	..	..	..	..
1—2	69	28	41	68	28	40	1	..	1	..	..	..
2—3	80	35	45	80	35	45	..	..	..	..	..	..
3—4	89	44	45	87	43	44	2	1	1	..	..	..
4—5	92	44	48	90	44	46	2	..	2	..	..	..
5—10	401	185	216	365	179	186	32	6	26	4	..	4
10—15	370	168	202	291	160	131	72	8	64	7	..	7
15—20	370	180	190	149	129	20	193	50	143	28	1	27
20—25	407	200	207	120	111	9	241	89	152	46	..	46
25—30	399	192	207	49	47	2	273	143	130	77	2	75
30—35	379	182	197	26	25	1	269	154	115	84	3	81
35—40	326	160	166	7	6	1	232	149	83	87	5	82
40—45	275	139	136	6	5	1	186	127	59	83	7	76
45—50	180	88	92	4	4	..	103	73	30	73	11	62
50—55	147	68	79	4	4	..	79	56	23	64	8	56
55—60	94	39	55	1	1	..	43	33	10	50	5	45
60—65	70	26	44	..	..	..	28	21	7	42	5	37
65—70	30	10	20	..	..	..	8	6	2	22	4	18
70 & over	68	27	41	1	..	1	14	10	4	53	17	36
						BRAHMO.						
All ages	1,554	880	674	847	445	402	655	409	246	52	26	26
0—5	76	31	45	76	31	45	..	..	..	..	..	..
0—1	37	14	23	37	14	23	..	..	..	..	..	..
1—2	13	6	7	13	6	7	..	..	..	..	..	..
2—3	13	6	7	13	6	7	..	..	..	..	..	..
3—4	9	3	6	9	3	6	..	..	..	..	..	..
4—5	4	2	2	4	2	2	..	..	..	..	..	..
5—10	114	55	59	111	53	58	3	2	1	..	..	..
10—15	237	132	105	230	127	103	7	5	2	..	..	..
15—20	249	137	112	237	128	109	12	9	3	..	..	..
20—25	231	112	119	132	67	65	99	45	54	..	..	..
25—30	172	98	74	27	19	8	144	78	66	1	1	..
30—35	108	79	29	12	6	6	92	71	21	4	2	2
35—40	91	58	33	7	5	2	72	48	24	12	5	7
40—45	112	75	37	5	5	..	97	64	33	10	6	4
45—50	90	64	26	6	4	2	82	59	23	2	1	1
50—55	26	18	8	1	..	1	25	18	7	..	..	..
55—60	11	7	4	1	..	1	10	7	3	..	..	..
60—65	11	5	6	1	..	1	6	3	3	4	2	2
65—70	12	3	9	1	..	1	4	..	4	7	3	4
70 & over	14	6	8	..	..	..	2	..	2	12	6	6
						ARYA.						
All ages	3	3	..	1	1	..	2	2	..	..	..	..
0—5	..	..	..	..	..	..	..	..	..	..	..	..
0—1	..	..	..	..	..	..	..	..	..	..	..	..
1—2	..	..	..	..	..	..	..	..	..	..	..	..
2—3	..	..	..	..	..	..	..	..	..	..	..	..
3—4	..	..	..	..	..	..	..	..	..	..	..	..
4—5	..	..	..	..	..	..	..	..	..	..	..	..
5—10	..	..	..	..	..	..	..	..	..	..	..	..
10—15	1	1	..	1	1	..	..	..	..	..	..	..
15—20	1	1	..	..	..	..	1	1	..	..	..	..
20—25	..	..	..	..	..	..	..	..	..	..	..	..
25—30	1	1	..	..	..	..	1	1	..	..	..	..
30—35	..	..	..	..	..	..	..	..	..	..	..	..
35—40	..	..	..	..	..	..	..	..	..	..	..	..
40—45	..	..	..	..	..	..	..	..	..	..	..	..
45—50	..	..	..	..	..	..	..	..	..	..	..	..
50—55	..	..	..	..	..	..	..	..	..	..	..	..
55—60	..	..	..	..	..	..	..	..	..	..	..	..
60—65	..	..	..	..	..	..	..	..	..	..	..	..
65—70	..	..	..	..	..	..	..	..	..	..	..	..
70 & over	..	..	..	..	..	..	..	..	..	..	..	..

IMPERIAL TABLE VII.—Age, sex and marital condition by religion.

Part A.—Calcutta.

Age-group.	All marital conditions.			Unmarried.			Married.			Widowed.		
	Both sexes.	Males.	Females.	Both sexes.	Males.	Females.	Both sexes.	Males.	Females.	Both sexes.	Males.	Females.
1	2	3	4	5	6	7	8	9	10	11	12	13
SIKH.												
All ages	**4,705**	**3,602**	**1,103**	**1,787**	**1,385**	**402**	**2,768**	**2,102**	**666**	**150**	**115**	**35**
0—5	435	267	168	424	261	163	11	6	5	..	..	..
0—1	*103*	*48*	*55*	*102*	*48*	*54*	*1*	..	*1*	..	..	..
1—2	*61*	*35*	*26*	*60*	*35*	*25*	*1*	..	*1*	..	..	..
2—3	*91*	*63*	*28*	*91*	*63*	*28*	..	..	..	..	..	..
3—4	*96*	*67*	*29*	*93*	*65*	*28*	*3*	*2*	*1*	..	..	..
4—5	*84*	*54*	*30*	*78*	*50*	*28*	*6*	*4*	*2*	..	..	..
5—10	329	218	111	291	185	106	36	31	5	2	2	..
10—15	331	233	98	250	172	78	80	60	20	1	1	..
15—20	579	430	149	235	212	23	342	216	126	2	2	..
20—25	776	584	192	232	217	15	538	361	177	6	6	..
25—30	729	584	145	154	144	10	562	427	135	13	13	..
30—35	599	497	102	110	104	6	473	378	95	16	15	1
35—40	358	304	54	45	45	..	299	246	53	14	13	1
40—45	240	207	33	28	28	..	196	165	31	16	14	2
45—50	130	117	13	9	9	..	106	97	9	15	11	4
50—55	96	85	11	5	5	..	74	68	6	17	12	5
55—60	50	41	9	3	2	1	31	28	3	16	11	5
60—65	21	15	6	..	..	..	11	10	1	10	5	5
65—70	10	6	4	1	1	..	1	1	..	8	4	4
70 & over	22	14	8	..	..	..	8	8	..	14	6	8
CHRISTIAN.*												
All ages	**47,558**	**26,307**	**21,251**	**24,858**	**14,107**	**10,751**	**20,009**	**11,548**	**8,461**	**2,691**	**652**	**2,039**
0—5	4,442	2,274	2,168	4,316	2,208	2,108	121	66	55	5	..	5
0—1	*1,065*	*551*	*514*	*1,042*	*540*	*502*	*22*	*11*	*11*	*1*	..	*1*
1—2	*778*	*401*	*377*	*759*	*391*	*368*	*19*	*10*	*9*	..	..	..
2—3	*884*	*446*	*438*	*857*	*432*	*425*	*26*	*14*	*12*	*1*	..	*1*
3—4	*859*	*432*	*427*	*832*	*417*	*415*	*26*	*15*	*11*	*1*	..	*1*
4—5	*856*	*444*	*412*	*826*	*428*	*398*	*28*	*16*	*12*	*2*	..	*2*
5—10	4,328	2,193	2,135	4,159	2,104	2,055	164	87	77	5	2	3
10—15	4,662	2,386	2,276	4,347	2,257	2,090	304	127	177	11	2	9
15—20	5,089	2,729	2,360	3,772	2,261	1,511	1,282	466	816	35	2	33
20—25	5,243	2,870	2,373	3,163	2,025	1,138	2,012	839	1,173	68	6	62
25—30	4,974	2,874	2,100	1,801	1,207	594	3,011	1,631	1,380	162	36	126
30—35	4,542	2,653	1,889	1,252	843	409	3,093	1,760	1,333	197	50	147
35—40	3,644	2,153	1,491	583	384	199	2,794	1,699	1,095	267	70	197
40—45	3,278	1,983	1,295	441	267	174	2,531	1,631	900	306	85	221
45—50	2,422	1,496	926	339	204	135	1,767	1,204	563	316	88	228
50—55	1,914	1,166	748	273	161	112	1,343	923	420	298	82	216
55—60	1,111	629	482	146	72	74	691	489	202	274	68	206
60—65	848	450	398	116	57	59	470	332	138	262	61	201
65—70	429	201	228	59	28	31	185	131	54	185	42	143
70 & over	632	250	382	91	29	62	241	163	78	300	58	242
JAIN.												
All ages	**3,185**	**2,381**	**804**	**929**	**605**	**324**	**2,096**	**1,687**	**409**	**160**	**89**	**71**
0—5	269	150	119	263	144	119	6	6	..	..	..	..
0—1	*58*	*34*	*24*	*58*	*34*	*24*	..	..	..	..	..	..
1—2	*52*	*35*	*17*	*51*	*34*	*17*	*1*	*1*	..	..	..	..
2—3	*48*	*26*	*22*	*46*	*24*	*22*	*2*	*2*	..	..	..	..
3—4	*56*	*28*	*28*	*54*	*26*	*28*	*2*	*2*	..	..	..	..
4—5	*55*	*27*	*28*	*54*	*26*	*28*	*1*	*1*	..	..	..	..
5—10	223	122	101	198	112	86	24	10	14	1	..	1
10—15	284	162	122	189	127	62	95	35	60	..	..	..
15—20	421	304	117	126	101	25	291	201	90	4	2	2
20—25	460	362	98	82	67	15	371	290	81	7	5	2
25—30	393	319	74	32	24	8	354	291	63	7	4	3
30—35	350	297	53	17	12	5	317	273	44	16	12	4
35—40	257	225	32	7	6	1	230	204	26	20	15	5
40—45	190	172	18	5	4	1	171	157	14	14	11	3
45—50	123	109	14	4	2	2	102	95	7	17	12	5
50—55	80	72	8	2	2	..	65	60	5	13	10	3
55—60	47	42	5	2	2	..	34	33	1	11	7	4
60—65	36	26	10	1	1	..	22	20	2	13	5	8
65—70	23	10	13	1	1	..	9	7	2	13	2	11
70 & over	29	9	20	..	..	..	5	5	..	24	4	20
SWETAMBARI.												
All ages	*139*	*131*	*8*	*42*	*41*	*1*	*91*	*86*	*5*	*6*	*4*	*2*
0—5	*7*	*6*	*1*	*7*	*6*	*1*	..	..	..	..	..	..
0—1	..	..	..	..	..	..	..	..	..	..	..	..
1—2	*2*	*2*	..	*2*	*2*	..	..	..	..	..	..	..
2—3	*1*	*1*	..	*1*	*1*	..	..	..	..	..	..	..
3—4	*2*	*1*	*1*	*2*	*1*	*1*	..	..	..	..	..	..
4—5	*2*	*2*	..	*2*	*2*	..	..	..	..	..	..	..
5—10	*7*	*7*	..	*6*	*6*	..	*1*	*1*	..	..	..	..
10—15	*13*	*12*	*1*	*10*	*10*	..	*3*	*2*	*1*	..	..	..
15—20	*19*	*19*	..	*9*	*9*	..	*10*	*10*	..	..	..	..
20—25	*19*	*19*	..	*5*	*5*	..	*14*	*14*	..	..	..	..
25—30	*18*	*16*	*2*	*3*	*3*	..	*15*	*13*	*2*	..	..	..
30—35	*17*	*15*	*2*	*2*	*2*	..	*15*	*13*	*2*	..	..	..
35—40	*14*	*14*	..	..	..	..	*14*	*14*	..	..	..	..
40—45	*9*	*9*	..	..	..	..	*9*	*9*	..	..	..	..
45—50	*5*	*4*	*1*	..	..	..	*4*	*4*	..	*1*	..	*1*
50—55	*5*	*5*	..	..	..	..	*4*	*4*	..	*1*	*1*	..
55—60	*3*	*3*	..	..	..	..	*2*	*2*	..	*1*	*1*	..
60—65	..	..	..	..	..	..	..	..	..	..	..	..
65—70	*1*	*1*	..	..	..	..	..	..	..	*1*	*1*	..
70 & over	*2*	*1*	*1*	..	..	..	..	..	..	*2*	*1*	*1*

* Includes 74 persons of Indefinite Beliefs (64 males, 10 females).

IMPERIAL TABLE VII.—Age, sex and marital condition by religion.

Part A.—Calcutta.

Age-group.	All marital conditions.			Unmarried.			Married.			Widowed.		
	Both sexes.	Males.	Females.	Both sexes.	Males.	Females.	Both sexes.	Males.	Females.	Both sexes.	Males.	Females.
1	2	3	4	5	6	7	8	9	10	11	12	13
						SWETAMBARI TERAPANTHI.						
All ages	*135*	*126*	*9*	*10*	*6*	*4*	*122*	*118*	*4*	*3*	*2*	*1*
0—5	*9*	*6*	*3*	*7*	*4*	*3*	*2*	*2*	..	..	..	..
0—1	*1*	..	*1*	*1*	..	*1*	..	..	..	..	..	..
1—2	*2*	*1*	*1*	*2*	*1*	*1*	..	..	..	..	..	..
2—3	..	..	..	..	..	..	..	..	..	..	..	..
3—4	*3*	*2*	*1*	*2*	*1*	*1*	*1*	*1*	..	..	..	..
4—5	*3*	*3*	..	*2*	*2*	..	*1*	*1*	..	..	..	..
5—10	*1*	..	*1*	..	..	..	..	..	..	*1*	..	*1*
10—15	*6*	*5*	*1*	*2*	*1*	*1*	*4*	*4*	..	..	..	..
15—20	*18*	*18*	..	*1*	*1*	..	*17*	*17*	..	..	..	..
20—25	*25*	*23*	*2*	..	..	..	*25*	*23*	*2*	..	..	..
25—30	*19*	*18*	*1*	..	..	..	*19*	*18*	*1*	..	..	..
30—35	*13*	*13*	..	..	..	..	*13*	*13*	..	..	..	..
35—40	*13*	*13*	..	..	..	..	*13*	*13*	..	..	..	..
40—45	*16*	*15*	*1*	..	..	..	*15*	*14*	*1*	*1*	*1*	..
45—50	*8*	*8*	..	..	..	..	*7*	*7*	..	*1*	*1*	..
50—55	*2*	*2*	..	..	..	..	*2*	*2*	..	..	..	..
55—60	*3*	*3*	..	..	..	..	*3*	*3*	..	..	..	..
60—65	*2*	*2*	..	..	..	..	*2*	*2*	..	..	..	..
65—70	..	..	..	..	..	..	..	..	..	..	..	..
70 & over	..	..	..	..	..	..	..	..	..	..	..	..
						JEW.						
All ages	**1,829**	**931**	**898**	**916**	**490**	**426**	**785**	**410**	**375**	**128**	**31**	**97**
0—5	198	102	96	192	100	92	6	2	4	..	..	..
0—1	*41*	*21*	*20*	*40*	*21*	*19*	*1*	..	*1*	..	..	..
1—2	*32*	*18*	*14*	*32*	*18*	*14*	..	..	..	..	..	..
2—3	*40*	*22*	*18*	*39*	*21*	*18*	*1*	*1*	..	..	..	..
3—4	*43*	*21*	*22*	*41*	*20*	*21*	*2*	*1*	*1*	..	..	..
4—5	*42*	*20*	*22*	*40*	*20*	*20*	*2*	..	*2*	..	..	..
5—10	213	115	98	203	112	91	10	3	7	..	..	..
10—15	219	126	93	201	116	85	18	10	8	..	..	..
15—20	198	102	96	134	66	68	63	36	27	1	..	1
20—25	189	88	101	97	42	55	92	46	46	..	..	..
25—30	151	73	78	34	17	17	113	55	58	4	1	3
30—35	131	61	70	17	9	8	108	50	58	6	2	4
35—40	121	52	69	11	8	3	103	44	59	7	..	7
40—45	117	58	59	10	8	2	96	49	47	11	1	10
45—50	90	54	36	9	7	2	63	42	21	18	5	13
50—55	73	42	31	5	4	1	49	33	16	19	5	14
55—60	43	21	22	1	1	..	27	18	9	15	2	13
60—65	33	15	18	1	..	1	18	12	6	14	3	11
65—70	22	9	13	1	..	1	10	5	5	11	4	7
70 & over	31	13	18	..	..	..	9	5	4	22	8	14
						ZOROASTRIAN.						
All ages	**1,199**	**692**	**507**	**560**	**324**	**236**	**578**	**339**	**239**	**61**	**29**	**32**
0—5	117	64	53	115	62	53	2	2	..	..	..	..
0—1	*18*	*8*	*10*	*18*	*8*	*10*	..	..	..	..	..	..
1—2	*14*	*7*	*7*	*14*	*7*	*7*	..	..	..	..	..	..
2—3	*27*	*16*	*11*	*27*	*16*	*11*	..	..	..	..	..	..
3—4	*32*	*19*	*13*	*31*	*18*	*13*	*1*	*1*	..	..	..	..
4—5	*26*	*14*	*12*	*25*	*13*	*12*	*1*	*1*	..	..	..	..
5—10	119	66	53	107	58	49	12	8	4	..	..	..
10—15	121	68	53	95	51	44	26	17	9	..	..	..
15—20	114	66	48	66	36	30	48	30	18	..	..	..
20—25	128	71	57	66	38	28	61	32	29	1	1	..
25—30	125	69	56	42	27	15	83	42	41	..	..	..
30—35	105	61	44	27	20	7	77	41	36	1	..	1
35—40	91	49	42	13	9	4	74	39	35	4	1	3
40—45	89	50	39	12	8	4	71	40	31	6	2	4
45—50	65	46	19	9	8	1	47	34	13	9	4	5
50—55	47	34	13	5	4	1	35	27	8	7	3	4
55—60	29	17	12	1	1	..	19	12	7	9	4	5
60—65	22	14	8	..	..	..	14	9	5	8	5	3
65—70	11	7	4	1	1	..	5	4	1	5	2	3
70 & over	16	10	6	1	1	..	4	2	2	11	7	4
						BUDDHIST.						
All ages	**3,021**	**2,420**	**601**	**1,152**	**955**	**197**	**1,801**	**1,448**	**353**	**68**	**17**	**51**
0—5	182	114	68	173	108	65	8	5	3	1	1	..
0—1	*40*	*28*	*12*	*40*	*28*	*12*	..	..	..	..	..	..
1—2	*28*	*19*	*9*	*28*	*19*	*9*	..	..	..	..	..	..
2—3	*33*	*21*	*12*	*33*	*21*	*12*	..	..	..	..	..	..
3—4	*40*	*23*	*17*	*36*	*20*	*16*	*3*	*2*	*1*	*1*	*1*	..
4—5	*41*	*23*	*18*	*36*	*20*	*16*	*5*	*3*	*2*	..	..	..
5—10	136	82	54	117	71	46	19	11	8	..	..	..
10—15	146	102	44	114	81	33	32	21	11	..	..	..
15—20	322	267	55	206	190	16	114	76	38	2	1	1
20—25	431	363	68	240	231	9	188	131	57	3	1	2
25—30	479	401	78	155	149	6	320	251	69	4	1	3
30—35	421	347	74	86	81	5	328	264	64	7	2	5
35—40	312	257	55	29	22	7	276	233	43	7	2	5
40—45	255	213	42	19	14	5	230	198	32	6	1	5
45—50	137	115	22	5	3	2	123	110	13	9	2	7
50—55	98	80	18	2	..	2	87	78	9	9	2	7
55—60	47	36	11	2	1	1	38	34	4	7	1	6
60—65	33	25	8	2	2	..	24	22	2	7	1	6
65—70	6	4	2	..	..	..	3	3	..	3	1	2
70 & over	16	14	2	2	2	..	11	11	..	3	1	2

IMPERIAL TABLE VII.—Age, sex and marital condition by religion.

Part A.—Calcutta.

Age-group.	All marital conditions.			Unmarried.			Married.			Widowed.		
	Both sexes.	Males.	Females.	Both sexes.	Males.	Females.	Both sexes.	Males.	Females.	Both sexes.	Males.	Females.
1	2	3	4	5	6	7	8	9	10	11	12	13
CONFUCIAN.												
All ages	**1,363**	**1,131**	**232**	**578**	**475**	**103**	**706**	**580**	**126**	**79**	**76**	**3**
0—5	150	123	27	150	123	27	..	..	..	..	..	..
0—1	*60*	*56*	*4*	*60*	*56*	*4*	..	..	..	..	..	..
1—2	*25*	*21*	*4*	*25*	*21*	*4*	..	..	..	..	..	..
2—3	*27*	*23*	*4*	*27*	*23*	*4*	..	..	..	..	..	..
3—4	*24*	*17*	*7*	*24*	*17*	*7*	..	..	..	..	..	..
4—5	*14*	*6*	*8*	*14*	*6*	*8*	..	..	..	..	..	..
5—10	56	30	26	45	22	23	11	8	3	..	..	..
10—15	84	59	25	56	39	17	28	20	8	..	..	..
15—20	158	127	31	80	65	15	78	62	16	..	..	..
20—25	176	146	30	71	60	11	105	86	19	..	..	..
25—30	163	131	32	48	42	6	111	85	26	4	4	..
30—35	184	154	30	59	56	3	114	87	27	11	11	..
35—40	167	148	19	47	46	1	100	83	17	20	19	1
40—45	99	92	7	17	17	..	65	58	7	17	17	..
45—50	50	47	3	5	5	..	32	30	2	13	12	1
50—55	34	33	1	..	..	..	26	25	1	8	8	..
55—60	22	21	1	..	..	..	17	17	..	5	4	1
60—65	13	13	..	..	..	..	12	12	..	1	1	..
65—70	4	4	..	..	..	..	4	4	..	..	..	..
70 & over	3	3	..	..	..	..	3	3	..	..	..	..
TRIBAL.												
All ages	**426**	**327**	**99**	**130**	**97**	**33**	**281**	**223**	**58**	**15**	**7**	**8**
0—5	49	29	20	46	27	19	3	2	1	..	..	..
0—1	*14*	*8*	*6*	*14*	*8*	*6*	..	..	..	..	..	..
1—2	*8*	*5*	*3*	*8*	*5*	*3*	..	..	..	..	..	..
2—3	*6*	*3*	*3*	*6*	*3*	*3*	..	..	..	..	..	..
3—4	*12*	*7*	*5*	*10*	*6*	*4*	*2*	*1*	*1*	..	..	..
4—5	*9*	*6*	*3*	*8*	*5*	*3*	*1*	*1*	..	..	..	..
5—10	23	14	9	14	9	5	9	5	4	..	..	..
10—15	23	14	9	12	8	4	11	6	5	..	..	..
15—20	46	35	11	30	27	3	16	8	8	..	..	..
20—25	63	53	10	23	23	..	40	30	10	..	..	..
25—30	72	59	13	3	2	1	67	57	10	2	..	2
30—35	53	43	10	1	..	1	51	43	8	1	..	1
35—40	33	26	7	..	..	..	31	25	6	2	1	1
40—45	27	23	4	..	..	..	25	22	3	2	1	1
45—50	16	14	2	..	..	..	14	13	1	2	1	1
50—55	9	8	1	..	..	..	7	7	..	2	1	1
55—60	6	5	1	1	1	..	4	3	1	1	1	..
60—65	5	4	1	..	..	..	2	2	..	3	2	1
65—70	..	..	..	..	..	..	..	..	..	..	..	..
70 & over	1	..	1	..	..	..	1	..	1	..	..	..

Part B.—Suburbs in 24-Parganas.

Age-group.	All marital conditions.			Unmarried.			Married.			Widowed.		
	Both sexes.	Males.	Females.	Both sexes.	Males.	Females.	Both sexes.	Males.	Females.	Both sexes.	Males.	Females.
1	2	3	4	5	6	7	8	9	10	11	12	13
ALL RELIGIONS.												
All ages	**63,975**	**36,983**	**26,992**	**24,350**	**15,820**	**8,530**	**31,222**	**19,730**	**11,492**	**8,403**	**1,433**	**6,970**
0—5	7,518	3,819	3,699	7,474	3,806	3,668	41	13	28	3	..	3
0—1	*1,766*	*911*	*855*	*1,766*	*911*	*855*	..	..	..	..	..	..
1—2	*1,359*	*699*	*660*	*1,355*	*699*	*656*	*4*	..	*4*	..	..	..
2—3	*1,518*	*759*	*759*	*1,511*	*758*	*753*	*7*	*1*	*6*	..	..	..
3—4	*1,457*	*720*	*737*	*1,443*	*715*	*728*	*13*	*5*	*8*	*1*	..	*1*
4—5	*1,418*	*730*	*688*	*1,399*	*723*	*676*	*17*	*7*	*10*	*2*	..	*2*
5—10	6,627	3,642	2,985	6,104	3,564	2,540	506	76	430	17	2	15
10—15	6,341	3,577	2,764	5,021	3,348	1,673	1,269	227	1,042	51	2	49
15—20	6,853	4,137	2,716	2,539	2,349	190	4,052	1,772	2,280	262	16	246
20—25	7,270	4,373	2,897	1,851	1,775	76	4,961	2,558	2,403	458	40	418
25—30	5,932	3,342	2,590	717	527	190	4,352	2,713	1,639	863	102	761
30—35	5,485	3,231	2,254	436	273	163	4,091	2,817	1,274	958	141	817
35—40	4,823	3,105	1,718	86	76	10	3,729	2,863	866	1,008	166	842
40—45	4,437	2,938	1,499	59	52	7	3,304	2,671	633	1,074	215	859
45—50	2,947	1,817	1,130	19	16	3	1,935	1,589	346	993	212	781
50—55	2,082	1,152	930	15	13	2	1,249	1,005	244	818	134	684
55—60	1,379	744	635	9	6	3	740	618	122	630	120	510
60—65	1,060	525	535	11	8	3	510	406	104	539	111	428
65—70	486	224	262	6	5	1	202	156	46	278	63	215
70 & over	735	357	378	3	2	1	281	246	35	451	109	342

IMPERIAL TABLE VII.—Age, sex and marital condition by religion.

Part B.—Suburbs in 24-Parganas.

Age-group.	All marital conditions.			Unmarried.			Married.			Widowed.		
	Both sexes.	Males.	Females.	Both sexes.	Males.	Females.	Both sexes.	Males.	Females.	Both sexes.	Males.	Females.
1	2	3	4	5	6	7	8	9	10	11	12	13
						MUSLIM.						
All ages	**12,478**	**7,080**	**5,398**	**4,883**	**3,143**	**1,740**	**6,211**	**3,605**	**2,606**	**1,384**	**332**	**1,052**
0—5	1,567	822	745	1,561	822	739	6	..	6	..	..	..
0—1	382	195	187	382	195	187	..	..	..	..	..	..
1—2	286	152	134	286	152	134	..	..	..	..	..	..
2—3	318	164	154	318	164	154	..	..	..	..	..	..
3—4	294	153	141	292	153	139	2	..	2	..	..	..
4—5	287	158	129	283	158	125	4	..	4	..	..	..
5—10	1,386	772	614	1,279	743	536	104	28	76	3	1	2
10—15	1,330	727	603	1,048	672	376	277	55	222	5	..	5
15—20	1,268	665	603	454	421	33	788	240	548	26	4	22
20—25	1,423	793	630	347	320	27	1,023	460	563	53	13	40
25—30	1,211	734	477	121	98	23	988	611	377	102	25	77
30—35	1,000	620	380	45	42	3	843	550	293	112	28	84
35—40	834	505	329	14	12	2	670	464	206	150	29	121
40—45	791	488	303	6	6	..	565	408	157	220	74	146
45—50	563	343	220	3	3	..	336	265	71	224	75	149
50—55	396	220	176	3	3	..	239	195	44	154	22	132
55—60	271	154	117	..	..	..	155	135	20	116	19	97
60—65	204	109	95	1	1	..	107	92	15	96	16	80
65—70	89	46	43	..	..	..	43	40	3	46	6	40
70 & over	145	82	63	1	..	1	67	62	5	77	20	57
						HINDU.						
All ages	**49,693**	**28,748**	**20,945**	**18,782**	**12,249**	**6,533**	**24,142**	**15,537**	**8,605**	**6,769**	**962**	**5,807**
0—5	5,764	2,887	2,877	5,731	2,878	2,853	30	9	21	3	..	3
0—1	1,320	677	643	1,320	677	643	..	..	..	..	..	..
1—2	1,038	528	510	1,034	528	506	4	..	4	..	..	..
2—3	1,166	575	591	1,160	575	585	6	..	6	..	..	..
3—4	1,133	550	583	1,124	547	577	8	3	5	1	..	1
4—5	1,107	557	550	1,093	551	542	12	6	6	2	..	2
5—10	5,107	2,785	2,322	4,693	2,737	1,956	400	47	353	14	1	13
10—15	4,854	2,756	2,098	3,830	2,586	1,244	979	168	811	45	2	43
15—20	5,427	3,383	2,044	1,992	1,870	122	3,201	1,501	1,700	234	12	222
20—25	5,671	3,469	2,202	1,434	1,407	27	3,834	2,035	1,799	403	27	376
25—30	4,533	2,478	2,055	566	408	158	3,215	1,996	1,219	752	74	678
30—35	4,319	2,495	1,824	373	218	155	3,112	2,168	944	834	109	725
35—40	3,862	2,515	1,347	67	61	6	2,958	2,328	630	837	126	711
40—45	3,527	2,367	1,160	49	44	5	2,656	2,205	451	822	118	704
45—50	2,286	1,409	877	14	12	2	1,539	1,284	255	733	113	620
50—55	1,609	884	725	11	10	1	956	772	184	642	102	540
55—60	1,053	551	502	6	5	1	557	460	97	490	86	404
60—65	794	374	420	8	6	2	372	291	81	414	77	337
65—70	353	152	201	6	5	1	138	101	37	209	46	163
70 & over	534	243	291	2	2	..	195	172	23	337	69	268
						SAKTA.						
All ages	*8,501*	*5,431*	*3,070*	*3,044*	*1,901*	*1,143*	*4,511*	*3,393*	*1,118*	*946*	*137*	*809*
0—5	897	451	446	896	451	445	1	..	1	..	..	..
0—1	220	104	116	220	104	116	..	..	..	..	..	..
1—2	166	80	86	166	80	86	..	..	..	..	..	..
2—3	176	89	87	176	89	87	..	..	..	..	..	..
3—4	175	90	85	174	90	84	1	..	1	..	..	..
4—5	160	88	72	160	88	72	..	..	..	..	..	..
5—10	778	462	316	725	462	263	53	..	53	..	..	..
10—15	764	456	308	617	446	171	141	10	131	6	..	6
15—20	1,153	841	312	299	282	17	827	559	268	27	..	27
20—25	1,095	772	323	187	186	1	867	586	281	41	..	41
25—30	560	266	294	165	42	123	310	215	95	85	9	76
30—35	545	296	249	144	22	122	297	258	39	104	16	88
35—40	683	488	195	7	6	1	559	468	91	117	14	103
40—45	888	712	176	4	4	..	762	690	72	122	18	104
45—50	520	393	127	..	..	..	408	371	37	112	22	90
50—55	214	110	104	..	..	..	121	95	26	93	15	78
55—60	150	70	80	..	..	..	72	59	13	78	11	67
60—65	109	41	68	..	..	..	43	34	9	66	7	59
65—70	42	17	25	..	..	..	14	12	2	28	5	23
70 & over	103	56	47	..	..	..	36	36	..	67	20	47
						VAISHNAVA.						
All ages	*1,903*	*999*	*904*	*783*	*463*	*320*	*780*	*473*	*307*	*340*	*63*	*277*
0—5	248	115	133	247	115	132	1	..	1	..	..	
0—1	46	19	27	46	19	27	..	..	..	..	..	..
1—2	47	22	25	47	22	25	..	..	..	..	..	..
2—3	56	27	29	55	27	28	1	..	1	..	..	..
3—4	50	24	26	50	24	26	..	..	..	..	..	..
4—5	49	23	26	49	23	26	..	..	..	..	..	..
5—10	215	120	95	199	119	80	16	1	15	..	..	..
10—15	197	115	82	157	111	46	38	4	34	2	..	2
15—20	178	88	90	68	65	3	101	23	78	9	..	9
20—25	174	73	101	40	40	..	117	29	88	17	4	13
25—30	161	82	79	33	4	29	105	72	33	23	6	17
30—35	176	110	66	35	6	29	115	101	14	26	3	23
35—40	151	95	56	4	3	1	98	84	14	49	8	41
40—45	125	71	54	..	..	..	73	64	9	52	7	45
45—50	80	41	39	..	..	..	47	37	10	33	4	29
50—55	61	30	31	..	..	..	29	25	4	32	5	27
55—60	54	20	34	..	..	..	17	13	4	37	7	30
60—65	39	14	25	..	..	..	9	6	3	30	8	22
65—70	15	7	8	..	..	..	..	..	..	15	7	8
70 & over	29	18	11	..	..	..	14	14	..	15	4	11

IMPERIAL TABLE VII.—Age, sex and marital condition by religion.

Part B.—Suburbs in 24-Parganas.

Age-group.	All marital conditions.			Unmarried.			Married.			Widowed.		
	Both sexes.	Males.	Females.	Both sexes.	Males.	Females.	Both sexes.	Males.	Females.	Both sexes.	Males.	Females.
1	2	3	4	5	6	7	8	9	10	11	12	13
SIKH.												
All ages	**8**	**8**	..	**4**	**4**	..	**4**	**4**	..	..	..	..
0—5	3	3	..	3	3	..	..	..	..	..	..	..
0—1	*1*	*1*	..	*1*	*1*	..	..	..	..	..	..	..
1—2	*1*	*1*	..	*1*	*1*	..	..	..	..	..	..	..
2—3	*1*	*1*	..	*1*	*1*	..	..	..	..	..	..	..
3—4	..	..	..	..	..	..	..	..	..	..	..	..
4—5	..	..	..	..	..	..	..	..	..	..	..	..
5—10	..	..	..	..	..	..	..	..	..	..	..	..
10—15	1	1	..	1	1	..	..	..	..	..	..	..
15—20	..	..	..	..	..	..	..	..	..	..	..	..
20—25	..	..	..	..	..	..	..	..	..	..	..	..
25—30	1	1	..	..	..	..	1	1	..	..	..	..
30—35	2	2	..	..	..	..	2	2	..	..	..	..
35—40	1	1	..	..	..	..	1	1	..	..	..	..
40—45	..	..	..	..	..	..	..	..	..	..	..	..
45—50	..	..	..	..	..	..	..	..	..	..	..	..
50—55	..	..	..	..	..	..	..	..	..	..	..	..
55—60	..	..	..	..	..	..	..	..	..	..	..	..
60—65	..	..	..	..	..	..	..	..	..	..	..	..
65—70	..	..	..	..	..	..	..	..	..	..	..	..
70 & over	..	..	..	..	..	..	..	..	..	..	..	..
CHRISTIAN.												
All ages	**915**	**501**	**414**	**484**	**281**	**203**	**326**	**179**	**147**	**105**	**41**	**64**
0—5	95	50	45	90	46	44	5	4	1	..	..	..
0—1	*29*	*14*	*15*	*29*	*14*	*15*	..	..	..	..	..	..
1—2	*17*	*9*	*8*	*17*	*9*	*8*	..	..	..	..	..	..
2—3	*19*	*11*	*8*	*18*	*10*	*8*	*1*	*1*	..	..	..	..
3—4	*17*	*9*	*8*	*14*	*7*	*7*	*3*	*2*	*1*	..	..	..
4—5	*13*	*7*	*6*	*12*	*6*	*6*	*1*	*1*	..	..	..	..
5—10	98	60	38	96	59	37	2	1	1	..	..	..
10—15	120	72	48	114	70	44	6	2	4	..	..	..
15—20	99	49	50	76	43	33	22	6	16	1	..	1
20—25	86	43	43	54	32	22	32	11	21	..	..	..
25—30	84	46	38	25	16	9	53	29	24	6	1	5
30—35	74	42	32	15	10	5	51	31	20	8	1	7
35—40	55	27	28	4	2	2	36	19	17	15	6	9
40—45	54	28	26	3	1	2	30	14	16	21	13	8
45—50	46	26	20	1	..	1	27	16	11	18	10	8
50—55	38	20	18	1	..	1	25	17	8	12	3	..
55—60	19	12	7	3	1	2	11	9	2	5	2	3
60—65	22	14	8	2	1	1	12	10	2	8	3	5
65—70	12	7	5	..	..	..	7	5	2	5	2	3
70 & over	13	5	8	..	..	..	7	5	2	6	..	6
JAIN.												
All ages	**9**	**7**	**2**	..	..	..	**9**	**7**	**2**	..	..	..
0—5	..	..	..	..	..	..	..	..	..	..	..	..
0—1	..	..	..	..	..	..	..	..	..	..	..	..
1—2	..	..	..	..	..	..	..	..	..	..	..	..
2—3	..	..	..	..	..	..	..	..	..	..	..	..
3—4	..	..	..	..	..	..	..	..	..	..	..	..
4—5	..	..	..	..	..	..	..	..	..	..	..	..
5—10	..	..	..	..	..	..	..	..	..	..	..	..
10—15	..	..	..	..	..	..	..	..	..	..	..	..
15—20	..	..	..	..	..	..	..	..	..	..	..	..
20—25	1	1	..	..	..	..	1	1	..	..	..	..
25—30	2	1	1	..	..	..	2	1	1	..	..	..
30—35	2	1	1	..	..	..	2	1	1	..	..	..
35—40	[illegible]	[illegible]	..	..	..	..	2	2	..	..	..	..
40—45	1	1	..	..	..	..	1	1	..	..	..	..
45—50	..	..	..	..	..	..	..	..	..	..	..	..
50—55	..	..	..	..	..	..	..	..	..	..	..	..
55—60	..	..	..	..	..	..	..	..	..	..	..	..
60—65	..	..	..	..	..	..	..	..	..	..	..	..
65—70	1	1	..	..	..	..	1	1	..	..	..	..
70 & over	..	..	..	..	..	..	..	..	..	..	..	..
BUDDHIST.												
All ages	**157**	**99**	**58**	**41**	**29**	**12**	**80**	**49**	**31**	**36**	**21**	**15**
0—5	25	16	9	25	16	9	..	..	..	..	..	..
0—1	*14*	*10*	*4*	*14*	*10*	*4*	..	..	..	..	..	..
1—2	*4*	*2*	*2*	*4*	*2*	*2*	..	..	..	..	..	..
2—3	*2*	*1*	*1*	*2*	*1*	*1*	..	..	..	..	..	..
3—4	*2*	*1*	*1*	*2*	*1*	*1*	..	..	..	..	..	..
4—5	*3*	*2*	*1*	*3*	*2*	*1*	..	..	..	..	..	..
5—10	5	4	1	5	4	1	..	..	..	..	..	..
10—15	5	3	2	4	3	1	1	..	1	..	..	..
15—20	8	6	2	5	4	1	3	2	1	..	..	..
20—25	6	5	1	2	2	..	4	3	1	..	..	..
25—30	18	12	6	..	..	..	17	11	6	1	1	..
30—35	18	12	6	..	..	..	17	11	6	1	1	..
35—40	11	6	5	..	..	..	8	4	4	3	2	1
40—45	9	7	2	..	..	..	7	5	2	2	2	..
45—50	11	8	3	..	..	..	7	5	2	4	3	1
50—55	9	6	3	..	..	..	6	4	2	3	2	1
55—60	7	4	3	..	..	..	2	1	1	5	3	2
60—65	8	4	4	..	..	..	3	1	2	5	3	2
65—70	9	3	6	..	..	..	3	1	2	6	2	4
70 & over	8	3	5	..	..	..	2	1	1	6	2	4

IMPERIAL TABLE VII.—Age, sex and marital condition by religion.

Part B.—Suburbs in 24-Parganas.

Age-group.	All marital conditions.			Unmarried.			Married.			Widowed.		
	Both sexes.	Males.	Females.	Both sexes.	Males.	Females.	Both sexes.	Males.	Females.	Both sexes.	Males.	Females.
1	2	3	4	5	6	7	8	9	10	11	12	13
						TRIBAL.						
All ages	**714**	**539**	**175**	**156**	**114**	**42**	**449**	**348**	**101**	**109**	**77**	**32**
0—5	64	41	23	64	41	23	..	..	..	..	..	..
0—1	*20*	*14*	*6*	*20*	*14*	*6*	..	..	..	..	..	..
1—2	*13*	*7*	*6*	*13*	*7*	*6*	..	..	..	..	..	..
2—3	*12*	*7*	*5*	*12*	*7*	*5*	..	..	..	..	..	..
3—4	*11*	*7*	*4*	*11*	*7*	*4*	..	..	..	..	..	..
4—5	*8*	*6*	*2*	*8*	*6*	*2*	..	..	..	..	..	..
5—10	31	21	10	31	21	10	..	..	..	..	..	..
10—15	31	18	13	24	16	8	6	2	4	1	..	1
15—20	51	34	17	12	11	1	38	23	15	1	..	1
20—25	83	62	21	14	14	..	67	48	19	2	..	2
25—30	83	70	13	5	5	..	76	64	12	2	1	1
30—35	70	59	11	3	3	..	64	54	10	3	2	1
35—40	58	49	9	1	1	..	54	45	9	3	3	..
40—45	55	47	8	1	1	..	45	38	7	9	8	1
45—50	40	30	10	1	1	..	25	18	7	14	11	3
50—55	30	22	8	..	..	..	23	17	6	7	5	2
55—60	29	23	6	..	..	..	15	13	2	14	10	4
60—65	32	24	8	..	..	..	16	12	4	16	12	4
65—70	22	15	7	..	..	..	10	8	2	12	7	5
70 & over	35	24	11	..	..	..	10	6	4	25	18	7

Part C.—Howrah City.

Age-group.	All marital conditions.			Unmarried.			Married.			Widowed.		
	Both sexes.	Males.	Females.	Both sexes.	Males.	Females.	Both sexes.	Males.	Females.	Both sexes.	Males.	Females.
1	2	3	4	5	6	7	8	9	10	11	12	13
						ALL RELIGIONS.						
All ages	**224,873**	**145,120**	**79,753**	**75,085**	**49,451**	**25,634**	**132,353**	**91,482**	**40,871**	**17,435**	**4,187**	**13,248**
0—5	21,199	11,133	10,066	20,653	10,790	9,863	527	339	188	19	4	15
0—1	*4,703*	*2,409*	*2,294*	*4,581*	*2,311*	*2,270*	*119*	*97*	*22*	*3*	*1*	*2*
1—2	*3,688*	*1,944*	*1,744*	*3,621*	*1,901*	*1,720*	*66*	*43*	*23*	*1*	..	*1*
2—3	*4,447*	*2,346*	*2,101*	*4,359*	*2,287*	*2,072*	*86*	*59*	*27*	*2*	..	*2*
3—4	*4,299*	*2,269*	*2,030*	*4,174*	*2,197*	*1,977*	*118*	*69*	*49*	*7*	*3*	*4*
4—5	*4,062*	*2,165*	*1,897*	*3,918*	*2,094*	*1,824*	*138*	*71*	*67*	*6*	..	*6*
5—10	18,963	10,665	8,298	16,892	9,876	7,016	2,031	783	1,248	40	6	34
10—15	19,643	11,028	8,615	14,910	9,440	5,470	4,636	1,568	3,068	97	20	77
15—20	23,654	14,699	8,955	9,496	7,920	1,576	13,639	6,664	6,975	519	115	404
20—25	27,853	18,533	9,320	7,309	6,682	627	19,613	11,630	7,983	931	221	710
25—30	28,064	19,927	8,137	2,903	2,487	416	23,704	17,022	6,682	1,457	418	1,039
30—35	24,652	18,056	6,596	1,458	1,236	222	21,594	16,342	5,252	1,600	478	1,122
35—40	18,398	13,265	5,133	588	447	141	15,800	[illegible]	3,408	2,010	516	1,494
40—45	14,748	10,487	4,261	383	280	103	12,256	9,690	2,566	2,109	517	1,592
45—50	9,515	6,523	2,992	197	126	71	7,246	5,921	1,325	2,072	476	1,596
50—55	7,299	4,718	2,581	160	82	78	5,130	4,212	918	2,009	424	1,585
55—60	4,238	2,487	1,751	55	27	28	2,587	2,118	469	1,596	342	1,254
60—65	3,078	1,732	1,346	35	21	14	1,811	1,448	366	1,229	263	966
65—70	1,468	759	709	19	13	6	776	608	168	673	138	535
70 & over	2,101	1,108	993	27	24	3	1,000	835	165	1,074	249	825
						MUSLIM.						
All ages	**48,286**	**31,863**	**16,423**	**14,161**	**9,570**	**4,591**	**31,344**	**21,320**	**10,024**	**2,781**	**973**	**1,808**
0—5	4,396	2,407	1,989	4,251	2,326	1,925	141	79	62	4	2	2
0—1	*843*	*459*	*384*	*818*	*444*	*374*	*22*	*14*	*8*	*3*	*1*	*2*
1—2	*749*	*411*	*338*	*733*	*402*	*331*	*16*	*9*	*7*	..	..	..
2—3	*934*	*524*	*410*	*909*	*510*	*399*	*25*	*14*	*11*	..	..	..
3—4	*947*	*521*	*426*	*911*	*502*	*409*	*35*	*18*	*17*	*1*	*1*	..
4—5	*923*	*492*	*431*	*880*	*468*	*412*	*43*	*24*	*19*	..	..	..
5—10	4,263	2,414	1,849	3,714	2,186	1,528	544	226	318	5	2	3
10—15	4,148	2,464	1,684	2,963	1,999	964	1,167	458	709	18	7	11
15—20	4,722	3,003	1,719	1,356	1,273	83	3,292	1,692	1,600	74	38	36
20—25	5,812	3,860	1,952	1,081	1,045	36	4,612	2,747	1,865	119	68	51
25—30	5,959	4,204	1,755	451	432	19	5,310	3,664	1,646	198	108	90
30—35	5,297	3,828	1,469	188	174	14	4,878	3,535	1,343	231	119	112
35—40	4,042	2,962	1,080	64	54	10	3,678	2,788	890	300	120	180
40—45	3,276	2,391	885	42	35	7	2,914	2,248	666	320	108	212
45—50	2,219	1,607	612	21	20	1	1,846	1,484	362	352	103	249
50—55	1,640	1,144	496	18	16	2	1,292	1,037	255	330	91	239
55—60	955	627	328	7	6	1	671	550	121	277	71	206
60—65	728	465	263	1	1	..	492	406	86	235	58	177
65—70	301	181	120	1	..	1	186	150	36	114	31	83
70 & over	528	306	222	3	3	..	321	256	65	204	47	157

IMPERIAL TABLE VII.—Age, sex and marital condition by religion.

Part C.—Howrah City.

Age-group.	All marital conditions.			Unmarried.			Married.			Widowed.		
	Both sexes.	Males.	Females.	Both sexes.	Males.	Females.	Both sexes.	Males.	Females.	Both sexes.	Males.	Females.
1	2	3	4	5	6	7	8	9	10	11	12	13
HINDU.												
All ages	**173,613**	**111,511**	**62,102**	**59,595**	**39,060**	**20,535**	**99,524**	**69,275**	**30,249**	**14,494**	**3,176**	**11,318**
0—5	16,460	8,542	7,918	16,065	8,286	7,779	381	255	126	14	1	13
0—1	*3,781*	*1,913*	*1,868*	*3,685*	*1,831*	*1,854*	*96*	*82*	*14*	..	..	..
1—2	*2,888*	*1,503*	*1,385*	*2,837*	*1,469*	*1,368*	*50*	*34*	*16*	*1*	..	*1*
2—3	*3,441*	*1,782*	*1,659*	*3,378*	*1,737*	*1,641*	*61*	*45*	*16*	*2*	..	*2*
3—4	*3,274*	*1,704*	*1,570*	*3,189*	*1,655*	*1,534*	*80*	*48*	*32*	*5*	*1*	*4*
4—5	*3,076*	*1,640*	*1,436*	*2,976*	*1,594*	*1,382*	*94*	*46*	*48*	*6*	..	*6*
5—10	14,442	8,098	6,344	12,928	7,543	5,385	1,479	551	928	35	4	31
10—15	15,253	8,418	6,835	11,724	7,308	4,416	3,451	1,098	2,353	78	12	66
15—20	18,621	11,519	7,102	7,950	6,518	1,432	10,230	4,925	5,305	441	76	365
20—25	21,703	14,487	7,216	6,072	5,526	546	14,823	8,808	6,015	808	153	655
25—30	21,769	15,529	6,240	2,386	2,011	375	18,133	13,210	4,923	1,250	308	942
30—35	19,058	14,041	5,017	1,229	1,034	195	16,469	12,650	3,819	1,360	357	1,003
35—40	14,131	10,158	3,973	509	381	128	11,926	9,384	2,542	1,696	393	1,303
40—45	11,275	7,972	3,303	327	234	93	9,178	7,335	1,843	1,770	403	1,367
45—50	7,145	4,825	2,320	164	97	67	5,288	4,361	927	1,693	367	1,326
50—55	5,545	3,506	2,039	133	58	75	3,754	3,119	635	1,658	329	1,329
55—60	3,223	1,825	1,398	44	19	25	1,876	1,540	336	1,303	266	1,037
60—65	2,305	1,242	1,063	29	17	12	1,293	1,023	270	983	202	781
65—70	1,138	562	576	15	11	4	575	446	129	548	105	443
70 & over	1,545	787	758	20	17	3	668	570	98	857	200	657
SAKTA.												
All ages	***1,213***	***749***	***464***	***454***	***327***	***127***	***646***	***405***	***241***	***113***	***17***	***96***
0—5	*142*	*76*	*66*	*141*	*76*	*65*	*1*	..	*1*	..	..	..
0—1	*19*	*10*	*9*	*19*	*10*	*9*	..	..	..	..	..	..
1—2	*27*	*16*	*11*	*27*	*16*	*11*	..	..	..	..	..	..
2—3	*32*	*17*	*15*	*32*	*17*	*15*	..	..	..	..	..	..
3—4	*34*	*17*	*17*	*33*	*17*	*16*	*1*	..	*1*	..	..	..
4—5	*30*	*16*	*14*	*30*	*16*	*14*	..	..	..	..	..	..
5—10	*130*	*78*	*52*	*114*	*76*	*38*	*13*	*2*	*11*	*3*	..	*3*
10—15	*122*	*76*	*46*	*91*	*72*	*19*	*27*	*4*	*23*	*4*	..	*4*
15—20	*133*	*84*	*49*	*52*	*50*	*2*	*79*	*34*	*45*	*2*	..	*2*
20—25	*160*	*102*	*58*	*38*	*37*	*1*	*119*	*65*	*54*	*3*	..	*3*
25—30	*135*	*89*	*46*	*11*	*10*	*1*	*116*	*78*	*38*	*8*	*1*	*7*
30—35	*96*	*65*	*31*	*4*	*4*	..	*82*	*60*	*22*	*10*	*1*	*9*
35—40	*68*	*47*	*21*	..	..	..	*58*	*45*	*13*	*10*	*2*	*8*
40—45	*68*	*42*	*26*	*2*	*1*	*1*	*52*	*39*	*13*	*14*	*2*	*12*
45—50	*43*	*25*	*18*	*1*	*1*	..	*29*	*22*	*7*	*13*	*2*	*11*
50—55	*35*	*22*	*13*	..	..	..	*25*	*21*	*4*	*10*	*1*	*9*
55—60	*28*	*16*	*12*	..	..	..	*18*	*14*	*4*	*10*	*2*	*8*
60—65	*23*	*12*	*11*	..	..	..	*13*	*10*	*3*	*10*	*2*	*8*
65—70	*15*	*7*	*8*	..	..	..	*9*	*7*	*2*	*6*	..	*6*
70 & over	*15*	*8*	*7*	..	..	..	*5*	*4*	*1*	*10*	*4*	*6*
VAISHNAVA.												
All ages	***54***	***28***	***26***	***24***	***15***	***9***	***24***	***11***	***13***	***6***	***2***	***4***
0—5	*7*	*3*	*4*	*7*	*3*	*4*	..	..	..	..	..	..
0—1	*1*	..	*1*	*1*	..	*1*	..	..	..	..	..	..
1—2	*1*	..	*1*	*1*	..	*1*	..	..	..	..	..	..
2—3	*1*	..	*1*	*1*	..	*1*	..	..	..	..	..	..
3—4	*2*	*1*	*1*	*2*	*1*	*1*	..	..	..	..	..	..
4—5	*2*	*2*	..	*2*	*2*	..	..	..	..	..	..	..
5—10	*5*	..	*5*	*3*	..	*3*	*1*	..	*1*	*1*	..	*1*
10—15	*3*	..	*3*	*2*	..	*2*	*1*	..	*1*	..	..	..
15—20	*4*	*2*	*2*	*2*	*2*	..	*1*	..	*1*	..	..	..
20—25	*4*	*2*	*2*	*1*	*1*	..	*3*	*1*	*2*	*1*	..	*1*
25—30	*7*	*4*	*3*	*1*	*1*	..	*5*	*3*	*2*	*1*	..	*1*
30—35	*5*	*3*	*2*	*1*	*1*	..	*4*	*2*	*2*	..	..	..
35—40	*6*	*5*	*1*	*3*	*3*	..	*3*	*2*	*1*	..	..	..
40—45	*8*	*6*	*2*	*4*	*4*	..	*3*	*2*	*1*	*1*	..	*1*
45—50	*2*	*1*	*1*	..	..	..	*1*	..	*1*	*1*	*1*	..
50—55	*1*	..	*1*	..	..	..	*1*	..	*1*	..	..	..
55—60	*1*	*1*	..	..	..	..	..	..	..	*1*	*1*	..
60—65	*1*	*1*	..	..	..	..	*1*	*1*	..	..	..	..
65—70	..	..	..	..	..	..	..	..	..	..	..	..
70 & over	..	..	..	..	..	..	..	..	..	..	..	..
SIKH.												
All ages	**164**	**133**	**31**	**49**	**38**	**11**	**113**	**94**	**19**	**2**	**1**	**1**
0—5	17	11	6	15	9	6	2	2	..	..	..	..
0—1	..	..	..	..	..	..	..	..	..	..	..	..
1—2	*3*	*2*	*1*	*3*	*2*	*1*	..	..	..	..	..	..
2—3	*4*	*2*	*2*	*4*	*2*	*2*	..	..	..	..	..	..
3—4	*5*	*4*	*1*	*4*	*3*	*1*	*1*	*1*	..	..	..	..
4—5	*5*	*3*	*2*	*4*	*2*	*2*	*1*	*1*	..	..	..	..
5—10	15	12	3	12	9	3	3	3	..	..	..	..
10—15	13	10	3	9	7	2	4	3	1	..	..	..
15—20	13	10	3	5	5	..	8	5	3	..	..	..
20—25	12	11	1	4	4	..	8	7	1	..	..	..
25—30	21	16	5	2	2	..	19	14	5	..	..	..
30—35	22	19	3	2	2	..	20	17	3	..	..	..
35—40	17	15	2	..	..	..	17	15	2	..	..	..
40—45	13	10	3	..	..	..	13	10	3	..	..	..
45—50	8	7	1	..	..	..	8	7	1	..	..	..
50—55	3	3	..	..	..	..	3	3	..	..	..	..
55—60	4	4	..	..	..	..	3	3	..	1	1	..
60—65	2	2	..	..	..	..	2	2	..	..	..	..
65—70	2	1	1	..	..	..	1	1	..	1	..	1
70 & over	2	2	..	..	..	..	2	2	..	..	..	..

IMPERIAL TABLE VII.—Age, sex and marital condition by religion.

Part C.—Howrah City.

Age-group.	All marital conditions.			Unmarried.			Married.			Widowed.		
	Both sexes.	Males.	Females.	Both sexes.	Males.	Females.	Both sexes.	Males.	Females.	Both sexes.	Males.	Females.
1	2	3	4	5	6	7	8	9	10	11	12	13
						CHRISTIAN.						
All ages	**2,517**	**1,409**	**1,108**	**1,210**	**729**	**481**	**1,157**	**643**	**514**	**150**	**37**	**113**
0—5	306	163	143	303	160	143	2	2	..	1	1	..
0—1	*73*	*34*	*39*	*72*	*33*	*39*	*1*	*1*	..	..	..	..
1—2	*46*	*26*	*20*	*46*	*26*	*20*	..	..	..	..	..	..
2—3	*66*	*37*	*29*	*66*	*37*	*29*	..	..	..	..	..	..
3—4	*66*	*36*	*30*	*64*	*34*	*30*	*1*	*1*	..	*1*	*1*	..
4—5	*55*	*30*	*25*	*55*	*30*	*25*	..	..	..	..	..	..
5—10	236	136	100	231	133	98	5	3	2	..	..	..
10—15	217	127	90	206	120	86	10	6	4	1	1	..
15—20	251	136	115	171	111	60	78	24	54	2	1	1
20—25	273	137	136	141	96	45	129	41	88	3	..	3
25—30	260	137	123	58	36	22	194	99	95	8	2	6
30—35	234	138	96	36	23	13	189	113	76	9	2	7
35—40	188	118	70	14	12	2	161	103	58	13	3	10
40—45	174	108	66	14	11	3	141	91	50	19	6	13
45—50	133	76	57	11	8	3	95	62	33	27	6	21
50—55	103	59	44	9	8	1	74	47	27	20	4	19
55—60	48	25	23	4	2	2	31	19	12	13	4	9
60—65	42	22	20	5	3	2	26	16	10	11	3	8
65—70	26	14	12	3	2	1	13	10	3	10	2	8
70 & over	26	13	13	4	4	..	9	7	2	13	2	11
						JAIN.						
All ages	**57**	**42**	**15**	**8**	**5**	**3**	**48**	**37**	**11**	**1**	..	**1**
0—5	3	1	2	2	..	2	1	1	..	..	..	..
0—1	*1*	..	*1*	*1*	..	*1*	..	..	..	..	..	..
1—2	..	..	..	..	..	..	..	..	..	..	..	..
2—3	..	..	..	..	..	..	..	..	..	..	..	..
3—4	*2*	*1*	*1*	*1*	..	*1*	*1*	*1*	..	..	..	..
4—5	..	..	..	..	..	..	..	..	..	..	..	..
5—10	..	..	..	..	..	..	..	..	..	..	..	..
10—15	5	4	1	2	1	1	3	3	..	..	..	..
15—20	10	8	2	2	2	..	8	6	2	..	..	..
20—25	10	9	1	1	1	..	9	8	1	..	..	..
25—30	9	7	2	1	1	..	8	6	2	..	..	..
30—35	6	3	3	..	..	..	6	3	3	..	..	..
35—40	5	4	1	..	..	..	5	4	1	..	..	..
40—45	1	1	..	..	..	..	1	1	..	..	..	..
45—50	2	1	1	..	..	..	2	1	1	..	..	..
50—55	3	2	1	..	..	..	3	2	1	..	..	..
55—60	3	2	1	..	..	..	2	2	..	1	..	1
60—65	..	..	..	..	..	..	..	..	..	..	..	..
65—70	..	..	..	..	..	..	..	..	..	..	..	..
70 & over	..	..	..	..	..	..	..	..	..	..	..	..
						ZOROASTRIAN.						
All ages	**84**	**64**	**20**	**31**	**24**	**7**	**51**	**40**	**11**	**2**	..	**2**
0—5	11	7	4	11	7	4	..	..	..	..	..	..
0—1	*4*	*3*	*1*	*4*	*3*	*1*	..	..	..	..	..	..
1—2	*2*	*2*	..	*2*	*2*	..	..	..	..	..	..	..
2—3	*1*	*1*	..	*1*	*1*	..	..	..	..	..	..	..
3—4	*2*	*1*	*1*	*2*	*1*	*1*	..	..	..	..	..	..
4—5	*2*	..	*2*	*2*	..	*2*	..	..	..	..	..	..
5—10	3	2	1	3	2	1	..	..	..	..	..	..
10—15	4	3	1	4	3	1	..	..	..	..	..	..
15—20	14	10	4	6	6	..	7	4	3	1	..	1
20—25	17	14	3	5	5	..	12	9	3	..	..	..
25—30	9	8	1			..	9	8	1	..	..	..
30—35	6	5	1	..	..	..	6	5	1	..	..	..
35—40	6	3	3	1	..	1	4	3	1	1	..	1
40—45	4	2	2	..	..	..	4	2	2	..	..	..
45—50	4	4	..	1	1	..	3	3	..	..	..	..
50—55	2	2	..	..	..	..	2	2	..	..	..	..
55—60	2	2	..	..	..	..	2	2	..	..	..	..
60—65	1	1	..	..	..	..	1	1	..	..	..	..
65—70	1	1	..	..	..	..	1	1	..	..	..	..
70 & over	..	..	..	..	..	..	..	..	..	..	..	..
						BUDDHIST.						
All ages	**49**	**41**	**8**	**9**	**8**	**1**	**40**	**33**	**7**	..	..	..
0—5	2	1	1	2	1	1	..	..	..	..	..	..
0—1	..	..	..	..	..	..	..	..	..	..	..	..
1—2	..	..	..	..	..	..	..	..	..	..	..	..
2—3	*1*	..	*1*	*1*	..	*1*	..	..	..	..	..	..
3—4	*1*	*1*	..	*1*	*1*	..	..	..	..	..	..	..
4—5	..	..	..	..	..	..	..	..	..	..	..	..
5—10	..	..	..	..	..	..	..	..	..	..	..	..
10—15	1	1	..	1	1	..	..	..	..	..	..	..
15—20	1	1	..	1	1	..	..	..	..	..	..	..
20—25	4	3	1	1	1	..	3	2	1	..	..	..
25—30	17	14	3	2	2	..	15	12	3	..	..	..
30—35	15	13	2	2	2	..	13	11	2	..	..	..
35—40	3	2	1	..	..	..	3	2	1	..	..	..
40—45	2	2	..	..	..	..	2	2	..	..	..	..
45—50	2	2	..	..	..	..	2	2	..	..	..	..
50—55	1	1	..	..	..	..	1	1	..	..	..	..
55—60	1	1	..	..	..	..	1	1	..	..	..	..
60—65	..	..	..	..	..	..	..	..	..	..	..	..
65—70	..	..	..	..	..	..	..	..	..	..	..	..
70 & over	..	..	..	..	..	..	..	..	..	..	..	..

IMPERIAL TABLE VII.—Age, sex and marital condition by religion.

Part C.—Howrah City.

Age-group.	All marital conditions.			Unmarried.			Married.			Widowed.		
	Both sexes.	Males.	Females.	Both sexes.	Males.	Females.	Both sexes.	Males.	Females.	Both sexes.	Males.	Females.
1	2	3	4	5	6	7	8	9	10	11	12	13
TRIBAL.												
All ages	**103**	**57**	**46**	**22**	**17**	**5**	**76**	**40**	**36**	**5**	..	**5**
0—5	4	1	3	4	1	3	..	..	..	..	..	..
0—1	*1*	..	*1*	*1*	..	*1*	..	..	..	..	..	..
1—2	..	..	..	..	..	..	..	..	..	..	..	..
2—3	..	..	..	..	..	..	..	..	..	..	..	..
3—4	*2*	*1*	*1*	*2*	*1*	*1*	..	..	..	..	..	..
4—5	*1*	..	*1*	*1*	..	*1*	..	..	..	..	..	..
5—10	4	3	1	4	3	1	..	..	..	..	..	..
10—15	2	1	1	1	1	..	1	..	1	..	..	..
15—20	22	12	10	5	4	1	16	8	8	1	..	1
20—25	22	12	10	4	4	..	17	8	9	1	..	1
25—30	20	12	8	3	3	..	16	9	7	1	..	1
30—35	14	9	5	1	1	..	13	8	5	..	..	..
35—40	6	3	3	..	..	..	6	3	3	..	..	..
40—45	3	1	2	..	..	..	3	1	2	..	..	..
45—50	2	1	1	..	..	..	2	1	1	..	..	..
50—55	2	1	1	..	..	..	1	1	..	1	..	1
55—60	2	1	1	..	..	..	1	1	..	1	..	1
60—65	..	..	..	..	..	..	..	..	..	..	..	..
65—70	..	..	..	..	..	..	..	..	..	..	..	..
70 & over	..	..	..	..	..	..	..	..	..	..	..	..

IMPERIAL TABLE VIII.—Marital condition of selected castes, tribes, races and Muslim social groups by sexes at age-groups.

This table corresponds to imperial table XIV of 1921 and gives for selected groups figures similar to those in imperial table VII. The age-groups differ in two ways from those both in imperial table VII and in imperial table XIV of 1921 : the ages shown are to the nearest and not to the last birthday, and the usual quinary groups have been abandoned in order to avoid to some extent the distortion in the figures introduced by the observed preference for certain digits.

2. The entries occur in two series, first those of Asiatic race and next Anglo-Indians and non-Asiatics. Amongst Indians the groups chosen are those given in the title page to imperial table VIII in volume V, part ii ; details are given separately for persons of primitive tribes professing different religions ; and subsidiary figures are given by race, tribe or province of origin for such Indian Christians as are not shown elsewhere in the table under their own tribe. Amongst non-Asiatics no record is given of 846 persons (male 611, female 235) who returned themselves as European without specifying their nationality or country of birth, and considerations of space have excluded from the table details for groups numbering less than ten for whom the following statement is given here :

CASTE, etc. and religion.	Sex.	All marital conditions and ages.	Marital condition and age.																				
			Unmarried.							Married.							Widowed.						
			All ages.	0—6.	7—13.	14—16.	17—23.	24—43.	44 & over.	All ages.	0—6.	7—13.	14—16.	17—23.	24—43.	44 & over.	All ages.	0—6.	7—13.	14—16.	17—23.	24—43.	44 & over.
1	2	3	4	5	6	7	8	9	10	11	12	13	14	15	16	17	18	19	20	21	22	23	24
Austrian—Christian ..	Males	2	1	..	..	..	..	..	1	1	..	..	..	..	..	1	..	..	..	..	..	..	..
	Females	5	1	..	..	1	..	..	..	3	..	..	..	1	..	2	1	..	..	..	..	..	1
Bulgarian—Christian ..	Males	..	..	..	..	..	..	..	..	..	..	..	..	..	..	..	..	..	..	..	..	..	..
	Females	4	2	1	..	..	1	..	..	1	..	..	..	1	..	..	1	..	..	..	..	..	1
Canadian—Christian ..	Males	5	3	..	2	1	..	..	..	2	..	..	..	1	..	1	..	..	..	..	..	..	..
	Females	3	1	..	1	..	..	..	..	2	..	..	..	..	1	1	..	..	..	..	..	..	..
Danish—Christian ..	Males	3	..	..	..	..	..	..	..	3	..	..	..	1	2	..	..	..	..	..	..	..	..
	Females	2	..	..	..	..	..	..	..	2	..	..	..	1	1	..	..	..	..	..	..	..	..
Fijian—Christian ..	Males	1	..	..	..	..	..	..	..	1	..	..	..	..	..	1	..	..	..	..	..	..	..
	Females	1	..	..	..	..	..	..	..	1	..	..	..	..	1	..	..	..	..	..	..	..	..
Maltese—Christian ..	Males	..	..	..	..	..	..	..	..	..	..	..	..	..	..	..	..	..	..	..	..	..	..
	Females	1	..	..	..	..	..	..	..	..	..	..	..	..	..	..	1	..	..	..	..	1	..
New Zealander—Christian ..	Males	1	..	..	..	..	..	..	..	1	..	..	..	..	..	1	..	..	..	..	..	..	..
	Females	..	..	..	..	..	..	..	..	..	..	..	..	..	..	..	..	..	..	..	..	..	..
Philippinese—Christian ..	Males	4	1	..	..	1	..	..	..	3	..	..	..	..	1	2	..	..	..	..	..	..	..
	Females	..	..	..	..	..	..	..	..	..	..	..	..	..	..	..	..	..	..	..	..	..	..
Syrian—Christian ..	Males	1	1	..	..	..	1	..	..	..	..	..	..	..	..	..	..	..	..	..	..	..	..
	Females	..	..	..	..	..	..	..	..	..	..	..	..	..	..	..	..	..	..	..	..	..	..

3. Figures for sub-castes of Brahmans are incomplete owing to the failure of 187,458 persons (male 123,816, female 63,642) to make any return of their sub-caste.

IMPERIAL TABLE VIII.—Marital condition of selected castes,

CASTE, etc. and religion.	Sex.	All marital conditions and ages.	Marital — Unmarried. All ages.	0—6	7—13	14—16	17—23	24—43	44 & over.
1	2	3	4	5	6	7	8	9	10
AGARWALA—Hindu ..	Males	**3,359**	**1,207**	321	335	158	266	121	6
	Females	**1,890**	**480**	251	153	44	20	12	..
BAIDYA—Hindu ..	Males	**11,118**	**6,331**	1,556	1,462	638	1,620	1,026	29
	Females	**7,894**	**3,419**	1,412	1,287	425	246	44	5
BAISHNAB—Hindu ..	Males	**8,807**	**3,951**	1,118	1,181	449	757	379	67
	Females	**9,483**	**2,318**	1,169	813	104	107	111	14
BAURI—Hindu ..	Males	**41**	**9**	1	4	1	2	..	1
	Females	**166**	**44**	17	24	3	..	..	..
BRAHMAN—Hindu ..	Males	**129,288**	**58,658**	14,266	14,021	6,388	12,891	8,513	579
	Females	**67,995**	**26,275**	12,347	10,654	1,964	768	391	151
ACHARYA ..	Males	*37*	*17*	*5*	*3*	*5*	*2*	*2*	..
	Females	*10*	*6*	*3*	*1*	*2*	..	..	..
AGRADANI ..	Males	*12*	*7*	*1*	*2*	*4*	..	..	..
	Females	*9*	*4*	*2*	*1*	*1*	..	..	..
BARNASANKAR ..	Males	*12*	*8*	..	*1*	*4*	*3*	..	..
	Females	..	..	..	..	..	..	..	..
BHAT ..	Males	*166*	*47*	*7*	*16*	*21*	*3*	..	..
	Females	*147*	*33*	*9*	*18*	*6*	..	..	..
BHUINHAR ..	Males	*1*	..	..	..	..	..	..	..
	Females	..	..	..	..	..	..	..	..
DRAVIDA ..	Males	*13*	*3*	*1*	..	..	*2*	..	..
	Females	*11*	*3*	*2*	*1*	..	..	..	..
GAUDADYA ..	Males	*33*	*21*	*8*	*4*	*2*	*5*	*2*	..
	Females	*37*	*11*	..	*1*	..	*4*	*6*	..
GAUDIYA ..	Males	*7*	*4*	..	*2*	*1*	*1*	..	..
	Females	..	..	..	..	..	..	..	..
KANYAKUBJA ..	Males	*187*	*99*	*15*	*49*	*31*	*4*	..	..
	Females	*9*	*2*	*1*	*1*	..	..	..	..
MAHARASHTRIYA ..	Males	*9*	*2*	*2*	..	..	..	..	..
	Females	*7*	*1*	..	*1*	..	..	..	..
MAITHILI ..	Males	*14*	*6*	*2*	*2*	*2*	..	..	..
	Females	*3*	..	..	..	..	..	..	..
NEPALI ..	Males	*18*	*5*	..	*3*	*2*	..	..	..
	Females	..	..	..	..	..	..	..	..
RARHI ..	Males	*4,077*	*1,443*	*402*	*393*	*154*	*320*	*170*	*4*
	Females	*3,193*	*1,208*	*493*	*457*	*161*	*66*	*28*	*3*
SARASWAT ..	Males	*40*	..	..	..	..	..	..	..
	Females	*4*	*2*	*1*	*1*	..	..	..	..
UTKAL ..	Males	*163*	*65*	*13*	*19*	*11*	*16*	*6*	..
	Females	*18*	*7*	*2*	*3*	*2*	..	..	..
VAIDIK ..	Males	*326*	*158*	*47*	*49*	*19*	*24*	*15*	*4*
	Females	*349*	*145*	*60*	*71*	*9*	*4*	..	*1*
VARENDRA ..	Males	*357*	*155*	*54*	*46*	*23*	*21*	*11*	..
	Females	*556*	*269*	*103*	*95*	*46*	*17*	*6*	*2*
BRAHMO—Hindu ..	Males	**880**	**445**	33	102	152	104	46	8
	Females	**674**	**402**	48	110	95	124	19	6
BHUMIJ—Tribal ..	Males	**53**	**13**	6	5	..	1	1	..
	Females	**19**	**4**	2	2	..	..	..	..
CHINESE—Christians only ..	Males	**70**	**27**	5	7	2	3	7	3
	Females	**77**	**42**	14	7	7	12	1	1
DOM—Hindu ..	Males	**2,740**	**912**	337	342	99	87	44	3
	Females	**1,852**	**513**	226	232	46	7	2	..
INDIAN CHRISTIAN—Christian ..	Males	**8,302**	**4,344**	965	1,155	542	1,048	539	95
	Females	**6,811**	**3,394**	924	970	512	527	374	87
ASSAMESE ..	Males	*12*	*1*	..	*1*	..	..	..	..
	Females	*1*	..	..	..	..	..	..	..
BENGALI ..	Males	*6,140*	*3,263*	*749*	*923*	*404*	*755*	*384*	*48*
	Females	*5,492*	*2,808*	*726*	*832*	*436*	*425*	*313*	*76*
BIHARI ..	Males	*307*	*152*	*21*	*51*	*6*	*29*	*31*	*14*
	Females	*194*	*66*	*20*	*10*	*9*	*14*	*11*	*2*
BURMESE ..	Males	*4*	*4*	..	..	..	*1*	*3*	..
	Females	*1*	..	..	..	..	..	..	..
CEYLONESE ..	Males	*5*	*2*	..	..	..	*1*	*1*	..
	Females	..	..	..	..	..	..	..	..
GOANESE ..	Males	*323*	*151*	*7*	*10*	*11*	*86*	*28*	*9*
	Females	*20*	*11*	*8*	*2*	*1*	..	..	..
JEW ..	Males	*45*	*16*	*2*	*3*	*3*	..	*6*	*2*
	Females	*25*	*12*	*2*	*3*	*3*	..	*3*	*1*
MADRASI ..	Males	*772*	*430*	*89*	*100*	*93*	*110*	*24*	*14*
	Females	*463*	*227*	*78*	*59*	*32*	*38*	*16*	*4*
MALABARI ..	Males	*2*	*2*	..	..	..	..	*2*	..
	Females	..	..	..	..	..	..	..	..
NEPALI ..	Males	*5*	*3*	..	*1*	..	*2*	..	..
	Females	*5*	*1*	..	..	..	*1*	..	..
ORIYA ..	Males	*87*	*28*	*3*	*2*	*3*	*3*	*14*	*3*
	Females	*13*	*5*	..	*2*	..	..	*3*	..
PUNJABI ..	Males	*115*	*50*	*11*	*11*	*4*	*11*	*12*	*1*
	Females	*62*	*31*	*14*	*9*	*2*	*4*	*2*	..
JALIYA KAIBARTTA—Hindu ..	Males	**4,362**	**1,913**	450	618	366	280	191	8
	Females	**3,623**	**887**	381	249	145	55	44	13
JAPANESE—Christian ..	Males	**43**	**17**	3	12	..	..	..	2
	Females	**31**	**11**	6	4	..	1	..	..
JOGI OR JUGI—Hindu ..	Males	**2,743**	**1,336**	461	405	135	243	84	8
	Females	**2,225**	**711**	399	251	21	22	18	..
KAYASTHA—Hindu ..	Males	**116,632**	**53,081**	13,150	12,214	5,576	13,360	8,365	416
	Females	**65,942**	**23,150**	10,485	9,904	1,727	625	358	51
KOCH—Hindu ..	Males	**35**	**23**	..	4	5	9	5	..
	Females	..	..	..	..	..	..	..	..
LEPCHA—All religions ..	Males	**88**	**21**	..	4	17	..	..	..
	Females	**6**	**3**	1	1	..	..	1	..
Hindu ..	Males	*88*	*21*	..	*4*	*17*	..	..	..
	Females	*5*	*2*	*1*	*1*	..	..	..	..
Christian ..	Males	..	..	..	..	..	..	..	..
	Females	*1*	*1*	..	..	..	..	*1*	..
MAHISHYA—Hindu ..	Males	**45,022**	**16,666**	3,825	4,548	2,156	4,369	1,657	111
	Females	**31,416**	**7,335**	4,321	2,548	125	164	330	47
MALAYAN—Christian ..	Males	**8**	**2**	1	..	1	..	..	..
	Females	**11**	**7**	2	2	..	3	..	..
" MUMIN " (JOLAHA)—Muslim ..	Males	**2,478**	**689**	203	244	59	128	51	4
	Females	**1,428**	**408**	221	153	19	5	9	1
MUNDA—All religions ..	Males	**287**	**115**	33	21	8	33	19	1
	Females	**131**	**59**	22	20	5	6	3	3
Tribal ..	Males	*130*	*25*	*4*	*2*	*3*	*12*	*4*	..
	Females	*24*	*8*	*3*	*2*	*1*	..	*2*	..
Christian ..	Males	*157*	*90*	*29*	*19*	*5*	*21*	*15*	*1*
	Females	*107*	*51*	*19*	*18*	*4*	*6*	*1*	*3*

tribes, races and Muslim social groups by sexes at age-groups.

condition and age.

Married.							Widowed.						
All ages.	0—6	7—13	14—16	17—23	24—43	44 & over	All ages.	0—6	7—13	14—16	17—23	24—43	44 & over
11	12	13	14	15	16	17	18	19	20	21	22	23	24
1,987	5	32	70	384	1,095	401	165	..	..	1	10	83	71
1,220	12	34	180	322	584	88	190	..	..	2	9	78	101
4,564	24	54	61	322	2,793	1,310	223	..	1	..	5	83	134
3,496	3	78	240	1,054	1,649	472	979	..	3	6	45	315	610
4,427	18	87	93	578	2,494	1,157	429	..	..	..	17	153	259
4,207	30	253	502	1,038	1,895	489	2,958	5	11	17	207	1,366	1,352
31	..	2	..	6	17	6	1	..	..	..	..	1	..
94	..	3	4	19	42	26	28	..	..	1	2	11	14
68,147	220	567	970	8,318	44,820	13,252	4,483	2	3	142	265	1,808	2,263
30,921	80	1,358	3,037	9,096	13,436	3,914	10,799	8	23	94	722	4,202	5,750
16	..	..	..	1	8	7	4	..	..	..	..	3	1
4	..	..	..	..	2	2	..	..	..	..	..	..	..
5	..	..	..	..	2	3	..	..	..	..	..	..	..
5	..	..	..	1	2	2	..	..	..	..	..	..	..
3	..	..	..	..	1	2	1	..	..	..	..	..	1
..	..	..	..	..	..	..	..	..	..	..	..	..	..
103	..	..	14	68	18	3	16	..	..	..	..	9	7
67	..	..	37	16	11	3	47	..	..	5	18	20	4
1	..	..	..	..	1	..	..	..	..	..	..	..	..
..	..	..	..	..	..	..	..	..	..	..	..	..	..
9	..	..	..	..	8	1	1	..	..	..	..	1	..
7	..	..	..	1	1	5	1	..	..	..	..	..	1
12	..	..	..	1	9	2	..	..	..	..	..	..	..
13	..	..	..	..	7	6	13	..	..	..	..	5	8
3	..	..	..	..	2	1	..	..	..	..	..	..	..
..	..	..	..	..	..	..	..	..	..	..	..	..	..
85	..	..	1	18	44	22	3	..	..	..	..	1	2
6	..	..	..	5	..	1	1	..	..	..	..	..	1
7	..	..	..	1	5	1	..	..	..	..	..	..	..
5	..	..	1	2	1	1	1	..	..	..	..	1	..
7	..	..	..	..	4	3	1	..	..	..	..	..	1
3	..	..	..	2	1	..	..	..	..	..	..	..	..
10	..	..	..	..	6	4	3	..	..	..	..	1	2
..	..	..	..	..	..	..	..	..	..	..	..	..	..
2,575	3	20	81	231	1,376	864	59	..	..	..	7	20	32
1,507	1	22	94	367	702	321	478	..	..	2	19	154	303
40	..	..	..	3	17	20	..	..	..	..	..	..	..
2	..	..	..	..	2	..	..	..	..	..	..	..	..
92	..	..	..	15	48	29	6	..	..	..	..	4	2
9	..	..	..	..	7	2	2	..	..	..	..	..	2
159	..	..	1	17	81	60	9	..	..	..	..	3	6
154	..	3	8	30	76	37	50	..	..	..	2	17	31
186	1	1	4	19	89	72	16	..	..	..	..	9	7
188	..	7	15	52	85	29	99	..	..	..	15	25	59
409	..	4	5	14	253	133	26	..	..	..	..	13	13
246	..	2	2	3	179	60	26	..	..	..	..	13	13
31	..	..	..	1	22	8	9	..	..	..	..	..	9
12	..	..	1	4	5	2	3	..	..	..	..	..	3
38	..	..	..	5	16	17	5	..	..	..	1	..	4
34	..	..	4	..	11	19	1	..	..	..	1	..	..
1,666	7	26	67	178	856	532	162	..	1	1	16	56	88
1,138	15	70	100	246	403	304	201	..	2	4	10	77	108
3,686	18	42	72	358	2,183	1,013	272	1	1	2	1	109	158
2,817	16	47	94	699	1,406	355	800	4	3	7	20	288	478
10	..	..	..	..	10	..	1	..	..	..	..	1	..
1	..	..	..	1	..	..	..	..	..	..	..	..	..
2,712	13	31	58	254	1,610	746	165	1	1	..	..	64	99
2,078	16	40	66	553	1,150	253	606	4	2	6	17	204	373
146	..	1	5	26	70	44	9	..	..	..	..	3	6
100	..	..	6	26	60	8	28	..	..	..	..	13	15
..	..	..	..	..	..	..	..	..	..	..	..	..	..
1	..	..	..	..	1	..	..	..	..	..	..	..	..
2	..	..	..	1	1	..	1	..	..	..	..	..	1
..	..	..	..	..	..	..	..	..	..	..	..	..	..
166	..	..	..	12	103	51	6	..	..	..	..	2	4
6	..	..	..	..	6	..	3	..	..	..	..	..	3
25	..	..	..	4	8	13	4	..	..	..	..	3	1
9	..	..	..	4	4	1	4	..	..	..	..	..	4
287	5	6	6	23	168	79	55	..	..	..	..	20	35
177	..	5	14	46	69	43	59	..	1	1	..	25	32
..	..	..	..	..	..	..	..	..	..	..	..	..	..
..	..	..	..	..	..	..	..	..	..	..	..	..	..
2	..	..	..	2	..	..	..	..	..	..	..	..	..
1	..	..	..	1	..	..	3	..	..	..	..	3	..
56	..	..	..	..	51	5	3	..	..	..	..	2	1
8	..	..	..	..	1	7	..	..	..	..	..	..	..
55	..	3	1	5	24	22	10	..	..	1	1	4	4
24	..	1	2	5	9	7	7	..	..	..	..	2	5
2,254	1	21	31	240	1,574	387	195	..	..	..	2	94	99
1,816	5	97	223	365	621	505	920	..	5	13	142	391	369
24	..	..	..	2	13	9	2	..	..	..	..	2	..
19	..	..	..	..	8	11	1	..	..	..	..	1	..
1,293	3	12	15	161	765	337	114	..	..	..	2	37	75
1,033	4	62	113	291	452	111	481	1	..	2	40	153	285
60,255	154	672	895	6,184	35,045	17,305	3,296	5	2	4	170	1,278	1,837
31,377	116	1,039	2,452	8,706	13,982	5,082	11,415	2	24	61	688	4,482	6,158
10	..	..	..	..	7	3	2	..	..	..	..	..	2
..	..	..	..	..	..	..	..	..	..	..	..	..	..
61	..	..	..	35	22	4	6	..	..	..	..	3	3
3	..	..	..	2	1	..	..	..	..	..	..	..	..
61	..	..	..	35	22	4	6	..	..	..	..	3	3
3	..	..	..	2	1	..	..	..	..	..	..	..	..
..	..	..	..	..	..	..	..	..	..	..	..	..	..
..	..	..	..	..	..	..	..	..	..	..	..	..	..
26,975	79	252	487	4,888	14,919	6,350	1,381	..	3	26	46	547	759
13,346	64	866	1,411	3,041	6,536	1,426	10,537	7	24	87	584	5,002	4,833
4	..	..	..	..	1	3	2	..	..	..	..	2	..
3	..	..	..	2	1	..	1	..	..	..	..	1	..
1,714	4	46	47	236	1,012	369	75	..	..	..	8	31	36
849	6	57	95	190	411	90	171	1	..	2	4	54	110
164	..	1	2	24	107	30	8	..	..	..	..	7	1
59	..	1	2	21	33	2	13	..	..	..	1	4	8
103	..	1	2	20	67	13	2	..	..	..	..	1	1
13	..	1	2	6	4	..	3	..	..	..	..	1	2
61	..	..	..	4	40	17	6	..	..	..	..	6	..
46	..	..	..	15	29	2	10	..	..	..	1	3	6

IMPERIAL TABLE VIII.—Marital condition of selected castes,

CASTE, etc. and religion.	Sex.	All marital conditions and ages.	Marital						
			Unmarried.						
			All ages.	0—6	7—13	14—16	17—23	24—43	44 & over.
1	2	3	4	5	6	7	8	9	10
NAMASUDRA—Hindu ..	Males	**2,475**	**986**	296	259	128	190	96	17
	Females	**1,804**	**431**	202	133	53	18	21	4
ORAON—All religions ..	Males	**475**	**130**	51	24	14	27	13	1
	Females	**231**	**83**	40	17	5	7	14	..
Tribal ..	Males	*290*	*56*	*24*	*7*	*5*	*13*	*7*	..
	Females	*92*	*19*	*12*	*5*	*1*	*1*	..	..
Christian ..	Males	*185*	*74*	*27*	*17*	*9*	*14*	*6*	*1*
	Females	*139*	*64*	*28*	*12*	*4*	*6*	*14*	..
PERSIAN—Christians only ..	Males	**19**	**16**	..	..	8	8	..	..
	Females	**26**	**11**	2	2	5	1	..	1
SANTAL—All religions ..	Males	**661**	**254**	71	72	12	67	28	4
	Females	**483**	**174**	67	37	22	36	11	1
Hindu ..	Males	*68*	*42*	*2*	*28*	*4*	*4*	*4*	..
	Females	*10*	*8*	*7*	*1*	..	..	..	..
Tribal ..	Males	*450*	*134*	*42*	*27*	*4*	*48*	*11*	*2*
	Females	*185*	*49*	*31*	*13*	*1*	*3*	*1*	..
Christian ..	Males	*143*	*78*	*27*	*17*	*4*	*15*	*13*	*2*
	Females	*288*	*117*	*29*	*23*	*21*	*33*	*10*	*1*
SAYYAD—Muslim ..	Males	**5,089**	**1,938**	438	690	203	386	209	12
	Females	**2,204**	**682**	316	255	65	32	8	6
SHAHA—Hindu ..	Males	**8,035**	**2,724**	550	756	428	471	512	7
	Females	**4,378**	**991**	511	371	42	42	22	3
SIAMESE—Christian ..	Males	..	..	..	..	..	..	..	..
	Females	**12**	..	..	..	..	..	..	..
ANGLO-INDIAN—Christian ..	Males	**9,111**	**5,277**	1,366	1,492	611	935	721	152
	Females	**9,358**	**4,890**	1,261	1,433	703	707	562	224
AMERICAN—Christian ..	Males	**129**	**73**	8	10	5	13	33	4
	Females	**62**	**30**	13	4	5	1	4	3
ARMENIAN—Christian ..	Males	**418**	**221**	64	49	33	36	35	4
	Females	**328**	**158**	54	41	28	16	16	3
AUSTRALIAN—Christian ..	Males	**17**	**4**	2	1	1	..	..	..
	Females	**15**	**9**	3	2	..	2	2	..
BELGIAN—Christian ..	Males	**30**	**23**	3	4	..	4	10	2
	Females	**2**	**1**	1	..	..	..	..	..
DUTCH—Christian ..	Males	**78**	**32**	5	2	2	5	9	9
	Females	**20**	**7**	4	..	..	..	2	1
ENGLISH—Christian ..	Males	**7,598**	**3,709**	843	565	332	540	1,152	277
	Females	**4,916**	**2,121**	774	521	209	300	228	89
FRENCH—Christian ..	Males	**118**	**61**	13	15	13	10	5	5
	Females	**104**	**57**	19	7	8	5	14	4
GERMAN—Christian ..	Males	**76**	**51**	8	4	1	15	20	3
	Females	**37**	**17**	3	7	1	..	3	3
GREEK—Christian ..	Males	**29**	**13**	1	2	1	1	6	2
	Females	**43**	**24**	15	8	1	..	..	..
IRISH—Christian ..	Males	**312**	**178**	32	41	20	44	31	10
	Females	**220**	**105**	39	30	10	12	7	7
ITALIAN—Christian ..	Males	**164**	**74**	1	4	4	5	60	..
	Females	**29**	**13**	6	3	3	..	..	1
NORWEGIAN—Christian ..	Males	**18**	**9**	..	..	..	3	6	..
	Females	..	..	..	..	..	..	..	..
PORTUGUESE—Christian ..	Males	**113**	**66**	17	17	7	11	12	2
	Females	**63**	**39**	16	15	3	3	2	..
RUSSIAN—Christian ..	Males	**11**	**6**	1	1	2	..	2	..
	Females	**13**	**6**	..	..	..	..	6	..
SCOTCH—Christian ..	Males	**701**	**268**	58	35	14	29	108	24
	Females	**307**	**120**	40	22	14	14	24	6
SOUTH AFRICAN—Christian ..	Males	**9**	**3**	..	..	..	2	1	..
	Females	**7**	**2**	..	1	1	..	..	..
SPANISH—Christian ..	Males	**37**	**33**	1	..	8	24	..	..
	Females	**9**	**4**	2	2	..	..	..	..
SWEDISH—Christian ..	Males	**35**	**14**	..	..	1	6	7	..
	Females	**1**	..	..	..	..	..	..	..
SWISS—Christian ..	Males	**16**	**6**	2	..	1	1	2	..
	Females	**6**	**3**	1	..	..	2	..	..
WELSH—Christian ..	Males	**62**	**47**	6	19	19	2	1	..
	Females	**4**	**1**	1	..	..	..	..	..

tribes, races and Muslim social groups by sexes at age-groups.

condition and age.

Married.							Widowed.						
All ages.	0—6	7—13	14—16	17—23	24—43	44 & over	All ages.	0—6	7—13	14—16	17—23	24—43	44 & over
11	12	13	14	15	16	17	18	19	20	21	22	23	24
1,389	7	27	34	247	754	320	100	..	..	..	6	36	58
888	6	83	115	216	298	170	485	..	1	10	38	255	181
270	..	1	3	55	176	35	39	..	..	..	..	16	23
117	..	..	4	18	79	16	15	..	..	..	2	5	8
210	..	*1*	*2*	*34*	*146*	*27*	*24*	..	..	..	..	*7*	*17*
61	..	..	*4*	*18*	*28*	*11*	*12*	..	..	..	*2*	*3*	*7*
60	..	..	*1*	*21*	*30*	*8*	*15*	..	..	..	..	*9*	*6*
56	..	..	..	..	*51*	*5*	*3*	..	..	..	..	*2*	*1*
3	..	..	..	..	3	..	..	..	..	..	..	..	..
8	..	..	..	1	4	3	7	..	..	..	..	6	1
351	2	6	5	25	216	97	56	..	..	..	..	4	52
216	1	6	9	51	102	47	93	..	..	2	6	31	54
26	..	..	*1*	*3*	*9*	*13*	..	..	..	..	..	..	..
1	..	..	..	..	*1*	..	*1*	..	..	..	..	..	*1*
267	*2*	*5*	*4*	*16*	*170*	*70*	*49*	..	..	..	..	*2*	*47*
109	*1*	*5*	*4*	*24*	*54*	*21*	*27*	..	..	*2*	*4*	*2*	*19*
58	..	*1*	..	*6*	*37*	*14*	*7*	..	..	..	..	*2*	*5*
106	..	*1*	*5*	*27*	*47*	*26*	*65*	..	..	..	*2*	*29*	*34*
2,979	15	74	145	356	1,668	721	172	..	..	1	9	71	91
1,235	8	79	111	276	556	205	287	1	1	1	41	75	168
4,910	3	25	93	553	2,124	2,112	401	..	2	1	20	136	242
2,889	5	127	206	843	1,076	632	498	..	1	3	81	183	280
..	..	..	..	..	..	..	..	..	..	..	..	..	..
12	..	..	..	..	8	4	..	..	..	..	..	..	..
3,579	..	..	26	287	443	1,123	255	..	..	..	4	81	170
3,651	..	..	99	664	2,062	826	817	..	..	..	43	222	552
50	..	..	..	3	23	24	7	..	..	..	..	2	5
28	..	..	..	3	17	8	4	..	1	..	..	1	2
185	..	..	..	2	88	95	12	..	..	..	..	4	8
124	..	..	8	8	58	50	46	..	..	..	..	10	36
13	..	..	..	..	4	9	..	..	..	..	..	..	..
6	..	..	..	..	2	4	..	..	..	..	..	..	..
3	..	..	..	2	..	1	4	..	..	..	..	..	4
1	..	..	..	..	..	1	..	..	..	..	..	..	..
42	..	..	..	3	24	15	4	..	..	..	..	..	4
12	..	..	..	3	6	3	1	..	..	..	..	..	1
3,748	22	26	15	397	1,767	1,521	141	..	..	..	1	53	87
2,440	23	19	42	292	1,335	729	355	..	..	2	14	95	244
45	..	..	..	2	24	19	12	..	..	..	2	5	5
29	..	..	1	3	17	8	18	..	..	..	1	11	6
23	..	..	..	4	8	11	2	..	..	..	..	..	2
18	..	..	..	1	7	10	2	..	..	..	..	1	1
16	..	..	..	..	9	7	..	..	..	..	..	..	..
16	..	..	..	..	1	15	3	..	..	..	..	2	1
123	..	..	..	11	55	57	11	..	..	..	..	1	10
87	..	..	1	14	36	36	28	..	..	..	..	7	21
86	..	..	..	..	44	42	4	..	..	..	..	3	1
11	..	..	..	3	6	2	5	..	..	..	1	2	2
9	..	..	..	2	3	4	..	..	..	..	..	..	..
..	..	..	..	..	..	..	..	..	..	..	..	..	..
46	..	..	..	7	25	14	1	..	..	..	..	..	1
22	..	..	..	5	16	1	2	..	..	..	..	1	1
2	..	..	..	..	2	..	3	..	..	..	..	3	..
4	..	..	..	..	3	1	8	..	..	..	..	3	..
412	..	..	1	58	171	182	21	..	..	..	..	9	12
170	..	2	2	11	81	74	17	..	..	1	1	3	12
6	..	..	..	..	3	3	..	..	..	..	..	..	..
5	..	..	..	..	4	1	..	..	..	..	..	..	..
4	..	..	..	..	3	1	..	..	..	..	..	..	..
3	..	..	..	3	..	..	2	..	..	..	1	1	..
19	..	..	..	..	3	10	2	..	..	..	..	..	2
1	..	..	..	..	1	..	..	..	..	..	..	..	..
10	..	..	..	..	8	2	..	..	..	..	..	..	..
3	..	..	..	..	1	2	..	..	..	..	..	..	..
12	..	..	..	..	5	7	3	..	..	..	..	3	..
3	..	..	..	..	1	2	..	..	..	..	..	..	..

IMPERIAL TABLE IX.—Census infirmities.

This table corresponds to imperial table XII of 1921. It shows the numbers returned as suffering from insanity, deaf-mutism, total blindness or "corrosive" leprosy. The table is divided into two parts. In part i the distribution is given by age and sex. In part ii the distribution is by wards and sex.

2. In each part of the table the entry under Total Afflicted is not always equal to the sum of corresponding entries under each affliction. This is because persons suffering from more than one affliction are shown under each. In the supplement printed after the table the numbers of persons thus entered more than once are shown by sexes according to age (part i) and according to ward (part ii). There are no persons suffering from more than one infirmity in Howrah and Suburbs of Calcutta in 24-Parganas.

Part i.—Distribution by age.

Age.	Population Afflicted.			Insane.			Deaf-mute.			Blind.			Leper.		
	Both sexes.	Males.	Females.	Both sexes.	Males.	Females.	Both sexes.	Males.	Females.	Both sexes.	Males.	Females.	Both sexes.	Males.	Females.
1	2	3	4	5	6	7	8	9	10	11	12	13	14	15	16
CALCUTTA WITH SUBURBS AND HOWRAH.															
All ages ..	**2,182**	**1,506**	**676**	**569**	**419**	**150**	**513**	**329**	**184**	**826**	**541**	**285**	**292**	**228**	**64**
0—5 ..	41	26	15	4	4	..	31	17	14	6	5	1	..	..	..
0—1 ..	..	..	..	..	..	..	..	..	..	..	..	..	..	..	..
1—2 ..	*3*	*1*	*2*	..	..	..	*3*	*1*	*2*	..	..	..	..	..	..
2—3 ..	*5*	*3*	*2*	*1*	*1*	..	*4*	*2*	*2*	..	..	..	..	..	..
3—4 ..	*15*	*9*	*6*	*1*	*1*	..	*11*	*6*	*5*	*3*	*2*	*1*	..	..	..
4—5 ..	*18*	*13*	*5*	*2*	*2*	..	*13*	*8*	*5*	*3*	*3*	..	..	..	..
5—10 ..	115	74	41	15	12	3	69	42	27	29	20	9	3	1	2
10—15 ..	152	101	51	26	20	6	79	49	30	40	27	13	9	6	3
15—20 ..	165	126	39	40	33	7	56	41	15	50	36	14	21	18	3
20—25 ..	188	143	45	60	50	10	52	36	16	51	37	14	27	21	6
25—30 ..	205	153	52	90	74	16	46	27	19	41	29	12	30	24	6
30—35 ..	196	140	56	84	66	18	41	24	17	38	24	14	33	26	7
35—40 ..	196	137	59	72	46	26	29	21	8	56	38	18	41	32	9
40—45	191	134	57	72	44	28	25	19	6	64	48	16	31	24	7
45—50 ..	144	100	44	39	27	12	22	15	7	63	42	21	23	18	5
50—55 ..	131	90	41	23	17	6	20	14	6	67	42	25	23	18	5
55—60 ..	128	79	49	15	9	6	18	12	6	76	44	32	20	15	5
60—65 ..	119	71	48	15	9	6	11	6	5	75	42	33	18	14	4
65—70 ..	65	42	23	8	5	3	5	2	3	44	28	16	8	7	1
70 & over ..	146	90	56	6	3	3	9	4	5	126	79	47	5	4	1
CALCUTTA.															
All ages ..	**1,586**	**1,099**	**487**	**422**	**308**	**114**	**342**	**219**	**123**	**583**	**382**	**201**	**257**	**201**	**56**
0—5 ..	25	18	7	3	3	..	18	12	6	4	3	1	..	..	..
0—1 ..	..	..	..	..	..	..	..	..	..	..	..	..	..	..	..
1—2 ..	*2*	*1*	*1*	..	..	..	*2*	*1*	*1*	..	..	..	..	..	..
2—3 ..	*2*	*1*	*1*	..	..	..	*2*	*1*	*1*	..	..	..	..	..	..
3—4 ..	*9*	*6*	*3*	*1*	*1*	..	*6*	*4*	*2*	*2*	*1*	*1*	..	..	..
4—5 ..	*12*	*10*	*2*	*2*	*2*	..	*8*	*6*	*2*	*2*	*2*	..	..	..	..
5—10 ..	77	50	27	11	8	3	50	31	19	14	11	3	3	1	2
10—15 ..	98	66	32	20	15	5	55	34	21	17	12	5	8	6	2
15—20 ..	106	82	24	27	22	5	40	30	10	21	15	6	20	17	3
20—25 ..	132	101	31	42	34	8	38	27	11	28	20	8	26	21	5
25—30 ..	156	116	40	66	53	13	35	20	15	32	23	9	25	21	4
30—35 ..	151	108	43	61	48	13	31	17	14	31	21	10	28	22	6
35—40 ..	147	101	46	54	35	19	17	11	6	44	29	15	34	26	8
40—45 ..	140	98	42	52	33	19	12	9	3	49	36	13	28	21	7
45—50 ..	107	77	30	29	21	8	13	8	5	48	34	14	20	16	4
50—55 ..	99	68	31	17	12	5	12	7	5	51	34	17	21	16	5
55—60 ..	99	61	38	13	8	5	10	7	3	61	35	26	16	12	4
60—65 ..	94	58	36	14	9	5	7	5	2	57	32	25	16	12	4
65—70 ..	50	34	16	8	5	3	3	1	2	31	21	10	8	7	1
70 & over ..	105	61	44	5	2	3	1	..	1	95	56	39	4	3	1
SUBURBS IN 24-PARGANAS.															
All ages ..	**187**	**128**	**59**	**54**	**42**	**12**	**37**	**19**	**18**	**94**	**66**	**28**	**2**	**1**	**1**
0—5 ..	5	1	4	..	..	..	5	1	4	..	..	..	..	..	..
0—1 ..	..	..	..	..	..	..	..	..	..	..	..	..	..	..	..
1—2 ..	..	..	..	..	..	..	..	..	..	..	..	..	..	..	..
2—3 ..	*1*	..	*1*	..	..	..	*1*	..	*1*	..	..	..	..	..	..
3—4 ..	*3*	*1*	*2*	..	..	..	*3*	*1*	*2*	..	..	..	..	..	..
4—5 ..	*1*	..	*1*	..	..	..	*1*	..	*1*	..	..	..	..	..	..
5—10 ..	19	13	6	2	2	..	7	4	3	10	7	3	..	..	..
10—15 ..	29	19	10	3	2	1	9	5	4	17	12	5	..	..	..
15—20 ..	30	22	8	4	4	..	4	2	2	22	16	6	..	..	..
20—25 ..	25	19	6	6	6	..	3	1	2	16	12	4	..	..	..
25—30 ..	17	12	5	10	8	2	4	2	2	3	2	1	..	..	..
30—35 ..	14	9	5	10	7	3	2	2	..	2	..	2	..	..	..
35—40 ..	10	7	3	7	4	3	1	1	..	1	1	..	1	1	..
40—45 ..	9	6	3	6	4	2	1	..	1	2	2	..	..	..	..
45—50 ..	4	2	2	3	2	1	..	..	..	1	..	1	..	..	..
50—55 ..	4	3	1	2	2	..	..	..	..	2	1	1	..	..	..
55—60 ..	5	3	2	..	..	..	1	1	..	3	2	1	1	..	1
60—65 ..	3	2	1	..	..	..	..	..	..	3	2	1	..	..	..
65—70 ..	4	2	2	..	..	..	..	..	..	4	2	2	..	..	..
70 & over ..	9	8	1	1	1	..	..	..	..	8	7	1	..	..	..
HOWRAH.															
All ages ..	**409**	**279**	**130**	**93**	**69**	**24**	**134**	**91**	**43**	**149**	**93**	**56**	**33**	**26**	**7**
0—5 ..	11	7	4	1	1	..	8	4	4	2	2	..	..	..	..
0—1 ..	..	..	..	..	..	..	..	..	..	..	..	..	..	..	..
1—2 ..	*1*	..	*1*	..	..	..	*1*	..	*1*	..	..	..	..	..	..
2—3 ..	*2*	*2*	..	*1*	*1*	..	*1*	*1*	..	..	..	..	..	..	..
3—4 ..	*3*	*2*	*1*	..	..	..	*2*	*1*	*1*	*1*	*1*	..	..	..	..
4—5 ..	*5*	*3*	*2*	..	..	..	*4*	*2*	*2*	*1*	*1*	..	..	..	..
5—10 ..	19	11	8	2	2	..	12	7	5	5	2	3	..	..	..
10—15 ..	25	16	9	3	3	..	15	10	5	6	3	3	1	..	1
15—20 ..	29	22	7	9	7	2	12	9	3	7	5	2	1	1	..
20—25 ..	31	23	8	12	10	2	11	8	3	7	5	2	1	..	1
25—30 ..	32	25	7	14	13	1	7	5	2	6	4	2	5	3	2
30—35 ..	31	23	8	13	11	2	8	5	3	5	3	2	5	4	1
35—40 ..	39	29	10	11	7	4	11	9	2	11	8	3	6	5	1
40—45 ..	42	30	12	14	7	7	12	10	2	13	10	3	3	3	..
45—50 ..	33	21	12	7	4	3	9	7	2	14	8	6	3	2	1
50—55 ..	28	19	9	4	3	1	8	7	1	14	7	7	2	2	..
55—60 ..	24	15	9	2	1	1	7	4	3	12	7	5	3	3	..
60—65 ..	22	11	11	1	..	1	4	1	3	15	8	7	2	2	..
65—70 ..	11	6	5	..	..	..	2	1	1	9	5	4	..	..	..
70 & over ..	32	21	11	..	..	..	8	4	4	23	16	7	1	1	..

IMPERIAL TABLE IX.—Census infirmities.

Part ii.—Distribution by wards.

Name of ward, etc.	Population Afflicted.			Insane.			Deaf-mute.			Blind.			Leper.		
	Both sexes.	Males.	Females.	Both sexes.	Males.	Females.	Both sexes.	Males.	Females.	Both sexes.	Males.	Females.	Both sexes.	Males.	Females.
1	2	3	4	5	6	7	8	9	10	11	12	13	14	15	16
CALCUTTA WITH SUBURBS AND HOWRAH ..	**2,182**	**1,506**	**676**	**569**	**419**	**150**	**513**	**329**	**184**	**826**	**541**	**285**	**292**	**228**	**64**
CALCUTTA WITH SUBURBS IN 24-PARGANAS ..	**1,773**	**1,227**	**546**	**476**	**350**	**126**	**379**	**238**	**141**	**677**	**448**	**229**	**259**	**202**	**57**
Calcutta ..	**1,586**	**1,099**	**487**	**422**	**308**	**114**	**342**	**219**	**123**	**583**	**382**	**201**	**257**	**201**	**56**
MUNICIPAL AREA ..	**1,580**	**1,095**	**485**	**422**	**308**	**114**	**340**	**217**	**123**	**580**	**381**	**199**	**256**	**200**	**56**
District No. I—Total ..	**374**	**246**	**128**	**110**	**83**	**27**	**83**	**52**	**31**	**160**	**95**	**65**	**25**	**20**	**5**
Ward No. 1 Shampukur ..	59	34	25	15	10	5	10	5	5	29	15	14	5	4	1
Ward No. 2 Kumartuli ..	51	35	16	16	12	4	15	11	4	20	12	8	..	..	..
Ward No. 3 Bartola ..	75	51	24	19	16	3	23	14	9	31	20	11	2	1	1
Ward No. 4 Sukea's Street ..	8	2	6	..	..	..	3	1	2	3	1	2	2	..	2
Ward No. 5 Jorabagan ..	29	24	5	6	4	2	6	4	2	12	11	1	6	6	..
Ward No. 6 Jorasanko ..	53	39	14	27	22	5	9	5	4	16	11	5	2	2	..
Ward No. 30 Belgachia ..	30	19	11	8	5	3	7	4	3	13	8	5	3	3	..
Ward No. 31 Satpukur ..	34	19	15	10	7	3	3	3	..	21	9	12	..	..	..
Ward No. 32 Cossipore ..	35	23	12	9	7	2	7	5	2	15	8	7	5	4	1
District No. II—Total ..	**317**	**208**	**109**	**90**	**60**	**30**	**90**	**54**	**36**	**122**	**81**	**41**	**17**	**15**	**2**
Ward No. 7 Burra Bazar ..	7	7	..	2	2	..	..	..	..	5	5	..	..	..	..
Ward No. 8 Kalootola ..	36	30	6	5	5	..	9	5	4	14	12	2	9	9	..
Ward No. 9 Muchipara ..	90	65	25	27	22	5	23	17	6	36	22	14	4	4	..
Ward No. 10 Bow Bazar ..	17	12	5	4	1	3	6	5	1	7	6	1	..	..	..
Ward No. 11 Paddapukur ..	63	37	26	27	14	13	25	12	13	11	11	..	..	..	..
Ward No. 12 Waterloo Street ..	1	1	..	..	..	..	..	..	..	1	1	..	..	..	..
Ward No. 28 Beliaghata ..	56	31	25	13	7	6	19	12	7	22	11	11	3	2	1
Ward No. 29 Maniktala ..	47	25	22	12	9	3	8	3	5	26	13	13	1	..	1
District No. III—Total ..	**465**	**348**	**117**	**94**	**69**	**25**	**78**	**45**	**43**	**143**	**110**	**33**	**157**	**128**	**29**
Ward No. 13 Fenwick Bazar ..	19	15	4	5	5	..	6	4	2	9	7	2	..	..	..
Ward No. 14 Taltola ..	31	31	..	5	5	..	2	2	..	24	24	..	..	..	..
Ward No. 15 Kalinga ..	9	5	4	1	..	1	3	1	2	5	4	1	..	..	..
Ward No. 16 Park Street ..	1	1	..	..	..	..	..	..	..	1	1	..	..	..	..
Ward No. 17 Batman Bustee ..	1	1	..	..	..	..	..	..	..	1	1	..	..	..	..
Ward No. 18 Tengra ..	220	163	57	28	19	9	18	4	14	33	24	9	143	118	25
Ward No. 19 Intally ..	78	53	25	28	22	6	23	13	10	22	14	8	8	5	3
Ward No. 20 Beniapukur ..	72	55	17	16	12	4	19	15	4	33	24	9	5	4	1
Ward No. 21 Ballygunge ..	34	24	10	11	6	5	7	6	1	15	11	4	1	1	..
District No. IV—Total ..	**424**	**293**	**131**	**128**	**96**	**32**	**89**	**66**	**23**	**155**	**95**	**60**	**57**	**37**	**20**
Ward No. 27 Tollygunge ..	43	28	15	15	12	3	11	8	3	17	8	9	..	..	..
Ward No. 22 Bhawanipur ..	100	71	29	34	26	8	29	19	10	35	24	11	2	2	..
Ward No. 23 Alipore ..	21	16	5	10	8	2	6	5	1	5	2	3	1	1	..
Ward No. 24 Ekbalpore ..	137	94	43	27	19	8	20	19	1	43	25	18	48	31	17
Ward No. 25 Watganj and Hastings ..	37	28	9	14	11	3	10	7	3	10	8	2	3	2	1
Ward No. 26 Garden Reach ..	86	56	30	28	20	8	13	8	5	45	28	17	3	1	2
FORT WILLIAM AND MAIDAN ..	**1**	..	**1**	..	..	..	..	..	..	**1**	..	**1**	..	..	..
PORT ..	**5**	**4**	**1**	..	..	..	**2**	**2**	..	**2**	**1**	**1**	**1**	**1**	..
Suburbs in 24-Parganas ..	**187**	**128**	**59**	**54**	**42**	**12**	**37**	**19**	**18**	**94**	**66**	**28**	**2**	**1**	**1**
Tollygunge ..	35	24	11	22	17	5	9	4	5	4	3	1	..	..	..
South Suburban Municipality ..	152	104	48	32	25	7	28	15	13	90	63	27	2	1	1
HOWRAH ..	**409**	**279**	**130**	**93**	**69**	**24**	**134**	**91**	**43**	**149**	**93**	**56**	**33**	**26**	**7**
Ward No. 1 ..	23	14	9	7	4	3	7	5	2	8	4	4	1	1	..
Ward No. 2 ..	11	8	3	3	2	1	4	2	2	2	2	..	2	2	..
Ward No. 3 ..	25	16	9	5	3	2	7	4	3	12	9	3	1	..	1
Ward No. 4 ..	04	50	14	12	8	4	18	14	4	20	10	4	14	12	2
Ward No. 5 ..	54	39	15	4	3	1	10	9	1	34	21	13	6	6	..
Ward No. 6 ..	67	45	22	20	17	3	20	13	7	26	14	12	1	1	..
Ward No. 7 ..	31	22	9	9	7	2	11	9	2	10	6	4	1	..	1
Ward No 8 ..	64	41	23	15	12	3	27	17	10	19	11	8	3	1	2
Ward No. 9 ..	25	18	7	3	3	..	15	9	6	5	4	1	2	2	..
Ward No. 10 ..	45	26	19	15	10	5	15	9	6	13	6	7	2	1	1

SUPPLEMENT TO IMPERIAL TABLE IX.—Persons in Calcutta suffering from more than one census infirmity.

Part i.—By age and sex.

Infirmity and age.	Both sexes.	Males.	Females.
1	2	3	4
Insane and Deaf-mute.			
All ages	**4**	**2**	**2**
5—10	**1**	1	..
10—15	**1**	..	1
20—25	**1**	..	1
50—55	**1**	1	..
Insane and blind.			
All ages	**2**	**1**	**1**
40—45	**1**	1	..
50—55	**1**	..	1
Insane and leper.			
All ages	**5**	**5**	..
10—15	**1**	1	..
15—20	**2**	2	..
20—25	**1**	1	..
25—30	**1**	1	..

Infirmity and age.	Both sexes.	Males.	Females.
1	2	3	4
Deaf-mute and blind.			
All ages	**2**	**2**	..
40—45	**1**	1	..
55—60	**1**	1	..
Deaf-mute and leper.			
25—30	**1**	..	**1**
Blind and leper.			
45—50	**2**	**1**	**1**
Insane, deaf-mute and leper.			
35—40	**1**	..	**1**

Part ii.—By wards.

Name of Municipal Ward.	Insane and deaf-mute.			Insane and blind.			Insane and leper.			Deaf-mute and blind.			Deaf-mute and leper.			Blind and leper.			Insane, deaf-mute and leper.		
	Both sexes.	Males.	Females.	Both sexes.	Males.	Females.	Both sexes.	Males.	Females.	Both sexes.	Males.	Females.	Both sexes.	Males.	Females.	Both sexes.	Males.	Females.	Both sexes.	Males.	Females.
1	2	3	4	5	6	7	8	9	10	11	12	13	14	15	16	17	18	19	20	21	22
CALCUTTA	**4**	**2**	**2**	**2**	**1**	**1**	**5**	**5**	..	**2**	**2**	..	**1**	..	**1**	**2**	**1**	**1**	**1**	..	**1**
Ward No. 5 Jorabagan	..	..	..	1	1	..	..	..	..	..	..	..	..	..	..	..	..	..	..	..	..
Ward No. 6 Jorasanko	..	..	..	..	..	..	1	1	..	..	..	..	..	..	..	..	..	..	..	..	..
Ward No. 8 Kalootola	..	..	..	..	..	..	1	1	..	..	..	..	..	..	..	..	..	..	..	..	..
Ward No. 13 Fenwick Bazar	..	..	..	..	..	..	..	..	..	1	1	..	..	..	..	..	..	..	..	..	..
Ward No. 18 Tengra	..	..	..	..	..	..	2	2	..	..	..	..	..	..	..	..	..	..	..	..	..
Ward No. 19 Intally	..	..	..	..	..	..	1	1	..	..	..	..	..	..	..	..	..	..	1	..	1
Ward No. 20 Beniapukur	..	..	..	..	..	..	..	..	..	..	..	..	..	..	..	1	..	1	..	..	..
Ward No. 23 Alipore	1	..	1	..	..	..	..	..	..	..	..	..	..	..	..	..	..	..	..	..	..
Ward No. 24 Ekbalpore	..	..	..	1	..	1	..	..	..	..	..	..	..	..	..	..	..	..	..	..	..
Ward No. 26 Garden Reach	2	1	1	..	..	..	..	..	..	..	..	..	1	..	1	..	..	..	..	..	..
Ward No. 28 Beliaghata	1	1	..	..	..	..	..	..	..	..	..	..	..	..	..	..	..	..	..	..	..
Ward No. 30 Belgachia	..	..	..	..	..	..	..	..	..	..	..	..	..	..	..	1	1	..	..	..	..
Ward No. 32 Cossipore	..	..	..	..	..	..	..	..	..	1	1	..	..	..	..	..	..	..	..	..	..

IMPERIAL TABLE X.—Occupation or means of livelihood.

This table corresponds (with modifications) to imperial table XVII of 1921. Particulars given in 1921 of the dependents of workers in each occupation have not been collected but persons shown as " workers " in 1921 have been shown separately as " earners " and " working dependents ". Tables were designed to show subsidiary occupations of earners with agricultural occupations and also for certain mixed occupations to give the numbers returning each occupation as principal or subsidiary means of livelihood : these tables would have furnished particulars to some extent comparable with details (not now given but given in 1921) showing those workers in each occupation who have some form of agricultural occupation as a subsidiary means of livelihood, but public economy has made it impossible to prepare them. In place of these details, however, the present table shows also the numbers of earners following each occupation as a subsidiary means of livelihood to some other. Figures are shown by sexes for Calcutta with Suburbs and Howrah, Calcutta, Suburbs in 24-Parganas and Howrah city.

2. The scheme by which occupations have been classified comprises four main classes, divided into twelve sub-classes, fifty-five orders, and one hundred and ninety-five groups. Figures have also been given for three subsidiary groups forming part of the groups shown as No. 44, No. 102 and No. 117 : these are No. *44A.—Jute pressing ;* No. *102A.—Persons concerned with inland water transport ;* and No. *117A.—Trade in jute textiles.* The main classes and sub-classes are the same as in 1921. Orders Nos. 3, 4 and 5 of 1921 (Mines ; Quarries of hard rocks : and Salt, etc.) have been re-constituted as two, viz., 3.—Metallic minerals : and 4.—Non-metallic minerals : this results in a reduction of the number of orders by one and consequent changes of numeration. Many groups have been combined, for instance under the order 14.—Building industries, and others have been re-arranged or sub-divided, particularly in sub-classes I and II dealing with the exploitation of animals, vegetation and minerals. The group now appearing as No. 183 (persons connected with places of public entertainment) under the order " Letters, arts and sciences" was classed in 1921 as No. 101 under the order " Other miscellaneous and undefined industries "; whilst witches and wizards, shown in 1921 with beggars and vagrants now find themselves in group No. 181 in the company of horoscope casters, astrologers, fortune-tellers and mediums ; but with these exceptions the changes in the allocation of groups amongst orders are few and of minor importance. The list below gives in detail the corresponding groups in the tables of 1921 and 1931 :—

Corresponding groups in the tables of—							
1931	1921	1931	1921	1931	1921	1931	1921
1	1	63	54, 55	108	114	154	156
2, 3, 4	3	64	56	109	115	155	157
5, 6, 8	2	65	52, 53, 57				
7	4, 5	66	58	110	116	156	158
9, 10, 11, 12, 14, 15	6	67	59	111	117	157	159
		68	61	112	118	158	160
13, 16	7	69	62	113	119	159	161
17	8	70	60, 63, 64	114	120	160	162
18, 19	9	71	65				
20	10			115	121	161	163
21	11	72	67	116	122	162	164
22, 23	12, 13, 14	73	68	117	123	163	165
24, 26	15	74	71	118	124	164	166
25	16	75	72	119, 120, 121, 122	125	165	167
27	17	76	74				
28	18					166	168
29, 30, 31, 32, 33, 34	21	77	73	123	126	167	169
		78, 79, 80	75	124	127	168	170
35	19	81	66, 69, 70	125	128	169, 170, 171, 173	171
36	20	82	78	126	129		
37, 38, 39, 41	22	83, 84	76, 77, 79	127, 128	130	172	172
40	23, 24						
42	25	85	80	129	136	174	173
43	26, 27	86	81	130	132, 134, 135	175	174
44	28	87	82	131	133	176	175
45	29, 30	88	83	132	131, 138	177	176
46	31, 32, 33	89	84	133	139	178, 179, 180, 181, 193	177, 189
47	34, 35						
48	36	90	85, 86, 87, 88, 89	134	Nil.		
49	37			135, 136, 137	137	182	178
50	38	91	90	138	140	183	101
51	39, 40	92	91	139	141	184	179
		93	92	140	142	185	180
52	41	94	93			186	183
53	42			141	143		
54	43	95	94, 95	142	144	187	181, 182
55	44	96	96	143	145	188	184
56	45	97	97	144	146	189	185
		98	98, 99	145	147	190	186
57	46	99	100			191	187
58	47			146	148		
59	48	100	102, 103	147	149	192	188
60	49	101	104	148	150	193	189 (see also 181 of 1931).
61	50	102	107, 110	149	151		
		103	105, 108	150	152		
62	51	104	106, 109			194	190
				151	153	195	191
		105	111	152	154		
		106	112	153	155		
		107	113				

3. Persons shown as working dependents under group No. 192 are convicted prisoners in jail undergoing rigorous imprisonment. Other inmates of jails, asylums and almshouses are shown as " earners principal occupation " in this group and their numbers are similarly shown in the totals of the order, sub-class and class in which they fall as well as in columns 4-5, 11-12 and 18-19 opposite "All occupations" : but in the statements at the head of each group of columns they are excluded from the total number of earners and included in the total of non-working dependents.

4. The following statement gives a description of Orders and groups for which no returns were made which are consequently omitted in the table :—

8.—Cultivators of *jhum*, *taungya* and other shifting areas.
9.—Cinchona.
10.—Cocoanut.
11.—Coffee.
12.—Ganja.
14.—Rubber.
20.—Collectors of lac.
24.—Birds, bees, etc.
25.—Silkworms.

3.—METALLIC MINERALS.

29.—Gold
30.—Iron.
31.—Lead, silver and zinc.
32.—Manganese.
33.—Tin and wolfram.
34.—Other metallic minerals.

4.—NON-METALLIC MINERALS.

36.—Petroleum.
37.—Building materials (including stone, materials for cement manufacture and clays).
39.—Precious and semi-precious stones.
41.—Other non-metallic minerals.

6.—HIDES, SKINS AND HARD MATERIALS FROM THE ANIMAL KINGDOM.

52.—Furriers and persons occupied with feathers and bristles, brush-makers.
53.—Workers (except button-makers) in bone, ivory, horn, shell, etc.

10.—CHEMICAL PRODUCTS PROPERLY SO CALLED AND ANALOGOUS.

69.—Manufacture and refining of mineral oils.

11.—FOOD INDUSTRIES.

77.—Brewers and distillers.
79.—Manufacturers of opium.
80.—Manufacturers of *ganja.*
81.—Other food industries.

18. TRANSPORT BY AIR.

101.—Persons connected with aerodromes and aeroplanes.

39.—TRADE OF OTHER SORTS.

149.—Dealers in rags, stable refuse, etc.

40.—ARMY.

154.—Indian States Armies.

44.—PUBLIC ADMINISTRATION.

160.—Service of Indian and foreign states.

IMPERIAL TABLE X.—

Group No.	Occupation (CLASS, Sub-class, ORDER and group).	Calcutta with Suburbs and Howrah. Total earners .. .. 709,473* Total working dependents .. 4,025 Total non-working dependents .. 772,084* Total population .. .. 1,485,582 — Total, both sexes.	Numbers following the occupation as — Principal occupation. Males.	Principal occupation. Females.	Working dependents. Males.	Working dependents. Females.	Subsidiary to another occupation. Males.	Subsidiary to another occupation. Females.	Cal[cutta] … Total earners .. Total working dependents Total non-working depend[ents] Total population .. — Total, both sexes.	Numbers following — Principal occupation. Males.	Principal occupation. Females.
1	2	3	4	5	6	7	8	9	10	11	12
	ALL OCCUPATIONS	725,194	654,707	55,557	3,868	157	10,427	478	616,335	562,281	43,795
	A.—PRODUCTION OF RAW MATERIALS	25,696	19,919	2,170	55	3	3,492	57	15,300	12,151	1,263
	I.—Exploitation of animals and vegetation	25,297	19,556	2,155	55	3	3,471	57	15,212	12,065	1,261
	1. PASTURE AND AGRICULTURE	23,506	18,028	1,937	50	3	3,431	57	14,799	11,714	1 232
	(a) Ordinary Cultivation	21,012	15,652	1,853	50	3	3,397	57	12,944	9,897	1,199
1	Non-cultivating proprietors taking rent in money or kind ..	10,857	7,792	1,400	4	..	1,619	42	8,738	6,538	1,084
2	Estate agents and managers of private owners	41	41	..	..	..	..	..	19	19	..
3	Estate agents and managers of government	4	4	..	..	..	..	..	4	4	..
4	Rent collectors, clerks, etc.	2,164	2,153	3	..	..	8	..	1,334	1,327	..
5	Cultivating owners	4,342	2,828	201	..	..	1,309	4	1,934	1,350	59
6	Tenant cultivators	716	547	88	..	..	74	7	1	1	..
7	Agricultural labourers	2,888	2,287	161	46	3	387	4	914	658	56
	(b) Cultivation of special crops, fruit, etc. (Planters, managers, clerks and labourers)	1,643	1,610	12	..	..	21	..	1,309	1,298	9
13	Pan-vine	122	113	7	..	..	2	..	122	113	7
15	Tea	34	33	1	..	..	..	..	11	10	1
16	Market gardeners, flower and fruit growers	1,487	1,464	4	..	..	19	..	1,176	1,175	1
	(c) Forestry	382	382	..	..	..	..	..	319	319	..
17	Forest officers, rangers, guards, etc.	100	100	..	..	..	..	..	100	100	..
18	Wood-cutters and charcoal-burners	209	209	..	..	..	..	..	146	146	..
19	Collectors of forest produce	73	73	..	..	..	..	..	73	73	..
	(d) Stock raising	468	383	72	..	..	13	..	226	199	24
21	Cattle and buffalo breeders and keepers	280	217	54	..	..	9	..	114	87	24
22	Breeders of transport animals	13	13	..	..	..	..	..	13	13	..
23	Herdsmen, shepherds and breeders of other animals	175	153	18	..	..	4	..	99	99	..
	(e) Raising of small animals and insects	1	1	..	..	..	..	..	1	1	..
26	Lac cultivation	1	1	..	..	..	..	..	1	1	..
	2.—FISHING AND HUNTING	1,791	1,528	218	5	..	40	..	413	351	29
27	Fishing and pearling	1,782	1,519	218	5	..	40	..	404	342	29
28	Hunting	9	9	..	..	..	..	..	9	9	..
	II.—Exploitation of minerals	399	363	15	..	..	21	..	88	86	2
	4.—NON-METALLIC MINERALS	399	363	15	..	..	21	..	88	86	2
35	Coal	392	360	11	..	..	21	..	85	83	2
38	Mica	6	2	4	..	..	..	..	2	2	..
40	Salt, saltpetre and other saline substances	1	1	..	..	..	..	..	1	1	..
	B.—PREPARATION AND SUPPLY OF MATERIAL SUBSTANCES	319,357	300,559	15,398	176	24	3,123	77	263,494	251,622	10,234
	III.—Industry	140,269	129,275	9,632	99	8	1,216	39	108,755	102,085	6,125
	5.—TEXTILES	34,313	30,642	3,337	3	..	327	4	15,436	13,906	1,441
42	Cotton ginning, cleaning and pressing	277	268	7	..	..	2	..	219	210	7
43	Cotton spinning, sizing and weaving	1,821	1,765	45	..	..	11	..	495	454	37
44	Jute pressing, spinning and weaving	31,754	28,171	3,263	3	..	313	4	14,424	12,965	1,376
44A	*Jute pressing*	*9,826*	*9,072*	*683*	*3*	..	*67*	*1*	*3,012*	*3,012*	..
45	Rope, twine, string and other fibres	122	109	12	..	..	1	..	60	49	11
46	Wool carding, spinning and weaving	14	14	..	..	..	..	..	5	5	..
47	Silk spinning and weaving	26	26	..	..	..	..	..	14	14	..
48	Hair (horse-hair), etc.	5	5	..	..	..	..	..	..	..	..
49	Dyeing, bleaching, printing, preparation and sponging of textiles ..	139	139	..	..	..	..	..	137	137	..
50	Lace, crepe, embroideries, fringes, etc., and insufficiently described textile industries	155	145	10	..	..	..	..	82	72	10
	6.—HIDES, SKINS AND HARD MATERIALS FROM THE ANIMAL KINGDOM	211	211	..	..	..	..	..	69	69	..
51	Workers in leather	211	211	..	..	..	..	..	69	69	..
	7.—WOOD	12,863	12,553	222	..	..	85	3	11,788	11,606	161
54	Sawyers	302	302	..	..	..	..	..	302	302	..
55	Carpenters, turners and joiners, etc.	10,089	9,956	64	..	..	66	3	9,418	9,354	43
56	Basket-makers and other workers woody materials, (including leaves) and thatchers and builders working with bamboo, reeds or similar materials	2,472	2,295	158	..	..	19	..	2,068	1,950	118
	8.—METALS	4,104	4,005	41	..	..	58	..	3,623	3,592	11
57	Smelting, forging and rolling of iron and other metals.. ..	189	187	2	..	..	..	..	127	127	..
58	Makers of arms, guns, etc.	76	76	..	..	..	..	..	76	76	..
59	Blacksmiths, other workers in iron and makers of implements ..	3,062	2,989	26	..	..	47	..	2,677	2,666	2
60	Workers in brass, copper and bell-metal	254	248	5	..	..	1	..	244	241	2
61	Workers in other metals (except precious metals)	447	429	8	..	..	10	..	423	406	7
62	Workers in mints, die-sinkers, etc.	76	76	..	..	..	..	..	76	76	..
	9.—CERAMICS	1,692	1,437	213	..	..	42	..	1,002	987	14
63	Potters and makers of earthen ware	606	538	41	..	..	27	..	304	296	8
64	Brick and tile makers	773	590	168	..	..	15	..	388	384	3
65	Other workers in ceramics	313	309	4	..	..	..	..	310	307	3
	10.—CHEMICAL PRODUCTS PROPERLY SO CALLED AND ANALOGOUS	1,535	1,450	81	..	..	..	4	1,377	1,299	74
66	Manufacture of matches, fireworks and other explosives ..	588	545	39	..	..	..	4	585	542	39
67	Manufacture of aerated and mineral waters and ice	96	95	1	..	..	..	..	91	90	1
68	Manufacture and refining of vegetable oils	481	457	24	..	..	..	..	371	348	23
70	Other chemical manufacturers	370	353	17	..	..	..	..	330	319	11

* Figures of earners exclude and those of non-working dependents include 791 inmates of jails, etc., all males shown in columns 4 and 5 opposite "All occupations," "class D," "sub-class XII," "order 53" and "group 192."

Occupation or means of livelihood.

cutta.				Suburbs in 24-Parganas.							Howrah City.							
.. **605,364 .. 3,715 ents .. **587,655 .. 1,196,734				Total earners .. 23,547 Total working dependents .. 1 Total non-working dependents .. 40,427 Total population .. 63,975							Total earners .. ***80,562 Total working dependents .. 309 Total non-working dependents .. ***144,002 Total population .. 224,873							
the occupation as				Numbers following the occupation as							Numbers following the occupation as							
Working dependents.		Subsidiary to another occupation.		Total, both sexes.	Principal occupation.		Working dependents.		Subsidiary to another occupation.		Total, both sexes.	Principal occupation.		Working dependents.		Subsidiary to another occupation.		Group No.
Males.	Females.	Males.	Females.		Males.	Females.	Males.	Females.	Males.	Females.		Males.	Females.	Males.	Females.	Males.	Females.	
13	14	15	16	17	18	19	20	21	22	23	24	25	26	27	28	29	30	31
3,594	**121**	**6,210**	**334**	**25,115**	**20,491**	**3,056**	**1**	..	**1,547**	**20**	**83,744**	**71,935**	**8,706**	**273**	**36**	**2,670**	**124**	
..	**3**	**1,861**	**22**	**4,774**	**3,346**	**346**	**1**	..	**1,070**	**11**	**5,622**	**4,422**	**561**	**54**	..	**561**	**24**	
..	**3**	**1,861**	**22**	**4,769**	**3,345**	**342**	**1**	..	**1,070**	**11**	**5,316**	**4,146**	**552**	**54**	..	**540**	**24**	
..	**3**	**1,828**	**22**	**4,722**	**3,321**	**324**	**1**	..	**1,065**	**11**	**3,985**	**2,993**	**381**	**49**	..	**538**	**24**	
..	**3**	**1,823**	**22**	**4,344**	**2,969**	**324**	**1**	..	**1,039**	**11**	**3,724**	**2,786**	**330**	**49**	..	**535**	**24**	
..	..	1,098	18	**778**	367	77	..	..	330	4	**1,341**	887	239	4	..	191	20	1
..	..	..	..	**4**	4	..	..	..	..	..	**18**	18	..	..	..	..	..	2
..	..	..	..	..	..	..	..	..	..	..	..	..	..	..	..	..	..	3
..	..	7	..	**544**	543	..	..	..	1	..	**286**	283	3	..	..	..	..	4
..	..	525	..	**1,395**	832	109	..	..	454	..	**1,013**	646	33	..	..	330	4	5
..	..	..	..	**252**	110	71	..	..	64	7	**463**	436	17	..	..	10	..	6
..	3	193	4	**1,371**	1,113	67	1	..	190	..	**603**	516	38	45	..	4	..	7
..	..	**2**	..	**179**	**161**	..	..	..	**18**	..	**155**	**151**	**3**	..	..	**1**	..	
..	..	2	..	..	..	..	..	..	..	..	..	..	..	..	..	..	..	13
..	..	..	..	**2**	2	..	..	..	..	..	**21**	21	..	..	..	..	..	15
..	..	..	..	**177**	159	..	..	..	18	..	**134**	130	3	..	..	1	..	16
..	..	..	..	**57**	**57**	..	..	..	..	..	**6**	**6**	..	..	..	..	..	
..	..	..	..	..	..	..	..	..	..	..	..	..	..	..	..	..	..	17
..	..	..	..	**57**	57	..	..	..	..	..	**6**	6	..	..	..	..	..	18
..	..	..	..	..	..	..	..	..	..	..	..	..	..	..	..	..	..	19
..	..	**3**	..	**142**	**134**	..	..	..	**8**	..	**100**	**50**	**48**	..	..	**2**	..	
..	..	3	..	**108**	102	..	..	..	6	..	**58**	28	30	..	..	..	..	21
..	..	..	..	..	..	..	..	..	..	..	..	..	..	..	..	..	..	22
..	..	..	..	**34**	32	...	..	..	2	..	**42**	22	18	..	..	2	..	23
..	..	..	..	..	..	..	..	..	..	..	..	..	..	..	..	..	..	
..	..	..	..	..	..	..	..	..	..	..	..	..	..	..	..	..	..	26
..	..	**33**	..	**47**	**24**	**18**	..	..	**5**	..	**1,331**	**1,153**	**171**	**5**	..	**2**	..	
..	..	33	..	**47**	24	18	..	..	5	..	**1,331**	1,153	171	5	..	2	..	27
..	..	..	..	..	..	..	..	..	..	..	..	..	..	..	..	..	..	28
..	..	..	..	**5**	**1**	**4**	..	..	..	..	**306**	**276**	**9**	..	..	**21**	..	
..	..	..	..	**5**	**1**	**4**	..	..	..	..	**306**	**276**	**9**	..	..	**21**	..	
..	..	..	..	**1**	1	..	..	..	..	..	**306**	276	9	..	..	21	..	35
..	..	..	..	**4**	..	4	..	..	..	..	..	..	..	..	..	..	..	38
..	..	..	..	..	..	..	..	..	..	..	..	..	..	..	..	..	..	40
15	**12**	**1,568**	**43**	**10,480**	**8 520**	**1,621**	..	..	**330**	**9**	**45,383**	**40,417**	**3,543**	**161**	**12**	**1,225**	**25**	
8	**8**	**508**	**21**	**5,765**	**4,433**	**1,127**	..	..	**197**	**8**	**25,749**	**22,757**	**2,380**	**91**	..	**511**	**10**	
..	..	**87**	**2**	**607**	**400**	**206**	..	..	**1**	..	**18,270**	**16,336**	**1,690**	**3**	..	**239**	**2**	
..	..	2	..	**8**	8	..	..	..	..	..	**50**	50	..	..	..	..	..	42
..	..	4	..	**54**	48	5	..	..	1	..	**1,272**	1,263	3	..	..	6	..	43
..	..	81	2	**508**	307	201	..	..	..	..	**16,822**	14,899	1,686	3	..	232	2	44
..	..	..	..	*383*	*182*	*201*	..	..	..	..	*6,431*	*5,878*	*482*	*3*	..	*67*	*1*	*44A*
..	..	..	..	..	..	..	..	..	..	..	**62**	60	1	..	..	1	..	45
..	..	..	..	..	..	..	..	..	..	..	**9**	9	..	..	..	..	..	46
..	..	..	..	**12**	12	..	..	..	..	..	..	..	..	..	..	..	..	47
..	..	..	..	..	..	..	..	..	..	..	**5**	5	..	..	..	..	..	48
..	..	..	..	..	..	..	..	..	..	..	**2**	2	..	..	..	..	..	49
..	..	..	..	**25**	25	..	..	..	..	..	**48**	48	..	..	..	..	..	50
..	..	..	..	**141**	**141**	..	..	..	..	..	**1**	**1**	..	..	..	..	..	
..	..	..	..	**141**	141	..	..	..	..	..	**1**	1	..	..	..	..	..	51
..	..	**21**	..	**753**	**686**	**10**	..	..	**57**	..	**322**	**261**	**51**	..	..	**7**	**3**	
..	..	..	..	..	..	..	..	..	..	..	..	..	..	..	..	..	..	54
..	..	21	..	**412**	374	..	..	..	38	..	**259**	228	21	..	..	7	3	55
..	..	..	..	**341**	312	10	..	..	19	..	**63**	33	30	..	..	..	..	56
..	..	**20**	..	**365**	**323**	**4**	..	..	**38**	..	**116**	**90**	**26**	..	..	..	..	
..	..	..	..	**13**	13	..	..	..	..	..	**49**	47	2	..	..	..	..	57
..	..	..	..	..	..	..	..	..	..	..	..	..	..	..	..	..	..	58
..	..	9	..	**323**	284	1	..	..	38	..	**62**	39	23	..	..	..	..	59
..	..	1	..	**9**	6	3	..	..	..	..	**1**	1	..	..	..	..	..	60
..	..	10	..	**20**	20	..	..	..	..	..	**4**	3	1	..	..	..	..	61
..	..	..	..	..	..	..	..	..	..	..	..	..	..	..	..	..	..	62
..	..	**1**	..	**467**	**258**	**178**	..	..	**31**	..	**223**	**192**	**21**	..	..	**10**	..	
..	..	..	..	**149**	103	29	..	..	17	..	**153**	139	4	..	..	10	..	63
..	..	1	..	**318**	155	149	..	..	14	..	**67**	51	16	..	..	..	..	64
..	..	..	..	..	..	..	..	..	..	..	**3**	2	1	..	..	..	..	65
..	..	..	**4**	**48**	**41**	**7**	..	..	..	..	**110**	**110**	..	..	..	..	..	
..	..	..	4	..	..	..	..	..	..	..	**3**	3	..	..	..	..	..	66
..	..	..	..	**2**	2	..	..	..	..	..	**3**	3	..	..	..	..	..	67
..	..	..	..	**6**	5	1	..	..	..	..	**104**	104	..	..	..	..	..	68
..	..	..	..	**40**	34	6	..	..	..	..	..	..	..	..	..	..	..	70

**Figures of earners exclude and those of non-working dependents include 712 inmates of jails, etc., all males shown in columns 11 and 12 opposite " All occupations" " class D," " sub class XII ", " order 53 " and " group 192 ".

***Figures of earners exclude and those of non-working dependents include 79 inmates of jails, etc., all males shown in columns 25 and 26 opposite " All occupations", " class D ", " sub-class XII ", " order 53 " and " group 192."

IMPERIAL TABLE X.—

Group No.	Occupation (**CLASS, Sub-class, ORDER** and group).	Calcutta with Suburbs and Howrah. — Total, both sexes.	Numbers following the occupation as — Principal occupation. — Males.	Principal occupation. — Females.	Working dependents. — Males.	Working dependents. — Females.	Subsidiary to another occupation. — Males.	Subsidiary to another occupation. — Females.	Cal[cutta] — Total, both sexes.	Numbers following — Principal occupation. — Males.	Principal occupation. — Females.
1	2	3	4	5	6	7	8	9	10	11	12
	III.—Industry—*concluded.*										
	11.—FOOD INDUSTRIES	**9,495**	**8,080**	**1,255**	**12**	..	**141**	**7**	**7,472**	**6,845**	**564**
71	Rice pounders and huskers and flour grinders	2,837	1,743	1,055	..	..	35	4	1,417	1,003	412
72	Grain parchers, etc.	32	31	1	..	..	..	..	19	19	..
73	Butchers	1,287	1,264	19	4	..	..	..	1,170	1,153	17
74	Makers of sugar, molasses and gurh	205	205	..	..	..	..	..	205	205	..
75	Sweetmeat and condiment makers	668	652	16	..	..	..	..	668	652	16
76	Toddy drawers	12	10	2	..	..	..	..	4	2	2
78	Manufacturers of tobacco	3,871	3,598	158	8	..	104	3	3,450	3,276	113
81	Other food industries	583	577	4	..	..	2	..	539	535	4
	12.—INDUSTRIES OF DRESS AND THE TOILET	**31,951**	**29,549**	**1,976**	**84**	..	**339**	**3**	**27,558**	**25,605**	**1,753**
82	Boot, shoe, sandal and clog makers	9,106	8,062	1,006	5	..	32	1	8,546	7,543	984
83	Tailors, milliners, dress-makers and darners	9,835	9,313	287	74	..	161	..	8,312	7,910	271
84	Embroiderers, hat-makers and makers of other articles of wear	744	732	8	..	..	4	..	631	626	5
85	Washermen and cleaners	7,862	7,211	539	5	..	107	..	6,375	5,958	387
86	Barbers, hair-dressers and wig-makers	4,404	4,231	136	..	..	35	2	3,694	3,568	106
	13.—FURNITURE INDUSTRIES	**1,423**	**1,404**	**19**	..	..	..	..	**1,423**	**1,404**	**19**
88	Cabinet-makers, carriage-painters, etc.	1,398	1,379	19	..	..	..	..	1,398	1,379	19
89	Upholsterers, tent-makers, etc.	25	25	..	..	..	..	..	25	25	..
	14.—BUILDING INDUSTRIES	**14,024**	**12,890**	**1,034**	..	..	**98**	**2**	**12,428**	**11,389**	**978**
90	Lime-burners, cement workers ; excavators and well-sinkers ; stone cutters and dressers ; brick layers and masons ; builders (other than of buildings made of bamboo or similar materials), painters, decorators of houses, tilers, plumbers, etc.	14,024	12,890	1,034	..	..	98	2	12,428	11,389	978
	15.—CONSTRUCTION OF MEANS OF TRANSPORT	**1,987**	**1,969**	**1**	..	..	**17**	..	**1,885**	**1,885**	..
91	Persons engaged in making, assembling or repairing motor vehicles or cycles	1,146	1,130	1	..	..	15	..	1,060	1,060	..
92	Carriage, cart, palki, etc., makers and wheel-wrights	130	128	..	..	..	2	..	117	117	..
93	Ship, boat, aeroplane builders	711	711	..	..	..	..	..	708	708	..
	16.—PRODUCTION AND TRANSMISSION OF PHYSICAL FORCE	**2,668**	**2,664**	**1**	..	..	**3**	..	**2,278**	**2,277**	**1**
94	Heat, light, electricity, motive power, etc.	2,668	2,664	1	..	..	3	..	2,278	2,277	1
	17.—MISCELLANEOUS AND UNDEFINED INDUSTRIES	**24,003**	**22,421**	**1,452**	..	**8**	**106**	**16**	**22,416**	**21,221**	**1,109**
95	Printers, engravers, book-binders, etc.	10,842	10,801	9	..	..	32	..	10,715	10,676	9
96	Makers of musical instruments	590	590	..	..	..	..	..	588	588	..
97	Makers of clocks and surgical or scientific instruments, etc.	474	470	..	..	..	4	..	321	320	..
98	Makers of jewellery and ornaments	3,717	3,663	30	..	..	24	..	3,433	3,382	30
99	Other miscellaneous and undefined industries (toy-making, taxidermy, etc.)	46	22	24	..	..	..	..	38	22	16
100	Scavenging	8,334	6,875	1,389	..	8	46	16	7,321	6,233	1,054
	IV.—Transport	**64,100**	**62,791**	**1,035**	**52**	**4**	**217**	**1**	**56,788**	**55,955**	**744**
	19.—TRANSPORT BY WATER	**22,579**	**22,460**	**39**	**34**	..	**46**	..	**22,120**	**22,054**	**37**
102	Ship-owners, boat-owners and their employees, officers, mariners, etc., ships' brokers, boatmen and towmen	19,488	19,405	6	34	..	43	..	19,055	19,025	4
102A	*Ship-owners, boat-owners and their employees, officers, mariners, etc., ships' brokers, boatmen, and towmen of sea-going vessels*	*12,623*	*12,540*	*6*	*34*	..	*43*	..	*12,052*	*12,022*	*4*
103	Persons (other than labourers) employed in harbours, docks, rivers and canals, including pilots	1,758	1,722	33	..	..	3	..	1,736	1,700	33
104	Labourers employed on harbours, docks, rivers and canals	1,333	1,333	..	..	..	..	..	1,329	1,329	..
	20.—TRANSPORT BY ROAD	**27,322**	**26,449**	**769**	..	**4**	**99**	**1**	**24,858**	**24,236**	**565**
105	Persons (other than labourers) employed on the construction and maintenance of roads and bridges	1	1	..	..	..	..	..	..	..	..
106	Labourers employed on the construction of roads and bridges	3,254	2,507	747	..	..	..	..	2,492	1,948	544
107	Owners, managers and employees (excluding personal servants) connected with mechanically driven vehicles (including trams)	7,918	7,899	4	..	..	14	1	7,726	7,707	4
108	Owners, managers and employees (excluding personal servants) connected with other vehicles	9,683	9,623	1	..	..	59	..	8,369	8,338	..
109	Palki, etc., bearers and owners	1,303	1,287	16	..	..	..	..	1,260	1,244	16
110	Pack elephant, camel, mule, ass and bullock owners and drivers	5	5	..	..	..	..	..	5	5	..
111	Porters and messengers	5,158	5,127	1	..	4	26	..	5,006	4,994	1
	21.—TRANSPORT BY RAIL	**10,701**	**10,414**	**202**	**18**	..	**67**	..	**6,616**	**6,498**	**118**
112	Railway employees of all kinds other than coolies	8,093	7,853	173	..	..	67	..	5,090	4,974	116
113	Labourers employed on railway construction and maintenance and coolies and porters employed on railway premises	2,608	2,561	29	18	..	..	..	1,526	1,524	2
	22.—POST OFFICE, TELEGRAPH AND TELEPHONE SERVICES	**3,498**	**3,468**	**25**	..	..	**5**	..	**3,194**	**3,167**	**24**
114	Post office, Telegraph and Telephone services	3,498	3,468	25	..	..	5	..	3,194	3,167	24
	V.—Trade	**114,988**	**108,493**	**4,731**	**25**	**12**	**1,690**	**37**	**97,951**	**93,582**	**3,365**
	23.—BANKS, ESTABLISHMENTS OF CREDIT, EXCHANGE AND INSURANCE	**3,157**	**2,980**	**42**	..	..	**132**	**3**	**2,944**	**2,791**	**27**
115	Bank managers, money-lenders, exchange and insurance agents, money changers and brokers and their employees	3,157	2,980	42	..	..	132	3	2,944	2,791	27
	24.—BROKERAGE COMMISSION AND EXPORT	**5,566•**	**5,484**	**46**	..	..	**34**	**2**	**5,197**	**5,125**	**40**
116	Brokers, commission agents, commercial travellers, workhouse owners and their employees	5,566	5,484	46	..	..	34	2	5,197	5,125	40
	25.—TRADE IN TEXTILES	**5,171**	**4,998**	**66**	..	..	**104**	**3**	**4,610**	**4,486**	**51**
117	Trade in piece goods, jute, wool, cotton, silk, hair and other textiles	5,171	4,998	66	..	..	104	3	4,610	4,486	51
117A	*Trade in jute*	*169*	*135*	..	..	..	*34*	..	*165*	*131*	..

cutta.				Suburbs in 24-Parganas.							Howrah City.							
the occupation as				Numbers following the occupation as							Numbers following the occupation as							
Working dependents.		Subsidiary to another occupation.		Total, both sexes.	Principal occupation.		Working dependents.		Subsidiary to another occupation.		Total, both sexes.	Principal occupation.		Working dependents.		Subsidiary to another occupation.		Group No.
Males.	Females.	Males.	Females.		Males.	Females.	Males.	Females.	Males.	Females.		Males.	Females.	Males.	Females.	Males.	Females.	
13	14	15	16	17	18	19	20	21	22	23	24	25	26	27	28	29	30	31
8	..	**50**	**5**	**1,513**	**842**	**646**	..	..	**25**	..	**510**	**393**	**45**	**4**	..	**66**	**2**	
..	..	..	2	**1,371**	718	628	..	..	25	..	**49**	22	15	..	..	10	2	71
..	..	..	..	**2**	1	1	..	..	..	..	**11**	11	..	..	..	..	..	72
..	..	..	..	**27**	26	1	..	..	..	..	**90**	85	1	4	..	..	..	73
..	..	..	..	..	..	..	..	..	..	..	..	..	..	..	..	..	..	74
..	..	..	..	..	..	..	..	..	..	..	..	..	..	..	..	..	..	75
..	..	..	..	**1**	1	..	..	..	..	..	**7**	7	..	..	..	..	..	76
8	..	50	3	**109**	93	16	..	..	..	..	**312**	229	29	..	..	54	..	78
..	..	..	..	**3**	3	..	..	..	..	..	**41**	39	..	..	..	2	..	81
..	..	**200**	..	**1,272**	**1,212**	**30**	..	..	**29**	**1**	**3,121**	**2,732**	**193**	**84**	..	**110**	**2**	
..	..	19	..	**88**	83	3	..	..	1	1	**472**	436	19	5	..	12	..	82
..	..	131	..	**762**	749	5	..	..	8	..	**761**	654	11	74	..	22	..	83
..	..	..	..	**4**	4	..	..	..	..	..	**109**	102	3	..	..	4	..	84
..	..	30	..	**281**	250	22	..	..	9	..	**1,206**	1,003	130	5	..	68	..	85
..	..	20	..	**137**	126	..	..	..	11	..	**573**	537	30	..	..	4	2	86
..	..	..	..	..	..	..	..	..	..	..	..	..	..	..	..	..	..	
..	..	..	..	..	..	..	..	..	..	..	..	..	..	..	..	..	..	88
..	..	..	..	..	..	..	..	..	..	..	..	..	..	..	..	..	..	89
..	..	**59**	**2**	**401**	**373**	**12**	..	..	**16**	..	**1,195**	**1,128**	**44**	..	..	**23**	..	
..	..	59	2	**401**	373	12	..	..	16	..	**1,195**	1,128	44	..	..	23	..	90
..	..	..	..	**37**	**36**	**1**	..	..	..	..	**65**	**48**	..	..	..	**17**	..	
..	..	..	..	**26**	25	1	..	..	..	..	**60**	45	..	..	..	15	..	91
..	..	..	..	**11**	11	..	..	..	..	..	**2**	..	..	..	..	2	..	92
..	..	..	..	..	..	..	..	..	..	..	**3**	3	..	..	..	..	..	93
..	..	..	..	**23**	**23**	..	..	..	..	..	**367**	**364**	..	..	..	**3**	..	
..	..	..	..	**23**	23	..	..	..	..	..	**367**	364	..	..	..	3	..	94
..	**8**	**70**	**8**	**138**	**98**	**33**	..	..	..	**7**	**1,449**	**1,102**	**310**	..	..	**36**	**1**	
..	..	30	..	**33**	33	..	..	..	..	..	**94**	92	..	..	..	2	..	95
..	..	..	..	..	..	..	..	..	..	..	**2**	2	..	..	..	..	..	96
..	..	1	..	**7**	7	..	..	..	..	..	**146**	143	..	..	..	3	..	97
..	..	21	..	..	..	..	..	..	..	..	**284**	281	..	..	..	3	..	98
..	..	..	..	**3**	..	3	..	..	..	..	**5**	..	5	..	..	..	..	99
..	8	18	8	**95**	58	30	..	..	..	7	**918**	584	305	..	..	28	1	100
..	**4**	**84**	**1**	**928**	**760**	**166**	..	..	**2**	..	**6,384**	**6,076**	**125**	**52**	..	**131**	..	
..	..	**29**	..	**60**	**58**	**1**	..	..	**1**	..	**399**	**348**	**1**	**34**	..	**16**	..	
..	..	26	..	**60**	58	1	..	..	1	..	**373**	322	1	34	..	16	..	102
..	..	*26*	..	*60*	*58*	*1*	..	..	*1*	..	*511*	*460*	*1*	*34*	..	*16*	..	*102A*
..	..	3	..	..	..	..	..	..	..	..	**22**	22	..	..	..	..	..	103
..	..	..	..	..	..	..	..	..	..	..	**4**	4	..	..	..	..	..	104
..	**4**	**52**	**1**	**771**	**608**	**162**	..	..	**1**	..	**1,693**	**1,605**	**42**	..	..	**46**	..	
..	..	..	..	..	..	..	..	..	..	..	**1**	1	..	..	..	..	..	105
..	..	..	..	**295**	134	161	..	..	..	..	**467**	425	42	..	..	..	..	106
..	..	14	1	**67**	67	..	..	..	..	..	**125**	125	..	..	..	..	..	107
..	..	31	..	**389**	387	1	..	..	1	..	**925**	898	..	..	..	27	..	108
..	..	..	..	**14**	14	..	..	..	..	..	**29**	29	..	..	..	..	..	109
..	..	..	..	..	..	..	..	..	..	..	..	..	..	..	..	..	..	110
..	4	7	..	**6**	6	..	..	..	..	..	**146**	127	..	..	..	10	..	111
..	..	..	..	**76**	**73**	**3**	..	..	..	..	**4,009**	**3,843**	**81**	**18**	..	**67**	..	
..	..	..	..	**34**	31	3	..	..	..	..	**2,969**	2,848	54	..	..	67	..	112
..	..	..	..	**42**	42	..	..	..	..	..	**1,040**	995	27	18	..	..	..	113
..	..	**3**	..	**21**	**21**	..	..	..	..	..	**283**	**280**	**1**	..	..	**2**	..	
..	..	3	..	**21**	21	..	..	..	..	..	**283**	280	1	..	..	2	..	114
7	..	**976**	**21**	**3,787**	**3,327**	**328**	..	..	**131**	**1**	**13,250**	**11,584**	**1,038**	**18**	**12**	**583**	**15**	
..	..	**124**	**2**	**95**	**84**	**4**	..	..	**7**	..	**118**	**105**	**11**	..	..	**1**	**1**	
..	..	124	2	**95**	84	4	..	..	7	..	**118**	105	11	..	..	1	1	115
..	..	**30**	**2**	**31**	**29**	..	..	..	**2**	..	**338**	**330**	**6**	..	..	**2**	..	
..	..	30	2	**31**	29	..	..	..	2	..	**338**	330	6	..	..	2	..	116
..	..	**70**	**3**	**23**	**23**	..	..	..	..	..	**538**	**489**	**15**	..	..	**34**	..	
..	..	70	3	**23**	23	..	..	..	..	..	**538**	489	15	..	..	34	..	117
..	..	*34*	..	..	..	..	..	..	..	..	*4*	*4*	..	..	..	..	..	*117A*

IMPERIAL TABLE X.—

Group No.	Occupation (CLASS, Sub-class, ORDER and group).	Calcutta with Suburbs and Howrah. Numbers following the occupation as: Total, both sexes.	Principal occupation. Males.	Principal occupation. Females.	Working dependents. Males.	Working dependents. Females.	Subsidiary to another occupation. Males.	Subsidiary to another occupation. Females.	Cal... Numbers following: Total, both sexes.	Principal occupation. Males.	Principal occupation. Females.
1	2	3	4	5	6	7	8	9	10	11	12
	V.—Trade—*concluded.*										
	26.—TRADE IN SKINS, LEATHER AND FURS	**1,335**	**1,309**	**11**	..	..	**15**	..	**1,128**	**1,106**	**7**
118	Trade in skins, leather, furs, feathers, horn, etc., and the articles made from these	**1,335**	1,309	11	..	..	15	..	**1,128**	1,106	7
	27.—TRADE IN WOOD	**1,060**	**1,000**	**28**	..	..	**32**	..	**787**	**759**	**25**
119	Trade in wood (not firewood)	**958**	915	11	..	..	32	..	**704**	693	8
120	Trade in barks	**37**	37	..	..	..	..	..	**29**	29	..
121	Trade in bamboos and canes	**44**	27	17	..	..	..	..	**41**	24	17
122	Trade in thatches and other forest produce	**21**	21	..	..	..	..	..	**13**	13	..
	28.—TRADE IN METALS	**595**	**582**	**8**	..	..	**5**	..	**511**	**501**	**8**
123	Trade in metals, machinery, knives, tools, etc.	**595**	582	8	..	..	5	..	**511**	501	8
	29.—TRADE IN POTTERY, BRICKS AND TILES	**131**	**129**	**1**	..	..	**1**	..	**107**	**106**	**1**
124	Trade in pottery, bricks and tiles	**131**	129	1	..	..	1	..	**107**	106	1
	30.—TRADE IN CHEMICAL PRODUCTS	**498**	**476**	**6**	..	..	**16**	..	**442**	**423**	**6**
125	Drugs, dyes, paints, petroleum, explosives, etc.	**498**	476	6	..	..	16	..	**442**	423	6
	31.—HOTELS, CAFES, RESTAURANTS, ETC.	**4,751**	**4,622**	**110**	**5**	..	**14**	..	**4,033**	**3,928**	**97**
126	Vendors of wine, liquors, aerated waters and ice	**586**	571	8	5	..	2	..	**277**	276	1
127	Owners and managers of hotels, cook shops, sarais, etc. (and employees)	**4,112**	3,998	102	..	..	12	..	**3,753**	3,649	96
128	Hawkers of drink and food-stuffs	**53**	53	..	..	..	..	..	**3**	3	..
	32.—OTHER TRADE IN FOOD-STUFFS	**37,642**	**34,228**	**2,713**	**12**	**12**	**656**	**21**	**31,858**	**29,589**	**1,850**
129	Grain and pulse dealers	**3,368**	3,039	302	..	1	23	3	**2,929**	2,767	142
130	Dealers in sweetmeats, sugar and spices	**3,155**	2,944	138	12	2	56	3	**2,413**	2,287	72
131	Dealers in dairy products, eggs and poultry	**5,339**	4,629	625	..	..	82	3	**4,369**	3,938	397
132	Dealers in animals for food	**153**	150	3	..	..	..	..	**152**	149	3
133	Dealers in fodder for animals	**352**	344	8	..	..	..	..	**334**	327	7
134	Dealers in other food-stuffs	**23,596**	21,454	1,627	..	9	494	12	**20,050**	18,517	1,222
135	Dealers in tobacco	**962**	951	10	..	..	1	..	**905**	898	7
136	Dealers in opium	**110**	110	..	..	..	..	..	**106**	106	..
137	Dealers in ganja	**607**	607	..	..	..	..	..	**600**	600	..
	33.—TRADE IN CLOTHING AND TOILET ARTICLES	**2,149**	**2,119**	**23**	..	..	**7**	..	**2,012**	**1,983**	**23**
138	Trade in ready-made clothing and other articles of dress and the toilet (hats, umbrellas, socks, ready-made shoes, perfumes, etc.)	**2,149**	2,119	23	..	..	7	..	**2,012**	1,983	23
	34.—TRADE IN FURNITURE	**853**	**842**	**6**	..	..	**5**	..	**803**	**797**	**4**
139	Trade in furniture, carpets, curtains and bedding	**238**	234	4	..	..	..	..	**233**	230	3
140	Hardware, cooking utensils, porcelain, crockery	**615**	608	2	..	..	5	..	**570**	567	1
	35.—TRADE IN BUILDING MATERIALS	**195**	**185**	**7**	..	..	**3**	..	**155**	**148**	**7**
141	Trade in building materials (other than bricks, tiles and woody materials)	**195**	185	7	..	..	3	..	**155**	148	7
	36.—TRADE IN MEANS OF TRANSPORT	**312**	**307**	**3**	..	..	**2**	..	**248**	**244**	**2**
142	Dealers and hirers in mechanical transport—motors, cycles, etc.	**168**	166	..	..	..	2	..	**151**	149	..
143	Dealers and hirers in other carriages, carts, boats, etc.	**12**	12	..	..	..	..	..	**4**	4	..
144	Dealers and hirers of elephants, camels, horses, cattle, asses, mules, etc.	**132**	129	3	..	..	..	..	**93**	91	2
	37.—TRADE IN FUEL	**2,120**	**1,904**	**149**	..	..	**64**	**3**	**1,525**	**1,433**	**8**
145	Dealers in firewood, charcoal, coal, cowdung, etc.	**2,120**	1,904	149	..	..	64	3	**1,525**	1,433	88
	38.—TRADE IN ARTICLES OF LUXURY AND THOSE PERTAINING TO LETTERS AND THE ARTS AND SCIENCES	**5,597**	**5,303**	**155**	..	..	**139**	..	**4,643**	**4,527**	**64**
146	Dealers in precious stones, jewellery (real and imitation), clocks, optical instruments, etc.	**1,639**	1,585	20	..	..	34	..	**1,249**	1,209	14
147	Dealers in common bangles, bead necklaces, fans, small articles, toys, hunting and fishing tackle, flowers, etc.	**244**	198	46	..	..	..	..	**195**	183	12
148	Publishers, book-sellers, stationers, dealers in music, pictures, musical instruments and curiosities	**3,714**	3,520	89	..	..	105	..	**3,199**	3,135	38
	39.—TRADE OF OTHER SORTS	**43,856**	**42,025**	**1,357**	**8**	..	**461**	**5**	**36,948**	**35,636**	**1,065**
150	General store-keepers and shop-keepers otherwise unspecified	**38,062**	36,468	1,160	8	..	421	5	31,682	30,586	889
151	Itinerant traders, pedlars and hawkers (of other than food, etc.)	**5,776**	5,541	195	..	..	40	..	**5,260**	5,044	176
152	Other traders (including farmers of pounds, tolls and markets)	**18**	16	2	..	..	..	..	**6**	6	..
	C.—PUBLIC ADMINISTRATION AND LIBERAL ARTS	**62,697**	**59,109**	**3,058**	**1**	..	**516**	**13**	**57,284**	**54,298**	**2,755**
	VI.—Public Force	**7,742**	**7,735**	..	..	..	**7**	..	**7,144**	**7,140**	..
	40.—ARMY	**1,754**	**1,754**	..	..	..	..	..	**1,753**	**1,753**	..
153	Army (Imperial)	**1,754**	**1,754**	..	..	..	..	..	**1,753**	1,753	..
	41.—NAVY	**9**	**9**	..	..	..	..	..	**9**	**9**	..
155	Navy	**9**	9	..	..	..	..	..	**9**	9	..
	42.—AIR FORCE	**3**	**3**	..	..	..	..	..	**3**	**3**	..
156	Air Force	**3**	3	..	..	..	..	..	**3**	3	..
	43.—POLICE	**5,976**	**5,999**	..	..	..	**7**	..	**5,379**	**5,375**	..
157	Police	**5,911**	5,907	..	..	..	4	..	**5,376**	5,372	..
158	Village watchmen	**65**	62	..	..	..	3	..	**3**	3	..

Occupation or means of livelihood.

cutta.				Suburbs in 24-Parganas.							Howrah City.							
the occupation as					Numbers following the occupation as							Numbers following the occupation as						Group No.
Working dependents.		Subsidiary to another occupation.		Total, both sexes.	Principal occupation.		Working dependents.		Subsidiary to another occupation.		Total, both sexes.	Principal occupation.		Working dependents.		Subsidiary to another occupation.		
Males.	Females.	Males.	Females.		Males.	Females.	Males.	Females.	Males.	Females.		Males.	Females.	Males.	Females.	Males.	Females.	
13	14	15	16	17	18	19	20	21	22	23	24	25	26	27	28	29	30	31
..	..	**15**	..	**201**	**198**	**3**	..	..	..	..	**6**	**5**	**1**	..	..	..	..	
..	..	15	..	201	198	3	..	..	..	..	6	5	1	..	..	..	..	118
..	..	**3**	..	**156**	**155**	**1**	..	..	..	..	**117**	**86**	**2**	..	..	**29**	..	
..	..	3	..	156	155	1	..	..	..	..	98	67	2	..	..	29	..	119
..	..	..	..	..	..	..	..	..	..	..	8	8	..	..	..	..	..	120
..	..	..	..	..	..	..	..	..	..	..	3	3	..	..	..	..	..	121
..	..	..	..	..	..	..	..	..	..	..	8	8	..	..	..	..	..	122
..	..	**2**	..	..	..	..	..	..	..	..	**84**	**81**	..	..	..	**3**	..	
..	..	2	..	..	..	..	..	..	..	..	84	81	..	..	..	3	..	123
..	..	..	..	..	..	..	..	..	..	..	**24**	**23**	..	..	..	**1**	..	
..	..	..	..	..	..	..	..	..	..	..	24	23	..	..	..	1	..	124
..	..	**13**	..	..	..	..	..	..	..	..	**56**	**53**	..	..	..	**3**	..	
..	..	13	..	..	..	..	..	..	..	..	56	53	..	..	..	3	..	125
..	..	**8**	..	**245**	**239**	**6**	..	..	..	..	**473**	**455**	**7**	**5**	..	**6**	..	
..	..	..	..	195	189	6	..	..	..	..	114	106	1	5	..	2	..	126
..	..	8	..	..	..	..	..	..	..	..	359	349	6	..	..	4	..	127
..	..	..	..	50	50	..	..	..	..	..	..	..	..	..	..	..	..	128
7	..	**402**	**10**	**1,693**	**1,321**	**263**	..	..	**109**	..	**4,091**	**3,318**	**600**	**5**	**12**	**145**	**11**	
..	..	20	..	111	75	35	..	..	1	..	328	197	125	..	1	2	3	129
7	..	47	..	81	74	7	..	..	..	..	661	583	59	5	2	9	3	130
..	..	32	2	407	291	100	..	..	16	..	563	400	128	..	..	34	1	131
..	..	..	..	..	..	..	..	..	..	..	1	1	..	..	..	..	..	132
..	..	..	..	1	1	..	..	..	..	..	17	16	1	..	..	..	..	133
..	..	303	8	1,060	847	121	..	..	92	..	2,486	2,090	284	..	9	99	4	134
..	..	..	..	33	33	..	..	..	..	..	24	20	3	..	..	1	..	135
..	..	..	..	..	..	..	..	..	..	..	4	4	..	..	..	..	..	136
..	..	..	..	..	..	..	..	..	..	..	7	7	..	..	..	..	..	137
..	..	**6**	..	**5**	**5**	..	..	..	..	..	**132**	**131**	..	..	..	**1**	..	
..	..	6	..	5	5	..	..	..	..	..	132	131	..	..	..	1	..	138
..	..	**2**	..	**22**	**19**	..	..	..	**3**	..	**28**	**26**	**2**	..	..	..	..	
..	..	..	..	..	..	..	..	..	..	..	5	4	1	..	..	..	..	139
..	..	2	..	22	19	..	..	..	3	..	23	22	1	..	..	..	..	140
..	..	..	..	**26**	**23**	..	..	..	**3**	..	**14**	**14**	..	..	..	..	..	
..	..	..	..	26	23	..	..	..	3	..	14	14	..	..	..	..	..	141
..	..	**2**	..	**31**	**30**	**1**	..	..	..	..	**33**	**33**	..	..	..	..	..	
..	..	2	..	3	3	..	..	..	..	..	14	14	..	..	..	..	..	142
..	..	..	..	..	..	..	..	..	..	..	8	8	..	..	..	..	..	143
..	..	..	..	28	27	1	..	..	..	..	11	11	..	..	..	..	..	144
..	..	**1**	**3**	**74**	**58**	**16**	..	..	..	..	**521**	**413**	**45**	..	..	**63**	..	
..	..	1	3	74	58	16	..	..	..	..	521	413	45	..	..	63	..	145
..	..	**52**	..	**343**	**332**	**4**	..	..	**7**	..	**611**	**444**	**87**	..	..	**80**	..	
..	..	26	..	251	242	2	..	..	7	..	130	131	4	..	..	1	..	146
..	..	..	..	7	5	2	..	..	..	..	42	10	32	..	..	..	..	147
..	..	26	..	85	85	..	..	..	..	..	430	300	51	..	..	79	..	148
..	..	**246**	**1**	**842**	**811**	**30**	..	..	..	**1**	**6,066**	**5,578**	**262**	**8**	..	**215**	**3**	
..	..	206	1	838	807	30	..	..	..	1	5,542	5,075	241	8	..	215	3	150
..	..	40	..	2	2	..	..	..	..	..	514	495	19	..	..	..	..	151
..	..	..	..	2	2	..	..	..	..	..	10	8	2	..	..	..	..	152
..	..	**221**	**10**	**1,992**	**1,791**	**112**	..	..	**89**	..	**3,421**	**3,020**	**191**	**1**	..	**206**	**3**	
..	..	**4**	..	**405**	**405**	..	..	..	..	..	**193**	**190**	..	..	..	**3**	..	
..	..	..	..	..	..	..	..	..	..	..	**1**	**1**	..	..	..	..	..	
..	..	..	..	..	..	..	..	..	..	..	1	1	..	..	..	..	..	153
..	..	..	..	..	..	..	..	..	..	..	..	..	..	..	..	..	..	
..	..	..	..	..	..	..	..	..	..	..	..	..	..	..	..	..	..	155
..	..	..	..	..	..	..	..	..	..	..	..	..	..	..	..	..	..	
..	..	..	..	..	..	..	..	..	..	..	..	..	..	..	..	..	..	156
..	..	**4**	..	**405**	**405**	..	..	..	..	..	**192**	**189**	..	..	..	**3**	..	
..	..	4	..	387	387	..	..	..	..	..	148	148	..	..	..	..	..	157
..	..	..	..	18	18	..	..	..	..	..	44	41	..	..	..	3	..	158

Group No.	Occupation (**CLASS, Sub-class, ORDER** and group).	Calcutta with Suburbs and Howrah.							Cal		
		Numbers following the occupation as							Numbers following		
		Total, both sexes.	Principal occupation.		Working dependents.		Subsidiary to another occupation.		Total, both sexes.	Principal occupation.	
			Males.	Females.	Males.	Females.	Males.	Females.		Males.	Females.
1	2	3	4	5	6	7	8	9	10	11	12
	VII.—Public Administration	**21,645**	**21,316**	**176**	..	..	**153**	..	**20,421**	**20,261**	**116**
	44.—PUBLIC ADMINISTRATION	**21,645**	**21,316**	**176**	..	..	**153**	..	**20,421**	**20,261**	**116**
159	Service of the State	**14,880**	14,700	77	..	..	103	..	**13,870**	13,753	77
161	Municipal and other local (not village) service	**6,761**	6,612	99	..	..	50	..	**6,551**	6,508	39
162	Village officials and servants other than watchmen	**4**	4	..	..	..	..	..	..	..	..
	VIII.—Professions and Liberal Arts	**33,310**	**30,058**	**2,882**	**1**	..	**356**	**13**	**29,719**	**26,897**	**2,639**
	45.—RELIGION	**6,503**	**6,197**	**226**	**1**	..	**78**	**1**	**5,498**	**5,253**	**203**
163	Priests, ministers, etc.	**5,878**	5,595	203	1	..	78	1	**4,927**	4.704	181
164	Monks, nuns, religious mendicants	**331**	322	9	..	..	..	..	**329**	320	9
165	Other religious workers	**4**	4	..	..	..	..	..	**4**	4	..
166	Servants in religious edifices, burial and burning grounds, pilgrim conductors, circumcisers, etc.	**290**	276	14	..	..	..	..	**238**	225	13
	46.—LAW	**9,415**	**9,383**	..	..	..	**32**	..	**8,998**	**8,969**	..
167	Lawyers of all kinds, including Quazis, Law Agents and Mukhtiars	**5,370**	5,354	..	..	..	16	..	**5,109**	5,093	..
168	Lawyers' clerks, petition-writers, etc.	**4,045**	4,029	..	..	..	16	..	**3,889**	3,876	..
	47.—MEDICINE	**7,870**	**6,489**	**1,314**	..	..	**57**	**10**	**7,028**	**5,793**	**1,202**
169	Registered medical practitioners including oculists	**3,057**	2,876	164	..	..	16	1	**2,661**	2,516	137
170	Other persons practising the healing arts without being registered	**1,489**	1,422	42	..	..	22	3	**1,300**	1,256	38
171	Dentists	**616**	615	1	..	..	..	..	**613**	612	1
172	Midwives, vaccinators, compounders, nurses, masseurs, etc.	**2,675**	1,543	1,107	..	..	19	6	**2,434**	1,389	1,026
173	Veterinary surgeons	**33**	33	..	..	..	..	..	**20**	20	..
	48.—INSTRUCTION	**6,413**	**5,348**	**944**	..	..	**120**	**1**	**5,373**	**4,449**	**868**
174	Professors and teachers of all kinds	**6,256**	5,224	917	..	..	114	1	**5,225**	4,334	841
175	Clerks and servants connected with education	**157**	124	27	..	..	6	..	**148**	115	7
	49.—LETTERS, ARTS AND SCIENCES (OTHER THAN 44)	**3,109**	**2,641**	**398**	..	..	**69**	**1**	**2,822**	**2,433**	**366**
176	Public scribes, stenographers, etc.	**478**	296	182	..	..	..	..	**476**	294	182
177	Architects, surveyors, engineers and their employees (not being State servants)	**155**	155	..	..	..	..	..	**120**	120	..
178	Authors, editors, journalists and photographers	**321**	303	6	..	..	12	..	**292**	274	6
179	Artists, sculptors and image-makers	**1,007**	948	14	..	..	45	..	**910**	895	9
180	Scientists (astronomers, botanists, etc.)	**2**	2	..	..	..	..	..	**2**	2	..
181	Horoscope-casters, astrologers, fortune-tellers, wizards, witches and mediums	**92**	90	2	..	..	..	..	**66**	65	1
182	Musicians (composers and performers other than military), actors, dancers, etc.	**961**	762	192	..	..	6	1	**897**	726	166
183	Managers and employees of places of public entertainments, race courses, societies, clubs, etc.	**61**	61	..	..	..	..	..	**52**	52	..
184	Conjurors, acrobats, reciters, exhibitors of curiosities and wild animals, etc.	**32**	24	2	..	..	6	..	**7**	5	2
	D.—MISCELLANEOUS	**317,444**	**275,120**	**34,931**	**3,636**	**130**	**3,296**	**331**	**280,257**	**244,210**	**29,543**
	IX.—Persons living on their income	**13,316**	**10,659**	**1,794**	..	..	**814**	**49**	**12,538**	**10,112**	**1,622**
	50.—PERSONS LIVING PRINCIPALLY ON THEIR INCOME	**13,316**	**10,659**	**1,794**	..	..	**814**	**49**	**12,538**	**10,112**	**1,622**
185	Proprietors (other than of agricultural land), fund and scholarships holders and pensioners	**13,316**	10,659	1,794	..	..	814	49	**12,538**	10,112	1,622
	X.—Domestic Service	**107,874**	**90,837**	**16,143**	**3**	**41**	**692**	**158**	**98,833**	**83,851**	**14,250**
	51.—DOMESTIC SERVICE	**107,874**	**90,837**	**16,143**	3	**41**	**692**	**158**	**98,833**	**83,851**	**14,250**
186	Private motor drivers and cleaners	**2,718**	2,699	5	..	..	14	..	**1,980**	1,975	1
187	Other domestic servants	**105,156**	88,138	16,138	3	41	678	158	**96,853**	81,876	14,249
	XI.—Insufficiently described occupations	**179,832**	**170,283**	**7,732**	**2**	**5**	**1,775**	**35**	**153,928**	**147,467**	**5,237**
	52.—GENERAL TERMS WHICH DO NOT INDICATE A DEFINITE OCCUPATION	**179,832**	**170,283**	**7,732**	**2**	**5**	**1,775**	**35**	**153,928**	**147,467**	**5,237**
188	Manufacturers, businessmen and contractors otherwise unspecified	**3,641**	3,589	15	..	..	37	..	**3,424**	3,380	14
189	Cashiers, accountants, book-keepers, clerks and other employees in unspecified offices, warehouses and shops	**95,070**	91,629	2,312	2	..	1,113	14	**89,114**	86,768	1,448
190	Mechanics otherwise unspecified	**7,760**	7,719	4	..	..	37	..	**4,347**	4,347	..
191	Labourers and workmen otherwise unspecified	**73,361**	67,346	5,401	..	5	588	21	**57,043**	52,972	3,775
	XII.—Unproductive	**16,422**	**3,341**	**9,262**	**3,631**	**84**	**15**	**89**	**14,958**	**2,780**	**8,434**
	53.—INMATES OF JAILS, ASYLUMS AND ALMS HOUSES	**4,506**	**791**	..	**3,631**	**84**	..	..	**4,374**	**712**	..
192	Inmates of jails, asylums and alms houses	**4,506**	791	..	3,631	84	..	..	**4,374**	712	..
	54.—BEGGARS, VAGRANTS AND PROSTITUTES	**11,900**	**2,534**	**9,262**	..	..	**15**	**89**	**10,583**	**2,067**	**8,434**
193	Beggars and vagrants	**3,843**	2,534	1,292	..	..	15	2	**3,064**	2,067	994
194	Procurers and prostitutes	**8,057**	..	7,970	..	..	..	87	**7,519**	..	7,440
	55.—OTHER UNCLASSIFIED NON-PRODUCTIVE INDUSTRIES	**16**	**16**	..	..	..	..	..	**1**	**1**	..
195	Other unclassified non-productive industries	**16**	16	..	..	..	..	..	**1**	1	..

Occupation or means of livelihood.

cutta.				Suburbs in 24-Parganas.							Howrah City.							
the occupation as				Total, both sexes.	Numbers following the occupation as						Total, both sexes.	Numbers following the occupation as						Group No.
Working dependents.		Subsidiary to another occupation.			Principal occupation.		Working dependents.		Subsidiary to another occupation.			Principal occupation.		Working dependents.		Subsidiary to another occupation.		
Males.	Females.	Males.	Females.		Males.	Females.	Males.	Females.	Males.	Females.		Males.	Females.	Males.	Females.	Males.	Females.	
13	14	15	16	17	18	19	20	21	22	23	24	25	26	27	28	29	30	31
..	..	**44**	..	**726**	**672**	**9**	..	..	**45**	..	**498**	**383**	**51**	..	..	**64**	..	
..	..	**44**	..	**726**	**672**	**9**	..	..	**45**	..	**498**	**383**	**51**	..	..	**64**	..	
..	..	40	..	685	642	..	..	..	43	..	325	305	..	..	..	20	..	159
..	..	4	..	41	30	9	..	..	2	..	169	74	51	..	..	44	..	161
..	..	..	..	..	..	..	..	..	..	..	4	4	..	..	..	..	..	162
..	..	**173**	**10**	**861**	**714**	**103**	..	..	**44**	..	**2,730**	**2,447**	**140**	**1**	..	**139**	**3**	
..	..	**41**	**1**	**165**	**139**	**7**	..	..	**19**	..	**840**	**805**	**16**	**1**	..	**18**	..	
..	..	41	1	163	137	7	..	..	19	..	788	754	15	1	..	18	..	163
..	..	..	..	1	1	..	..	..	..	..	1	1	..	..	..	..	..	164
..	..	..	..	..	..	..	..	..	..	..	..	..	..	..	..	..	..	165
..	..	..	..	1	1	..	..	..	..	..	51	50	1	..	..	..	..	166
..	..	**29**	..	**128**	**127**	..	..	..	**1**	..	**289**	**287**	..	..	..	**2**	..	
..	..	16	..	80	80	..	..	..	..	..	181	181	..	..	..	..	..	167
..	..	13	..	48	47	..	..	..	1	..	108	106	..	..	..	2	..	168
..	..	**26**	**7**	**267**	**211**	**46**	..	..	**10**	..	**575**	**485**	**66**	..	..	**21**	**3**	
..	..	7	1	99	77	22	..	..	..	..	297	283	5	..	..	9	..	169
..	..	6	..	27	21	..	..	..	6	..	162	145	4	..	..	10	3	170
..	..	..	..	..	..	..	..	..	..	..	3	3	..	..	..	..	..	171
..	..	13	6	130	102	24	..	..	4	..	111	52	57	..	..	2	..	172
..	..	..	..	11	11	..	..	..	..	..	2	2	..	..	..	..	..	173
..	..	**55**	**1**	**205**	**172**	**25**	..	..	**8**	..	**835**	**727**	**51**	..	..	**57**	..	
..	..	49	1	197	164	25	..	..	8	..	834	726	51	..	..	57	..	174
..	..	6	..	8	8	..	..	..	..	..	1	1	..	..	..	..	..	175
..	..	**22**	**1**	**96**	**65**	**25**	..	..	**6**	..	**191**	**143**	**7**	..	..	**41**	..	
..	..	..	..	..	..	..	..	..	..	..	2	2	..	..	..	..	..	176
..	..	..	..	4	4	..	..	..	..	..	31	31	..	..	..	..	..	177
..	..	12	..	2	2	..	..	..	..	..	27	27	..	..	..	..	..	178
..	..	6	..	28	28	..	..	..	..	..	69	25	5	..	..	39	..	179
..	..	..	..	..	..	..	..	..	..	..	..	..	..	..	..	..	..	180
..	..	..	..	10	10	..	..	..	..	..	16	15	1	..	..	..	..	181
..	..	4	1	37	12	25	..	..	..	..	27	24	1	..	..	2	..	182
..	..	..	..	9	9	..	..	..	..	..	..	..	..	..	..	..	..	183
..	..	..	..	6	..	..	..	..	6	..	19	19	..	..	..	..	..	184
3,579	**106**	**2,560**	**259**	**7,869**	**6,834**	**977**	..	..	**58**	..	**29,318**	**24,076**	**4,411**	**57**	**24**	**678**	**72**	
..	..	**769**	**35**	**146**	**99**	**44**	..	..	**3**	..	**632**	**448**	**128**	..	..	**42**	**14**	
..	..	**769**	**35**	**146**	**99**	**44**	..	..	**3**	..	**632**	**448**	**128**	..	..	**42**	**14**	
..	..	769	35	146	99	44	..	..	3	..	632	448	128	..	..	42	14	185
..	**20**	**587**	**125**	**2,193**	**1,778**	**405**	..	..	**10**	..	**6,848**	**5,208**	**1,488**	**3**	**21**	**95**	**33**	
..	**20**	**587**	**125**	**2,193**	**1,778**	**405**	..	..	**10**	..	**6,848**	**5,208**	**1,488**	**3**	**21**	**95**	**33**	
..	..	4	..	174	172	2	..	..	..	..	564	552	2	..	..	10	..	186
..	20	583	125	2,019	1,606	403	..	..	10	..	6,284	4,656	1,486	3	21	85	33	187
1	**2**	**1,202**	**19**	**5,261**	**4,855**	**361**	..	..	**45**	..	**20,643**	**17,961**	**2,134**	**1**	**3**	**528**	**16**	
1	**2**	**1,202**	**19**	**5,261**	**4,855**	**361**			**45**		**20,643**	**17,961**	**2,134**	**1**	**3**	**528**	**16**	
..	..	30	..	27	27	..	..	..	..	..	190	182	1	..	..	7	..	188
1	..	885	12	1,295	1,221	74	..	..	..	..	4,661	3,640	790	1	..	228	2	189
..	..	..	..	435	422	1	..	..	12	..	2,978	2,950	3	..	..	25	..	190
..	2	287	7	3,504	3,185	286	..	..	33	..	12,814	11,189	1,340	..	3	268	14	191
3,578	**84**	**2**	**80**	**269**	**102**	**167**	..	..	..	..	**1,195**	**459**	**661**	**53**	..	**13**	**9**	
3,578	**84**	..	..	..	..	..	..	..	..	..	**132**	**79**	..	**53**	..	..	..	
3,578	84	..	..	..	..	..	..	..	..	..	132	79	..	53	..	..	..	192
..	..	**2**	**80**	**269**	**102**	**167**	..	..	..	..	**1,048**	**365**	**661**	..	..	**13**	**9**	
..	..	2	1	202	102	100	..	..	..	..	577	365	198	..	..	13	1	193
..	..	..	7	67	..	67	..	..	..	..	471	..	463	..	..	..	8	194
..	..	..	..	..	..	..	..	..	..	..	**15**	**15**	..	..	..	..	..	
..	..	..	..	..	..	..	..	..	..	..	15	15	..	..	..	..	..	195

IMPERIAL TABLE XI.—Occupations of selected castes, tribes or races by sexes.

This table corresponds to imperial table XXI of 1921 and shows the distribution amongst certain broad occupational sub-classes of the earners of selected groups. Figures are shown first for those following the traditional occupation of the group (if any) and subsequently for those with other means of livelihood. The numbers following the traditional occupation are not repeated in the appropriate column of the distribution by sub-classes: for instance Mahishyas are shown as cultivators and those returned as cultivators appear in columns 8 and 9 but not again in columns 18 and 19. Where a sub-class comprises more occupations than that traditional to a group the figures under it similarly exclude those shown in columns 8 and 9 as following the traditional occupation: thus the traditional occupation of Baidyas is given as physicians and persons so returned are shown in columns 8 and 9; the returns for this caste under columns 52 and 53 include only those who follow other professions than medicine given in the heading to these columns, viz., persons whose profession is the law or teaching.

2. The table contains some additional information not given in 1921. The classification then made into workers and dependents has been extended to show "earners" "working dependents" and "non-working dependents". Figures are also given of the number of working dependents as well as earners following the traditional occupation of their group. The religion of groups chosen is given and for primitive tribes separate details are shown of those professing different religions.

3. The table is arranged to show first Indians, then Other than Indians. The figures for Indian Christians appearing as serial No. 13 in the table include details for Christians of the primitive tribes also separately given under the tribal name. Particulars of the detailed classes forming the groups shown in the table as Indian Christians (serial No. 13), Europeans and allied races (serial No. 35) and Others—Other than Indians—(serial No. 36) are shown partly in the statement below which gives their distribution under columns 16-65 of the table. There being no traditional or caste occupation for these groups no entries fall under columns 2 and 12-15 of the table.

Serial entry in the table and actual return.	Earners.		Working dependents.		Non-working dependents
	Males.	Females.	Males.	Females.	Both sexes.
1	2	3	4	5	6
13 Indian Christians ..	**4,538**	**1,280**	**1**	..	**9,294**
Assamese ..	11	..	..	..	2
Bengali ..	3,412	1,020	1	..	7,199
Bihari ..	163	31	..	..	307
Burmese ..	3	..	..	..	2
Ceylonese ..	4	..	..	..	1
Goanese ..	305	..	..	..	38
Jew ..	30	3	..	..	37
Lepcha ..	..	1	..	..	..
Madrasi ..	221	82	..	..	932
Malabari ..	..	..	..	..	2
Munda ..	90	21	..	..	153
Nepali ..	5	3	..	..	2
Oraon ..	110	18	..	..	196
Oriya ..	57	..	..	..	43
Punjabi ..	26	5	..	..	146
Santal ..	101	96	..	..	234
35 European and allied races	**5,372**	**954**	**225**	..	**10,478**
American ..	71	11	..	..	109
Armenian ..	161	45	..	..	540
Australian ..	4	3	..	..	25
Austrian ..	1	1	..	..	5
Belgian ..	12	..	..	..	20
Bulgarian ..	..	..	..	..	4
Canadian ..	1	..	..	..	7
Dane ..	2	2	..	..	1
Dutch ..	51	4	..	..	43

Serial entry in the table and actual return.	Earners.		Working dependents.		Non-working dependents
	Males.	Females.	Males.	Females.	Both sexes.
1	2	3	4	5	6
English ..	3,616	630	225	..	8,043
European (unspecified)	374	121	..	..	351
French ..	53	30	..	..	139
German ..	23	5	..	..	85
Greek ..	18	4	..	..	50
Irish ..	212	43	..	..	277
Italian ..	145	3	..	..	45
Maltese ..	..	1	..	..	..
New Zealander ..	1	..	..	..	..
Norwegian ..	14	..	..	..	4
Portuguese ..	63	4	..	..	109
Russian ..	4	10	..	..	10
Scotch ..	436	33	..	..	539
South African ..	7	..	..	..	9
Spanish ..	26	4	..	..	16
Swedish ..	21	..	..	..	15
Swiss ..	9	..	..	..	13
Welsh ..	47	..	..	..	19
36 Others ..	**88**	**31**	..	..	**185**
Chinese ..	41	7	..	..	99
Fijian ..	1	..	..	..	1
Japanese ..	33	9	..	..	32
Malayan ..	5	3	..	..	11
Persian ..	3	7	..	..	35
Philippinese ..	4	..	..	..	..
Siamese ..	..	5	..	..	7
Syrian ..	1	..	..	..	..

Further details for these groups are given in the supplement printed after the table.

IMPERIAL TABLE XI.—

Serial No.	Caste, tribe or race and religion.	Traditional occupation.	Population dealt with. Earners. Males.	Earners. Females.	Working dependents. Males.	Working dependents. Females.	Non-working dependents. Both sexes.	Number of earners whose traditional caste occupation was returned as their Principal means of livelihood. Males.	Principal means of livelihood. Females.	Subsidiary means of livelihood. Males.	Subsidiary means of livelihood. Females.
	1	2	3	4	5	6	7	8	9	10	11
1	**INDIANS**										
2	Bagdi ..	Cultivators, fishermen, labourers and menial servants.	2,590	1,453	2	2	4,879	762	633	3	..
3	Baidya ..	Physicians ..	5,012	262	1	..	13,737	547	52	16	..
4	Barui ..	Betel-leaf growers ..	1,266	179	6	21	1,468	253	3	..	..
5	Bauri ..	Cultivators, earth workers and palki bearers.	24	35	..	..	148	1	..	..	..
6	Bhumij (Tribal) ..	Nil ..	34	7	..	1	30	..	..	..	..
7	Brahman ..	Priests ..	78,617	2,788	25	..	115,853	5,420	43	171	1
8	Chamar ..	Tanners and leather workers ..	18,433	1,414	7	6	12,585	3,723	43	..	..
9	Dhobi ..	Washermen ..	6,571	657	6	..	6,953	4,867	455	6	..
10	Dom ..	Basket and mat makers, scavengers and drummers.	1,615	536	1	..	2,440	901	300	..	4
11	Goala ..	Herdsmen and milkmen ..	24,737	1,874	..	..	13,800	2,781	329	..	..
12	Hari ..	Menials and scavengers ..	466	226	..	7	737	170	142	..	..
13	Indian Christian ..	Nil ..	4,538	1,280	1	..	9,294	..	..	..	..
14	Jaliya-Kaibartta ..	Fishermen and boatmen ..	1,918	735	..	..	5,332	938	280	2	..
15	Jogi or Jugi ..	Weavers ..	1,457	147	..	..	3,364	37	4	6	2
16	Kamar ..	Metal workers and blacksmith ..	4,209	611	4	..	5,603	1,208	16	7	..
17	Kayastha ..	Writers ..	67,465	5,236	3	2	109,868	6,948	60	22	..
18	Kumhar ..	Potters ..	2,036	211	..	..	2,763	565	64	..	..
19	Lepcha (Hindu) ..	Cultivators ..	62	..	..	2	29	..	..	..	..
20	Lepcha (Christian) ..	Nil ..	..	1	..	..	..	..	..	..	..
21	Mahishya ..	Cultivators ..	30,009	8,059	2	10	38,358	2,425	66	13	..
22	"Mumin" (Jolaha) (Muslim) ..	Weavers ..	1,825	143	1	..	1,937	29	..	14	..
23	Muchi ..	Tanners, and leather workers and drummers.	9,682	466	..	3	4,901	5,770	69	..	..
24	Munda (Tribal) ..	Nil ..	110	17	..	..	27	..	..	..	..
25	Munda (Christian) ..	Nil ..	90	21	..	..	153	..	..	..	..
26	Namasudra ..	Nil ..	1,616	416	4	..	2,243	..	..	..	..
27	Napit ..	Barbers ..	7,756	826	15	1	7,439	3,435	130	2	..
28	Oraon (Tribal) ..	Nil ..	229	60	..	..	93	..	..	..	..
29	Oraon (Christian) ..	Nil ..	110	18	..	..	196	..	..	..	..
30	Santal (Tribal) ..	Nil ..	363	120	..	..	152	..	..	..	..
31	Santal (Christian) ..	Nil ..	101	96	..	..	234	..	..	..	..
32	Sayyad (Muslim) ..	Nil ..	3,359	146	17	1	3,870	..	..	..	..
33	**OTHER THAN INDIANS**										
34	Anglo-Indian ..	Nil ..	4,102	1,308	..	2	13,057	..	..	..	..
35	European and allied races ..	Nil ..	5,372	954	225	..	10,478	..	..	..	..
36	Others ..	Nil ..	88	31	..	..	185	..	..	..	..

Recorded principal occupation of earners other than the traditional

Serial No.	Caste, tribe or race and religion.	III.—Industries. Owners, managers, clerks, etc. Males.	Owners, managers, clerks, etc. Females.	Artizans and other workers. Males.	Artizans and other workers. Females.	IV.—Transport. Owners, managers, ships' officers, etc. Males.	Owners, managers, ships' officers, etc. Females.	Labourers, boatmen, carters, palki bearers, etc. Males.	Labourers, boatmen, carters, palki bearers, etc. Females.	V.—Trade. Males.	V.—Trade. Females.	VI.—Public Force. Commissioned and gazetted officers. Males.	Commissioned and gazetted officers. Females.	Others. Males.	Others. Females.
	1	32	33	34	35	36	37	38	39	40	41	42	43	44	45
1	**INDIANS**														
2	Bagdi ..	13	4	1,010	213	7	..	104	7	178	108	..	..	15	..
3	Baidya ..	451	2	102	4	86	..	35	..	484	7	39	..	66	..
4	Barui ..	39	..	237	5	6	..	44	..	206	2	3	..	8	..
5	Bauri ..	1	..	..	1	..	..	..	..	3	1	..	..	..	..
6	Bhumij (Tribal) ..	..	..	..	..	..	..	..	..	..	..	..	..	..	..
7	Brahman ..	3,041	8	4,570	78	1,774	3	1,549	7	9,811	163	158	..	1,927	2
8	Chamar ..	49	10	5,605	652	27	..	1,268	25	404	64	..	..	71	..
9	Dhobi ..	10	..	385	62	8	..	53	3	337	26	..	..	11	..
10	Dom ..	..	3	152	105	..	..	30	12	28	7	..	..	17	3
11	Goala ..	205	3	3,747	172	61	..	1,627	13	2,144	73	2	..	251	..
12	Hari ..	..	..	81	20	1	..	25	1	28	..	..	..	5	..
13	Indian Christian ..	98	5	226	21	113	13	171	4	603	55	12	..	255	1
14	Jaliya-Kaibartta ..	57	4	179	50	6	1	87	1	159	39	..	..	1	..
15	Jogi or Jugi ..	84	5	310	20	4	..	22	..	352	12	..	..	8	..
16	Kamar ..	109	2	965	112	25	..	112	1	654	24	..	..	25	..
17	Kayastha ..	1,904	21	4,716	109	793	..	551	15	10,933	190	128	..	822	1
18	Kumhar ..	34	..	520	15	9	..	26	..	297	7	..	..	3	..
19	Lepcha (Hindu) ..	..	..	31	..	..	..	..	..	..	..	..	..	..	..
20	Lepcha (Christian) ..	..	..	..	..	..	..	..	..	..	..	..	..	..	..
21	Mahishya ..	577	48	6,971	1,248	185	27	657	1	4,589	457	31	..	295	..
22	Muchi ..	2	..	1,352	194	334	..	338	..	58	42	..	..	25	2
23	"Mumin" (Jolaha) (Muslim) ..	55	..	934	91	44	..	123	1	142	8	1	..	2	..
24	Munda (Tribal) ..	..	..	11	..	..	2	13	4	12	..	..	..	..	..
25	Munda (Christian) ..	..	..	7	..	3	4	5	1	6	..	..	..	17	..
26	Namasudra ..	53	..	353	37	13	..	138	..	227	39	..	..	1	1
27	Napit ..	126	..	901	55	37	1	88	..	710	46	1	..	25	..
28	Oraon (Tribal) ..	..	..	..	..	..	..	27	11	9	5	..	..	..	..
29	Oraon (Christian) ..	..	..	2	1	..	1	1	..	10	1	..	..	13	..
30	Santal (Tribal) ..	..	..	7	16	..	..	34	34	17	11	..	..	..	..
31	Santal (Christian) ..	..	..	4	1	1	1	3	1	8	..	1	..	21	..
32	Sayyad (Muslim) ..	72	..	394	24	65	..	109	1	735	17	2	..	116	..
33	**OTHER THAN INDIANS**														
34	Anglo-India ..	211	12	354	43	231	103	129	11	667	99	11	..	64	..
35	European an allied races ..	567	25	74	11	231	55	77	2	676	144	101	..	1,239	2
36	Others ..	19	..	24	3	3	..	..	..	6	9	9	..	6	..

Occupations of selected castes, tribes or races by sexes.

Number of working dependents following the traditional occupation of their caste.		Number of earners returning their traditional occupation as their principal means of livelihood who had some subsidiary occupation.		Recorded principal occupation of earners other than the traditional occupation of their caste by sub-classes.																Serial No.
				I.—Exploitation of animals and vegetation.												II.—Extraction of minerals.				
				Income from rent of land.		Cultivation of all kinds.		Agents and managers of landed estates, planters, forest officers and their clerks, rent collectors.		Field labourers, wood cutters, etc.		Raisers of livestock, milkmen and herdsmen.		Fishers and huntsmen.		Owners, managers, clerks, etc.		Labourers.		
Males.	Females.	Males.	Females.	Males.	Females.	Males.	Females.	Males.	Females.	Males.	Females.	Males.	Females.	Males.	Females.	Males.	Females.	Males.	Females.	
12	13	14	15	16	17	18	19	20	21	22	23	24	25	26	27	28	29	30	31	
																				1
1	..	12	1	7	5	..	..	2	..	63	11	2	1	11	25	..	..	3	..	2
..	..	5	..	122	18	44	1	49	1	..	..	..	..	..	..	2	..	25	..	3
..	..	2	..	4	2	3	1	3	..	46	11	..	3	..	..	..	..	3	..	4
..	..	..	..	..	..	..	..	..	..	2	..	..	..	..	1	..	..	3	..	5
..	..	..	..	..	..	17	..	..	..	13	6	..	..	..	..	..	..	..	..	6
14	..	327	1	1,576	270	357	29	405	1	35	2	18	2	3	..	432	..	45	2	7
7	1	114	1	35	3	20	11	5	..	48	96	17	1	6	..	..	..	15	6	8
..	..	54	1	11	4	2	..	3	..	10	..	..	..	..	1	..	1	22	..	9
4	..	3	..	8	..	4	..	..	..	26	8	..	..	..	..	..	..	1	..	10
9	..	31	1	246	. 45	112	5	46	..	258	6	846	3	5	1	6	..	276	..	11
..	..	..	..	..	..	1	4	3	..	19	..	..	..	4	..	..	..	..	..	12
..	..	..	..	126	11	45	13	4	1	34	12	5	..	21	2	..	..	1	..	13
2	..	4	1	2	13	6	1	..	..	31	1	..	2	17	..	..	..	6	..	14
..	..	..	..	17	7	23	..	1	..	4	1	..	2	..	..	..	..	5	..	15
24	..	13	..	4	19	24	1	2	..	7	1	2	..	1	..	..	..	2	2	16
43	..	256	..	1,911	283	315	18	613	2	96	1	14	1	11	..	122	..	2	..	17
..	..	2	..	8	2	6	..	2	..	11	..	..	..	..	..	..	..	7	..	18
..	..	..	..	..	..	..	..	..	..	..	..	..	..	..	..	..	..	..	..	19
..	..	..	..	..	..	..	..	..	..	..	..	..	..	..	..	..	..	..	..	20
111	..	190	..	263	122	..	..	109	..	475	17	23	16	99	9	5	..	4	3	21
..	..	..	..	2	..	7	..	1	..	..	..	2	2	1	2	5	..	6	..	22
..	..	26	..	6	5	42	..	..	..	2	2	7	..	15	..	..	..	1	..	23
..	..	..	..	..	..	8	..	..	..	14	..	..	..	..	..	..	..	..	..	24
..	..	..	..	..	..	..	..	..	..	..	..	..	..	..	..	..	..	..	..	25
..	..	..	..	16	6	142	5	1	..	37	..	..	..	11	..	..	..	..	..	26
6	..	46	..	46	19	14	..	1	2	19	5	..	2	2	..	..	..	..	1	27
..	..	..	..	..	..	17	..	..	..	28	8	..	..	..	..	..	..	..	..	28
..	..	..	..	..	..	..	..	..	..	..	..	..	..	..	..	..	..	..	..	29
..	..	..	..	..	..	22	..	..	..	19	11	..	..	..	..	..	..	..	..	30
..	..	..	..	..	2	..	..	..	..	..	..	..	..	..	..	..	..	..	..	31
..	..	..	..	79	11	133	2	4	5	45	..	1	..	6	..	..	..	45	..	32
																				33
..	..	..	..	13	13	1	2	..	2	..	..	..	..	..	1	47	..	..	2	34
..	..	..	..	10	20	3	..	30	3	..	..	2	..	..	..	42	..	74	..	35
..	..	..	..	..	..	..	..	..	..	..	..	..	..	..	..	..	..	1	..	36

occupation of their caste by sub-classes.

VII.—Public Administration.				VIII.—Arts and professions.						IX.—Persons living on their income.		X.—Domestic service.		XI.—Insufficiently described occupations.				XII.—Unproductive.		Serial No.
Gazetted officers.		Others.		Religion.		Law, Medicine and Teaching.		Others.						Contractors, clerks, cashiers, etc., otherwise unspecified.		Labourers unspecified.		Beggars, prostitutes, criminals and inmates of jails.		
Males.	Females.	Males.	Females.	Males.	Females.	Males.	Females.	Males.	Females.	Males.	Females.	Males.	Females.	Males.	Females.	Males.	Females.	Males.	Females.	
46	47	48	49	50	51	52	53	54	55	56	57	58	59	60	61	62	63	64	65	
																				1
..	..	13	..	2	1	9	10	4	3	24	38	72	171	88	17	178	13	23	193	2
59	15	661	5	69	15	384	56	88	3	99	6	385	42	1,166	16	34	..	15	19	3
..	..	30	..	1	..	17	..	6	1	11	2	82	33	138	..	122	1	4	10	4
..	..	..	..	..	..	..	..	..	..	..	..	1	24	..	..	13	7	..	1	5
..	..	..	..	..	..	..	..	..	..	..	..	2	..	..	..	2	1	..	..	6
435	..	4,124	11	587	161	3,880	95	1,524	59	1,669	269	13,755	927	18,882	65	2,388	42	245	546	7
..	..	377	14	..	..	2	..	8	27	753	18	1,227	193	312	8	4,429	227	32	16	8
2	..	48	..	..	..	8	..	3	1	179	7	233	67	175	..	195	11	9	19	9
11	..	20	2	76	..	..	..	3	1	18	2	81	58	35	2	184	24	10	9	10
15	..	581	1	1	..	102	2	64	10	66	61	5,520	770	1,603	25	4,131	81	41	274	11
..	..	19	..	..	..	..	..	..	2	1	..	67	46	3	..	37	6	2	5	12
104	..	66	16	35	30	268	341	66	261	256	73	859	270	961	96	168	23	41	31	13
2	..	25	..	..	..	5	..	5	6	34	9	97	207	97	1	161	32	3	88	14
3	..	19	..	10	..	28	2	15	..	28	7	127	51	273	2	78	4	9	30	15
1	..	45	..	..	..	34	2	27	2	37	24	305	284	298	2	315	12	7	107	16
207	2	7,485	5	108	..	2,861	108	973	118	1,329	267	6,845	2,559	14,843	105	2,861	88	74	1,283	17
2	..	23	..	..	..	24	..	1	1	21	3	141	77	185	7	147	12	4	23	18
..	..	..	..	..	..	..	..	16	1	1	..	10	..	4	..	..	..	..	..	19
..	..	..	..	..	..	..	..	..	1	..	..	..	..	..	..	..	..	..	..	20
21	..	787	1	5	9	479	6	382	16	146	216	3,685	3,978	3,790	28	3,922	300	84	1,491	21
..	..	30	6	..	..	..	..	5	16	74	8	640	46	185	..	696	68	100	8	22
..	..	2	2	1	2	5	..	6	..	16	6	83	7	15	..	227	17	8	6	23
..	..	..	..	..	..	..	..	..	..	..	..	19	2	..	..	33	9	..	..	24
1	..	..	..	..	..	..	..	..	3	2	4	24	7	19	2	6	..	..	..	25
1	..	20	..	..	..	25	..	9	1	7	8	218	165	165	2	167	7	12	145	26
20	..	90	..	..	..	59	..	72	1	157	17	857	336	537	56	550	17	9	138	27
..	..	..	..	..	..	..	..	..	..	..	..	23	5	..	..	125	31	..	..	28
1	..	..	..	..	..	..	3	..	1	..	3	4	6	23	1	54	1	2	..	29
..	..	..	..	..	..	..	..	..	..	..	..	35	15	..	..	229	33	..	..	30
..	..	..	..	..	1	1	14	..	35	3	2	39	28	18	11	2	..	..	..	31
20	..	127	1	7	1	139	3	9	3	81	20	575	44	349	5	213	3	33	6	32
																				00
78	1	277	77	38	12	163	264	69	162	133	56	183	103	1.374	318	51	1	8	26	34
207	..	191	25	26	24	153	209	75	192	80	27	181	70	1,245	101	81	..	6	44	35
1	..	1	..	..	..	1	1	..	5	..	3	1	5	14	4	2	..	..	1	36

SUPPLEMENT TO IMPERIAL TABLE XI.—Details of groups not shown separately in the table.

Entry in table with detailed return and reference to column of table.	Males.	Females.
1	2	3
13 Indian Christian		
Assamese total earners	**11**	..
40, 41 ..	9	..
50,51 ..	2	..
Bengali total earners	**3,412**	**1,020**
16,17 ..	125	9
18,19 ..	45	13
20, 21 ..	4	..
22, 23 ..	34	12
24 25 ..	5	..
26 27 ..	21	2
30 31 ..	1	..
31, 33 ..	46	4
34, 35 ..	196	19
36, 37 ..	44	2
38, 39 ..	102	..
40, 41 ..	441	8
42, 43 ..	6	..
44, 45 ..	183	1
46, 47 ..	73	..
48, 49 ..	55	16
50, 51 ..	27	26
52, 53 ..	240	309
54, 55 ..	39	204
56, 57 ..	248	62
58, 59 ..	623	205
60, 61 ..	763	77
62, 63 ..	57	22
64, 65 ..	34	29
Bihari total earners ..	**163**	**31**
32, 33 ..	1	..
34, 35 ..	3	..
36, 37 ..	3	..
38, 39 ..	1	..
40, 41 ..	32	8
42, 43 ..	1	..
44, 45 ..	1	..
46, 47 ..	23	..
48, 49 ..	10	..
50, 51 ..	..	1
52, 53 ..	10	3
54, 55 ..	5	6
56, 57 ..	1	..
58, 59 ..	19	9
60, 61 ..	36	2
62, 63 ..	12	..
64, 65 ..	5	2
Burmese total earners	**3**	..
50, 51 ..	3	..
Ceylonese total earners	**4**	..
40, 41 ..	2	..
60, 61 ..	2	..
Goanese total earners	**305**	..
16,17 ..	1	..
32, 33 ..	30	..
34, 35 ..	7	..
36, 37 ..	58	..
38, 39 ..	47	..
42, 43 ..	1	..
44, 45 ..	18	..
46, 47 ..	6	..
52, 53 ..	9	..
54, 55 ..	6	..
58, 59 ..	37	..
60, 61 ..	53	..
62, 63 ..	32	..
Jew total earners ..	**30**	**3**
20, 21 ..	..	1
40, 41 ..	27	..
42, 43 ..	1	..
50, 51 ..	2	2
Lepcha total earners	..	**1**
54, 55 ..	..	1
Madrasi total earners	**221**	**82**
32, 33 ..	19	1
34, 35 ..	7	..
36, 37 ..	4	6
38, 39 ..	6	2
40, 41 ..	57	33
44, 45 ..	1	..
48, 49 ..	1	..
52, 53 ..	8	12
54, 55 ..	16	10
56, 57 ..	..	2
58, 59 ..	66	13
60, 61 ..	31	3
62, 63 ..	5	..
Munda total earners	**90**	**21**
34, 35 ..	7	..
36, 37 ..	3	4
38, 39 ..	5	1
40, 41 ..	6	..
44, 45 ..	17	..
46, 47 ..	1	..
54, 55 ..	..	3
56, 57 ..	2	4
58, 59 ..	24	7
60, 61 ..	19	2
62, 63 ..	6	..

Entry in table with detailed return and reference to column of table.	Males.	Females.
1	2	3
13 Indian Christian—*concld.*		
Nepali total earners ..	**5**	**3**
40, 41 ..	1	1
58, 59 ..	..	2
60, 61 ..	4	..
Oraon total earners ..	**110**	**18**
34, 35 ..	2	1
36, 37 ..	..	1
38, 39 ..	1	..
40, 41 ..	10	1
44, 45 ..	13	..
46, 47 ..	1	..
52, 53 ..	..	3
54, 55 ..	..	1
56, 57 ..	..	3
58, 59 ..	4	6
60, 61 ..	23	1
62, 63 ..	54	1
64, 65 ..	2	..
Oriya total earners ..	**57**	..
32, 33 ..	2	..
38, 39 ..	4	..
44, 45 ..	1	..
56, 57 ..	2	..
58, 59 ..	44	..
60, 61 ..	4	..
Panjabi total earners	**26**	**5**
38, 39 ..	2	..
40, 41 ..	10	4
42, 43 ..	2	..
50, 51 ..	1	..
54, 55 ..	..	1
58, 59 ..	3	..
60, 61 ..	8	..
Santal total earners ..	**101**	**96**
16, 17 ..	..	2
34, 35 ..	4	1
36, 37 ..	1	1
38, 39 ..	3	1
40, 41 ..	8	..
42, 43 ..	1	..
44, 45 ..	21	..
50, 51 ..	..	1
52, 53 ..	1	14
54, 55 ..	..	35
56, 57 ..	3	2
58, 59 ..	39	28
60, 61 ..	18	11
62, 63 ..	2	..
35 European and allied races		
American total earners	**71**	**11**
32, 33 ..	19	1
36, 37 ..	3	..
38, 39 ..	1	..
40 41 ..	12	..
46, 47 ..	2	..
48, 49 ..	3	1
50, 51 ..	..	3
52, 53 ..	8	4
54, 55 ..	..	1
56, 57 ..	4	..
60, 61 ..	19	1
Armenian total earners	**161**	**45**
16, 17 ..	2	1
18, 19 ..	1	..
20, 21 ..	15	..
30, 31 ..	1	..
32, 33 ..	32	..
34, 35 ..	1	5
36, 37 ..	3	3
38, 39 ..	5	..
40, 41 ..	31	6
46, 47 ..	9	..
48, 49 ..	8	2
50, 51 ..	3	..
52, 53 ..	2	17
54, 55 ..	3	1
56, 57 ..	4	5
58, 59 ..	7	1
60, 61 ..	34	..
64, 65 ..	..	4
Australian total earners	**4**	**3**
24, 25 ..	2	..
40, 41 ..	..	1
52, 53 ..	1	..
54, 55 ..	1	2
Austrian total earners	**1**	**1**
40, 41 ..	1	..
64, 65 ..	..	1
Belgian total earners	**12**	..
36, 37 ..	2	..
48, 49 ..	2	..
50, 51 ..	3	..
56, 57 ..	3	..
60, 61 ..	2	..
Canadian total earners	**1**	..
60, 61 ..	1	..
Dane total earners ..	**2**	**2**
38, 39 ..	1	..
40, 41 ..	..	2
46, 47 ..	1	..
Dutch total earners ..	**51**	**4**
32, 33 ..	12	..
40, 41 ..	13	..
52, 53 ..	2	2
56, 57 ..	11	..
58, 59 ..	11	1
60, 61 ..	2	1

Entry in table with detailed return and reference to column of table.	Males.	Females.
1	2	3
35 European and allied races—*contd.*		
English total earners	**3,616**	**630**
16, 17 ..	8	17
18, 19 ..	1	..
20, 21 ..	10	3
28, 29 ..	40	..
30, 31 ..	70	..
32, 33 ..	225	7
34, 35 ..	45	4
36, 37 ..	138	40
38, 39 ..	31	2
40, 41 ..	446	110
42, 43 ..	35	..
44, 45 ..	1,146	..
46, 47 ..	105	..
48, 49 ..	128	17
50, 51 ..	12	14
52, 53 ..	101	126
54, 55 ..	38	135
56, 57 ..	55	17
58, 59 ..	100	50
60, 61 ..	873	76
62, 63 ..	9	..
64, 65 ..	..	12
European (unspecified) total earners.	**374**	**121**
16, 17 ..	..	2
32, 33 ..	153	12
40, 41 ..	35	3
42, 43 ..	36	..
44, 45 ..	11	..
48, 49 ..	..	4
50, 51 ..	..	5
52, 53 ..	..	45
54, 55 ..	..	22
56, 57 ..	..	1
58, 59 ..	..	10
60, 61 ..	139	17
French total earners	**53**	**30**
20, 21 ..	1	..
36, 37 ..	4	3
38, 39 ..	2	..
40, 41 ..	13	3
44, 45 ..	2	2
46, 47 ..	5	..
52, 53 ..	5	4
54, 55 ..	3	2
58, 59 ..	3	..
60, 61 ..	13	..
62, 63 ..	2	..
64, 65 ..	..	16
German total earners	**23**	**5**
36, 37 ..	1	1
40, 41 ..	4	2
42, 43 ..	2	..
52, 53 ..	2	..
54, 55 ..	..	1
56, 57 ..	..	1
58, 59 ..	3	..
60, 61 ..	11	..
Greek total earners ..	**18**	**4**
32, 33 ..	13	..
34, 35 ..	2	..
40, 41 ..	2	1
60, 61 ..	1	..
64, 65 ..	..	3
Irish total earners ..	**212**	**43**
20, 21 ..	2	..
32, 33 ..	4	1
34, 35 ..	3	2
36, 37 ..	1	6
38, 39 ..	4	..
40, 41 ..	11	7
42, 43 ..	16	..
44, 45 ..	14	..
46, 47 ..	73	..
48, 49 ..	11	..
50, 51 ..	4	..
52, 53 ..	17	6
54, 55 ..	1	16
56, 57 ..	2	1
58, 59 ..	4	2
60, 61 ..	6	2
62, 63 ..	33	..
64, 65 ..	6	..
Italian total earners	**145**	**3**
30, 31 ..	1	..
34, 35 ..	3	..
36, 37 ..	27	..
38, 39 ..	19	..
40, 41 ..	14	1
42, 43 ..	1	..
44, 45 ..	1	..
48, 49 ..	..	1
54, 55 ..	17	..
58, 59 ..	26	1
60, 61 ..	13	..
62, 63 ..	23	..
Maltese total earners	..	**1**
60, 61 ..	..	1
New Zealander total earners.	**1**	..
18, 19 ..	1	..
Norwegian total earners	**14**	..
36 37 ..	8	..
52, 53 ..	2	..
60, 61 ..	4	..

Entry in table with detailed return and reference to column of table.	Males.	Females.
1	2	3
35 European and allied races—*concld.*		
Portuguese total earners	**63**	**4**
32, 33 ..	1	..
34, 35 ..	1	..
36, 37 ..	2	..
38, 39 ..	1	..
40, 41 ..	3	2
42, 43 ..	1	..
44, 45 ..	6	..
48, 49 ..	20	..
50, 51 ..	1	..
52, 53 ..	2	1
54, 55 ..	5	..
56, 57 ..	1	..
58, 59 ..	12	1
60, 61 ..	6	..
62, 63 ..	1	..
Russian total earners	**4**	**10**
40, 41 ..	1	..
54, 55 ..	3	2
64, 65 ..	..	8
Scotch total earners ..	**436**	**33**
20, 21 ..	2	..
28, 29 ..	2	..
30, 31 ..	2	..
32, 33 ..	108	4
34, 35 ..	19	..
36, 37 ..	39	2
38, 39 ..	1	..
40 41 ..	76	3
42, 43 ..	3	..
44, 45 ..	18	..
46, 47 ..	12	..
48, 49 ..	19	..
50, 51 ..	3	2
52, 53 ..	10	4
54, 55 ..	1	10
56, 57 ..	..	2
58, 59 ..	15	4
60, 61 ..	103	2
62, 63 ..	3	..
South African total earners.	**7**	..
60, 61 ..	7	..
Spanish total earners	**26**	**4**
36, 37 ..	1	..
38, 39 ..	12	..
40, 41 ..	..	3
42, 43 ..	2	..
44, 45 ..	1	..
52, 53 ..	1	..
60, 61 ..	8	1
62, 63 ..	1	..
Swedish total earners	**21**	..
40, 41 ..	11	..
62, 63 ..	10	..
Swiss total earners ..	**9**	..
40, 41 ..	3	..
42, 43 ..	1	..
54, 55 ..	3	..
60, 61 ..	2	..
Welsh total earners ..	**47**	..
36, 37 ..	2	..
42, 43 ..	4	..
44, 45 ..	40	..
60, 61 ..	1	..
36 Others		
Chinese total earners	**41**	**7**
30, 31 ..	1	..
32, 33 ..	1	..
34, 35 ..	22	1
36, 37 ..	3	..
40, 41 ..	6	[illegible]
44, 45 ..	3	..
54, 55 ..	..	2
58, 59 ..	..	1
60, 61 ..	3	..
62, 63 ..	2	..
Fijian total earners ..	**1**	..
46, 47 ..	1	..
Japanese total earners	**33**	**9**
32, 33 ..	17	..
34, 35 ..	1	1
40, 41 ..	..	2
42, 43 ..	9	..
48, 49 ..	1	..
56, 57 ..	..	3
60, 61 ..	5	3
Malayan total earners	**5**	**3**
34, 35 ..	1	..
40, 41 ..	..	1
44, 45 ..	3	..
54, 55 ..	..	1
58, 59 ..	..	1
60, 61 ..	1	..
Persian total earners	**3**	**7**
32, 33 ..	1	..
40, 41 ..	..	1
52, 53 ..	1	1
58, 59 ..	..	3
60, 61 ..	1	1
64, 65 ..	..	1
Philippinese total earners	**4**	..
60, 61 ..	4	..
Siamese total earners	..	**5**
34, 35 ..	..	1
40, 41 ..	..	2
54, 55 ..	..	2
Syrian total earners ..	**1**	..
58, 59 ..	1	..

NOTE.—Imperial Table XII has not been printed.

IMPERIAL TABLE XIII.—Literacy by religion, age-groups and sex.

This table corresponds to imperial table VIII of 1921. It shows by sexes figures for those literate (able to write a letter to a friend and to read the reply), illiterate and literate in English. Details are given by age-groups for all religions found, and for the four areas of (1) Calcutta with suburbs in 24-Parganas and Howrah, (2) Calcutta, (3) suburbs of Calcutta in 24-Parganas and (4) Howrah. The age-groups are the same as shown in volume V, part ii.

2. The figures for Hindus include 3 Aryas (male) and 1,554 Brahmos (male 880, female 674). All of these are in Calcutta and details for them are given below :—

Age.		Total population.			Literate.			Illiterate.			Literate in English.		
		Both sexes.	Males.	Females.	Both sexes.	Males.	Females.	Both sexes.	Males.	Females.	Both sexes.	Males.	Females.
1		2	3	4	5	6	7	8	9	10	11	12	13
ARYA.													
All ages	..	**3**	**3**	..	**3**	**3**	..	..	..	..	**1**	**1**	..
10—15	..	**1**	1	..	**1**	1	..	..	..	..	..	..	..
15—20	..	**1**	1	..	**1**	1	..	..	..	..	..	..	..
20 & over	..	**1**	1	..	**1**	1	..	..	..	..	**1**	1	..
BRAHMO.													
All ages	..	**1,554**	**880**	**674**	**1,218**	**712**	**506**	**336**	**168**	**168**	**841**	**521**	**320**
0—5	..	**76**	31	45	..	..	..	**76**	31	45	..	..	..
5—10	..	**114**	55	59	**84**	50	34	**30**	5	25	**25**	13	12
10—15	..	**237**	132	105	**212**	121	91	**25**	11	14	**103**	55	48
15—20	..	**249**	137	112	**237**	125	112	**12**	12	..	**168**	94	74
20 & over	..	**878**	525	353	**685**	416	269	**193**	109	84	**545**	359	186

3. Nine Jains (male 7, female 2) in the suburbs in 24-Parganas have not been shown separately. All are aged 20 and over and their distribution is as follows : Literate 5 (male 4, female 1) ; Illiterate 4 (male 3, female 1) ; There is one Jew (male) aged 20 and over in the suburbs in 24-Parganas who is literate and literate in English.

4. Figures for Christians include both Indians and other than Indians. Details distinguishing the races are given below :—

Age.		Indian Christians.						Christians other than Indians.					
		Literate.			Literate in English.			Literate.			Literate in English.		
		Both sexes.	Males.	Females.	Both sexes.	Males.	Females.	Both sexes.	Males.	Females.	Both sexes.	Males.	Females.
1		2	3	4	5	6	7	8	9	10	11	12	13
CALCUTTA.													
All ages	..	**7,853**	**4,327**	**3,526**	**5,831**	**3,195**	**2,636**	**25,746**	**14,408**	**11,338**	**24,475**	**13,592**	**10,883**
5—10	..	**664**	332	332	**443**	232	211	**1,849**	885	964	**1,753**	829	924
10—15	..	**982**	469	513	**724**	346	378	**2,262**	1,107	1,155	**2,154**	1,047	1,107
15—20	..	**1,281**	602	679	**971**	457	514	**2,891**	1,619	1,272	**2,746**	1,529	1,217
20 & over	..	**4,926**	2,924	2,002	**3,693**	2,160	1,533	**18,744**	10,797	7,947	**17,822**	10,187	7,635
SUBURBS IN 24-PARGANAS.													
All ages	..	**222**	**138**	**84**	**45**	**26**	**19**	**321**	**169**	**152**	**321**	**169**	**152**
5—10	..	**17**	8	9	**4**	2	2	**20**	8	12	**20**	8	12
10—15	..	**25**	11	14	**4**	2	2	**42**	19	23	**42**	19	23
15—20	..	**30**	17	13	**5**	3	2	**57**	27	30	**57**	27	30
20 & over	..	**150**	102	48	**32**	19	13	**202**	115	87	**202**	115	87
HOWRAH.													
All ages	..	**268**	**165**	**103**	**220**	**136**	**84**	**1,603**	**888**	**715**	**1,559**	**858**	**701**
5—10	..	**24**	12	12	**19**	9	10	**144**	89	55	**140**	88	52
10—15	..	**26**	13	13	**20**	10	10	**165**	97	68	**159**	94	65
15—20	..	**30**	19	11	**23**	14	9	**193**	100	93	**187**	97	90
20 & over	..	**188**	121	67	**158**	103	55	**1,101**	602	499	**1,073**	579	494

5. Further details of Indian Christians by racial, tribal or provincial affiliations are given in imperial table XIV.

IMPERIAL TABLE XIII.—Literacy by religion, age-groups and sex.

Religion.	Age.	Total population. Both sexes.	Total population. Males.	Total population. Females.	Literate. Both sexes.	Literate. Males.	Literate. Females.	Illiterate. Both sexes.	Illiterate. Males.	Illiterate. Females.	Literate in English. Both sexes.	Literate in English. Males.	Literate in English. Females.
1	2	3	4	5	6	7	8	9	10	11	12	13	14
(1) CALCUTTA WITH SUBURBS IN 24-PARGANAS AND HOWRAH.													
ALL RELIGIONS.	**All ages** ..	**1,485,582**	**997,051**	**488,531**	**560,220**	**428,865**	**131,355**	**925,362**	**568,186**	**357,176**	**259,137**	**218,460**	**40,677**
	0—5 ..	130,144	67,950	62,194	..	..	..	130,144	67,950	62,194	..	..	..
	5—10 ..	120,973	67,805	53,173	37,179	22,986	14,193	83,799	44,819	38,980	15,000	10,903	4,097
	10—15 ..	124,285	73,152	51,133	51,215	32,737	18,478	73,070	40,415	32,655	23,706	17,613	6,093
	15—20 ..	158,737	107,316	51,421	72,476	53,731	18,745	86,261	53,585	32,676	36,115	29,807	6,308
	20 & over ..	951,438	680,828	270,610	399,350	319,411	79,939	552,088	361,417	190,671	184,316	160,137	24,179
HINDU.	**All ages** ..	**1,045,599**	**688,105**	**357,494**	**413,141**	**311,428**	**101,713**	**632,458**	**376,677**	**255,781**	**191,768**	**167,962**	**23,806**
	0—5 ..	96,842	50,141	46,701	..	..	..	96,842	50,141	46,701	..	..	..
	5—10 ..	86,621	47,994	38,627	29,349	17,998	11,351	57,272	29,996	27,276	10,995	8,367	2,628
	10—15 ..	87,575	50,656	36,919	39,973	25,217	14,756	47,602	25,439	22,163	17,994	13,842	4,152
	15—20 ..	110,693	73,788	36,905	54,055	39,469	14,586	56,638	34,319	22,319	27,476	23,403	4,073
	20 & over ..	663,868	465,526	198,342	289,764	228,744	61,020	374,104	236,782	137,322	135,303	122,350	12,953
MUSLIM.	**All ages** ..	**371,919**	**268,254**	**103,665**	**102,943**	**90,901**	**12,042**	**268,976**	**177,353**	**91,623**	**31,454**	**29,852**	**1,602**
	0—5 ..	26,930	14,392	12,538	..	..	..	26,930	14,392	12,538	..	..	..
	5—10 ..	28,538	16,733	11,805	4,649	3,376	1,273	23,889	13,357	10,532	1,426	1,240	186
	10—15 ..	30,441	19,106	11,335	7,100	5,371	1,729	23,341	13,735	9,606	2,314	2,047	267
	15—20 ..	40,648	29,202	11,446	12,881	11,063	1,818	27,767	18,139	9,628	4,194	3,936	258
	20 & over ..	245,362	188,821	56,541	78,313	71,091	7,222	167,049	117,730	49,319	23,520	22,629	891
SIKH.	**All ages** ..	**4,877**	**3,743**	**1,134**	**2,134**	**1,863**	**271**	**2,743**	**1,880**	**863**	**448**	**401**	**47**
	0—5 ..	455	281	174	..	..	..	455	281	174	..	..	..
	5—10 ..	344	230	114	90	67	23	254	163	91	29	22	7
	10—15 ..	345	244	101	136	108	28	209	136	73	47	37	10
	15—20 ..	592	440	152	271	223	48	321	217	104	65	55	10
	20 & over ..	3,141	2,548	593	1,637	1,465	172	1,504	1,083	421	307	287	20
CHRISTIAN.	**All ages** ..	**50,990**	**28,217**	**22,773**	**36,013**	**20,095**	**15,918**	**14,977**	**8,122**	**6,855**	**32,451**	**17,976**	**14,475**
	0—5 ..	4,843	2,487	2,356	..	..	..	4,843	2,487	2,356	..	..	..
	5—10 ..	4,662	2,389	2,273	2,718	1,334	1,384	1,944	1,055	889	2,379	1,168	1,211
	10—15 ..	4,999	2,585	2,414	3,502	1,716	1,786	1,497	869	628	3,103	1,518	1,585
	15—20 ..	5,439	2,914	2,525	4,482	2,384	2,098	957	530	427	3,989	2,127	1,862
	20 & over ..	31,047	17,842	13,205	25,311	14,661	10,650	5,736	3,181	2,555	22,980	13,163	9,817
JAIN.	**All ages** ..	**3,251**	**2,430**	**821**	**1,731**	**1,521**	**210**	**1,520**	**909**	**611**	**569**	**533**	**36**
	0—5 ..	272	151	121	..	..	..	272	151	121	..	..	..
	5—10 ..	224	122	102	85	63	22	139	59	80	22	20	2
	10—15 ..	288	166	122	130	96	34	158	70	88	47	42	5
	15—20 ..	431	312	119	259	222	37	172	90	82	99	88	11
	20 & over ..	2,036	1,679	357	1,257	1,140	117	779	539	240	401	383	18
JEW.	**All ages** ..	**1,830**	**932**	**898**	**1,131**	**594**	**537**	**699**	**338**	**361**	**843**	**454**	**389**
	0—5 ..	198	102	96	..	..	..	198	102	96	..	..	..
	5—10 ..	213	115	98	138	68	70	75	47	28	81	47	34
	10—15 ..	219	126	93	160	88	72	59	38	21	99	61	38
	15—20 ..	198	102	96	146	72	74	52	30	22	110	52	58
	20 & over ..	1,002	487	515	687	366	321	315	121	194	553	294	259
ZORO-ASTRIAN.	**All ages** ..	**1,283**	**756**	**527**	**836**	**533**	**303**	**447**	**223**	**224**	**702**	**445**	**257**
	0—5 ..	128	71	57	..	..	..	128	71	57	..	..	..
	5—10 ..	122	68	54	62	28	34	60	40	20	51	23	28
	10—15 ..	125	71	54	68	32	36	57	39	18	60	28	32
	15—20 ..	128	76	52	82	52	30	46	24	22	67	39	28
	20 & over ..	780	470	310	624	421	203	156	49	107	524	355	169
BUDDHIST.	**All ages** ..	**3,227**	**2,560**	**667**	**1,744**	**1,514**	**230**	**1,483**	**1,046**	**437**	**640**	**585**	**55**
	0—5 ..	209	131	78	..	..	..	209	131	78	..	..	..
	5—10 ..	142	87	55	43	27	16	99	60	39	9	8	1
	10—15 ..	151	105	46	79	61	18	72	44	28	21	18	3
	15—20 ..	331	274	57	207	177	30	124	97	27	76	70	6
	20 & over ..	2,394	1,963	431	1,415	1,249	166	979	714	265	534	489	45
CONFUCIAN.	**All ages** ..	**1,363**	**1,131**	**232**	**446**	**331**	**115**	**917**	**800**	**117**	**253**	**244**	**9**
	0—5 ..	150	123	27	..	..	..	150	123	27	..	..	..
	5—10 ..	56	30	26	41	23	18	15	7	8	8	8	..
	10—15 ..	84	59	25	60	44	16	24	15	9	20	20	..
	15—20 ..	158	127	31	78	58	20	80	69	11	39	37	2
	20 & over ..	915	792	123	267	206	61	648	586	62	186	179	7
TRIBAL.	**All ages** ..	**1,243**	**923**	**320**	**101**	**85**	**16**	**1,142**	**838**	**304**	**9**	**8**	**1**
	0—5 ..	117	71	46	..	..	..	117	71	46	..	..	..
	5—10 ..	56	37	19	4	2	2	52	35	17	..	..	..
	10—15 ..	58	34	24	7	4	3	51	30	21	1	..	1
	15—20 ..	119	81	38	15	11	4	104	70	34	..	..	..
	20 & over ..	893	700	193	75	68	7	818	632	186	8	8	..
(2) CALCUTTA.													
ALL RELIGIONS.	**All ages** ..	**1,196,734**	**814,948**	**381,786**	**473,589**	**302,558**	**111,031**	**723,145**	**452,390**	**270,755**	**227,858**	**190,620**	**37,238**
	0—5 ..	101,427	52,998	48,429	..	..	..	101,427	52,998	48,429	..	..	..
	5—10 ..	95,388	53,498	41,890	30,523	18,618	11,905	64,865	34,880	29,985	12,960	9,252	3,708
	10—15 ..	98,301	58,547	39,754	42,665	27,033	15,632	55,636	31,514	24,122	20,589	15,069	5,520
	15—20 ..	128,230	88,480	39,750	61,850	46,022	15,828	66,380	42,458	23,922	32,115	26,397	5,718
	20 & over ..	773,388	561,425	211,963	338,551	270,885	67,666	434,837	290,540	144,297	162,194	139,902	22,292
HINDU.	**All ages** ..	**822,293**	**547,846**	**274,447**	**340,637**	**256,223**	**84,414**	**481,656**	**291,623**	**190,033**	**164,515**	**143,116**	**21,399**
	0—5 ..	74,618	38,712	35,906	..	..	..	74,618	38,712	35,906	..	..	..
	5—10 ..	67,072	37,111	29,961	23,568	14,215	9,353	43,504	22,896	20,608	9,221	6,899	2,322
	10—15 ..	67,468	39,482	27,986	32,593	20,314	12,279	34,875	19,168	15,707	15,262	11,571	3,691
	15—20 ..	86,645	58,886	27,759	45,096	33,007	12,089	41,549	25,879	15,670	24,015	20,388	3,627
	20 & over ..	526,490	373,655	152,835	239,380	188,687	50,693	287,110	184,968	102,142	116,017	104,258	11,759
MUSLIM.	**All ages** ..	**311,155**	**229,311**	**81,844**	**91,540**	**81,432**	**10,108**	**219,615**	**147,879**	**71,736**	**29,657**	**28,124**	**1,533**
	0—5 ..	20,967	11,163	9,804	..	..	..	20,967	11,163	9,804	..	..	..
	5—10 ..	22,889	13,547	9,342	3,990	2,914	1,076	18,599	10,633	8,266	1,345	1,166	179
	10—15 ..	24,963	15,915	9,048	6,202	4,720	1,482	18,761	11,195	7,566	2,158	1,902	256
	15—20 ..	34,658	25,534	9,124	11,562	10,009	1,553	23,096	15,525	7,571	3,940	3,693	247
	20 & over ..	207,678	163,152	44,526	69,786	63,789	5,997	137,892	99,363	38,529	22,214	21,363	851

IMPERIAL TABLE XIII.—Literacy by religion, age-groups and sex.

Religion.	Age.	Total population.			Literate.			Illiterate.			Literate in English.		
		Both sexes.	Males.	Females.	Both sexes.	Males.	Females.	Both sexes.	Males.	Females.	Both sexes.	Males.	Females.
1	2	3	4	5	6	7	8	9	10	11	12	13	14
	(2) CALCUTTA.												
SIKH.	**All ages** ..	**4,705**	**3,602**	**1,103**	**2,064**	**1,799**	**265**	**2,641**	**1,803**	**838**	**432**	**385**	**47**
	0—5 ..	435	267	168	..	..	..	435	267	168	..	..	..
	5—10 ..	329	218	111	86	65	21	243	153	90	28	21	7
	10—15 ..	331	233	98	133	106	27	198	127	71	46	36	10
	15—20 ..	579	430	149	265	218	47	314	212	102	64	54	10
	20 & over ..	3,031	2,454	577	1,580	1,410	170	1,451	1,044	407	294	274	20
CHRISTIAN.	**All ages** ..	**47,558**	**26,307**	**21,251**	**33,599**	**18,735**	**14,864**	**13,959**	**7,572**	**6,387**	**30,306**	**16,787**	**13,519**
	0—5 ..	4,442	2,274	2,168	..	..	..	4,442	2,274	2,168	..	..	..
	5—10 ..	4,328	2,193	2,135	2,513	1,217	1,296	1,815	976	839	2,196	1,061	1,135
	10—15 ..	4,662	2,386	2,276	3,244	1,576	1,668	1,418	810	608	2,878	1,393	1,485
	15—20 ..	5,089	2,729	2,360	4,172	2,221	1,951	917	508	409	3,717	1,986	1,731
	20 & over ..	29,037	16,725	12,312	23,670	13,721	9,949	5,367	3,004	2,363	21,515	12,347	9,168
JAIN.	**All ages** ..	**3,185**	**2,381**	**804**	**1,698**	**1,490**	**208**	**1,487**	**891**	**596**	**559**	**523**	**36**
	0—5 ..	269	150	119	..	..	..	269	150	119	..	..	..
	5—10 ..	223	122	101	85	63	22	138	59	79	22	20	2
	10—15 ..	284	162	122	129	95	34	155	67	88	47	42	5
	15—20 ..	421	304	117	255	218	37	166	86	80	97	86	11
	20 & over ..	1,988	1,643	345	1,229	1,114	115	759	529	230	393	375	18
JEW.	**All ages** ..	**1,829**	**931**	**898**	**1,130**	**593**	**537**	**699**	**338**	**361**	**842**	**453**	**389**
	0—5 ..	198	102	96	..	..	..	198	102	96	..	..	..
	5—10 ..	213	115	98	138	68	70	75	47	28	81	47	34
	10—15 ..	219	126	93	160	88	72	59	38	21	99	61	38
	15—20 ..	198	102	96	146	72	74	52	30	22	110	52	58
	20 & over ..	1,001	486	515	686	365	321	315	121	194	552	293	259
ZORO-ASTRIAN.	**All ages** ..	**1,199**	**692**	**507**	**771**	**476**	**295**	**428**	**216**	**212**	**657**	**405**	**252**
	0—5 ..	117	64	53	..	..	..	117	64	53	..	..	..
	5—10 ..	119	66	53	59	26	33	60	40	20	50	22	28
	10—15 ..	121	68	53	65	29	36	56	39	17	58	26	32
	15—20 ..	114	66	48	69	42	27	45	24	21	58	32	26
	20 & over ..	728	428	300	578	379	199	150	49	101	491	325	166
BUDDHIST.	**All ages** ..	**3,021**	**2,420**	**601**	**1,660**	**1,435**	**225**	**1,361**	**985**	**376**	**630**	**576**	**54**
	0—5 ..	182	114	68	..	..	..	182	114	68	..	..	..
	5—10 ..	136	82	54	43	27	16	93	55	38	9	8	1
	10—15 ..	146	102	44	78	60	18	68	42	26	21	18	3
	15—20 ..	322	267	55	203	173	30	119	94	25	75	69	6
	20 & over ..	2,235	1,855	380	1,336	1,175	161	899	680	219	525	481	44
CONFUCIAN.	**All ages** ..	**1,363**	**1,131**	**232**	**446**	**331**	**115**	**917**	**800**	**117**	**253**	**244**	**9**
	0—5 ..	150	123	27	..	..	..	150	123	27	..	..	..
	5—10 ..	56	30	26	41	23	18	15	7	8	8	8	..
	10—15 ..	84	59	25	60	44	16	24	15	9	20	20	..
	15—20 ..	158	127	31	78	58	20	80	69	11	39	37	2
	20 & over ..	915	792	123	267	206	61	648	586	62	186	179	7
TRIBAL.	**All ages** ..	**426**	**327**	**99**	**44**	**44**	**..**	**382**	**283**	**99**	**7**	**7**	**..**
	0—5 ..	49	29	20	..	..	..	49	29	20	..	..	..
	5—10 ..	23	14	9	..	..	..	23	14	9	..	..	..
	10—15 ..	23	14	9	1	1	..	22	13	9	..	..	..
	15—20 ..	46	35	11	4	4	..	42	31	11	..	..	..
	20 & over ..	285	235	50	39	39	..	246	106	50	7	7	..
	(3) SUBURBS IN 24-PARGANAS.												
ALL RELIGIONS.	**All ages** ..	**63,975**	**36,983**	**26,992**	**14,062**	**11,294**	**2,768**	**49,913**	**25,689**	**24,224**	**5,561**	**4,942**	**619**
	0—5 ..	7,518	3,819	3,699	..	..	..	7,518	3,819	3,699	..	..	..
	5—10 ..	6,627	3,642	2,985	1,049	744	305	5,578	2,898	2,680	256	188	68
	10—15 ..	6,341	3,577	2,764	1,403	1,013	390	4,938	2,564	2,374	418	306	112
	15—20 ..	6,853	4,137	2,716	1,862	1,448	414	4,991	2,689	2,302	635	517	118
	20 & over ..	36,636	21,808	14,828	9,748	8,089	1,659	26,888	13,719	13,169	4,252	3,932	321
HINDU.	**All ages** ..	**49,693**	**28,748**	**20,945**	**11,746**	**9,501**	**2,245**	**37,947**	**19,247**	**18,700**	**4,735**	**4,315**	**420**
	0—5 ..	5,764	2,887	2,877	..	..	..	5,764	2,887	2,877	..	..	..
	5—10 ..	5,107	2,785	2,322	912	658	254	4,195	2,127	2,068	218	165	53
	10—15 ..	4,854	2,756	2,098	1,193	878	315	3,661	1,878	1,783	338	255	83
	15—20 ..	5,427	3,383	2,044	1,524	1,195	329	3,903	2,188	1,715	502	422	80
	20 & over ..	28,541	16,937	11,604	8,117	6,770	1,347	20,424	10,167	10,257	3,677	3,473	204
MUSLIM.	**All ages** ..	**12,478**	**7,080**	**5,398**	**1,676**	**1,407**	**269**	**10,802**	**5,673**	**5,129**	**455**	**428**	**27**
	0—5 ..	1,567	822	745	..	..	..	1,567	822	745	..	..	..
	5—10 ..	1,386	772	614	96	68	28	1,290	704	586	14	13	1
	10—15 ..	1,330	727	603	137	101	36	1,193	626	567	34	30	4
	15—20 ..	1,268	665	603	240	201	39	1,028	464	564	70	64	6
	20 & over ..	6,927	4,094	2,833	1,203	1,037	166	5,724	3,057	2,667	337	321	16
SIKH.	**All ages** ..	**8**	**8**	**..**	**4**	**4**	**..**	**4**	**4**	**..**	**..**	**..**	**..**
	0—5 ..	3	3	..	..	..	..	3	3	..	..	..	..
	5—10 ..	..	..	..	..	..	..	..	..	..	..	..	..
	10—15 ..	1	1	..	..	..	..	1	1	..	..	..	..
	15—20 ..	..	..	..	..	..	..	..	..	..	..	..	..
	20 & over ..	4	4	..	4	4	..	..	..	..	..	..	..
CHRISTIAN.	**All ages** ..	**915**	**501**	**414**	**543**	**307**	**236**	**372**	**194**	**178**	**366**	**195**	**171**
	0—5 ..	95	50	45	..	..	..	95	50	45	..	..	..
	5—10 ..	98	60	38	37	16	21	61	44	17	24	10	14
	10—15 ..	120	72	48	67	30	37	53	42	11	46	21	25
	15—20 ..	99	49	50	87	44	43	12	5	7	62	30	32
	20 & over ..	503	270	233	352	217	135	151	53	98	234	134	100
BUDDHIST	**All ages** ..	**157**	**99**	**58**	**44**	**40**	**4**	**113**	**59**	**54**	**4**	**3**	**1**
	0—5 ..	25	16	9	..	..	..	25	16	9	..	..	..
	5—10 ..	5	4	1	..	..	..	5	4	1	..	..	..
	10—15 ..	5	3	2	1	1	..	4	2	2	..	..	..
	15—20 ..	8	6	2	3	3	..	5	3	2	1	1	..
	20 & over ..	114	70	44	40	36	4	74	34	40	3	2	1

IMPERIAL TABLE XIII.—Literacy by religion, age-groups and sex.

Religion.	Age.	Total population.			Literate.			Illiterate.			Literate in English.		
		Both sexes.	Males.	Females.	Both sexes.	Males.	Females.	Both sexes.	Males.	Females.	Both sexes.	Males.	Females
1	2	3	4	5	6	7	8	9	10	11	12	13	14
	(3) SUBURBS IN 24-PARGANAS.												
TRIBAL.	**All ages**	**714**	**539**	**175**	**43**	**30**	**13**	**671**	**509**	**162**	..	..	..
	0—5	64	41	23	..	..	..	64	41	23	..	..	..
	5—10	31	21	10	4	2	2	27	19	8	..	..	..
	10—15	31	18	13	5	3	2	26	15	11	..	..	..
	15—20	51	34	17	8	5	3	43	29	14	..	..	..
	20 & over	537	425	112	26	20	6	511	405	106	..	..	..
	(4) HOWRAH.												
ALL RELIGIONS.	**All ages**	**224,873**	**145,120**	**79,753**	**72,569**	**55,013**	**17,556**	**152,304**	**90,107**	**62,197**	**25,718**	**22,898**	**2,820**
	0—5	21,199	11,133	10,066	..	..	..	21,199	11,133	10,066	..	..	..
	5—10	18,963	10,665	8,298	5,607	3,624	1,983	13,356	7,041	6,315	1,784	1,463	321
	10—15	19,643	11,028	8,615	7,147	4,691	2,456	12,496	6,337	6,159	2,699	2,238	461
	15—20	23,654	14,699	8,955	8,764	6,261	2,503	14,890	8,438	6,452	3,365	2,893	472
	20 & over	141,414	97,595	43,819	51,051	40,437	10,614	90,363	57,158	33,205	17,870	16,304	1,566
HINDU.	**All ages**	**173,613**	**111,511**	**62,102**	**60,758**	**45,704**	**15,054**	**112,855**	**65,807**	**47,048**	**22,518**	**20,531**	**1,987**
	0—5	16,460	8,542	7,918	..	..	..	16,460	8,542	7,918	..	..	..
	5—10	14,442	8,098	6,344	4,869	3,125	1,744	9,573	4,973	4,600	1,556	1,303	253
	10—15	15,253	8,418	6,835	6,187	4,025	2,162	9,066	4,393	4,673	2,394	2,016	378
	15—20	18,621	11,519	7,102	7,435	5,267	2,168	11,186	6,252	4,934	2,959	2,593	366
	20 & over	108,837	74,934	33,903	42,267	33,287	8,980	66,570	41,647	24,923	15,609	14.619	990
MUSLIM.	**All ages**	**48,286**	**31,863**	**16,423**	**9,727**	**8,062**	**1,665**	**38,559**	**23,801**	**14,758**	**1,342**	**1,300**	**42**
	0—5	4,396	2,407	1,989	..	..	..	4,396	2,407	1,989	..	..	..
	5—10	4,263	2,414	1,849	563	394	169	3,700	2,020	1,680	67	61	6
	10—15	4,148	2,464	1,684	761	550	211	3,387	1,914	1,473	122	115	7
	15—20	4,722	3,003	1,719	1,079	853	226	3,643	2,150	1,493	184	179	5
	20 & over	30,757	21,575	9,182	7,324	6,265	1,059	23,433	15,310	8,123	969	945	24
SIKH.	**All ages**	**164**	**133**	**31**	**66**	**60**	**6**	**98**	**73**	**25**	**16**	**16**	..
	0—5	17	11	6	..	..	..	17	11	6	..	..	..
	5—10	15	12	3	4	2	2	11	10	1	1	1	..
	10—15	13	10	3	3	2	1	10	8	2	1	1	..
	15—20	13	10	3	6	5	1	7	5	2	1	1	..
	20 & over	106	90	16	53	51	2	53	39	14	13	13	..
CHRISTIAN.	**All ages**	**2,517**	**1,409**	**1,108**	**1,871**	**1,053**	**818**	**646**	**356**	**290**	**1,779**	**994**	**785**
	0—5	306	163	143	..	..	..	306	163	143	..	..	..
	5—10	236	136	100	168	101	67	68	35	33	159	97	62
	10—15	217	127	90	191	110	81	26	17	9	179	104	75
	15—20	251	136	115	223	119	104	28	17	11	210	111	99
	20 & over	1,507	847	660	1,289	723	566	218	124	94	1,231	682	549
JAIN.	**All ages**	**57**	**42**	**15**	**28**	**27**	**1**	**29**	**15**	**14**	**10**	**10**	..
	0—5	3	1	2	..	..	..	3	1	2	..	..	..
	5—10	..	..	..	..	..	..	..	..	..	..	..	..
	10—15	5	4	1	1	1	..	4	3	1	..	..	..
	15—20	10	8	2	4	4	..	6	4	2	2	2	..
	20 & over	39	29	10	23	22	1	16	7	9	8	8	..
ZORO-ASTRIAN.	**All ages**	**84**	**64**	**20**	**65**	**57**	**8**	**19**	**7**	**12**	**45**	**40**	**5**
	0—5	11	7	4	..	..	..	11	7	4	..	..	..
	5—10	3	2	1	3	2	1	..	..	..	1	1	..
	10—15	4	3	1	3	3	..	1	..	1	2	2	..
	15—20	14	10	4	13	10	3	1	..	1	9	7	2
	20 & over	52	42	10	46	42	4	6	..	6	33	30	3
BUDDHIST.	**All ages**	**49**	**41**	**8**	**40**	**39**	**1**	**9**	**2**	**7**	**6**	**6**	..
	0—5	2	1	1	..	..	..	2	1	1	..	..	..
	5—10	..	..	..	..	..	..	..	..	..	..	..	..
	10—15	1	1	..	..	..	..	1	1	..	..	..	..
	15—20	1	1	..	1	1	..	..	..	..	..	..	..
	20 & over	45	38	7	39	38	1	6	..	6	6	6	..
TRIBAL.	**All ages**	**103**	**57**	**46**	**14**	**11**	**3**	**89**	**46**	**43**	**2**	**1**	**1**
	0—5	4	1	3	..	..	..	4	1	3	..	..	..
	5—10	4	3	1	..	..	..	4	3	1	..	..	..
	10—15	2	1	1	1	..	1	1	1	..	1	..	1
	15—20	22	12	10	3	2	1	19	10	9	..	..	..
	20 & over	71	40	31	10	9	1	61	31	30	..	..	..

IMPERIAL TABLE XIV.—Literacy of selected castes, tribes, races and Muslim social groups, by sexes.

This table corresponds to imperial table IX of 1921 and gives for selected groups figures similar to these in imperial table XIII but without classification by age. The entries occur in two series, first those of Asiatic race and next Anglo-Indians and non-Asiatics. Amongst Indians the groups chosen are those given in the title page of imperial table XIV in volume V, part ii ; details are given separately for persons of primitive tribes professing different religions ; and subsidiary figures are given by race, tribe or province of origin for such Indian Christians as are not shown elsewhere in the table under their own tribe.

2. Figures for sub-castes of Brahmans are incomplete owing to the failure of 187,458 persons (male 123,816, female 63,642) to make any return of their sub-caste.

3. Amongst non-Asiatics no record is given of 846 persons (male 611, female 235) who returned themselves as European without specifying their nationality or country of birth, and considerations of space have excluded from the table details for groups numbering less than ten for whom the following statement is given here :—

Race, etc., and religion.	Total population.			Literate.			Illiterate.			Literate in English.		
	Both sexes.	Male.	Female.	Both sexes.	Male.	Female.	Both sexes.	Male.	Female.	Both sexes.	Male.	Female.
1	2	3	4	5	6	7	8	9	10	11	12	13
Austrian—Christian	7	2	5	4	1	3	3	1	2	4	1	3
Dulgarian—Christian	4	..	4	4	..	4	..	..	..	1	..	1
Canadian—Christian	8	5	3	7	4	3	1	1	..	7	4	3
Danish—Christian	5	3	2	5	3	2	..	..	..	5	3	2
Fijian—Christian	2	1	1	2	1	1	..	..	..	2	1	1
Maltese—Christian	1	..	1	..	..	..	1	..	1	..	..	..
New Zealander	1	1	..	1	1	..	..	..	..	1	1	..
Philippinese—Christian	4	4	..	4	4	..	..	..	..	4	4	..
Syrian—Christian	1	1	..	1	1	..	..	..	..	1	1	..

IMPERIAL TABLE XIV.—Literacy of selected castes, tribes, races and Muslim social groups, by sexes.

Caste, etc., and religion.	Total population.			Literate.			Illiterate.			Literate in English.		
	Both sexes.	Male.	Female.	Both sexes.	Male.	Female.	Both sexes.	Male.	Female.	Both sexes.	Male.	Female.
1	2	3	4	5	6	7	8	9	10	11	12	13
AGARWALA—Hindu ..	**5,249**	3,359	1,890	**1,793**	1,497	296	**3,456**	1,862	1,594	**412**	373	39
BAGDI—Hindu ..	**8,926**	4,463	4,463	**1,076**	695	381	**7,850**	3,768	4,082	**263**	167	96
BAIDYA—Hindu ..	**19,012**	11,118	7,894	**13,672**	8,822	4,850	**5,340**	2,296	3,044	**9,630**	7,375	2,255
BAISHNAB—Hindu ..	**18,290**	8,807	9,483	**5,045**	3,798	1,247	**13,245**	5,009	8,236	**1,538**	1,339	199
BARUI—Hindu ..	**2,940**	1,832	1,108	**910**	681	229	**2,030**	1,151	879	**302**	270	32
BAURI—Hindu ..	**207**	41	166	**17**	12	5	**190**	29	161	**5**	5	..
BRAHMAN—Hindu ..	**197,283**	129,288	67,995	**117,586**	86,486	31,100	**79,698**	42,802	36,896	**63,898**	55,154	8,744
ACHARYA ..	*47*	*37*	*10*	*21*	*17*	*4*	*26*	*20*	*6*	*9*	*8*	*1*
AGRADANI ..	*21*	*12*	*9*	*14*	*8*	*6*	*7*	*4*	*3*	*7*	*5*	*2*
BAKNASANKAR ..	*12*	*12*	..	*10*	*10*	..	*2*	*2*	..	*7*	*7*	..
BHAT ..	*313*	*166*	*147*	*70*	*46*	*24*	*143*	*120*	*123*	*28*	*25*	*3*
BHUINHAR ..	*1*	*1*	..	..	..	..	*1*	*1*	..	..	..	..
DRAVIDA ..	*24*	*13*	*11*	*10*	*5*	*5*	*14*	*8*	*6*	*6*	*4*	*2*
GAUDADYA ..	*70*	*33*	*37*	*42*	*21*	*21*	*28*	*12*	*16*	*8*	*6*	*2*
GAUDIYA ..	*7*	*7*	..	*5*	*5*	..	*2*	*2*	..	*3*	*3*	..
KANYAKUBJA ..	*196*	*187*	*9*	*122*	*122*	..	*74*	*65*	*9*	*36*	*36*	..
MAHARASHTRIYA	*16*	*9*	*7*	*12*	*7*	*5*	*4*	*2*	*2*	*7*	*5*	*2*
MAITHILI ..	*17*	*14*	*3*	*9*	*9*	..	*8*	*5*	*3*	*1*	*1*	..
NEPALI ..	*18*	*18*	..	*5*	*5*	..	*13*	*13*	..	..	..	..
RARHI ..	*7,270*	*4,077*	*3,193*	*4,867*	*2,983*	*1,884*	*2,403*	*1,094*	*1,309*	*2,303*	*1,597*	*706*
SARASWAT ..	*44*	*40*	*4*	*31*	*30*	*1*	*13*	*10*	*3*	*8*	*8*	..
UTKAL ..	*181*	*163*	*18*	*33*	*31*	*2*	*148*	*132*	*16*	*2*	*2*	..
VAIDIK ..	*675*	*326*	*349*	*393*	*214*	*179*	*282*	*112*	*170*	*201*	*152*	*49*
VARENDRA ..	*913*	*357*	*556*	*642*	*271*	*371*	*271*	*86*	*185*	*360*	*180*	*180*
BHUMIJ—Tribal ..	**72**	53	19	**2**	1	1	**70**	52	18	..	..	..
CHAKMA—Hindu ..	..	..	..	..	..	..	..	..	..	..	..	..
CHAMAR—Hindu ..	**32,445**	24,738	7,707	**2,759**	2,511	248	**29,686**	22,227	7,459	**274**	250	24
CHINESE—Christians only	**147**	70	77	**104**	47	57	**43**	23	20	**94**	40	54
DHOBI—Hindu ..	**14,187**	9,288	4,899	**1,970**	1,664	306	**12,217**	7,624	4,593	**333**	301	32
DOM—Hindu ..	**4,592**	2,740	1,852	**187**	141	46	**4,405**	2,599	1,806	**14**	9	5
GARO—Tribal ..	**7**	4	3	**1**	1	..	**6**	3	3	..	..	..
GOALA—Hindu ..	**40,411**	31,020	9,391	**11,216**	9,875	1,341	**29,195**	21,145	8,050	**2,791**	2,639	152
HARI—Hindu ..	**1,436**	777	659	**130**	101	29	**1,306**	676	630	**35**	27	8
INDIAN CHRISTIAN—Christian ..	**15,113**	8,302	6,811	**8,192**	4,524	3,668	**6,921**	3,778	3,143	**5,671**	3,150	2,521
ASSAMESE ..	*13*	*12*	*1*	*3*	*3*	..	*10*	*9*	*1*	*1*	*1*	..
BENGALI ..	*11,632*	*6,140*	*5,492*	*6,946*	*3,738*	*3,208*	*4,686*	*2,402*	*2,284*	*4,840*	*2,614*	*2,226*
BIHARI ..	*501*	*307*	*194*	*207*	*135*	*72*	*294*	*172*	*122*	*118*	*70*	*48*
BURMESE ..	*5*	*4*	*1*	*1*	..	*1*	*4*	*4*	..	*1*	..	*1*
CEYLONESE ..	*5*	*5*	..	..	..	..	*5*	*5*	..	..	..	..
GOANESE ..	*343*	*323*	*20*	*85*	*83*	*2*	*258*	*240*	*18*	*74*	*72*	*2*
JEW ..	*70*	*45*	*25*	*15*	*13*	*2*	*55*	*32*	*23*	*15*	*13*	*2*
MADRASI ..	*1,235*	*772*	*463*	*374*	*230*	*144*	*861*	*542*	*319*	*267*	*150*	*117*
MALABARI ..	*2*	*2*	..	*2*	*2*	..	..	..	..	*2*	*2*	..
NEPALI ..	*10*	*5*	*5*	*6*	*4*	*2*	*4*	*1*	*3*	*6*	*4*	*2*
ORIYA ..	*100*	*87*	*13*	*18*	*17*	*1*	*82*	*70*	*12*	*9*	*9*	..
PUNJABI ..	*177*	*115*	*62*	*81*	*54*	*27*	*96*	*61*	*35*	*40*	*17*	*23*
JALIYA KAIBARTTA—Hindu ..	**7,985**	4,362	3,623	**1,479**	1,206	273	**6,506**	3,156	3,350	**327**	266	61
JAPANESE—Christian	**74**	43	31	**45**	28	17	**29**	15	14	**43**	26	17
JOGI OR JUGI—Hindu	**4,968**	2,743	2,225	**1,623**	1,275	348	**3,345**	1,468	1,877	**592**	571	21
KALU—Hindu ..	**3,040**	1,742	1,298	**814**	654	160	**2,226**	1,088	1,138	**125**	112	13
KAMAR—Hindu ..	**10,427**	6,474	3,953	**4,104**	3,140	964	**6,323**	3,334	2,989	**1,430**	1,320	110
KAYASTHA—Hindu ..	**182,574**	116,632	65,942	**106,231**	73,630	32,601	**76,343**	43,002	33,341	**61,884**	51,479	10,405
KUMHAR—Hindu ..	**5,010**	3,135	1,875	**1,298**	1,069	229	**3,712**	2,066	1,646	**540**	519	21
LEPCHA—All religions ..	**94**	88	6	**2**	2	..	**92**	86	6	..	..	..
Hindu ..	*93*	*88*	*5*	*2*	*2*	..	*91*	*86*	*5*	..	..	..
Christian ..	*1*	..	*1*	..	..	..	*1*	..	*1*	..	..	..
MAHISHYA—Hindu ..	**76,438**	45,022	31,416	**24,563**	20,069	4,494	**51,875**	24,953	26,922	**9,246**	8,581	665
MALAYAN—Christian ..	**19**	8	11	**9**	6	3	**10**	2	8	**5**	4	1
"MUMIN" (JOLAHA)—Muslim ..	**3,906**	2,478	1,428	**468**	446	22	**3,438**	2,032	1,406	**56**	56	..
MUNDA—All religions ..	**794**	594	200	**189**	143	46	**605**	451	154	**85**	60	25
Hindu ..	*376*	*307*	*69*	*42*	*35*	*7*	*334*	*272*	*62*	*2*	*2*	..
Tribal ..	*154*	*130*	*24*	*25*	*20*	*5*	*129*	*110*	*19*	*1*	*1*	..
Christian ..	*264*	*157*	*107*	*122*	*88*	*34*	*142*	*69*	*73*	*82*	*57*	*25*
NAMASUDRA—Hindu ..	**4,279**	2,475	1,804	**1,395**	1,098	297	**2,884**	1,377	1,507	**441**	406	35
NAPIT—Hindu ..	**16,037**	10,929	5,108	**4,899**	3,876	1,023	**11,138**	7,053	4,085	**1,471**	1,256	215
ORAON—All religions ..	**1,074**	812	262	**192**	140	52	**882**	672	210	**122**	84	38
Hindu ..	*368*	*337*	*31*	*35*	*34*	*1*	*333*	*303*	*30*	*8*	*7*	*1*
Tribal ..	*382*	*290*	*92*	*28*	*22*	*6*	*354*	*268*	*86*	*2*	*2*	..
Christian ..	*324*	*185*	*139*	*129*	*84*	*45*	*195*	*101*	*94*	*112*	*75*	*37*
PERSIAN—Christians only	**45**	19	26	**36**	16	20	**9**	3	6	**34**	16	18
SANTAL—All religions ..	**1,144**	661	483	**249**	112	137	**895**	549	346	**111**	72	39
Hindu ..	*78*	*68*	*10*	..	..	..	*78*	*68*	*10*	..	..	..
Tribal ..	*635*	*450*	*185*	*46*	*39*	*7*	*589*	*411*	*178*	*7*	*6*	*1*
Christian ..	*431*	*143*	*288*	*203*	*73*	*130*	*228*	*70*	*158*	*104*	*66*	*38*
SAYYAD—Muslim ..	**7,293**	5,089	2,204	**2,839**	2,238	601	**4,454**	2,851	1,603	**1,221**	1,082	139
SHAHA—Hindu ..	**12,413**	8,035	4,378	**4,804**	3,892	912	**7,609**	4,143	3,466	**2,427**	2,299	128
SIAMESE—Christian ..	**12**	..	12	**10**	..	10	**2**	..	2	**8**	..	8
SUNRI—Hindu ..	**2,845**	1,876	969	**932**	710	222	**1,913**	1,166	747	**270**	264	6
ANGLO-INDIAN—Christian ..	**18,469**	9,111	9,358	**13,757**	6,728	7,029	**4,712**	2,383	2,329	**13,371**	6,478	6,893
AMERICAN—Christian ..	**191**	129	62	**153**	102	51	**38**	27	11	**135**	86	49
ARMENIAN—Christian ..	**746**	418	328	**421**	187	234	**325**	231	94	**377**	169	208
AUSTRALIAN—Christian	**32**	17	15	**23**	9	14	**9**	8	1	**23**	9	14
BELGIAN—Christian ..	**32**	30	2	**20**	18	2	**12**	12	..	**20**	18	2
DUTCH—Christian ..	**98**	78	20	**75**	64	11	**23**	14	9	**73**	63	10
ENGLISH—Christian ..	**12,514**	7,598	4,916	**10,867**	6,797	4,070	**1,647**	801	846	**10,801**	6,761	4,040
FRENCH—Christian ..	**222**	118	104	**177**	94	83	**45**	24	21	**153**	74	79
GERMAN—Christian ..	**113**	76	37	**103**	70	33	**10**	6	4	**99**	67	32
GREEK—Christian ..	**72**	29	43	**34**	24	10	**38**	5	33	**34**	24	10
IRISH—Christian ..	**532**	312	220	**410**	245	165	**122**	67	55	**388**	225	163
ITALIAN—Christian ..	**193**	164	29	**114**	92	22	**79**	72	7	**110**	89	21
NORWEGIAN—Christian	**18**	18	..	**1**	1	..	**17**	17	..	**1**	1	..
PORTUGUESE—Christian ..	**176**	113	63	**121**	74	47	**55**	39	16	**117**	70	47
RUSSIAN—Christian ..	**24**	11	13	**17**	6	11	**7**	5	2	**17**	6	11
SCOTCH—Christian ..	**1,008**	701	307	**854**	594	260	**154**	107	47	**823**	565	258
SOUTH AFRICAN—Christian ..	**16**	9	7	**9**	5	4	**7**	4	3	**8**	4	4
SPANISH—Christian ..	**46**	37	9	**9**	2	7	**37**	35	2	**9**	2	7
SWEDISH—Christian ..	**36**	35	1	..	..	..	**36**	35	1	..	..	..
SWISS—Christian ..	**22**	16	6	**20**	14	6	**2**	2	..	**19**	13	6
WELSH—Christian ..	**66**	62	4	**52**	48	4	**14**	14	..	**52**	48	4

IMPERIAL TABLE XV.—Language—Part I.—Mother tongue by locality and sex.

This table corresponds to No. X of 1921. Part I only is here printed : part II is new at this census and is omitted in the interests of economy. The table printed shows a distribution by mother tongue of the population of Calcutta with suburbs and Howrah, Calcutta, suburbs in 24-Parganas and Howrah City.

2. The languages are shown in the following order : First come A.—Languages of Bengal (including Hindustani), Nepal and Sikkim ; next come languages of the neighbouring provinces, B.—Assam ; C.—Bihar and Orissa and D.—Burma ; next come languages of E.—Other parts of India and F.—Other Asiatic countries ; finally come G.—European languages. Within their groups languages are generally shown in alphabetical order, but Hindustani follows Bengali out of its proper place.

Serial No.	Language.	Calcutta with suburbs in 24-Parganas and Howrah City.			Calcutta.			Suburbs in 24-Parganas.			Howrah City.		
		Both sexes.	Males.	Females.	Both sexes.	Males.	Females.	Both sexes.	Males.	Females.	Both sexes.	Males.	Females.
	1	2	3	4	5	6	7	8	9	10	11	12	13
1	**ALL LANGUAGES** ..	**1,485,582**	**997,051**	**488,531**	**1,196,734**	**814,948**	**381,786**	**63,975**	**36,983**	**26,992**	**224,873**	**145,120**	**79,753**
2	**A.—Languages of Bengal, Nepal and Sikkim** ..	**1,362,721**	**906,512**	**456,209**	**1,088,351**	**734,948**	**353,403**	**61,232**	**34,778**	**26,454**	**213,138**	**136,786**	**76,352**
3	Bengali ..	822,861	499,570	323,291	648,451	402,043	246,408	53,170	28,537	24,633	121,240	68,990	52,250
4	Hindustani ..	535,023	403,367	131,656	436,123	330,149	105,974	8,023	6,205	1,818	90,877	67,013	23,864
5	*Hindi* ..	*412,750*	*316,537*	*96,213*	*329,687*	*253,878*	*75,809*	*6,529*	*5,188*	*1,341*	*76,534*	*57,471*	*19,063*
6	*Urdu* ..	*122,242*	*86,816*	*35,426*	*106,427*	*76,266*	*30,161*	*1,494*	*1,017*	*477*	*14,321*	*9,533*	*4,788*
7	*Chhatrisgarhi* ..	*31*	*14*	*17*	*9*	*5*	*4*	..	..	..	*22*	*9*	*13*
8	Bhotia ..	55	37	18	55	37	18	..	..	..	..	..	..
9	*Bhotia of Tibet (Tibetan)* ..	*39*	*26*	*13*	*39*	*26*	*13*	..	..	..	..	..	..
10	*Bhotia, unspecified* ..	*16*	*11*	*5*	*16*	*11*	*5*	..	..	..	..	..	..
11	Gurung ..	2	2	..	2	2	..	..	..	..	..	..	..
12	Mro ..	1	1	..	1	1	..	..	..	..	..	..	..
13	Murmi ..	7	5	2	7	5	2	..	..	..	..	..	..
14	Naipali (Khas-kura) ..	4,752	3,513	1,239	3,693	2,694	999	39	36	3	1,020	783	237
15	Newari ..	8	8	..	8	8	..	..	..	..	..	..	..
16	Khambu ..	2	2	..	2	2	..	..	..	..	..	..	..
17	Rong (Lepcha) ..	10	7	3	9	7	2	..	..	..	1	..	1
18	**B.—Languages of Assam** ..	**308**	**276**	**32**	**308**	**276**	**32**	..	..	..	..	..	..
19	Assamese ..	160	132	28	160	132	28	..	..	..	..	..	..
20	Khasi ..	124	120	4	124	120	4	..	..	..	..	..	..
21	Meithei (Manipuri) ..	24	24	..	24	24	..	..	..	..	..	..	..
22	**C.—Languages of Bihar and Orissa** ..	**47,500**	**43,030**	**4,470**	**39,688**	**36,286**	**3,402**	**1,937**	**1,722**	**215**	**5,875**	**5,022**	**853**
23	Kherwari ..	1,638	940	698	1,148	607	541	345	247	98	145	86	59
24	*Bhumij* ..	*18*	*9*	*9*	..	..	..	*18*	*9*	*9*	..	..	..
25	*Mundari* ..	*432*	*296*	*136*	*353*	*226*	*127*	*31*	*29*	*2*	*48*	*41*	*7*
26	*Santali* ..	*1,188*	*635*	*553*	*795*	*381*	*414*	*296*	*209*	*87*	*97*	*45*	*52*
27	Kurukh (Oraon) ..	940	723	217	405	279	126	318	263	55	217	181	36
28	Oriya ..	44,922	41,367	3,555	38,135	35,400	2,735	1,274	1,212	62	5,513	4,755	758
29	**D.—Languages of Burma** ..	**119**	**93**	**26**	**119**	**93**	**26**	..	..	..	..	..	..
30	Arakanese ..	12	12	..	12	12	..	..	..	..	..	..	..
31	Burmese ..	107	81	26	107	81	26	..	..	..	..	..	..
32	**E.—Languages of other parts of India** ..	**32,576**	**22,578**	**9,998**	**28,846**	**20,402**	**8,444**	**91**	**80**	**11**	**3,639**	**2,096**	**1,543**
33	Gujarati ..	4,121	2,717	1,404	3,883	2,534	1,349	1	1	..	237	182	55
34	Kanarese ..	41	25	16	39	25	14	..	..	..	2	..	2
35	Kashmiri ..	39	37	2	39	37	2	..	..	..	..	..	..
36	Malayalam ..	243	195	48	236	192	44	..	..	..	7	3	4
37	Marathi ..	1,101	889	212	1,031	835	196	41	34	7	29	20	9
38	*Konkani* ..	*35*	*14*	*21*	*35*	*14*	*21*	..	..	..	..	..	..
39	Panjabi ..	9,654	7,591	2,063	9,209	7,250	1,959	12	12	..	433	329	104
40	Pashto ..	756	708	48	710	662	48	31	31	..	15	15	..
41	Rajsthani ..	7,481	5,027	2,454	7,397	4,956	2,441	2	..	2	82	71	11
42	*Marwari* ..	*7,474*	*5,021*	*2,453*	*7,397*	*4,956*	*2,441*	*2*	..	*2*	*75*	*65*	*10*
43	Sindhi ..	381	302	79	359	286	73	..	..	..	22	16	6
44	*Kachchhi* ..	*159*	*126*	*33*	*155*	*122*	*33*	..	..	..	*4*	*4*	..
45	Tamil ..	2,744	1,493	1,251	2,554	1,401	1,153	..	..	..	190	92	98
46	Telugu ..	6,015	3,594	2,421	3,389	2,224	1,165	4	2	2	2,622	1,368	1,254
47	**F.—Languages of Asiatic countries outside India** ..	**6,726**	**4,731**	**1,995**	**6,388**	**4,521**	**1,867**	**156**	**98**	**58**	**182**	**112**	**70**
48	Arabic ..	817	629	188	764	629	135	..	..	..	53	..	53
49	Armenian ..	520	208	312	517	208	309	..	..	..	3	..	3
50	Chinese ..	3,226	2,593	633	3,028	2,460	568	156	98	58	42	35	7
51	Persian ..	415	285	130	333	209	124	..	..	..	82	76	6
52	Hebrew ..	1,195	593	602	1,195	593	602	..	..	..	..	..	..
53	Japanese ..	535	408	127	533	407	126	..	..	..	2	1	1
54	Sinhalese ..	15	15	..	15	15	..	..	..	..	..	..	..
55	Turkish ..	3	..	3	3	..	3	..	..	..	..	..	..
56	**G.—European languages** ..	**35,632**	**19,831**	**15,801**	**33,034**	**18,422**	**14,612**	**559**	**305**	**254**	**2,039**	**1,104**	**935**
57	English ..	34,953	19,428	15,525	32,393	18,043	14,350	548	299	249	2,012	1,086	926
58	French ..	170	72	98	154	62	92	7	4	3	9	6	3
59	Italian ..	159	144	15	157	142	15	..	..	..	2	2	..
60	Portuguese ..	84	27	57	84	27	57	..	..	..	..	..	..
61	Danish ..	2	2	..	2	2	..	..	..	..	..	..	..
62	Dutch ..	65	57	8	60	54	6	4	2	2	1	1	..
63	Flemish (with Belgian) ..	2	2	..	2	2	..	..	..	..	..	..	..
64	Gaelic ..	8	8	..	8	8	..	..	..	..	..	..	..
65	German ..	52	18	34	42	13	29	..	..	..	10	5	5
66	Greek ..	50	17	42	59	17	42	..	..	..	..	..	..
67	Hungarian ..	1	1	..	1	1	..	..	..	..	..	..	..
68	Norwegian ..	1	1	..	..	..	..	..	..	..	1	1	..
69	Russian ..	37	19	18	33	16	17	..	..	..	4	3	1
70	Spanish ..	38	35	3	38	35	3	..	..	..	..	..	..
71	Swedish ..	1	..	1	1	..	1	..	..	..	..	..	..

IMPERIAL TABLE XV—Language Part II.

(Not printed.)

IMPERIAL TABLE XVI.—Religions by locality and sex.

This table corresponds to imperial table VI of 1921 and shows details of all the religions returned. Seventy-five persons of indefinite belief are included amongst Christians. All these are of European or allied races. One (male) was returned from Howrah city as Atheist; and the remaining 74 were returned from Calcutta under the following designations :—

Religion returned.	Both sexes.	Male.	Female.	Religion returned.	Both sexes.	Male.	Female.
1	2	3	4	1	2	3	4
Theosophist ..	26	19	7	Sceptic ..	11	9	2
Freethinker ..	17	17	..	Atheist ..	3	3	..
Agnostic ..	16	15	1	Deist ..	1	1	..

2. Details of sects were recorded but were either imperfectly returned or were not utilised in full as a measure of public economy No sect was returned by 1,022,226 Hindus (male 674,679, female 347,547). One person (male) in Paddapukur (Ward 11 of Calcutta) returned himself as a Saiva : the remainder returned the following sects here distinguished as brahmanic and non-brahmanic :—

Locality.	Brahmanic.						Non-Brahmanic.					
	Sakta.			Vaishnava.			Arya Samaj.			Brahmo Samaj.		
	Both sexes.	Male.	Female.	Both sexes.	Male.	Female.	Both sexes.	Male.	Female.	Both sexes.	Male.	Female.
1	2	3	4	5	6	7	8	9	10	11	12	13
CALCUTTA WITH SUBURBS AND HOWRAH.	**15,910**	**9,659**	**6,251**	**5,905**	**2,883**	**3,022**	**3**	**3**	..	**1,554**	**880**	**674**
CALCUTTA WITH SUBURBS IN 24-PARGANAS.	**14,697**	**8,910**	**5,787**	**5,851**	**2,855**	**2,996**	**3**	**3**	..	**1,554**	**880**	**674**
Calcutta ..	**6,196**	**3,479**	**2,717**	**3,948**	**1,856**	**2,092**	**3**	**3**	..	**1,554**	**880**	**674**
MUNICIPAL AREA ..	**6,196**	**3,479**	**2,717**	**3,948**	**1,856**	**2,092**	**3**	**3**	..	**1,554**	**880**	**674**
District No. I ..	**2,663**	**1,631**	**1,032**	**2,393**	**1,273**	**1,120**	**3**	**3**	..	**1,203**	**703**	**500**
Ward No. 1 Shampukur ..	1,272	749	523	369	230	139	..	..	..	3	3	..
Ward No. 2 Kumartuli ..	3	3	..	31	31	..	..	..	..	..	..	..
Ward No. 3 Bartola ..	955	579	376	1,192	567	625	..	..	..	17	17	..
Ward No. 4 Sukea's Street	..	..	..	..	..	..	..	..	..	1,041	628	413
Ward No. 5 Jorabagan ..	144	100	44	308	193	115	..	..	..	..	..	..
Ward No. 6 Jorasanko ..	203	149	54	118	77	41	..	..	..	142	55	87
Ward No. 30 Belgachia ..	12	12	..	75	26	49	..	..	..	..	..	..
Ward No. 31 Satpukur ..	74	39	35	300	149	151	3	3	..	..	..	..
District No. II ..	**1,737**	**1,121**	**616**	**720**	**358**	**362**	..	..	..	**93**	**56**	**37**
Ward No. 7 Burra Bazar ..	14	14	..	..	..	..	..	..	..	..	..	..
Ward No. 8 Kalootola ..	116	116	..	23	23	..	..	..	..	..	..	..
Ward No. 9 Muchipara ..	933	510	423	359	135	224	..	..	..	80	56	24
Ward No. 10 Bow Bazar ..	5	..	5	..	..	..	..	..	..	2	..	2
Ward No. 11 Paddapukur ..	448	342	106	172	113	59	..	..	..	..	..	..
Ward No. 28 Beliaghata ..	23	23	..	5	5	..	..	..	..	..	..	..
Ward No. 29 Maniktala ..	198	116	82	161	82	79	..	..	..	11	..	11
District No. III ..	**6**	**6**	..	..	..	..	..	..	..	**131**	**58**	**73**
Ward No. 15 Kalinga ..	6	6	..	..	..	..	..	..	..	27	11	16
Ward No. 19 Intally ..	..	..	..	..	..	..	..	..	..	10	10	..
Ward No. 20 Beniapukur ..	..	..	..	..	..	..	..	..	..	4	..	4
Ward No. 21 Ballygunge ..	..	..	..	..	..	..	..	..	..	90	37	53
District No. IV ..	**1,790**	**721**	**1,069**	**835**	**225**	**610**	..	..	..	**127**	**63**	**64**
Ward No. 27 Tollygunge ..	527	221	306	268	123	145	..	..	..	..	..	..
Ward No. 22 Bhawanipur ..	499	73	426	98	..	98	..	..	..	95	48	47
Ward No. 23 Alipore ..	407	237	170	137	67	70	..	..	..	..	..	..
Ward No. 24 Ekbalpore ..	51	32	19	41	24	17	..	..	..	32	15	17
Ward No. 26 Garden Reach	306	158	148	291	11	280	..	..	..	..	..	..
Suburbs in 24-Parganas ..	**8,501**	**5,431**	**3,070**	**1,903**	**999**	**904**	..	..	..	..	..	..
Tollygunge ..	244	142	102	135	67	68	..	..	..	..	..	..
South Suburban Municipality	8,257	5,289	2,968	1,768	932	836	..	..	..	..	..	..
HOWRAH ..	**1,213**	**749**	**464**	**54**	**28**	**26**	..	..	..	..	..	..
Ward No. 1 ..	515	286	229	15	10	5	..	..	..	..	..	..
Ward No. 5 ..	157	144	13	..	..	..	..	..	..	..	..	..
Ward No. 6 ..	484	289	195	7	7	..	..	..	..	..	..	..
Ward No. 9 ..	..	..	..	1	1	..	..	..	..	..	..	..
Ward No. 10 ..	57	30	27	31	10	21	..	..	..	..	..	..

3. The great majority of Muslims are Sunnis by sect and no particulars have been compiled for other sects except the Shias. For them and for Christians, distinguished as Roman Catholic, Romo-Syrian, Other Syrian and Others, details are given in supplement No. I printed after the table.

4. Of the Jains only 274 returned their sect, viz., Swetambari 139 (male 131, female 8) and Swetambari Terapanthi 135 (male 126, female 9). All are found in Calcutta and their distribution by wards is as follows :—

Sect and ward.	Both sexes.	Male.	Female.	Sect and ward.	Both sexes.	Male.	Female.
1	2	3	4	1	2	3	4
Jain Swetambari ..	**139**	**131**	**8**	**Jain Swetambari Terapanthi** ..	**135**	**126**	**9**
Ward No. 3 ..	23	19	4	Ward No. 7 ..	135	126	9
Ward No. 7 ..	105	104	1				
Ward No. 11 ..	10	7	3				
Ward No. 24 ..	1	1	..				

5. In the interests of public economy no table has been prepared corresponding to imperial table XV of 1921. The racial distribution of Christians is shown by sect and sex in a summary form in supplement No. II printed after the table.

IMPERIAL TABLE XVI.—

Serial No.	Locality.	All religions.			Hindu.			Muslim.			Christian.		
		Both sexes.	Male.	Female.	Both sexes.	Male.	Female.	Both sexes.	Male.	Female.	Both sexes.	Male.	Female.
	1	2	3	4	5	6	7	8	9	10	11	12	13
1	**CALCUTTA WITH SUBURBS AND HOWRAH.**	**1,485,582**	**997,051**	**488,531**	**1,045,599**	**688,105**	**357,494**	**371,919**	**268,254**	**103,665**	**50,990**	**28,217**	**22,773**
2	**CALCUTTA WITH SUBURBS IN 24-PARGANAS.**	**1,260,709**	**851,931**	**408,778**	**871,986**	**576,594**	**295,392**	**323,633**	**236,391**	**87,242**	**48,473**	**26,808**	**21,665**
3	**Calcutta** ..	**1,196,734**	**814,948**	**381,786**	**822,293**	**547,846**	**274,447**	**311,155**	**229,311**	**81,844**	***47,558**	***26,307**	***21,251**
4	**MUNICIPAL AREA** ..	**1,158,044**	**778,559**	**379,485**	**806,169**	**533,370**	**272,799**	**292,601**	**210,996**	**81,605**	**44,307**	**23,433**	**20,874**
5	**District No. I** ..	**380,265**	**244,356**	**135,909**	**333,346**	**212,132**	**121,214**	**43,923**	**30,703**	**13,220**	**2,007**	**837**	**1,170**
6	Ward No. 1 Shampukur ..	**66,633**	40,571	26,062	**62,724**	37,787	24,937	**3,689**	2,661	1,028	**50**	11	39
7	Ward No. 2 Kumartuli ..	**38,294**	23,968	14,326	**37,318**	23,067	14,251	**905**	869	36	**12**	6	6
8	Ward No. 3 Bartola ..	**67,107**	41,066	26,041	**59,416**	35,895	23,521	**7,330**	4,980	2,350	**222**	102	120
9	Ward No. 4 Sukea's Street	**54,101**	35,227	18,874	**44,081**	28,564	15,517	**9,418**	6,392	3,026	**539**	223	316
10	Ward No. 5 Jorabagan ..	**39,355**	28,320	11,035	**38,393**	27,507	10,886	**778**	696	82	**76**	42	34
11	Ward No. 6 Jorasanko ..	**46,116**	29,847	16,269	**41,022**	26,061	14,961	**4,861**	3,700	1,161	**110**	8	102
12	Ward No. 30 Belgachia ..	**22,252**	14,228	8,024	**14,796**	9,751	5,045	**6,717**	4,168	2,549	**665**	255	410
13	Ward No. 31 Satpukur ..	**19,194**	11,934	7,260	**15,292**	9,388	5,904	**3,725**	2,421	1,304	**143**	92	51
14	Ward No. 32 Cossipore ..	**27,213**	19,195	8,018	**20,304**	14,112	6,192	**6,500**	4,816	1,684	**190**	98	92
15	**District No. II** ..	**287,035**	**204,746**	**82,289**	**184,108**	**128,368**	**55,740**	**86,435**	**65,836**	**20,599**	**9,244**	**5,161**	**4,083**
16	Ward No. 7 Burra Bazar ..	**18,690**	16,815	1,875	**13,653**	12,241	1,412	**3,299**	3,005	294	**492**	416	76
17	Ward No. 8 Kalootola ..	**48,998**	39,545	9,453	**17,092**	13,071	4,021	**28,232**	23,858	4,374	**404**	235	169
18	Ward No. 9 Muchipara ..	**80,604**	57,880	22,724	**56,834**	40,009	16,825	**21,794**	16,747	5,047	**1,820**	1,003	817
19	Ward No. 10 Bow Bazar ..	**21,075**	16,029	5,046	**10,231**	7,760	2,471	**6,313**	5,653	660	**2,747**	1,450	1,297
20	Ward No. 11 Paddapukur ..	**35,323**	23,191	12,132	**31,333**	20,538	10,795	**1,512**	1,383	129	**2,338**	1,183	1,155
21	Ward No. 12 Waterloo Street	**6,711**	5,860	851	**4,112**	3,946	166	**816**	776	40	**1,233**	729	504
22	Ward No. 28 Beliaghata ..	**33,235**	19,541	13,694	**25,702**	15,124	10,578	**7,317**	4,272	3,045	**158**	114	44
23	Ward No. 29 Maniktala ..	**42,399**	25,885	16,514	**25,151**	15,679	9,472	**17,152**	10,142	7,010	**52**	31	21
24	**District No. III** ..	**219,153**	**151,464**	**67,689**	**94,738**	**66,957**	**27,781**	**95,384**	**68,692**	**26,692**	**25,997**	**13,884**	**12,113**
25	Ward No. 13 Fenwick Bazar	**30,975**	25,686	5,289	**12,565**	10,619	1,946	**13,631**	12,357	1,274	**4,115**	2,293	1,822
26	Ward No. 14 Taltola ..	**38,427**	27,660	10,767	**14,331**	9,831	4,500	**18,128**	14,276	3,852	**5,410**	3,245	2,165
27	Ward No. 15 Kalinga ..	**14,052**	10,063	3,989	**4,597**	3,528	1,069	**5,481**	4,444	1,037	**3,708**	1,952	1,756
28	Ward No. 16 Park Street ..	**5,438**	4,121	1,317	**1,506**	1,418	88	**1,115**	1,076	39	**2,577**	1,469	1,108
29	Ward No. 17 Baman Bustee	**2,679**	2,056	623	**854**	782	72	**612**	592	20	**1,061**	592	469
30	Ward No. 18 Tengra ..	**11,772**	7,444	4,328	**8,013**	5,049	2,964	**3,497**	2,242	1,255	**195**	117	78
31	Ward No. 19 Intally ..	**44,224**	28,125	16,099	**26,395**	17,159	9,236	**13,682**	9,270	4,412	**3,889**	1,527	2,362
32	Ward No. 20 Beniapukur ..	**40,587**	25,648	14,939	**12,710**	8,741	3,969	**24,820**	15,277	9,543	**2,956**	1,553	1,403
33	Ward No. 21 Ballygunge ..	**30,999**	20,661	10,338	**13,767**	9,830	3,937	**14,418**	9,158	5,260	**2,086**	1,136	950
34	**District No. IV** ..	**271,591**	**177,993**	**93,598**	**193,977**	**125,913**	**68,064**	**66,859**	**45,765**	**21,094**	**7,059**	**3,551**	**3,508**
35	Ward No. 27 Tollygunge ..	**40,730**	24,400	16,330	**36,378**	21,531	14,847	**3,270**	2,112	1,158	**428**	254	179
36	Ward No. 22 Bhawanipur ..	**79,684**	50,564	29,120	**70,697**	44,412	26,285	**4,446**	3,473	973	**2,338**	1,060	1,320
37	Ward No. 23 Alipore ..	**30,020**	21,350	8,670	**22,373**	15,346	7,027	**6,053**	5,098	955	**1,372**	727	
38	Ward No. 24 Ekbalpore ..	**32,822**	21,664	11,158	**16,584**	11,205	5,379	**14,584**	9,633	4,951	**1,595**	781	814
39	Ward No. 25 Watganj and Hastings.	**32,463**	23,884	8,579	**22,280**	15,937	6,343	**8,871**	7,233	1,638	**1,054**	555	499
40	Ward No. 26 Garden Reach	**55,872**	36,131	19,741	**25,665**	17,482	8,183	**29,635**	18,216	11,419	**272**	174	98
41	**FORT WILLIAM AND MAIDAN**	**3,083**	**2,661**	**422**	**1,282**	**1,116**	**166**	**341**	**308**	**33**	**1,383**	**1,185**	**198**
42	**PORT** ..	**33,702**	**31,831**	**1,871**	**13,874**	**12,400**	**1,474**	**17,276**	**17,070**	**206**	**1,868**	**1,689**	**179**
43	**CANALS** ..	**1,905**	**1,897**	**8**	**968**	**960**	**8**	**937**	**937**	..	..	..	..
44	**Suburbs in 24-Parganas** ..	**63,975**	**36,983**	**26,992**	**49,693**	**28,748**	**20,945**	**12,478**	**7,080**	**5,398**	**915**	**501**	**414**
45	Tollygunge ..	**24,476**	14,800	9,676	**17,231**	10,642	6,589	**6,457**	3,652	2,805	**267**	133	134
46	South Suburban Municipality	**39,499**	22,183	17,316	**32,462**	18,106	14,356	**6,021**	3,428	2,593	**648**	368	280
47	**HOWRAH** ..	**224,873**	**145,120**	**79,753**	**173,613**	**111,511**	**62,102**	**48,286**	**31,863**	**16,423**	****2,517**	****1,409**	**1,108**
48	Ward No. 1 ..	**20,763**	13,938	6,825	**17,761**	11,750	6,011	**2,993**	2,183	810	**4**	3	1
49	Ward No. 2 ..	**6,514**	4,143	2,371	**6,073**	3,841	2,232	**423**	291	132	**10**	6	4
50	Ward No. 3 ..	**14,905**	9,626	5,279	**12,105**	7,767	4,338	**2,630**	1,758	872	**132**	76	56
51	Ward No. 4 ..	**31,882**	22,830	9,052	**21,418**	15,784	5,634	**8,657**	6,018	2,639	**1,606**	874	732
52	Ward No. 5 ..	**29,410**	18,734	10,676	**14,934**	9,862	5,072	**14,105**	8,678	5,427	**348**	183	165
53	Ward No. 6 ..	**33,790**	19,650	14,140	**31,133**	18,022	13,111	**2,634**	1,610	1,024	**14**	9	5
54	Ward No. 7 ..	**26,338**	17,613	8,725	**23,423**	15,528	7,895	**2,822**	2,048	774	**73**	20	53
55	Ward No. 8 ..	**37,497**	23,907	13,590	**27,510**	17,006	10,504	**9,769**	6,757	3,012	**177**	118	59
56	Ward No. 9 ..	**12,937**	8,627	4,310	**9,651**	6,592	3,059	**3,103**	1,893	1,210	**82**	62	20
57	Ward No. 10 ..	**10,837**	6,052	4,785	**9,605**	5,359	4,246	**1,150**	627	523	**71**	58	13

*Includes 74 persons of indefinite belief (64 males and 10 females).
**Includes one male of indefinite belief.

Religions by locality and sex.

Sikh.			Jain.			Buddhist.			Jew.			Confucian.			Zoroastrian.			Tribal.			Serial No.
Both sexes.	Male.	Female.	Both sexes.	Male.	Female.	Both sexes.	Male.	Female.	Both sexes.	Male.	Female.	Both sexes.	Male.	Female.	Both sexes.	Male.	Female.	Both sexes.	Male.	Female.	
14	15	16	17	18	19	20	21	22	23	24	25	26	27	28	29	30	31	32	33	34	
4,877	**3,743**	**1,134**	**3,251**	**2,430**	**821**	**3,227**	**2,560**	**667**	**1,830**	**932**	**898**	**1,363**	**1,131**	**232**	**1,283**	**756**	**527**	**1,243**	**923**	**320**	1
4,713	**3,610**	**1,103**	**3,194**	**2,388**	**806**	**3,178**	**2,519**	**659**	**1,830**	**932**	**898**	**1,363**	**1,131**	**232**	**1,199**	**692**	**507**	**1,140**	**866**	**274**	2
4,705	**3,602**	**1,103**	**3,185**	**2,381**	**804**	**3,021**	**2,420**	**601**	**1,829**	**931**	**898**	**1,363**	**1,131**	**232**	**1,199**	**692**	**507**	**426**	**327**	**99**	3
4,542	**3,451**	**1,091**	**3,149**	**2,356**	**793**	**2,562**	**1,968**	**594**	**1,803**	**912**	**891**	**1,363**	**1,131**	**232**	**1,199**	**692**	**507**	**349**	**250**	**99**	4
285	**207**	**78**	**534**	**340**	**194**	**57**	**49**	**8**	**22**	**8**	**14**	..	..	..	**51**	**43**	**8**	**40**	**37**	**3**	5
39	31	8	**130**	80	50	**1**	1	..	..	..	..	..	..	..	..	..	..	..	..	..	6
5	2	3	**51**	23	28	**2**	1	1	..	..	..	..	..	..	..	..	..	**1**	..	1	7
31	22	9	**101**	60	41	**3**	3	..	..	..	..	..	..	..	..	..	..	**4**	4	..	8
2	2	..	**34**	21	13	**5**	3	2	..	..	..	..	..	..	**22**	22	..	..	..	..	9
33	25	8	**71**	46	25	..	..	..	..	..	..	..	..	..	..	..	..	**4**	4	..	10
68	41	27	**36**	19	17	**15**	14	1	..	..	..	..	..	..	..	..	..	**4**	4	..	11
17	16	1	..	..	..	**5**	5	..	**22**	8	14	..	..	..	**20**	16	4	**10**	9	1	12
..	..	..	**3**	2	1	**17**	17	..	..	..	..	..	..	..	..	..	..	**14**	14	..	13
90	68	22	**108**	89	19	**9**	5	4	..	..	..	..	..	..	**9**	5	4	**3**	2	1	14
504	**381**	**123**	**2,141**	**1,744**	**397**	**1,570**	**1,259**	**311**	**1,088**	**539**	**549**	**1,298**	**1,089**	**209**	**637**	**361**	**276**	**10**	**8**	**2**	15
51	49	2	**1,174**	1,088	86	**6**	4	2	**13**	10	3	..	..	..	**2**	2	..	..	..	..	16
293	213	80	**370**	231	139	**539**	428	111	**394**	216	178	**1,298**	1,089	209	**376**	204	172	..	..	..	17
19	14	5	**80**	59	21	**38**	37	1	**5**	3	2	..	..	..	**11**	6	5	**3**	2	1	18
46	28	18	**410**	295	115	**576**	472	104	**571**	261	310	..	..	..	**181**	110	71	..	..	..	19
..	..	..	**50**	29	21	**39**	31	8	**25**	13	12	..	..	..	**25**	13	12	**1**	1	..	20
50	48	2	**25**	25	..	**371**	286	85	**80**	36	44	..	..	..	**22**	12	10	**2**	2	..	21
25	15	10	**25**	11	14	..	..	..	..	..	..	..	..	..	**5**	2	3	**3**	3	..	22
20	14	6	**7**	6	1	**1**	1	..	..	..	..	..	..	..	**15**	12	3	**1**	..	1	23
736	**568**	**168**	**417**	**246**	**171**	**558**	**396**	**162**	**642**	**333**	**309**	**52**	**34**	**18**	**497**	**277**	**220**	**132**	**77**	**55**	24
30	25	5	**35**	20	15	**160**	124	36	**140**	69	71	**27**	14	13	**267**	160	107	**5**	5	..	25
27	17	10	**173**	86	87	**179**	110	69	**18**	8	10	**18**	13	5	**143**	74	69	..	..	..	26
3	3	..	**7**	6	1	**38**	24	14	**182**	89	93	..	..	..	**36**	17	19	..	..	..	27
63	59	4	**10**	7	3	**30**	21	9	**119**	61	58	..	..	..	**18**	10	8	..	..	..	28
8	6	2	**3**	3	..	**36**	26	10	**95**	49	46	..	..	..	**10**	6	4	..	..	..	29
..	..	..	**10**	9	1	**2**	2	..	..	..	..	..	..	..	..	..	..	**55**	25	30	30
18	12	6	**122**	80	42	**34**	26	8	**21**	12	9	..	..	..	**23**	10	13	**40**	29	11	31
21	15	6	**25**	16	9	**12**	10	2	**36**	29	7	**7**	7	..	..	..	..	..	..	..	32
566	431	135	**32**	19	13	**67**	53	14	**31**	16	15	..	..	..	..	..	..	**32**	18	14	33
3,017	**2,295**	**722**	**57**	**26**	**31**	**377**	**264**	**113**	**51**	**32**	**19**	**13**	**8**	**5**	**14**	**11**	**3**	**167**	**128**	**39**	34
604	466	138	**18**	9	9	**16**	12	4	**11**	11	..	..	..	..	..	..	..	**5**	5	..	35
2,111	1,572	539	**12**	..	12	**44**	26	18	**11**	..	11	..	..	..	..	..	..	**25**	21	4	36
73	57	16	..	..	..	**140**	115	25	**9**	7	2	..	..	..	..	..	..	..	..	..	37
3	2	1	**15**	9	6	**19**	17	2	..	..	..	..	..	..	..	..	..	**22**	17	5	38
9	7	2	**12**	8	4	**124**	67	57	..	..	..	**13**	8	5	**6**	5	1	**94**	64	30	39
217	191	26	..	..	..	**34**	27	7	**20**	14	6	..	..	..	**8**	6	2	**21**	21	..	40
22	**15**	**7**	**36**	**25**	**11**	**19**	**12**	**7**	..	..	..	..	..	..	..	..	..	..	..	..	41
141	**136**	**5**	..	..	..	**440**	**440**	..	**26**	**19**	**7**	..	..	..	..	..	..	**77**	**77**	..	42
..	..	..	..	..	..	..	..	..	..	..	..	..	..	..	..	..	..	..	..	..	43
8	**8**	..	**9**	**7**	**2**	**157**	**99**	**58**	**1**	**1**	..	..	..	..	..	..	..	**714**	**539**	**175**	44
..	..	..	**9**	7	2	**156**	08	58	..	..	..	..	..	..	..	..	..	**356**	628	88	45
8	8	..	..	..	..	**1**	1	..	**1**	1	..	..	..	..	..	..	..	**358**	271	87	46
164	**133**	**31**	**57**	**42**	**15**	**49**	**41**	**8**	..	..	..	..	..	..	**84**	**64**	**20**	**103**	**57**	**46**	47
..	..	..	..	..	..	..	..	..	..	..	..	..	..	..	**5**	2	3	..	..	..	48
..	..	..	**8**	5	3	..	..	..	..	..	..	..	..	..	..	..	..	..	..	..	49
..	..	..	**9**	7	2	**11**	8	3	..	..	..	..	..	..	..	..	..	**18**	10	8	50
164	133	31	..	..	..	**8**	7	1	..	..	..	..	..	..	**14**	7	7	**15**	7	8	51
..	..	..	..	..	..	**1**	1	..	..	..	..	..	..	..	**17**	10	7	**5**	..	5	52
..	..	..	..	..	..	..	..	..	..	..	..	..	..	..	**9**	9	..	..	..	..	53
..	..	..	..	..	..	..	..	..	..	..	..	..	..	..	**20**	17	3	..	..	..	54
..	..	..	**4**	..	4	**10**	9	1	..	..	..	..	..	..	**5**	5	..	**22**	12	10	55
..	..	..	**36**	30	6	**19**	16	3	..	..	..	..	..	..	**14**	14	..	**32**	20	12	56
..	..	..	..	..	..	..	..	..	..	..	..	..	..	..	..	..	..	**11**	8	3	57

SUPPLEMENT No. I TO IMPERIAL TABLE XVI.—Sects of Muslims and Christians.

Locality.	Muslim.			Christian.											
	Shia.			Roman Catholic.			Romo-Syrian.			Other Syrian.			Others.		
	Both sexes.	Male.	Female.	Both sexes.	Male.	Female.	Both sexes.	Male.	Female.	Both sexes.	Male.	Female.	Both sexes.	Male.	Female.
1	2	3	4	5	6	7	8	9	10	11	12	13	14	15	16
CALCUTTA WITH SUBURBS AND HOWRAH.	**314**	**277**	**37**	**22,401**	**12,081**	**10,320**	**355**	**103**	**252**	**154**	**65**	**89**	**28,080**	**15,968**	**12,112**
CALCUTTA WITH SUBURBS IN 24-PARGANAS.	**274**	**247**	**27**	**21,379**	**11,503**	**9,876**	**355**	**103**	**252**	**152**	**65**	**87**	**26,587**	**15,137**	**11,450**
Calcutta ..	**274**	**247**	**27**	**20,948**	**11,275**	**9,673**	**355**	**103**	**252**	**152**	**65**	**87**	***26,103**	***14,864**	***11,239**
MUNICIPAL AREA ..	**274**	**247**	**27**	**20,120**	**10,545**	**9,575**	**355**	**103**	**252**	**152**	**65**	**87**	**23,680**	**12,720**	**10,960**
District No. I ..	**73**	**73**	..	**422**	**133**	**289**	**36**	**16**	**20**	**11**	**10**	**1**	**1,538**	**678**	**860**
Ward No. 1 Shampukur ..	73	73	..	2	2	..	..	..	..	..	..	..	48	9	39
Ward No. 2 Kumartuli ..	..	..	..	8	4	4	..	..	..	..	..	..	4	2	2
Ward No. 3 Bartola ..	..	..	..	12	5	7	..	..	..	9	9	..	201	88	113
Ward No. 4 Sukea's Street	..	..	..	75	34	41	..	..	..	..	..	..	464	189	275
Ward No. 5 Jorabagan ..	..	..	..	7	1	6	..	..	..	..	..	..	69	41	28
Ward No. 6 Jorasanko ..	..	..	..	6	2	4	..	..	..	..	..	..	104	6	98
Ward No. 30 Belgachia ..	..	..	..	206	19	187	36	16	20	1	..	1	422	220	202
Ward No. 31 Satpukur ..	..	..	..	33	20	13	..	..	..	1	1	..	109	71	38
Ward No. 32 Cossipore ..	..	..	..	73	46	27	..	..	..	..	..	..	117	52	65
District No. II ..	**174**	**166**	**8**	**4,292**	**2,317**	**1,975**	**319**	**87**	**232**	**134**	**49**	**85**	**4,499**	**2,708**	**1,791**
Ward No. 7 Burra Bazar ..	..	..	..	306	273	33	..	..	..	..	..	..	186	143	43
Ward No. 8 Kalootola ..	..	..	..	258	137	121	..	..	..	..	..	..	146	98	48
Ward No. 9 Muchipara ..	165	160	5	713	396	317	..	..	..	1	1	..	1,106	606	500
Ward No. 10 Bow Bazar ..	..	..	..	1,314	526	788	319	87	232	132	48	84	982	789	193
Ward No. 11 Paddapukur ..	9	6	3	1,243	748	495	..	..	..	..	..	..	1,095	435	660
Ward No. 12 Waterloo Street	..	..	..	449	232	217	..	..	..	..	..	..	784	497	287
Ward No. 28 Beliaghata ..	..	..	..	6	3	3	..	..	..	1	..	1	151	111	40
Ward No. 29 Maniktala ..	..	..	..	3	2	1	..	..	..	..	..	..	49	29	20
District No. III ..	..	..	..	**12,552**	**6,640**	**5,912**	..	..	..	**6**	**5**	**1**	**13,439**	**7,239**	**6,200**
Ward No. 13 Fenwick Bazar	..	..	..	2,473	1,349	1,124	..	..	..	..	..	..	1,642	944	698
Ward No. 14 Taltola ..	..	..	..	3,392	2,083	1,309	..	..	..	2	1	1	2,016	1,161	855
Ward No. 15 Kalinga ..	..	..	..	2,017	1,121	896	..	..	..	..	..	..	1,691	831	860
Ward No. 16 Park Street ..	..	..	..	591	279	312	..	..	..	2	2	..	1,984	1,188	796
Ward No. 17 Baman Bustee	..	..	..	315	213	102	..	..	..	..	..	..	746	379	367
Ward No. 18 Tangra ..	..	..	..	162	96	66	..	..	..	..	..	..	33	21	12
Ward No. 19 Intally ..	..	..	..	2,555	990	1,565	..	..	..	..	..	..	1,334	537	797
Ward No. 20 Beniapukur ..	..	..	..	606	294	312	..	..	..	2	2	..	2,348	1,257	1,091
Ward No. 21 Ballygunge ..	..	..	..	441	215	226	..	..	..	..	..	..	1,645	921	724
District No. IV ..	**27**	**8**	**19**	**2,854**	**1,455**	**1,399**	..	..	..	**1**	**1**	..	**4,204**	**2,095**	**2,109**
Ward No. 27 Tollygunge ..	8	8	..	63	37	26	..	..	..	1	1	..	364	216	148
Ward No. 22 Bhawanipur ..	..	..	..	305	200	105	..	..	..	..	..	..	2,033	860	1,173
Ward No. 23 Alipore ..	..	..	..	1,299	677	622	..	..	..	..	..	..	73	50	23
Ward No. 24 Ekbalpore ..	..	..	..	790	340	450	..	..	..	..	..	..	805	441	364
Ward No. 25 Watganj and Hastings.	..	..	..	307	148	159	..	..	..	..	..	..	747	407	340
Ward No. 26 Garden Reach	19	..	19	90	53	37	..	..	..	..	..	..	182	121	61
FORT WILLIAM AND MAIDAN	..	..	..	**412**	**354**	**58**	..	..	..	..	..	..	**971**	**831**	**140**
PORT ..	..	..	..	**416**	**376**	**40**	..	..	..	..	..	..	**1,452**	**1,313**	**139**
Suburbs in 24-Parganas ..	..	..	..	**431**	**228**	**203**	..	..	..	..	..	..	**484**	**273**	**211**
Tollygunge ..	..	..	..	111	54	57	..	..	..	..	..	..	156	79	77
South Suburban Municipality	..	..	..	320	174	146	..	..	..	..	..	..	328	194	134
HOWRAH ..	**40**	**30**	**10**	**1,022**	**578**	**444**	..	..	..	**2**	..	**2**	***1,493**	***831**	**662**
Ward No. 1 ..	..	..	..	..	..	..	..	..	..	..	..	..	4	3	1
Ward No. 2 ..	31	21	10	3	1	2	..	..	..	..	..	..	7	5	2
Ward No. 3 ..	..	..	..	..	..	..	..	..	..	..	..	..	132	76	56
Ward No. 4 ..	..	..	..	761	413	348	..	..	..	2	..	2	843	461	382
Ward No. 5 ..	9	9	..	212	128	84	..	..	..	..	..	..	136	55	81
Ward No. 6 ..	..	..	..	8	6	2	..	..	..	..	..	..	6	3	3
Ward No. 7 ..	..	..	..	7	5	2	..	..	..	..	..	..	66	15	51
Ward No. 8 ..	..	..	..	2	..	2	..	..	..	..	..	..	175	118	57
Ward No. 9 ..	..	..	..	..	..	..	..	..	..	..	..	..	82	62	20
Ward No. 10 ..	..	..	..	29	25	4	..	..	..	..	..	..	42	33	9

*Includes persons of indefinite belief.

SUPPLEMENT No. II TO IMPERIAL TABLE XVI.—Christians by race.

Race and sect.	Calcutta with suburbs in 24-Parganas and Howrah.			Calcutta with suburbs in 24-Parganas.			Calcutta.			Suburbs in 24-Parganas.			Howrah.		
	Both sexes.	Male.	Female.	Both sexes.	Male.	Female.	Both sexes.	Male.	Female.	Both sexes.	Male.	Female.	Both sexes.	Male.	Female.
1	2	3	4	5	6	7	8	9	10	11	12	13	14	15	16
EUROPEANS AND ALLIED RACES.															
All sects ..	**16,905**	**10,503**	**6,402**	**16,083**	**10,054**	**6,029**	**15,913**	**9,961**	**5,952**	**170**	**93**	**77**	**822**	**449**	**373**
Roman Catholic ..	**5,222**	2,941	2,281	**4,973**	2,810	2,163	**4,861**	2,748	2,113	**112**	62	50	**249**	131	118
Romo-Syrian ..	**69**	41	28	**69**	41	28	**69**	41	28	..	..	..	..	..	..
Other Syrian ..	**38**	22	16	**38**	22	16	**38**	22	16	..	..	..	..	..	..
Others ..	**11,576**	7,499	4,077	**11,003**	7,181	3,822	**10,945**	7,150	3,795	**58**	31	27	**573**	318	255
ANGLO-INDIANS															
All sects ..	**18,469**	**9,111**	**9,358**	**17,251**	**8,457**	**8,794**	**16,863**	**8,246**	**8,617**	**388**	**211**	**177**	**1,218**	**654**	**564**
Roman Catholic ..	**11,043**	5,330	5,713	**10,392**	4,977	5,415	**10,176**	4,859	5,317	**216**	118	98	**651**	353	298
Romo-Syrian ..	**255**	55	200	**255**	55	200	**255**	55	200	..	..	..	..	..	..
Other Syrian ..	**68**	11	57	**66**	11	55	**66**	11	55	..	..	..	**2**	..	2
Others ..	**7,103**	3,715	3,388	**6,538**	3,414	3,124	**6,366**	3,321	3,045	**172**	93	79	**565**	301	264
INDIANS															
All sects ..	**15,113**	**8,302**	**6,811**	**14,637**	**7,997**	**6,640**	**14,280**	**7,800**	**6,480**	**357**	**197**	**160**	**476**	**305**	**171**
Roman Catholic ..	**5,923**	3,677	2,246	**5,801**	3,583	2,218	**5,698**	3,535	2,163	**103**	48	55	**122**	94	28
Romo-Syrian ..	**19**	7	12	**19**	7	12	**19**	7	12	..	..	..	..	..	..
Other Syrian ..	**39**	30	9	**39**	30	9	**39**	30	9	..	..	..	..	..	..
Others ..	**9,132**	4,588	4,544	**8,778**	4,377	4,401	**8,524**	4,228	4,296	**254**	149	105	**354**	211	143
OTHERS															
All sects ..	**428**	**236**	**192**	**428**	**236**	**192**	**428**	**236**	**192**	..	..	..	..	..	..
Roman Catholic ..	**213**	133	80	**213**	133	80	**213**	133	80	..	..	..	..	..	..
Romo-Syrian ..	**12**	..	12	**12**	..	12	**12**	..	12	..	..	..	..	..	..
Other Syrian ..	**9**	2	7	**9**	2	7	**9**	2	7	..	..	..	..	..	..
Others ..	**194**	101	93	**194**	101	93	**194**	101	93	..	..	..	..	..	..

IMPERIAL TABLE XVII.—Caste, tribe or Muslim social group, race and nationality.

This table corresponds to imperial table XIII of 1921. It is primarily intended to show the caste of Hindus and the tribe of primitive peoples, but shows also the social group of Muslims and the race or nationality or both so far as they were returned by others than these three classes of the population. It is divided into two parts. Part A is confined to Asiatics and shows for Indians the caste, tribal or similar group and for others the available details of race, etc. It gives also details of the locality of origin of Indians for whom a caste return was replaced by a geographical description (e. g., "Bilaspuri") and who belong to no primitive tribe. The religion of each group shown is indicated and where members of the same group were returned under different religions subsidiary figures are given for each religion returned. Part B gives for Anglo-Indians and for other than Asiatic such details as are available of their race or nationality or both, and shows separately British subjects and others : but no direct question as to nationality was included in the census schedule and the returns of nationality are based on birthplace and cannot claim absolute accuracy. Racial (e.g., "Welsh"), national (e.g., "German") and even merely geographical descriptions (e.g. "Philippinese" and "Fijian" which provide no certain clue to either race or nationality) appear in this part of the table and the student must make the best he can of the rather indefinite information offered to him.

2. Part A of the table contains a group of those Hindus who returned no caste : this includes in addition to outcastes and some prostitutes also a number of persons who repudiate the caste system on principle or refused for some other reason to return their caste. There is also a group including such inadequate or erroneous caste returns as could not be identified. Amongst Muslims the groups given in detail are Beharas, Moghuls, 'Mumin' (Jolahas), Pathans, Sayyads and Shekhs : other sections numbered in all 56,953 distributed as under.

	Calcutta with suburbs in 24-Parganas and Howrah.	Suburbs in 24-Parganas.	Howrah.
Both sexes ..	**56,953**	**12,277**	**44,676**
Males ..	36,545	6,958	29,587
Females ..	20,408	5,319	15,089

3. The racial, tribal or geographical affiliation of Indian Christians as a class can be conveniently ascertained from imperial tables VIII, XIV and XIX and is not here repeated.

4. In the table Tribal Christians appear twice—once under their own tribal name and once in the total of Indian Christians. Allowing for this double entry and counting in all muslims the detailed figures for Asiatic races include 1,437,426 persons (male 968,140, female 469,286) out of a total of 1,450,749 (male 977,695, female 473,054). The difference is accounted for as follows :—

Race, tribe, caste, etc. and religion.	Calcutta with suburbs in 24-Parganas and Howrah.			Calcutta.			Suburbs in 24-Parganas.			Howrah.		
	Both sexes.	Males.	Females.	Both sexes.	Males.	Females.	Both sexes.	Males.	Females.	Both sexes.	Males.	Females.
1	2	3	1	5	6	7	8	9	10	11	12	13
TOTAL NOT SHOWN IN TABLE	**13,323**	**9,555**	**3,768**	**13,000**	**9,300**	**3,700**	**18**	**16**	**2**	**305**	**239**	**66**
1 Confucians ..	**1,363**	1,131	232	**1,363**	1,131	232	..	..	..	..	..	..
2 Jews ..	**1,830**	932	898	**1,829**	931	898	**1**	1	..	..	..	..
3 Jains ..	**3,251**	2,430	821	**3,185**	2,381	804	**9**	7	2	**57**	42	15
4 Sikhs ..	**4,877**	3,743	1,134	**4,705**	3,602	1,103	**8**	8	..	**164**	133	31
5 Zoroastrians ..	**1,283**	756	527	**1,199**	692	507	..	..	..	**84**	64	20
6 Sinhalese—Buddhist ..	**10**	10	..	**10**	10	..	..	..	..	..	..	..
7 'Hindustani'—Buddhist ..	**58**	13	45	**58**	13	45	..	..	..	..	..	..
8 Bengali—Buddhist ..	**632**	529	103	**632**	529	103	..	..	..	..	..	..
9 Bihari—Buddhist ..	**12**	10	2	**12**	10	2	..	..	..	..	..	..
10 Other—Buddhist ..	**7**	1	6	**7**	1	6	..	..	..	..	..	..

The race of all these is clear from the entries given with the exception of No. 10 and possibly No. 1, which however refer almost certainly to Japanese and Chinese.

IMPERIAL TABLE XVII.—Caste, tribe, race or nationality.

Race, tribe, caste, etc. and religion.		Calcutta with suburbs in 24-Parganas and Howrah.			Calcutta.			Suburbs in 24-Parganas.			Howrah.		
		Both sexes.	Males.	Females.	Both sexes.	Males.	Females.	Both sexes.	Males.	Females.	Both sexes.	Males.	Females.
1		2	3	4	5	6	7	8	9	10	11	12	13
TOTAL POPULATION	..	**1,485,582**	**997,051**	**488,531**	**1,196,734**	**814,948**	**381,768**	**63,975**	**36,983**	**26,992**	**224,873**	**145,120**	**79,753**
A.—ASIATIC RACES	..												
Agaria	..	**51**	46	5	**46**	46	..	..	..	..	**5**	..	5
Agarwala	..	**5,249**	3,359	1,890	**4,694**	3,002	1,692	**4**	3	1	**551**	354	197
Aguri	..	**789**	578	211	**699**	511	188	**2**	..	2	**88**	67	21
Arakanese—Buddhist	..	**11**	11	..	**11**	11	..	..	..	..	..	..	..
Armenian—Christian	..	**746**	418	328	**738**	415	323	..	..	..	**8**	3	5
Arora	..	**130**	108	22	**130**	108	22	..	..	..	..	..	..
Arya	..	**3**	3	..	**3**	3	..	..	..	..	..	..	..
Babhan	..	**19**	10	9	**19**	10	9	..	..	..	..	..	..
Bagdi	..	**8,926**	4,463	4,463	**5,365**	2,579	2,786	**1,449**	801	648	**2,112**	1,083	1,029
Bahelia	..	**37**	26	11	**34**	23	11	**1**	1	..	**2**	2	..
Baidya	..	**19,012**	11,118	7,894	**17,498**	10,167	7,331	**459**	271	188	**1,055**	680	375
Baisbaniya	..	**5,108**	3,193	1,915	**2,940**	2,003	937	**131**	121	10	**2,037**	1,069	968
Baishnab	..	**18,290**	8,807	9,483	**13,895**	6,760	7,135	**1,433**	701	732	**2,962**	1,346	1,616
Baiti	..	**89**	61	28	**30**	28	2	**5**	3	2	**54**	30	24
Baniya	..	**9,100**	5,936	3,164	**9,100**	5,936	3,164	..	..	..	..	..	..
Barui	..	**2,940**	1,832	1,108	**1,817**	1,204	613	**42**	23	19	**1,081**	605	476
Bauri	..	**207**	41	166	**180**	22	158	**22**	14	8	**5**	5	..
Bediya	..	**149**	110	39	**61**	49	12	..	..	..	**88**	61	27
Behara—Muslim	..	**1**	..	1	**1**	..	1	..	..	..	..	..	..
Beldar	..	**416**	208	208	**384**	179	205	..	..	..	**32**	29	3
Bhar	..	**1,684**	1,294	390	**1,149**	922	227	..	..	..	**535**	372	163
Bhatiya	..	**253**	106	147	**243**	105	138	**1**	1	..	**9**	..	9
Bhogta	..	**12**	12	..	..	..	..	..	..	..	**12**	12	..
Bhotia of Bhutan (Drupka)	..	**249**	211	38	**249**	211	38	..	..	..	..	..	..
Bhotia of Nepal (Shar-pa)	..	**114**	46	68	**114**	46	68	..	..	..	..	..	..
Bhotia of Sikkim (Denjonpa)	..	**10**	10	..	**10**	10	..	..	..	..	..	..	..
Bhotia (unspecified)—Buddhist	..	**13**	8	5	**13**	8	5	..	..	..	..	..	..
Bhuinhar	..	**178**	172	6	**178**	172	6	..	..	..	..	..	..
Bhuinmali	..	**72**	43	29	**28**	27	1	..	..	..	**44**	16	28
Bhuiya	..	**2,517**	2,098	419	**1,439**	1,112	327	**87**	56	31	**991**	930	61
Bhuj	..	**47**	47	..	**47**	47	..	..	..	..	..	..	..
Bhumij—All religions	..	**108**	75	33	**31**	17	14	**72**	53	19	**5**	5	..
Hindu	..	*36*	*22*	*14*	*31*	*17*	*14*	..	..	..	*5*	*5*	
Tribal	..	*72*	*53*	*19*	..	..	..	*72*	*53*	*19*	..		
Bidur	..	**5**	5	..	**5**	5	..	..	..	..	..	..	..
Bilaspuri	..	**23**	11	12	**11**	11	..	..	..	..	**12**	..	12
Bind	..	**409**	205	204	**353**	152	201	**1**	1	..	**55**	52	3
Brahman	..	**197,283**	129,288	67,995	**159,104**	105,886	53,218	**8,527**	4,878	3,649	**29,652**	18,524	11,128
Brahmo	..	**1,554**	880	674	**1,554**	880	674	..	..	..	..	..	..
Burmese—Buddhist	..	**92**	68	24	**92**	68	24	..	..	..	..	..	..
Chain	..	**13**	13	..	**4**	4	..	..	..	..	**9**	9	..
Chamar	..	**32,445**	24,738	7,707	**24,867**	18,920	5,947	**682**	454	228	**6,896**	5,364	1,532
Chasadhoba	..	**352**	272	80	**142**	142	..	**4**	4	..	**206**	126	80
Caste inadequately returned	..	**943**	916	27	**936**	909	27	**3**	3	..	**4**	4	..
Caste not returned	..	**13,589**	7,956	5,633	**2,676**	1,279	1,397	**10**	10	..	**10,903**	6,667	4,236
Chinese—Buddhist	..	**1,653**	1,341	312	**1,456**	1,209	247	**156**	98	58	**41**	34	7
„ —Christian	..	**147**	70	77	**147**	70	77	..	..	..	..	..	..
Dalihara	..	**3**	..	3	**3**	..	3	..	..	..	..	..	..
Damai	..	**33**	2	31	**33**	2	31	..	..	..	..	..	..
Dhanuk	..	**198**	186	12	**129**	122	7	**12**	12	..	**57**	52	5
Dhenuar	..	**9**	..	9	**9**	..	9	..	..	..	..	..	..
Dhobi	..	**14,187**	9,288	4,899	**11,252**	7,463	3,789	**634**	456	178	**2,301**	1,369	932
Dhunia	..	**268**	157	111	**268**	157	111	..	..	..	..	..	..
Dom	..	**4,592**	2,740	1,852	**3,757**	2,214	1,543	**80**	47	33	**755**	479	276
Dosadh	..	**8,481**	6,395	2,086	**6,324**	4,789	1,535	**238**	197	41	**1,919**	1,409	510
Gandhabanik	..	**12,296**	8,080	4,216	**10,239**	6,630	3,609	**202**	131	71	**1,855**	1,319	536
Gareri	..	**174**	114	60	**114**	77	37	**53**	30	23	**7**	7	..
Garo	..	**7**	4	3	**7**	4	3	..	..	..	..	..	..
Ghasi	..	**214**	170	44	**157**	118	39	..	..	..	**57**	52	5
Ghatwal	..	**78**	69	9	**72**	63	9	..	..	..	**6**	6	..
Goala	..	**40,411**	31,020	9,391	**30,770**	24,051	[illegible]	[illegible]	[illegible]	[illegible]	[illegible]	[illegible]	[illegible]
Gond	..	**1**	1	..	..	..	..	..	..	..	**1**	1	..
Gonr	..	**412**	297	115	**127**	80	47	**117**	91	26	**168**	126	42
Gonrhi	..	**85**	63	22	**83**	62	21	..	..	..	**2**	1	1
Gorait	..	**47**	44	3	**45**	42	3	..	..	..	**2**	2	..
Gujrati	..	**216**	100	116	**212**	96	116	..	..	..	**4**	4	..
Gurung	..	**332**	275	57	**322**	268	54	..	..	..	**10**	7	3
Halalkhor	..	**360**	236	124	**302**	236	66	..	..	..	**58**	..	58
Halwai	..	**1,176**	838	338	**1,010**	711	299	**25**	25	..	**141**	102	39
Hari	..	**1,436**	777	659	**1,073**	590	483	**26**	12	14	**337**	175	162
Indian Christian	..	**15,113**	8,302	6,811	**14,280**	7,800	6,480	**357**	197	160	**476**	305	171
Jalia—Kaibarta (Adi-Kaibartta)	..	**7,985**	4,362	3,623	**3,756**	2,088	1,668	**177**	115	62	**4,052**	2,159	1,893
Japanese—Buddhist	..	**490**	379	111	**488**	378	110	..	..	..	**2**	1	1
Christian	..	**74**	43	31	**74**	43	31	..	..	..	..	..	..
Jhalo-Malo and Malo	..	**1,010**	767	243	**921**	736	185	..	..	..	**89**	31	58
Jimdar	..	**27**	14	13	..	..	..	**16**	7	9	**11**	7	4
Jogi or Jugi	..	**4,968**	2,743	2,225	**3,297**	1,804	1,493	**935**	514	421	**736**	425	311
Kachari	..	**184**	149	35	**184**	149	35	..	..	..	..	..	..
Kachhi	..	**43**	41	2	**31**	30	1	..	..	..	**12**	11	1
Kahar and Rawani Kahar	..	**21,151**	16,832	4,319	**17,296**	13,888	3,408	**202**	143	59	**3,653**	2,801	852
Koiri	..	**4,033**	3,479	554	**2,861**	2,552	309	**187**	155	32	**985**	772	213
Kalal	..	**16**	..	16	**16**	..	16	..	..	..	..	..	..
Kalu and Teli	..	**21,030**	13,816	7,214	**15,864**	10,750	5,114	**902**	547	355	**4,264**	2,519	1,745
Kalwar	..	**4,940**	3,357	1,583	**3,683**	2,478	1,205	**26**	11	15	**1,231**	868	363
Kamar	..	**10,427**	6,474	3,953	**8,468**	5,281	3,187	**453**	245	208	**1,506**	948	558
Kami	..	**2**	1	1	**2**	1	1	..	..	..	..	..	..
Kan	..	**20**	20	..	**20**	20	..	..	..	..	..	..	..
Kandh	..	**92**	76	16	**92**	76	16	..	..	..	..	..	..
Kandu	..	**1,554**	1,298	256	**960**	797	163	**27**	27	..	**567**	474	93
Kansari	..	**4,824**	2,571	2,253	**4,692**	2,475	2,217	**1**	..	1	**131**	96	35
Kaora	..	**5,741**	3,100	2,641	**2,907**	1,499	1,408	**1,926**	1,038	888	**908**	563	345
Kapali	..	**644**	395	249	**453**	289	164	**21**	15	6	**170**	91	79
Kapuria	..	**44**	40	4	**44**	40	4	..	..	..	..	..	..
Karan	..	**457**	409	48	**326**	317	9	**131**	92	39	..	..	..
Karenga	..	**174**	146	28	**76**	74	2	**35**	34	1	**63**	38	25

IMPERIAL TABLE XVII.—Caste, tribe, race or nationality.

Race, tribe, caste, etc. and religion.	Calcutta with suburbs in 24-Parganas and Howrah.			Calcutta.			Suburbs in 24-Parganas.			Howrah.		
	Both sexes.	Males.	Females.	Both sexes.	Males.	Females.	Both sexes.	Males.	Females.	Both sexes.	Males.	Females.
1	2	3	4	5	6	7	8	9	10	11	12	13
Kaur ..	**110**	87	23	**110**	87	23	..	..	..	..	..	..
Kayastha ..	**182,574**	116,632	65,942	**160,630**	103,354	57,276	**4,471**	2,833	1,638	**17,473**	10,445	7,028
Kewat ..	**399**	276	123	**256**	197	59	**14**	14	..	**129**	65	64
Khambu—Buddhist ..	**2**	2	..	**2**	2	..	..	..	..	..	..	..
Khami ..	**52**	52	..	**52**	52	..	..	..	..	..	..	..
Khandait ..	**9,723**	8,373	1,350	**7,081**	6,085	996	**861**	694	167	**1,781**	1,594	187
Kharia ..	**122**	18	104	**3**	..	3	..	..	..	**119**	18	101
Khas ..	**1**	1	..	**1**	1	..	..	..	..	..	..	..
Khasi ..	**6**	4	2	**6**	4	2	..	..	..	..	..	..
Khatik ..	**465**	319	146	**299**	157	142	**1**	1	..	**165**	161	4
Khetri ..	**1,048**	860	188	**1,025**	860	165	..	..	..	**23**	..	..
Kochh ..	**35**	35	..	**35**	35	..	..	..	..	..	..	..
Konai ..	**54**	40	14	**48**	34	14	..	..	..	**6**	6	..
Kora ..	**161**	131	30	**48**	23	25	..	..	..	**113**	108	5
Kotal ..	**13**	8	5	**13**	8	5	..	..	..	..	..	..
Kotari ..	**3**	..	3	**3**	..	3	..	..	..	..	..	..
Kumhar ..	**5,010**	3,135	1,875	**3,177**	1,968	1,209	**1,279**	773	506	**554**	394	160
Kurmi ..	**12,966**	9,954	3,012	**9,628**	7,392	2,236	**371**	271	100	**2,967**	2,291	676
Lalbegi ..	**2,571**	2,135	436	**2,433**	2,000	433	**26**	26	..	**112**	109	3
Lepcha—All religions ..	**102**	94	8	**101**	94	7	..	..	..	**1**	..	1
Hindu ..	*93*	*88*	*5*	*93*	*88*	*5*	..	..	..	..	..	..
Buddhist ..	*8*	*6*	*2*	*8*	*6*	*2*	..	..	..	..	..	..
Christian ..	*1*	..	*1*	..	..	..	..	..	..	*1*	..	*1*
Limbu—All religions ..	**28**	24	4	**14**	10	4	**9**	9	..	**5**	5	..
Hindu ..	*23*	*19*	*4*	*14*	*10*	*4*	*9*	*9*	..	..	..	..
Buddhist ..	*5*	*5*	..	..	..	..	..	..	..	*5*	*5*	..
Lodha ..	**81**	69	12	**50**	46	4	**3**	3	..	**28**	20	8
Lohar ..	**796**	667	129	**559**	465	94	**8**	7	1	**229**	195	34
Madrasi ..	**779**	481	298	**667**	408	259	..	..	..	**112**	73	39
Magura ..	**2**	..	2	**2**	..	2	..	..	..	..	..	..
Mahar ..	**3**	3	..	**3**	3	..	..	..	..	..	..	..
Mahato ..	**122**	98	24	**122**	98	24	..	..	..	..	..	..
Mahasri ..	**138**	77	61	**130**	77	53	..	..	..	**8**	..	8
Mahishya ..	**76,438**	45,022	31,416	**46,215**	28,128	18,087	**10,239**	5,122	5,117	**19,984**	11,772	8,212
Mahali ..	**49**	33	16	**46**	33	13	..	..	..	**3**	..	3
Mal ..	**702**	636	66	**364**	326	38	..	..	..	**338**	310	28
Malakar ..	**809**	579	230	**809**	579	230	..	..	..	..	..	..
Malayan—Christian ..	**19**	8	11	**19**	8	11	..	..	..	..	..	..
Mali ..	**2,262**	1,624	638	**1,437**	1,027	410	**73**	57	16	**752**	540	212
Mallah ..	**2,939**	2,792	147	**2,322**	2,282	40	**3**	3	..	**614**	507	107
Mangar ..	**25**	1	24	**25**	1	24	..	..	..	..	..	..
Marathi ..	**552**	485	67	**542**	479	63	..	..	..	**10**	6	4
Marwari ..	**4,023**	2,636	1,387	**3,714**	2,438	1,276	**11**	..	11	**298**	198	100
Mech ..	**15**	15	..	**15**	15	..	..	..	..	..	..	..
Methor ..	**8,430**	5,122	3,308	**7,301**	4,527	2,774	**110**	64	46	**1,019**	531	488
Mogul—Muslim ..	**3,135**	2,603	532	**3,135**	2,603	532	..	..	..	..	..	..
Moyra ..	**9,988**	7,110	2,878	**8,484**	6,039	2,445	**260**	156	104	**1,244**	915	329
Muchi ..	**15,052**	11,881	3,171	**12,943**	10,422	2,521	**569**	395	174	**1,540**	1,064	476
Mudaliar ..	**4**	4	..	..	..	..	..	..	..	**4**	4	..
Mumin (Jolaha)—Muslim ..	**3,906**	2,478	1,428	**788**	531	257	**3**	1	2	**3,115**	1,946	1,169
Munda—All religions ..	**794**	594	200	**627**	458	169	**63**	49	14	**104**	87	17
Hindu ..	*376*	*307*	*69*	*274*	*232*	*42*	*16*	*4*	*12*	*86*	*71*	*15*
Tribal ..	*154*	*130*	*24*	*89*	*69*	*20*	*47*	*45*	*2*	*18*	*16*	*2*
Christian ..	*264*	*157*	*107*	*264*	*157*	*107*	..	..	..	..	..	..
Murmi ..	**11**	11	..	**11**	11	..	..	..	..	..	..	..
Musahar ..	**129**	85	44	**66**	37	29	..	..	..	**63**	48	15
Nagar ..	**29**	..	29	**29**	..	29	..	..	..	..	..	..
Nagesia ..	**6**	3	3	..	..	..	..	..	..	**6**	3	3
Naik ..	**45**	44	1	**30**	30	..	..	..	..	**15**	14	1
Namasudra ..	**4,279**	2,475	1,804	**3,808**	2,201	1,607	**295**	169	126	**176**	105	71
Napit ..	**16,037**	10,929	5,108	**12,208**	8,534	3,674	**860**	450	410	**2,969**	1,945	1,024
Nepali ..	**2,032**	1,521	511	**1,826**	1,397	429	..	..	..	**206**	124	82
Nepali—Buddhist ..	**115**	69	46	**113**	67	46	**1**	1	..	**1**	1	..
Newar—All religions ..	**110**	101	9	**72**	66	6	..	..	..	**38**	35	3
Hindu ..	*102*	*93*	*9*	*64*	*58*	*6*	..	..	..	*38*	*35*	*3*
Buddhist ..	*8*	*8*	..	*8*	*8*	..	..	..	..	..	..	..
Nuniya ..	**2,996**	2,492	504	**2,208**	1,860	348	**318**	237	81	**470**	395	75
Oraon—All religions ..	**1,140**	878	262	**498**	337	161	**375**	308	67	**267**	233	34
Hindu ..	*368*	*337*	*31*	*85*	*72*	*13*	*89*	*89*	..	*194*	*176*	*18*
Tribal ..	*382*	*290*	*92*	*79*	*56*	*23*	*286*	*219*	*67*	*17*	*15*	*2*
Buddhist ..	*66*	*66*	..	*66*	*66*	..	..	..	..	..	..	..
Christian ..	*324*	*185*	*139*	*268*	*143*	*125*	..	..	..	*56*	*42*	*14*
Oriya ..	**2,165**	2,020	145	**2,165**	2,020	145	..	..	..	..	..	..
Paharia ..	**3**	..	3	**3**	..	3	..	..	..	..	..	..
Paharia—Buddhist ..	**2**	2	..	**2**	2	..	..	..	..	..	..	..
Pan ..	**60**	35	25	**9**	5	4	..	..	..	**51**	30	21
Panjabi ..	**319**	272	47	**312**	272	40	..	..	..	**7**	..	7
Pasi ..	**4,410**	3,333	1,077	**2,451**	1,885	566	**590**	354	236	**1,369**	1,094	275
Pathan—Muslim ..	**14,683**	11,846	2,837	**14,683**	11,846	2,837	..	..	..	..	..	..
Patni ..	**161**	79	82	**132**	63	69	..	..	..	**29**	16	13
Patra ..	**1**	1	..	**1**	1	..	..	..	..	..	..	..
Patwa ..	**92**	58	34	**70**	45	25	..	..	..	**22**	13	9
Persian (Christians only) ..	**45**	19	26	**45**	19	26	..	..	..	..	..	..
Pod ..	**6,389**	3,706	2,683	**2,015**	1,339	676	**3,615**	1,912	1,703	**759**	455	304
Rai ..	**21**	12	9	**21**	12	9	..	..	..	..	..	..
Rajbangshi ..	**2,806**	1,618	1,188	**2,014**	1,173	841	**130**	53	77	**662**	392	270
Rajput ..	**36,584**	30,640	5,944	**30,673**	25,734	4,939	**782**	571	211	**5,129**	4,335	794
Raju ..	**27**	27	..	**27**	27	..	..	..	..	..	..	..
Rajwar ..	**986**	816	170	**868**	751	117	**37**	25	12	**81**	40	41
Routia ..	**13**	6	7	..	..	..	..	..	..	**13**	6	7
Sadgop ..	**17,395**	9,266	8,129	**13,851**	7,496	6,355	**672**	152	520	**2,872**	1,618	1,254
Sayyad—Muslim ..	**7,293**	5,089	2,204	**6,600**	4,638	1,962	**198**	121	77	**495**	330	165

IMPERIAL TABLE XVII.—Caste, tribe, race or nationality.

Race, tribe, caste, etc. and religion.	Calcutta with suburbs in 24-Parganas and Howrah.			Calcutta.			Suburbs in 24-Parganas.			Howrah.		
	Both sexes.	Males.	Females.	Both sexes.	Males.	Females.	Both sexes.	Males.	Females.	Both sexes.	Males.	Females
1	2	3	4	5	6	7	8	9	10	11	12	13
Solanki ..	**320**	131	189	**188**	50	138	..	..	..	**132**	81	51
Sankari ..	**432**	336	96	**432**	336	96	..	..	..	..	..	..
Santal—All religions ..	**1,150**	667	483	**736**	392	344	**309**	222	87	**105**	53	52
Hindu ..	*78*	*68*	*10*	*41*	*41*	..	..	..	..	*37*	*27*	*12*
Tribal ..	*635*	*450*	*185*	*258*	*202*	*56*	*309*	*222*	*87*	*68*	*26*	*40*
Buddhist ..	*6*	*6*	..	*6*	*6*	..	..	..	..	..	..	..
Christian ..	*431*	*143*	*288*	*431*	*143*	*288*	..	..	..	..	..	..
Sannyasi ..	**92**	36	56	**88**	32	56	..	..	..	**4**	4	..
Sarak ..	**12**	..	12	**12**	..	12	..	..	..	..	..	..
Savar ..	**3,827**	3,318	509	**3,574**	3,123	451	..	..	..	**253**	195	58
Shaha ..	**12,413**	8,035	4,378	**11,673**	7,495	4,178	**75**	46	29	**665**	494	171
Shekh—Muslim ..	**285,948**	209,693	76,255	**285,948**	209,693	76,255	..	..	..	..	..	..
Siamese (Christians only) ..	**12**	..	12	**12**	..	12	..	..	..	..	..	..
Sindhi ..	**2**	..	2	**2**	..	2	..	..	..	..	..	..
Subarnabanik ..	**36,516**	21,033	15,483	**33,745**	19,668	14,077	**277**	198	79	**2,494**	1,167	1,327
Sudha ..	**29**	29	..	**29**	29	..	..	..	..	..	..	..
Sudra ..	**1,315**	932	383	**784**	553	231	..	..	..	**531**	379	152
Sukli ..	**51**	40	11	**51**	40	11	..	..	..	..	..	..
Sunri ..	**2,845**	1,876	969	**2,236**	1,486	750	**115**	72	43	**494**	318	176
Sutradhar ..	**6,411**	3,719	2,692	**5,477**	3,138	2,339	**45**	25	20	**889**	556	333
Swarnakar ..	**3,117**	1,835	1,282	**2,349**	1,389	960	**143**	86	57	**625**	360	265
Syrian (Christians only) ..	**1**	1	..	**1**	1	..	..	..	..	..	..	..
Tambuli ..	**3,605**	2,072	1,533	**3,264**	1,880	1,384	**35**	20	15	**306**	172	134
Tamil ..	**5**	..	5	**5**	..	5	..	..	..	..	..	..
Tanti and Tatwa ..	**23,822**	13,567	10,255	**20,170**	11,161	9,009	**252**	146	106	**3,400**	2,260	1,140
Telegu ..	**69**	12	57	**69**	12	57	..	..	..	..	..	..
Telinga ..	**1,528**	748	780	**269**	179	90	**7**	7	..	**1,252**	562	690
Tharu ..	**159**	159	..	**159**	159	..	..	..	..	..	..	..
Tibetan—Buddhist ..	**37**	26	11	**37**	26	11	..	..	..	..	..	..
Tili ..	**13,654**	8,121	5,533	**8,307**	4,742	3,565	**285**	225	60	**5,062**	3,154	1,908
Tiyar ..	**1,044**	421	623	**275**	133	142	**526**	184	342	**243**	104	139
Toto ..	**2**	2	..	**2**	2	..	..	..	..	..	..	..
Turaha ..	**489**	378	111	**240**	210	30	..	..	..	**249**	168	81
Turi ..	**287**	226	61	**282**	221	61	..	..	..	**5**	5	..
Vaskar ..	**287**	137	150	**287**	137	150	..	..	..	..	..	..
Yakka ..	**23**	..	23	**23**	..	23	..	..	..	..	..	..
B.—NON-ASIATIC RACES*												
i British subjects												
Anglo-Indian ..	**18,469**	9,111	9,358	**16,863**	8,246	8,617	**388**	211	177	**1,218**	654	564
Australian ..	**32**	17	15	**31**	16	15	..	..	..	**1**	1	..
Canadian ..	**8**	5	3	**7**	5	2	..	..	..	**1**	..	1
English ..	**12,514**	7,598	4,916	**11,750**	7,202	4,548	**159**	87	72	**605**	309	296
Figian ..	**2**	1	1	**2**	1	1	..	..	..	..	..	..
Irish ..	**532**	312	220	**488**	288	200	..	..	..	**44**	24	20
Maltese ..	**1**	..	1	**1**	..	1	..	..	..	..	..	..
New Zealander ..	**1**	1	..	**1**	1	..	..	..	..	..	..	..
Scotch ..	**1,008**	701	307	**894**	622	272	..	..	..	**114**	79	35
South African ..	**16**	9	7	**16**	9	7	..	..	..	..	..	..
Welsh ..	**66**	62	4	**66**	62	4	..	..	..	..	..	..
ii Other than British subjects.												
American ..	**191**	129	62	**173**	114	59	..	..	..	**18**	15	3
Austrian ..	**7**	2	5	**7**	2	5	..	..	..	..	..	..
Belgian ..	**32**	30	2	**32**	30	2	..	..	..	..	..	..
Bulgarian ..	**4**	..	4	**4**	..	4	..	..	..	..	..	..
Dane ..	**5**	3	2	**5**	3	2	..	..	..	..	..	..
Dutch ..	**98**	78	20	**92**	74	18	**4**	2	2	**2**	2	..
European unspecified ..	**846**	611	235	**846**	611	235	..	..	..	..	..	..
French ..	**222**	118	104	**205**	109	96	**7**	4	3	**10**	5	5
German ..	**113**	76	37	**103**	71	32	..	..	..	**10**	5	5
Greek ..	**72**	29	43	**72**	29	43	..	..	..	..	..	..
Italian ..	**193**	164	29	**190**	161	29	..	..	..	**3**	3	..
Norwegian ..	**18**	18	..	**17**	17	..	..	..	..	**1**	1	..
Philippinese ..	**4**	4	..	**4**	4	..	..	..	..	..	..	..
Portuguese ..	**176**	113	63	**175**	112	63	..	..	..	**1**	1	..
Russian ..	**24**	11	13	**20**	10	10	..	..	..	**4**	1	3
Spaniard ..	**46**	37	9	**46**	37	9	..	..	..	..	..	..
Swede ..	**36**	35	1	**36**	35	1	..	..	..	..	..	..
Swiss ..	**22**	16	6	**22**	16	6	..	..	..	..	..	..

*Excluding 75 Europeans of indefinite belief viz., 74 in Calcutta (male 64, female 10), 1 male in Howrah city.

IMPERIAL TABLE XIX.—Europeans and allied races and Anglo-Indians by age and sex.

This table corresponds to imperial table XVI of 1921. It shows figures in part A for Europeans and allied races (e.g., Americans, South Africans, etc.) distinguishing (1) British subjects from (2) Others and in part B for Anglo-Indians. All Europeans and persons of allied races whose birthplace is Great Britain or a British Colony or Dependency are included amongst the British subjects unless the contrary was expressly stated in the returns. Figures for wards of Howrah city have been shown separately for the first time in this table.

2. The age-groups differ in some respects from those adopted in 1921. A rough method of adjustment by which the figures for the two years can be compared is suggested in the title page to the same table in vol. V, part II. In using the unadjusted figures allowance should be made for the fact that the age was taken in 1931 to the nearest and in 1921 at the last birthday.

3. The details of Armenians included in the table are separately shown below :—

	Calcutta with Suburbs and Howrah City.			Calcutta.			Howrah.		
	Both sexes.	Male.	Female.	Both sexes.	Male.	Female.	Both sexes.	Male.	Female.
1	2	3	4	5	6	7	8	9	10
All ages ..	**746**	**418**	**328**	**738**	**415**	**323**	**8**	**3**	**5**
0—6	118	64	54	118	64	54	..	..	..
7—13	90	49	41	89	48	41	1	1	..
14—16	69	33	36	68	32	36	1	1	..
17—23	62	38	24	61	37	24	1	1	..
24—43	211	127	84	208	127	81	3	..	3
44 & over	196	107	89	194	107	87	2	..	2

IMPERIAL TABLE XIX.—Europeans and allied races and Anglo-Indians by age and sex.

A.—Europeans by age and sex (1) British Subjects.

(A) Europeans and allied races (including Armenians). (1) British Subjects.

Name of ward, etc.	Total: Both sexes	Total: Male	Total: Female	All ages: Both sexes	All ages: Male	All ages: Female	0—13: Male	0—13: Female	14—16: Male	14—16: Female	17—23: Male	17—23: Female	24—33: Male	24—33: Female	34—43: Male	34—43: Female	44—53: Male	44—53: Female	54 and over: Male	54 and over: Female
1	2	3	4	5	6	7	8	9	10	11	12	13	14	15	16	17	18	19	20	21
CALCUTTA WITH SUBURBS AND HOWRAH.	**35,449**	**19,679**	**15,770**	**15,278**	**9,439**	**5,839**	**1,035**	**862**	**256**	**305**	**1,299**	**838**	**2,764**	**1,283**	**1,924**	**1,221**	**1,388**	**681**	**773**	**649**
CALCUTTA WITH SUBURBS IN 24-PARGANAS.	**33,408**	**18,575**	**14,033**	**14,482**	**9,007**	**5,475**	**963**	**781**	**239**	**290**	**1,255**	**790**	**2,669**	**1,198**	**1,817**	**1,150**	**1,319**	**645**	**745**	**621**
Calcutta	**32,850**	**18,271**	**14,579**	**14,324**	**8,921**	**5,403**	**954**	**767**	**235**	**288**	**1,246**	**769**	**2,645**	**1,183**	**1,798**	**1,137**	**1,307**	**642**	**736**	**617**
MUNICIPAL AREA	**29,898**	**15,650**	**14,248**	**11,860**	**6,725**	**5,135**	**880**	**676**	**211**	**281**	**629**	**735**	**1,712**	**1,120**	**1,487**	**1,090**	**1,154**	**632**	**652**	**601**
District No. I	**1,004**	**465**	**539**	**339**	**179**	**160**	**16**	**28**	**5**	**10**	**11**	**22**	**44**	**42**	**50**	**26**	**37**	**23**	**16**	**9**
Ward No. 1 Shampukur	5	2	3	1	1	..	..	..	..	..	..	..	1	..	..	..	..	..	..	..
Ward No. 2 Kumartuli	10	5	5	2	1	1	..	..	..	..	..	..	..	1	1	..	..	..	..	..
Ward No. 3 Bartola	7	2	5	5	1	4	..	..	..	1	..	1	1	1	..	1	..	..	..	..
Ward No. 4 Sukea's Street	106	58	48	29	17	12	..	2	..	..	1	2	6	4	3	1	5	2	..	1
Ward No. 5 Jorabagan	59	29	30	56	26	30	2	8	3	4	3	4	3	6	9	5	5	2	1	1
Ward No. 6 Jorasanko	11	4	7	5	1	4	..	..	..	..	1	..	..	2	..	..	..	2	..	..
Ward No. 30 Belgachia	603	239	364	67	21	46	3	2	..	1	3	10	4	14	4	9	4	6	3	4
Ward No. 31 Satpukur	100	62	38	92	57	35	10	10	2	1	1	2	12	9	19	6	10	6	3	1
Ward No. 32 Cossipore	103	64	39	82	54	28	1	6	..	3	2	3	17	5	14	4	13	5	7	2
District No. II	**6,835**	**3,707**	**3,128**	**1,326**	**857**	**469**	**78**	**92**	**20**	**36**	**88**	**59**	**255**	**94**	**177**	**103**	**163**			**34**
Ward No. 7 Burra Bazar	477	412	65	222	189	33	9	6	4	7	30	3	102	4	22	9	13	3		1
Ward No. 8 Kalootola	304	184	120	26	18	8	3	..	2	1	2	1	4	3	4	1	1	1	2	1
Ward No. 9 Muchipara	869	476	393	225	145	80	26	15	9	3	15	13	30	16	38	15	20	13	7	5
Ward No. 10 Bow Bazar	2,481	1,277	1,204	147	86	61	10	19	2	7	16	11	22	10	17	9	14	3	5	2
Ward No. 11 Paddapukur	1,566	674	892	147	51	96	12	27	..	12	5	16	4	18	4	12	21	3	5	8
Ward No. 12 Waterloo Street	1,101	660	441	536	353	183	17	25	3	6	20	15	88	39	88	54	90	28	47	16
Ward No. 28 Beliaghata	10	6	4	4	2	2	..	..	..	..	..	..	1	1	..	..	..	..	1	1
Ward No. 29 Maniktala	27	18	9	19	13	6	1	..	..	..	..	..	4	3	4	3	4	..	..	..
District No. III	**17,232**	**8,927**	**8,305**	**7,060**	**3,961**	**3,099**	**584**	**386**	**133**	**146**	**391**	**454**	**942**	**621**	**891**	**701**	**651**	**416**	**369**	**375**
Ward No. 13 Fenwick Bazar	3,571	1,930	1,641	1,425	844	581	149	80	44	21	106	80	204	118	155	135	120	79	66	68
Ward No. 14 Taltola	2,906	1,491	1,415	443	204	239	51	57	10	16	20	29	16	39	25	36	39	31	43	31
Ward No. 15 Kalinga	2,830	1,487	1,343	852	455	397	73	54	20	18	44	78	104	67	86	72	66	47	62	61
Ward No. 16 Park Street	2,426	1,367	1,059	1,996	1,142	854	108	15	21	47	101	174	299	140	315	230	209	132	89	116
Ward No. 17 Baman Bustee	904	513	391	660	340	320	60	55	10	12	32	30	65	73	74	77	69	45	30	28
Ward No. 18 Tengra	122	76	46	61	37	24	12	3	2	..	3	2	5	4	7	11	3	3	5	1
Ward No. 19 Intally	2,311	867	1,444	255	135	120	30	23	3	8	15	12	24	30	29	19	19	10	15	18
Ward No. 20 Beniapukur	955	518	437	371	201	170	43	25	19	19	28	21	41	30	28	37	23	19	19	19
Ward No. 21 Ballygunge	1,207	678	529	997	603	394	58	74	4	5	42	28	184	120	172	84	103	50	40	33
District No. IV	**4,827**	**2,551**	**2,276**	**3,135**	**1,728**	**1,407**	**202**	**170**	**53**	**89**	**139**	**200**	**471**	**363**	**369**	**260**	**303**	**142**	**191**	**183**
Ward No. 27 Tollygunge	205	130	75	168	108	60	13	11	2	..	3	7	38	25	32	13	17	4	3	..
Ward No. 22 Bhawanipur	1,177	659	518	811	468	343	34	48	6	5	51	48	139	86	119	94	86	19	33	43
Ward No. 23 Alipore	1,131	549	582	698	401	297	49	55	18	6	17	39	106	80	97	73	88	29	26	15
Ward No. 24 Ekbalpore	1,266	648	618	486	229	257	62	31	8	43	23	36	43	41	42	31	23	29	28	46
Ward No. 25 Watganj and Hastings	839	424	415	771	386	385	19	16	16	30	39	63	108	123	50	37	69	38	85	78
Ward No. 26 Garden Reach	209	141	68	201	136	65	25	9	3	5	6	7	37	8	29	12	20	23	16	1
FORT WILLIAM AND MAIDAN	**1,218**	**1,054**	**164**	**1,212**	**1,049**	**163**	**56**	**57**	**11**	**4**	**365**	**17**	**536**	**40**	**64**	**30**	**11**	**5**	**6**	**10**
PORT	**1,734**	**1,567**	**167**	**1,252**	**1,147**	**105**	**18**	**34**	**13**	**3**	**252**	**17**	**397**	**23**	**247**	**17**	**142**	**5**	**78**	**6**
Suburbs in 24-Parganas	**558**	**304**	**254**	**158**	**86**	**72**	**9**	**14**	**4**	**2**	**9**	**21**	**24**	**15**	**19**	**13**	**12**	**3**	**9**	**4**
Tollygunge	176	87	89	50	24	26	6	9	..	..	4	5	10	8	1	1	2	1	1	2
South Suburban Municipality	382	217	165	108	62	46	3	5	4	2	5	16	14	7	18	12	10	2	8	2
HOWRAH	**2,041**	**1,104**	**937**	**796**	**432**	**364**	**72**	**81**	**17**	**15**	**44**	**48**	**95**	**85**	**107**	**71**	**69**	**36**	**28**	**28**
Ward No. 1	4	3	1	2	1	1	..	..	..	..	..	..	..	1	..	..	1	..	..	..
Ward No. 2	3	1	2	2	..	2	..	1	..	..	..	..	..	..	..	..	..	1	..	..
Ward No. 3	52	33	19	32	22	10	1	1	..	2	..	1	9	3	10	2	2	1	..	..
Ward No. 4	1,510	821	689	474	256	218	48	54	14	11	29	28	46	42	56	46	45	17	18	20
Ward No. 5	240	109	131	104	45	59	16	14	2	2	7	6	5	20	4	5	6	5	5	7
Ward No. 7	55	15	40	51	15	36	1	6	..	..	..	11	5	8	5	5	2	6	2	..
Ward No. 8	122	87	35	122	87	35	6	5	1	..	6	1	29	11	30	12	12	5	3	1
Ward No. 9	55	35	20	9	6	3	..	..	..	..	2	1	1	..	2	1	1	1	..	..

IMPERIAL TABLE XIX: part A (2) and B.—Europeans other than British subjects and Anglo-Indians by age and sex.

(A) Europeans and allied races (including Armenians)—*concld.*

(2) Others.

Name of ward, etc.	All ages.			0—13		14—16		17—23		24—33		34—43		44—53		54 and over.	
	Both sexes.	Male.	Female.	Male.	Female.	Male.	Female.	Male.	Female.	Male.	Female.	Male.	Female.	Male.	Female.	Male.	Female.
1	22	23	24	25	26	27	28	29	30	31	32	33	34	35	36	37	38
CALCUTTA WITH SUBURBS AND HOWRAH.	**1,702**	**1,129**	**573**	**116**	**119**	**26**	**32**	**238**	**58**	**291**	**136**	**207**	**118**	**162**	**50**	**89**	**60**
CALCUTTA WITH SUBURBS IN 24-PARGANAS.	**1,675**	**1,111**	**564**	**115**	**118**	**26**	**32**	**235**	**58**	**287**	**133**	**204**	**115**	**159**	**48**	**85**	**60**
Calcutta	**1,663**	**1,104**	**559**	**115**	**118**	**26**	**32**	**234**	**58**	**284**	**131**	**203**	**113**	**158**	**47**	**84**	**60**
MUNICIPAL AREA	**1,310**	**756**	**554**	**111**	**117**	**22**	**32**	**118**	**58**	**175**	**130**	**137**	**111**	**123**	**47**	**70**	**59**
District No. I	**54**	**37**	**17**	**7**	..	**2**	..	**13**	**2**	**7**	**7**	**4**	**4**	**1**	**3**	**3**	**1**
Ward No. 3 Bartola	1	..	1	..	..	..	..	..	..	..	1	..	..	..	..	..	..
Ward No. 4 Sukea's Street	1	..	1	..	..	..	..	..	..	..	..	..	1	..	..	..	..
Ward No. 30 Belgachia	36	28	8	6	..	2	..	12	2	4	3	3	2	..	1	1	..
Ward No. 32 Cossipore	16	9	7	1	..	..	..	1	..	3	3	1	1	1	2	2	1
District No. II	**263**	**165**	**98**	**21**	**15**	**2**	**14**	**15**	**12**	**36**	**26**	**37**	**18**	**27**	**7**	**27**	**6**
Ward No. 7 Burra Bazar	1	..	1	..	..	..	..	..	..	..	..	..	1	..	..	..	..
Ward No. 8 Kalootola	9	7	2	..	..	..	..	1	1	..	..	5	1	1	..	..	..
Ward No. 9 Muchipara	15	8	7	1	..	..	..	1	2	3	4	2	1	1	..	..	..
Ward No. 10 Bow Bazar	38	29	9	..	1	..	..	6	4	8	2	7	1	4	1	4	..
Ward No. 11 Paddapukur	49	17	32	6	7	1	12	1	2	1	5	2	2	3	1	3	3
Ward No. 12 Waterloo Street	150	103	47	14	7	1	2	6	3	24	15	21	12	17	5	20	3
Ward No. 28 Belliaghata	1	1	..	..	..	..	..	..	..	..	..	..	..	1	..	..	..
District No. III	**802**	**459**	**343**	**71**	**74**	**15**	**15**	**78**	**32**	**100**	**77**	**87**	**73**	**79**	**31**	**29**	**41**
Ward No. 13 Fenwick Bazar	245	105	140	29	39	5	8	21	14	26	24	15	26	7	15	2	14
Ward No. 14 Taltola	114	80	34	17	12	5	2	16	..	12	2	17	7	8	6	5	5
Ward No. 15 Kalinga	95	55	40	4	9	2	3	2	5	16	7	9	9	18	1	4	6
Ward No. 16 Park Street	171	122	49	6	9	..	1	23	8	21	10	28	13	32	2	12	6
Ward No. 17 Baman Bustee	52	39	13	6	..	3	..	8	..	8	2	4	4	6	3	4	4
Ward No. 19 Intally	36	20	16	6	2	..	1	3	2	3	3	5	5	2	2	1	1
Ward No. 20 Beniapukur	23	17	6	..	1	..	..	4	1	6	4	3	..	4	..	..	..
Ward No. 21 Ballygunge	66	21	45	3	2	..	..	1	2	8	25	6	9	2	2	1	5
District No. IV	**191**	**95**	**96**	**12**	**28**	**3**	**3**	**12**	**12**	**32**	**20**	**9**	**16**	**16**	**6**	**11**	**11**
Ward No. 27 Tollygunge	2	1	1	..	..	..	..	1	..	..	1	..	..	..	..	..	..
Ward No. 22 Bhawanipur	105	53	52	4	17	3	3	8	6	24	13	4	7	5	3	5	3
Ward No. 23 Alipore	42	20	22	5	7	..	..	3	2	4	4	1	4	5	2	2	3
Ward No. 24 Ekbalpore	40	19	21	3	4	..	..	..	4	4	2	4	5	5	1	3	5
Ward No. 25 Watganj and Hastings ..	2	2	..	..	..	..	..	..	..	..	..	..	..	1	..	1	..
FORT WILLIAM AND MAIDAN	**5**	**4**	**1**	..	..	..	..	..	..	**1**	..	**1**	**1**	**2**	..	..	..
PORT	**348**	**344**	**4**	**4**	**1**	**4**	..	**116**	..	**108**	**1**	**65**	**1**	**33**	..	**14**	**1**
Suburbs in 24-Parganas	**12**	**7**	**5**	..	..	..	..	**1**	..	**3**	**2**	**1**	**2**	**1**	**1**	**1**	..
Tollygunge	3	2	1	..	..	..	..	1	..	1	1	..	..	..	..	..	..
South Suburban Municipality	9	5	4	..	..	..	..	..	..	2	1	1	2	1	1	1	..
HOWRAH	**27**	**18**	**9**	**1**	**1**	..	..	**3**	..	**4**	**3**	**3**	**3**	**3**	**2**	**4**	..
Ward No. 4	22	13	9	1	1	..	..	2	..	3	3	1	3	2	2	4	..
Ward No. 5	3	3	..	..	..	..	..	1	..	1	..	1	..	..	..	..	..
Ward No. 9	2	2	..	..	..	..	..	..	..	..	..	1	..	1	..	..	..

IMPERIAL TABLE XIX: part A (2) and B.—Europeans other than British subjects and Anglo-Indians by age and sex—*concld.*

(B) Anglo-Indians.

Name of ward, etc.	All ages.			0—3		4—6		7—13		14—16		17—19		20—29		30—39		40—49		50—59		60—69		70 & over.	
	Both sexes.	Male.	Female.	Male.	Female.	Male.	Female.	Male.	Female.	Male.	Female.	Male.	Female.	Male.	Female.	Male.	Female.	Male.	Female	Male.	Female.	Male.	Female.	Male.	Female.
1	39	40	41	42	43	44	45	46	47	48	49	50	51	52	53	54	55	56	57	58	59	60	61	62	63
CALCUTTA WITH SUBURBS AND HOWRAH.	**18,469**	**9,111**	**9,358**	**764**	**706**	**602**	**555**	**1,492**	**1,433**	**637**	**802**	**690**	**722**	**1,649**	**1,789**	**1,332**	**1,229**	**967**	**890**	**522**	**651**	**282**	**341**	**174**	**240**
CALCUTTA WITH SUBURBS IN 24-PARGANAS.	**17,251**	**8,457**	**8,794**	**704**	**641**	**551**	**513**	**1,372**	**1,371**	**603**	**771**	**635**	**672**	**1,538**	**1,665**	**1,206**	**1,158**	**905**	**828**	**502**	**619**	**271**	**322**	**170**	**234**
Calcutta	**16,863**	**8,246**	**8,617**	**680**	**630**	**537**	**495**	**1,345**	**1,357**	**590**	**763**	**626**	**660**	**1,497**	**1,631**	**1,178**	**1,133**	**886**	**808**	**490**	**602**	**255**	**311**	**162**	**227**
MUNICIPAL AREA ..	**16,728**	**8,169**	**8,559**	**676**	**627**	**534**	**495**	**1,337**	**1,344**	**583**	**757**	**620**	**656**	**1,483**	**1,622**	**1,163**	**1,126**	**875**	**802**	**484**	**595**	**252**	**309**	**162**	**226**
District No. I ..	**611**	**249**	**362**	**22**	**15**	**11**	**4**	**12**	**14**	**5**	**105**	**27**	**47**	**49**	**88**	**28**	**38**	**15**	**17**	**12**	**23**	**5**	**9**	**63**	**2**
Ward No. 1 Shampukur ..	4	1	3	..	1	..	1	..	..	..	..	..	..	..	..	1	1	..	..	..	..	..	..	..	..
Ward No. 2 Kumartuli ..	8	4	4	..	..	..	1	..	..	..	1	1	..	1	..	..	1	2	1	..	..	..	..	..	..
Ward No. 3 Bartola ..	1	1	..	..	..	..	..	..	..	..	..	1	..	..	..	..	..	..	..	..	..	..	..	..	..
Ward No. 4 Sukea's Street..	76	41	35	5	1	4	1	5	7	..	4	2	2	9	7	7	2	4	3	3	4	2	3	..	1
Ward No. 5 Jorabagan ..	3	3	..	..	..	1	..	..	..	..	..	..	..	..	..	2	..	..	..	..	..	..	..	..	..
Ward No. 6 Jorasanko ..	6	3	3	..	..	..	..	1	..	1	..	..	..	..	1	..	1	..	..	..	..	1	1	..	..
Ward No. 30 Belgachia ..	500	190	310	15	9	5	1	6	7	4	100	23	44	38	80	17	31	9	13	8	19	2	5	63	1
Ward No. 31 Satpukur ..	8	5	3	2	2	1	..	..	..	..	..	..	1	1	..	1	..	..	..	..	..	..	..	..	..
Ward No. 32 Cossipore ..	5	1	4	..	2	..	..	..	..	..	..	..	..	..	..	..	2	..	..	1	..	..	..	..	..
District No. II ..	**5,246**	**2,685**	**2,561**	**226**	**209**	**175**	**173**	**449**	**367**	**245**	**188**	**223**	**185**	**527**	**541**	**366**	**306**	**245**	**218**	**127**	**201**	**79**	**75**	**23**	**98**
Ward No. 7 Burra Bazar ..	254	223	31	7	3	5	1	115	4	64	..	7	4	14	10	7	8	4	..	..	1	..	..	..	..
Ward No. 8 Kalootola ..	269	159	110	11	26	6	3	28	11	11	13	18	6	48	17	19	10	7	11	7	6	3	6	1	1
Ward No. 9 Muchipara ..	629	323	306	13	14	29	19	76	43	32	28	36	41	88	81	15	34	14	21	15	14	4	7	1	4
Ward No. 10 Bow Bazar ..	2,296	'1,162	1,134	97	108	84	93	137	196	93	84	93	81	229	209	174	143	137	102	58	69	46	31	14	18
Ward No. 11 Paddapukur ..	1,370	606	764	87	51	43	40	72	93	31	54	54	31	112	196	97	79	59	55	29	96	17	24	5	45
Ward No. 12 Waterloo Street	415	204	211	11	7	8	17	21	20	14	9	13	21	34	28	52	29	23	29	18	15	9	6	1	30
Ward No. 28 Beliaghata ..	5	3	2	..	..	..	..	..	..	..	..	1	..	..	..	1	2	1	..	..	..	..	..	..	..
Ward No. 29 Maniktala ..	8	5	3	..	..	..	..	..	..	..	..	1	1	2	..	1	1	..	..	..	..	..	1	1	..
District No. III ..	**9,370**	**4,507**	**4,863**	**360**	**368**	**253**	**291**	**693**	**799**	**308**	**397**	**332**	**345**	**815**	**858**	**679**	**699**	**542**	**489**	**307**	**324**	**149**	**192**	**69**	**101**
Ward No. 13 Fenwick Bazar	1,901	981	920	81	82	41	52	203	116	90	42	64	68	163	188	138	136	101	93	61	64	28	45	11	34
Ward No. 14 Taltola ..	2,349	1,207	1,142	103	117	88	75	165	141	67	57	85	86	226	215	176	175	145	116	79	84	53	49	20	27
Ward No. 15 Kalinga ..	1,883	977	906	58	47	57	58	127	102	65	43	89	68	202	164	153	171	131	122	62	64	23	45	10	22
Ward No. 16 Park Street ..	259	103	156	2	3	6	4	7	7	8	12	4	24	21	45	12	18	24	26	12	10	3	5	4	2
Ward No. 17 Baman Bustee	192	134	58	3	6	1	2	37	6	39	2	12	3	14	7	13	13	10	8	4	9	1	2	..	..
Ward No. 18 Tengra ..	61	39	22	2	1	1	1	6	3	3	1	4	1	9	2	3	8	7	3	1	1	3	..	..	1
Ward No. 19 Intally ..	2,020	712	1,308	69	75	46	81	100	388	23	236	49	65	121	151	124	122	86	88	53	60	26	32	15	10
Ward No. 20 Beniapukur ..	561	300	261	35	31	10	17	41	28	8	..	23	20	52	60	49	37	36	29	27	22	12	13	7	4
Ward No. 21 Ballygunge ..	144	54	90	7	6	3	1	7	8	5	4	2	10	7	26	11	19	2	4	8	10	..	1	2	1
District No. IV ..	**1,501**	**728**	**773**	**68**	**35**	**95**	**27**	**183**	**164**	**25**	**67**	**38**	**79**	**92**	**135**	**90**	**83**	**73**	**78**	**38**	**47**	**19**	**33**	**7**	**25**
Ward No. 27 Tollygunge ..	35	21	14	6	..	3	2	..	1	..	..	1	2	1	3	7	2	2	3	..	1	1	..	..	..
Ward No. 22 Bhawanipur ..	261	138	123	12	2	7	4	18	11	6	6	11	19	23	38	23	17	21	12	9	4	7	3	1	7
Ward No. 23 Alipore ..	391	128	263	9	7	12	13	39	127	5	38	5	13	24	25	16	20	8	14	9	5	1	1	..	..
Ward No. 24 Ekbalpore ..	740	400	340	38	24	70	8	121	19	12	20	18	42	41	62	34	41	35	45	16	36	9	25	6	18
Ward No. 25 Watganj and Hastings ..	66	36	30	3	2	3	..	4	6	2	3	3	3	3	5	9	3	5	3	4	1	..	4	..	..
Ward No. 26 Garden Reach	8	5	3	..	..	..	..	1	..	..	..	..	..	..	2	1	..	2	1	..	..	1	..	..	..
FORT WILLIAM AND MAIDAN	**1**	**1**	**..**	..	..	..	..	..	..	..	..	1	..	..	..	..	..	..	..	..	..	..	..	..	..
PORT ..	**134**	**76**	**58**	**4**	**3**	**3**	**..**	**8**	**13**	**7**	**6**	**5**	**4**	**14**	**9**	**15**	**7**	**11**	**6**	**6**	**7**	**3**	**2**	**..**	**1**
Suburbs in 24-Parganas	**388**	**211**	**177**	**24**	**11**	**14**	**18**	**27**	**14**	**13**	**8**	**9**	**12**	**41**	**34**	**28**	**25**	**19**	**20**	**12**	**17**	**16**	**11**	**8**	**7**
Tollygunge ..	123	61	62	2	3	1	5	1	2	..	1	..	5	11	9	8	10	12	11	10	7	13	6	3	3
South Suburban Municipality	265	150	115	22	8	13	13	26	12	13	7	9	7	30	25	20	15	7	9	2	10	3	5	5	4
HOWRAH	**1,218**	**654**	**564**	**60**	**65**	**51**	**42**	**120**	**62**	**34**	**31**	**55**	**50**	**111**	**124**	**126**	**71**	**62**	**62**	**20**	**32**	**11**	**19**	**4**	**6**
Ward No. 1 ..	2	2	..	..	..	..	..	..	..	..	..	..	..	1	..	..	..	..	..	1	..	..	..	..	..
Ward No. 2 ..	1	1	..	..	..	..	..	..	..	..	..	..	..	..	..	1	..	..	..	..	..	..	..	..	..
Ward No. 3 ..	20	11	9	1	..	..	..	1	..	..	1	2	1	2	1	1	3	3	2	1	..	..	..	..	1
Ward No. 4 ..	1,014	552	462	45	56	43	34	108	56	31	23	44	40	99	102	107	53	45	53	16	25	10	5	4	5
Ward No. 5 ..	133	61	72	11	8	7	8	7	4	2	4	4	7	5	17	13	13	9	5	2	4	1	2	..	..
Ward No. 7 ..	4	..	4	..	..	..	..	..	..	..	..	..	1	..	1	..	1	..	..	..	1	..	..	..	..
Ward No. 9 ..	44	27	17	3	1	1	..	4	2	1	3	5	1	4	3	4	1	5	2	..	2	..	2	..	..

B.G. Press—1932-33—6626A—700.